Design – Build – Run

(Continues)

Part V: Conclusion

Design – Build – Run

Design – Build – Run

Applied Practices and Principles for Production-Ready Software Development

Dave Ingram

WILEY

Wiley Publishing, Inc.

Design – Build – Run: Applied Practices and Principles for Production-Ready Software Development

Published by
Wiley Publishing, Inc.
10475 Crosspoint Boulevard
Indianapolis, IN 46256
www.wiley.com

Copyright © 2009 by Wiley Publishing, Inc., Indianapolis, Indiana

Published simultaneously in Canada

ISBN: 978-0-470-25763-0

Manufactured in the United States of America

10 9 8 7 6 5 4 3 2 1

Library of Congress Cataloging-in-Publication Data

Ingram, Dave, 1968-

Design – build – run : applied practices and principles for production-ready software development / Dave Ingram.
    p. cm.
  Includes index.
  ISBN 978-0-470-25763-0 (pbk.)
    1. Computer software—Development.   2. Systems software.   I. Title.
  QA76.76.D47I543 2009
  005.1—dc22

                                                   2008052155

For general information on our other products and services please contact our Customer Care Department within the United States at (877) 762-2974, outside the United States at (317) 572-3993 or fax (317) 572-4002.

Trademarks: Wiley, the Wiley logo, Wrox, the Wrox logo, Wrox Programmer to Programmer, and related trade dress are trademarks or registered trademarks of John Wiley & Sons, Inc. and/or its affiliates, in the United States and other countries, and may not be used without written permission. All other trademarks are the property of their respective owners. Wiley Publishing, Inc., is not associated with any product or vendor mentioned in this book.

Wiley also publishes its books in a variety of electronic formats. Some content that appears in print may not be available in electronic books.

I would like to dedicate this book to my fiancée, Sarah, and our cats, Barney (deceased) and Zebedee, whose love, support, and patience has been unfaltering throughout this project.

About the Author

Dave Ingram is a Senior Manager and a Senior Technology Architect within the Architecture Group at one of the world's largest consulting firms. He is responsible for implementing streamlined development lifecycles, build and test approaches, including best practice, for large-scale, mission-critical software systems. Throughout his 22-year career in the software industry, he has been involved in many development projects, including games and game engines, third and fourth generation language development as well as very large-scale and high-volume architecture and application development. He has worked for many large international corporations; written white papers and training materials for analysts, developers, and architects; and is a Chartered Member (MBCS CITP) of the British Computer Society.

Credits

Acquisitions Editors
Chris Webb
Carol Kessel

Development Editor
John Sleeva

Technical Editor
John Masters

Production Editor
Kathleen Wisor

Copy Editor
Nancy Rapoport

Editorial Manager
Mary Beth Wakefield

Production Manager
Tim Tate

Vice President and Executive Group Publisher
Richard Swadley

Vice President and Executive Publisher
Barry Pruett

Associate Publisher
Jim Minatel

Project Coordinator, Cover
Lynsey Stanford

Proofreader
Nancy Carrasco

Indexer
J & J Indexing

Acknowledgments

Writing a book is a huge undertaking, especially when you have a day job too. I have worked on this book through the night, weekends, and also on holiday. I would like to say thank you to Sarah's family, who have been very supportive and very understanding, especially when I've had to miss family events. I would also like to thank my best friend, David "John" Steele, for all his support over the years and his hard work, help, and input. I would like to thank my close friend, John Masters, for acting as Technical Editor and I'd like to thank everybody at Wiley Publishing for all their hard work and efforts. I would especially like to thank Chris Webb for moving my original proposal forward.

It goes without saying that without the support and encouragement from a number of colleagues I would not have had the enthusiasm to write a book. This list that follows is by no way exhaustive but I would like to say thank you to Paul Billing, Keith Haviland, Nigel Barnes, Iain Henderson, Liv Sandbaek, Phil Tomkins, and Lee Murdoch.

Finally, I would like to thank my mum (Ann), my dad (William, deceased) and my brother (Derek) for supporting me throughout my very early years of computing and learning to program.

Contents

Contents

Contents

Contents

Contents

Contents

Part V: Conclusion

Introduction

Dear reader, thank you for choosing this book and welcome to *Design – Build – Run: Applied Practices and Principles for Production-Ready Software Development*. Software construction is a complicated process. It is enjoyable, but it is also very hard work, from start to finish. It invariably involves working very long hours (usually weekends), attending countless meetings and discussions, and rushing to meet the deadlines. In fact, the same goes for writing a book. You do it, however, because you believe in it. You're creating something new, and that's exciting. It is also very challenging but that just fuels our desire to get it done, get it done right, and get it right the first time. In my opinion there's simply nothing better than seeing a system you've worked on go-live. Of course, afterwards you always look back and think how you could have done it better, and that's what makes you advance as individuals and us as an industry overall.

I'm not taking anything away from the great achievement of getting a software system live, but going live is not an indication that the project was a true success. The fact is that some systems still go-live when they're not entirely fit for purpose. Some may not work functionally or have *all* the required functionality. Some may not work technically. They may failover frequently, or they may be slow or difficult to use, support, and/or maintain. In a lot of cases, projects go-live after experiencing huge delays and massive budget overruns and it is hard to see these as true success stories. A true success story is a project that delivers a system with all the required functionality, on time and within budget.

So, what is the secret to success? Why is it that some software projects are a huge success and others are considered a failure? Is it the design? Is it the process? Is it the planning or the estimating? Is it the people or the skills? Is it the quality of the product? The very short answer is that it is usually a combination of these factors that leads to the success or failure ranking of a project. As developers, you play a huge part in the process; everything you do can have a positive or negative effect on the overall outcome of a project.

A software system is not just a software application. *A software system* is *the sum of all its parts*. A system encompasses all the *applications*, all the *environments*, all the *processes*, and all the *tools* that go along with it. For a system to be production-ready, all these facets need to be production-ready, too. For a project to be successful, all the aspects of production readiness and the processes required to get there need to be fully understood and taken into account during the decision-making process. The software development lifecycle is a *system*. It consists of *applications*, *environments*, *processes*, and *tools* and the outputs of this process are the software systems that you develop. Everything needs to work in harmony to be truly successful.

This book is neither a project management reference nor a technology- or language-specific set of *best practices*. Although the examples in this book use Microsoft technologies, they can equally apply to other languages and technologies. This book is a guide to designing and building production-ready software from the start. This means understanding the impact of the choices you make and building software and processes that are fit for all the purposes they need to be.

Today's mission-critical systems need to work and they need to work very well. Having a thorough understanding of what is involved in designing, building, and running large-scale software systems is a key factor in success and that is exactly what this book will provide you with.

Whom This Book Is For

This book focuses primarily on the technical aspects of production-ready software development and, as such, it is directed more toward software developers and development team leaders. Software architects and designers will also learn a great deal from reading this book, as the journey from design to production covers a wide variety of principles and practices.

To really get the most out of this book, you should be familiar with software design and development practices. You should be able to read flow charts and UML diagrams. You should also be familiar with software development and the concepts of unit testing and integration testing. Knowledge of more advanced topics such as code coverage, code analysis, and performance analysis is an advantage but not necessary. Knowledge of performance counters and the Windows Event Log will also help, but again, it is not necessary.

This book will enable you to build your skills by providing real-world knowledge and practical advice to take into the field to build truly award-winning solutions.

What This Book Covers

This book covers all the topics relating to building production-ready systems, which includes understanding the build process and the tools you need to develop and test your applications. It covers all the quality characteristics your system needs to meet and what you can do to ensure that you meet them. The book also covers all the environments and circumstances your system could be used in and how you can ensure that it is fit for these purposes. Most important, it covers the practices and patterns you can leverage during design and development to improve your software quality, lower the total cost of ownership, and ensure that it is truly production-ready.

This book is restricted to the "construction" phase of the development lifecycle, which, for the purposes of this book will encompass design, build, unit testing, and integration testing. Other areas of the development lifecycle are referred to but only where necessary to provide context or where the key concepts are relevant.

The book looks at what is involved in determining the development processes, the environments involved, and the processes and tools. You are going to look at how and where to set the build quality bar and, more important, how you will achieve it through effective use of the skills, tools, and technologies you have.

In particular, I am going to focus on the patterns and practices that you can use to design and build your software to better support the following:

❑   The functional and technical quality characteristics for all its users and uses

❑   The data centers and environments it can be deployed to and how it can be used in them

❑   The operations and application maintenance functions, including monitoring, reporting, batch, issue diagnosis, support and resolution, and maintenance of the solution

How This Book Is Structured

The book is structured in such a way that each chapter introduces key concepts or considerations that flow through to the next. That is not to say that this book can't be used as a reference, but I suggest that initially you follow the book chapter-by-chapter to get the most out of it:

❑ In Part I, you look at what production readiness means and all the quality characteristics your software needs to meet. You will examine the tools and technologies you're going to use by weighing the pros and cons of each and understanding the financial and quality impact of what you're going to do or not going to do. You set out your responsibilities as a developer and development team and ensure that you have everything in place to ensure success.

❑ In Part II, you then look at the entire production spectrum. You will look at the environments and the data centers. You will look at service delivery and operations, and you'll look at monitoring, alerting, reporting, and batch. You will examine incident investigation and application maintenance.

❑ In Part III, you will look at the conceptual design for the case study used throughout the remainder of this book. The chapters look at the conceptual design, planning the architecture, and modeling the application components. The case study is used to draw out a number of techniques and considerations and to lead into the patterns and practices discussions.

❑ In Part IV, you will then examine some key patterns and practices that ensure you design and build your systems so that they are production-ready and support all that you have seen so far. You will examine designing for batch and reporting. You will move on to designing for performance, designing for resilience, designing for monitoring, designing for incident investigation, designing for application maintenance, and designing for testing. This part closes off with designing for deployment.

❑ In Part V, you take a quick look at the some of the implications of applying the patterns and practices to your projects and the steps you can take to address them. This part uses the code associated with this book to demonstrate profiling the code and assessing the output as well as running the tests and assessing code coverage.

What You Need to Use This Book

To review and build the prototype solution, you will need the following:

❑ Any windows operating system capable of running Microsoft Visual Studio 2008

❑ Microsoft Visual Studio 2008

Conventions

To help you get the most from the text and keep track of what's happening, I've used a number of conventions throughout the book.

> **Boxes like this one hold important, not-to-be forgotten information that is directly relevant to the surrounding text.**

Tips, hints, tricks, and asides to the current discussion are offset and placed in italics like this.

As for styles in the text:

❑ I *highlight* new terms and important words when I introduce them.

❑ I show keyboard strokes like this: Ctrl+A.

❑ I show file names, URLs, and code within the text like so: `persistence.properties`.

❑ I present code in two different ways:

```
In code examples we highlight new and important code with a gray background.
The gray highlighting is not used for code that's less important in the present
context, or has been shown before.
```

Source Code

As you work through the examples in this book, you may choose either to type in all the code manually or to use the source code files that accompany the book. All of the source code used in this book is available for download at `http://www.wrox.com`. Once at the site, simply locate the book's title (either by using the Search box or by using one of the title lists) and click the Download Code link on the book's detail page to obtain all the source code for the book.

Because many books have similar titles, you may find it easiest to search by ISBN; this book's ISBN is 978-0-470-25763-0.

Once you download the code, just decompress it with your favorite compression tool. Alternately, you can go to the main Wrox code download page at `http://www.wrox.com/dynamic/books/download.aspx` to see the code available for this book and all other Wrox books.

Errata

We make every effort to ensure that there are no errors in the text or in the code. However, no one is perfect, and mistakes do occur. If you find an error in one of our books, like a spelling mistake or faulty piece of code, we would be very grateful for your feedback. By sending in errata you may save another reader hours of frustration and at the same time you will be helping us provide even higher quality information.

To find the errata page for this book, go to `http://www.wrox.com` and locate the title using the Search box or one of the title lists. Then, on the book details page, click the Book Errata link. On this page you can view all errata that has been submitted for this book and posted by Wrox editors. A complete book list including links to each book's errata is also available at `www.wrox.com/misc-pages/booklist.shtml`.

If you don't spot "your" error on the Book Errata page, go to `www.wrox.com/contact/techsupport.shtml` and complete the form there to send us the error you have found. We'll check the information and, if appropriate, post a message to the book's errata page and fix the problem in subsequent editions of the book.

p2p.wrox.com

For author and peer discussion, join the P2P forums at p2p.wrox.com. The forums are a Web-based system for you to post messages relating to Wrox books and related technologies and interact with other readers and technology users. The forums offer a subscription feature to e-mail you topics of interest of your choosing when new posts are made to the forums. Wrox authors, editors, other industry experts, and your fellow readers are present on these forums.

At http://p2p.wrox.com you will find a number of different forums that will help you not only as you read this book, but also as you develop your own applications. To join the forums, just follow these steps:

1. Go to p2p.wrox.com and click the Register link.

2. Read the terms of use and click Agree.

3. Complete the required information to join as well as any optional information you wish to provide and click Submit.

4. You will receive an e-mail with information describing how to verify your account and complete the joining process.

You can read messages in the forums without joining P2P but in order to post your own messages, you must join.

Once you join, you can post new messages and respond to messages other users post. You can read messages at any time on the Web. If you would like to have new messages from a particular forum e-mailed to you, click the Subscribe to this Forum icon by the forum name in the forum listing.

For more information about how to use the Wrox P2P, be sure to read the P2P FAQs for answers to questions about how the forum software works as well as many common questions specific to P2P and Wrox books. To read the FAQs, click the FAQ link on any P2P page.

Part I

Production-Ready Software

1

"Production" Readiness

Developing and implementing a software system is a complicated and tricky business. In fact, "developing" and "implementing" are really two different but very interrelated disciplines. For the purposes of this book, "implementing a software system" refers to the activities and processes required to get a software system from an initial concept into live service or production, whereas "developing a software system" refers to the activities and processes of actual software construction and proving. Although the two disciplines are interrelated, they can also be very far apart. Just because a piece of software has been developed doesn't necessarily mean it will be implemented. Many software projects don't even get off the ground or are shelved part way through. This is especially true when the overall project isn't or hasn't been planned, executed, and delivered well. While the development is essential, the implementation is paramount. That said, the project needs to have a sound business case, and the project needs to be firmly planned, executed, and delivered.

This chapter looks at the high-level criteria for production readiness as it relates to both software development and its ultimate implementation. This chapter is organized into the following sections:

❑ **What Is Production Readiness?** On the one hand, production readiness assesses whether your system meets all the necessary criteria for live service. On the other hand, production readiness also refers to your readiness to produce or manufacture software. This section reviews the high-level activities involved in the system development lifecycle and how they map to some mainstream software development methodologies. Software systems, whether large or small, include a variety of *applications, environments, processes,* and *tools,* as well as a number of different *users.* The foundation criteria for software *development* and *implementation* are:

   ❑ Applications must be fit for purpose.

   ❑ Environments must be fit for purpose.

   ❑ Processes and tools must be fit for purpose.

   ❑ Users must be trained.

❏ **Why Is Production Readiness Important?** Some software projects fail or are seen to be a failure. You need to do everything that you can to ensure that your software development and implementation projects are successful. This section discusses some of the most important and common contributors to project failure, including poor scope, poor planning and execution, and poor quality.

❏ **The Production-Readiness "Process"** — This section builds on the previous ones to provide some foundation principles for software development and implementation, which provide the basis of the production-readiness "process." I've put "process" in quotes because it is not really a formal process; rather, it is a mindset. You need to really think about what you're going to do, how you're going to it, and who you're doing it for.

In this chapter, I don't look at specific technologies or vendors, nor do I go into a huge amount of detail. This chapter provides a high-level overview of the production-readiness landscape and some of the high-level actions to achieve it. At the end of this chapter, I'll recap on what's been covered and as the book progresses, I will cover some of these items in more detail to show how everything fits together to achieve the primary goal — successful software *development* and *implementation*.

What Is Production Readiness?

The term *production readiness* will mean different things to different people. In the world of software systems implementation, the term refers to whether a software system is ready for live service. In its simplest form, this means "Is the system ready for implementation?" It doesn't matter whether you're developing software for external clients, for internal purposes, for general sale, or even for yourself — the question remains the same.

The word *production* also means to produce or manufacture. In achieving production readiness for your system, you need to ensure that you're not only ready for its final implementation, but that you're also ready for everything that leads up to it.

Modern software systems encompass many different applications, environments, processes, and tools, as well a wide variety of users and uses. To fully assess whether a system is ready for go-live or production, you must truly understand the production-readiness criteria. You should ask yourself the following questions:

❏ Are your applications fit for purpose?

❏ Are your environments fit for purpose?

❏ Are your processes and tools fit for purpose?

❏ Are your users trained and ready?

Production readiness is underpinned by the criteria associated with these questions. However, it is very difficult to answer yes or no to any of these questions without fully understanding their true and entire meaning. For instance, what is meant by "Are your environments fit for purpose?" or "Are your users trained and ready?" Successful software development and implementation depend entirely on how well you *define, agree*, and *understand* all the necessary criteria.

When you start development and unit testing, you need a fit-for-purpose development environment. You need a development machine that has all the right applications and tools installed on it. You need to know how to use these properly, and, finally, you need to know what you're doing and how you're going to do it. In short, you've just taken a little step in defining some criteria to assess your own readiness to start producing software.

I've called this chapter "'Production' Readiness" to capture this dual meaning of the word *production* and to highlight the very essence of this book: You must be ready for production and you must assess and ensure your production readiness every step of the way, whether it is *development* or *implementation*. Producing software is your job, irrespective of who you do it for. The activities involved in software development are shown in Figure 1-1.

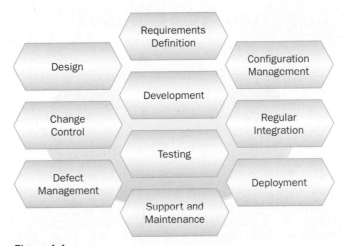

Figure 1-1

How well you *plan, execute,* and *deliver* these activities will determine the outcome of your project. The activities will be explained in more detail throughout this book. However, having a set of production-readiness criteria that relates to software development is just as important as a set of criteria for assessing the end result for implementation. The following provides a brief overview of each of the activities shown in the diagram:

❑ **Requirements definition** — This activity relates to analyzing the problem and defining and solidifying the requirements for the solution. Requirements are often categorized into functional requirements and non-functional requirements. Functional requirements document the solution's features and functions from a usage perspective. They can include business rules, calculations, and other functional and transaction-processing rules. Non-functional requirements document the solution's technical characteristics rather than functional processing.

Non-functional requirements are often referred to as "technical requirements" or the quality characteristics that the system must incorporate.

❑ **Design** — The design of a software system is typically performed in multiple stages. The design starts out at a high-level and subsequent phases and activities break the information down and provide additional low-level information. Traditionally, software design involves functional specification, technical specification, architecture specification, and so forth.

❑ **Development** — This is the actual business of "coding" and "building" the solution. In a custom-built application there will be a large proportion of coding, whereas a solution that involves third-party products generally has a mix of coding, configuration, or customization. Third-party products can often have their own proprietary programming language, although some do support extensions that can be developed in mainstream languages and tools, such as C# and Java.

❑ **Regular integration** — *Continuous integration* is a process whereby developers check-in their code and the very act of checking in triggers the solution to be built and regression tested. This ensures that all the code and artifacts are continually integrated and work together. Best practices have for a long time stated that build and regression testing should be performed at least once a day. The business of integration is about bringing all the components and artifacts together, compiling them, and running the regression tests. This is typically referred to as *software builds*. Although *continuous integration* is a good thing in certain situations, I'm more inclined to use the term "regular integration" to cover all situations. Bringing the artifacts together at regular intervals reduces the number of integration issues and the effort required to fix them.

❑ **Testing** — The testing that's performed on most software development projects includes unit testing, integration testing, and system testing. Unit testing validates that a single unit of software works correctly. A unit is typically a single class, module or method/function. Integration testing validates that a set of units work together in an integrated fashion. Integration testing can often be referred to as "assembly testing" because the set of units is generally referred to as an "assemblage" or "assembly." This is not to be confused with a .NET Assembly or Dynamic Link Library (DLL), which is also a collection of classes, interfaces, and so forth. System testing validates that the entire solution works correctly. System testing is often subdivided into multiple activities, including functional testing, technical testing, and acceptance testing, where each focuses on particular aspects of the system. Regression testing, mentioned earlier, executes as many of the test scenarios as possible from unit, integration, and system testing. "Smoke" testing is also often used to test the system end-to-end prior to passing the software on for further testing, and, as such, the test scenarios are more aligned to, and a subset of, the formal functional (and possibly technical) test scenarios.

❑ **Deployment** — This covers a few discrete activities. The first activity, release management, deals with the business of determining what constitutes a release, e.g., the actual contents of the release package. The second activity is packaging the release so that it can be deployed to a particular environment. And the third activity is the actual deployment, installation, configuration, and verification of the software (and content) of a release in a particular environment.

❑ **Configuration management** — In terms of software development, configuration management refers to the repository that is used to store documentation, source code, and other artifacts relating to the system or solution being implemented.

❑ **Change control** — As projects progress, changes to functionality and requirements are often identified. Including these changes in the overall scope of the project or release is referred to as *change control*. Incorporating change is typically based on an impact analysis that determines the costs and timescales associated with incorporating the change. These costs and timescales can be reviewed to determine whether there is a sufficiently valid business case for the change. It depends on the chosen development methodology, but traditionally a "change" refers to "a change to the signed-off requirements." Changes that are identified late in the cycle can have a dramatic affect on costs and timescales. Agile development methodologies embrace change, even late in the development cycle. However, changes still need to be validated for their business relevance and their impact in terms of costs and timescales.

❑ **Defect management** — Defects are identified during testing and review activities and can be raised at any point in the project lifecycle. A defect is not a change because the system (or solution) doesn't do what it is supposed to do according to the requirements and specifications. Defect management is the business of managing defects and their implementation within the system. It is not uncommon for some defects to be debated by the project team because they're actually a change to the requirements, and not really a defect at all.

❑ **Support and maintenance** — Once a system is in live service, it will need to be supported and maintained effectively. Back-end support concentrates on ensuring that the system is up and running and performing how it should. The system is also backed up and kept in good working order by the support team. Support also involves incident management and investigation when the system fails for some reason or another. Where defects are identified, or additional functionality is required, these will typically be implemented by the application maintenance team, which can sometimes be the support team too. Support, and more importantly maintenance activities, can be quite far-reaching and involve all the activities previously mentioned. Front-end support typically deals with user queries. Part of production readiness is ensuring that the system can be supported and maintained properly.

There are many formal and informal methodologies that can be adopted for software development, ranging from the traditional waterfall-style methods through to agile and spiral development methods. In almost all cases, the methodology will encompass the primary activities shown in Figure 1-1. However, the extent to which the activities are performed is entirely dependent on the methodology.

Figure 1-2 shows a very simple and high-level block plan based on the waterfall development approach. The plan is not complete and the phases do not represent a true scale. The diagram is used simply to highlight the key activities in the project lifecycle and when they are required and/or performed.

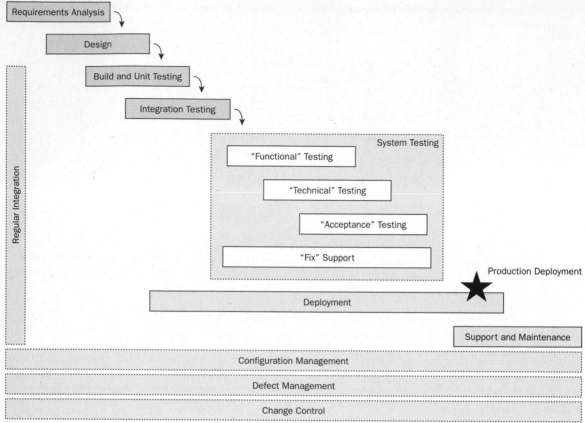

Figure 1-2

The waterfall approach focuses on phase containment. That is, one phase should not begin until the previous one is complete. For example, the development or build phases should not begin until the design phase is complete and signed off. Design should not start until the requirements are agreed and signed off. However, the sample plan shows the activities overlapping — for example, design overlapping with the build and unit test phases. It is very often the case that the development team will start building certain elements of the solution prior to the entire design being complete. For example, framework and utility components can often be started very early in the lifecycle. Functional testing can start when enough of the application is in place. Integration testing can continue while this is ongoing to finalize the design or development of other components. The plan shows functional testing, technical testing, and acceptance testing overlapping with one another, while the development team provides fix support — a very common scenario in the waterfall approach. In the early days of the project lifecycle, one phase drops into the other nicely, or at least it is meant to. It is important that each phase be ready for production (e.g. manufacture), and the waterfall approach provides some time to plan and mobilize for the follow-up phases. For example, during requirements analysis, you can prepare for design; in design, you can prepare for development; and so on.

The waterfall approach can also be used with iterative development, whereby the system is developed over a number of "iterations" or "releases." Each release delivers a certain amount of functionality that realizes business benefits and can be implemented in live service while future releases are under construction. Each release would typically encompass all the activities previously highlighted. There could be many releases being developed in parallel (as shown in Figure 1-3), which can be very difficult to manage.

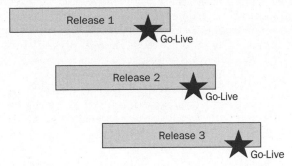

Figure 1-3

The release strategy is not associated with the methodology; it is associated with the project and the business priorities. Multiple releases all running in parallel have an impact on how you mobilize your projects and should be considered early. You'll see throughout this book how multiple releases affect some of the activities that you perform.

Although the high-level plan shown in Figure 1-2 would look somewhat different for an "agile" approach, the activities performed are again similar to those shown in Figure 1-1. A sample construction iteration outline is shown in Figure 1-4. The outline does not follow any specific agile development methodology. It is simply used to demonstrate the similarity in the activities and tasks that are performed during the project lifecycle.

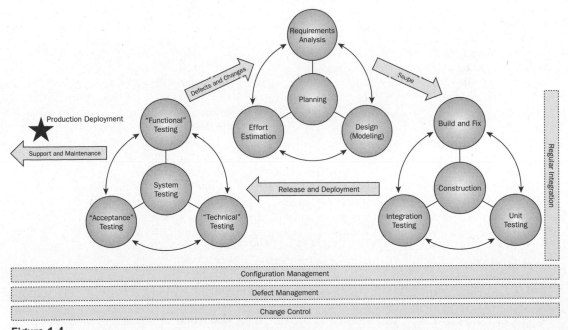

Figure 1-4

Agile software development methodologies focus primarily on developing working software rather than writing documentation (specifications and so forth). The software is developed over multiple iterations. Each of the iterations lasts for a fairly short period of time, usually somewhere between 4 to 8 weeks, and produces a working version of the system. An agile iteration would normally include requirements gathering and prioritization, as well as estimating and planning. A certain amount of design and modeling is also required. The code needs to be developed, tested, and fixed where defects are identified. The output at the end of the iteration doesn't necessarily contain all the features and functions required for live service. However, there's usually a discussion by the stakeholders, as to whether the functionality would realize true business benefits. If so, the project team has further discussions and plans meetings around what needs to be implemented to ensure the software is production-ready and can be deployed into live service. The necessary production readiness activities and requirements are then prioritized for the next iteration. Given that agile development methods focus on developing working software at (almost) every stage, it is even more important that all the applications, environments, processes, tools, and users be ready.

The plans have shown that in both methodologies the activities pretty much remain the same. The degree and quality to which each of the activities is performed ultimately determine the quality and readiness of the outputs. Deciding where to set the quality bar depends entirely on the budget and time constraints of the project, as discussed later. If the right processes and practices are in place, tuned, and understood, then all development can follow the same practice and provide the same level of quality even during fix and later application maintenance.

The applications, environments, processes, and tools that underpin all these activities must be fit for purpose. The development methodology, along with the activities it encompasses, is simply a component of the overall scope of the project. As you can see from the figures, the development methodology ultimately plays its part in the overall *preparation, execution,* and *delivery* of the project.

This chapter, and this book, promote and examine production readiness as it relates to both the actual *development* of a software system and its ultimate *implementation*. It focuses primarily on the activities involved in the project and what developers, architects, and team leaders can do to help ensure a successful outcome. To achieve your goals for production readiness, you need to ensure that:

❑ Your applications are fit for purpose.

❑ Your environments are fit for purpose.

❑ Your processes and tools are fit for purpose.

❑ Your users are trained.

"Fit for purpose" doesn't necessarily mean best of breed. It simply means that everything must be fit for the purpose its intended for. If you were working on next-generation software, it is quite likely that you'd require the best of breed as well.

Applications Must Be Fit for Purpose

A software system doesn't normally just involve a single application — for example, the one you're producing. Many other applications are usually involved. Some will be custom built and others will be off-the-shelf and configured or customized. It is important that all of these be fit for purpose. The system is really only as strong as its weakest links. It doesn't help to say "It's the database. It just keeps falling over." Or "The logs don't actually tell me anything . . . . " All of your applications need to be production-ready and meet all the necessary quality characteristics (which are discussed in the next chapter). Your system is usually built from many custom and third-party applications. This is referred to as the "solution stack." Which applications are included in the final state solution stack will depend entirely on the size and scale of the system being implemented. Figure 1-5 shows a sample final state solution stack for the purposes of this book.

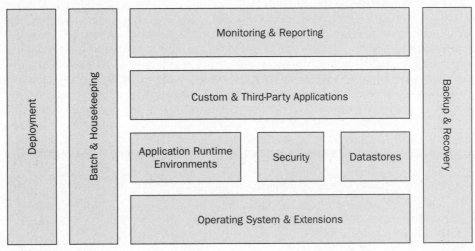

Figure 1-5

You need to ensure that all the chosen applications, as well as the ones you develop, display the necessary quality characteristics. The systems that you implement today will undoubtedly contain the ones you develop yourself. However, they also include many other applications, as described here:

❑ **The operating system and extensions** — This is pretty obvious but it is worth mentioning as everything else sits on top of the operating system and, if it is inherently flawed in some way, this could impact your system. You must determine and understand which aspects and features of the operating system you are using so that you can ensure they are properly tested and evaluated for production readiness. The requirements of the system and the applications need to be mapped to the features of the operating system and extensions. For example, a system may provide failover capabilities and in a Windows environment, some of these could make use of Windows Clustering Services. In this case, you need to ensure they meet the needs of the system. For instance, you might have a requirement whereby the system needs to failover in 20 seconds. If the underlying services do not support this requirement, you're going to have a problem. Understanding all the applications you have in the stack will enable you to determine which ones can be clustered properly. Some third-party applications might not support clustering at all and, as such, alternative failure and recovery solutions need to be put in place to ensure that they are fit for purpose. Furthermore, knowing which specific features of the operating system your application is going to use enables you to better develop your application. For example, knowing which application components will run as services, clustered applications, or a combination of both will enable you to determine what you can and should incorporate during development and testing.

❑ **The Application Runtime Environment and extensions** — This is again pretty obvious, but whichever runtime environments your applications are going to run within must also be fit for

11

purpose. You need to understand the requirements of your applications to determine that the appropriate runtime environment is in place and is tested appropriately. Third-party applications often have specific system requirements that stipulate specific runtime versions to be used. For example, a third-party Customer Relationship Management (CRM) system might stipulate that the .NET Framework version 2.0 should be used. Understanding these requirements will ensure that you have compatible runtimes in place. If your custom applications are built to run on the .NET Framework version 3.5, you might have a problem running both applications on the same machine. Trying to run applications on an inappropriate runtime can cause issues and delays. Choosing applications that can all run on the same version of a runtime is often the best way forward. Understanding the runtime environment enables you to determine what you can incorporate during development. For instance, knowing which application components will run within Internet Information Services (IIS) will help you to determine what you can and should incorporate during development and testing. Furthermore, knowing the exact version of the runtime will enable you to avoid using incompatible, deprecated, or even unsupported features during development, which can also cause issues further down the line.

❑ **The data stores** — Again, this sounds pretty obvious, but the data stores (or databases) will be used by many of the applications and tools you put in place. The database needs to support all the requirements and needs of the applications and tools that use it. You need to map the requirements of the applications to the features of the database. Applications that all use the same database engine can help to reduce costs because you do not have to deal with multiple database technologies, although this is sometimes not possible. Knowing the features of the database that you are going to use will help you to determine what you can and should do during development and testing. For instance, the system might utilize multiple databases to improve performance and separate functionality. All these databases will require some form of housekeeping, purging of old data, re-indexing, and perhaps even recompiling stored procedures for optimal performance. Understanding the types of databases and engines that you are going to use will help you to better design, build, and run your system.

❑ **The security and encryption solutions** — Some systems are often required to use an external security or authentication system — for example, using Microsoft's Active Directory to store user- and role-based information. These applications will again have their own requirements and considerations for design, development, and implementation. It is important that all of these applications be production-ready and scaled appropriately for the entire system. The project may also need to use an isolated encryption server or service. Hardware encryption/decryption is quite common in large-scale secure systems, and it will also have its own considerations and usage scenarios. It is important to understand these external systems because, again, they need to be scaled and used appropriately. A single instance could cause a bottleneck in the final solution, and finding this out toward the go-live date could be a very costly business to rectify.

❑ **The batch solution** — Even in these days of 24/7 availability and service-orientated architectures (SOA), batch can still form a large part of an overall solution. Batch is traditionally thought of as an overnight process, with a lot of number crunching and data processing — and this is still the case in a lot of systems. However, batch covers many different types of jobs. Batch jobs and processes can be as fundamental as clearing out old data or taking the system down in readiness for routine housekeeping. It is important to ensure that the batch solution is fit for purpose and meets all the necessary quality characteristics. The "batch window" (the time in which all batch jobs must be completed) is ever decreasing due to the high availability demands of today's systems. In some situations, the batch window is almost non-existent and the majority of the system must remain up and running while batch or routine maintenance is performed. You need to ensure that your batch solution takes the batch window into account. Understanding the batch solution and its features will help you to develop better batch jobs and frameworks within your applications. Knowing which application components will run as batch or background processes will also determine what you can and should do during design, development, and testing.

❑ **The reporting and analytics solutions** — I've often said, "It's not what you put into a system, it's what you get out of it." The truth is that the two are related. "Rubbish in, rubbish out" is an old saying. The reporting solution and the resultant reports also need to be fit for purpose. The information in the reports is used for many different purposes by many different people. Some reports can be used to make financial or investment decisions; others might be used to assess performance; and some can be used during incident investigation. The reporting solution needs to be understood so that you can determine what you can and should do during design, development, and testing. For instance, reports can often be executed against a replicated database and a report can be as simple as running a SQL query. There are also third-party reporting applications, such as SQL Server Reporting Services which allow you to design, build and execute custom reports. These reporting applications require specific knowledge, not only on how to develop reports but also how to implement the overall reporting solution. Knowing which reports you need to produce and how and where they will run will help you to better design, build, and test your application. There are also many applications that provide web analytics. These applications very often analyze web logs and provide usage and trend analysis reports. The use of these applications also introduces the need for additional development and training. The applications will have their own hardware and software requirements, as well as various deployment considerations. Additional batch jobs or scripts might be required to copy the log files from various servers to a central location for processing, analyzing, and reporting.

❑ **The monitoring solution** — All your applications and infrastructure will require monitoring. You need to know when something goes wrong in order to investigate and correct it. You may also need to know when something good happens in the system. The monitoring solution needs to be fit for purpose. If the monitoring solution is unstable or ineffective, you risk entering a black hole. You don't know what the application is doing because you don't know what the monitoring solution is doing. Monitoring is often divided into different levels and can involve different monitoring applications. Understanding the various applications involved will help you to determine what you can and should do during development and testing. For instance, most monitoring solutions are capable of extracting information from the Windows Event Log, WMI (Windows Management Instrumentation) events, and performance counters, which you can use to provide better monitoring and instrumentation capabilities in your applications.

❑ **The backup (and recovery) solution** — A number of artifacts go along with the applications you put in place, each artifact having its own backup requirements. Understanding what needs to be backed up and when is important. Your backup strategy needs to be fit for purpose. You saw earlier that the batch window is ever decreasing, and backups are generally included in this window. You need to ensure that you back up only what you have to. For instance, if you lose a server, you can generally re-image it or a new one (apply the base operating system, applications and configuration) much faster than restoring from a backup. Furthermore, most companies send backup tapes off-site at regular intervals. You may need to take this into account, as the time it takes to get a backup restored could also cover the time it takes to get the tape back. Understanding the recovery strategy also helps to better design the application for recoverability.

❑ **The deployment solution** — You have many applications that need to be deployed to your different environments. Your deployment solution needs to support all these requirements and needs. If you can't get the software out in the environment, you're not going to be able to run it. Understanding the deployment requirements and applications will help you to better design, build, and test your applications. Automated deployment tools still require configuration and customization, and knowing what needs to be installed and where will help you to better design, build, and test the solution.

There are usually many other applications apart from those listed, and these include applications such as anti-virus software that will also need to be production-ready. However, I am not going to cover all of these in this book. The key point is that all the applications and solutions (including your own) need to be production-ready and display all the necessary quality characteristics in every environment that they are going to be used in.

I've chosen to highlight the preceding areas because it is in these areas that we as software designers and developers can have a major impact, both positively and negatively, during the project lifecycle. Understanding the purpose of these applications, what they are used for, and how they integrate with the system is a key factor which will improve the quality and success of your software. For example, it is very important to understand all the features that are being used in the applications and that they are fully documented (and supported) by the appropriate vendor. It is not uncommon to use *undocumented features* directly or indirectly, which can cause issues for the entire project further down the line. It can lead to applications not being supported. It can lead to upgrade and maintenance issues, as well as different behaviors in testing and production environments.

Environments Must Be Fit for Purpose

Applications don't usually jump straight from the development environment into the production environment without going through other environments and additional testing. Throughout the project lifecycle there are a number of different environments used along the way. Production or live service environments are generally not a single environment either; they can often involve a disaster recovery counterpart and a pre-production counterpart. Every environment you design and use must be fit for purpose and meet the necessary quality characteristics. It is important that each environment is scaled and configured appropriately for its use. In some cases, it is not possible to test certain features of the system without having access to an environment that is sized and scaled appropriately and contains all the required features and functionality. For instance, testing the clustering failure and recovery scenarios requires an environment with multiple clustered servers.

Your environments all have their own requirements and specific uses. Depending on the size and scale of the project, the number of environments will vary and some environments may be shared and used for multiple purposes, which also introduces its own set of considerations. Figure 1-6 shows just a few very basic and common environment configurations.

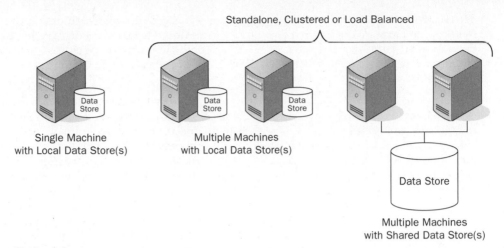

Figure 1-6

Whether an environment is a single machine or multiple machines; whether the servers are standalone, clustered, or load balanced; and whether they have local or shared data stores is entirely dependent on what the environment is being used for. However, the environment configuration will typically bring its own considerations for management, usage, and maintenance. The development methodology will generally dictate the various activities that are performed during the project lifecycle, and these activities will require an environment in which they can be performed (including all the required access, applications, and other required resources). It is possible that some of these activities will be performed in the same environment, which may also need to be considered. The following lists some of the environments required to perform the preceding activities:

❑   **Design environment** — The design environment is used to produce the system and solution designs. It is an environment that is often taken for granted; however, the design environment needs to be fit for purpose and sized and scaled appropriately. Modern software design tools are becoming more and more prevalent and require increasing amounts of memory. The size and scale of the design environments will depend entirely on the design tools and technologies being used. In the race for better quality and reduced timescales, software design tools often produce a lot of code and templates, which can help to reduce the development timescales. However, this would also need to be considered and assessed. It is possible that the code generated by the tool doesn't meet the coding standards of the project. It could be configurable, but then again, it could also require a large amount of rework following its generation. In addition, when a machine doesn't have enough memory or when it is not fast enough to support the design activities, the effects can ripple through the project, affecting development as well as hindering the design activities. There may be multiple design applications, each of which has its own requirements and constraints that need to be considered when defining the design environment.

❑   **Development environment** — The development environment is primarily used to write and fix your code, write reports and batch jobs, configure applications, and perform unit testing and integration testing. It is the environment that you use on a day-to-day basis to get your job done. If this environment is not fit for purpose, you really don't have a chance of developing anything. That is not to say that it has to be the most powerful environment available. It needs to be sized and scaled appropriately. The tools and technologies that are being used determine the development environment requirements. Development machines are often multi-purpose and this needs to be taken into account. For instance, some development machines may be used to develop architecture and application components; some machines may be used to develop batch components or reports; and still other machines may be used to develop packaging and deployment solutions. The development environment needs to support the requirements of its usage and the tools that will be used in it.

❑ **Regular integration environment** — The regular integration and build environment needs to be fit for purpose; otherwise, you're not going to be able to build a complete software release. The build process usually involves compiling everything from the bottom up and includes compiling the tools and tests you've developed as well. Understanding the build process often helps during design and development to ensure that components are placed in the correct libraries or assemblies, as this can affect the way the solution is built, packaged, and deployed. For example, you could have a code generator that generates data access objects from the database. If this is built correctly, it should really use common low-level framework components for logging, tracing, and instrumentation. This really means that the common low-level framework components need to be built before the code generator. But, if these common low-level components rely on some generated database access objects, a cyclic dependency between the components results, which can lead to trouble. The number of applications that need to be built and the dependencies can sometimes require more than one machine to be used to build the various components of the solution. This can often reduce the time it takes to build a complete release. Where this book refers to the *build environment*, it is also essentially referring to the regular integration environment. Builds and releases can be executed on a daily or weekly basis, depending on the project's needs. They can also be taken more frequently, if required. Committing artifacts, building, and regression testing regularly reduce the number of failed or broken builds and issues. There are many practices for the regular integration "process," but they typically stipulate the following three principles:

❑ **Maintaining a source repository and checking in code and artifacts at regular intervals** — Typically, the latest code is taken into the build, although other techniques and labeling can also be employed to mark files as "ready to build." The source code repository stores all the source code and related artifacts.

❑ **Automating the build** — The application build shouldn't really require manual intervention or processes, unless, of course, it fails for some reason. There are a lot of tools to help with automating builds and releases. However, these tools often need configuration and often require custom scripting and development, which needs to be considered.

❑ **Automatically testing the release** — The built software should be tested, and this testing should be automated to reduce manual effort. This is referred to as *regression testing*.

❑ **Configuration management environment** — Although this environment is typically accessed from other environments, I've listed it separately because it is a very important environment and one that does need to be fit for purpose and meet all the necessary quality characteristics. If this environment isn't backed up, there's a possibility of losing all the source code and other project artifacts. If it is unstable or connectivity to it is slow, it could cause delays to the project by increasing down time.

❑ **Regression test environment** — The regression test environment is used to test the application to a *suitable* degree. However, it could be the same environment as the regular integration environment. I much prefer to use a "clean machine" because it ensures that nothing is lingering on the build machine that's not included in the release. It is not always possible to test everything in the regression test environment, so it is good to have an understanding of what the limitations are. Ideally, as much as possible will be tested in this environment, so it needs to be sized and scaled accordingly. The number of tests that need to be run and the time it takes end-to-end will determine whether more than one machine needs to be used to execute different tests in parallel. Wherever possible, all regression testing should be automated to reduce manual effort, and the regression test data should be aligned to that of a functional test and/or technical test to avoid unnecessary issues in other environments or later testing.

❏ **Test environments** — Test environments are where the application will be put through its paces, functionally and technically. You need to ensure that these are fit for purpose and scaled appropriately. Understanding the different test environments will help you to understand your deployment requirements and your test tool requirements. Each test has its own purpose, and as such the applications and environment may be configured in different ways to support these requirements. The size and scale of the project, as well as the methodology, will typically dictate the number of test activities or phases and the environments required to perform them in. Some test environments need to compress multiple days of testing into one day to save time and effort. For instance, lifecycle testing usually involves testing Day 0 (the day prior to go-live), Day 1 (the day of go-live), Day 2 (the day after), and so on. For example, a transaction entered on Day 1 that is not processed (for any reason) may need to be picked up and processed on Day 2. Another example is data expiration whereby a record has a specific expiry date or elapsed time. The application needs to be able to support this level of testing and it can sometimes be as simple as allowing the application to have a specific date/time configuration rather than relying on the system clock or, even worse, having to test in "real time."

❏ **Training environments** — The training environments are often forgotten but provide an invaluable service. Training environments can sometimes be referred to as *sandboxes* — environments where users can experiment using the applications and try out features and functions. The training environments can also help to pull together the training documentation and other associated artifacts. It is important to understand the training requirements and the potential training environment requirements. A training environment can sometimes be as simple as a single desktop machine, although it could also be a full-scale, production-like environment.

❏ **Production environments** — The production environments are ultimately where the system belongs. There may be disaster recovery environments and pre-production environments that can and often are used in the event of failures in the live environment. The pre-production environment can be thought of as a separate test environment because of its usage, although I prefer to include it as a production environment because it is typically more controlled and can be used as a production fall-back in certain situations. You need to ensure that the production environments are fit for purpose. The production environments will generally have their own configuration settings, and sometimes the first time you get to test something is in a production environment. For instance, usernames and credentials will often be different across the production environments. The access rights of these users and credentials need to be clearly stated to avoid unnecessary issues after deployment.

❏ **Operations and support environments** — Although these can be considered part of the production environments, I've listed them separately because they, too, must be fit for purpose. A system that is monitoring another system needs to be fit for purpose. It is no good if the operations and support environments don't meet all the necessary quality criteria. If the monitoring environment isn't robust, you won't be able to tell whether your own system is up and running. If the batch environment isn't robust, you won't be able to perform routine maintenance of your applications and environments.

❑ **Application maintenance environments** — The application maintenance environments are actually the same as the development environments. I've again listed these separately because they must be fit for purpose. Once a system has been handed over to live support and application maintenance, changes will probably need to be made and the environment must be fit for purpose and support all the necessary activities for development, testing, and deployment.

There may be other environments that have specific requirements and uses; however, most environments fit into one of the preceding categories. The key message is that all of your environments need to be understood, sized, and scaled appropriately, and display the required quality characteristics to ensure that you can smoothly progress through the project lifecycle. In addition, not all of them need to be on separate hardware. There are many situations where the same physical hardware is used for multiple activities, which also has its own considerations.

Processes and Tools Must Be Fit for Purpose

Throughout the project lifecycle there are a number of processes that need to be followed and a number of tools that are associated with them. Each process has its own purpose and often there are tools associated with them to enhance productivity. If the tools don't work or do not display the same quality characteristics of a production-ready solution, they can negatively impact the ability to perform a given task. In the same way, the processes need to be robust and streamlined to avoid unnecessary work or re-work. Figure 1-1 showed a number of different activities and processes that will be performed on a typical software development project. Each process will typically involve the use of a number of different tools and technologies. The following processes and tools must be fit for purpose:

❑ **Requirements analysis and tracking processes and tools** — You need to capture your requirements and constraints, and they need to be documented, agreed on, and accessible. You need to ensure that the requirements also capture the relevant quality characteristics to avoid issues later on. The appropriate processes and tools need to be in place to ensure that the solution requirements are tracked and implemented accordingly. It should be possible to trace your requirements through all the project artifacts to ensure that all have been captured and implemented accordingly.

❑ **Design processes and tools** — The design process involves ensuring that your requirements are validated and that your designs meet those requirements. The tools that you use can be as simple as diagrams and documents. Alternatively, you may be using some advanced Model Driven Engineering (MDE) or CASE (Computer-Aided Software Engineering) tools and techniques. MDE and CASE tools are used to model the software design. In most cases, these tools can be used to generate code and other artifacts, such as database scripts and even documentation. The tools you use must be fit for purpose and not impact your ability to design software. The process you are going to use for design needs to be in place, along with the appropriate review checkpoints. Your estimates need to take your process into account to avoid potential overruns or missed milestones. Design covers the application functionality, the hardware architecture, and the software architecture. Understanding the requirements and the design is crucial during the development process. That does not mean things are not going to change as you move on, but it ensures that everyone is working from the same page. If things change, you will need to update your designs, so the tools and processes need to be fit for this purpose as well.

❑ **Development processes and tools** — The development process is where you are going to do your coding. You've seen that development involves architecture, application, batch, reporting, deployment, and tools development. These areas may involve a variety of different tools and it is important that all the development tools and processes be fit for purpose. Timescales can be increased dramatically by not having the right tools and processes in place. Your tools need to display the required quality characteristics of a production-ready application. To avoid slippages, your estimates need to take into account your development tools and processes. Understanding the development requirements is paramount to supporting the development activities. You also need to ensure that the components you develop during construction are fit for purpose and ready to build; otherwise, you could experience issues when you submit your development work into the build process.

❑ **Configuration management processes and tools** — The tools and processes that you use to manage your source code and other development and test artifacts need to be in place and fit for purpose. Not being able to check in or check out can have an impact on development and test timescales. The version/source control system may also have its own database and housekeeping recommendations or requirements. It is important that these are also understood to ensure that the source control system is kept in good shape and doesn't adversely affect your ability to develop and test. Releases are often developed in parallel, involving branching and merging activities. It is important that all these factors are understood to ensure that the source control tools and processes support these requirements as well as all the other required quality characteristics. If implemented incorrectly, branching and merging can be a painful business, so the process needs to be defined, understood, and executed well to avoid failures and delays.

❑ **Regular integration processes and tools** — It is important to define and understand this process so that you avoid failed builds and don't have to go back around the loop. The tools you use to build a release must be fit for purpose and have the required quality characteristics. If you can't build a release, you can't get it into the deployment process. Ensuring that you provide ready-to-build components and artifacts is vital to the successful building of a release. You need to ensure that your components work with the latest versions, and that your components are tested and that the tests work with the latest versions. Submitting incorrect or non-ready-to-build components has a negative impact on the build process and your ability to get the appropriate components into the deployment process.

❑ **Deployment processes and tools** — The deployment process covers everything from including all the final artifacts in a deployment package to getting releases into the environments with all the correct set-ups and configurations ready for use. It is important that the tools you use are fit for purpose and that you get your software out where it is required. The requirements of the environments need to be understood to ensure that the relevant artifacts are deployed, including binaries, tests, documentation, and data (including base data and test data). A lot of time can be wasted installing and re-installing releases because of incorrect options or settings being selected.

❑ **Testing processes and tools** — The testing process is where the software will be tested. It is important that the tools and processes used to test the software be fit for purpose. Simple things such as trying to bring the environment up can impact testing negatively. You need to ensure that you have all the productivity tools and processes in place so that testing can continue without environment or process issues. That's not to say that there will not be defects in your code, but it will ensure smoother testing of your software without unnecessary issues, and help you to find the real issues to concentrate on and fix.

❑ **Defect tracking processes and tools** — Software is very rarely defect-free, although we strive to achieve it. Having a good defect tracking system in place helps you understand the defects you need to take into account and plan for. It is important that this system is also fit for purpose and displays the required quality characteristics. The defect tracking system is often customized to the project's needs, so understanding these needs helps greatly. These needs will also change as the project progresses, so you need to be able to react to this and change accordingly. Understanding the defect tracking system and what information needs to be included in a defect will help to improve your ability to react to them. There's nothing worse than trying to work on fixing a defect and finding that there isn't enough information to go on.

❑ **Change control processes and tools** — Things change as you move through the development lifecycle, and having a good change control process and the tools to support it is a key factor for success. Understanding and implementing a formal change control process and adhering to it will enable you to avoid unnecessary delays and improve the transparency of changes. Delays are often suffered during development by working on out-of-date information. Sometimes it is better to complete a development piece prior to taking updates into account, but knowing that it is going to change assists in planning and estimating and improves the entire process.

❑ **Application support and maintenance processes and tools** — Your system needs to be supported in the event that any issues arise that need to be fixed. This is not just for your own applications; it includes third-party applications, as well. You need to have the right processes and tools in place to assist with support queries. You can greatly improve the supportability of the applications you develop; however, third-party applications are not always the same. Understanding the support requirements of these will help you to define your support processes and the productivity tools that you should put in place. I've never had a support call in which the support person didn't ask for the version numbers of the operating system, patches, the hardware it is running on, the version of the application, the logs files, and so on. These are basic support requirements, and having robust and streamlined processes to obtain this information will help you better react to support calls and incidents.

There are potentially many other processes and tools involved during software development and implementation. However, the preceding list captures all the processes discussed in this book.

Users Must Be Trained

It is important that all the users of your system be educated correctly and sufficiently. There are a number of users of the system and each has his or her own agenda and work to do. Understanding the requirements of your users is important to the success of your project.

Education can be as simple as providing productivity guides and documentation, or it can be instructor-led training courses on the environments, applications, languages, and/or technologies. The processes that you put in place need to be well-documented so that everyone understands them and, more importantly, follows them.

A lot of different people and roles are involved in a software implementation project. Figure 1-7 shows just some of the roles and responsibilities that can be involved in an end-to-end software implementation project.

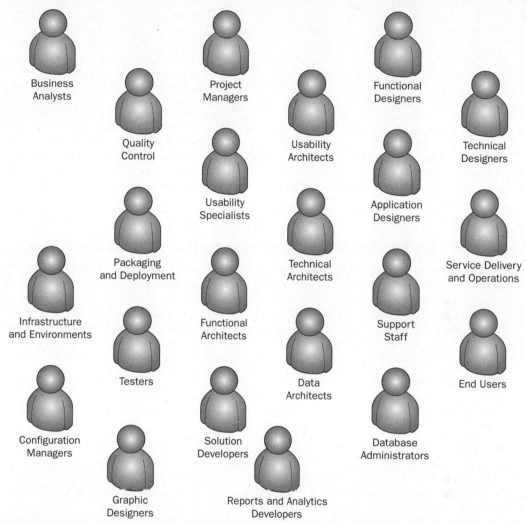

Figure 1-7

Although Figure 1-7 doesn't depict every person and role, as you can see, it is possible for a number of different people to be involved in the overall project, all of which need to understand the applications, tools, and processes that they use. Furthermore, in many cases a single individual can perform many roles, which could require knowledge of many different applications, tools, and processes.

It is important that everyone involved in the project know how to use the *applications, environments, processes*, and *tools* that they are going to use throughout the project. The documentation and education that you put in place will generally be multi-purpose — that is, it will be used by a variety of different people. There are, of course, documents that are specific to a particular process or technology and, as such, target a particular group of users. Understanding your users and their needs is an important part of production readiness, and having access to the relevant documentation is equally important. Your project will have a variety of documentation, including:

❑ **Project documentation and guides** — This set of documentation includes a variety of materials, including the project overview and business case, the requirements and specifications (both functional and technical), architecture diagrams and documentation, the project plans, and the organization structure. These documents are important for you to understand what you are building and why. It is important that they contain all the relevant information to allow you to do your job properly.

❑ **Application and technology guides** — This set of documentation covers all your applications and technologies. Third-party applications come with their own documentation that can be supplemented with your own additions and extensions. These may be as simple as installation and configuration guides. These documents need to contain the information necessary to ensure that whoever is using them can get up to speed quickly and efficiently. For example, one such guide would be about how to configure application-specific clustering, including the specific naming standards that must be adhered to and which prerequisites must be in place.

❑ **Environment guides** — The environment guides provide an overview of the environments you are using, how they are scaled, what they are used for and when. The information can come from many sources, such as architecture diagrams and other specifications. You need to understand the environments and how to use them, which may be as simple as knowing how to get access to the functional test environment. The important thing is that the information is available and includes everything required to use the environment effectively.

❑ **Process and productivity guides** — There are a number of processes that will be created and followed during the project. It is important that these processes be understood to ensure that everyone is working from the same page and understands what to do and when to do it. You will have a development process, a build process, a unit test process, an integration test process, as well as many more throughout the project. The process guides need to document the process and procedures in plain language to ensure that everyone can follow them.

❑ **Tool guides** — Understanding the tools, what they are used for, how to use them, and when to use them is important. This set of documentation covers all your tools and the specifics of how you are going to use them for your own purposes. These documents may cover how to use the source control system, how to use the defect tracking system, and how to use the unit test tools and integration test tools. The important thing is that all the tools are well-documented so that users of these tools can understand their purpose and use them effectively.

❑ **Completion reports and handover documents** — Part of the overall development cycle involves producing completion reports. Depending on the methodology chosen, each phase or activity may involve a hand-off between phases or teams. The completion criteria for the activity or phase will need to be met, and the completion report documents how this has been achieved — for example, documenting the test results, reviews and profiling results. The handover documentation will typically also include the number of defects that have been raised and addressed within the current activity. It may also include outstanding defects or other items that have not been addressed and need to be carried over to a further release.

❑ **Release notes** — Although release notes strictly belong within the handover documentation category, I've pulled them out separately as they are very important documents. In summary, a release note typically includes the current version, system requirements, installation instructions, and resolved issues as well as known issues. Whenever you produce a release, an associated release note should be produced to go along with it. Although automated deployment tools might be available to help with the installation, the release note still needs to show the contents of the overall release.

There will probably be other useful documents that are produced throughout the project lifecycle. However, I've chosen the preceding because during design, development, and early testing, you can have a dramatic impact on their production and readiness. As this book progresses, you'll see how some of these documents are used and the people that will use them.

Having these documents and guides in place helps to reduce the time and effort you spend on education and one-on-one training. You might have many developers or testers starting on your project, and being in a position to provide them with an induction pack will greatly help to reduce your costs and improve their readiness to start developing or testing. All the documentation that you produce needs to be fit for purpose to ensure that everyone is ready to do their jobs. The documentation will be used throughout the project and will form a valuable part in the handover to live service.

It is also important to note that I'm not necessarily suggesting that all of this information be captured in formal "documents." Online help files, wikis, and other electronic-based methods can be employed to reduce overheads and improve the overall level of communication, collaboration, and education within the team. A *wiki* is really a set of web pages that can be read and/or updated by project resources. A wiki can often save a lot of documentation effort by focusing on the actual information that's required by the reader. I personally like guides and certain other documentation to be very article-based and quick to the point, and to provide all the necessary information and step-by-step instructions to perform a task.

I'm a firm believer in the "project portal" concept. It is great to have a single project website where people can go to find out information about the project, which can include status, plans, designs, specifications, process guides, training guides, induction guides, and so on. In my opinion, the project portal is essentially a one-stop shop for everyone and everything to do with the project. I try to think of the content as "day one developer," which basically just means that I imagine what a new resource would need to get up-to-speed when they first come to the project, aside from access and an environment to work in. It is not a full time-and-motion study, but it works very well to ensure that inducting a new resource is efficient and successful. If a new resource can get up-to-speed quickly, all resources should be up-to-speed. A well-laid-out portal can provide a rich user experience and ensure that everyone has access to the latest status, plans, information, templates, and project documentation. Setting up and maintaining a project portal, however, offer up their own challenges that need to be factored into the scope, budgets, and timescales. And, of course, it too, needs to be fit for purpose and production-ready.

Why Is Production Readiness Important?

Failure is *not* an option. I can only assume that almost all projects start off with this stance. Most of the projects that I've worked on certainly have. The trouble is that a number of projects do fail or are seen to be a failure in the eyes of customers or stakeholders. The question is not "Why do they fail?" The ultimate question is "How do we succeed?" A cursory search on the Internet would yield an abundance of results on both these subjects. However, I'm not going to go into the statistics and findings of these studies. I'm going to provide my personal point of view on what I think are the main causes of failure and what I think are the key factors for success. To answer the second question "How do we succeed?" it is often necessary to examine your past mistakes, understand what went wrong, and put measures in place so that it doesn't happen again — which is just commonsense. In recent times, there have been some very newsworthy software outages, some of which have cost millions of dollars in lost revenues and crashing stock prices. Mission-critical systems can't sustain serious outages in live service. In some extreme circumstances, the outages have cost many high-ranking personnel their jobs and sometimes their careers. It is not always so bad, however. On the less extreme side, a project can be seen as a failure because of delays and budget overruns. A successful project is typically referred to as one that delivers all the required scope, on time and on budget. To achieve this goal requires you fully to understand the scope, timescales, and budgets for the project.

> *My first experience of "commercial" software development: I remember back to around the mid-80s when I wrote a program for a small business in my hometown. The program was written on a BBC Model B computer in BBC BASIC. The owner of the firm told me what he wanted the program to do, and I thought I could write it in a couple of days and said I'd do it for £50. For a couple of evenings I wrote the initial version and tested it (as best as I could) on the machine in his office. The following day he came in and "played around" with it. When I arrived that evening, he dictated his "improvements" and it took me literally weeks to include them. After which, I never heard from him again and I didn't get any more money for doing the additional work! I'm not trying to be funny, but the moral of the story is to get it right up front (or at least as best you can) because success is not solely based on customer satisfaction! It can cost an awful lot of time and effort to satisfy the customer. In a fix-priced agreement it is important to understand the implications of this very early on.*

It is a fact that some software implementation projects fail. There are many different reasons for why these projects fail. Sometimes a project is simply scrapped because it doesn't have a truly viable business case. Others are scrapped because of budget cuts, contractual disputes, and poor implementation. In my personal experience on the shop floor, projects fail or are seen to be a failure for these three reasons:

❑ **Poor scope** — Scope really refers to the requirements, constraints, and quality of the project, software, or even task. When the scope is poorly defined, the outcome can't be assessed effectively, the effects of which can have far-reaching consequences. Poorly defined or missing requirements as well as changes in scope lead to "scope creep." This can contribute to a project's failure by increasing costs and timescales and potentially delaying go-live. Changes or corrections to scope can also be caused by an incorrect or erroneous interpretation. For instance, consider what a response might be to the following extreme statement: "You told me you wanted an online store. You never actually said you wanted it to run on UNIX." Interpretation only works when the recipient of the final product actually agrees with what has been interpreted and delivered. If not, it has the potential to cause major disputes. More often than not, requirements and constraints are missing or misinterpreted and not sufficiently clarified, which results in an incorrect or incomplete solution. Furthermore, assumptions, like interpretation, can also lead to incorrect or incomplete deliveries, for example, "Oh, I thought that *you* were going to write that bit," or "I assumed it only needed to work with Internet Explorer."

Poor scope is not just about the functionality of the software, either. Poorly defined processes and tasks also affect the overall outcome of a project. For example, not stipulating the relevant quality criteria and reviews can also affect the final result. Having a well-defined and agreed scope will help to avoid these types of common problems. The quality criteria apply to all components of the delivery, including documentation, source code, and all other areas and artifacts. For instance, a technical specification can be seen as defective or sub-standard if it doesn't include certain elements, such as class diagrams, interaction diagrams, and component walkthroughs. The developer may not be in a position to develop the solution without such information. The impact and effort to include these items can then have a big impact on the budget and timescales. In this example, the elements that need to be included in the document are simply part of the scope of work. Minor failings can build up over time and cause overruns and slippages, which can ultimately result in the project being seen as a failure. Rework is a costly business. For the purposes of this book, the term "scope" also includes all the applications, environments, processes, and tools. I'm also bundling customer and/or stakeholder involvement under this heading because without the appropriate level of involvement, it is nearly impossible to define (and agree on) the appropriate scope for a project, solution, or task. A very clear scope allows for much better preparation, execution, and delivery.

❑ **Poor planning and execution** — This heading includes a variety of different tasks and the environments they need to be performed in. One of the most common planning errors is setting or agreeing to unrealistic timescales. Although aggressive timescales can sometimes positively and constructively stretch project resources, unrealistic timescales can often break them. Unrealistic timescales can totally compromise quality and functionality. For instance, the documentation may not be as complete as it could be, there may be a major rush to start coding, and the quality may be dropped over the race to deliver. In this scenario, the plans are based on when a task needs to be finished and not how long it will realistically take to perform (according to a reasonable set of estimates). Plans should be based on realistic estimates, and the estimates should be based on a very clear scope and understanding. Furthermore, just because one particular person can complete a given task to the specific scope in a given timeframe, doesn't necessarily mean that someone else can.

This leads to another common planning error: inappropriate resource planning and staffing — that is, insufficient numbers of resources, assigning the wrong resources to the tasks, or using insufficiently trained personnel. Other typical planning mistakes are — failing to include all the required tasks in the plan, overlapping tasks without fully understanding their dependencies, and not building in the appropriate review, hand-over, and potential corrective activities. When the plans are agreed and in place, they need to be executed. That doesn't mean that the plan won't change — you often need to make adjustments — it just means that there is a solid way forward and changes can be incorporated according to the agreed process. It is also not worth denying that poor workmanship can lead to poor execution. There are a lot of reasons why certain resources don't perform very well. It can certainly happen when the resources aren't sufficiently trained or qualified. Therefore, it is important to ensure that all resources be sufficiently trained and educated to perform the required tasks. Finally, unnecessary downtime can occur when there are conflicts and major differences of opinion. Disputes can often cause delays and overruns when rework is needed. The entire team needs to understand and subscribe to the scope and the plans.

❑ **Poor quality** — Poor quality can occur for many reasons, including insufficient quality controls and insufficient scope, insufficient planning and "squeezed" timescales (as previously mentioned). Inappropriate resource allocation can also lead to poor quality — for example, using inexperienced resources when experienced personnel are required. The term "quality" refers to more than just code quality; it encompasses all the components of the delivery. If the technical specification is poor, it typically results in delays and multiple iterations before it is acceptable. In the worst case, it results in a poor implementation, especially when the gaps or errors are not caught early enough.

Poor quality is generally uncovered during testing, reviews and/or checkpoints. When testing and reviews take place early and regularly, it is much easier to manage the outcome and corrective workload. There's a very good opportunity for planning the corrective actions that need to be taken — for instance, categorizing the defects into their appropriate severity, prioritizing in order of implementation, and/or justifying and discounting them. Re-work and updates can be a costly and time-consuming task, especially when a lot of issues are discovered and even more so when they're discovered very late in the process. It can be even more costly when the issues are raised by an external body, which could be the customer or another organization and perhaps sometimes even both. There are costs and implications associated with the time and effort required to go through the issues, assess and agree on them (where necessary), and then plan and address them. It might not be possible to address all the issues within the timescales and/or budgets, which could incur severe commercial penalties and/or delay go-live dates. The implications can be very far-reaching and it is really not worth getting caught in these situations. Defining the scope early, and understanding and agreeing on the criteria for quality and regular check-pointing and correction will avoid unnecessary disputes. Quality is an extremely important part of the overall implementation, which is why I truly believe it is a component of scope. A poorly defined scope, that doesn't encompass quality, can lead to a perception of failure. Testing will uncover defects. If it didn't, you wouldn't need to test. Testing should really be done early and frequently to ensure that as many defects as possible are captured and addressed (where necessary) as early as possible.

The Production-Readiness "Process"

Production readiness is all-encompassing. It includes everything to do with your system and ensuring that you are ready for development as well as live service through all of your processes and practices. It is not actually a formal process. It is really just a collection of foundation principles for successful software development and implementation, including:

❑ Good preparation

❑ Good execution

❑ Good delivery

These are all just umbrella terms that encompass many discrete and varied tasks, although they all play a vital role in the production readiness process, which simply underpins these primary success factors by specifying the steps — *prepare, execute,* and *deliver* (see Figure 1-8).

Figure 1-8

"Why do you need to prepare? Just do it!" Although this might seem like a good idea, racing ahead unprepared can cause major issues further down the line. There's no point in hiring a bunch of developers when there aren't enough development machines for them to work on. Similarly, it would be dangerous to start development on an application when the architecture and frameworks aren't sufficiently in place or the designs are inadequate. There's clearly a balance to the amount of upfront preparation that should be performed on a project, iteration, or task. However, the preparation really does need to consider what must be in place and what the scope is to ensure effective execution and delivery. You look at this in more detail later.

It is important to do the most critical upfront work as soon as possible to ensure that everything is fit for purpose and ready when it is required. This book places its focus on the elements of scope, execution, and delivery. As the book progresses, you'll see more on the tasks and activities that underpin these high-level, production-readiness steps. In the meantime, the following provides a brief overview of the steps in the process:

❑   **Prepare** — This step involves planning and defining the scope, including the applications, environments, processes, and tools, as well as defining the associated inputs, standards, checks, and outputs. It covers the definition of the acceptance criteria between one process and another. It also includes the definition of timescales and costs associated with each of these elements and the necessary checks and governance required for them.

❑   **Execute** — This step encompasses the actual execution of the plans and processes. It is the physical work being carried out on the production line (including any additional planning). For construction, this would cover the development team accepting inputs, producing designs, having them reviewed and agreed, coding, testing, packaging, releasing, and so forth. For testing this would include all the inputs required to produce test scripts, execute tests, and so on.

❑   **Deliver** — This step refers to the hand-off between processes and teams. In terms of software implementation, this would ultimately include handing over the solution to a support team or an application maintenance team once the system is in live service. Hand-offs are performed at many points in the development cycle, and one of the key areas is handing over a solution to a test team for testing or acceptance.

The activities should not be overly prescriptive, nor should they slow down the overall process. The processes and activities should always aim to reduce overheads and improve the performance of the overall project and the team. The processes that are implemented should be reviewed regularly and continually improved.

The Project Management Triangle

The commercial world of software implementation is typically all about squeezing as much as possible into given budgets and timescales. It is very rare that you're given a free hand and unlimited budgets to do what you want. Projects are typically constrained by a set of defined boundaries — *scope*, *budget*, and *timescales*, as shown in Figure 1-9. This is generally referred to as the *project management triangle*.

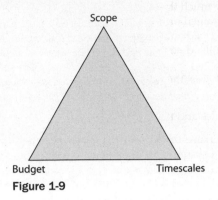

Figure 1-9

The figure shows the traditional project constraints and the axes are defined as follows:

❑ **Scope** — Refers to the requirements (functional and non-functional), constraints, and quality characteristics. In some cases, quality is treated as a separate dimension; however, as I've mentioned before, I treat quality as nothing more than a component of the overall scope.

❑ **Timescales** — Refers to the overall project timeline, from start to finish.

❑ **Budget (or costs)** — Refers to the amount of money available or required to complete the project.

The figure is drawn as an equilateral triangle, which simply reinforces the basic premise that changes to a single axis will affect the other two in a similar and consistent way. Although this point could very well be argued, an increase in the scope of a project will generally *increase* costs and timescales, whereas a reduction in scope will generally *decrease* costs and timescales (see Figure 1-10).

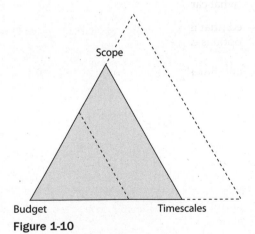

Figure 1-10

It is really just a matter of how much the changes affect the overall project. There's a theory that *two of these boundaries* can be constrained or fixed, but not all three (especially when initiating and planning a project). When everything is agreed and finalized, all three boundaries are typically set and the project is then underway. The following list details some of the various options when setting these boundaries:

❑ If the scope is fixed (that is, the solution must meet all the specified scope), the following options can be assessed:

  ❑ Both the timescales and the budgets must be aligned according to the scope.

  ❑ The timescale remains fixed and the budget is set to allow for more resources and parallel activities. This works on the principle that by using more people, the tasks can be done in a shorter timeframe. However, this in itself is sometimes challenging to achieve, given staffing and task dependencies. It is also possible that the budget or costs can be balanced elsewhere if performing the specific tasks in a shorter timeframe will reduce costs further down the line or in other areas.

  ❑ The budget remains fixed and the timescales are set accordingly. This generally works on the assumption that by using fewer resources, the task (or tasks) will take longer to complete but the costs will remain the same. For example, if you assume each resource costs $100 per day, a task (or set of tasks) that takes five person days will cost $500. If the task can be completed with five people, it could theoretically be completed in a single day. Using only a single resource, it would take five days. However, in both cases the cost is the same.

❑ If the timescales are constrained (that is, the software must be delivered on a specified date), the following options can be assessed:

  ❑ Both the scope and the budgets must be aligned according to the timescales.

  ❑ The scope remains fixed and the budget is set accordingly — again, using more (or less) people to achieve a particular result.

  ❑ The budget remains fixed and the scope is set accordingly. This works on the basis of delivering only what can be achieved within the timeframe and budget.

❑ If the budgets are fixed (that is, the software must be delivered within a specific amount of costs), the following options can be assessed:

  ❑ Both the scope and timescales are aligned accordingly.

  ❑ The scope remains fixed and the timescales are set accordingly. This works because you use far fewer resources over a longer period of time to deliver the appropriate scope.

  ❑ The timescales are fixed and the scope is set accordingly. Again, this works because you set the scope to what can be delivered within the budget and timescales.

If a successful project is considered to be one that delivers *all the scope, on time* and *on budget*, to ensure this, the scope, budget and timescales need to be very clearly defined and understood. In my opinion, it really all starts with scope. Figure 1-11 shows the high-level components of scope related to software development and implementation.

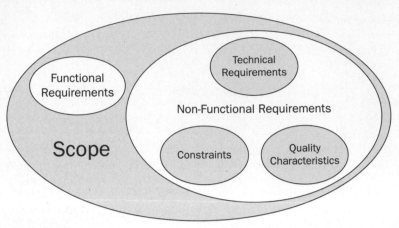

Figure 1-11

The scope will typically dictate the budgets and timescales. If the budgets and timescales are reduced, this could have an impact on the scope. I know I've labored on this point, but clearly defining the entire scope will ensure that everyone is on the same page and under no delusions or assumptions about what will be delivered and how it will be delivered, and its quality characteristics. The following provides a brief overview of the components of scope:

❑ **Functional requirements** — As the name implies, functional requirements define a set of functions for a software system, application, or its components. Functional requirements describe the functional behavior of the system. Functional requirements often include business rules, calculations, and processing requirements that describe how the software must work or behave from a functional perspective. Requirements are often born out of use-cases and high-level analysis and design activities.

❑ **Non-functional requirements** — Non-functional requirements, which can also be referred to as *technical requirements*, typically stipulate criteria for how the software should execute — for example, the system's expected performance characteristics, resource utilization, or security measures. Non-functional requirements are often referred to as the "ilities" primarily because they all end in "ility" — for example, reliability, scalability, availability, usability, maintainability, and so on. There's a fine line between functional requirements, technical requirements, and the quality characteristics of a software system. In fact, non-functional requirements are very often referred to as the *quality goals, quality attributes,* or *quality characteristics*. These types of overlapping terms and meanings are rife within the software industry, so I feel that it is really not worth getting hugely hung up on labeling and categorizing them and trying to define a truly perfect boundary. However, in terms of a software implementation project, the technical requirements could encompass execution qualities such as reliability and availability, whereas the quality characteristics could include the static and evolutionary aspects such as documentation, maintainability, and scalability. In the end, as far as I'm concerned, it is all just scope — functional, technical, or otherwise.

❑ **Quality characteristics** — The quality characteristics often encompass the non-functional requirements of a system. For instance, code quality can be seen as a technical or non-functional requirement and can be categorized under the readability or maintainability characteristics. But what really defines code quality? How is it measured, proven, and accepted? Chapter 2 examines some of the common quality characteristics and how they apply to not just the software but the entire system (which, as you've already seen, encompasses *applications, environments* and *processes,* and *tools*). For example, a manual process that doesn't "scale" can easily impact a project. It is not just about the software, although the final application not being able to scale for future demand can also impact the project.

❏ **Constraints** — Requirements can also be referred to as *constraints,* so you again face overlapping terminology. However, I categorize requirements as the business rules, the functionality and features of the system, as well as the technical aspects of the system. Constraints, on the other hand, are restrictions on the degree of flexibility and freedom around implementing the system. For example, constraints could include, cost and budget, location, environment, tools and technologies, methodologies and process, resources, and timescales. A simple rule-of-thumb that I use when differentiating a requirement from a constraint is to determine whether it pertains to *how* and *when* the system will be implemented, as opposed to *what* is being implemented and *what* it needs to do.

While it is a very good idea to categorize all the various attributes of scope, it is actually far more important to ensure that they are captured, agreed, and fully understood. To help achieve success, your *preparation, execution,* and *delivery* need to capture all the attributes within your *scope, timescales,* and *budgets.*

Summary

In this first chapter you've seen that production readiness relates to both software development and implementation. It is about the quality and readiness of everything to do within the project and solution. If you're unfamiliar with some of the terms used in this chapter, don't worry — they'll be discussed further as the book progresses. Your application is just one part of an entire system, and you've seen what the individual parts can consist of, how they can be used, and who can use them. As you continue reading, you will start to see how everything fits together. However, keeping these factors for success in the back of your mind will help you to improve your own capabilities, help others to improve theirs, and should positively impact the overall outcome of the project.

The following are the key points to take away from this chapter:

❏ **There are a core set of "development" and "implementation" activities.** Irrespective of the chosen development approach, there are a core set of activities that are performed during the project lifecycle. The activities discussed in this chapter include:

    ❏ Requirements definition

    ❏ Design

    ❏ Development

    ❏ Regular integration

    ❏ Deployment

    ❏ Testing

    ❏ Configuration management

    ❏ Change control

- ❏ Defect management
- ❏ Support and maintenance

❏ **Failure is *not* an option.** Good planning, good execution, and good delivery will help to ensure successful development and implementation of software projects. As soon as the project starts, you're in a "production mode" of some sort, and any tools, technologies, environments, or processes that are being used need to be fit for purpose to avoid unnecessary delays moving forward. Considering all the production readiness and development readiness criteria will help you to *prepare* better, *execute* better, and *deliver* better, resulting in a truly fit-for-purpose system.

❏ **Clearly define the scope of the project, solution, or task.** Only when you know the true scope of a project, system, or task can you really determine what needs to be done, how it can be done, and the associated budgets and timescales. A successful project *delivers all the required scope on time and on budget*. Scope should include all the following for all your applications, environments, processes, and tools:

- ❏ Functional requirements
- ❏ Technical requirements
- ❏ Quality characteristics
- ❏ Constraints

❏ **Production readiness is all-encompassing.** It is is not just about producing production-ready code and testing it thoroughly. It encompasses everything to do with your system. You need to ensure that everything is fit for purpose and ready for production usage.

❏ **Applications must be fit for purpose.** Identify as many of the other applications early in the lifecycle, as this will help to ensure that the solution stack is well-defined and all the appropriate steps can be taken to assess, design, develop, document, and implement them. It is also important to understand all the features and functions of the applications being used, and that they are documented and supported to avoid potential issues later in the cycle. The applications highlighted and discussed in this chapter include:

- ❏ Operating system and extensions
- ❏ Application Runtime Environments and extensions
- ❏ The data stores
- ❏ The security and encryption solution
- ❏ The batch solution
- ❏ The reporting and analytics solutions
- ❏ The monitoring solution
- ❏ The backup and recovery solutions
- ❏ The deployment solutions
- ❏ Your own custom applications

❏ **Environments must be fit for purpose.** Key environments should be identified early. The environments should be sized and scaled appropriately for their purpose and ready to use when they are required. The environment includes all the necessary hardware, software, access, and networking components. The environments highlighted and discussed in this chapter include:

❏ The design environments

❏ The development environments

❏ The regular integration and build environment

❏ The configuration management environment

❏ The regression test environments

❏ The test environments

❏ The training environments

❏ The production environments (including pre-production and disaster recovery)

❏ The support and operations environments

❏ The application maintenance environments

❏ **Processes and tools must be fit for purpose.** Ensure that all the processes that need to be followed are documented and fully understood. Where necessary, tools should be used to improve the overall performance and outcome of the process. The processes and tools discussed in this chapter support the "development" and "implementation" activities.

❏ **Users must be trained.** Your users include many different people, including designers, developers, infrastructure and release personnel, testers, support staff, as well as end users. Each of these user groups needs to be trained, and there's a variety of documentation that can be put in place to help with this. Your documentation needs to cover all your applications, environments, processes, and tools — not just the application you are developing. Documentation doesn't need to be exhaustive, but it does need to be fit for purpose, and a project portal, online help, and wikis can help to speed up its production and usage. The high-level user groups and roles discussed in this chapter include:

❏ Business analysts

❏ Designers

❏ Developers

❏ Testers

❏ Configuration management

❏ Release management

❏ Service delivery and operations

❏ Application maintenance

❏ Customers and business users

The types of documentation and education material discussed in this chapter include:

❏ Project documentation and guides (including requirements, quality, and constraints)

❏ Application and technologies guides (covering all your applications)

❑   Environment guides (covering all your environments)

❑   Process and productivity guides (covering all your processes)

❑   Tools guides (covering all your tools)

❑   Completion reports

❑   Release notes

❑   **Your systems involve multiple applications, environments, processes and tools.** You need to ensure that all of them are industrial strength and meet all the required quality characteristics for production readiness.

The following chapter examines some of the quality characteristics that should be considered for all your environments, applications, processes, tools, and documentation.

2

The Quality Landscape

No software system is completely and utterly defect-free. The testing and reviewing that you perform will always highlight defects and deficiencies in your outputs. The level of testing and reviewing that you actually perform and when you perform it dictate how many defects can be highlighted and fixed before the system is put into live service or production. The preparation, execution, and delivery that you perform should really ensure that quality is maintained throughout the project. The software quality landscape encompasses the categories and measures for defining and maintaining software quality. The measures are intended to reduce the number of defects that are found out late in the process and to produce high-quality code and artifacts throughout the project. There's no doubt that quality has costs associated with it, but the extent to which it actually costs needs to be understood, controlled, and minimized without compromising the final result. I mentioned in the previous chapter that I consider quality to be a component of scope, and the software quality characteristics contain the high-level categories for each of the quality areas. The total number of defects and their scale should be reduced as much as possible during construction to avoid unnecessary delays, excessive numbers of defects during formal testing, and cost overruns. To support these principles, you need to implement and employ tools and processes that help to maintain quality throughout the project.

This chapter is organized into the following sections:

❑   **The Quality Characteristics** — Provides an overview of the individual quality characteristics, including correctness and completeness, usability, accessibility, reliability and stability, performance, efficiency, availability, integrity and security, operability and supportability, deployability, configurability, maintainability, readability, reusability, modularity, flexibility and extensibility, and testability.

❑   **Why Quality (and Scope) Matter** — Takes a look at a robust construction phase and the activities performed to get a realistic picture of what's involved in quality construction. This section also covers how budgets and timescales are affected if the appropriate scope isn't factored in accordingly. I then look at what potentially lies beyond the construction phase, including overlapping test phases, the profile of defects during testing, turning around defects, hot-fixing, technical tuning and re-factoring, and sweeping. I describe how some of these activities lead to a drop in the quality bar and outline a number of practices that you can employ to improve and maintain quality and productivity.

❑ **Quality Comes at a Price** — Provides an overview of the financial matters involved in quality construction, and a basis for understanding the financial implications to assist in the decision-making process. The section also looks at calculating the potential cost of defects and performing cost/benefit analyses, and, finally, looks at the implications of realistic estimating to ensure that the scope, budget, and timescales are set and agreed on.

In this chapter you'll get an overview of the quality characteristics and some of the activities you can perform to improve the quality of your software and projects as well as understanding the costs and benefits associated with them. As the book progresses, I'll cover some of these items in more detail.

Before diving in, I'd like to share a short story with you that is quite poignant at this point. It was a marvelous day when my editor told me that my proposal for this book had been accepted and that I should start work immediately. I asked him if the final contract had been sent and he told me that it had been. However, he said there was an issue — the courier's online tracking system was reporting an "Incorrect Address" error, although we confirmed that the contract had been addressed correctly. I took it upon myself to telephone the courier company to follow up with them. I gave the representative (rep) my tracking number and she replied, "Okay, I'm just waiting for the details to load on my screen." There was a lengthy pause. The rep then said, "I'm sorry about this, but my system is running really slow today." "No worries," I replied. After another lengthy pause, the representative said, "I'm really sorry. Do you mind if I transfer you to someone else as my computer just froze?"

With reference to the preceding short story, I actually wondered whether this sort of thing (the computers running slowly and freezing up) happened quite often or whether it was simply a one-time event. If the situation occurs on a regular basis, I can only imagine the frustration of the users and customers, and how it would erode confidence in the overall quality of the solution. There's nothing worse than having to use an application or service that you don't have confidence in. The quality characteristics and, more important, ensuring that the solution actually meets them, will help to instill confidence in the solution.

The Quality Characteristics

The quality characteristics are often born out of a set of guiding principles, which set the scene or vision for the solution. The guiding principles are a set of high-level statements that outline the intent of the solution. Typically, there are around ten or so guiding principles for any undertaking, although this varies greatly depending on what they refer to. Some organizations use guiding principles to set out what matters to them, their employees, and their customers. Projects generally use guiding principles to set out key capabilities and characteristics of the solution. If the project is implementing a new version of an existing application, the guiding principles will often include capabilities that are an improvement over the previous version. For example, if scalability is limited or non-existent in the existing system, one guiding principle for the new system may be "highly scalable." The principles do not describe the exact functionality; instead, they capture a high-level manifesto that underpins the vision and goals for the future state solution. The following are examples of guiding principles:

❏ **Positive user experience** — Positively impact the user experience and satisfaction of the system while retaining and satisfying the business goals and requirements. Providing a rich and satisfying user experience is not just good for the customer — it's good for business and the company. With respect to websites and a global population, however, there are potentially millions of users, all of whom will have their own point of view on how user friendly the site is. The designer needs to come up with an easy-to-use interface while providing all the relevant functionality.

❏ **Flexible** — Support for a growing, changing, and adapting marketplace by providing the ability to add new functionality quickly and easily. The ability to react quickly to changes in the market and provide new functionality quickly and easily is a factor for success. The solution should be flexible enough without dramatically impacting costs and timescales when it comes to adding new functionality.

❏ **High performance** — Support for global transaction levels and volumes. With a worldwide population the site could be accessed by millions of users, so performance is a key principle that should underpin the design. The end-to-end transaction time is crucial to end users. It's very frustrating sitting around waiting for pages to refresh, especially when you have no idea of what is happening in the background.

❏ **Cost effective** — Efficient and cost effective to operate, support, maintain and enhance. The system shouldn't introduce an unnecessary burden on the support organization. The solution needs to be generally easy to operate. The system needs to be relatively easy to maintain. Additional features and enhancements will be added over time. During analysis and design a number of features will be deemed out of scope, all of which could be candidates for a future release.

❏ **Highly secure** — The system may capture personal information about customers. If this information were to get into the wrong hands, it could not only be newsworthy but it could seriously affect the customers, the organization's reputation, market share, and bottom-line figures. The system should implement highly secure protocols for data capture, viewing, extraction, and amendment. The system will maintain and protect customer and user privacy and information at all times.

❏ **New technologies** — The system should be built and tested using the latest generation of technologies.

The guiding principles are usually mapped to a set of business benefits and drivers that can be realized through the adoption of the solution. For instance, one business driver may be to reduce manual effort (and costs) by 20 percent. In such a case, automation would feature quite high on the software implementation agenda.

The overall solution doesn't just include code. Contrary to popular belief, software developers don't just develop code. They're responsible for many other tasks, including reviewing documentation, writing technical designs and other documentation, writing test scripts, testing software, preparing presentations, and showing results. They implement development processes and practices. They write code and scripts; develop test data; and design configuration files, components, and applications. They're also responsible for helping other people, handing over their solution and documentation as well as doing a whole bunch of other things. Improving the quality of our system means applying the same due diligence to everything you do and not just focusing on the quality of your code. If you take a step back and think about what you are doing and why you are doing it, you can not only improve the quality of your code but everything else around it. Beautifully crafted code can be let down by poor, inaccurate, or incomplete documentation or tools. In these days of agile, rapid application development and model-driven engineering techniques, there's still a reasonable proportion of the job that doesn't involve actual coding. As I mentioned in the previous chapter, the use of wikis can really help to reduce the amount of "formal" documentation that is produced. However, it still needs to be fit for purpose.

Continuous improvement is about ensuring that everything you do is high quality and displays a number of different quality characteristics. The following table briefly summarizes the essence of each quality characteristic. I've used the term *it* and not *application, software,* or *system* because I believe that these terms somewhat imply source code or source-related artifacts, and, as you've seen, production readiness applies to applications, environments, processes, and tools, which involve more than just source code — the quality characteristics can apply to everything you produce, although not every characteristic will apply to a particular deliverable.

Correctness and completeness	Correctness and completeness represent the extent to which it delivers what it should. Correctness and completeness are derived from the scope — that is, the requirements and constraints whether documented or otherwise.
Usability	Usability is the ease of which it can be used. This is not to say that all things will be easy to use, but "usability" refers to the overall ease of use from a variety of different user groups and perspectives.
Accessibility	Accessibility is the extent to which it can support a variety of different users. This doesn't just mean supporting users with disabilities. It includes a variety of subject areas, including alternative languages and users in different locations.
Reliability and stability	Reliability and stability represent the ability for it to perform its functions under normal (and adverse) conditions. This includes repeatability and predictability, in that it should produce the same results under the same conditions. This also includes all failure and recovery and disaster recovery situations.
Performance (Speed/Users)	Performance is the speed at which it performs its functions under normal and adverse conditions and load. In order to gauge true performance, the number of users, locations, and transactions also need to be considered. The term "performance" is often used to include other characteristics; however, I've chosen to separate the definition as I've included the other characteristics individually.
Efficiency	Efficiency is the extent to which it utilizes resources. Resources include system resources (such as CPU, memory, disk) as well as human resources and other resources (such as printers, paper, and the environment).
Availability	Availability is the extent to which it is available and ready for use. Different users have different expectations of availability that should be taken into account.

Scalability	The ability to which it can scale to meet future demand or growth needs.
Integrity and security	Integrity is the extent to which it prevents unauthorized or improper use or distribution.
Operability and supportability	Operability is the extent to which it can be operated and kept up-and-running (functioning and in a healthy state). Supportability is the extent to which it can be effectively supported.
Deployability	Deployability is the extent to which it can be deployed. There are typically many users and environments involved in the project, and deployability is vital to getting the right artifacts out to the right people and places.
Configurability and adaptability	Configurability is the extent to which it can be configured or adapted for different scenarios and situations.
Maintainability	Maintainability is the extent to which it can be maintained and enhanced as the project progresses.
Readability	Readability is the ease of which it can be read or understood. There are many different users and groups of users, so readability is often seen from a number of different perspectives.
Reusability	Reusability is the extent to which it can be reused, in whole or in part, and for other purposes or in other areas.
Modularity	Modularity is the extent to which it is broken up into component parts or building blocks. Modularity often breeds re-use by providing smaller artifacts that can be pieced together into a larger solution.
Flexibility and extensibility	Flexibility and extensibility is the extent to which its usage can be changed or extended. Unlike maintainability and configurability, flexibility and extensibility deal with changing its usage and extending it beyond its original scope.
Testability	Testability is the extent to which it can be tested, proven, and quantified. If it can't be quantified, it can't be proven to work. Certain situations call for a pragmatic risk assessment based on skills and knowledge to avoid lengthy and costly testing that covers very extreme and unlikely circumstances.

The degree or extent to which each of these characteristics applies depends entirely on what they are being applied to. For instance, documentation needs to be correct and complete, readable, and usable, as well as reusable and maintainable. Documentation may also need to be integral and secure. This could be as simple as including a security classification on the document. Tools will generally need to be more configurable and extensible, given the number of potential uses, environments, and situations they will be used in. Architecture and framework components will generally be more reusable. Processes also need to be usable, efficient, and scalable to cope with future demand. A process that doesn't scale can impact a project greatly. For example, assume that you have a single DBA who is responsible for developing all database artifacts. If there's an influx of database requirements, it's likely that one person could be overloaded, which can have an impact on timescales. If your project team is distributed across multiple locations, the applications, environments, processes, and tools would also need to accommodate this.

It would take a very large table to list all the individual items that we use and produce, along with their associated quality characteristics. It's worth thinking about each of these characteristics and how they could apply to what you're producing or implementing.

There are many quality characteristics, and a search on the Internet would return many results on the subject. I've included the preceding characteristics because they cover the entire system and they're the primary characteristics I'll focus on within this book.

Why Quality (and Scope) Matter

Studies have shown that the cost of fixing bugs later in the lifecycle is generally higher than finding and fixing them earlier on. In the previous chapter, you saw that projects can fail or be seen to be a failure because of poor quality and poor scope.

I'm a firm believer that no system is completely defect-free and the short story I mentioned at the start of this chapter would go some way to support this statement. That's not to say that your processes shouldn't strive to achieve zero defects; it simply means that you're probably not going to achieve a truly perfect solution. In any case, you'd first need to define exactly what a "perfect solution" means. It will almost certainly mean different things to different people. If you can stand back and say, "It's my best work yet," then you're probably in a good place. That doesn't mean to say that you couldn't identify some areas of improvement or refinement. The problem is that you don't always get the time to revisit your work in the way that you would like. You test and review during the project to ensure that as many defects are captured and fixed as possible, although there's always the opportunity for some defects to slip through the net. In fact, software is very often shipped along with a set of "known issues." These known issues have been identified and are not seen as show-stoppers for the release. Minor defects are often carried over into future releases. The defects may affect a small area of the overall solution or occur only under very specific circumstances. There may be issues with documentation and other artifacts that are also not seen as critical.

Quality is in the eye of the beholder, and it really depends on what is perceived as quality and what is perceived as a defect. The word "defective" has many meanings, but the most applicable for this section are "lacking a part," "incomplete," and/or "faulty." If the scope isn't defined sufficiently, not only is the scope incomplete, it's extremely likely that the end result will be, too. Your primary goal is to ensure that your software and the associated artifacts are accepted by the recipient, whomever that may be and whatever it is you're delivering.

Quality (and scope) matter because *you* need to produce the final state solution. If the applications, environments, processes, and tools to achieve this don't enable you to do it effectively, you're in a bit of trouble before you've even started. A development environment that crashes every five minutes will have an impact on your ability to program. If the source control system is down, you can't access your artifacts. If it's not backed up, you run the risk of losing everything. Furthermore, if the scope isn't agreed to and understood, you have no idea what you're supposed to be producing, how you're supposed to be producing it, and what you're ultimately meant to be delivering.

Quality (and scope) matter because whether it's source code, configuration files, database artifacts, test scripts, test data or documentation you're producing and delivering, it's typically subject to some form of inspection, review, and acceptance. This could be a peer review, a team lead review, or even an external review. It's no good writing huge specifications only to find that the requirements are wrong, or the specification is incomplete or there's not enough detail. Furthermore, let's assume that you're developing a solution for a third-party organization and you develop the components to adhere to your own internal standards and practices. If the solution is subsequently reviewed by the external party, all manner of issues could be found with it. In my experience, these types of issues can have a very dramatic effect on the overall outcome of the project and its perceived quality. It's no good finding out that all the documentation and code will need to be re-factored because they're not acceptable.

You need to estimate the effort involved in developing and testing the item to meet this acceptance. The level of testing will depend on the solution, but, ultimately, all the testing and acceptance is to ensure that the final product is fit for purpose. Again, it's no good finding out that the system should support automatic recovery when it hasn't been implemented. Although agile development techniques attempt to address this by ensuring that construction iterations produce a working solution, what's a working solution? End users may consider this as the solution incorporates all the functionality they require to perform their job. Support and operations staff may consider this as it meets all the necessary operability criteria. The application maintenance team may consider this as the software meets all of its maintenance criteria.

The most important thing in software development is to understand (and agree on) all the relevant quality characteristics and include them in the overall scope.

Construction Quality Echoes throughout the Project

Improving quality means improving everything you do from start to finish. This means ensuring that what comes out of the construction activities is fit for purpose. Initially, this means that it (the software) can be passed on to the test team for further testing and verification with the *minimum amount* of fuss, issues, and rework. You don't want your test activities to be *defect bound*, meaning that there are either too many issues to continue or there are show-stopping issues. However, you don't want to push the development out so far that it balloons the costs and timescales of the project.

The beginning of this chapter looked at some of the quality characteristics your systems should display. Now let's consider some of the processes and practices that you can employ during construction to improve the quality of your software and outputs, these activities include:

- ❑ Reviewing functional and technical designs and/or requirements
- ❑ Producing low-level technical designs and specifications for review and acceptance prior to coding
- ❑ Developing and reviewing components and documentation
- ❑ Developing and reviewing unit test plans, scripts, test data, and test harnesses
- ❑ Executing and reviewing unit tests and results
- ❑ Submitting components and artifacts for review and release
- ❑ Developing and reviewing integration test plans, scripts, data, and test harnesses
- ❑ Executing and reviewing integration tests and results
- ❑ Documenting completion reports

The exact order in which these activities are performed depends on your chosen development approach, and the degree to which any of these activities is performed determines the quality of the outputs from construction.

Figure 2-1 shows a hypothetical but structured construction process based on the preceding activities. The process outlined does not strictly follow any specific methodology; however, it covers the key activities listed as well as indicating an initial flow (and order) and incorporates review checkpoints.

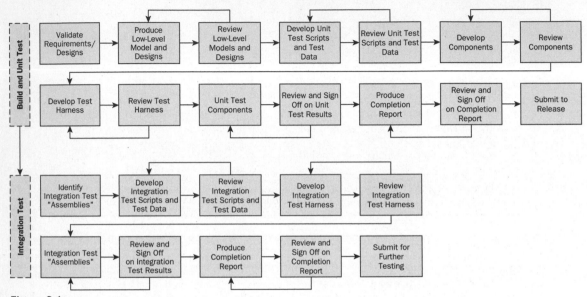

Figure 2-1

Although the process outlined might appear quite lengthy and regimented, it's really a question of how quickly each of the steps can be performed. You may already be performing these activities on your projects, although perhaps not in the same order as the plan shows or in a structured manner. For example, when you're developing your code, you typically review your code by reading through it. However, when you write down the individual tasks, it can really help to identify productivity enhancements and structured approaches. With the right tools and processes in place, there's no reason why the tasks and activities can't be executed in a relatively straightforward and expeditious manner. The process and the tools are all just another part of the overall scope of work.

As I mentioned earlier, the degree to which each of these activities is performed is truly where the quality bar lies. Setting the quality bar involves assessing the processes, practices, and tools, and evaluating these against costs and timescales. That said, a very high quality bar generally means a high quality solution.

The level and quality of testing and reviews you perform will ultimately determine the number of defects known or perhaps unknown in the construction outputs. Your mission, therefore, should be *to catch as many defects as early as possible and assess/fix them accordingly*. To achieve this goal, you will need to put some industrial-strength processes and tools in place, while balancing them against budgets and timescales.

The development methodology and approach will typically stipulate what the inputs and outputs of the activities are. In addition, the activities may not be performed in the order shown. Figure 2-1 depicts two high-level processes, one for "Build and Unit Test" and one for "Integration Test." These activities are described in the following sections and would generally apply to all components in the production-ready solution. This includes all framework and architecture components, application components, batch processes, reports, tools, scripts, and so forth.

The Build and Unit Test Process

The following describes the activities shown in Figure 2-1:

❑ **Validate requirements/designs.** First and foremost, you need to ensure that the requirements and designs meet the needs of the development team. That's not to say that if you think the design or requirements are poor or could be done better that you shouldn't flag it. You need to ensure that the inputs to the development phase are complete and unambiguous, and are sufficient for you to perform development, unit testing, and integration testing. During requirements and design validation, it's best to keep a log of queries, risks, and issues that may arise from the review, and to ensure that these are tracked and managed appropriately. These queries will need to be addressed before the construction can be fully closed off on the component. The requirements and designs should map back to the quality characteristics and include all the relevant items. The actual content of the requirements or design will depend entirely on the type of component that needs to be built and tested. However, the following provides a reasonable starting point:

  ❑ **Functional design/requirements** — A detailed description of the component and what it is meant to do. This could consist of use cases, activity diagrams, flow diagrams, and textual descriptions to describe the component in detail. The functional aspects may also include various logging, usability, accessibility, and security information.

  ❑ **Technical requirements and considerations** — A detailed description of the component's technical characteristics, such as failure and recovery scenarios, exception processing, and performance considerations. The technical requirements and considerations may also include areas covering configuration, scalability, resilience, and so forth. The requirements should map back to the relevant quality characteristics.

  ❑ **Monitoring requirements and considerations** — A detailed description of the component's monitoring characteristics, such as instrumentation requirements and logging and tracing requirements.

  ❑ **Operability considerations** — A detailed description of the component's operability considerations — for instance, whether the component is controlled by batch or how the component is started/stopped and managed.

❑ **Develop unit test scripts and test data.** The unit test plan contains the list of tests that are going to be carried out. Ideally, tests should be grouped into the following categories:

  ❑ **Functional tests** — Covering the necessary functionality outlined in the functional requirements.

  ❑ **Technical tests** — Covering the technical requirements including performance. Where it's not possible to conduct certain tests because of environment limitations, these need to be logged so that they can be carried out later.

  ❑ **Monitoring tests** — Covering the monitoring requirements, including all instrumentation updates and logs.

  ❑ **Operability tests** — Covering operability requirements. Again, limitations in the environment that don't support certain tests need to be flagged for execution in a later test activity.

Each group of tests should be further divided into successful scenarios and failure scenarios. Each test must contain a detailed description of the test being carried out and the relevant input data and expected results. The expected results should include the following (where appropriate):

- ❏ Return values and output values (including any external updates, such as file system, database, and so on)

- ❏ Instrumentation and diagnostic outputs (including events, tracing, performance counters, and so on)

There may be other outputs for the particular unit that should also be captured.

- ❏ **Review unit test scripts and test data.** The unit test plans and data are reviewed against the Develop Unit Test Scripts and Test Data Checklist. The checklist is essentially based on the preceding recommendations and practices — for example, ensuring that the unit tests are present and correct and contain all the necessary conditions and expected results, and that the test data being used is appropriate. The reviewer then provides comments back to the developer for further clarification and/or updates. Where necessary, the reviewer should work with the developer to ensure a full understanding of the comment and its impact. Communication is paramount in software development.

- ❏ **Develop components.** The components are developed according to the functional and technical requirements and specifications. While developing components, you should consider the items for the Develop Components Checklist:

  - ❏ All code must conform to the coding standards and guidelines.

  - ❏ All code is checked for performance and technical issues.

  - ❏ All comments adhere to the commenting standards and documentation-generation guidelines.

  - ❏ All functional and technical queries must be addressed.

  - ❏ All additional/modified exceptions and contextual information must be agreed on.

  - ❏ All modified input/output values must be agreed on.

  - ❏ All instrumentation and diagnostic updates must be agreed on.

  - ❏ All implementation updates and deviations must be agreed on.

- ❏ **Review components.** The components are reviewed according to the functional and technical requirements and specifications, as well as the Develop Components Checklist, and comments are provided for further updates. Again, the checklist is based on the outlined recommendations and practices. It is important to ensure that any modifications to the specification are agreed on by the relevant groups of people, such as end-users, business staff, support staff and so forth. It is equally important that this information is passed on to other teams, such as the testing team, to ensure that they are captured and incorporated appropriately.

❏ **Develop unit test harness.** The test harness is developed in accordance with the unit test plan. During development of the test harness, the following also needs to be ensured:

  ❏ All code must conform to the coding standards and guidelines.

  ❏ All code is checked for performance and technical issues.

  ❏ All comments adhere to the commenting standards and documentation generation guidelines.

  ❏ All unit test conditions have the necessary test classes and methods.

  ❏ All input data matches the unit test plan.

  ❏ All output data and expected results match the unit test plan.

  ❏ All actual results are verified (where possible, this should not involve manual effort).

  ❏ Any unexpected results or conditions cause the tests to fail.

❏ **Review unit test harness.** The test harness is reviewed according to the unit test plan and the Develop Test Harness Checklist, and comments are provided for further updates.

❏ **Unit test components.** The components are unit tested and verified. During this activity the following needs to be ensured:

  ❏ All unit tests pass and provide all the relevant assertions.

  ❏ All code is covered. Where code can't be tested for whatever reason, it must be flagged so that it can be tested later or removed if not required.

  ❏ All changes to expected results or actual results are agreed on.

  ❏ All changes to implementation are agreed on.

❏ **Review and sign off on unit test.** The unit test results are reviewed and signed off on according to the Unit Test Checklist, which is based on the preceding recommendations. Comments are provided for further updates.

❏ **Produce completion report.** The completion report is compiled and includes the following:

  ❏ Updated log with all queries addressed where possible and all open queries or additional testing requirements documented.

  ❏ Completed unit test plan and test data.

  ❏ Unit test harness source code and artifacts. These also include the actual results extraction scripts and tools. You may be able to use these later.

  ❏ Component source code and artifacts such as configuration files.

  ❏ Source code compliance reports. The compliance reports are generated from the static code analysis tools and the performance analysis tools. The compliance reports cover all source code, including the unit test harness and the component source code.

  ❏ Unit test results, including all instrumentation extracts and logs.

  ❏ Code coverage report detailing what code has been covered. Where it's not possible to cover certain aspects, a detailed synopsis is provided.

❑ Performance and technical reports detailing analysis of components and database elements.

❑ Review comments showing where each comment has been addressed or a detailed synopsis of why it has not been addressed.

❑ All documentation, whether generated automatically or otherwise.

❑ **Review and sign off on completion report.** The completion report is reviewed and signed off on according to the Completion Report Checklist, and comments are provided for further updates.

❑ **Submit to release.** Once the completion report has been reviewed and signed off on, everything is in place and can be submitted into a formal release according to the release process. Each release package will have different configurations and include different artifacts; as such, all artifacts included in the completion report should be included in the configuration management system and submitted to build (where appropriate).

The scope encompasses the activities, tasks, and outputs of the chosen construction process. The activities are intended to deliver a high-quality solution to the further test phases. Later in this chapter, you look at the costs associated with quality, and these can be applied more importantly to the costs associated with poor quality. Whether it's a tool, a core architecture component, or anything else for that matter, the construction quality needs to be met and maintained through the lifetime of the project or solution. Although I'm not dictating the actual approach, the essence of the tasks and activities should be considered carefully. This is just one area where quality and scope are interrelated. The more activities involved in construction, the longer it's likely to take and cost. However, to balance this out, savings can be made further down the line by reducing testing and fix effort as well as support and maintenance effort.

Code Quality 101

It can sometimes be very difficult to agree on the necessary quality characteristics because of different points of view. For instance, in the previous chapter I posed the question, "What defines code quality?" Code quality can again mean different things to different people. However, as far as I'm concerned the following are just a few of the key principles and practices of "code quality 101":

❑ Conforming to naming conventions, coding standards, and best practice architectural and language patterns

❑ Well-structured and commented code for maintainability and readability

❑ Employing layering, isolation, and encapsulation techniques to promote re-use and to reduce duplicated code sections

❑ Modular code that is not overly complex, not too difficult to understand and test, such as not including large classes, large methods, and multiple nested conditions

❑ Not including any redundant code, unused libraries, and/or parameters

❑ Using configuration values instead of hard-coded values and "magic numbers"

❑ Using interfaces, late instantiation techniques and "mock" objects or stubs/simulators to support thorough testing

❑ Including exception handling and resilience patterns

❑   Including logging, tracing, and diagnostics for operability and supportability

❑   Efficient use of system resources and tuned for "production" performance

I'm using "code quality 101" to refer to the very basic principles and practices for quality code. "101" has long been used by teaching institutes and training vendors to identify the first and most basic course in a series.

It is entirely possible that the artifact could meet all its requirements without ever incorporating any of the above, especially if they're not defined and included within the scope. For example, I could ask someone to write a simple tool for use during incident investigation. It definitely depends on the person as to whether all, some, or none of the preceding would be taken into account. More important, it really depends on how I set the scope for the task. In the software industry, we often take "best practice" for granted. We sometimes assume that because these practices are well known, every program will (and must) conform to them and that every developer will incorporate them. However, I may not actually require all the "best practice" for a particular task. There's the infamous "throw-away code" situation. This is when something needs to be done very quickly and it's only required for a very short-lived period. In this situation, performing "all" the best practices isn't always necessary; however, the item still needs to be fit for purpose. The item is simply a means to an end. However, I often find that "throw-away code" isn't just a means to an end, and if I need it now, then I need to really understand whether it's needed in the future.

There can be very differing opinions on what "best practice" actually is and what it means. As the software industry progresses, new practices and patterns are always identified and become "the thing to do." If the quality is included in the scope, then a system that meets its completion criteria will also meet all its true quality criteria. The following provides some additional context for some of the code quality items presented in the preceding list:

❑   **Standards and guidelines** — Development standards ensure that all developers are writing similar code and artifacts that adhere to a given set of standards. These need to include commenting standards, naming conventions, configuration, exception handling, instrumentation, and logging and architecture usage. The standards also need to cover the rudimentary practices for performance and other technical characteristics. These standards and procedures should cover all languages and technologies, such as database artifacts, source code, and scripting languages. In addition, the standards need to be followed for everything that this developed, including tools and productivity scripts.

❑   **Reusable components and layering** — During development, you will develop a number of different components — some for the core application, some for batch, some for reporting, and some for tools. Layering the architecture and components so that you can reuse as much as possible for many different purposes will reduce overhead and improve the overall quality of the solution. For instance, a logging component should be able to be used everywhere to ensure consistency throughout the system. Ensuring that architecture components are application independent greatly improves reusability. Often architecture components are built with the assumption that they are going to be used by the core application and, as such, are not so adaptable to other uses such as batch, reporting, and tools. Batch and reporting generally involve developing *generic services*. For example, a common batch component is one that can execute a stored procedure and write the results to a file. This functionality could be reused by your test tools to extract actual results from the database for comparison against expected results. Furthermore, these scripts could be used in live environments to extract data for issue investigation.

❑ **Configuration values and settings** — Your system is going to need to deal with a number of different environments and situations, and one size doesn't fit all. You need to have an appropriate level of configuration to support this. Your instrumentation and logging should be highly configurable to support the different levels required in the different environments. You should also ensure that database connectivity is highly configurable for the same reasons. Low-level configuration components can be used to standardize access to configuration values and settings, parts of which can often be generated from the configuration files and they can also be reused by tools and other components.

❑ **Instrumentation and diagnostics** — You need to ensure that the appropriate level of instrumentation and diagnostics is in place in your applications and tools so that when issues arise, they can be tracked down quickly and efficiently. Test tools are often thought of as a means to an end and don't often include logging or instrumentation. However, including logging and instrumentation in the tools themselves enables you to measure their own performance and effectively diagnose any bugs in them. Incorporating reusable instrumentation and logging classes within the architecture allows you to make use of them everywhere. You must also ensure that instrumentation and logging don't adversely affect performance. The instrumentation needs to be configurable so that it can be tuned for different environments. This is to ensure that you are in a position to react to issues and turn them around quickly. It is equally important that you test and validate the instrumentation and logging outputs to ensure that they are correct. When you get to the real issues with your system, the quality of your instrumentation and diagnostics will count more than anything else. Having productivity tools and scripts to gather and extract logs, instrumentation, and events allows you to verify their correctness during testing and can be reused during live service incident investigation. Instrumentation and logging should be highly configurable so that the most appropriate levels can be calibrated in each environment.

The following sections take a slightly closer look at some of the practices I've mentioned in the build and unit test process, namely:

❑ Code profiling and peer reviews

❑ Code coverage

❑ Unit testing

❑ Documentation generation

Code Profiling and Peer Reviews

There are many tools to assess code quality. These tools can automatically highlight various errors with the code. Some tools work by analyzing the code from a static point of view, whereas others examine the solution while it's actually running. However, it may not be possible for all your code to be automatically profiled. For instance, you might be using a custom package that doesn't support it. Therefore, documented standards and "Mark One Eyeball" (or manual) reviews are typically the only way of checking the quality. In fact, manual reviews and checks should still be performed to ensure complete quality.

As much as your processes and tools allow you to perform your own quality checks, a peer review will uncover many different issues. Peer reviews should be performed throughout the development process, and should focus on all areas, not just code. Peer reviews should cover unit test plans and data, integration test plans and data, source code, and other artifacts, as well as release readiness reports. A peer review checklist should be used and updated as they are conducted. Peer review comments should be documented thoroughly and managed appropriately. Where common issues are found, they should be filtered through to the productivity and process guides to provide more information. It often helps to have a Top 10 list of common issues to avoid future occurrences.

> Mark One Eyeball *is a basic military term that refers to visual reconnaissance instead of using any high-tech means when on maneuvers or out searching.*

Using code analysis and code profiling tools can help to ensure adherence to standards and highlight potential performance issues with the code. It also helps with peer reviews because the outputs from the profiler are the starting point for the review. If the report shows a large number of errors that can't be explained, it is a fairly reasonable indication that the code isn't ready.

Static code analysis generally checks the code against coding standards, abstraction and dependencies, configuration settings, and other statically identifiable issues. For example, the profiler may detect the keyword new inside a loop and raise a warning. Static code profilers can often find potential areas for bugs, memory leaks, and so on. They often point out many naming standard errors, unused libraries, methods and parameters, and hard-coded values.

One very important aspect of code profiling is the "cyclomatic complexity" reporting features. In short, cyclomatic complexity is a measurement of how complex the code is and the number of test cases required to achieve coverage. The measurement is based on the number of branches and paths in the code. The more branches and paths in the code, the more complex it is.

Dynamic code profiling takes place when the code is actually executing. The tools typically look at the resource utilization of the application, memory, CPU, database, and so on. They can often highlight actual memory leaks and inefficient code. The output reports are used to tune the application accordingly.

These tools often require up-front configuration and may not support all languages and technologies used in the project. As such, they should be complemented with peer reviews to ensure that the code adheres to the appropriate standards.

Code profiling should be used carefully, and often some components need to deviate from the standards for very good reasons. These components need to be noted, understood, and incorporated. In general, using these tools early on can provide some useful insights and help to improve code quality during construction. When the technical test fully ramps up and starts probing, you can bet your bottom dollar that it won't be long before a profiler is wheeled out to "inspect" the solution. Having them used up front will really help to avoid re-work later. The technical testing often encounters very convoluted issues that code profiling can often help to diagnose.

Code profiling should be automated and easy to execute. It's more likely to be used if it can be executed easily. The results need to be captured for analysis and possible correction. It's important that the team understand the outputs of the report in order to address the issues. Writing a guide for executing and analyzing code profiling is a good place to start.

In addition to code profiling tools, stored procedures and other database artifacts can be profiled to identify potential bottlenecks in the data layer. This is typically achieved by running an execution plan against the stored procedure for various scenarios. The report will show how efficient the procedure is and will often highlight areas for improvement.

It's important that the scope includes the use of these tools (where determined) and, more important, the details of the underlying rules. All too often there's a debate over which configuration is the right one and which rules should be switched on or off.

Code Coverage

Using a code coverage tool effectively is a great way to determine how much of the source code is executed during testing. The outputs can be used to determine whether additional tests need to be developed to hit more code or, in some cases, the results can identify redundant code. The code coverage tool typically injects instrumentation into the code so that when a test is executed the tool can examine how much code has been executed. I typically refer to these as *covered builds*. The code is measured on a number of criteria that includes but is not limited to:

❑ **Function (methods)** — Measures the methods that are executed.

❑ **Statement** — Measures the statements in each method that are executed.

❑ **Condition** — Measures the conditions that are executed.

❑ **Path** — Measures the conditional paths that are executed.

❑ **Entry/exit** — Measures the number of permutations of entry and exit for the function (method).

It may not be possible to automatically check code coverage for your entire solution; therefore, the unit test approach needs to be documented and understood so that the development team produces and executes scripts that cover the required amount of code. The code review approach needs to be documented and understood so that Mark One Eyeball reviews confirm this has been achieved. Where possible, the unit test approach and review should be aligned to the rules outlined previously.

Mission-critical systems often require 100 percent of the code to be covered. If you commit to achieving 100 percent code coverage during unit testing, you'll need to include tests for every condition and every possible scenario. To ensure this happens, you may need many additional test classes, stubs and/or mock/simulator objects, as well as the conditions and scripts.

Developers often write defensive code — for instance, including `if` statements and `null` checks. While this may be seen to add to the robustness of the solution, you actually need to test that they work. If you have high code coverage criteria then you will need to devise tests and data in such a way that each scenario can be fully tested. I personally believe that every line of code you write should be tested thoroughly.

Achieving 100 percent code coverage during unit testing doesn't mean the application works the way it should or that it even displays all the necessary quality characteristics. It's just one part of the scope and quality. Maintaining unit tests and integration tests can be a costly business and, therefore, it's important that they do exactly what they should — to ensure that the system works correctly.

Unit Testing

Although the concept of unit testing has existed for a long time, there are differing views on what unit testing should actually test and how it should be performed. Traditionally, unit testing has been categorized as a "white-box test" that tests the smallest part in the solution, such as a single method. The term "white-box" is used because you can see the actual code that is going to be executed by the method. However, in test driven approaches, the tests are initially based on the designs (functional and technical) and the public interfaces exposed by classes because the actual code hasn't been written at the time the test cases are being devised. In either case, unit testing should be aligned with code coverage in that the tests should be devised to cover the following aspects of the unit:

❑   Statements

❑   Conditions

❑   Paths

❑   Entry/exit permutations

Unit tests are independent of each other, that is, they shouldn't rely on the outcome or state from a previous test. Unit tests should support being executed in any order.

Unit tests aren't really supposed to span outside the boundaries of the actual class being tested — for instance, if the class being tested contains a method that makes a call to another referenced class, the unit test spills into the referenced class. To support testing the unit in complete isolation, an interface should be defined and a "mock" object should be developed and used during unit testing. This approach can improve the overall quality of unit testing because the mock object can be written to simulate various conditions.

Mock objects are often referred to as *stubs* or *simulators*. The complexity and features of the mock object will depend entirely on its purpose. In most cases, the mock object needs to contain conditions for each of the possible calls and permutations from the consumer. The development and test effort required for this needs to be captured in the overall budgets and timescales. Furthermore, a lot of time, effort, and money can be wasted trying to determine whether it is the code that doesn't work or the mock object that is not functioning correctly. It is not always possible to keep the mock object simple but the more you try to, the easier it is to test and fix.

The level and approach to unit testing is entirely dependent on the system being implemented. In some cases, unit testing is a form of integration testing in that some objects are not stubbed and as such they are called as part of the overall test. Although this can be seen as wrong in the purest view, it is important that the approach is agreed to by all the stakeholders, rather than having a debate about it afterwards. A classic example is instrumentation and diagnostics. It is perfectly possible to mock these objects and make gathering the output for completion much easier. However, using the real object early on (where possible) will ensure that the system works the way it should in production. This is nothing more than striking a balance between reality and theory. These decisions and the unit testing approach need to be documented and included in the scope, as they will have an effect on the budgets and timescales.

There are many tools that help to automate unit testing rather than you having to execute scripts manually. I'm definitely a fan of automated unit testing. The business of executing tests manually is simply a chore and it also means that an automated regression test capability can't be employed, which affects the regular integration approach and adds unnecessary delays on the project.

Documentation Generation

Using documentation generation tools helps with the production of system documentation for handover and future development purposes. Documentation is generated from the *comments* in the code and can be a lot easier than writing it by hand. The generated documentation typically includes:

❑   Namespaces and namespace hierarchy

❑   Class, interface, delegate, and enumeration lists and descriptions

❏   Public property, method, and parameter lists and descriptions

❏   Return value and exception lists and descriptions

The output is usually a compiled help file that contains links to make it easier to navigate. However, these tools do not support all languages and technologies and often require up-front configuration to be used effectively.

Your commenting standards need to stipulate what needs to be included in your code to support documentation generation, and your process guides need to contain step-by-step instructions on how to produce the relevant system documentation.

> *Many other practices can be employed during the construction phase and some of these are highlighted later. The practices listed here are simply a core set of practices that should be considered during build and unit test to ensure high-quality outputs. While the amount of work may have increased during construction, the savings further down the line will be truly beneficial.*

The Integration Test Process

The integration test process and activities are very similar to their unit testing counterparts, so I won't go into the details again. Integration testing is generally considered *black-box testing*. The tests are designed to call the *assembly* through a *public* interface on the first class (or object) in the assembly, and assert the expected results. The tests are designed to cover the main integration scenarios between the individual components. Running integration tests and examining the code coverage often highlights areas where additional tests could be developed or where there's redundant code in the solution. Redundant code isn't always picked up by static code profilers because they typically check only to see if there are references (or calls) to classes and methods within the solution. The code coverage output shows exactly what was executed and called. However, this assumes that you have a very thorough set of integration tests.

Successful integration tests start with identifying the assemblies in the solution. It is important to get the right level of granularity when performing integration tests. Integration testing can be performed in many ways. However, in a lot of cases, integration tests start by testing the system with real components where stubs or mock objects were being used for unit testing. This has the effect of testing the flow through all the components below it. Each layer is tested in turn, moving up to the very top layer. This is typically referred to as a *bottom up* approach. However, in some cases, an assembly can be an entire vertical slice of an application — for example, the Create New Account function. It is important to identify and agree on the assemblies and the approach early so that they can be tested appropriately and avoid issues later in the lifecycle.

It's very important to remember that integration testing may also need to use mock, stub, or simulator components. Although this might seem to be a contradiction in terms, integration testing doesn't always test the entire solution. For example, suppose you're using a third-party component for username/password authentication. There may be constraints whereby you can't use the actual component during integration testing. For example, it might require some backend features that aren't available. Therefore, it will need to be "stubbed" or "simulated" during development and integration testing.

The integration tests are again organized into the following various categories and test both success and failure scenarios:

- ❑ Functional tests
- ❑ Technical tests
- ❑ Monitoring tests
- ❑ Operability tests

It is important during integration testing that the entry/exit testing be thorough and that it exercise all the various permutations and possible outputs to ensure that the assembly is fit for purpose. Testing a single permutation will only go so far in assessing the quality of the build.

> *The construction process should focus on capturing and correcting as many defects as possible prior to formal testing. What comes out of construction will ultimately determine how straightforward the remainder of the project goes. When there's a mass of defects raised beyond construction, it is not long before someone says "How many of these could have been detected earlier?"*

Defects Affect Testing and Ongoing Development

You saw in the previous chapter that you can potentially have multiple test activities and/or phases running in parallel. Each of the test teams will generally want their fixes as soon as possible. Functional testing may argue that the system needs to be functionally correct and performance doesn't matter at *this* point. Performance can always be enhanced and tweaked later, or so the argument goes. Technical testing, on the other hand, may argue that the system needs to be technically correct. Obviously, both sets of requirements need to be met to ensure that the system is production-ready. The fixes need to be managed, prioritized, and implemented according to their allotted priority. Furthermore, functional and technical test phases can often be broken into multiple streams of testing, with each stream concentrating on a particular area or part of the system. For instance, technical tests might split, with one stream concentrating on failure and recovery scenarios, while another focuses on monitoring and operability tests. Functional tests may be split into functional areas or application slices. For example, one area deals with creating new accounts while another area deals with online shopping or cart management.

Once you start testing (and acceptance activities), defects start getting raised and fix turnaround time becomes paramount. Fix turnaround time is the total time it takes to perform all the necessary activities to get a fix out to the required environment. There could be multiple teams of people that are potentially unproductive because of show-stopping defects. Testing and acceptance is basically halted until certain issues are resolved. This can impact not only deadlines, but also costs. If customers are involved in the testing and there are major defects, it can also cause further perception issues with respect to the product's quality. If the development team is impacted by a large number of defects that need to be fixed, it can also cause further delays and cost overruns to outstanding development efforts, such as the inclusion of additional functionality.

When formal testing begins, there are usually many issues that need to be addressed before testing is fully up and running. These early issues are generally not related to the actual application or its functionality. However, there is a fine line between the two.

Regardless of whether you are conducting unit, integration, or system testing, the profile of defects generally follows the path outlined in Figure 2-2.

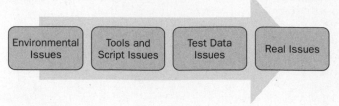

Figure 2-2

Each of these high-level defect categories is discussed in the list that follows:

❑ **Environmental issues** — These issues concern getting the test environment up-and-running. Assuming that the test hardware is in place, these issues are more concerned with access to the environment, deploying the application in the environment, ensuring the correct configuration settings are in place, installing the test data, and bringing the application into a testable state.

❑ **Tools and script issues** — These issues concern executing actual test scripts, getting the test tools up-and-running, injecting transactions manually or automatically from the tools and scripts, and determining the results. The scripts may have been developed separately from the test tools and this is the first time they've been put together. The tools themselves may be new, and "operator error" may come into the equation. Other issues can be encountered when trying to compare results — for example, actual results can't be extracted or compared properly.

❑ **Test data issues** — With the environment and script issues resolved to a degree, you typically start to experience issues with the test data. Test data issues can cover a wide variety of scenarios, including the following:

    ❑ Not all the test data is installed.

    ❑ There's too much test data to load in the test environment.

    ❑ The data is actually incorrect or incomplete.

❑ **Real issues (bugs)** — Once the testing activities are truly up-and-running, you start to identify the real bugs in the system. That's not to say that you won't find anymore bugs in the environment, test tools, or test data, but you've gotten yourself into a position to be able to test and uncover the real issues that need to be dealt with.

Testing is the primary proving ground for the solution. No matter which approach is actually taken, the software must ultimately meet all its functional and technical requirements; therefore, the tests that are carried out need to ensure that this is achieved. The quality of the software and the testing is going to be the biggest area of concern when testing begins. Having fit-for-purpose and production-ready applications, environments, processes, and tools, as well as trained test (and fix) resources, will greatly improve the quality and performance of your testing.

Fixing Defects Quickly Can Reduce Quality

When testing halts because of show-stopping issues, the development or fix teams need to turn around defects fast. In situations like this, the quality can start to drop because you need to get fixes out to the test streams very quickly. All the good stuff you put in place during development typically gets put to the side in order to drop a fix to a test team quickly. There isn't enough time to update the design; have it reviewed and signed off on; update the code; update all the unit tests; update the integration tests; update the regression tests; run them all; ensure code coverage remains the same; profile the code for memory leaks, performance, and adherence to standards; generate the documentation; collate all the results; and have it all reviewed and signed off before delivering a fix into the build process; have it go round the entire build and regression cycle; and finally getting it installed in a test environment. That said, not all defects will need to go back as far as the requirements or design stages, and everything will depend on the criticality of the defect. In addition, the level of tooling that is used can dramatically reduce the overall time to deliver a fix while retaining the appropriate levels of quality. In most cases, the quality can drop when:

❑ Testing is blocked

❑ Tuning and re-factoring are required

These scenarios are discussed in the following sections.

When Testing Is Blocked

When either show-stopping issues occur or a large number of fixes need to be delivered during testing, the development team generally turns into a rapid response unit and really needs to turn around fixes very quickly to keep the test teams up and running and on track. This is often achieved by short-cutting the quality process to get the fix out the door and sweeping up the other items later. Interestingly enough, it is exactly the same situation with issues that are encountered during live service, although these are generally tested more thoroughly prior to being deployed.

An example of this situation is the infamous "one-liner" — a very simple change needs to be made to one line of code that will only take two seconds to implement. The test manager is breathing down your neck about how many people are waiting for the fix, and the development manager is embarrassed at how such a simple issue wasn't found during build, unit, and/or integration testing.

In these types of situations, it's not very long before the decision is made to compile the solution and drop a few "hot-fixed" DLLs into the environment to keep everyone happy and everything running smoothly. Another very common example of hot-fixing is the even more infamous "don't know, can't reproduce" type of issue. You've looked at the code, the data, the scripts, the logs, and everything else, and you just don't have a clue what's going on. This invariably leads to adding more trace statements to the component in the hope that this will provide an insight into what is going on so that the defect can be found and fixed. This again is very often the case during technical testing and early live service because in general verbose logging and tracing is turned off to improve the overall performance of the system.

The rationale for hot-fixing when applied to a test phase goes along the lines of "If people can't do anything anyway, we can't really make the situation any worse, so let's give it a go." Issues encountered during live service may still shortcut the full quality process, but to a much lesser degree than during test. More often than not, the fix will be tested and proven, put into a formal release and regression tested prior to being deployed to the production environment.

A formal hot-fix or "patch" process should be identified early to ensure that it delivers quality artifacts and doesn't necessarily leave an abundance of tasks to be carried out later. It's equally important that all hot-fixes or patches are uniquely identified and have a release note, just like any other software release.

When Tuning and Re-Factoring Are Required

During development the full end-to-end product is not typically technically tested in its entirety. For instance, certain failure and recovery scenarios may need to be tested in a specific environment. Load testing may also require a specific environment. Only when the complete system is tested in a live (or live-like) environment, with live data and live situations, do you get a true indication of the system's actual technical characteristics, such as performance, stability, and recovery. This is also true of some functional characteristics, but these will generally be dealt with in the normal way, unless of course they happen to be show-stoppers. It's not often that components need to be completely re-factored as a result of functional inadequacies, although it has been known to happen. Core algorithms and calculations can be so badly written that they simply have to be rewritten.

When a component isn't functionally or technically satisfactory, it may be tuned or sometimes re-factored completely. This can often be to the detriment of its functionality but more so to the detriment of its quality. The component is a bottleneck to the continuation of technical testing and needs to be fixed and fixed quickly. The really technical folks know all about tuning, but explaining this in a defect report will take too long and the turnaround time is not quick enough. In some cases, this leads to a situation in which the technical team makes local updates to the component to continue testing.

Furthermore, this technical tuning and re-factoring exercise generally doesn't include updating the documentation, updating the unit tests, updating the integration tests, and so on, and once again the quality drops, leaving everything else to be swept up later.

A formal approach to tuning and re-factoring should be agreed on so that whatever happens, the components maintain their quality. Clearly, the more that you can do during the construction phase to ensure that the components are technically correct, the better. Not having very large and unwieldy components in the solution can help. The smaller the component, the less there is to change.

When Quality Drops, Sweeping Is Left

Sweeping is a slang term to describe tidying up the system and bringing it back up to its original quality bar. How high you set that bar will depend on what needs to be done. However, with respect to the construction process outlined earlier in this chapter, sweeping would actually involve all the following tasks:

- ❏ Updating designs and other documentation
- ❏ Sweeping the code and updating comments, updating logging and tracing, updating exception handling, and generally tidying up the code
- ❏ Updating and correcting unit tests and integration tests, as well as associated documentation, scripts, and test data
- ❏ Re-executing all the quality and performance tools to ensure that adherence to standards and profiles and code coverage is achieved

In fact, sweeping is everything you would do during the construction phase, albeit in a usually compressed timeframe (which, again, can affect the overall quality of the outputs).

The rationale behind sweeping can be summarized as follows:

❑ When the level of defects drops, the fix team can split their time between fixing bugs and tidying up everything else.

❑ As long as the "smoke" tests that are included within the regression testing pass, the solution is "good to go" even if the unit tests and integration tests don't pass. The cost implications of sweeping are not always detrimental to the overall financial state of the project; however, depending on the size of the system and the level to which the quality has dropped, it can take a large effort to bring it back up again. Sweeping exercises really need to be planned and executed effectively; otherwise, they can introduce more defects and again reduce the overall quality of the solution.

There are two main reasons for bringing the quality bar back up. The first is that when the system goes into live running and maintenance, it needs to meet the original quality characteristics so that it can be supported and maintained efficiently. The second reason is that most projects have multiple releases, and when you pass all the artifacts to the next team, everything needs to meet the required quality so that they can use them to effectively design and develop the next release.

The bottom line: Wherever possible, quality should be maintained throughout the project and not left to a sweeping or cleanup operation.

More Tips for Improving and Maintaining Quality

In the previous section you saw the typical profile of defects once the software leaves construction, and their potential impact. You need to use this information to your advantage to improve the quality of your processes, tools, and applications. You've also seen some practices that you can employ during construction to ensure your systems meet the necessary quality characteristics. These included thorough unit testing and integration testing, as well as including instrumentation and diagnostics. The following are some additional tips for improving construction quality and the construction process:

❑ **Work with the test teams.** While you're in development, the test teams are busy working away on their own agenda and that's usually developing their own test plans, test scripts, and test data. First, you need to ensure that what you are doing is in line with their expectations and that you are working from the same sets of requirements and designs. If you are developing to version 1 of a document and the test teams are working off of version 2, what you will deliver is not going to match their expectations and you'll encounter issues (see the "Define releases and their content" bullet later in this list). Another benefit of this relationship is getting a bird's-eye view of the types of tests that will be executed and the input data and expected results. You should use this as much as possible during development (see the following bullet).

❑ **Use common test data.** Where possible, you should use a common set of test data during unit testing and integration testing to avoid issues later in the lifecycle. It is often not possible to replicate the exact quantity of the test data — for instance, technical test will generally use much larger sets of test data to fully stress the system, but you should look to use a reduced set of the same data. Identifying common configuration and transaction data greatly reduces test data issues during functional and technical tests, and simplifies test scripts and tools.

❑ **Separate data and databases.** There are a number of different environments and processes that you need to support and having effective data and database management in place will help. As mentioned previously, using common test data assists with this greatly, but you will still need to support different data and databases in different environments. Separating data and databases enables you to deploy only the required databases, artifacts, and data required. You don't want test tables, test views, or test tool databases deployed along with the primary database into the production environment.

❏ **Use common test scripts and scenarios.** In the same way that you should try to use a common set of test data, you should also try to minimize the number of different test scripts that are used. This is especially true for integration testing when you are testing a set of components. Technical tests will usually isolate a single integrated set of components and put them through their paces. Where you can, you should align your tests to get early insights into the technical characteristics. Obviously, the tests are conducted in different environments and, as such, the expected results may need to be tweaked, but aligning yourself against what will come next can greatly reduce the number of issues you encounter. It's the same for functional tests; although functional tests will ripple through functionality in a more end-to-end fashion, you can still align yourself nicely to reduce the impact. Your unit tests and integration tests should be automated and exercise as much of the system as possible via the binaries and not rely on manual effort.

❏ **Use common test tools, stubs, and simulators.** Where possible, the test tools that are going to be used during functional and technical testing should be used during the development phase. This irons out a number of issues with the tools early on and eases the testing processes. Using off-the-shelf tools enables you to configure them appropriately for your testing needs. By developing your own test tools, you can ensure that you capture the requirements of the test teams to ensure that they are fit for purpose. In some situations, you might be using third-party or other applications that are not available during development, and you'll need to develop a stub or simulator to exercise certain functionality. You should try and use a common stub or simulator for all testing activities. Where possible, you should use the actual third-party components to avoid downstream issues.

❏ **Track releases and features.** Requirements and designs change during the project lifecycle, and often it's not possible to incorporate a change immediately. You need to keep track of what features are in each release (the Release Note) to ensure that test teams install the appropriate release for the tests that they are performing. If a tester is following a test script for something that's not included within the release, this script isn't going to pass and an issue will be raised against the software. Release planning also tracks which defects have been fixed in which release. Patches and hot-fixes should also be tracked, just like any other release.

❏ **Define releases and their content.** A release doesn't just include DLLs. It can include configuration files, database scripts, productivity scripts, data, test scripts (including expected results), and documentation. Everything that is required for a particular purpose needs to be included in a release that can be installed quickly and easily with all the right artifacts and configuration. Copying files from one place to another is often tedious and time consuming. The installation package should be complete and should not require access to network drives, source control, or any other repository. This allows the consumer to install the software and artifacts in a completely independent and isolated environment. Things move on and source control or network drives have the *latest* view. If the test scripts have been updated because of a change or enhancement, they may no longer work with a previous release and the latest release may not be at the correct stage to be deployed. The packaging solution should have different configurations for each purpose, such as developer testing, functional testing, and technical testing, as well as supporting custom configuration to allow picking and choosing of what is to be installed. Silent installation should also be supported to reduce manual intervention and support productivity tools and scripts (see the upcoming bullet "Develop productivity tools and scripts").

❑ **Separate test matter from production.** Throughout development you may introduce different release types, such as Debug, Test, Final, and so on. This ensures that only the relevant components and artifacts are compiled and included in the resulting binaries. It avoids including test statements in a final release and allows you to have specific features in test releases, enabling you to better test some of the more complex functionality of the system. However, you need to ensure that switching between release types doesn't impact your ability to find, fix, and test. You don't want to be messing about too much installing different releases to ensure that the code works correctly. Functional and technical testing will generally use final releases to remove all ambiguity. However, there may be instances where functional testing can't use all the "live" components; therefore, stubs and simulators might need to be used. It's worth thinking about how the number of different code bases can be reduced, a topic I'll discuss further in Chapter 23.

❑ **Perform regular integration and automated builds.** Performing regular builds ensures that everything that is *ready to build* is included in a single build and doesn't affect anything else. The build process should be automated as much as possible as this will be used moving forward to deliver into the release process. It is important that every developer knows what ready to build means, what is required, and how to submit their artifacts into the process. This avoids unnecessary issues, including missing files and compilation errors, when everything is brought together. The regular build process should build all the various compiled release types as well as *covered builds* for each of them.

❑ **Fully regression test build and releases** — Once everything has been brought together into a single build, it should be *fully* regression tested. At first this will consist of executing all the unit tests. However, it could also include some rudimentary "smoke" tests. Moving forward, the regression pack would include and execute the integration tests, and, ultimately, it will be extended to cover a magnitude of tests, including functional tests and technical tests, collectively referred to as "smoke" tests. The regression test tools need to be extensible to be able to support different test scenarios. Unit tests and integration tests may need to run against a particular release configuration and its *covered* counterpart, whereas the functional and technical tests will need to run against a final release. The interesting thing here is that you can run all the functional tests and technical tests against a *covered* build and see how much code is exercised, as it often provides very useful results. Once the quality bar has dropped and the unit tests don't work or the integration tests don't work, the only tests left are the functional and technical regression tests, which can start to become the single measure of quality. The regression tests have usually been built up into a really wide reaching set, covering a wide variety of functionality and technical features, so they should be capable of validating more of the system from a live-like fashion. The tests are generally automated, so in some cases they won't cover the more manually intensive tests. However, they are a good indication of "functional" quality if all the tests pass. If the system passes these regression tests, it is generally good enough to be deployed, or that's the idea anyway. In many cases, this can be true — just because the unit tests pass doesn't mean that they are functionally or technically correct. Once the quality bar is dropped, there is no way of telling whether it's the code that doesn't work or the tests that are wrong. It's usually the tests that are broken, as the code has been "smoke" tested in the environment and proven to work. So, the broken unit or integration tests now need to match the code along with everything else that needs to be addressed. Misaligned code and unit/integration tests should be frowned upon. However, having a rich set of regression tests and an extensible regression capability will allow the product to be tested in a variety of ways, preferably in parallel to get a true measure of its "overall" quality.

❑ **Define a ready-to-build and ready-to-release process.** Before anything is submitted to a build or a release, it must pass all the required quality checks. First, the process will need to include steps that ensure all the source code compiles and runs with the latest code base. Additional steps in the process will involve ensuring that all the relevant tests have been executed (and passed); all the required results are in place (including log files, instrumentation reports, and event logs); all the necessary documentation has been generated and is correct; all the test scripts, expected results, and actual results are in place and match; all the necessary profiling reports are in place and meet the required quality level; all requirements and design comments have been incorporated or addressed; and that all peer review comments have been incorporated or addressed.

❑ **Develop and use templates containing TODO statements.** Copying and pasting is very dangerous during development. Logging statements, instrumentation, and comments are not updated properly, leading to poor quality documentation and code. Providing a set of base templates with TODO notes helps to ensure that all your components follow an agreed pattern — for instance, `TODO — put your implementation here`. TODO notes need to be checked and then removed from the code prior to delivery to build to avoid any confusion later down the line. The templates also need to adhere to the standards and guidelines.

❑ **Develop productivity tools and scripts.** Do it regularly manually and it should be automated. Reducing the amount of manual effort by providing tools and scripts not only reduces the number of issues but increases the speed at which the task can be done. For instance, turning an environment around from development testing to functional testing can involve installing a different release with different test data and scripts. Gathering log files, databases extracts, and other artifacts supports many purposes and should be automated. For example, after running the unit tests, you want to capture all the log files, events logs, and performance counters to include in build completion. These tools and scripts can also be used during testing and live running to assist in issue identification and resolution.

❑ **Using code generation techniques** — Generating code through the use of code generators often speeds up development by effectively automating laborious tasks. Code generators are often used to generate data access components because they can be driven from the database schema. You need to ensure that not only the code generators themselves adhere to all the required quality characteristics, but that the code they produce also adheres to them. In the cases of Model Driven Engineering, code is generated from the design. The generated code needs to meet all the required quality characteristics. Generated code needs to be reviewed, profiled, and used in exactly the same way as if it were written by hand.

❑ **Continuously improve.** Finally, everything you do during the development phase must be reviewed regularly and streamlined. You must maintain the quality bar and not get into situations where you're lagging behind due to ineffective processes. Wherever possible, you need to improve the performance of your tools and processes so that they can be used throughout the lifecycle effectively. Running things in parallel helps to keep the total end-to-end time down, and reducing the number of dependencies between tasks, tests, and steps means that given a suitable environment, you can run multiple tests and processes in parallel.

In the next chapter, "Preparing for 'Production'", you'll examine some more of the activities that should be considered prior to launching into formal coding.

Quality Comes at a Price

This section looks at some of the financial implications of quality and, more important, the costs associated with a lack of quality. Quality generally comes at a price, although an abundance of activities can be performed that are low cost and very high gain, assuming that they are put in place early. I'm not going to use a lot of statistics in this section because I think we are all generally aware of the cost implications of getting things wrong up front, and there are more than ample books and references that cover this subject. This section discusses some of the financial aspects that should be considered during the decision-making process. Once you understand all the processes and the financial implications, you can ensure that the Project Management Triangle is accurate. You'll use the construction process and some of the tips outlined earlier to assess the relevant costs and savings. The fact that you're a developer doesn't mean that you shouldn't be aware of the financial impact you can have on a project.

While you might not be a financier, the decisions that you make and the actions that you take affect the financial health of the project and the system as a whole. These decisions and actions need to be justified and cost effective for now and in the future.

Calculating the Potential Cost of Defects

Given that it's difficult to predict the future and the number of defects that you might encounter, a simple cost-benefit analysis needs to take best-guess and real-world estimates into account. For example, it would be extremely naive to assume that there would be no defects in the system following the construction phase. It would also be naive to assume that the system will go into production completely defect-free. However, there are usually many test phases or activities between construction and production that will result in the production release having far fewer defects than the first release that came out of construction. Therefore, it's prudent to assume a certain level of defects following initial construction. Many studies have been conducted into this subject, although I am not going to go into these here. Suffice it to say that defects will be present in the solution. However, the number and complexity of defects can't be determined up front. The further the project gets through testing, the more subtle the issues can become and the more thought they require on how to resolve them.

Let's look at a very simple defect model to try and calculate the cost of defects and use this information to determine whether "code quality 101" could be cost effective. To keep the math simple, assume that the cost of each developer is $10 per hour, and that each developer works a standard 8-hour day. If adhering to "code quality 101" were to cost $160 (that is, 2 days), it would need to save at least $160 further down the line to be cost effective. This figure does not include the initial set-up and implementation costs. This is where the educated guesswork comes in and defect modeling is one way of achieving a possible figure.

The following table shows some high-level defect categories and hypothetical effort/costs associated with them:

Defect Category	Fix Effort / Cost	Brief Explanation
Very Simple	.5 hour / $5	Assume a very simple change to a class that doesn't require any test script updates, such as updating or correcting the comments or tidying up the code. The estimate includes the time it takes to check out the code, make the change, execute all the quality checks and processes, check in the change, and submit the change into a release.
Simple	2 hours / $20	Assume a simple change to a class that requires one test script update and expected results change. Assume that this change also needs to be factored into further testing.
Medium	4 hours / $40	Assume a reasonable defect with multiple test changes and conditions that need to be factored throughout.
Complex	40 hours / $400	Assume a fairly sizable re-factoring exercise of a reasonably sized component.
Very Complex	160 hours / $1600	Assume a rewrite of a fairly complex component.

No two applications are the same and as such each application will generally have it's own specific effort estimates. However, by using the categories in the preceding table, you can put together a sliding scale or model of defect totals and associated costs that can show various positions throughout the project lifetime.

Figure 2-3 shows a hypothetical defect model based on the preceding inputs.

Defect Model	Very Simple		Simple		Medium		Complex		Very Complex		Total Cost per Defect Count
$ Cost per Defect	$5.00		$20.00		$40.00		$400.00		$1,600.00		
Percentage of Overall Defects	50%		30%		15%		3%		2%		
30	15	$75.00	9	$180.00	4.5	$180.00	0.9	$360.00	0.6	$960.00	$1,755.00
100	50	$250.00	30	$600.00	15	$600.00	3	$1,200.00	2	$3,200.00	$5,850.00
500	250	$1,250.00	150	$3,000.00	75	$3,000.00	15	$6,000.00	10	$16,000.00	$29,250.00
1,000	500	$2,500.00	300	$6,000.00	150	$6,000.00	30	$12,000.00	20	$32,000.00	$58,500.00
5,000	2,500	$12,500.00	1,500	$30,000.00	750	$30,000.00	150	$60,000.00	100	$160,000.00	$292,500.00

Figure 2-3

The defect model shown is used to highlight the basic analysis. It does not take into account any other resource downtime and it does not take into account individual component complexities or developer skills. As such, it provides a very static average used for example purposes only.

The defect model in Figure 2-3 has two main rows, *$ Cost per Defect* and *Percentage of Overall Defects*, which can apply to a single class, component, or assembly, or it provides an average across all the components and assemblies.

❑ **$ Cost per Defect** — Contains a cost for each high-level defect category, as outlined in the preceding table. The table sets the scene for the defect model by examining the different categories and associating a baseline cost with each one.

❑ **Percentage of Overall Defects** — Contains a figure that represents the percentage of defects assumed in this category. For example, this model is estimating that 50 percent of the overall defects will be in the category Very Simple. It estimates that 2 percent will be in the Very Complex category.

The two rows provide the basis of the remaining calculations in the model and as such should be based on educated best guesses or real-world estimates from previous calibration exercises.

The remaining rows in the model show a total number of defects in the first column, and then each category column shows how may defects in the category it represents and the total cost for this category. For example, the row estimating a total of 30 overall defects calculates the following statistics:

❑ 15 very simple defects, at a total cost of $75

❑ 9 simple defects, at a total cost of $180

❑ 4.5 medium defects, at a total cost of $180

❑ 0.9 complex defects, at a total cost of $360

❑ 0.6 very complex defects, at a total cost of $960

The statistics total up to $1,755, which could be spent fixing 30 defects according to the various percentage splits. It's clearly not possible to actually have 0.9 or 0.6 defects, so these will probably roll up to whole units and increase the costs again. These figures are clearly only representative of the overall percentage within the defect category.

So, assuming the defect model is somewhat realistic and based on some real-world examples, it would show that the "code quality 101," which was estimated to cost $160, needs to potentially capture and fix the equivalent of eight simple defects to make it cost-effective. I guess you need to ask yourself "How many simple defects would the result have if I didn't adhere to any code quality at all?" Remember that defects are not just functional or execution issues. A review of the code could have highlighted thirty two very simple defects that would need to be addressed. When it comes to maintaining the system and adding new functionality, it could take someone a long while to "get their head around the code," which would also increase the costs. Although it was possible to arrive at this conclusion based solely on the information in the preceding table, it is a useful exercise to produce a basic model because it can be used to ratify the overall categories and percentages. It is also very useful at the end of each phase to examine how close the estimates were to the actual figures and update them accordingly.

Using a defect model such as this or any other model really helps to determine the foundation of the cost-benefit analysis. Cost-benefit analysis is discussed in more detail shortly. It is important that the model be based on real-world findings or estimates to ensure that the figures are as accurate as possible.

It is actually astonishing when you plug in real-world figures and see just how much you can potentially save by performing a few rudimentary activities up front. It is also astonishing to see just how much some defects can really cost further down the line.

This is just one simple example of calculating a cost-benefit figure that is related to potential defects and fix effort. There are other situations where defect modeling could be inappropriate and another model is required. For example, when choosing to use an existing component instead of custom component, building a solution will involve determining the amount of effort required to design, build, and implement the custom solution, as well as balancing these against the costs associated with product selection, procurement, licensing, implementation, and usage of the existing component.

Basic Financial Analysis

To meet the ever-increasing challenge of production-ready development, it's clear that some pretty industrialized tools, processes, and practices need to be put in place, and there are costs associated with doing this. Having a basic understanding of some of the financial implications helps to bolster the decision-making process. Financial discussions should always be held up front to avoid budget increases and to avoid unnecessary disputes later.

Let's look at two financial measures to bear in mind during development: the total cost of ownership (TCO) and the cost of poor quality (COPQ).

❑ Total cost of ownership (TCO) is a financial statement that covers the costs associated with the entire system, from its initial development and implementation to its final decommission. The following list is a representative view of what is generally included within a TCO statement:

 ❑ Costs associated with initial development and implementation

 ❑ Costs associated with running the system (infrastructure, electricity, floor space, and so on)

 ❑ Costs associated with the system's usage, support, and maintenance

 ❑ Costs associated with training (including project staff, users, and support staff)

 ❑ Costs associated with failures and outages (planned and unplanned)

 ❑ Costs associated with performance and response time issues (degradation)

 ❑ Costs associated with reputation loss and recovery

 ❑ Costs associated with decommission

❑ The cost of poor quality (COPQ) is the sum of the costs associated with producing defective material, including but not limited to:

 ❑ Costs associated with finding and fixing the defect

 ❑ Costs associated with lost opportunities

 ❑ Costs associated with loss of resources due to fixing the defect

There are many other financial controls and disciplines that should be carefully considered when setting the quality bar for a project. However, the preceding financial elements cover what you need to demonstrate best practice in the quality landscape.

Any practice that is used during the project increases the *costs associated with initial development and implementation* in the TCO statement. However, the additional costs should be met or bettered in savings or potential savings in the other areas. For instance, the following is a very simple example:

❑ If the cost of integration testing (and fixing) an assembly or sub-assembly is $500, then it must save at least $500 or have the potential to save at least $500 in other areas further down the line to make it a worthwhile practice.

Depending on the size of the functional and technical test teams, this cost could be easily realized by reducing the amount of time and effort spent idle as a result of defects. This is especially true if the assembly is architectural in nature and resides lower down in the stack, affecting a number of components higher up.

Cost-Benefit Analysis

It is often prudent to perform a rudimentary cost-benefit analysis to determine whether a process or practice should be implemented. The primary purpose of the cost-benefit analysis is to calculate the difference between what the solution will cost to put in versus the amount of money it will save by implementing it. Any practice increases costs associated with development and implementation, so you want to concentrate on where these can reduce additional costs.

The following table shows a very high-level mapping. To keep this section relatively brief, I have chosen to map a handful of best practices that are close to my heart, but you can easily see the purpose of the exercise. The table is only partly completed and as we progress throughout this book there are many other practices that can be included that help to reduce costs. For instance, a fault-tolerant design would be included with *costs associated with failures and outages*.

Total Cost of Ownership	Best Practice	Brief Explanation
Costs associated with the system's usage, support, and maintenance	Instrumentation and diagnostics Standards and guidelines Process and productivity guides (including generated documentation) Productivity tools and scripts Templates and TODO statements Configuration Build and regression testing	In addition to all the project documentation, the best practices listed improve the overall support and maintenance staff's productivity and knowledge of the system and how to support, maintain, and deploy it.
Costs associated with training (including project staff, users, and support staff)	Process and productivity guides (including documentation generation)	The documentation produced will help each individual user group understand the system and the processes and tools surrounding it.

(continued)

(continued)

Total Cost of Ownership	Best Practice	Brief Explanation
Costs associated with failures and outages (planned and unplanned)	Common test foundation (data, scripts, regression) Unit and integration testing Static Code Profiling and Peer review	Thorough testing at an early stage with common data and scenarios will help to reduce the number of potential defects. Static code profiling and peer reviews will ensure that the components are thoroughly reviewed prior to release.
Costs associated with performance and response time issues (degradation)	Performance profiling Unit and integration testing (performance cycles)	The cursory code profiling and performance cycles will help to identify potential performance bottlenecks and issues early.

This type of exercise should be conducted in full against any other financial measures that are in place. As mentioned at the start of this chapter, the TCO and COPQ measures provide a good basis for this sort of analysis. COPQ is not mapped in this section, although it would be quite simple to produce.

The simple mapping provides two important purposes:

❏ It shows how the initiative can be used to reduce costs.

❏ It highlights any gaps that might need to be plugged by introducing a particular initiative or practice to reduce costs further.

Once the basic mapping has been done, additional cost-benefit analysis can be performed to further bolster the information presented. The important thing to remember is that everything you do during the project and especially the construction phase is to try and reduce costs (and defects) further down the line.

Best Practice Analysis

This section simply bolsters the previous one by examining some of the best practices and the tools that are associated with them. Providing a simple set of pros and cons is very useful when determining where to set the quality bar for construction. It is important to note that best practices aren't without drawbacks. Bearing in mind these drawbacks and taking effective action and putting the appropriate controls in place are vital to a successful construction process.

The following C# code snippet would be very easy to write and manually test:

```csharp
public void OutputMessage( string message )
{
    Console.WriteLine("OutputMessage: {0}", message);
}
```

If some basic exception handling and logging is added, the code might look like something like this:

```
public void OutputMessage( string message )
{
    try
    {
        Console.WriteLine("OutputMessage: {0}", message);
    }
    catch( Exception e )
    {
        Console.WriteLine("OutputMessageException: {0}", e );
    }
}
```

In this very simple example, the code is now harder to fully test because the exception handling and logging section also needs to be tested. In this example, handling the exception is nothing more than catching it, and logging is simply outputting the error message to the console (without any contextual information, e.g. the message being passed in).

A very simple solution to testing the exception handling is to introduce a special test `message` argument and a compiler directive such as `TEST`. A compiler directive is essentially a command used by the source code compiler. In this case, the command is a conditional directive to determine whether the condition evaluates to true. If it does, the code will be compiled and included in the compiled version. If the condition evaluates to false, the code will not be compiled and included.

```
public void OutputMessage( string message )
{
    try
    {
        #if TEST

        if( message == "EXCEPTION_TEST" )
        {
            throw new Exception( message );
        }

        #endif

        Console.WriteLine("OutputMessage: {0}", message);

    }
    catch( Exception e )
    {

        Console.WriteLine("OutputMessageException: {0}", e );
    }
}
```

Using these conditional directives would allow two different versions of the code to be compiled — one for normal testing and one for exception testing. Furthermore, including the special test value allows a single version for testing, which can be built upon. There are many different ways of dealing with this type of problem, including the use of interfaces to swap in special test components. When a development team ramps up, a common approach needs to be in place to avoid multiple ways of doing the same thing. Designing for testing is covered later in this book, so I'm not going to go into the details and alternatives right now.

In this simple example, there is nothing really special happening in the exception handling section, so a simple test is probably good enough to test it. However, this is a prime example of the 80/20 rule: 80 percent of the time is spent proving 20 percent of the functionality. The 80/20 rule also applies to other development practices, such as coding standards and commenting. Once these are applied, the sample source code might look something like this:

```
<summary>
    The OutputMessage method is used to display a message on the console
</summary>
<arguments>
    <argument name="message">Message to be displayed. In test mode, when the
    input message contains 'EXCEPTION_TEST' an internal exception will be
    raised.</argument>
</arguments>
public void OutputMessage( string message )
{
    try
    {
        #region TEST_CODE

        #if TEST

        // check for test mode message
        if( message == "EXCEPTION_TEST" )
        {

            // throw a new exception based on the incoming message
            throw new Exception( message );
        }

        #end if

        #endregion

        // Functional Requirement 101 - Output Message to Console
        Console.WriteLine("OutputMessage: {0}", message);

    }
    catch( Exception e )
    {

        // Technical Requirement 101 - Output Exception to Console
        Console.WriteLine("OutputMessageException: {0}", e );

    }
}
```

Although this is an extremely basic example, it highlights some of the important factors that need to be taken into account when defining the construction process and setting the quality bar. Of course, the preceding code snippet probably wouldn't ever be used in a real-world scenario.

The following table lists some pros and cons with a few of the practices I've discussed and includes some basic high-level actions associated with them. As has been mentioned, in general terms, any additional practice that is introduced will increase development effort to some degree. However, I've chosen not to include *increases development effort* in the cons because the drawbacks of not including the best practices far outweigh including them.

Best Practice	Pros	Cons	Actions
Coding standards (including naming conventions and coding conventions)	Makes the code easier to read and follow. Provides a consistent basis for all coding and scripting.	All developers need to understand and follow the guidelines. Code needs to be checked for adherence and non-compliance. Needs to be updated and maintained as new practices are introduced.	Must have: A coding standards and guidelines document and induction guide. Tools and guidelines for checking adherence and non-conformance. A process whereby new practices can be introduced and re-factoring can be taken into account.
Commenting	Makes the code easier to understand, follow, and maintain.	Needs to be updated when the code changes. Needs to be reviewed for correctness and meaningfulness.	Must have: Clear guidelines that when code is updated, comments are updated accordingly. Review checklist that includes commenting checks.
Exception handling, including defensive coding	Protects the system against unknown or invalid circumstances and situations.	Needs to be tested and asserted. Needs to be reviewed for compliance to standards.	Must have: Guidelines and templates for exception handling coding. A development and test framework for testing exceptions. Review checklist that includes exception-handling checks.
Event logging and tracing	Helps with issue investigation and resolution. Helps with monitoring and alerting.	Can affect performance if not implemented efficiently. Needs to be tested and asserted. Needs to be reviewed for correctness and completeness.	Must have: Guidelines and templates for logging and tracing usage. A development and test framework for testing logging and tracing. Review checklist that includes logging and tracing checks.

(continued)

(continued)

Best Practice	Pros	Cons	Actions
Instrumentation	Helps with support monitoring and alerting.	Can affect performance if not implemented efficiently. Needs to be tested and asserted. Needs to be reviewed for correctness and completeness.	Must have: Guidelines and templates for instrumentation implementation. A development and test framework for testing instrumentation. Review checklist that includes instrumentation checks.

You need to fully understand the implications in terms of cost (and timescales) of the practices being proposed or introduced. It's all too easy to jump on to the latest thinking or a cool tool that's been announced. Doing the homework and some background analysis will clarify specific benefits and what else needs to be implemented to support the practice's usage. The following table lists some of the pros and cons of the tools associated with these practices. I'll leave it to you to determine which actions you would put in place to counter the cons, although some of the manual processes were touched on earlier.

Tool	Pros	Cons
Static code analysis	Automates the process of checking code against the coding standards. Allows developers to check work and correct issues prior to formal review, saving valuable review time. Reviewers can re-execute the tool to ensure conformance and validate exceptions.	Specific coding standards need to be configured unless the out-of-the-box configuration is adequate (in most cases, it isn't). Needs to be updated and maintained as new practices are introduced. Static code analysis does not remove the need for formal reviews.
Code profiling	Helps to identify potential performance and technical issues prior to formal review or build (including database element profiling). This reduces the amount of review time and potential defects.	Specific profiling needs to be configured unless the out-of-the-box configuration is adequate (in most cases, it only goes so far). Code and database profiling does not remove the need for formal reviews.
Test coverage analysis	Code coverage identifies areas of code that have not been tested. This analysis can be used to develop further tests or remove areas of redundant code.	Striving to meet 100 percent coverage can increase development and test times if the appropriate practices are not already in place. An appropriate benchmark needs to be established. The 80/20 rule applies here in that 80 percent of the time can be spent trying to cover 20 percent of the code. Some tests may need to be run against different configuration settings to achieve a true representation of code coverage.

Tool	Pros	Cons
Documentation generation	Generating the documentation from the code saves you from having to write it manually and avoids rework, and keeps the code and documentation in-line.	The generated documentation often needs to be updated with class diagrams and interaction diagrams generated from other tools, which need to be carefully understood and configured. This can require manual effort in documentation production.
Automated tests	Manual testing is often a laborious task and mistakes can be made. Once a series of tests has been automated, it reduces manual effort and provides a solid foundation for regression testing.	The tests and expected results need to be maintained throughout to ensure changes and updates are reflected correctly. This is especially true of user interface testing. As soon as fields move or additional fields are added, you can sometimes see a dramatic effect on the user interface test scripts. The tools often require complex configuration, which needs to be managed and maintained.

Some of these tools can be purchased and some can be developed in-house. In either case, they need to be configured appropriately and managed as a part of the overall solution and justified accordingly. That said, I'm a firm believer in using these types of tools for any and all development projects.

Estimates and Estimating

One final quality input to the planning process is the estimates. Build and unit test estimates should cover the resources and time required to build a component and unit test it. The estimates are highly dependent on the level of quality, the effectiveness and efficiency of the development and test processes, procedures and tools, and the skill level of the developer. Estimating is a true discipline and getting ready for development as early as possible helps to ensure better estimates.

Estimating is essentially answering the question "How long will it take?" and its counterpart question "How much will it cost?" For the purpose of this exercise, I am going to use a very simple case to demonstrate the value of realistic estimating. The challenge question is as follows:

❑ How long will it take to produce a simple console application in C# that takes a single string argument and displays the message on the screen?

You may be thinking of a figure right now, based on the preceding example code snippets. The answer to this question is that it really depends. However, for the purposes of this exercise, I'm going to put a stake in the ground and say 15 minutes for a very simple solution with manual testing and minimum best practice. 15 minutes is a realistic estimate to perform the following tasks:

1. Open Visual Studio.

2. Create a new console application.

3. Add a `Console.WriteLine` statement that outputs the argument.

4. Compile the solution and generate an EXE file.

5. Open a command window.

6. Change the directory to the location of the generated EXE.

7. Run the EXE, passing an argument on the command line.

8. Check that the correct argument is displayed in the output.

There's nothing special about this and it's a viable solution to the problem and one that would probably be used in a C# training course. You saw an example of this earlier, albeit not as a form console application. In this instance, the estimate takes into account only a basic implementation and covers coding and very minimal testing. This example is used only to bolster the importance of understanding all the processes and practices I've covered so far and including them in the estimating process.

Once the quality bar is in place and you've done the up-front work, you can put some realistic estimates in place by walking through the process. The process and tools dictate the *minimum development time* and the component's complexity, and developer skill dictates the *maximum development time*. The more efficient the processes and tools are, the lower the minimum, and the less complex the components are and the better and faster developers are, the lower the maximum. The *mean development time* is middle ground between the most experienced developer and the least experienced developer. For instance, if it takes a highly skilled developer one day to complete a task and it takes two days for a less skilled developer, the *mean development time* would be approximately 1.5 days, the difference between the two. Over time, the actual development times can be recorded to improve estimating, although the estimates still need to factor into the *minimum development time* for the process, as it may have changed.

Figure 2-4 shows a mapping between developer skill and component complexity.

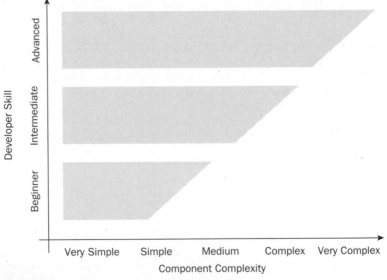

Figure 2-4

Minimizing the number of complex or very complex components allows for less highly skilled developers to work on them. The ideal solution is to keep all components within the range of Very Simple to Medium, allowing the maximum number of developers to work on them, although this needs to be balanced with development progression. Advanced developers want to work on complex programs, junior developers want to advance to intermediate programs, and so on.

If there are complex or very complex components in the solution, advanced developers are required on the team. The project plan will determine how many developers are required and the appropriate level of skill. It is generally easier to get beginner and intermediate developers than it is to get advanced developers. Keeping the solution simple means more people can work on it, and having the right processes and practices in place helps to keep everything on track and consistent.

In my experience, nothing takes less than the minimum development time individually. Volumes of scale need to be applied to achieve this. For instance, a rules engine may involve hundreds of rules components. If there are 100 simple rules, components that are around one or two lines of core code each and the appropriate templates are used. The time per component may dip below the minimum because of the volumes and parallelism involved. This, however, should not necessarily be relied on when estimating, as it can often cause a development bottleneck that needs to be reviewed carefully.

To arrive at a true estimate, you need to fill in the gaps in the process. For example, if you look at steps of developing test scripts and testing data from the development process, the process might look something like this (I've simplified the steps for this example):

1. Copy the unit test template to the appropriate component folder under unit test conditions.

2. Fill in the component name, developer, team, and reviewer fields.

3. Fill in the test conditions according to the test condition checklist.

4. Save the unit test conditions.

5. Conduct a formal review according to test condition checklist.

Steps 3 and 5 are the hardest to estimate. Step 3 is difficult because you need to know how many conditions there are, and Step 5 is based on the number of conditions. In general, conditions that can be met by input values and output values are far easier to test than internal conditions. Complexity is typically based on the number of conditions, which also include the input values and the different combinations, the number of branches in the component, the nesting of the branches, and the outputs or expected results.

The following pseudo code contains one input, `AccountType`, which has two possible values, `Administrator` and `User`. The code has two branches, one for valid account types and one invalid account types.

```
FUNCTION VALIDATE_ACCOUNT_TYPE( AccountType )

    VALID_ACCOUNT_TYPE = FALSE

    IF AccountType = "Administrator" OR AccountType = "User" THEN

        SET VALID_ACCOUNT_TYPE = TRUE

    ELSE

        RAISE BUSINESS EVENT: INVALID_ACCOUNT_TYPE + AccountType
```

```
          SET VALID_ACCOUNT_TYPE = FALSE

     END IF

     RETURN VALID_ACCOUNT_TYPE

END FUNCTION
```

The pseudo code doesn't contain any error handling or other outputs, so it acts as a very simple case. The functional test conditions would include those listed in the following table:

Condition	Description	Input Value	Expected Results
1	Valid administrator account type	Administrator	Return value = TRUE.
2	Valid user account type	User	Return value = TRUE.
3	Invalid account type	XXX	Return value = FALSE. INVALID_ACCOUNT_ TYPE event raised with XXX

The basic test conditions in the preceding table would obtain 100 percent code coverage. They also take into account the event being raised and the contextual information. The INVALID_ACCOUNT_TYPE event could be verified manually; however, it's still an expected result of the condition and not just that the method returns false.

When estimating how long it will take to build and test a component, you should take into account the number of conditions, input values, and expected results, as described in the following table. Functional designs sometimes don't take into account exception handling and logging (unless there are very specific requirements), as these are thought of as technical characteristics that should be documented in the technical or detailed design documents.

Condition	Category	Description	Input Value	Expected Results
1	Functional	Valid administrator account type	Administrator	Return value = TRUE.
2	Functional	Valid user account type	User	Return value = TRUE.
3	Functional	Invalid account type	XXX	Return value = FALSE. INVALID_ACCOUNT_ TYPE event raised with XXX.

Condition	Category	Description	Input Value	Expected Results
4	Performance	10,000 * valid administrator account type	Administrator	Return value = TRUE. < 5ms response time
5	Performance	10,000 * valid user account type	User	Return value = TRUE. < 5ms response time
6	Performance	10,000 * mixed valid administrator and user account types	2,000 * administrator 8,000 * user	Return value = TRUE. < 5ms response time
7	Monitoring / Incident Investigation	Invalid account type YYY	YYY	Return value = FALSE. INVALID_ACCOUNT_ TYPE event raised with YYY.
8	Monitoring / Incident Investigation	Invalid account type ZZZ	ZZZ	Return value = FALSE. INVALID_ACCOUNT_ TYPE event raised with ZZZ.
9	Monitoring / Incident Investigation Performance	10,000 * mixed invalid YYY and ZZZ account types	2,000 * YYY 8,000 * ZZZ	Return value = FALSE. 2,000 * INVALID_ ACCOUNT_TYPE event raised with YYY. 8,000 * INVALID_ ACCOUNT_TYPE event raised with ZZZ. < 5ms response time.

This may seem like an over-the-top set of test conditions for such a small component. However, they could be extended even further to take into account logging and other technical features.

The key message is to ensure that the level of testing is included in the scope and that the testing stresses the component appropriately, whether at the unit level or integration level, prior to it leaving construction. It should be firmly understood that not all issues will be resolved during construction, but the level of build quality and testing should underpin the quality bar for progressing further. The level of testing and the criteria should be taken into account when estimating.

Summary

This chapter covered the quality characteristics you need to bear in mind with everything that you do and implement. You've also seen what is involved in construction quality and the processes and practices you can employ to ensure your outputs are of a high quality. You've seen how you can better prepare yourself for testing and issue resolution. You might not be able to totally eradicate these situations, but you should do whatever you can up front to minimize them and keep costs and timescales under control. Quality needs to be factored into the scope so that the budgets and timescales can be realistically set and agreed on.

The following are the key points to take away from this chapter:

- **The quality characteristics apply to everything you do.** Quality is not just about code quality; it applies to all the artifacts that you produce and deliver. You should think about how each of the individual characteristics could apply to the particular item or artifact you are producing.

- **Construction quality echoes throughout the project.** You need to ensure that your construction processes and practices are tuned to produce high-quality outputs and deliverables. Some key activities and practices include:

  - Validating requirements and designs and documenting queries and questions that need to be addressed before the component can be closed off completely

  - Producing and reviewing low-level models and designs

  - Developing and reviewing unit test scripts and test data to ensure breadth and depth of test coverage

  - Developing and reviewing components (application, architecture and framework, batch, reporting, and so on)

  - Developing and reviewing test harnesses, including mock objects, test stubs, and simulators

  - Executing thorough unit tests and ensuring that all the relevant outputs are captured and verified

  - Identifying assemblies (collections of related components) and ensuring the appropriate level of granularity

  - Executing thorough integration tests and ensuring that all the relevant outputs are captured and verified

  - Compiling completion reports that document the evidence and outcomes of the activities carried out

  - Submitting artifacts into a release and ensuring that all the relevant artifacts are included in a release

  - Performing peer reviews and quality checks throughout the process

- **Include quality characteristics in the overall scope.** It is important to agree on the quality characteristics up front and include them in the overall scope. It's particularly important to ensure that all quality characteristics are captured and the processes reflect them. In addition, where tools are used, the configuration should be agreed on to avoid any disputes. The best practices include:

❏ Ensuring code quality by defining standards, guidelines, and templates

❏ Promoting re-use and layering to support testing and improve component re-use throughout the solution

❏ Using code generation techniques and ensuring that the resulting code meets all the coding standards and is profiled and reviewed as if it were crafted by hand

❏ Using automated static and dynamic code profiling to ensure code quality and to identify potential issues early

❏ Including instrumentation and diagnostics in all your components

❏ Using automated code coverage tools to identify the amount of code covered during testing

❏ Automatically generating documentation from code comments

❏ **Avoid an influx of issues during testing.** It is important to ensure that your test tools, test environments, and processes are fit for purpose and ready when you need them. You need to try to avoid an influx of:

❏ Environment issues

❏ Tool and script issues

❏ Test data issues

❏ Real bugs

❏ **Turning around defects quickly can affect quality.** You need to incorporate processes and practices that allow sustained quality and support rapid turnaround when testing is blocked. The processes that can potentially reduce quality include:

❏ Hot-fixing or patching

❏ Technical tuning and re-factoring

❏ **Improve and maintain quality throughout.** You can improve the overall quality of the system in a number of ways. The following lists the key activities discussed in addition to those already mentioned:

❏ Work with the test teams.

❏ Re-use common test data, scripts, and scenarios.

❏ Re-use common test tools, stubs, and simulators.

❏ Reduce the number of release configurations to avoid delays and installing and re-installing different releases for different testing activities.

❏ Automate as much as possible. Do it twice manually, and it should be automated.

❏ Review processes and practices and continuously improve them where possible.

❏ **Quality comes at a price.** Nothing is for free. You need to understand the implications in terms of cost (and timescales) of the choices that you make. The estimates need to be based on realistic figures and the processes will actually determine the average amount of time required. However, proven and well-implemented processes and practices can help to reduce the costs. The costs need to be understood, agreed to, and included in the overall scope to ensure that the Project Management Triangle is set.

❑ **Identify and correct as many defects as early as possible.** The testing and verification that you perform during the construction phase should try to catch as many defects as possible. This will avoid costly and time-consuming "wash-up" sessions, whereby defects are scrutinized to determine whether they could have been detected during construction or earlier.

The following chapter examines some of the processes that should be considered and put in place early to ensure that you are fully prepared for production, e.g. the development and implementation of quality software products.

3

Preparing for "Production"

This chapter examines some of the key areas you should consider when setting up your software-development production line. With a well-oiled production line, you should be able to develop anything and get high quality products out the end. We're not concentrating so much on the final solution, although its size and scale will affect some of the decisions you make. As with any kind of manufacturing, you need the right raw materials, the right processing, and the right quality controls.

There are many processes that you need to establish before starting full-on production (e.g., development) to ensure that you are in a position to produce high quality outputs and I tend to use the word "defining" for a lot of the activities described. In the majority of cases, I am actually referring to "defining and implementing." As with most things in life, we're very often constrained by certain factors, and software development is no different. Aside from timescales and budgets, we can also be constrained by a particular methodology, technology, or policy, for example. When setting up your factory, you must understand whether there are any specific constraints that the production line must follow. If not, then you're free to implement your own. Think of these as the formal regulations for your production line. In the construction industry, buildings must be inspected at regular intervals. There may be regulations whereby your code will be inspected at regular intervals by an external party. The regulations can be set by your own company, the consumer, an official body or third-party, or, finally, by yourself. However, before you start making your own regulations, you need to determine if there are regulations that you *must* adhere to.

You're going to look at some of the types of applications, environments, processes, and tools that should be assessed and put in place (where appropriate). Everything you've seen so far needs to be cost effective and implemented in a controlled and orderly fashion. This chapter focuses primarily on getting your software production line established.

This chapter is organized into the following sections:

❑ **Preparation Is Paramount** — Examines the high-level activities that you perform during the project and shows how they can be broken down to ensure they are mobilized effectively. It also discusses the key constraints that should be identified when mobilizing any activities.

❑ **Development Mobilization** — Discusses the specifics regarding the activities, choices, and decisions that should be taken into account when mobilizing the development activities. This includes ensuring that you have the right inputs and that they are well-defined, ensuring that you have all the right processes and practices in place, and ensuring the outputs from the development activities are fit for purpose.

❑ **Build, Release, and Regular Integration Mobilization** — The build and regular integration activities are vital to ensuring that you can build and release your software. This section discusses this process along with some of the different releases and their typical contents.

❑ **Test Mobilization** — Testing is where you're going to prove your application works the way it should. Having solid foundations in place for testing will help your project. This section looks at some of the specifics in mobilizing your testing activities.

❑ **Defect Management (and Fix) Mobilization** — Testing, as well as other activities, is going to raise defects. This section looks at defect management, including the workflow and the contents of defects, and discusses some ways of how defects can be categorized for management (and reporting) purposes.

❑ **Configuration Management Mobilization** — You need to store all your artifacts somewhere, and this section discusses the configuration-management system and processes. It looks at some of the items that you can choose to place under configuration management and how they can be organized to meet the needs of the project. It also discusses branching and merging, which may be required.

❑ **Change Control Mobilization** — Things are going to change, so you need to be ready to assess changes appropriately. You also need to ensure that the change process is followed.

I am not going to cover the analysis and design mobilization activities, although you should also consider them accordingly. The activities outlined in this chapter will give you some ideas for identifying and defining analysis and design mobilization. Mobilizing your project effectively is a key factor for success and the activities discussed in this chapter should be included within the overall scope of the project to ensure that the costs and timescales are accounted for.

Preparation Is Paramount

Chapter 1 discussed the high-level activities involved in software development and implementation. You also looked at the production-readiness process and saw that your applications, environments, processes, and tools must be fit for purpose and your users must be trained and ready. All of these are brought together and shown in Figure 3-1.

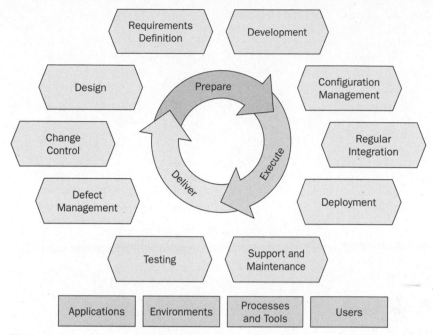

Figure 3-1

Hindsight is a wonderful thing. So is learning from our triumphs and mistakes. When planning your project, you need to remember your past experiences and look at what was good and what wasn't so good. You need to improve everything each time until you have the ideal process. Although the process will differ from project to project and organization to organization, the best time to reflect on past experience is early on. Once your project is off and running, the time to change and the impact of change generally increases, although you should reflect at very regular intervals and improve where necessary.

You want to give your projects the best chance of success and a good way of achieving this is to ensure that you are prepared for each of the activities in Figure 3-1. You need to think about what you're going to do and how you're going to do it. This can be thought of as *mobilization*. Before starting actual development, you should mobilize the development activities — for example, ensuring that the best practice is in place, ensuring the developers have been on the right training or fit the right profile, and so on.

The ultimate goal of setting up your production line is to get as much of it as possible defined and working up front, before full-scale production starts. The purpose of the mobilization activity is really to iron out the processes, practices, and procedures, to plug as many gaps as possible, and to provide a solid foundation before launching into it full-scale. Every activity in the development lifecycle has its own prerequisites and ideally needs to be mobilized, stabilized, and documented. On a normal production line, you wouldn't want to start production of millions of units, only to find half way through there was a flaw in the process.

Remember that even with these mobilization activities in place, you probably won't get it right the first time. Tweaks and adjustments will need to be made throughout the project in order to fully refine the process. Depending on the number of mobilization activities and the time required, you could perform them simultaneously. For instance, if you want to use an agile approach to construction, you'd need to mobilize quite a few activities beforehand.

As a developer, you are used to breaking down problems into their component parts, and preparation is no different. You need to look at what you will be doing during these activities and break it down into discrete tasks. Your success ultimately is based on how well you *prepare*, *execute*, and *deliver* the activities throughout the project lifecycle. This section (and chapter) looks at some of these high-level preparation activities.

I recently took my car to the garage after I, unfortunately, scraped and dented a panel. I was told that because there was nowhere to blend the paint, it required a complete re-spray. Although the design of the car is beautiful, it's a shock to the system when you're told that what appears to be a minor repair is actually a major one because of the car's design, not to mention the expense of it. I use this story for two important reasons. First, a total re-spray is all about the preparation. Actually spraying the car takes little time in comparison to the sanding down, pulling out all the little dinks and chinks, and making good anything else. Second, it's a costly business when it seems like a simple matter to be addressed. It's just a minor dent, right? These two principles apply to software development. What may seem like a simple change can have huge cost implications if not considered early enough in the process. Considering the solution and the way it will be implemented, tested, deployed, and operated is nothing more than preparation. The actual development can be very little in comparison if the foundations are set correctly.

Breaking Down the Activities

To define a really low-level set of requirements (functional or technical), some form of design activity needs to be conducted. Similarly, to flesh out the design in more detail, some form of development activity will need to be conducted. This usually involves building a prototype or a reference application that models the basic functionality. Let's not forget that the testing activities often raise a series of changes based on real usage of the system. This is the nature of software development. It's very hard to get it right on paper, and it's very hard to get it right the first time.

Figure 3-2 shows each of the key activities split in two parts. Each part has a high-level and a low-level or detailed counterpart that provides more detailed information.

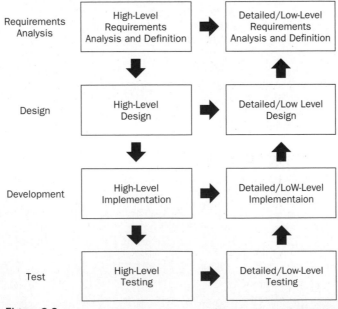

Figure 3-2

These activities essentially apply to everything you do and use. For example, you need to record your system's functional and technical requirements somewhere. This task itself actually starts off with requirements analysis. You need to understand the requirements for your Requirements Management Solution (RMS). You then need to design a suitable solution to your problem, develop it, and test it. Each of these activities is a process of refinement. You start off with a high-level concept and refine it as you progress. Similarly, you need to store your system's source code and configuration. This again starts with analyzing the requirements for the Configuration Management Solution (CMS). Again, you'll produce a high-level design, develop the solution, test it, and so on.

In this instance, your consumers are the folks who are going to use all these items. In the case of the RMS, this will probably be everyone involved in the project. You need to assess and define each of the quality characteristics and ensure that the solution meets them. You also need to ensure that all the consumers (users) can access the solution and understand how to use it.

Identifying the Constraints

I find the best place to start when mobilizing any activities is to identify the constraints. Constraints are always a very good place to start because they don't normally have any bearing on the functionality or technical aspects of the system or sub-systems — they simply shape the way the final state solution is implemented. Gathering, understanding, and defining the constraints serve as the starting point for building your software-development production line.

Figure 3-3 shows (and the following sections discuss) the high-level categories of the constraints you need to understand, plan for, or put in place yourself.

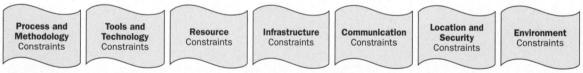

Figure 3-3

Constraints can be specified in both high-level and low-level form. For example, a high-level constraint could be "Code coverage must be checked and reported," whereas a low-level constraint would be "Code coverage must be 100 percent during unit testing and checked using code coverage version 8.7." The more detailed the constraints, the better.

Process and Methodology Constraints

You must first determine (and understand) the methodology that the overall project will follow. The methodology generally stipulates what the phases and/or activities are within the project, what each phase encompasses (including its inputs and outputs), and how the phases interact (and possibly overlap) with each other.

There are many formal methodologies (and you can define your own custom approaches), some of which were highlighted in the previous chapters. The size, scale, and complexity of the project (or activity) typically dictate the approach that should be taken. You're in the very early stages of setting up your development factory, and you have a number of "activities" to initiate.

It's possible that your "implementing the Requirements Management Solution" project could follow a very strict waterfall model, especially if the solution is going to be used for many other projects. Each phase would follow the previous phase, such as analysis, requirements definition, design, build, test, deployment, and so on. For example, analysis would involve talking to stakeholders and gathering their high-level requirements. It would also involve gathering the user's high-level requirements. The high-level requirements would be defined, documented, and reviewed as part of the requirements definition activity. The requirements would be fed into the design activities, and so on, and so forth.

Alternatively, "implementing the Requirements Management Solution" could follow a far more rapid development approach, especially if it's only for a single project. For example, it could be as simple as performing a cursory search on the Internet for some "best practice requirements gathering" tips, pulling together a template spreadsheet, storing it on a shared drive, and telling everyone where it is.

The approach could also be anywhere in between the two extremes. Every project is different, so the reality is that most projects use a mix of methodologies without necessarily knowing it or putting it in place formally. Large, mission-critical projects that have multiple sub-projects may follow a structured waterfall approach overall. However, some of the sub-projects and activities may follow more agile and rapid development approaches. For instance, tools development will more often than not follow a more agile approach. It's quite likely that scripts will be developed around the Configuration Management Solution to extract files and feed them into the Regular Integration Solution. These development activities could essentially follow a strict waterfall approach, although more than likely they won't.

The term *mission-critical* refers to items and software that are crucial to the successful completion of a project. It also means the items and software are vital to the organization's mission. It is, therefore, possible (although perhaps somewhat tenuous) to classify your mobilization activities as "mission-critical." Without a development environment and development tools, you can't develop any software at all. While every project is different, there are some high-level categories listed below:

❏ **Non-critical systems** — Systems that are not critical to the success of the project or organization

❏ **Mission-critical systems** — System that are critical to the success of the project or organization

❏ **Life-critical systems** — Systems that are critical to safety and lives

We rely on software and systems so much today that it's often hard to categorize under the "non-critical systems" heading. You need to determine whether the project and/or organization can succeed without it. Identifying what is mission-critical is the first step.

There are no hard-and-fast rules as to the development approach that should be taken for each system type. The system and the approach need to be assessed for their suitability. Each methodology will have its pros and cons. Although I could make some general recommendations for each, it's really a process of discussion and agreement. The project might have the opportunity to define its own development approach; however, organizations often have their own formal approaches to software development that must be followed. It is important to determine and understand whether there are any rigid constraints that *must* be adhered to regarding the software development approach. If the organization doesn't stipulate a formal approach, the project needs to define its own approach.

In addition to software development approaches, organizations often have their own internal processes that must be followed. This is another critical factor in your scope and preparation activities. It's not uncommon for organizations to stipulate external or third-party reviews and penetration tests, in which case you need to understand this process and ensure that it's planned for.

Furthermore, many organizations incorporate the following processes:

❑ **Procurement** — Anything that you want to buy may have to go through the organization's procurement process. This might mean using the organization's preferred suppliers and vendors instead of your own. This could result in not being able to purchase the items you need and force you to seek alternatives. If this is the case, it's very important to engage the procurement team early and understand the process, timescales, and constraints.

❑ **Recruitment** — I'll discuss resource constraints shortly, but a number of organizations have their own recruitment processes. Mobilizing your team might require new resources to be hired. If this is the case, the recruitment team needs to be engaged early to understand the process. In addition, you might want to engage outside specialists or contractors, a process that could come under the heading of recruitment or procurement, so it's well worth understanding.

❑ **Policy compliance** — Organizations usually have a number of internal policies that need to be adhered to. For example, an organization may have strict guidelines regarding the use of freeware, shareware, open source software, or even the use of trial licenses. The policy may have to be adhered to even if the software isn't a part of the final solution. Information exchange is another area that could require strict policy compliance. It's very important that you understand any policies or regulations that you *must* adhere to during the project.

There may be other categories of process and methodology constraints, but in summary, you need to ensure that you fully understand any and all of them. If none are in place, you are free to implement your own approach, assuming it is agreed on by the organization.

Tools and Technology Constraints

Most organizations have their own preferred tools and technologies. For example, there may be a constraint to use a particular configuration-management tool, load-testing tool, or profiling tool. It is quite rare that you get to choose everything from scratch, although it does sometimes happen. You generally get the opportunity to fill in the gaps with a combination of custom tools and scripts along with some other purchased tools. If there are no formal constraints, you're free to implement your own tools and technologies, again, assuming they are agreed on by the organization.

One particular constraint to watch out for is the use of "internal" components. For example, you may be integrating with the Order Management System (OMS), and the team responsible for the OMS has developed a specific integration component. If you're required to use any of these, you must ensure that they are fit for purpose and that you understand exactly how they are used, what they are used for, and, most importantly, whether they actually work. Specifications are no substitute for the real thing. What is the real thing? You need to get hold of it, install it, and make sure it works the way *you* need it to work. You may also find that you need to stub it or even simulate it (if suitable stubs and simulators aren't already available). When "internal" components *must* be used, it's worth engaging the teams responsible for them and understanding as much as possible regarding their installation, configuration, usage (in all situations), and, most importantly, support and maintenance. You may need to raise defects or changes against the component, so you should fully understand these processes, too. It's exactly the same for third-party products, as well.

The tools and technology constraints need to be listed along with:

❑ The exact version that must be used.

❑ What they are used for.

❑ Whom they are used by (designer, developer, tester, and so on).

❑ Instructions for obtaining them, installing them, and accessing them. It's equally important to determine whether they are hosted centrally or locally on the user's machine.

❑ Specific usage guidelines.

❑ Any licensing model and associated costs.

❑ The number of licenses required and available, and how to extend or obtain new ones and how long this takes.

❑ The current license keys and their expiry dates.

❑ Whether they require configuration, customization, or enhancement.

❑ The system requirements, deployment and backup requirements, and best practices.

❑ The support arrangements (office hours, out-of-hours, and so on).

All this information will help when mobilizing the activities and defining the additional tasks that may be required.

Resource Constraints

You need to understand if there are any key resources that must be utilized. In this case, you're mainly looking at human resources that need to be engaged. For example, a lot of companies have a central technical architecture or DBA function. It's often a constraint that all designs and outputs are reviewed and signed off by them. In some cases, this can sometimes create a bottleneck for projects. If you're producing large numbers of items, the individual or team could be overloaded. The resource constraints should be identified and documented. When attempting to identify resource constraints, you should ask yourself (and the organization) the following questions:

❑ Whom do I need to engage?

❑ Why am I engaging them?

❑ How do I engage them?

❑ What lead time do I need to give them?

❑ What do I need to provide them with?

❑ What are they going to provide back to me?

❑ How long can I expect them to take to complete their activities?

❑ What do I do if they are late or delayed?

It is imperative that you mitigate these risks and ensure that the project can continue even if it is waiting on sign-offs. If the team is going to continue with their core activities, this is referred to as *proceeding at risk*. Development that starts before the designs have been signed off is a very clear risk and needs to be carefully balanced. Developers can begin a number of activities while waiting for formally signed-off designs and other documentation; however, the delay could have a more far-reaching impact on the timescales.

If you're doing the project on behalf of another organization, it might be a constraint that all development staff pass their in-house test or have to be certified to a certain level before being able to work on the project. It may also be a constraint that all people working on the project must be cleared by security. This could apply equally to contractors and other temporary staff within your own organization.

The following questions help to quantify these constraints:

❑ What skills do the development staff, contractors, and/or temporary staff need?

❑ Are any specific qualifications/certifications required?

❑ Are there any specific processes to obtain them?

The final resource constraint is working hours and availability. A lot of companies (and regulations) stipulate maximum working hours. You need to understand this because not only will it affect how you manage your own people, it will also affect how you engage others. For instance, if the support organization works a set of core working hours, you may have to coordinate well in advance any out-of-hours arrangements.

All the resource constraints need to be listed and captured appropriately so that they can be carried forward throughout the mobilization activities (and, of course, the remainder of the project).

Infrastructure Constraints

Production hardware and related infrastructure is typically installed in a data center or server room. In addition, there may be constraints for specific hardware to be purchased and used. It is well worth understanding the number of servers required and the infrastructure constraints. Space is often at a premium, and sometimes to reduce the number of servers there's a constraint to consolidate and host multiple applications on the same server. This can have an effect on your solution design. In addition, you may need to buy additional infrastructure components and this can have a dramatic effect on costs. You will also need storage space for all your applications and this will need to be backed up too.

If all servers need to be housed in a central data center, you need to ensure that your team can access them. Your team could be spread across multiple locations, and their inability to access the servers via a remote access solution could be a problem. Furthermore, if work is going to be carried out across multiple locations, you need to know where the servers are located and define the appropriate connectivity. If all development machines are located in the U.K. and developers are located around the globe, it's critical that high-speed communications and tools are in place to avoid inefficient teams.

Where multi-site development takes place, the processes and tools also need to support this. When different teams are using different processes it causes major headaches for the project. You also need to consider security because data transmitted out of the country could also breach regulations or the company's internal policies. Even transferring data between networks could be a breach.

Time-zone differences can also cause problems for distributed projects. For instance, when should the backups kick off? It's not that uncommon when you're testing the system and see that it's running slowly, only to find that a backup is running at the same time. It's usually only after many hours of investigation that you find this out. Backups should be performed when no one is working on the system to ensure consistency and to not impact the project. It's not just backups that can impact testing and distributed teams like this; anti-virus software and other background tasks can affect the team in similar ways. It's important to understand when background tasks will be executed and what the task's potential impact will be.

The following questions will help you to identify or define infrastructure constraints:

- ❏ How much hardware do we need?
- ❏ Do we need to buy specific hardware?
- ❏ Where does it need to be located?
- ❏ Is there enough room (and resources) at this location?
- ❏ When is it required?
- ❏ Who will be using it?
- ❏ What is it used for?
- ❏ How should it be installed?
- ❏ How should it be accessed and from where?
- ❏ How should it be maintained and supported?

There are a lot more questions that you could ask to determine whether there were any other specific constraints regarding infrastructure. However, the preceding list provides an overview of what you're trying to define and ensure.

Communication Constraints

We're all used to communicating by telephone, live messaging software, and e-mail in our daily lives. We're also used to surfing the Net to find out information and browse articles. A lot of companies block certain sites, as well as disallow live messaging software. Your organization may have its own messaging software (instant, e-mail, or both). Although e-mail is commonplace, a lot of organizations don't allow instant messaging software and web-cams for communication. Some companies don't even allow pen drives in the building. So, transferring and sharing large artifacts has to be done on the network, thus preventing them and any classified material from being shipped outside the organization.

Although these items might seem rudimentary, they can sometimes affect how quickly you can mobilize and get up-and-running. Effective communications need to be in place right from the start. This is especially true if the team is distributed across multiple locations and/or time-zones.

It's important to understand how the team and its members need to communicate with each other and to ensure that the processes and tools are available or alternative methods are defined and in place.

Environment Constraints

You need to understand whether any shared environment constraints need to be considered. It is often necessary to install the software in an environment that is shared with other projects. For example, the pre-production environment might be shared across a number of different projects and initiatives. It is important to understand and document the process for using the environment as well as the person or persons you need to contact to reserve timeslots within which you can perform your activities. The following questions help to gather and document environment constraints:

❑ Do we need to share any environments with anyone else?

❑ Who is the main contact for the environment?

❑ How do we go about booking timeslots?

❑ How do we escalate issues with this environment?

Environment constraints can also include office and desk space. The number of "bums on seats" that you need may differ from the space available. There may also be a policy that prohibits desk sharing. You need to ensure that the project resources can be located effectively and that there's room for expansion (where necessary). Location and security constraints are discussed shortly.

Technical environments can also be constrained because of infrastructure constraints. You need to ensure that you capture any and all environment constraints so that you can effectively plan and mobilize your activities. To do so, answer the following questions:

❑ Which environments do we need to use?

❑ How many of them do we need?

❑ What should they be used for?

❑ How should they be sized and scaled?

❑ How should they be used?

❑ How should they be maintained and supported?

Location (and Security) Constraints

Location constraints include any specific locations where activities *must* be performed. Location opening and access times can cause problems — for example, if access to the building is only available during typical business hours or access to the data center is only allowed outside of hours. These constraints could impact when certain tasks are performed.

It is important to answer the following questions to understand the locations of resources, the activities that will be carried out, and the tools that will be required and used:

❑ Who needs to be where?

❑ What are they going to be doing there?

❑ What hours can they be there?

❑ What do they need to do their job?

❑ How long do they need to be there?

❑ Are there any security constraints at this location?

The final location constraints are travel and visa requirements. In a globally distributed team, resources are often required to travel to different locations to perform various tasks. Traveling to certain countries requires a number of injections that often take time to organize and are spread out over time. In addition, visa applications can often take a long time to obtain. It's worth asking the following questions:

- ❑ Will this person need to travel? If so, to where?
- ❑ Will this require any injections?
- ❑ Will this person need a visa?
- ❑ Are there any specific visa requirements that could be a problem?
- ❑ How do we go about getting a visa?
- ❑ How long does it take?

You should plan for this accordingly, and it's also worth discussing with the individual, just in case he or she has any prior commitments or thinks it could be a problem.

> Although there may be other constraints, the important thing is that they are all identified, documented, and well understood. Equally important, as you will see later, is that you do not need to know the answers to all the preceding questions to be able to proceed with a particular activity. Once you have a core set of constraints defined, you can start to outline the low-level processes and practices you need, and fine-tune them accordingly.

Development Mobilization

Development mobilization activities ensure that the actual development activities are completely defined and ready to use. The output of development mobilization feeds into a number of other mobilization activities. For example, once you've defined the inputs that you need for development, these will be fed into the design mobilization activities to ensure that they're accounted for. There can be a number of tasks carried out in this mobilization activity that could be split into parallel streams, where necessary.

The previous chapter looked at a high-level development plan and the activities involved. I also discussed scope in the previous chapters, so I'm not going to dwell on what has already been covered. Ultimately, the scope defines the inputs, approach, and outputs of construction. The next chapter looks at some of the inputs and outputs of construction. In this section, I'm simply going to provide some clarity for the scope and approach that will be taken during the formal development activities.

Defining the Development Scope

Initially, it is important to clarify the scope and approach of development. You need to ensure that the development team understands:

- ❑ What it needs to be doing
- ❑ How it's supposed to be doing it
- ❑ What it's using to do it

❑ When it needs to complete it

❑ What it needs to deliver at the end

It is important that all the artifacts that the development team is responsible for are clearly stated and understood. It really depends on the types of systems being developed, but the following provides a list of some high-level items that could be within the development scope for a medium-sized solution:

❑ **Technical designs** — It is important to understand whether the technical designs need to be signed off before development begins. If so, you might need to mitigate for delays. You could proceed at risk, which would need to be mitigated because the technical design could be reviewed and come back with an abundance of comments, which could have a dramatic impact on the overall development timescales. Having an agreed template in place for each of the component types in the solution will help. The template should contain all the relevant sections that need to be completed and the guidelines for completing them. You should consider developing a single technical design for each component type and ensure that it captures all the necessary information required by the development team as well as by the stakeholders. The initial technical designs will provide a basis for the remaining component designs and can be used as examples.

❑ **Database components** — Although most developers are somewhat familiar with the basics of database development, not everyone is a full-fledged DBA. There's a lot of tuning, indexing, security, and other technical tricks that can't always be performed within the development environment or by the development team. For example, identifying the index that should be clustered is generally easy, but determining how the tables and indexes should be split across the file system is something else. In these situations, it is important to understand whether the development team is responsible for making recommendations, implementing the actual solution, or simply providing support and input.

❑ **Framework and common service components** — The development teams could be split so that one team is working on framework components and the other is working on application components. It is important to have a clear line of division, to document who's responsible for what, and to ensure that everyone understands their respective responsibilities. If the development team is responsible for developing framework components, this needs to be factored into the scope. It will also need to be factored into the solution design. If the development team is not responsible for framework components, which are probably inputs to the process, they will need to be very clearly tested, documented, and understood.

❑ **Integration with third-party components** — It is important that any integration with components developed outside the core development team be clearly understood. This even goes for framework components developed by another team. Major problems and delays can arise when it is taken for granted that something works or is supposed to work. More often than not, there's a requirement to use a third-party product or a custom solution. If this is the case, then it needs to be thoroughly tested and prototyped beforehand to ensure that it can be used by the development team. If not, it may need to be simulated, which could take time to develop, especially if the product is complex.

❑ **Test stubs and simulators** — It is important to understand whether the development team is going to need to develop stubs and simulators. As previously mentioned, these can take a while to develop, depending on their complexity. Where possible, the stubs and simulators should be developed as early as possible and tested so that they can be used by the development team without undue impact. The development team will undoubtedly need to develop stubs for unit testing purposes.

❑ **Application components** — The application components are typically the "bread and butter" of the application development team.

❑ **Batch components and scripts** — I discuss batch in more detail later, but it is important to understand whether the development team is responsible for developing batch processes and batch jobs. If the application requires batch jobs or background processes, it's important to clearly define which jobs the development team is responsible for, how they need to be developed, and how they need to be tested. For example, it may be a requirement that all logs are shipped to a central system for auditing. First, the format of the logs would definitely need to be agreed to. Second, you'd need to understand whether it was a "push" or "pull" implementation, both of which have their implications on the development team.

❑ **Reports** — I discuss reports in more detail later, but, again, it is important to understand and document the reports that need to be produced by the development team and how they need to be implemented and tested.

❑ **Automated unit and integration tests** — It is very important to determine up front whether automated tests need to be developed. Furthermore, it needs to be noted where automated tests can't be developed — for example, where they're not supported by the applications being used. The development team should be developing automated tests and the level of code coverage should also be established early.

❑ **Test data and test scenarios** — Test data and test scenarios are often tricky. I mentioned in the previous chapter that common test data and scenarios should be used where possible. It's important to ensure that all the necessary applications, tools, and environments are available to do this. It's also important to ensure that changes to common test data don't create a bottleneck in the process.

❑ **Configuration values** — You're probably used to including configuration values in your software instead of hard-coded values. However, when it comes to deploying the software in other environments, the configuration settings need to be fully understood and calibrated for their optimum values. Consider the MaximumQueueDepth configuration value, for example. What is it? What should it be set to in the production environment? What happens when it is reached? Changing the value could have a dramatic effect on the solution and its performance characteristics. During technical testing, these will typically be calibrated for production. You need to understand whether the development team is responsible for making recommendations or simply documenting the settings and their ranges. In most cases, it's the latter. However, you don't want to get into tricky situations if someone were to ask "What should this value be set to in production?" It's important to ensure that you know what you're responsible for and when the values will be assessed and calibrated. The component may also have very specific configuration requirements which have been specified by the design team. For instance, the design team could specify that the low-level SQL components implement wait-retry logic and that the wait time and retry count are configurable. These values could be very different across the various environments. The wait-retry pattern is discussed in Chapter 19, "Designing for Resilience."

❑ **Release, packaging, and deployment** — It is important to understand whether the development team is responsible for developing or even managing the packing and deployment solution. With distributed teams and differing time zones, it may be necessary for each development team to understand the solution, and thus manage releases and builds, rather than just submitting artifacts into a central process.

❏ **Release notes (including installation procedures)** — If the team is responsible for releasing, packaging, and deploying the solution, they'll almost certainly be required to produce release notes. It's important to establish the content of the release notes early to ensure that they contain all the relevant information.

❏ **Operational procedures** — It is vitally important to understand which operational procedures the development team is responsible for (if any) — for example, how and when the application should be backed up, which procedures need to be followed during a backup and restore, and what to do in failure scenarios. Writing operational documentation is a lengthy process and should be factored into the scope, if required.

> **Many more items could be included within the scope. The preceding list is only representative and should be used as a guideline. The primary objective is to define and agree on as much of the development scope, as early as possible, to avoid surprises and delays.**

Clearly defining the requirements of each of these items will help to ensure that everyone is on the right track. You're likely not going to get everything right the first time, but it's important to at least understand what the team is responsible for and try to exercise the process early.

Defining the Inputs

I am going to discuss the inputs to construction in the next chapter (and throughout this book), so I won't spend much time on them here. The following list represents just a handful of the possible inputs into the construction process:

❏ **Functional and non-functional requirements** — It is important that the development team understand the functional and the non-functional requirements, including the quality characteristics and constraints. Functional specifications might include (or incorporate) the functional requirements, and technical specifications might include (or incorporate) the technical requirements. For instance, a functional requirement such as "the system must support user security" can be incorporated in the functional specifications by including user administration pages and functions. However, it is sometimes harder to capture all the non-functional requirements, quality characteristics, and constraints in a single technical or detailed specification. For instance, where are you going to capture (and document) the constraint "the unit tests must achieve 100 percent code coverage"? Technical requirements and quality characteristics often affect a number of components in the solution. For instance, the requirement "the system must be capable of processing 1000 records per second" would need to be considered across a variety of components. All requirements and constraints need to be fully documented and understood by the development team.

❏ **Use-case diagrams** — A use-case diagram shows the primary actor (user) and the functions he or she can perform when using the system.

❏ **Use cases** — The use cases are typically a textual representation of the step-by-step flow and interactions between an actor (the user) and the system. The use cases also document the major alternative flows in the application's functionality. It is very important in use cases to capture (and highlight) any manual steps that are involved in the overall process. These can often become the subject of debate later in the lifecycle.

❑ **Navigation map / site map** — The site map is another visual representation of the application or website. The site map highlights the individual pages and paths to those pages. It can be used to highlight areas of inconsistency, as well as the journeys through the system.

❑ **Storyboards** — Storyboards are a sequence of illustrations often used in media, filmmaking, and other "visual" industries. Producing storyboards can be a tricky business when it comes to business applications, but I find them very useful because they complement the use cases. The storyboards walk through the end-to-end flow of the system and can be used to agree the functionality with the stakeholders, as well as highlight areas for further consideration, such as page transitions, caching, and additional application functionality.

❑ **Page layouts and specifications** — The page specifications show the individual pages (or forms) in either high- or low-resolution. High-resolution page specifications can be produced using development and modeling tools, whereas low-resolution specifications can be produced in any package that supports basic drawing functionality. The page specifications not only show a layout of the page, but they also document the controls on the page, such as how the controls interact with each other, and how the user interacts with the controls and what the controls do.

❑ **Style and usability guidelines** — The style guidelines complement the page layouts and, typically, include information about:

   ❑ Standard fonts, styles, and colors

   ❑ Standard graphics and positioning requirements

   ❑ Standard usability criteria (ensuring tab order is correct, and so on)

❑ **Component models and specifications** — The component models and specifications are similar to the page specifications, although they document the components. The high-level component specifications describe the purpose of the component, whereas the low-level component specifications go into much greater detail regarding the component, its members (properties and methods), and usage. Component specifications can include as much or as little detail as necessary, including:

   ❑ Component diagrams and hierarchy

   ❑ Simple textual descriptions

   ❑ Member outlines (property and method descriptions)

   ❑ Class diagrams

   ❑ Activity, sequence, or interaction diagrams

   ❑ Configuration requirements

   ❑ Logging and diagnostic requirements

   ❑ Specific quality characteristics, such as automatic recovery in the event of a failure, wait-retry logic, or other specific patterns and practices

❑ **Report specifications** — Report specifications are also very similar to page specifications. Reports can contain lists of records, grouped records, charts, and graphs. A report specification would typically document the following:

  ❑ The report selection criteria (and controls)

  ❑ The output (along with sample results)

❑ **Batch job specifications** — Batch job specifications document various background or offline tasks that need to be performed. A batch job specification can be as simple as stating the basic function of the job. For example, it can state "The Remove Old Records job is used to remove the old records from the database." However, this doesn't describe what constitutes "old records," although this may be described in the requirements. Batch is also discussed in more detail later in this book. A reasonable batch job specification would include:

  ❑ The name and purpose of the job

  ❑ Its processing rules and criteria

  ❑ Its dependencies on other jobs

❑ **Data model** — The data model can be specified as logical or physical. The logical data model typically outlines the tables and the relationships (constraints) between them. The logical data model is described using business terminology and is technology (and implementation) independent. The logical data model doesn't generally include the specification of indexes, views, triggers, and stored procedures. The logical data model feeds in to the physical data model design, which is an important distinction because the physical data model would typically include the following:

  ❑ Tables and relationships

  ❑ Indexes (clustered and non-clustered)

  ❑ Views

  ❑ Stored procedures

  ❑ Security and roles

  ❑ File system usage and storage requirements

  It is important to understand and agree on who will be responsible for the design, development, and implementation of all the database artifacts.

❑ **Reference data** — The reference data typically encompasses the base data for the solution — for example, the items in a "Security Question" drop-down list or the product categories for an online store. The reference data is based on the data model, which may contain as little or as much data as necessary. The more data specified, however, the better. This saves you from having to make up base data for testing purposes.

❑ **Test scenarios and test data** — The test scenarios and test data include specific areas of testing that need to be covered and their input data, conditions, and expected results. There may be specific processing and calculations that must be thoroughly tested for which a series of test conditions and scenarios must be executed. You may also be sharing common scripts and data, and as such, they are an input into the construction activities.

❏ **Third-party components** — It is important that all the components that the development team needs to use are captured in the scope and inputs. This includes specific usage scenarios and guidelines as well as any stubs or simulators required for thorough testing. The following list represents a few items that can be considered inputs:

❏ Architecture and framework components

❏ Integration components

❏ Third-party components

❏ **Architecture blueprints and deployment diagrams** — It is important that the development team understand the holistic architecture and the overall deployment concept. These inputs can describe the architecture at either a logical or physical level. The blueprint will highlight the following components and how they are interconnected:

❏ Client computers

❏ Network components

❏ Servers

❏ Storage devices

These items help to flesh out the "requirements and design validation" steps in the construction process. The tasks should be complemented with checklists for each of the items to ensure that all the information is specified, and the associated query log should be used in conjunction with the checks.

Depending on the project and the team, the inputs will vary, but the preceding lists provide a good starting point. The key is to define and document the specific inputs that are required for each type of component and task, along with any required supplementary information.

This activity focuses on answering the question "Is there enough information to build the component?" If there isn't, the inputs need to be revised.

Defining the Process

The previous chapter showed a high-level construction plan, which would also be part of defining the construction process. It also includes all the constraint groups discussed earlier, as well as all the activities on the plan. The important thing is to ensure that these are documented appropriately and understood. This includes any mitigating actions that might need to be taken into account to reduce risk — for example, if there are specific skill-level requirements, listing specific training courses that can provide the relevant level of skills. If there are potential resource bottlenecks, clearly identify them and state what actions will be taken — for example, that development will go on at risk, that other development activities will be performed, or even that training will be scheduled during the period.

Based on the technology constraints and the component groups, the following activities define the hardware and software required to effectively develop, unit test, and integration test each of the components in the scope:

❑ **Gathering and compiling the system requirements for all the applications and tools being used, and defining the development architecture and infrastructure** — Each development machine needs to be fit for purpose and support the applications and tools that are going to be used.

❑ **Developing software installation and configuration guides** — The software needs to be installed and configured appropriately. As new team members come on board, they can use these instructions to set up their development environment appropriately. Alternatively, the information can be used for managing the roll-out of the applications from a central source.

❑ **Developing usage guides for common tasks** — In many cases, these documents are included with the software. However, they should be complemented with your own, specific usage guides. In addition, the tools developed internally need usage guides.

❑ **Defining the maintenance and governance structure** — This establishes who maintains each tool and document. As previously mentioned, you're probably not going to get everything right the first time, so be prepared to update and refine some of these activities. Setting out how this will take place and what needs to be updated will greatly improve efficiency.

These activities should highlight any specific workstation requirements for particular development activities. They should also highlight areas where shared databases or other shared infrastructure components are required.

The list is not exhaustive, but it gives you an idea of what to prepare for. I'd like to re-iterate that these items do not need to be all encompassing or overwhelming. Simple things that don't require much effort can save time in the future. However, performing a number of simple tasks can add up in time and effort. If you're going to do them, they need to be factored into the scope to ensure that you have sufficient time and money to implement them. In fact, that advice applies to all the subjects in this chapter.

Defining the Best Practices and Patterns

To mobilize construction, you must define the best practices and patterns. For each component group, the best practices and patterns should be documented (ideally using implementation specific examples), including the following items:

❑ Design guidelines (layering, encapsulation, re-use, and so on)

❑ Coding standards (naming conventions, formatting, and architectural patterns and practices)

❑ Commenting standards

❑ Exception handling and logging patterns

❑ Diagnostic patterns

❑ Common service usage (Data access, configuration settings)

❑ Other specific or unique patterns and practices

❑ Best practice unit and integration testing

❑ Testing tools and their usage

❑ Code coverage tools and their usage

❑   Best practice (static) analysis tools and usage guidelines

❑   Best practice (performance) analysis tools and usage guidelines

❑   Documentation-generation tools and usage guidelines

As you can imagine, some of the tasks in this activity can take a while to implement. Therefore, start them as early as possible to ensure a reasonable development buffer. Use comments to document the custom-built tools so that the usage documentation can be generated from the code, which saves valuable time and effort when updates are required. For example, simply update the comments and re-generate the documentation. However, it is not always possible to do this, so you may need additional time to produce "formal" documentation for the tools.

Defining the Core Activities

Defining the core activities involves setting out the tasks for each component group. Defining core activities is nothing more than defining the most basic high-level tasks that each member of the team needs to perform. These tasks include the following:

❑   Installing and configuring the development environment

❑   Getting the most recent or a specific version of the solution from the source repository

❑   Compiling and building the entire solution

❑   Running the unit tests and verifying the results

❑   Running the integration tests and verifying the results

❑   Running the profiling tools and verifying the results

The preceding activities ensure that every developer can obtain, compile, and verify the solution prior to starting his or her daily activities. The following sets out some basic tasks that the developers need to perform as part of their daily routine:

❑   Creating new components (the term "components" refers to any and all items in the solution):

   ❑   Creating the new component in the configuration-management system

   ❑   Copying and renaming the exemplar template files (exemplars are discussed shortly)

   ❑   Adding the component to the overall solution

   ❑   Completing all the TODO items

   ❑   Plumbing or configuring the component into the overall solution

   ❑   Updating existing scripts and productivity tools to include the new components

   ❑   Submitting the component into the build and release processes

❑   Developing tests:

   ❑   Defining unit test/integration test conditions and scenarios

   ❑   Creating unit test/integration test data

   ❑   Creating automated unit/integration tests and adding them to the solution

- ❏ Updating components and tests:
    - ❏ Obtaining component (and test) artifacts from the source repository (checking out)
    - ❏ Commenting changes
    - ❏ Verifying changes
    - ❏ Updating the component and test artifacts in the source repository (checking in)
- ❏ Documenting the completion of activities. The completion report would provide evidence that all the activities had been completed appropriately. For example, a completion report could include the following:
    - ❏ Evidence that all code review comments have been addressed
    - ❏ Confirmation that all queries have been successfully clarified and incorporated
    - ❏ Documented test results (including code coverage and profiling outputs)
    - ❏ Outstanding activities that need to be carried through to later phases
    - ❏ The actual time spent completing all the activities, which can be used to calibrate future estimates
- ❏ Submitting for (and performing) review and acceptance:
    - ❏ Peer reviews
    - ❏ Technical/group reviews
    - ❏ External reviews
    - ❏ Sign offs (including who signs off what)
- ❏ Submitting components into a release

The preceding are all very basic tasks, but if someone is new to a project or organization these are just a few things they need to know. When the development team ramps up and your organization takes on new developers, it will save a significant amount of time if you can simply point them to a Wiki where they can get all the information. Of course, you're always on hand to assist them if they get stuck.

The last part in defining the activities is to define the daily routine. The routine should capture the specific actions needed to ensure that the development effort is consistent and streamlined. I've listed a few possible actions here, but it will depend on the individual project:

1. At the start of the day developers will always get the "latest" view from the version-control system, compile it, and verify it before starting any new work. This ensures that at the start of the day every developer is working from a single, consistent baseline. There may be exceptions to this rule when a developer may require a specific version.

2. All code must be backed up overnight. This protects the project and the development team against loss or damage. The source code repository will invariably be backed up far more frequently than developer workstations. This means that each developer needs to check in (or shelve) his or her code at the end of the day. This also protects the development team from not being able to access vital files when the developer, who has them checked out, is not available. Tasks that spread over multiple days need to be managed. Although the code may not be "ready to build," it needs to be safely stored overnight to protect against loss or damage. Losing work is

costly to a project. Then again, it is costly to have team members sitting idle because they can't access the files they need. This problem needs to be managed, along with the next point, because the code must compile at all times. There's no perfect solution, but some version control systems support "parking" or "shelving" code and artifacts. This allows developers to shelve their work on the source control system and have it backed up without having to check it in.

3. All code is verified against the latest version prior to being checked in. This helps to protect the development team from getting code that does not compile or build. Checking in code or artifacts that do not work or do not compile may disrupt development, causing downtime. The development process and practices should include clear instructions on how to use the configuration management-system and what to do prior to checking in anything. Breaking the build is painful and costly, so all developers must do what they can to ensure this doesn't happen.

The basic idea is to try to document as much as possible to ensure that each and every developer has the necessary information to get on with the actual business of developing software. If the project is producing a formal pilot, this can be a great time to prove all these processes and the others in this chapter.

Defining the Templates and Exemplars

During mobilization it's important to ensure that each output artifact is outlined appropriately in the scope. For instance, if you're going to be producing technical designs, what sections should they include? Should they include class diagrams and complete sequence diagrams? Should they contain pseudo code?

An exemplar is a fully completed unit, whereas a template is a shell that needs to be completed. I find that defining initial templates, completing them, and going round the loop a couple of times naturally creates an exemplar and a template at the same time. Another difference between an exemplar and a template is that a template normally contains TODO statements, whereas an exemplar doesn't because exemplars include and follow all the best practices and patterns. The exemplars provide the basis for "real-world" references for the team instead of it being hypothetical. Reusing exemplars across projects can greatly improve productivity and development time.

Where possible, at least one of each of the items in the scope (where required) should be developed up front to provide the basis for the exemplar and template pattern. If the outputs are documentation-based, ideally there should be at least one exemplar or template document per group that contains all the relevant sections and instructions for how to complete them (if it's a template). This can then be agreed on by the consumer to avoid delays later in the project.

If the outputs are code-based, the exemplars and templates should ideally cover the following:

❑ One or more exemplar/template per component group

❑ One or more complete unit test exemplar/template per component group

❑ One or more complete integration test exemplar/template per component group

❑ One or more complete smoke test exemplars/templates

This output documents and indicates what the developer should do to complete his or her work.

You should use comments to fully document the exemplars and templates, which will save time producing documentation. You can even generate all the usage guides from the exemplar and template code comments.

Producing the exemplars and even the templates will help to ratify the process end-to-end and will act as the foundation for the actual construction process. As you produce each of the exemplars and templates, you'll also start to identify improvements and refinements to the inputs.

The development mobilization activities take each of the exemplars through the process to prove not only the process but the exemplar, as well, and to flesh out as much detail as possible. Not only is there a fully documented and functional development process at the end of it, there is a set of exemplars and templates that are used for reference purposes and that provide the basis for all new components. If any innovative approaches are identified, they should also be adopted to reduce overheads.

Wrapping It Up

Finally, wrapping up construction involves defining the exit criteria and the outputs from construction. As you've seen, development completion is a major milestone and all the artifacts need to be brought together so that you can show your results.

Closing off development starts by defining the contents of the completion report and matching the contents against the exit criteria. The process outlined in the previous chapter showed the individual developer completion summaries. The following provides a high-level list of items that can be included in the overall construction completion report:

- ❏ Input inventory
- ❏ Query log inventory
- ❏ Technical design inventory
- ❏ Component inventory
- ❏ Unit test inventory
- ❏ Integration test inventory
- ❏ Code coverage statistics
- ❏ Code profiling statistics
- ❏ Defect summary
- ❏ Financial summary (estimates vs. actual)

In addition to the preceding, there are, of course, the final releases themselves. You should keep the development completion reports and artifacts under version control so that you can refer to them at a later stage, if necessary. It's important that everything is included in the report, including the release, so that a clean machine can be used to verify the contents and even compile, build, and run everything.

While all these activities are going on, you need to document any and all known issues or areas for improvement to move forward. If something adverse was seen during the mobilization activities and hasn't been specifically fixed, it should be noted and assessed because the last thing you want is it to happen again when there's potentially a number of developers impacted.

All these activities are prime examples of where an agile or rapid development approach can be adopted. The activities should be done incrementally so that at every stage there is a working version that can be reviewed and taken forward as, and when, required.

Ideally, all this information would be available on the project portal so that every developer has easy access to the relevant documentation and associated process diagrams. The primary goal is to ensure that as many aspects as possible are covered. If there is a gap, plug it with a process and tool or guideline. The path of least resistance is generally the easiest, so let's concentrate on developing and not having to waste time with undefined or inefficient processes and tools. These activities not only help to build better quality software, but the documentation can be re-used again and again when handing over to live service and the application maintenance teams. This saves a huge amount of time and effort.

Thus far, this chapter has walked through development mobilization in quite a lot of detail. The remainder of this chapter is dedicated to the other key mobilization activities, including:

- ❑ Build, release, and regular integration
- ❑ Test
- ❑ Fix (defect management)
- ❑ Configuration management
- ❑ Change control

Build, Release, and Regular Integration Mobilization

Although build and release can be considered as two separate entities (that is, the tasks can be separated and executed in parallel), I've chosen to include them together. The purpose of build, release, and regular integration is to take all the development artifacts and compile them into a single release.

Releases will have different requirements, so they will have different packaging inputs. The build and release processes should take what has already been defined and execute all the best practice tools, as well as all the unit tests and integration tests, thereby providing the initial regression testing capability.

Builds should be done on a regular basis to bring everything together. The build cycle and inputs change as the project progresses. Initially, the latest version of the solution is taken into a build. As testing starts, a more structured approach to individual fixes or groups of fixes needs to be adopted. The build and regular integration processes should define the relevant approaches.

The activities that will be conducted are similar to those in the development mobilization phase, so I am not going to go into details that have been previously discussed, but instead I'll focus on the specifics that relate to build, release, and regular integration. The following describes the key activities involved:

❑ **Defining the process constraints** — The build process constraints should list all the tools and technologies that will be used to build and produce releases, as well as the packaging solution.

❑ **Defining the architecture** — The tools required to build, regression test, and release software often require a lot of configuration, so it's worth starting this process very early. Furthermore, the custom tools that are needed to install certain components should be developed as early as possible. For instance, creating and installing the database might involve a custom tool to execute various scripts. The architecture should include everything that is required to get the artifacts out of the configuration-management system, compile them, package them into releases, test them, and, finally, deploy them to an environment. In some cases, this also involves running post-installation scripts that change various values in configuration files or the database (e.g. environment-specific values). The build and release architecture components need to support silent installation or configured installation to streamline deployment into large-scale environments. This saves you from having to install a release manually. Ideally, the high-level (automatic) actions that should be supported include the following:

   ❑ Gathering all the artifacts from the source repository (that are Ready-to-Build or Ready-To-Release)

   ❑ Compiling the solutions according to their dependencies and release configurations

   ❑ Statically profiling the code and outputting the results

   ❑ Generating the documentation from the comments

   ❑ Executing all the unit tests and validating the results

   ❑ Executing all the integration tests and validating the results

   ❑ Executing any additional regression tests and validating the results

   ❑ Measuring code coverage during testing and outputting the results

   ❑ Dynamically profiling the code during testing and outputting the results

   ❑ Packaging the components into their respective releases (Ready-to-Release)

   ❑ Running as much in parallel as possible

❑ **Defining build scope and inputs** — The build scope defines the components and artifacts that are taken into the build process. The build process compiles all the necessary artifacts into binaries. The release will generally contain the resultant binaries, although some releases may include the original source code files (for example, if a code review might need to be performed). It is a good idea to identify the components that require compilation or other prerequisite steps prior to being included in a release. For example, stored procedures are usually stored as text files and are not compiled as part of the build process. However, they may be required to generate code, so a build database will need to be implemented first so that the code generator can be executed and the resultant code can be included in the build.

❑ **Defining release scope and inputs** — The release scope defines the components and artifacts that are taken into the packaging process. The release scope maps the items in the configuration-management system and maps the outputs from the build process to a particular release configuration. Releases contain a number of different items, as I've mentioned before, and the purpose of the release scope is to define and implement the packaging of these into their associated releases. The following provides a starting point for the different types of releases:

- Unit and integration test releases

- Functional test releases

- Technical test releases

- Acceptance test releases

- Review releases

- Production releases (including disaster recovery)

Although typically the items included with a release differ, each release contains the specific configuration and artifacts for its given purpose. The release should contain everything that goes along with it, including the following:

- Documentation (including generated documentation)

- Test scripts and test data

- Configuration files

- Database scripts

- Post-installation scripts and other productivity scripts

- Custom tools (environment-specific tools, test tools, and so on)

- Binaries and libraries

- Source code (only where appropriate or required)

- Release notes

- **Defining ready-to-build/ready-to-release processes** — In terms of the build and release, the ready-to-build process dictates how files and artifacts should be labeled or marked in the configuration-management system so that they can be easily extracted by the build process and included in a build. Often the latest files are taken. If you are using continuous integration tools and techniques, the very act of checking in a file will trigger a build. These should be complemented with the developer procedures and practices to ensure that only pre-approved artifacts are submitted to a build or release. The ready-to-build process goes hand-in-hand with the ready-to-release process. Just because something is ready to build doesn't mean that it is ready to release. For example, a large development piece of work may contain many different elements, each of which will be ready to build at different times, although they should all be released at the same time. The high-level activities include:

    - Defining the base-line ready-to-build process

    - Defining the defect/change specific build process

    - Defining the base-line ready-to-release process

    - Defining the defect/change specific release process

    - Developing and configuring the build and release tools

The build and release process will be used throughout the lifetime of the project, so it's worth getting it as good as possible. It will be handed over to support and maintenance, so a well-documented and easily understood process helps greatly.

Test Mobilization

The test mobilization first needs to focus on the unit and integration testing, which is followed by the initial regression testing (which encompasses the unit and integration tests). Then, it is followed by the additional test activities of the project (functional testing, technical testing, and so on). Smoke tests are often included in the regression tests, which mirror certain functional and technical tests. This allows the regression test capability to be enhanced throughout the project to include more tests and scenarios into the overall suite.

Again, the activities are very similar to those discussed previously, so I am only going to concentrate on the specifics around testing. The quality processes and review processes should be defined as well as the specific activities.

❑ **Defining process constraints** — The test process constraints should list the tools and technologies that will be used to test the application. Testing involves a number of different tools used for various test scenarios. Each testing activity uses a combination of test tools, which generally includes:

❑ Unit testing tools

❑ User interface testing tools

❑ Load or stress testing tools

❑ Custom test and verification tools

❑ Actual results and an expected results comparison

❑ Requirement/test condition and test script management tools

❑ Test execution and progress reporting tools

❑ Defect management tools

It is also important to understand, define, and document the testing activities that will use the defect-tracking system. Typically, unit testing doesn't track the defects because the developer normally runs the tests and corrects the defects. It is more likely that test defects are tracked, starting with integration testing.

It is important to ensure that, wherever possible, the testing activities are performed with "verbose" logging turned on. This greatly enhances the fix analysis and turnaround times and it alleviates defects going backwards and forwards.

❑ **Defining the architecture** — In addition to the overall testing architecture, there are four specific areas of interest:

    ❑ **Regression testing** — The regression testing architecture should be capable of executing a variety of tests (and tools) so that as much hands-free testing as possible can be performed on a release prior to it actually being released. The regression architecture needs to be extensible so that additional tests can be added easily. This allows the regression capability to be extended, including more scope and project progresses.

    ❑ **Test stubs and simulators** — In the testing architecture, specific stubs or simulators are required when actual components are not available or otherwise difficult to test. The stubs and simulators should mimic the real components as much as possible, as well as provide specific scenario-based functionality. For instance, it may be possible for the real component to raise an exception under certain circumstances. Thus, it is important for the stub to be configured by a test scenario to work the same way. However, a lot of time and effort can be spent investigating and correcting issues with complicated stubs and simulators, which are really only used to test the application. Your focus needs to be on testing the actual application and ensuring that it interacts with the real component. Keeping stubs and simulators fairly simple avoids issues with using them. Whenever third-party components or integration is required, it is vital that these touch points are tested as much as possible and stubs and simulators can sometimes help to focus the testing effort.

    ❑ **Custom test tools and scripts** — Another important part of the testing architecture is the custom test tools. The custom test tools should integrate into the regression architecture and not require human interaction, where possible. It's often very easy to build custom test tools that have a user interface, but because this requires manual input, test cycles need to be executed manually. Scripts are often required to "wrap" and integrate with the test tools. For instance, after each test, you gather the log files, diagnostic outputs, and database updates, and then place them somewhere safe (so they're not overwritten by the next test run). Other scripts may be used to gather all the test results and store them in the repository.

    ❑ **Actual and expected results comparison tools** — It is also very important to consider how actual results are gathered and compared to expected results, which often involves custom development or customization of third-party tools. Some actual results are much easier to extract than others. The extraction and comparison tools should also be fully automated. However, this adds additional complexity to the tools, which is another important reason for starting ahead of time and identifying them, purchasing them, or developing them in-house.

❑ **Defining the test scope** — The test scope is usually derived from the lifecycle and lists the types of testing to be undertaken. The following list reiterates the testing activities that have been discussed:

    ❑ Unit testing

    ❑ Integration testing

    ❑ Regression testing (including Smoke testing)

    ❑ Functional testing

    ❑ Technical testing

    ❑ Acceptance testing

Another important part of the test scope is to ensure that all the various component groups are included within the test scope. For example, if the application has batch components or reports, these need to be fully tested as well. You've already seen the component types and groups that will be developed. It is important that these are all mapped so that the scope of each set of tests is clearly defined. As a best practice, unit and integration testing should include a broad range of scenarios to identify defects early. For instance, performance testing a method gives an indicative timing that can be verified against the overall performance requirements to determine whether it is/or could be a potential bottleneck in the end-to-end process. If these tests are relatively straightforward to develop, there's no reason why they shouldn't be included. I'm not saying that they are the be-all and end-all, but they can help. Similarly, testing batch components with a realistic set of data gives an indication of whether the component needs to be re-factored or at least support configurable parallel processing. If running a job on a developer workstation takes an hour, something probably needs to be addressed.

❑ **Defining the test scenarios** — The test scenarios map to the test scope and the component types, defining the high-level test groups that will be conducted. The test scenarios map to the quality characteristics, including the following examples:

   ❑ Correctness tests (both positive and negative)

   ❑ Performance tests

   ❑ Failure and recovery tests

   ❑ Monitoring tests

   ❑ Operability tests

   ❑ Usability tests

   ❑ Penetration tests

The test cycles determine the high-level grouping for the individual test scenarios and conditions.

❑ **Defining the test inputs** — The test inputs are similar to those listed in the development section, such as requirements, use-cases, and so forth. The inputs map to the test cycles and test scope. However, different test activities will require different test inputs, and listing these will help to define the input verification criteria as well as define the entry and exit criteria.

❑ **Defining entry and exit criteria** — The entry and exit criteria stipulate the conditions that need to be met before the activity begins and before the activity is complete. Entry and exit criteria are entirely dependent on the project and the activities that need to be performed. The following are some common exit criteria and the potential issues with using them:

   ❑ **Percentage of code covered** — As mentioned previously, I don't actually believe this to be a true measure of quality. If only combining functional and technical tests achieves 100 percent code coverage, then you have a winner. It means that your tests exercise the entire code-base and that's just grand. Achieving 100 percent code coverage elsewhere only shows that you have a set of tests (and stubs) that exercise all the code, not that all the code is actually used in the final solution. However, it may very well be a constraint to achieve 100 percent code coverage in unit test.

   ❑ **Number and complexity of scenarios and/or conditions successfully executed and passed (or outstanding)** — This stipulates the number or percentage of test scenarios that must be completed — for example, 50 percent complex, 75 percent medium, and 100 percent simple. The numbers can equally be reversed. However, if reaching the exit criteria comes down to "pairing off" two complex scenarios, the easier of the two is the most likely place to focus all the test (and/or development) effort. Clearly, the remaining scenarios and conditions need to be addressed at some point.

❑ **Number and severity of defects open** — This is often used when an activity can end with only a certain number of defects open — such as, no critical, no high, x medium and y low. Clearly, both x and y need to be addressed at some point.

This scenario is very similar to the previous one. To explain, let's assume that during a functional test activity, a "low" defect can be a simple spelling mistake on a page. Let's also assume that a "low" defect could also be one that only happens under very extreme circumstances. Now, assume that you can "exit" with 30 "low" defects. If there are 31 open at the time you need to exit, what's going to happen? The most probable action is to fix the defect with the very least amount of development effort. In this instance, it's going to be the spelling mistake. The fact remains that the other defect could have far greater consequences later on. This measure depends on how defects are classified — a subject discussed in greater detail shortly.

❑ **Specific transactions executed and passed** — This is a good measure when you want to ensure that particular functionality or routes through the system have been clearly exercised. The transactions may not include all the individual permutations, but they've tested the flow in a variety of scenarios. Regression "smoke" tests are one such activity where this criterion is applied.

As mentioned previously, no system is completely free of defects. In order to start a particular test phase, you want to be in a position for it to continue without being adversely impacted. Thus, the earlier you identify more defects the better. The chosen methodology determines the number of test activities and when they are performed in the lifecycle. Each test activity has its own agenda, and the entry and exit criteria needs to be carefully considered and defined. Putting the appropriate entry and exit criteria in place helps to define clear boundaries for each testing activity. That still doesn't mean that the test phases won't overrun and overlap with each other. The more that you can do up front to ensure quality outputs from the construction page will help to reduce the testing downtime.

❑ **Defining the test completion report** — This is similar to development completion because testing completion complements development. All the testing artifacts need to be brought together into a single package for review and sign-off. The following provides a simple list of what might be included in the test completion report:

❑ Inputs inventory

❑ Test condition and scenario inventory

❑ Test execution statistics (tests executed, passed, and outstanding)

❑ Defect summary

❑ Financial summary (estimates vs. actual)

❑ **Defining the test exemplars and templates** — The test mobilization activities should implement a series of exemplars and templates that exercise all the testing capabilities and tools. The exemplars should be organized and grouped according to the test scope and activities. They should also contain multiple scenarios and conditions that exercise the various test data and the actual and expected results comparisons. This level of coverage will greatly improve the overall efficiency when the actual testing begins. You should be able to reduce the number of issues encountered and get straight to the real bugs.

❑ **Defining the test data and management approach** — The test data and associated management is critical to all test activities. As testing progresses, the test data is added to and improved. Test data management should make this easy, as well as deployment and installation of test data in the environments. The test data starts getting defined right back at the start of the project. Capturing as much test and reference data as possible provides a great start, but managing the data for the different test activities and cycles is somewhat harder — the sheer volume and the different combinations can be unwieldy. There are many environments, each of which will probably involve multiple activities and scenarios. The tools and processes for managing the test data need to be piloted very early, which is why test mobilization starts way up front. That doesn't mean it's complete; it just means you start it very early to define practices. The following are the high-level items that you should consider:

❑ Defining the test data management approach

❑ Defining the base reference data

❑ Defining the base test data

❑ Developing test data installation tools and usage guides

The test data should be based around real data and transaction scenarios. You should also test using expected production volumes of transactions and data. For instance, if the production environment is going to be potentially processing millions of requests or transactions, the test data should contain a similar number (if not more to really stress the system). There are tools that can generate test data and the use of these should be considered. Using live-like test data right from the start (unit test) can really help to flush out issues. However, it does also mean that there could be very large data sets, which could be a problem in smaller environments. The key is to use as much data as possible, as this will stress the system and provide more indicative performance figures.

Common test data should be identified and used across multiple phases of testing to reduce the overhead of both installation and management. As the project progresses, the situation will only get worse, and having to make multiple changes and script updates will severely hinder progress.

❑ **Defining rapid turnaround approach** — The lack of rapid turn-around scripts is often something that gets in the way of testing. There is often a need to turn around an environment from one test activity to another. Regression testing will exercise the release using various test data sets and scenarios, including going from functional testing to technical testing. This is usually performed by installing a release with a different configuration and underlying test data. Because this can often be a time-consuming exercise, it is better to have a rapid turnaround approach that reduces the overall time between installations and configurations.

Taking a set of exemplar test scenarios and conditions end-to-end will define the best practices and uncover areas where further tooling may be required to streamline the activities even more. In the end, your results will be used by all the testers (including developers). In addition, you'll create a series of exemplars and templates that can be used by all. These will also be handed over to support and maintenance, where they will be well-defined which will help ease the transition.

Defect Management (and Fix) Mobilization

Defect management (and fix) mobilization is going to be very important. As you've seen, once the formal test activities are initiated, you're going to see a number of defects raised. However, defects can be raised at any point during the project lifecycle. For example, designers can raise defects against the requirements; developers can raise defects against the design; and testers can raise defects against the solution. Of course, a lot of this depends on the methodology and approach.

As defects are encountered and raised, they need to be tracked, verified, and resolved. Defect management also encompasses management reporting. At various points throughout the project it's important to understand the number of "open" defects, their severity and priority, and so on. The reports help to shape how the project progresses. If entry and exit criteria are based on the number and severity of defects, the reports will help to compile the current picture and provide status reporting. It's important to understand the reporting requirements because they will help to shape the defect-tracking system and guide how it should be used. Each team may also have specific reporting requirements.

While individuals normally raise defects, it is possible that your tools can also raise defects automatically. For example, the regular integration system can raise a defect automatically to indicate a broken build, or the regression test tools can automatically raise a defect indicating the tests have failed. It's important to understand these integration points and the requirements of the defect-tracking system's Application Programming Interface (API). Custom reports may also need to make use of the API.

This section looks at the high-level defect management, fix mobilization activities, and some of the elements required to track and manage defects successfully.

Defining Process Constraints

The defect-management process constraints should list the tools and technologies that will be used for tracking and managing defects throughout the project. This will mainly consist of the defect-tracking tool as well as any custom or other tools that surround it. The defect-tracking tool may also need to integrate with other tools and applications, which need to be listed and accounted for.

The defect-tracking system will invariably require customization that is specific to the project. Using the out-of-the-box configuration can sometimes be like "trying to fit a square peg in a round hole." The process is defined by how the tool works, rather than how the process should work. Off-the-shelf tools typically allow customization of defect contents (the data elements) and workflow (state transitions). You need to ensure that the defect-tracking system is fit for purpose and that everyone understands how to use it properly.

The size and scale of the fix team depends entirely on the project and the technologies being used. I typically recommend that the fix team start at 100 percent of the development team size. However, if you've done everything you can to capture and fix many defects early, this percentage should be greatly reduced, very quickly. As the project progresses, this can be further assessed and reduced, as appropriate. The fix team doesn't need to be standing idle waiting for defects to be raised, it can be working on future enhancements or releases. However, when defects are raised, their priorities over existing work needs to be managed accordingly. If an agile approach is taken, the development team and fix team is usually one and the same. It's important to ensure that the defect-tracking system supports all the required users.

Defining the Process

As the project progresses, the requirements on the defect-tracking system will change. In the early days, it's all about the tracking of defects raised by the design, development, and test teams. Later on, it's about which defects are in which releases. Then, finally, it's about providing project wide management defect information. In the run-up to go-live, stakeholders will be particularly interested in the number of "open" defects, what they are, and whether they affect the go-live date. They'll also be interested in ensuring that *all* other defects raised throughout the project have been closed and verified appropriately.

Defect management can be quite stressful at times, especially when testing is blocked and defects need to be turned around quickly. Having a clearly defined process in place will help to ensure that defects are tracked and managed efficiently. Defining the process involves the following high-level activities:

- ❏ Defining the workflow and state transitions
- ❏ Defining the contents of a defect
- ❏ Defining the management report requirements

As you progress through these sections, you'll get an idea of what's involved, as well as some of the best practices for defect management.

Defining the Workflow

The defect-management workflow must have the appropriate transitions and mandatory entries to ensure that the correct procedure is followed. You must also ensure that the transitions support the appropriate alternative flows to avoid unnecessary overhead and confusion.

The defect-management workflow follows a defect from the point at which it has been raised to the point at which it is resolved (or rejected). Because defects can be raised at any point in the project, the people involved in the activities can be members of any one of the teams in the project, and the defects can relate to any of the parts of the solution. For example, a technical designer might raise a defect against a functional design document. It's important to remember that defects aren't just raised against code. To help with defining the workflow, let's look at some high-level, "popular" usage scenarios:

- ❏ Starting with the most popular, testers raise defects during testing and verification. The system has been through construction (including unit testing, integration testing, and whatever else led to this), and it's being tested as part of a formal test activity.
- ❏ Developers may raise defects against the solution design or any of the inputs into the construction process. For instance, a use case may have a missing step, or in the worst case, the design may not be able to be implemented as stated. If the development team is using third-party

components (for example, one they're not responsible for developing), then it's likely that they'll be raising defects when the components don't work correctly.

❏ The development team may raise defects against its own components. Formal defect tracking isn't generally used during unit testing. However, during integration testing there could be a problem with another component. Developers may even notice something in the solution that they think needs to be addressed. For example, they may come across a class that they think hasn't been implemented correctly or needs to be re-factored. This is a fairly common situation during development and fix. Furthermore, the defect may have nothing to do with what they are currently working on or even responsible for.

The actors work together in a customer- and supplier-style relationship. The customer raises the defect, while the supplier deals with it, although the customer and supplier can be the same team, as you've seen in the preceding scenarios. There are many other scenarios, but the focus here is primarily on development and fix. You can extrapolate from the examples and apply them to other areas of the lifecycle. The scenarios listed are very common and each has its own specific considerations for management.

Before looking at the workflow, let's look at a very simple scenario to set the scene:

1. You click on the Create New Account link.

2. The Create New Account page is displayed.

3. You verify the page layout and contents, and you notice a defect:

   ❏ Defect 1: There is a missing "mandatory field indicator" next to "Security Question."

4. You start to complete the form and notice some more defects:

   ❏ Defect 2: The tab order is all over the place.

   ❏ Defect 3: The username field allows only 15 characters, instead of 16 as stated in the entry tip or hint.

5. You click the submit button and are presented with a technical error:

   ❏ Defect 4: Technical error on submission.

6. You are now unable to continue with your script. Out of due diligence, you check the log files. You also try a couple of transactions on some other pages, and they all work fine. You head off to get a coffee while rebooting the entire system. You return and uninstall and re-install the software and run through the scenario again. The same thing happens again. You lean over to Sarah who is also testing and ask her to quickly run through the same scenario. Aha! It happens on her machine, too. This must be a defect!

Figure 3-4 shows a high-level sample workflow that highlights the common activities and transition points.

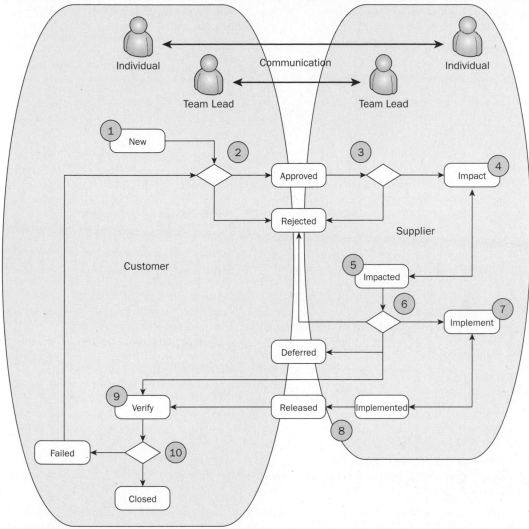

Figure 3-4

I've simplified the diagram so that it really only shows the actors and the main points in the workflow, rather than all the alternative flows that could be required. The workflow steps are as follows:

1. **New** — The defect is raised by an individual (or it could be a sub-system) and is given a basic state of *new* or something similar. When defects are raised, it is crucial that they contain all the relevant information so that you can estimate, locate, and fix the issue. The following is some of the key information that should be captured:

    ❑   Exact steps to reproduce

    ❑   Release and associated configuration installed

- ❏ Test script, test data, and inputs
- ❏ Screenshots of the end-to-end process
- ❏ Logs (verbose, where possible), events, and other diagnostics
- ❏ Database extracts (including reference data and transactional data)

The information listed is generally related to code-based defects. Tools and scripts should be developed to assist with obtaining this information so that it can easily be added to the defect. These tools and scripts will also be useful during any incident investigation.

For management reporting and tracking purposes, when the defect is raised, it should include the *activity* in which it was detected — for example, "Integration Test," "Functional Test," "Technical Test," or "Acceptance Test." When these activities are broken down into separate streams, the stream should also be included — for instance, "Operability Test," "Performance Test," and so forth. These can easily be obtained from the approach and the plan.

Although it is very possible that the exact nature (root cause) is known, this should be managed carefully when raising defects. It's easy to state something potentially incorrect or incomplete — for example, "The data model must have indexes." Well, yes, it probably should, but which data model? The tools may have an underlying database. Does this mean that they also must have indexes? It would probably help. It's therefore important when raising defects that specific *components* be identified (where possible). Generic defects can be useful, but they often require a lot of analysis. For example, consider the infamous "The logging is insufficient" or "The error handling isn't good enough" generic defects. A large-scale solution could have hundreds of components, perhaps thousands. These kinds of defects linger; you can never really close them properly until the system's gone live. Even then it could still be a problem in certain cases. Where possible, the defect should be descriptive and cite specific cases. Another common scenario is stating the resolution (or stating an incorrect resolution) — for example, "The *for* loop in *xyz* should be replaced with a *while* loop." Although it may be true, there may be a very good reason for the way something has been done. If someone doesn't know any better, he or she may simply implement this change and find that the solution no longer works the way it should. A detailed impact analysis *should* determine the resolution. The last one that really grinds my gears is asking questions (and having conversations) through the defect-management tool — for example, "Can the startup scripts be made easier?"

The defect should state what the problem is and how it was encountered. The impact analysis will state how to resolve it, the exact root cause, and the activity that introduced it (design, construction, and so on).

Guidelines should be developed to assist people when raising defects to avoid unnecessary cleansing and potentially sending them around the loop for no reason at all. These are all part of the defect management best practices. The approval process should ensure that all the necessary due diligence has been performed and the defect is good to go through the system. Defects are often visible to the entire project team (including stakeholders), and it's important that people raise defects in a professional manner. Stating that "This system needs re-writing" isn't professional. Defects are very different from changes, and proposed changes to functionality should be raised and discussed outside of the defect-tracking process. Throughout the project it is often necessary to control *who* can raise new defects.

Finally, when defects are raised, they're typically assigned a severity. You must have very strict guidelines on how to assess and assign severities. Defects may also have a priority and again it's very important to have guidelines for assessing and assigning this, too. This should avoid the situation where everything's a "Sev 1, P1." Severity and Priority are discussed shortly.

2. **Approval** — All defects raised should be validated by an authorized approver. In most cases, this would be the individual's team leader. The following represents a handful of tasks the team leader might perform:

    ❑   Ensure that the defect conforms to the standards and guidelines.

    ❑   Ensure that all the relevant information is specified, correct, and contains valid values.

    ❑   Ensure that the defect has all the relevant attachments.

    ❑   Validate that there's sufficient evidence that points to a defect — for example, it's not operator error, or the script, data, or environment. Furthermore, the team leader should do his or her best to ensure that it's not a change to the requirements or design.

    ❑   Verify that the "severity" (and possibly "priority") is assigned appropriately, and if not change them as necessary (according to the appropriate process). The priority may be affected by other outstanding defects that are higher priority.

    ❑   Reject the defect. There should be very strict guidelines for approving defects. Where a defect doesn't meet the strict guidelines, it should be rejected. The guidelines should include all necessary steps, as well as any other specifics.

    ❑   Approve the defect. The approval process should be clearly documented and understood to avoid debate. The defect should have all the necessary information and it's important to correctly identify the phase or activity in which the defect is raised.

3. **Approved** — The "approved" defects are taken into the "supplier" workflow (for example, fix). The fix team leader reviews the defect. The review follows the same steps as outlined earlier. The customer and supplier can work together on this to ensure a consistent picture and avoid many "rejected" defects. The defect is assigned to an individual or team for *impact analysis*. This step may involve discussions with multiple teams to determine the best person or team to perform the impact analysis. At this point in the process, it's good to get an idea of the *estimated time to impact*. Although this will be high-level, it provides a basis for planning. It will also help with the management reporting and financial summaries at completion, as well as continuous improvement.

4. **Impact** — The individual (or team) that the defect has been assigned to performs an impact assessment. The impact process involves reviewing all the information on the defect, re-creating the issue, and providing an assessment on how to resolve the issue. In many cases, the hardest part of impacting a defect is re-creating it. All too often there's not enough detail included in the defect report, which is why you're really trying to ensure that they're properly explained. The productivity scripts will really help to ensure that all the information can be easily gathered and attached to the defect. Even with all this information, it might be necessary to work with the individual or team that raised the defect. This is indicated on the workflow diagram as "communication." The fact is that sometimes people just don't talk to each other, which can lead

to one of my pet peeves, mentioned previously: communicating through the defect-tracking tool. For example:

```
[10:00][Developer] I can't reproduce it. Can you send me the logs?
[10:05][Tester]    I've attached logs.
[10:40][Developer] I can't find the logs you're referring to.
[11:00][Tester]    They're called "xyz.log".
[11:30][Developer] Oh yeah. Thanks.
[13:30][Developer] Can you try again with verbose logging on?
[15:30][Tester]    How do I do that?
...
```

This wastes valuable time (as you can see from the sample timestamps) because the developer and tester are not constantly monitoring the defect-tracking tool, which leads to large gaps between questions and replies. Alternative communication methods should be used, such as "Pick up the phone and work through the problem." The defect-tracking tool is not a discussion board; it should be used to describe the defect, its resolution, and key decisions. If you want to use the tool for this purpose, the defect description and root cause analysis (including key decision points) should be kept separate from any discussion threads. Otherwise, the conversational information might appear on management reports.

Assessing the impact of defects should be a very thorough process. It's important that the assessment is sufficiently detailed and I've listed just a handful of useful tips for assessing the impact:

❑ What's the problem? Provide additional context to the original defect description to describe exactly what the problem is.

❑ How did it come about? This simply adds context to how the defect came about. For example, the root cause analysis might be due to the design not being signed off and the development team proceeding at risk. The root cause analysis is not to point blame but to feed into the continuous improvement process to reduce the number of defects in the future.

❑ What's the solution? Provide a detailed analysis of the solution and what impact this may have on other areas of the system.

❑ Is it a big change? If so, what risks are associated with it?

❑ Will it require a change to any of the inputs into the construction phase? If so, which ones?

❑ Will it require a change to the test scripts/test data? If so, which ones?

❑ What needs to be updated? Provide a list of the things that will need updating (including documentation, classes, methods, unit tests, integration tests, scripts, data, tools, and so on).

❑ Will it require more than one person to work on it? If so, how many and from what departments

❑ Will it require changing or updating any batch jobs or reports? If so, which ones?

❑ Will it require updates to support or operational procedures? If so, which ones?

When possible, scripts and tools should be developed or used to help provide a more detailed impact assessment. For example, tools that walk the code tree can find areas where methods are called and this can provide information on which test cases might need to change. During an impact assessment it's very common for the following exception scenarios to arise:

❑ There's not enough detail on the defect (despite going through *two* approvals).

❑ You can't reproduce the defect.

❑ It's a problem with the test script or test data.

❑ It's not a defect; it is expected functionality.

❑ It's a defect relating to another part of the solution that is not managed by *this* team (which can also include environment and tooling issues).

❑ It's a defect that relates to both *this* part of the solution and other parts of the solution managed by other teams (which can also include environment and tooling issues).

❑ It has already been fixed.

It is important that the person who assesses the impact record the amount of time that he or she spent investigating and assessing the impact of the defect. When the defect is fully understood, it's equally important for the impact assessor to provide an estimated time to fix (and test) it. This information will help with planning, management reporting and financial summaries at completion, as well as continuous improvement.

5. **Impacted** — Once the defect has been fully impacted, it can be reviewed, checked, and moved through the workflow. It depends on the outcome of the impact assessment as to how the defect will be moved on. The diagram shows a few of the alternative transitions, including:

❑ **Impact** — If the assessment is not satisfactory, it may be necessary to re-impact the defect. Furthermore, it is important that the defect be impacted by all the relevant teams. For instance, during an initial assessment it might be noted that a database change needs to be made. This change may need to be impacted by many people, depending on how far-reaching the change is. For example, it might involve changing multiple test scripts and test data.

❑ **Verify** — The defect may no longer be present in the latest release. Therefore, the defect needs to be assigned for retesting against the latest release. Alternatively, the defect may be related to an existing defect, and, as such, has been fixed with the original. The defect needs to be marked as such and associated with the original for tracking.

❑ **Rejected** — After a detailed impact analysis, the defect may be rejected. It is possible that it's rejected because it isn't actually a defect. In some cases, defects are rejected because they can't be reproduced. Strict guidelines should be developed around rejecting impacted defects, and the parties involved should agree that the defect is actually a candidate for rejection. This avoids having to revisit rejected defects later on.

❑ **Deferred** — Based on the impact analysis, there's a possibility that the fix to a defect may be deferred to later in the project lifecycle. High-risk, low-gain defects typically fall into this category.

6. **Assignment** — The defect is assigned out to the various parties for implementation. This could be a single individual, but it could be a number of different teams based on the impact. One common scenario is to send a defect for implementation, and at some point during the process it's noted that the impact analysis wasn't done correctly. Then another team needs to impact it or perform a greater impact analysis. The defect-tracking tool (or process) should be capable of supporting this multiple distribution/multiple state scenario.

7. **Implement** — The implementation should start by validating the defect, its impact, and its proposed resolution. Taking a step back will help to ensure that you're not about to do something that you shouldn't be doing. During this review and validation exercise, an alternative resolution might be identified to the one originally specified and agreed. This is a very common scenario because things may have moved on in development since the original

assessment was performed. Furthermore, the initial assessment may have missed something that is uncovered during the detailed implementation. Changes to the originally proposed implementation need to be approved and documented in the tracking tool, along with the updated estimates.

Once the defect has been implemented, the actual time taken to implement should be recorded for reporting purposes. It provides realistic figures for the amount of time spent fixing defects. This can be compared against the estimates to provide a basis for improvement. In addition, the "fixed in activity" should be recorded to support management reporting.

8. **Release** — When all the implementation activities are complete, they can be reviewed, agreed on, and submitted into a release. This will follow all the same practices and processes for ready-to-build and ready-to-release. The defect-tracking tool should keep track of the release that a defect has been incorporated in. This avoids wasted effort retesting and verifying defects in the wrong release.

9. **Verify** — The defect is retested against the particular release that includes its resolution. It should have been noted during the impact analysis whether the test scripts and test data needed to be updated, and these should be verified. If necessary, the teams and individuals should work together to ensure that everything is present and correct. This will avoid defects going around the loop again when they may not need to — for instance, failing the implementation when the test script wasn't updated correctly or the wrong release has been installed.

Depending on the outcome of the verification the defect can take one of two routes:

❏ **Failed** — If the resolution hasn't successfully resolved the issue, the defect needs to be marked as failed. Particularly difficult defects may go around this loop quite a few times, and it's important that all additional or new information is added to the defect each time.

It is very important to document the defect-failure process to avoid a defect being failed when, in fact, it should be a completely new defect. This happens a lot, too, and it's sometimes unavoidable. It happens primarily because the individual doesn't know the exact nature of the failure or doesn't look into it. As far as he or she is concerned, the transaction they are performing still doesn't work. In the scene at the start of this section, you experienced a "technical error" on submission of a new account. If you still get a technical error on submission, you're likely to say that the defect hasn't been fixed, despite the fact that an entirely new problem is causing the technical error this time. This links right back to the start of the process and actually re-enforces my previous messages. I mentioned that you might have different releases for different purposes. This is a prime example. The "technical error" page in production will probably show a generic message and not contain error information. However, in testing it would be a good idea for it to show a proper error message. That way, instead of a defect being raised with "Technical Error on Submission of Create New Account," you can have something more distinguishable, such as "Connection String Error on submission of Create New Account." You now stand a much better chance of closing this defect and opening a new "Account Table Not Found Error on submission of Create New Account." This can also be achieved if the test team reviews the events and logs to obtain the exact error, and includes a reasonable headline for the defect. However, this would require detailed guidelines and instructions for the test team to follow.

❏ **Closed** — Once the defect has been successfully retested and verified, it can be closed. When a defect is closed, the activity in which it was closed should be recorded. Some defects are put on hold due to their severity or nature, and, therefore, might not be resolved in the same activity that they were raised in. This information also helps with management reporting.

There's one other very important thing to consider when looking at defect management. You might have multiple releases running in parallel on the project. This was highlighted previously. It's possible that a defect needs to be impacted across multiple teams and releases. In addition, you will need to ensure that the defect-management system caters for multiple releases (or branches) to avoid the defects getting muddled up.

This completes the walk-through of the process. Quite a lot is involved, so it's well worth getting a foundation process in place early. Identifying the roles and responsibilities will also help when defining the security model and checks required throughout the process.

Defining the Severity and Priority of Defects

This is probably the most controversial area in defect management. The fact is that defects need to be fixed because they indicate that the system doesn't "work" as it should. The problem is classifying defects in terms of their *impact* and the *order* in which they need to be fixed. These are traditionally referred to as the defect "severity" and "priority," respectively.

Severity is usually expressed in terms of Critical, High, Medium, and Low. Severity can also be expressed numerically — for example, 1, 2, 3, and 4. Similarly, priority is usually expressed in the same way — that is, High, Medium, or Low, or numerically.

How do I classify my defects? Well, first there needs to be very clear guidelines on how to assess and assign the classification. Second, it depends entirely on the approach to classifying defects. The following table shows some high-level severity classifications from the testing activity perspective and from the "system" perspective:

Severity	Classification From the "Testing" Perspective	Classification From the "System" Perspective
Critical	The defect blocks the closure of a complete test phase.	The defect causes the entire system to be unusable.
High	The defect blocks the closure of a complete test suite.	The defect causes part of the system to be unusable.
Medium	The defect blocks the closure of a complete test scenario.	The defect affects the usability or user experience.
Low	The defect isn't currently blocking the continuation of execution.	The defect doesn't affect usability or transaction processing.

And the following table shows a "lowest impact" classification of the defects raised in our little scenario using these definitions:

Defect	Classification From the "Testing" Perspective	Classification From the "System" Perspective
Defect 1: There is a missing "mandatory field indicator" next to "Security Question".	Low	Medium
Defect 2: The tab order is all over the place.	Low	Medium
Defect 3: The username field only allows 15 characters, instead of 16 as stated in the entry tip or hint.	Low	Medium
Defect 4: Technical error on submission.	Medium	High

From the system perspective, none of the defects cause the entire system to be unusable; therefore, none of them are critical. A very severe technical error could cause the entire system to crash, and this would be classified as "Critical" (using these definitions).

So, what does this tell you? It definitely tells you that Defect 4 is affecting a test case or scenario. It's also telling you that Defect 4 is causing a part of the system to be unusable. However, when looking at the other rows in the table, the testing side is telling you, "There's not much to worry about here," and the system side is telling you, "We've got some usability issues." In such a case, you need to ask yourself "Do you want to go-live (on the Internet) with defects 1, 2, or 3 outstanding?"

I'd prefer to see them all fully addressed before go-live. If you look at the defects, it doesn't appear that there will be much effort involved in fixing them. Or will there? You could have generated all the screens from configuration automatically, or you could have created them manually. Either way, you need to understand exactly what's involved in fixing them.

From a testing perspective, the preceding tables show that execution can actually continue because the defects 1, 2, and 3 don't really have an effect on execution. However, they do (and will) have an effect on closure of the scenario. Defect 3 will have an effect on your ability to confirm the boundaries. You can also classify them all as "Medium" in the first instance. However, you need to distinguish the order in which they should be prioritized. In this example, clearly defect 4 is what you want to continue testing. The priority can change, but this is your starting position. The following table shows a potential starting point to ascertain the severity and set priority from the testing perspective:

Defect	Severity	Priority
Defect 1: There is a missing "mandatory field indicator" next to "Security Question".	Medium	Low
Defect 2: The tab order is all over the place.	Medium	Low
Defect 3: The username field only allows 15 characters, instead of 16 as stated in the entry tip or hint.	Medium	Medium
Defect 4: Technical error on submission.	Medium	High

Why classify from the *testing* perspective? Your solution is made up of many applications, processes, and tools. Let's assume you're using a tool that injects transactions into the system. The tool and the application open just fine. You load your transaction set and click "Inject." Nothing happens. What's the problem?

❏ Is it a defect in the tool?

❏ Is it a defect in the application?

❏ Is it a defect in the transaction set/script?

❏ Is it a defect in the set-up (including environment, configuration, and test data)?

The problem is that you really don't know without performing some potentially detailed analysis. It depends how the test team is structured, but you can't expect the test team to perform a detailed and thorough investigation before raising the defect. For example, the test team might simply follow test scripts and instructions and not have the experience and knowledge to investigate issues. There's definitely a case for providing them with some "Top 10 Tips" that they can try in any situation. However, the root cause may still not be highlighted. Now you're a bit stuck when it comes to classifying the defect from the *system* perspective. This is precisely why defects are often classified from the *testing* perspective, in the first instance. It's just like saying, "I don't know what the problem is! It just doesn't work the way it's expected to. It's stopping me from completing this activity, so I need it fixed ASAP!"

Some test teams, such as the technical test team, are used to conducting detailed analysis, which can highlight the defect's impact to the system as well as their own testing activities. If the defect relates to a test tool, a test script, or test data, then the defect impacts their testing activities and not the final state solution. It's not uncommon for the technical test team to provide detailed impact assessments for defects that relate to the final state solution. However, the assessments still need to be ratified and agreed to.

This situation highlights that, although the "impact" to the tester can be assessed immediately, it is not always possible to determine the impact on the actual system — at least until the detailed impact analysis has been performed.

As a developer, you're used to incident investigation, especially on your own systems. However, if you had a problem with a third-party product, how would you classify a defect on the vendor's tracking system? You would typically classify it from your own perspective, not theirs, although it depends on their classifications, too. It generally means specifying the severity it has on you and the priority you think it should be given by them.

Let's examine another scenario. Suppose that you try to start a test tool and it simply doesn't start. You now have a very clear "problem definition" and can attribute a fault specifically to the test tool. However, it still doesn't change the impact it has on the activity. Using the testing perspective, "severity" and "priority," is a great way to manage defects according to test activities, but it's not very good for managing defects according to whether the system can go-live without them being addressed or for managing defects according to the actual severity of the defect.

People usually want to know the number and severity of defects related to the final state solution, as well as the defects that potentially impact the project's timelines and budgets. Therefore, it is prudent to ensure that *all* situations are provided for. As defects are fully "impacted," you can keep track of whether they actually relate to the final solution, whether they are required for go-live, and their impact on the solution. Using this approach you're starting off with the following end goals in mind:

❑ All critical go-live issues must be addressed.

❑ All "customer-facing" issues must be assessed as to when and how they can occur and what procedures/corrective actions need to be in place to deal with them.

❑ All issues relating to business processes and/or back-office processes need to be assessed, and suitable procedures/corrective actions need to be put in place.

You still need to define the "go-live" severity classifications. This can be used in your management reports. At any point, you can run your reports and determine what needs to be fixed to allow the current activities to continue unhindered, as well as what you need to ensure is fixed for go-live.

Because defects can be raised at almost any point in the lifecycle and against any part of the solution, you can generalize the sample classifications so that they are not specific to testing. The following table lists the sample "activity severity" classifications:

Activity Severity	Classification
Critical	The defect will block the closure of an entire activity.
High	The defect will block the closure of multiple tasks in an activity.
Medium	The defect will block the closure of an individual task in an activity.
Low	The defect isn't currently blocking closure.

There's one last scenario that I'd like to go through. Suppose that you're implementing a fix and notice that there's a problem with another class or method that's not part of the work you're doing. How do you raise and classify what you've found? Ultimately, it's "Low" severity and "Low" priority because it neither has an impact on what you're currently doing, nor is it a part of the scope you're working on. This means that you can at least capture defects that are not specific to the tasks you are performing, irrespective of its potential impact on the solution. If you're using defect severities for exit criteria, these might be included in the criteria. However, this must not discourage (authorized) people from "raising" what they find according to the proper guidelines. I always find it best to have a discussion before raising a formal defect in the tool even though it's reasonable to assume that the defect will be uncovered sometime in the future. At the very least, you always have a list of defects that were caught outside of any formal activities that may need to be assessed.

Whatever the severity and/or priority classifications are, there should be very strict guidelines on how to assess and assign them. Ensuring that the defect severities and priorities are appropriately classified, understood, and followed will help to ensure the fix process is consistent and efficient.

> **There are many ways and views of categorizing defects, and there may be strict constraints that need to be followed. The key is to ensure that the chosen severities are well-defined, documented, and followed accordingly.**

Defining the Contents of Defect

The contents of a defect will differ from project to project. The mandatory fields are stipulated to ensure that defects contain all the relevant information. The documentation and usage guides should clearly state what fields are required and how to appropriately select or complete them at each stage. It also breeds best practice and avoids defects with no information or limited context. The key fields should be mandatory and used for management reporting. The following are some sample high-level field groups based on the previous discussion:

❑ **State** — Indicates the state of the defect within the overall process (New, Approved, Impact, Impacted, Implement, Implemented, Failed, Closed, and so on).

❑ **Severity and/or Priority** — Indicates the defect's severity and priority. This could be from the testing perspective initially and then changed to the system perspective once a detailed analysis had been performed. Alternatively, both perspectives could be tracked against the defect, which would ease tracking and management.

❑ **Headline** — The headline should capture the "essence" of the defect, such as "Account Table Not Found Error on submission from Create New Account."

❑ **Overview and Description (and associated information)** — This provides the detailed description of the defect along with the steps to re-create it and all other information discussed earlier, including the components affected (if known).

❑ **Detected in Release** — This should contain the release or version number that the defect was detected in. The fix team would use the same release when attempting to re-create the issue. Furthermore, if this value indicated a much older release, the fix team may simply attempt to re-create the issue in the latest release.

❑ **Raised in Activity/Stream** — Identifies the activity where the defect was found (Design, Development, Functional Testing, Technical Testing, and so on). The values could be broken down to provide for individual streams such as Operability Testing, Failure and Recovery Testing, and so on.

❑ **Raised Against Activity/Stream** — This would indicate the activity or stream responsible for introducing the defect and thus the team that the defect should be assigned to for impact assessment. It's not always possible to identify the root cause until a thorough impact has been performed. For instance, when a defect is raised by a test team, this value might indicate "Online Application" or "Functional Design." The activities and streams would be dictated by the development approach and structure.

❑ **Impact Analysis and Root Cause Analysis** — This provides all the information about the defect's root cause and its resolution.

❑ **Deferred to Activity/Stream** — This is very useful when defects are being discussed. Not everything is fixed within the activity the defects are raised in. Often defects are deferred to another release or phase.

❑ **Resolved in Activity/Stream** — This would indicate the activity or stream where the defect was resolved. For example, if the functional test team actually fixed the issue because it was a script issue, this value might be "Functional Test." However, if it was an application issue that was resolved during technical testing, this value might contain "Technical Testing" or "Operability Testing." Again, the development approach would dictate the activities and streams in the overall project.

❏ **Resolved in Release** — This would contain the release or version number where the defect has been resolved. This value would be assigned when the fix (or fixes) was included in a formal release as part of the build and release processes.

❏ **Estimated and Actual Times** — It is important that the estimated and actual times be properly used and completed with realistic figures. All too often these fields are not mandatory or are completed with unrealistic figures that result in a planning nightmare. This is especially true when there are large numbers of defects or limited resources. The defect description and associated information should be detailed enough so that a realistic estimate can be arrived at. The estimated and actual figures are used for management reporting and continuous improvement.

The defect would also include all the necessary dates and times associated with the activities — for example, date raised, date impacted, and so on.

This is not an exhaustive list of fields and elements, but it captures the highlights. During the defect management and fix mobilization activities, the defect modeling can be performed. Having all the right information included within the defects will help to refine your management reporting and help you to continually improve the project.

Defining the Management Reports

The management reports will be used for both defect scheduling and post activity analysis. When an activity finishes, the reports can be used to determine the number of defects that were raised, closed, failed, and so on. A number of reports will be required during the project, and it is worth trying to identify them early on. This will ensure that the tracking tool has the correct fields and that the process can ensure they are captured. The following are a few high-level report types:

❏ Defects by Activity (Raised In, Resolved In, Root Cause Activity)

❏ Defects by Release (Raised Against Release, Resolved In Release)

❏ Defects by State

❏ Defects by Severity

❏ Defects by Deferred To

❏ Defects by Components Affected (Raised Against, Resolved In, and so on)

❏ Actual and Estimated Time (Impact, Implementation)

The reports will generally be used for daily and weekly meetings, as well as activity completion analysis. As with everything in the book, reports such as these will be required, so it's best to try and define as much up front as possible, while at the same time defining the process and best practice.

The defect-tracking process will generally last a long time, during which it will be refined. It may also be handed over to the support and maintenance team. All the documentation and configuration will assist with the handover activities. The defect-tracking tools can be experimented with while the development, test, and build mobilization exemplars are being developed.

Configuration Management Mobilization

Configuration management is critical in software development. It is used to store, manage, and version control everything produced throughout the project lifecycle. The project will create and use thousands of artifacts. In the mobilization activities, you'll have created a whole series. Some will be required in all environments, and some will be different in other environments. All these need to be kept safe, version controlled, and easily accessible and deployable.

Defining Process Constraints

The configuration-management process constraints should list the tools and technologies that will be used for storing, managing, and version controlling artifacts throughout the project. This will mainly consist of the configuration-management tool, as well as any custom or other tools that surround it. The configuration-management tool may also need to integrate with other tools and applications, and these need to be listed and accounted for.

The development tools often tightly integrate with the configuration-management system. This makes it easy for developers to check in and check out directly from the development IDE. You might be using tools to manage your requirements, test cases, test scripts, and test results, and these tools might integrate with the configuration-management system or implement their own version tracking. The defect and change tracking tools may also integrate with the configuration-management system. It's also possible that the project management tools also integrate with the configuration-management system.

The configuration-management system requires configuration, the amount of which depends entirely on the sophistication of the tool. In some cases, this can mean far tighter control over the changes and files that can be accessed. For instance, some configuration-management systems require the definition of activities and tasks before anything can be added, checked in, or checked out. You might have a "Build Create New Account Component" activity assigned to a particular developer. The developer will use this activity when he or she is checking their code in or out. All changes are then tracked under this activity so that you can see the files that have changed. The project management tool may integrate with the configuration-management system and automatically create a series of "activities" based on the project plan. This can be very useful for defect management, too. The defect-tracking tool may integrate with the configuration-management system and support the automatic creation of work items or "activities." That way, you can see all the changes associated with a single defect. If you want to make use of these kinds of features, you should think about them up front and plan them into the process accordingly.

The configuration-management system retains a history of changes to the artifacts, and traditionally "configuration management" is associated with "change control" or "change management." For the purposes of this book and this section, "configuration management" refers to the actual configuration-management system itself, rather than to the change-control process (which is discussed later).

The high-level activities, aside from defining the constraints, include:

❑ Defining the contents and individual repositories, which detail what you're going to store under configuration management and whether the contents will be separated using multiple repositories

❑ Defining the structure of each of the individual repositories

Defining the Contents and Repositories

Every application and every environment has its own configuration-management requirements. For example, the core operating system will reside on every computer, although it may be a different version in certain environments and may require different configuration for different purposes. The tools and applications that are used may only be required in certain environments, but again they may have a different configuration depending on what they are being used for. The test data can be different across the environments, and the database installation and configuration may be different, too. The configuration-management solution is used to store and manage these items.

You need to determine which files you're going to store and how you're going to store them within the configuration-management solution. Ideally, the configuration-management system would be used to store everything. However, some projects and companies also favor the use of network drives and other storage areas for artifacts that don't change very frequently — for instance, if the operating system doesn't change. That is, you might be upgrading to a new version at some point in the project, but in general you're not making changes to the operating system code or documentation. Therefore, do you really want to store the operating system's DVD image (ISO files, and so on) under version control? This question also goes for other third-party product media.

The configuration-management system retains a history of the changes to a file. Each time a file is checked in, the previous version on the file is kept. The fact that you're not frequently changing the files means they take relatively the same amount of disk space as they would on a network drive. In addition, it's often practical to have a server or base image. These images can be used to install and set up a server very quickly. Traditionally the software was installed from the ground up (usually manually) and could take a long time, depending on the number of applications to install and the configuration tasks. Disk images are essentially a backup or clone of the entire machine. If you're introducing a new server or need to restore an existing server, you can use an image to rapidly deploy everything. At lot of organizations and projects choose this approach to reduce manual errors and improve turnaround time. It's typically the production hardware that's imaged, although some companies use it for any critical servers or environments. For example, software houses will typically use this approach for development and test machines and environments. The time to build a new development machine is greatly reduced. There's no reason why you can't store the images within your configuration-management system.

You are making changes to the operating system and third-party product's configuration, so these files should definitely be kept under version control because the changes are very specific to *this* project. If applications do not easily support configuration management — for example, it's hard to determine which files contain the "variable" settings — the scripted installation or installation and configuration documentation should be kept under configuration management.

Furthermore, you'll be making many releases of your software throughout the project. Depending on the size of the project, there could be thousands of builds and hundreds of releases. Do you really want to store all these packages under configuration management? You need to keep all of them for historical purposes. Again, a lot of companies or projects choose to store these within the configuration-management system. The releases need to be kept neat and tidy so that obtaining and installing them is straightforward. One way of doing this is to keep them available via the project portal. They can be organized in such a way that they don't present a 1,000-item list with all the releases from Release 1 through to Release 1,000. The important thing is that they are backed up and kept safe. If you think about it, the project portal resides on the file system, and the files that are uploaded to it are placed on shared disk. So, as long as the shared file system is backed up, you can always restore your releases.

Using the configuration-management system to store items that don't really change is an alternative approach to using network drives. The configuration-management system will provide a consistent and central location for *all* your artifacts. You can distribute items from the configuration management system to the project portal.

Configuration-management systems support multiple repositories, with each repository essentially being a separate "database." So, you have the choice of using a single repository or multiple repositories. Using multiple repositories can help to separate artifacts, such as those discussed, as well as provide individual teams with their own repository. For example, technical testing may have enormous datasets that need to be version controlled. These could be stored in a "technical test" repository, for instance.

The following are a few examples of potential configuration-management repositories:

❑ **Infrastructure, Builds, and Releases** — This repository can be used to store all infrastructure-related items, including disk images, ISO files, and so on. It can also be used to store all the builds and releases.

❑ **Development** — This repository can be used to store all items for the development team.

❑ **Configuration** — This repository can be used to store all the configuration items across the project.

The remainder of this section takes a quick look at the following:

❑ Defining the structure

❑ Defining the branching and merging approach

Defining the Structure

Typically, the core development artifacts would include the following:

❑ **Database scripts** — The database scripts would include CREATE DATABASE, CREATE TABLE, CREATE VIEW, and CREATE PROCEDURE, for instance.

❑ **Source code files** — The source code files include all files associated with the solution, including .sln, .cs, .aspx, and so on.

❑ **Configuration files** — Configuration files include all .config files and other custom configuration files.

❑ **Productivity scripts** — Productivity scripts include all environment set-up scripts, instrumentation scripts, and log file-gathering scripts.

❑ **Test scripts and test data** — Test scripts and test data include all test configuration scripts, set-up and teardown scripts, data installation scripts, execution scripts, data extraction scripts, and comparison scripts.

❑ **Documentation** — The documentation includes all process guides, productivity guides, test plans, query logs, comment sheets, and other documentation.

It's generally good practice to separate out items that require different versions across environments. It should be relatively straightforward to pull out of this list what is initially most likely to require different versions. Starting with the most obvious, these are:

- ❏ **Configuration files** — The configuration files are most likely to require different versions for different purposes and environments. For instance, the `web.config` used for development may be very different from the one used in technical testing and production. Furthermore, technical testing may have different versions for different test activities.

- ❏ **Database scripts** — Certain database scripts, such as those containing `CREATE DATABASE` statements, will be different because technical test and production databases often make use of multiple disks and file systems. The databases will be installed differently across environments. There may also be other database scripts that are different across activities and environments.

- ❏ **Productivity scripts** — Certain productivity scripts will be different across environments. For example, technical testing is likely to have more servers, and the productivity scripts may need to support this. For example, in development and testing, your basic defect information gathering tool (or script) may only use a single server. However, this will need to be enhanced (or wrapped) for use in the technical test and production environments, where multiple servers could be used.

- ❏ **Testing scripts and test data** — Certain test scripts will be different. For instance, functional testing may only start certain components in the solution (therefore, the environment start-up will be different), whereas technical testing will probably start up everything. In addition, the number of servers and deployment of components might be different. The test data is also likely to be different. In development and functional testing, a core set of data may be used, whereas technical testing may have multiple sets of data for different scenarios. Technical testing is also likely to have extremely large data sets for load testing and soak testing. Soak testing is typically performed using a significant volume or data injected over an extended period of time. For example, the system may perform exactly as expected when tested with a few thousand transactions injected over an hour or so; however, when tested with millions of transactions injected at expected load over a few days, the application may display abnormal behaviors or characteristics that need to be investigated and corrected.

The number of environments will differ from project to project, but as long as there is more than one, the key is to identify what is most likely to be different across them. These "different" files need to be managed and tracked appropriately.

For the moment, let's look at the `web.config` files. When you add new configuration values or make changes to these files, it's possible that you'll need to update a number of different versions. You need to determine how you are going to manage this and where these "different" files are stored.

The configuration-management structure is really nothing more than a simple folder structure under which everything is stored. Organizing the folder structure is a personal choice and depends on the project. As the project progresses, the structure may change, which is why most structures start out with the basics required for development and are subsequently modified throughout the remainder of the project. There are often tools and scripts created to extract artifacts from the configuration-management system, and as such these are closely tied to the structure. These can be used to extract everything for a particular release or everything for a particular environment. The tools may look for certain versions or may just get the latest version. If the structure of the configuration-management system changes, these tools also need to be updated. It's a good idea to try to start off with a reasonable structure to streamline this process.

You have a couple of choices for where you could store the different `web.config` files:

❑ You could store copies of them in their respective repositories. For example, technical tests have their own copies, functional tests have their own copies, and so forth.

❑ You could store all the individual copies in a single "Configuration" repository.

Alternatively, you could choose to not store copies of them at all but instead implement some other mechanism for maintaining the individual configuration. It's possible in certain configuration files to have separate sections for different environments and purposes, which can sometimes make things easier, although it can also complicate the configuration file and lead to time being wasted changing values in the wrong place. This needs to be balanced against multiple configuration files and the associated maintenance.

Anyway, let's say that during development (or fix) you add a new configuration value to this file. This change *may* need to be propagated through each of these copies. I use the term *may* because the system may provide default behaviors if a particular configuration value is found. (This subject is discussed later in this book.) With respect to the updates to the configuration files, you have some choices at this point:

❑ The development team updates all the respective copies.

❑ The individual teams are responsible for the updates to their own copies.

If the individual teams are responsible for their own updates, this needs to be managed via the process. If the development team is responsible for the updates, it needs access to each file and/or repository.

Storing the files in a central repository can often make updates much easier, enabling you to note the differences between the files. Configuration-management tools generally support "diff" capabilities. A "diff" usually highlights the differences between two files side-by-side. If all the files are within the same repository, it's much easier to "diff" the files between development and technical testing, for example.

If the files are stored in a central repository, you have a lot of choices for how you can organize them within a folder structure. The following are just two sample structures:

❑ Filename\Activity\Purpose

❑ Activity\Purpose\Filename

(Note that if the files are not stored centrally, you still need to determine the overall structure.) Figure 3-5 illustrates the preceding sample organizational structures.

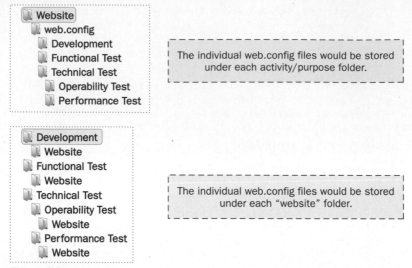

Figure 3-5

In the preceding examples, the basic structure could be extended to include other configuration files, database scripts, tools, test scripts, test data, and so on. When you're making changes to the database schema, it can often help to have things in a central repository because schema changes can affect all the test data (depending on how you're managing test data, of course).

An environment can be as small as a single computer for a specific purpose. Most development machines are a single computer, as are most test environments. Not all development machines are used for the same purpose, and neither are all test environments. One might be used to develop batch components, whereas another might be used to develop architecture components. If different configuration or files are required, ideally they should be separated in the configuration-management system.

There are many ways to slice-and-dice the configuration-management structure. If possible, the number of different versions of artifacts should be kept to a minimum to avoid maintenance overheads, and, if possible, development and testing should be conducted on a live-like configuration.

In addition to the core development artifacts, all the other components and files associated with the system need to be under configuration management, including the following:

- ❑ Construction tools, configuration, and scripts
- ❑ Build projects, configuration, and scripts
- ❑ Packaging projects, configuration, and scripts
- ❑ Deployment projects, configuration, and scripts
- ❑ Test tools, configuration, and scripts
- ❑ Development exemplars and templates
- ❑ Test exemplars and templates

❏ Batch configuration, schedules, and scripts

❏ Reports and data extracts

❏ Reference data and test data

The preceding is not an exhaustive list, but it gives you an idea of what to consider and how it can be best organized for all purposes. What you store and manage under configuration management depends entirely on your project and what you (or the project) develop/change.

Defining the Branching and Merging Approach

To complicate matters, I mentioned previously that systems development often involves multiple releases, which is something else you need to consider when looking at configuration management. When Release 2 comes along and is (potentially) running in parallel with Release 1, things start to get a little complicated. It's at this point that "branching and merging" often occurs. Figure 3-6 shows an example of a branching and merging timeline.

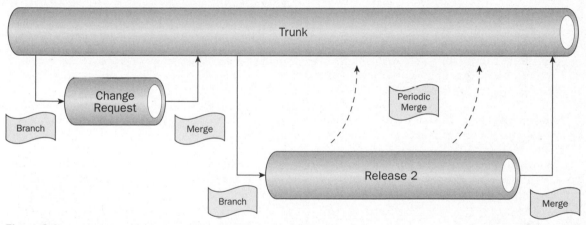

Figure 3-6

Essentially, the main branch (or "trunk") stores all the project artifacts. It is typically created at the start of the project with Release 1. The figure shows a change request coming in at some point during the development of Release 1. It is sometimes required to implement change requests off the main branch to isolate the changes and maintain consistency. The situation can be even more complicated if the change request were to overlap with the development of Release 2. Changes are made in the individual branches and subsequently merged back into the main trunk. Longer running branches may perform periodic merges, as appropriate.

You should remember the following:

❏ When a release goes into production, the source code and all other artifacts associated with it should be kept separate from any other development activities. The reason for this is to ensure that there is a "fix-on-fail" branch of the system. If there is an issue in live service that needs to be addressed, you need to be able to fix it on an exact copy of the production system. You must ensure that you don't muddle up changes and potentially deploy part of Release 2 into production.

❑ When defects are encountered during testing, they might need to be impact assessed for each release and branch. For example, if Release 1 testing raises a defect, it will be assessed for its impact on the Release 1 branch. It may also need to be assessed for its impact on the Release 2 branch (and others) to determine if it's a problem there, too. It's possible that there are multiple (and differing) impacts for a single defect. For example, Release 2 may have changed the code in such a way that a different impact and resolution is required than that for Release 1. Furthermore, issues that are detected in live service will almost certainly require impact assessment against any other development branches and releases. Figure 3-6 shows the fix-on-fail branch potentially merging back into the main trunk. However, this would typically require a detailed impact analysis to ensure that the files changed were identical (prior to the change) across all releases and branches.

Branches can usually be taken from any point in tree, although some projects favor branching and merging the entire project — for example, if Release 2 is a complete copy of Release 1. Alternatively, branching can be done at lower levels within the structure. It's entirely dependent on the project, the purpose of the branch, and the duration.

Release 2 will be updating in a separate location files that have been branched from a specific version of the Release 1 files. Updates may still be being made to the Release 1 files, and these changes need to be merged into the Release 2 versions where appropriate.

The individual teams need to work together to determine which changes should be merged. This is another important reason for using a configuration-management tool, as doing this manually and tracking all changed files would be an arduous task.

It's a good idea to understand this early on. If you're using a single repository, keeping everything under a single, top-level release folder (for example, `Within-a-Click\Release 1`) makes things a lot easier because a new folder for release 2 can be added, and so on.

Change Control Mobilization

That things are going to change is a fact and part of the nature of software development. New ideas and new ways of thinking will constantly come about. When users are testing, they'll often identify areas where improvements can be made. It's vital to a project that an appropriate change-control process is in place and that everyone understands and adheres to it.

I've discussed the differences between defects and changes. Changes follow a very similar workflow to defects, although changes usually involve financial discussions. I mentioned in Chapter 1 that it depends on the methodology but changes are often considered "a change to the signed-off requirements" and as such have more impact on budgets and timescales. When there are changes in "scope," these need to be impacted and estimated accordingly.

It is important that everyone understand and follow the change-control process. It is all too easy during development to start changing things without going through the proper channels. The change-control process is there to ensure that all changes go through the relevant process and are either approved or rejected. When approved, the changes can be scheduled into the development lifecycle and released accordingly.

Where possible, tools can and should be used to assist in the impact and estimating of changes in the same way that tools are used to impact defects. It is rare that a change will require a completely new application or architecture stack, so the existing estimating models will also provide a good starting point. If the change is something completely new, it may require a full bottom up/top down design and impact.

You saw in the previous section that a change could be implemented on its own branch to ensure that it doesn't conflict with mainstream development. After the change has been completed, it can be merged into the main trunk, as required.

The high-level steps for change control mobilization include:

❑ **Defining the process constraints** — As with all mobilization activities, this involves listing the tools and technologies (as well as any other constraints). The tools used for change control are often very similar to those used in defect management. They can sometimes integrate with the configuration-management system to ensure "activities" and work items are defined, as well.

❑ **Defining the process** — This involves defining the workflow, processes, and activities that need to be performed when dealing with changes. The workflow typically follows a similar path to defect management. The "impact" activity can include activities such as requirements analysis, design, and commercial discussions. The impact will also need to determine the impact to the overall project timeline and the associated risks.

I'm not going to go into these activities in detail because, as you can see, they are very similar to those already discussed. The important thing is to ensure that change is accounted for in the overall project.

Summary

This chapter examined some of the mobilization activities that can improve your readiness for full-scale implementation. The important thing to remember is that these activities will usually happen naturally throughout the project. It's better to have a handle on them early to avoid unnecessary delays and ensure that everything fits together nicely. As you've seen, a lot of the activities, processes, and tools are very closely coupled. Thinking about how your production line is going to operate will help you to ensure it operates smoothly and the results are of high quality. If you were building the entire system (including the production line) for someone else, it's likely that all these outputs and processes would be handed over to them.

The samples and suggestions outlined in this chapter should be used for reference purposes and not necessarily followed verbatim. Every project is different and will have its own specific requirements and best fit.

The following are the key points to take away from this chapter:

❏ **Mobilize early** — The best time to mobilize an activity is before it actually starts full-scale. Major changes to the processes, tools, and activities will have a far greater impact if they are already being used by large numbers of people. Mobilizing early ensures that everyone has a clearly defined process to follow and the appropriate tools to use.

❏ **Capture the constraints** — The most important part of mobilization is to ensure that all the relevant constraints are captured. You don't want to go off down your own path only to find that there's an existing process that you *must* follow. The constraints and categories discussed in this chapter included:

  ❏ Process and methodology

  ❏ Tools and technology

  ❏ Resources

  ❏ Infrastructure

  ❏ Communication

  ❏ Location (and security)

  ❏ Environment

❏ **Define the processes and tools** — You need to think about what you're doing, whom you're doing it for, and when it will be required. The key to effective mobilization is to cover as much as possible. Thinking about the individual processes and tools, how they interact with each other, and how they will be used will ensure that you have a good foundation for success. During your mobilization activities, you can create a number of exemplars and templates that can be used throughout the project. The mobilization activities discussed in this chapter included the following:

  ❏ **Development** — Development mobilization needs to capture the entire scope of the development activities — the inputs and the outputs. The inputs to development will be discussed in more detail in the next chapter and throughout this book.

  ❏ **Build and regular integration** — You need to ensure that you can build and release effectively. There could be many different releases, containing many different things, for many different purposes.

  ❏ **Test** — The testing activities will prove your system, so it important to ensure that you've defined the right test activities, their scope, and their outputs.

  ❏ Defect management — Defects are going to be raised throughout the lifecycle, and you need to be ready to track and manage these appropriately. You need to ensure that you have the right workflow in place and that the defects contain the right level of information. You can categorize defects in many ways depending on the requirements of the project/activity.

  ❏ **Configuration management** — The configuration-management system is used to store all your project artifacts. You need to determine what you're going to store within it and how it's going to be structured in terms of repositories and trees. You may also need to take into account branching and merging, and ensure that you cater for this.

❑ **Change control** — You need to ensure that you have the appropriate tools and processes in place to ensure changes are tracked and managed appropriately.

The number of applications, processes, and tools will depend entirely on the size and scale of the project. Setting up and configuring the applications and tools requires time and effort, which needs to be factored into the scope.

❑ **Continuously improve** — Just because you've mobilized the activity doesn't mean it will be perfect. It may need the odd tweak here and there. You need to regularly review the processes and tools and make improvements, as necessary.

The following chapter discusses the last subject in the overall production-readiness landscape — the inputs to the development activities to ensure the build team has everything it needs to produce quality software products.

The Ins and Outs of Construction

In the previous chapters, I've outlined a series of activities and actions that you should consider for each and every project you undertake. Although each project will be different, the underlying principles and foundations for production readiness remain the same. You've seen how these activities can improve the quality of the software that you develop, as well as improve the overall process of development and implementation. You've seen that all your applications, environments, processes, and tools need to be fit for purpose, and you've looked at the high-level software quality characteristics. The previous chapter touched on the high-level categories of inputs into the construction process. This chapter completes the high-level overview of the production-readiness landscape by taking a closer look at some of these inputs and discussing how to refine them to ensure you have the right level of detail for construction purposes. That's not to say that you'll get everything 100 percent right the first time, but you can at least give yourself the best shot at success. The more detail you have, the better your scope will be defined, the better your estimates will be, and the better your overall results will be. It is always going to be a balance between what you do up front and what you leave until later in the lifecycle.

This chapter is organized into the following sections:

❑ **Thinking Out-of-the-Box** — Regardless of whether you're developing software for in-house use, external use, or even off-the-shelf purchase, there are some key contents to a software package, and these include:

  ❑ The "back of the box," which typically shows the key features of the software, the business or usage benefits, key statistics, and other high-level sales collateral.

  ❑ The "media," which are essentially the DVDs or CDs that contain the actual software, help files, and installation files.

  ❑ The "User Guide," which provides all the instructions for using the software effectively and performing the day-to-day tasks.

❏ The "Operations Manual" or "Administrators Guide," which provides all the instructions and information for planning deployment, installation, configuration, and for monitoring and operating the software.

This section looks at how you can map everything you do to these basic contents. By thinking about what would come "out-of-the-box," you can shape the high-level roadmap of the project and its ultimate development and implementation.

❏ **Considering the Design** — This section looks at some of the high-level design considerations and how these will clearly have a domino effect on the remainder of the project. The more that you can define up front, the better the overall scope will be. Starting with a very simple picture, you can begin to extrapolate a number of areas that will require further analysis, discussion, and decisions. The high-level categories of considerations include:

❏ **Accessibility** — Examines how the software is or can be accessed by the widest number of users. For the purposes of this book, accessibility is not just about catering for people with disabilities; it is about catering for the entire user community or population.

❏ **Implementation** — Examines how the design choices can have an effect on the way the overall solution is developed and implemented. A single design choice can have a far-reaching impact on the overall budget and timescales. Minimizing the complexity and functionality of the solution can often help to reduce costs and timescales, although the application needs to be fit for purpose and there is a clear balance between the two.

❏ **Support and maintenance** — Examines the key points that should be considered for support and maintenance when looking at the design of the solution and the individual components. The software ultimately needs to be supported and maintained throughout its lifetime, so it is important to understand the support and maintenance implications of the overall design.

❏ **Custom built vs. off-the-shelf** — Examines some of the specific considerations when deciding whether to use third-party products or components.

In addition to the preceding areas, this section also lists some high-level general considerations when looking at the overall solution design.

❏ **The Analysis and Design Outputs** — This section discusses in detail how to use the following outputs of the analysis and design activities to further define the project and the out-of-the-box contents. The analysis and design outputs are the primary inputs into the construction activities. Good inputs can provide the basis for realistic estimates and, in turn, provide the very basis of the construction outputs (for example, the completed solution).

❏ Scope (the items that are in or out of scope)

❏ Requirements (both functional and non-functional)

❏ Use-case diagrams and use cases

❏ Navigation maps

❏ Storyboards

❏ Page layouts and specifications

❏ The data dictionary and logical data model

❏ Architecture and application component specifications

Thinking Out-of-the-Box

In keeping with the style of this book, let's start at the end and work backwards. While the Internet and software downloads have become the norm, you can think of a software package as a virtual box. Figure 4-1 shows the basic contents of a software package, as described in the introduction to this chapter.

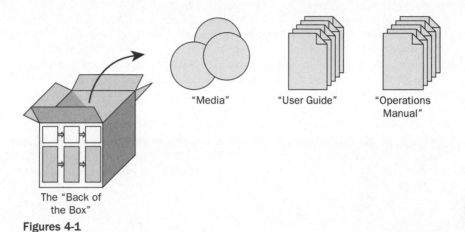

"Media"   "User Guide"   "Operations Manual"

The "Back of the Box"

Figures 4-1

With these core contents in mind, it helps to shape the overall project, its scope, its benefits, and its ultimate delivery. It also promotes my personal vision of thinking about the recipient of the software and assuming that they've just obtained the software. You can apply the "out-of-the-box" thinking to any piece of software that you develop, including tools and productivity scripts. The documentation would need to be very thorough and provide all the information required. Using the contents of the box as an outline of the key deliverables can provide a good starting point for the application design and development roadmap. Almost everything that you produce would ultimately be included within these (and supporting) documents. Thinking about the contents of these documents early on can save you the time and effort of producing multiple sets of documentation for similar purposes. As the project progresses, the documentation becomes more and more defined. I'm not suggesting that all architects and developers become technical authors. However, a large part of our job is to develop "documentation," and if we start in the right place, this can only help us to finish in the right place, too.

The following sections discuss the key focus areas shown in Figure 4-1.

The "Back of the Box"

Many years ago, I designed a database engine called DB*i*. I started by pulling together a simple data sheet that highlighted the key features and benefits of the engine. I envisioned that this would ultimately provide the content for the "back of the box." You've already seen in the previous chapters that software requirements are typically born out of a set of guiding principles that are generally underpinned by a set of key business drivers. The external business drivers, guiding principles, and key features of the software provide input into the "back of the box", data sheets, and other sales material.

Most projects will start out by producing lightweight presentations that capture the essence of the resulting software and its ultimate goals. For example, one business driver or product differentiator could be based on the performance of the solution. If you think about a packaged solution, this could be translated into response time guiding principles and statistics. The sales and marketing collateral might contain a statement, such as "Sub-second response time*." However, as with any marketing materials, the asterisk (*) normally indicates that certain conditions apply. In this example, it would probably indicate that the statistics would apply only to an environment similar to that where the statistics were calculated. Not all organizations are the same, of course, so the statistics could differ. Another guiding principle for the solution could be "High transaction throughput." Again, this would probably be included in the sales collateral as something similar to "Supports *10,000** transactions-per-second" (once it had been proven). The performance statistics would typically be measured in the server room with a specific configuration and environment. Alternative configurations and environments would typically differ in performance, hence another asterisk.

Almost everything that you produce in the early stages of the project is about presenting and visualizing the "end result" and its primary benefits. For a packaged solution, the "back-of-the-box" or datasheets would capture all of the key items and messages to provide the best chance of securing a sale. By thinking about these marketing messages, it can help you to outline (and prioritize) the key features and benefits for the solution.

The "Media"

Software is typically distributed on CDs or DVDs. A lot of software can also be purchased and/or downloaded via the Internet. In either case, the software needs to be installed in the environment in which it is going to be used and there needs to be very clear installation and configuration instructions. While the installation instructions for a packaged piece of software might be included in the user manual or a separate installation manual, the contents remain the same. The installation and configuration instructions need to be very clear and easy to follow. Furthermore, thinking about how the user is going to go about installing the software helps to shape the packaging and deployment processes and tools. If the software is going to be installed using a traditional installer, you will need to design the individual steps, selections, and entries. If you're going to use a simple extract file, then the user needs to know how to extract the software. In either case the user needs to know what has been installed and to where. It is very important to think about how your software will be distributed and what is included in each and every package.

The "User Guide"

During the analysis and design activities, the key features and functions of the solution are solidified, along with the appropriate quality characteristics. I've discussed some of the inputs to the construction activities, including use-case diagrams, use cases, and so on. In a packaged solution, the "User Guide" would capture all the features and functions of the solution, as well as all the introductory matter. It would document the features and how to use them in a step-by-step fashion. For example, in terms of the case study used later in this book, the User Guide might contain a section called "Creating a New Account," which would take the user through the end-to-end process of creating a new account. The User Guide would almost certainly contain screen shots, walkthroughs, display messages, and so forth.

It would also provide alternative flows and errors, including validation error messages. The User Guide also provides the foundations for testing the solution. A "functional design" can be thought of as the User Guide — initially starting with low-resolution graphics and progressing to a fully completed, high-resolution version. The User Guide would be used by end users of the system to complete their day-to-day activities. Furthermore, the User Guide would normally be available online through help files or HTML pages. The User Guide would also provide the basis for training and education.

You can essentially reduce the overall number of documented inputs and outputs by thinking about the primary User Guide output. I've often said that it should be possible to write a piece of software from the User Guide (and/or the Administrators Guide), and that it is a very good starting point for the application design activities. As the project progresses, the User Guide becomes increasingly refined as decisions and turning points are reached.

For a moment, assume that your application is an Application Programming Interface (API) or set of framework components. Your User Guide, in this instance, would contain component models and overviews, interfaces and usage guides, and scenarios. Each component would be fully documented along with the properties and methods — what their purpose is, what processing they perform, and how to use them appropriately. It would also contain all the necessary prerequisites and exceptions that could occur. In this example, the User Guide can be thought of as the "Developer's Guide" and maps almost directly to the "technical design," starting with a high-level outline and progressing to a fully completed developer's guide. The guide would be used primarily by the development or application maintenance team to get a full understanding of the system and how it works under the covers.

The "Operations Manual"

The Operations Manual (or Administrators Guide), which is discussed in more detail later in this book, would almost certainly contain information on deployment planning, the application itself, and the architecture (including the individual servers and components). It would contain information regarding networking and security, as well as the fault-tolerant features that can be employed. The installation and configuration instructions would document the various steps involved and the individual configuration settings, including their purpose and how to set them appropriately. The Operations Manual would also contain information and instructions on routine maintenance tasks, such as batch and housekeeping, operational procedures (starting, stopping, and so on), as well as specific procedures to monitor and tune the system effectively, and produce technical reports. Another key item in the Operations Manual would be all the error messages and error conditions, including information on what causes them to happen and what should be done to correct them. Typically, the content of the Operations Manual is derived from all the architecture diagrams, technical requirements, quality characteristics, and operational procedures. The Operations Manual would be used by the support staff, including service delivery and operations.

Considering the Design

It was a very long time ago when I first started having thoughts about writing a book about software development. I finally decided what I wanted to say by simply having a picture in my head similar to the one shown in Figure 4-2.

Figures 4-2

They say a picture is worth a thousand words, and it is true. The picture in Figure 4-2 took me approximately 20 minutes to produce. Trin Tragula, a character in *The Hitchhiker's Guide to the Galaxy*, by Douglas Adams, extrapolated the whole of creation from one small piece of fairy cake and created the "Total Perspective Vortex." In a similar way, it is possible to extrapolate and complete an entire *membership* design from the one simple picture presented. However, it is a totally different scenario to actually develop and implement the final solution.

Presenting the picture is similar to saying the actual words "membership system." The concept of a membership system is pretty common, and most seasoned web users, designers, and developers could easily list the general features and functions, as well as provide a series of handmade mockups like the one shown. Similarly if I were to say the words "online store," a team of users, designers and developers could take just these two words and start shaping something out. Every online store has very similar features — product browsing and searching, shopping cart, ordering and payment, and so on. It is only really the products and services offered that differ. Similarly, most membership systems have the same features, too — the ability to create a new account or profile, update your account details, change your password, obtain your password when you've forgotten it, and so on. However, each and every designer and developer would have their own view on what should be implemented, how it should look, and how it should behave. Design is the creative part of your job, and you want to secure and exhibit this creativity to achieve the best results for the consumer and yourself. As you start to break down the solution into its components parts, you start to get a better idea of what's involved in its development and implementation. It is simply a question of when the right time to do the design is and where you want to stop.

The code name Within-a-Click came to me while watching a mini-documentary by George Lucas called "Within a Minute: The Making of Episode III." It is a really fascinating documentary about everything that goes on behind the scenes to create just 1 minute of production film (which is actually staggering, by the way). Similarly, this book shows what can be involved behind the scenes to produce a fully production-ready "system" that is ready for implementation. So, I thought the name was rather fitting and appropriate. If you took only the sample picture in Figure 4-2 and fleshed out everything as if it were a full-scale system, you'd find that there's a lot more to it than "painting a pretty picture" in 20 minutes or so.

Not presented in Figure 4-2 or in the statement "membership system" are all the additional functional and technical elements that need to be considered in the design and implementation. The earlier chapters of this book outlined some of these areas. Going from a single picture to a fully production-ready solution is a much larger problem. You'll probably already have an idea of how you would personally go about implementing a solution. Perhaps you've read a book with a typically suitable starting point (or at the very least some useful tips). There are also third-party products and frameworks that would enable you to implement this type of functionality relatively quickly. But would the final state solution display all the quality characteristics discussed previously? Would it be built using the processes and practices outlined previously? Would it be accepted by the stakeholders and user community?

This section starts with the example in Figure 4-2 and builds from it a series of design and implementation considerations. First, there are a few immediate considerations that I'd like to pick out from Figure 4-2, and these are shown in Figure 4-3.

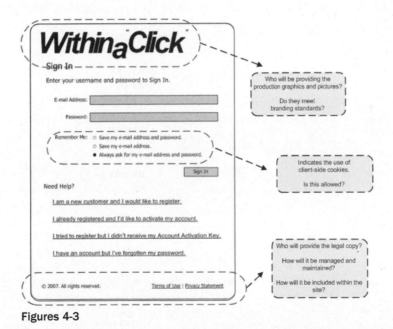

Figures 4-3

Figure 4-3 shows some initial considerations with the conceptual page. Although it looks good and could be shown to a user or stakeholder, there are some areas that need further design, discussion, and planning. You can also see that a number of other pages and functions would need to be incorporated into the overall solution. The conceptual page provides quite a lot of information to work with and expand upon. For example, the page shows links to other pages and functionality — such as the creation of a new account, the activation of a new account, and so forth — which would need to be fleshed out in more detail.

There is often a tendency to dive into the code without fully examining and understanding all the aspects of the final solution. Although there are many methodologies that promote rapid development, you should not simply forge ahead without a common and consistent objective. The cost of rework can be enormous if there is too much chopping and changing. A reasonable balance needs to be met between what is understood and what will require further consideration and clarification. It is important to also understand what can be determined later in the lifecycle without adversely impacting timescales and budgets. You don't need to nail down everything up front, but you do need to understand how it fits into the overall picture and process.

The page mockup contains the following links:

❑ **Terms of Use** — Almost all websites have a Terms of Use (TOU) page that lists the terms and conditions for using the site and the content it contains. The TOU page typically contains acceptance of terms, description of services, usage limitations, use of services, and legal copyrights and/or trademarks. The information in the TOU page is composed by the business (including the legal department, as necessary). Most sites have a link to the Terms of Use page at the bottom of each page.

❑ **Privacy Statement** — The privacy statement provides users with details of when and how their information is captured and how it is used. Most companies are committed to protecting the privacy of their customers and not sharing customer details with third-parties without the customers' express consent. The privacy statement should be drafted by the business (and the legal department, where necessary) and a link should be included on every page.

❑ **Copyright** — A copyright statement may also be necessary on every page for legal purposes.

I included these design elements only because they are often implemented (or at least specified) by other people and are also likely to change as the project progresses. It is important to understand the dependencies you have on other teams and other people. Your job could be as simple as including a link to another page, but then again it might not. It would not be a good idea to get to the point where all the development and testing had been completed only to find out that the legalities hadn't been included. The cost of including these late could be enormous and endanger go-live.

It is very easy to get carried away when drawing a conceptual page layout, especially when there are so many examples and real-world websites to get ideas from; however, it is an entirely different thing to develop the functionality behind it, test the solution, and deploy the final result into production. Leaving out certain features will reduce costs but could also have an adverse effect on the user experience. For instance, a simple "breadcrumb trail" can be very useful on websites to help the user navigate more easily as well as to understand where they are on the site. A breadcrumb might contain something like "Home > Create New Account". Breadcrumb trails can be either static (i.e. plain text) or links which would allow the user to navigate using them. Incorporating complex and difficult to implement features will increase costs. What might seem like "cool" features can also have a dramatic effect on costs, especially if they're not completely understood. It is all well and good to think "most sites include them, so it is definitely possible to do it, and it can't be that hard." However, it really can be very hard sometimes and there could be a lot of stumbling blocks to overcome, so it is best to have an understanding of what's involved before showing designs to users and stakeholders.

Figure 4-4 shows a typical sign-up (Create New Account) page that contains some typical elements found on modern sites today, the development implications of which could be quite far reaching.

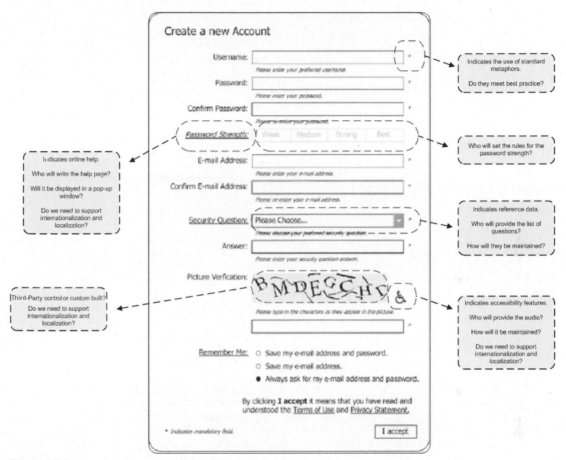

Figures 4-4

This section does not discuss the specifics of actually implementing a page like the one shown in Figure 4-4. This section simply looks at the design considerations and their potential impact.

Anyone familiar with creating a new account on a website would probably immediately recognize and understand the features and their use. However, the conceptual page raises some interesting questions.

First, the page includes some standard usage guidelines and indicators, such as the asterisk character (*) to indicate mandatory entries, the "wheelchair" icon to indicate disability features, and links to online help pages. In this example page, the asterisks are actually specified at the end of the field. Is this placement "best practice" for disability accessibility? The page definitely shows that accessibility has been considered because it includes the wheelchair icon. However, to answer the question of whether the asterisk is in the right place, you really need to understand the best practices for accessibility design and the tools that people with disabilities use. There are many books and articles that are solely dedicated to this subject, so I'm not going to go into all the details of accessibility — but in this example, the asterisks are actually placed incorrectly. The mandatory field indicator should really be included within, or alongside the entry label. I've highlighted this subject because it is very important to ensure that you fully understand the implications of what you're designing and implementing. Including accessibility features incorrectly could require an awful amount of rework. There's no point in including disability or accessibility features within the scope without truly understanding their implications.

Second, the conceptual page also indicates another group of related functionality. The page contains password entry fields, a link to password help, and a password strength indicator. Figure 4-5 shows a typical help page describing strong passwords.

Strong Passwords

Make it lengthy. Each character that you add to your password increases the protection that it provides many times over. Your passwords should be 8 or more characters in length; 14 characters or longer is ideal.

This system supports use of the space bar in passwords, so you can create a phrase made of many words (a "pass phrase"). A pass phrase is often easier to remember than a simple password, as well as being longer and harder to guess.

Combine letters, numbers, and symbols. The greater variety of characters that you have in your password, the harder it is to guess.

Dos and Don'ts

- Do include punctuation marks and/or numbers.

- Do use a mix of capital and lowercase letters.

- Do substitute zero for "O", $ for "S", 1 for "l" and so forth.

- Don't use a password that is easily guessable.

- Don't include any personal information (such as account numbers or pins)

Figures 4-5

The online help would naturally need to be kept in-sync with the password field validation rules. The password strength indicator could also be affected by changes in validation rules. It is important to consider how these features will be included in the solution, and how changes to them will be supported throughout the lifecycle. It would be quite easy to change the validation rules on a web page. However, when they affect other components and pages, additional activities are required. All these artifacts are interrelated, so understanding these types of dependencies is another crucial factor in the design and planning activities.

Third, another part of the design activity is to understand the features and elements of the system and assess whether they should be custom-built or third-party products, both of which will require further investigation and thorough testing. For example, in an effort to prevent automated programs from using a website maliciously, some websites implement a picture-verification scheme, a sample of which was shown in Figure 4-4. This type of control could be custom developed or a third-party control could be used. In either case, it is prudent to consider the accessibility requirements, as well. There may also need to be an audio version of the picture-verification scheme, which is a perfect segue to the next point.

I already mentioned that it is important to understand the accessibility requirements and I also mentioned for the purposes of this book that accessibility wasn't just about supporting users with disabilities. The wheelchair icon next to the picture-verification control indicates that there is an alternative audio file for users with visual disabilities. When using this type of control and alternative audio, you need to consider internationalization and localization, as well. You may now need to support multiple languages/locales, not only within the control, but within all the localized audio, as well. The controls also have an impact on automated testing. The controls and their functionality is specifically designed to stop automated programs from completing transactions. The audio will also need to be verified manually, so you need to understand who will test and ultimately "sign-off" on it. If you're supporting internationalization and localization, it is important to understand who's providing the language support and copy (text). It is equally important to know how this will be incorporated on the site or within the application.

As you can already see, the domino effect starts to come into play and everything becomes interrelated. A couple of simple additions on a picture that took under half-an-hour to draw has created potentially hours if not weeks of work. From these examples, it is clear that the introduction of one thing starts to introduce other areas that need to be taken into account and that's why you need to really get the scope defined and agreed on. At its lowest level, the system needs to meet its business requirements and I often find that the simplest design is often the best place to start before overlaying it with complex or possibly unknown functionality. Proposing features that are not fully understood can lead to delays and overruns, as well as to disputes. I know I've mentioned this a few times, but the discussion over requirements versus design is the biggest area of interpretation. You need to come up with a design that you know can be implemented within the agreed time and budget constraints. Alternatively, you could agree that the budget and time constraints are in-line with the proposed solution. However, in either approach you need to be sure you know how long it is going to take and how much it is going to cost. Consider the age-old question, "How long is a piece of string?" Which is often used as a response to how long something will take to complete. Estimating is a complicated business and, as such, starting with the simplest solution provides a solid foundation for estimating. It is not a very a good idea to propose features for which the implementation period is unknown. Being able to research and pilot technologies can help to further bolster your estimates, but this needs to be very clearly stipulated and agreed on. There is no point in putting together a design for which you can't realistically estimate the delivery timescales and costs, especially if you are constrained by them.

I'm a firm believer in system prototyping and researching. A prototype doesn't necessarily need to be a coded version, although for some technologies and functionality it is pretty much unavoidable. It could be on paper or a whiteboard for known features and functionality. Taking some simple conceptual pages like the ones shown and working through all the activities is a great way to flesh out even more detail. It is also the perfect time to pilot all of the mobilization activities previously discussed, customize the tools, shape the processes, implement the patterns and practices, and produce some high-quality exemplars and templates. A few basic page layouts and a handful of considerations are often enough to "walk through the system" and capture some more details to shape the scope of the solution. Even with a well-known concept such as a membership system, there's a lot more to consider than just core functionality.

Using features that similar websites include need to be very well understood and incorporated appropriately. As you've seen, using something like a picture-verification control can have far-reaching consequences. With just a couple of simple diagrams, it is possible to extrapolate the entire application in your head but not necessarily detail it as a full-scale implementation project.

The purpose of the analysis and design activities is to provide all the teams with a solid foundation to move forward. Spending too much time up front trying to nail down everything can be counter-productive, whereas spending too little time up front can result in a huge amount of rework later. The most important thing is that the inputs provide enough information for the teams to continue without undue impact. It is also worth mentioning at this point that "up front" simply means before you actually start full-scale development (or implementation) of the solution.

During the analysis and design activities, you also want to keep in mind certain additional high-level agenda items, including:

- Security and access
- Reference data
- The data model
- Configuration and settings
- Test data
- Test scenarios and conditions
- Reliability, stability, performance, and operability criteria

I've categorized the primary "design" considerations into four very high-level categories, each of which you've had an introduction to:

- **Accessibility** — The accessibility considerations focus mainly on how the system can be as accessible to as many people as possible and whether each aspect has a valid business case and is actually required. As you've seen, accessibility can introduce many other areas of consideration.

- **Implementation** — The implementation considerations focus on how the system will be built, tested, and deployed.

- **Support and maintenance** — The support and maintenance considerations focus on how the system will be supported and maintained, not only in live service but throughout the project lifecycle.

- **Custom built vs. off-the-shelf** — Determining whether to build something in-house or to use an existing solution has its own specific considerations.

The following sections examine each of these high-level categories. In addition, I'll discuss some other high-level considerations that may also need to be factored in to the overall design. These could also have an impact on some of the other choices and decisions that you need to make early on.

Accessibility Considerations

The accessibility of the system is the key to achieving the business goals. However, each goal needs to have a valid business case and each function or aspect needs to be carefully considered as to whether or not it is required. The following list provides some very high-level considerations:

❑   **Internationalization and localization** — Internationalization and localization refer to adapting the solution to support non-native languages and regions. Localization adapts the software for a specific region where the language and terminology may be slightly different to other parts of the country or language. Internationalization and localization should not involve any underlying code changes, as this will have an impact on costs, not to mention the configuration management overheads. You would need to manage (and deploy) multiple versions of the base code-set for different languages. If the screens and pages are generated, this may not be an issue. However, there will be different aspects of the software that will be specific to a language or locale that will need to be managed accordingly. It is important to understand whether the site and potentially the administration features of the application will need to support multiple languages. The low-level design can incorporate features that will make internationalization and localization easier, but implementing these features will cost time and effort, not only during the design activities but in the build and test activities, too. Although you're not at the low-level at this moment, it is worth thinking about so that the conceptual design can include it in the scope of work, earmark it for a future release, or exclude it completely. The conceptual design needs to be very clear on what is in and out of scope. In many cases, if something is not specifically stipulated, it is deemed out of scope, although this in itself should be clearly stated. It may not be a requirement right now, but it could very well be in the future, and this will need to be stated. The following represents just a few additional design considerations:

   ❑   Pages, labels, and fields will need to be sized to accommodate different languages.

   ❑   All static page elements, messages, and possibly graphics will need to be uniquely identified and stored in resource files, configuration files, or the database. If graphics contain text, multiple versions may be required. It is not generally advisable to include text in graphics.

   ❑   All external communications (e-mail, and so on) may also need to support multiple languages.

   ❑   Unicode (or an alternative) will need to be used throughout the solution, and string processing will need to take into account different lengths.

   ❑   Contextual information may change its placement in different languages. Messages (and the code) would need to take this into account if used.

   ❑   Multiple versions of the pages may need to be developed to display in different languages — for instance, left-to-right, right-to-left, and so on.

❑   **Disability inclusion** — Accessibility means adapting the solution so that it can be used and accessed by as many people as possible. You need to know whether the site or application needs to support any specific accessibility features. There are many standards, guidelines, and resources for implementing features that allow people with disabilities to access the site. The costs to implement features to support accessibility will depend entirely on the design of the site and the solution. The design will need to be balanced against the rich user experience guiding principle. Assistive technologies include screen readers, scanning software, audio content, and other features. Designing for accessibility will have an impact on implementation and test costs, depending on the features that are incorporated. For example, if audio content is required, it will need to be recorded, stored, and tested to ensure that it is acceptable. It is also often required to support individual user preferences. For instance, black text on a white background can cause issues and difficulties for some users. It may be necessary to display content in different colors based on individual user preferences. All of these considerations will open up the design and have an impact on timescales and costs. The following represents some additional design considerations:

- ❏ Custom audio may need to be provided, especially in the case of picture matching.

- ❏ ALT tags will need to be provided for all non-text page elements.

❏ **Multi-channel** — For the purposes of this book, the term "multi-channel" refers to supporting multiple external device types, such as PDAs (personal digital assistants), mobile phones, as well as computer-based browsers. Supporting multiple devices can have an impact on the design and implementation of the solution. This needs to be balanced with the rich user experience. A user may come in from a variety of different devices, so the site will need to adapt to the device accordingly. Images often take a while to download over a good network connection, let alone a mobile phone or PDA. There's the question of the screen size and placement of controls on the page to avoid excessive scrolling. Multi-channel can also imply supporting multiple browser types and versions. I find that the best sites are tailored specifically for mobile devices and commonly performed tasks.

❏ **Secure Sockets Layer (SSL)** — SSL is a secure protocol that encrypts all data between a web server and a client. It prevents anyone else from knowing the information that has been sent over the connection. SSL requires certificates that are issued by third-party authorities known as a *Certificate Authority* (CA). The CA certificate guarantees to the customer that the site is registered and that they are the identity they declare. Secure transactions are sent using the HTTPS protocol. Although this is a somewhat technical consideration, it is useful to identify transactions that will need to use the HTTPS protocol.

This list represents a handful of high-level accessibility considerations. These will have an effect on the way you implement, support, and maintain the system. Each aspect should have a valid business case and, where necessary, each aspect should be formally included in the scope. These considerations will also have an effect on other choices that you need to make, especially around third-party product selection, as these products would also need to incorporate and support the decisions already made.

Implementation Considerations

The implementation considerations mainly focus on the design choices and how they affect the solution's implementation from a development, test, and deployment perspective. The following list represents the high-level implementation considerations:

❏ **Development considerations** — When looking at a particular feature or function of the solution, it is worth thinking about the effect it will have on development. Development considerations are far reaching and can range from the level of skill required by the development team to what developers would need to complete the implementation. What may seem like a simple design element may incur a huge development effort. It may require licenses or software to be installed on the developer's machine. It may require very specific and detailed knowledge that may also require third-party training or consultancy. I've mentioned that development includes all aspects of the system, including architecture, scripts, and tools, all of which need to be considered when designing the solution to ensure that everything is captured appropriately and balanced against the costs and timescales. Stubs and simulators provide a good example for development considerations. The stub needs to mimic as much of the functionality of the real component as possible to ensure coverage. Developing the stub could very well take longer than the time it takes to develop the component itself. The stub may also be used during testing, which means that you are testing something that isn't really a live component, so how confident will you be when you get to use the real component?

It is equally important to take into account that the term "development" isn't just about code. Development can also include creating legal copy, including foreign language support and audio, training materials, and so forth.

❑ **Test considerations** — Looking at how a particular feature or design element would be tested is a really good idea. If you are going to be using automated tools and scripts to provide a regression capability, you need to ensure that the feature can be tested in this way. Limiting the amount of human intervention required greatly reduces costs. In the past, automated regression wasn't always a consideration. You wrote the code, ran it, put in a few values, and showed your boss the results, and that was it — the component was done. Today, however, development has moved on. There is much more of a focus on testing and quality control. A very simple design element can have a big impact on testing. You'll see this later, but consider the e-mailing of Activation Keys to a user's e-mail address. How would this be tested? How would the results be captured? How would the remaining membership process be tested? All these features will need testing and preferably support the automated regression capability. There are clearly some areas where manual testing would be required — for example, accessibility features such as audio and commentary. Testing has an impact on costs and timescales, and you need to know which areas and functions need to be tested manually and which areas can be automated, and the effort involved in each.

❑ **Deployment considerations** — I touched on deployment earlier but it is worth keeping in mind when looking at the design of the solution. Although this is somewhat lower level than the other considerations, simple design decisions can have a big effect on the deployment of the solution and will need to be incorporated in the costs. The more moving parts in the solution, the more effort there is in packaging and deployment. Deployment needs to be balanced alongside everything else. The solution will need to be deployed across a number of development, test, and production estates.

In addition to the preceding very general considerations, the following items are equally important:

❑ Changes in mandatory and optional fields are very common throughout the lifecycle of a project. Where possible, you should consider this during design and implementation and make it easier to change. If this were implemented as post submission validation, it would be relatively straightforward. However, it is further complicated by the indication that a required field indicator should be also used on the screen, although this is not too much trouble. Subtle choices like this need to be considered because they can have an effect on costs and timescales.

❑ Copy text will change. Copy is really any "static" text on the page, including titles, control labels, help text and subtitles, and so on. In this example, it may be something as simple as the "E-mail Address" labels. The business may decide that they would prefer "Email Address" or "E-Mail Address," and so on. Incorporating features that make it easier to change copy text is a good idea and can also help with internationalization and localization.

❑ Similar to copy text, graphics and drawings will change. Changing the size of a picture can affect all the controls on the page, shifting them one way or another and potentially causing misalignment. The pictures may also have an effect on storage space.

❑ It is also not uncommon for the layout of pages and screens to change throughout a project's lifecycle. What may seem like a simple change can have a dramatic impact, especially when using automated test tools that rely on control placement to operate correctly.

❑ Messages will also be subject to change as the project progresses. Anything that is customer- or user-facing will have a tendency to change. Putting in place features to limit the impact of these changes is a good idea.

The preceding list presents some general considerations when designing the system from both a functional and technical perspective. All the considerations mentioned here go hand-in-hand with the quality characteristics mentioned previously. The conceptual design needs to meet the requirements while balancing the costs and timescales against the implementation.

Support and Maintenance Considerations

The support and maintenance considerations focus on how the design choices will affect the way in which the solution is supported, not just in live service, but throughout the project. The following provides some high-level information on these subjects:

❑ **Support considerations** — There are many different layers of support. From an end user's point of view, the customer service organization is there to assist them in their queries. For example, if a customer doesn't receive the item they ordered, he or she might want to raise this with customer service. Then there's system support, which you will learn more about later. Support costs money, and keeping in mind the areas that may require specific support will help to shape the administrative aspects of the system, as well as to shape the design to reduce the number of areas that may potentially require support calls. Self help is a great way to reduce support costs, but this again needs to be implemented and balanced with the other costs. Self help can range from simple help pages and wizards to automated tools and diagnostic programs. Remember, users are not just the end customers; they also include the business and the support users.

❑ **Maintenance considerations** — It is very likely that the system will be enhanced throughout its lifetime, so reducing the amount of effort required to maintain the solution helps to reduce maintenance costs. One of the guiding principles for maintenance (and support) is its cost-effectiveness. Putting something in place that has excessive support and maintenance costs is contrary to this guiding principle. It is very hard to determine which maintenance activities will take place, but as the design unfolds, areas for consideration will become apparent. For instance, a feature may be deemed too radical or unnecessary in the first instance. However, taking a step back and thinking about what would need to be done to incorporate it later can provide some useful hooks into reducing the maintenance overhead.

Custom Built vs. Off-the-Shelf

Let's take a closer look at the preceding picture-verification example and ask a couple of questions:

❑ **How much will it cost to buy?** This is going to be a difficult question to answer without some further research. You'd need to find out what companies provide such controls. This is referred to as *vendor selection* and can be a time-consuming endeavor. In many cases, your customer may have preferred supplier agreements that could impact your selection. Support agreements, which involve contractual negotiation, may need to be put in place. The component will need to be tested and proven to implement the required functionality. The impact of these activities could dramatically affect your estimates and ability to implement your stated solution. I'm not ruling this out as an option; it is just something that needs to be considered and flagged when pulling together the design. Using third-party components, whether purchased, freeware, or shareware, will invariably involve this level of investigation and research. If a control or technology has been used before, some of these activities can be expedited. There has to be a good case for using the technology. In this instance, the requirements do not actually stipulate the use of such functionality, but it may provide an additional level of security that is worth the costs. It may also be prudent to provide a cost for custom building and implementing similar functionality, although again this could be an unnecessary expense if the application doesn't need this level of functionality and security.

❑ **How many licenses will it require?** This will greatly depend on the pricing of the control. Many companies waive development and test licenses, and instead concentrate on production licenses. The license agreement and structure needs to be carefully considered for any third-party application or component, as it can have a dramatic effect on overall costs. The licenses may need to be renewed regularly if a lifetime license can't be purchased, which has an impact on ongoing costs.

❑ **How will it affect development and test?** In the case of the picture verification control, it will certainly have an impact on testing as well as on development. As mentioned previously, the entire purpose of the control is to ensure that automated programs can't make use of the site and submit requests. This will greatly impact automated testing suites. You would need to consider being able to turn this functionality off and on to avoid this impact, or you might want to develop and use test stubs, both of which have an impact on costs.

❑ **How will it affect support and maintenance?** If the site suffers a problem deemed to be related to the control, rapid fix turnaround would be necessary. The company (supplying the control) may not have 24/7 support operations, a fact that would need to be considered during contract negotiations. Without the source code, it may be necessary to have verbose logging turned on, which could affect performance. The log files generated by the component would also need to be understood, managed, and purged. If licenses change when they are renewed, it has an impact on deployment. Another classic example I've seen is when the license expires. The site stops working properly because the license expired and wasn't renewed, or the new license wasn't applied correctly.

The questions equally apply to any other third-party components and products. You've seen how such a simple concept can evolve into something much, much larger, and there will be enough to implement and test without adding additional unnecessary effort. These are just a few questions that can affect the way you design and implement any given solution. It is important to understand what you are proposing and that you're not just entering a trial-and-error phase. Applying these kinds of questions to the design will greatly help to ensure that a deliverable solution is proposed. It is very easy during design to look at other sites and applications and grab ideas that are very good but could prove difficult during implementation. Of course, if the project is taking a prototypical approach, this may be perfectly acceptable.

General Design Considerations

There are a reasonable number of more general considerations that should be taken into account when considering the overall solution, including but not limited to the following:

❑ **Auditing** — In certain sensitive situations, such as military, financial, and other secure applications, it is prudent (and often required) to keep an audit trail for all transactions and changes. The audit trail typically keeps an account of all the changes to record and who made the change. Although this might seem very straightforward, the implementation may be more far reaching. For example, changes to reference data may need to be performed through a specific user interface and not directly in the database. The database may need to be locked-down very securely to prevent unauthorized changes. Data in the database may require specific auditing rules. You may also need to pass the user identity through all the components and layers to ensure that it is properly recorded against the transaction being performed.

❑ **Housekeeping and cleanup** — The database may be holding a huge number of records, and you need to understand how long these records need to be kept. For instance, you could have a process that removes incomplete transactions that are older than 30 days. This will help to keep the number of records in the database down. Furthermore, you would want to consider how long to keep the audit trail records. You could potentially remove all audit records that refer to a previous state. For example, all records that pertain to an in-flight or transient transaction could be removed once the transition is completed. In addition to the database, other areas of cleanup or housekeeping may be required.

❑ **Security and access** — Security should be considered right from the start of the design. The system should be restricted to authorized user access only. Where possible, a role- or group-based security model should be considered. A role or group uses "access rights" to specify which functions can be performed. For example, an access right could be "Reference Data Update" or "Security Question Reference Data Update." The access rights depend entirely on the solution. A role can have many access rights assigned to it. For instance, the role of "Administrator" could have access rights for "User Account Create" and "User Account Update." Managing permissions based on a group or role is much easier than managing them on an individual user basis. A user can be assigned many roles.

❑ **Transactions and transaction boundaries** — Given that an exception or an incident could occur at any moment, you need to understand where the transaction boundaries are. A transaction encompasses a number of steps or actions into a single unit of work. The entire transaction is either committed successfully or aborted. The transaction retains consistency across all the individual actions. Transactions are mainly thought of in terms of database actions, although distributed transactions can manage the single transaction across multiple applications and technologies. Transaction management is often tricky, and getting the boundaries right can have a domino effect. In many cases, the simplest approach is to say that if one step fails, all steps fail. If any step fails, the actions that have already been performed should be rolled back and the user should be presented with an appropriate error message and given the option to re-submit the transaction. A common cause of system failures and outages is transaction boundaries that are not appropriately managed, so it is worth thinking about how the end-to-end transaction works and the effect this has on the existing data and the user. For example, if it is not possible to roll back a particular action, it is vitally important to understand its overall impact. It might be possible to move the action to the end of the overall transaction so that it is the last thing to be committed. If an exception occurs at this point, it wouldn't have actually performed its action and all the previous actions would be rolled back.

❑ **Reference data validity** — Reference data validity determines the period when an element of reference data is valid. For example, if you have password complexity rules stored in the database, when a new account is created the system would need to use the valid rules. Invalid rules would need to remain in the database for consistency purposes, but all new accounts would use the latest valid rules. This applies to all reference data, including security questions, payment methods, and so on.

There are other functional considerations that may impact the design of the application. For example, if the password rules are no longer valid, the system may wish to force users to change their password to the new rules. Alternatively, the system could force the change when users update their accounts. This adds overheads to the application as well as the development and test effort. New password rules could be the subject of a news item and an article that would inform users that the password rules have changed. The business may also want reports on reference data usage and account usage to determine the impact of a particular change or proposed removal. For instance, if a certain payment method doesn't offer competitive fees, the organization may wish to know how many people use this payment method, the last time they used it, and the last time their account was accessed.

❑ **Immediate and scheduled updates** — In most applications, transactions and updates are made immediately to the live database. There may need to be validity constraints that stop the reference data item from being seen or used. Mission-critical systems often require any change to reference data to be carefully reviewed before it is applied or activated in the live database. This introduces a workflow and role complexities. Who is allowed to create the reference data? Who is allowed to authorize the reference data activation? The audit trail needs to keep a very clear record of the steps and the people performing the actions. The security roles are typically configured to force collusion between individuals in order to promote invalid updates. That is, a user is generally not allowed to create and authorize or promote the same record into the live database. This means that whoever is authorizing the update must coordinate with the creator to promote invalid data. It is possible for the authorizer to make a mistake, and this would need to be dealt with by the organization.

❑ **Workflow** — Workflow is closely related to the security and role-based features of the application. Workflow clearly needs to take into account the steps and activities involved in a particular task. For instance, using the example of reference data updates from the previous point, a business user updates a reference data record that needs to be approved. The application might assign this approval to a particular user. In this instance, it would be good for an administration interface to provide task list functionality so that when the user logs in he or she can see a list of activities to perform, such as reviews, approvals, or updates. A user may be out sick or on vacation, so a task could be sitting in his or her "To Do" list not being dealt with. Group assignments help in these situations. The task is assigned to a group of users. For instance, a new user record that requires approval would appear in the task list for anyone who has "new user approval" privileges. The first person to pick up the task would take ownership of the approval and perform the necessary tasks. It is important that the task allocation and assignment in these instances use a good locking approach to avoid multiple resources performing the same task at the same time.

❑ **Concurrency and transaction isolation** — Many requests will be going into the database, a fact that becomes even more apparent when you move on to batch and reporting. *Concurrency* refers to multiple transactions being processed at the same time and possibly interacting with and/or blocking each other. Transaction isolation is used to control the database's transaction-locking behavior, although concurrency should also be considered with all technologies and products being used and not just the database.

I mentioned previously that database access is notoriously prone to timeouts, and the most common application cause of this is locking and deadlocks. If a process needs to obtain a record that is already locked by another process, the database engine will typically wait until the record is unlocked by the first process. If the lock is not removed within the specified timeout period, the process that is waiting will experience a timeout exception. When two (or more) processes are waiting on each other to complete their tasks, a deadlock is experienced because neither process can complete. It is important to think about the different processes that are executing, the records they are reading and updating, and how potential locks and deadlocks could be avoided. The wait-retry pattern, which is discussed in Chapter 19, would allow both processes to retry the transaction a number of times before actually failing. However, this doesn't stop a lock or a deadlock from occurring in the first place. If the processes are tripping over each other, you'll simply experience more wait-retries and not resolve the root cause of the problem. And it is not just writing to the database that can cause locks; some SELECT statements can also cause a lock to be put in place, which can also cause timeouts. When reading from the database, you should carefully consider the transaction isolation level; there are usually two choices:

❑ **Read committed** — Reading committed data implies waiting for the data to be fully committed before it is read. For example, a query may be selecting records from a table while another process is writing to the table. When the query reaches the record being written, it will wait until the record has been committed fully before reading it and continuing. There is a nuance here, however. Once a record has been read and the query moves on, the data can be changed in the database, which will not be reflected in the query results. Reading committed data needs to be thought about very carefully and used only when it is absolutely necessary. Waiting for data to be committed is a common cause of timeouts.

❑ **Read uncommitted** — Reading uncommitted is commonly known as a *dirty read*. The query will read whatever data is in the database without it being fully committed. This is useful because the read is not subject to any locks; however, it does mean that processing the resulting data needs to be considered carefully because the record in the result may no longer be valid. For example, assume that you have a background process reading entries from a database e-mail registration queue and sending Activation Keys. If the process is reading uncommitted records, it is possible that it could read a record that is subsequently rolled back for some reason or another. In this instance, the user would receive an error message on the screen and an e-mail containing an Activation Key.

Last, there are a couple of final technical considerations I'd like to cover:

❑ The technical requirements could (and often do) apply to both the online application and the administration application. An administration application will generally provide richer functionality to a lesser number of users, but the transactions can also be quite database-intensive. It is important to consider the technical requirements across the board (unless otherwise stated) to ensure the conceptual design addresses them.

❑ Sensitive information will need to be stored encrypted so that it is not visible to third-parties. Sensitive information includes passwords, security question answers, and other personal information. It may even extend to e-mail addresses. There are many encryption algorithms that should be considered, with each having its own place within the solution.

❏   Malicious actions can seriously impact an organization. Misuse can be something as simple as pressing Ctrl+F5 repeatedly to force a roundtrip to the web server to refresh. This has the effect of slowing down the system for other users. It can also include black-box programs that repeatedly try to penetrate the system and access secure information or bring the site down. When considering a solution, you should always consider how it could be misused and try to plug the gap.

❏   Where necessary, supporting browser controls such as Forward, Back, and F5 and Ctrl+F5 functionality will greatly improve the site's usability. In addition, supporting as many different browsers as possible is also a good idea, especially for Internet-based applications and access.

The preceding list is not exhaustive, but it provides a basis for consideration when looking at the design of the solution. The following sections look at two very simple examples of design choices and their potential impact on the overall project and solution.

Date and Time Entries and Validation

In most case, dates and times need to be in the future, but how far in the future? For instance, assume a record has a Valid From date and a Valid To date. Specifying a Valid To date/time 1 second after the Valid From date/time would be technically possible (although the item would have probably expired by the time it was submitted to the database), but is it a realistic business scenario? Furthermore, is it realistic to assume that someone would do this anyway? Only a tester would do it to ensure that the implementation wasn't actually "greater than or equal to." It is a very common scenario and there are a number of ways of dealing with it. The following are a couple of potential solutions:

❏   Don't include the dates and times at all. This is always an option if the dates are potentially unnecessary and using them could introduce additional overheads and complexity.

❏   Where possible, remove the time portion and use only a date to ensure that a record is valid for a least one whole day. For example, if the "valid from date" is deemed "greater than or equal to" and the "valid to date" is deemed "less than or equal to," then comparing a record with a value of "10/12/2008" against valid from and valid to dates that were also "10/12/2008" would always return `true` (for example, the record is valid).

❏   Keep the dates and times but do nothing about user entry validation. Again, this wouldn't be a problem, but it really wouldn't look that good, either. It would look like due care and attention hadn't been paid to the design of the solution. The user could make a simple mistake that could go unnoticed. For instance, publishing a new record with an expiration date in the past would mean that it wasn't ever made available. This could cost the business hugely, and although the fault lies with the user, the developer and the system would bear the brunt of the retort.

❏   Provide a simple warning to the user that the dates are incorrect. For example, display the message "The date you have specified is in the past" and allow the user to change the value or proceed with the date and time entered. This gives the user the opportunity to correct the situation or simply ignore the warning. It is important to understand what the user is doing and in this scenario the user might be working on historical records where all the dates and times would naturally be in the past. A validation scheme that doesn't allow anything to be saved unless the dates and times are in the future can affect the work that the user is carrying out. If it is not possible to perform any updates to historical records, this scenario can be ignored and a full validation scheme should be put in place.

❑ Provide a simple "greater than" validation scheme — for example, the Valid To date must be greater than the Valid From date. This provides a simple validation implementation, although it doesn't support the example provided earlier whereby the Valid To could be 1 second greater than the Valid From value. If the user does specify a Valid To date that is less than or equal to the Valid From date, the system would force the user to correct the situation. If they proceed with a 1-second validity period, they are clearly at fault.

❑ Provide a configurable "greater than" validation scheme. This would typically involve configuration values that would stipulate how far apart the dates must be — for example, the Valid From date must be greater than the system date by at least one day and the Valid To must be greater that the Valid From by at least 1 day. This option provides a reasonable level of validation but may not always hold true. For example, if the configuration value is set too low, the same situation could arise where it is possible for the user to enter dates and times with 1 second validity periods. The drawback with this option is that it introduces granularity consequences. For example, should the value be in years, months, weeks, days, hours, minutes, or seconds?

❑ Implement an elaborate, configurable "greater than" entry scheme. When the user is typing values into the form, changing one value would automatically change the other by the configured amount. You see this sometimes in calendar-based programs. You set up a meeting for 1 hour and moving the start time automatically moves the end time. In addition, the Valid From date would always need to be greater than the system date. The underlying validation of both dates would still need to be performed to keep the application consistent.

❑ Change the Valid To field so that it is an "expires after" value — for example, the record expires after n days, and so on. This means that the user doesn't specify a Valid To date and time; they simply indicate how long the record is valid for. The validity period could be from the date at which the record was saved or from a Valid From date. The preceding Valid From considerations still apply.

There are probably even more choices. The choice of solutions depends on the situation, of course. Although this seems like a minor detail, it shows how something so simple can introduce a number of further considerations. A simple statement like "the Valid To must be greater than the Valid From" can have far reaching consequences for development and testing. Choosing an approach and defining a very clear scope will help to ensure that everyone is on the same page. I like to get these out of the way up front because there are many times when the comparison code isn't right and has to be revisited — for example, using "greater than" when it should be "less than" or vice versa and/or including "equal to" when it shouldn't be. Little validation mistakes like this can cost large amounts of wasted time and effort.

Using a Custom Calendar

Back in the days prior to the year 2000, everyone was panicking that planes would fall out of the sky and computers would crash and lose everything. Everyone set about testing their systems for what was known as Y2K compliance. The problem with testing the system's functionality was that you needed to put the system into a specific date (31 December 1999 23:59:59) and see what happened when the clock changed. It was easy for people that could change their system clock or if their application supported a custom date and time. For everyone else, it was a bit of a pain. Having a way of setting a custom date and time for the application can greatly simplify testing, especially when things need to happen at certain times. It also helps when multiple days of testing need to be compressed into a single day.

I like to go by the following "rules of thumb" when using a custom date and time:

❏ All diagnostic logging, tracing, and events remain in true system date and time, as issues can arise when the logs jump from one date to another. The logs will need to contain information up to the point at which the custom date is obtained. It would become confusing if the date and time (in the log) changed once the custom date was obtained.

❏ Use the custom date and time setting only when required (for example, during testing and test releases). A rogue configuration value in the database or configuration file can cause serious problems in production.

Typically, the custom calendar has only one method: the Now method. The Now method simply returns a date and time based on a configuration value. The implementation of the component can be slightly more involved than just returning a configuration value, depending on what you want to do. For instance, it may be good enough to simply specify a static date and time in the configuration file and have the Now method return it to the consumer. The date and time would always be the same, irrespective of when it was called. Another option is to have a baseline start date and time. In this instance, the clock starts ticking from the point at which the method is invoked. Therefore, after 10 minutes have elapsed, the Now value is 10 minutes ahead of the baseline start. The former example tends to be the most used. However, the latter can really help with testing, especially if you have a timed component — for example, a component that runs every 5 minutes until 6 P.M. A static date and time can't help here, but a running clock can. It can be set to 17:50 and the component will execute twice until 6 P.M. Furthermore, the program can be tested at 09:00 real time, while you have your morning coffee. The custom calendar eliminates the need to change the actual system clock, which can be a problem in managed environments.

The use of such components should be understood and considered very carefully. For example, third-party components may use the system clock and not support custom configuration. Therefore, when testing with an integrated solution, you may find that different dates and times are actually used. This could cause issues when investigating incidents or even when comparing actual results with expected results.

It is important to think about components like this up front, as they can save a lot of time and effort during testing. However, they may not be able to be used by everything. If you don't realize you need this component until you've started testing, it is going to be far too late.

I've mentioned these two subjects, date and time validation and using a custom calendar, to highlight the importance of considering the solution thoroughly and as early as possible. As the book progresses, I'll uncover more areas that should be considered early during the analysis and design activities.

The Analysis and Design Outputs

The design elements are the inputs into the development and test activities. Design is not just about designing the core application; it is also about designing the environments, tools, and processes. This section looks at some design elements that *can* be used as inputs into the development activities. The design elements can be broken down into two parts: functional design elements and technical design elements. The functional design elements focus on the functions of the system, whereas the technical elements focus on how it is going to provide them.

These items can either be fed from or feed into the requirements. As the design builds up, these will become more apparent. The primary analysis and design outputs discussed in this section include:

❑   Scope

❑   Requirements (both functional and non-functional)

❑   Use-case diagrams and use cases

❑   Navigation maps

❑   Storyboards

❑   Page layouts and specifications

❑   The data dictionary

❑   Architecture and application component specifications

Scope

As mentioned previously, it is important to set the scope early on. The scope is one of the most important outputs of the analysis and design activities. With everything considered and in its place, the scope enables you to avoid wasting time looking into unnecessary areas and features. The scope is intended to set out what's going to be included and what's not going to be included. It is important to word the scope in an unambiguous way. You don't want things coming back to haunt you further down the line. I've listed some example scope items here:

❑   Internationalization and localization

❑   Accessibility support

❑   Specific multi-channel processing

❑   Secure Sockets Layer (SSL)

❑   Online help

❑   Remember-me functionality

❑   Picture verification

❑   Password strength indicator

❑   Password history

It is vitally important to determine what's "in scope" and what's "out of scope." The out-of-scope features can often feed into future releases of the project. Depending on the project, some of these features may be considered early so that some rudimentary foundations can be put in place to avoid an implementation headache in following releases. This typically involves designing and implementing some form of framework that can support the features, but the actual features are not implemented until later.

Requirements

Requirements are a way of specifying what the application needs to do. Typically, requirements are written using statements containing words such as "shall" or "should" or "must." They can be high- or low-level statements, but the important thing is that each requirement can be proven and mapped to a particular area of the application. It is also important that requirements be uniquely labeled so that they can be tracked and traced throughout the project. A single low-level requirement should not specify more than one piece of functionality. When it comes to development and testing, it is far easier to track and determine whether a requirement has been met if it describes a discrete function. As the project progresses, it is far better to have a reasonably defined set of requirements and boundaries to work from. That does not mean that an exhaustive list of requirements needs to be drawn up before anything can be done. Going from high-level requirements to low-level requirements often involves some form of elaboration exercise and this is also a part of the mobilization and conceptual design stages.

There has long been a discussion about the differences between requirements and design. To support a fluid design process, the high-level requirements as well as the high-level or conceptual design should capture the essence of the features that are really necessary so that they can be taken forward and implemented accordingly. A low-level requirement restricts the level of interpretation and places concrete restrictions on the design and implementation.

Getting the requirements right up front doesn't necessarily mean getting the design right; it simply means that a reasonable set of requirements are in place prior to design and development. Writing requirements is a complicated business and getting the wording right often involves numerous iterations. The initial overview and high-level requirements provide a solid starting point for the refinement process. A complete set of very detailed requirements would take a very long time to produce, especially if they covered every aspect of the application, including its usage, support, and operation.

Some development methodologies require all the requirements to be detailed enough (and signed-off) to start design, whereas others take a more agile approach and promote change to ensure that the application delivers the functionality required. The key is that both approaches need a starting point, whether it be a diagram, an idea, a vision statement, or a few high-level guiding principles. The actual process of software implementation starts at this point, and the journey will take its own course as it progresses through its lifecycle.

Requirements relate to the entire system, which includes applications, environments, processes, and tools. High-level and low-level requirements and constraints should really be kept separate and not be mixed in the same lists. There are some basic characteristics that each detailed requirement or constraint should adhere to, and the following table lists my personal "top 5."

Description	Explanation
Each requirement should be uniquely identified.	Tracking requirements through the lifecycle is much easier if each requirement is uniquely identified.
Each requirement should be concise and precise, specified in plain language, and contain no ambiguity or vagueness.	Requirements that contain wordy descriptions or unknown language often require much further reading and investigation. Furthermore, abbreviations should not be used. The requirement should not be vague or invite ambiguity or interpretation. Ambiguity should not be confused with the need for a more low-level specification. For instance, the requirement "The system must include an online store" is not ambiguous in itself. It is clearly a high-level requirement that requires further specification.
Each requirement should specify only one thing.	Requirements that specify more than one thing are difficult to track and trace throughout the project. I tend to use a simple rule of thumb that says, "If it takes more than one test case to prove the requirement, then it is a candidate for separation." For example, "The system should accept the following payment types . . ." Each payment type would need to be fully tested. You couldn't sign-off on this requirement until all payment types were fully functional. It would also make it harder to move certain payment types into a future release. It is much easier (although longer) to have each payment type listed as a separate requirement for traceability and management.
Each requirement should be mandatory.	Although this may appear to be a very "black and white" view, optional requirements help to define the scope, budgets, and timescales in the early stages of a project. Optional requirements should be estimated and either included in the scope, moved to a future release, or discarded. When all the requirements have been reviewed, the scope should be clearly set and all requirements become mandatory.
Each requirement should have an owner.	It is the owner's responsibility to sign-off the requirement and ultimately agree that it has been met. Requirements without owners lead to debate and confusion.

Requirements should be grouped into different categories, such as functional requirements, technical requirements, and so on. Grouping the requirements just makes things easier moving forward for planning and testing.

The requirements map directly to the quality characteristics outlined in Chapter 2. However, the characteristics break down into two discrete groups:

❑ The first series of requirements provides rules for a system that is running or executing in live service. Examples of these requirements include functional requirements, usability, accessibility, reliability and stability, performance, efficiency, availability, integrity and security, and operability and supportability.

❑ The second series of requirements relate to internal and surrounding characteristics. Examples of these requirements include scalability, deployability, configurability, maintainability, readability, reusability, modularity, flexibility, extensibility, and testability.

Regardless of whether the requirements are considered functional or technical, the fact remains that the system must display *all* the characteristics. In the remainder of this section I'm going to focus on some of the technical requirements because these are often not clearly defined or, in some cases, not present, and it is vitally important that they are in-place and quantifiable. All requirements must be tested and proven in order to state that the system actually meets them.

During development, unit testing, and integration testing, numerous tests can be carried out that can give some real indications of the system's technical quality and characteristics. It is important to note that these are indications and that all technical characteristics should be fully proven during technical testing and acceptance testing. The technical testing and acceptance testing activities generally raise the most complex defects, which, as you've already seen, can sometimes involve complete re-factoring of components. Therefore, it is important to execute some key technical indication tests during unit testing and integration testing. It stands to reason that the associated technical requirements need to be defined so that they can be provided as inputs.

The following are some of the key requirements that should be provided, along with some typical examples and explanations:

❑ **Reliability and stability** — Reliability and stability refer to how the system functions under normal and adverse conditions. Reliability includes the measure of how predicable the system is. For example, given exactly the same input values and conditions, the system should produce exactly the same results time and time again. This is not always the case, as reliability can be impacted by coding or design flaws. One such coding flaw is a memory leak, which can sometimes be spotted by code profilers but is better spotted by running repeated tests over and over again. These repeated tests can also be used later to gauge performance.

Stability includes the measure of how the system deals with adverse conditions. Many things can cause adverse conditions, so the system should be robust and gracefully continue or exit, as appropriate. Typical high-level, fault-tolerant requirements that might be stipulated are as follows:

❑ Where there are single points of failure in the production system, they must be clearly identified and the risk of these must be reduced to allow the system's availability and other requirements to be met.

❑ The system must be reliable and deal with adverse conditions gracefully — for example, by failing over to an alternative server or by retrying transactions, and so on.

Reliability and stability requirements generally don't detail specific issues unless there is something particular that needs to be supported. One way of dealing with fault tolerance in your software is to ensure that all components include exception handling, although, where possible, this requirement should be broken down into discrete requirements on a component-by-component basis during component design. For example, let's look at a typical common database access component that would execute some form of data access request and return a response. This type of transaction is susceptible to database timeouts, connectivity issues, and network blips. If the exception is caught, the component should wait a while and the transaction should be re-tried. In most cases, the transaction would go through without failure. Of course, this depends entirely on the issue raised. The database could be failing over, connectivity could be completely lost, and so on. The Wait-Retry pattern, discussed later in this book, is just one example of where the component specification can break down the reliability and stability requirement into some specifics that can be taken into account during development and unit and integration testing.

❑ **Performance** — The performance requirements stipulate the speed at which the system should operate under normal and adverse conditions. This also related to the number of concurrent users and the transaction mix. The following are examples of typical high-level performance requirements:

   ❑ The system must perform an average screen response for each simple operation of better than 2 seconds, with no transaction taking more than 15 seconds, assuming no reported network problems. An example of a simple operation is viewing the home page.

   ❑ The system must perform an average screen response for each complex operation of better than 5 seconds, with no transaction taking more than 15 seconds, assuming no reported network problems. An example of a complex operation is signing in to the system.

   ❑ The system must support at least 3,000 concurrent users.

These requirements need to be broken down and modeled, which involves end-to-end transaction modeling. For example, if the system is using an external authentication server, the time it takes to service requests and its concurrency needs to be factored in. In addition, just because the system needs to support 3,000 concurrent users doesn't mean that they will all be performing the same transaction at the same time. This is where the transaction modeling mix needs to be factored in. For example, start by breaking up the user transactions into their respective categories, such as logging on, searching, updating an account, and logging off. The next step is to look at when, and how many times, these transactions are performed. In a single session, the user would log in and log out once. However, given the user base, are there particular times when users would typically log in? A corporate portal might be accessed at particular times during the day, such as between 08:30 and 10:00, between 12:00 and 13:30, and so on. It is important to understand the transaction mix, and modeling typical usage helps to gather all the scenarios. During testing, all the figures will depend on the hardware performance and the number of servers involved, as well as what else is running on them.

This is why the figures should be benchmarked against the requirements during unit testing and assembly testing. You can use the figures to highlight any concerns or possible re-factoring. For example, let's say the sign-in flow on a single workstation, using an authentication stub and a local database, takes an end-to-end time of 3 seconds. This would raise the odd eyebrow because you would really expect this to be much quicker than 3 seconds. It would be worth investigating why it took so long on a local machine with a local database and a stub. However, if it took 0.2

milliseconds, it would probably be within tolerance. Providing a guideline tolerance is also very useful because it can be included in the expected results.

❏ **Efficiency** — Efficiency refers to how well the system makes use of resources. The following are some typical efficiency requirements:

 ❏ All database servers will have processor utilization, measured over any 5 minute period, of less than 80 percent for 95 percent of the time.

 ❏ All database servers will have fixed memory utilization, measured over any 5 minute period, of less than 60 percent for 95 percent of the time.

 ❏ All web, application, and administration servers will have processor utilization, measured over any 5 minute period, of less than 70 percent for 95 percent of the time.

 ❏ All web, application, and administration servers will have fixed memory utilization, measured over any 5 minute period, of less than 90 percent for 95 percent of the time.

These requirements are highly dependent on what other components are running on the individual servers and when they run. Chapter 5 looks into the hardware and software topology of a production environment. Performing rudimentary tests during unit testing and integration testing will give an indication of the system's efficiency. This is especially true of long-running or high-volume transaction processing, which can utilize a lot of memory and processor capacity.

I have mentioned previously that requirements don't just pertain to the core application. Tools and other support elements should not lock up the processor so that nothing else can be done while they are running.

❏ **Availability** — Availability refers to the extent to which the system provides its services under normal and adverse conditions. The following are some typical availability requirements:

 ❏ The system must provide 24/7 access to all functionality and facilities (*exceptions to be defined*). The system must be available for a minimum of 99.5 percent of each calendar month, excluding planned outages.

 ❏ Based on this requirement, the entire system would have approximately only 4 hours of downtime per month. This means that all batch processes must execute while the system is up and running. (Batch is discussed in Chapters 10 and 16.) It also means that the system must be highly available and, therefore, highly resilient.

 ❏ The system should continue to operate even if one or more of its interfacing systems is fully or partially unavailable, with restrictions in functionality limited to the services that are unavailable and with no significant restrictions in performance.

 ❏ You can test the second requirement somewhat by using stubs or simulators to mimic certain failures to test the system under certain circumstances. If possible, you should test real components in real situations.

❏ **Scalability** — Scalability refers to how the system can be enlarged to support future usage or demand. Typical scalability requirements include:

 ❏ The system must be scalable to at least 6,000 concurrent users with only hardware additions, software license extensions, and configuration. This requirement means that the solution must scale without requiring any code changes. For example, no change to the core system code and/or product set should be required.

❏　　This requirement means that there must be nothing in the code or product set that restricts it to the number of users.

❏　　The system must be designed so that processes do not take exponentially longer as a result of increases in users, database size, transactions, and so on.

❏　　This requirement means that you should also test using a larger number of concurrent users to compare the transaction times. It also means that multiple processes and batch jobs might need to run in parallel in order to reduce the overall processing time.

❏　**Integrity and security** — The security requirements should stipulate the roles and functions that can be performed — for example, "Only marketing personnel can create straw polls," or "Only system administrators can create internal users." These are considered functional security requirements. Technical security requirements should stipulate credentials that the system should use when running, as well as basic credentials required to perform certain support or maintenance operations. It is important that the system components do not run using the "Local System" account or administrator accounts. This is also true for third-party components. During unit testing and integration testing, the components should be tested using the appropriate credentials.

❏　**Operability and supportability** — The operability criteria are often set by the service delivery and operations team. (You learn more about them in Chapter 7.) Operability and supportability refer to how easy is it to operate and support the system. Manual operations should be limited to only exceptional circumstances, and monitoring capabilities should be included within the system (as discussed in Chapters 8 and 20).

❏　**Configurability** — Configurability refers to how much the system can be configured rather than coded. It is much easier to make a configuration change than it is to change the code. There should be no hard-coded values in the system; it should use properly defined configuration values. Configuration needs to be balanced against performance. There's a view that obtaining configuration values can impact performance. However, proper coding guidelines and usage guides should be in place to ensure that obtaining configuration values does not adversely impact the system's performance. Stipulating specific configuration values avoids any misinterpretation.

The preceding list is only representative of some of the technical requirements that should be considered. If there are other specific requirements or groups of requirements, these should also be provided as inputs so that they can be taken into account. The preceding list represents some key requirement types that should be taken into account during development, unit testing, and integration testing in order to provide some benchmarking figures.

It doesn't really matter if these requirements are stipulated externally by the customer, internally, or a combination. The specific requirements should be listed and provided as inputs to the phases so that they can be addressed.

Use-Case Diagrams and Use Cases

Use-case diagrams express the different actors, their roles, and the actions they can perform with the system. Use cases provide a textual breakdown of the actions that the actor performs to achieve a desired result. The use cases help to shape the actions that the system must perform. This section looks at the high-level use-case diagram for the case study in this book, as well as one of its use cases. These will be repeated again in Chapter 13 because there's a lot of material between now and then. However, it will give you an idea of these inputs and some additional considerations. It also gives you a sneak peek at what's coming up later. However, I will not be going into the specifics of the case study in this chapter: I'm simply going to examine the inputs into the construction process.

Use-Case Diagrams

In their simplest form, use-case diagrams provide a clear picture of the various actors and actions they can perform.

Figure 4-6 shows a simple use-case diagram for the case study used in this book.

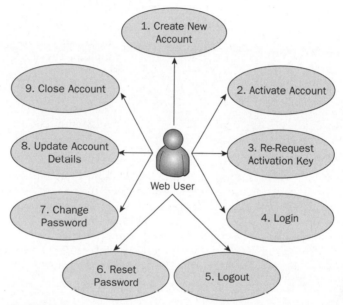

Figures 4-6

Although this is a very simple use-case diagram, it shows the primary actor and the actions he or she can perform within the system. It helps to start building up the security and authorization model. For instance, the diagram shows the "5. Logout" action, so it basically stands to reason that the user must be logged in to perform this function. However, it is not explicitly stated in the diagram. The diagram also shows "Reset Password" and "Change Password," which might seem like one and the same action. However, the user may have forgotten their password, so the site needs to allow for this. The Reset Password flow allows "anonymous" users to authenticate using an alternative means and then change their password using the standard Change Password functionality. The Change Password functionality is also available to logged-in users. In addition, it is not possible to determine from the diagram whether a "logged in" user can perform the "1. Create New Account" action. Breaking the information down into discrete parts will help define the full security and authorizations required. This would be useful because it shows you exactly which actions each type of user can perform. These can be associated with the various pages and transactions.

Figure 4-7 shows the completed sample use-case diagram by splitting out the different actors and the actions they can perform. In this example, the figure now shows what an "anonymous Web user" can perform as well as what a "logged-in Web user" can perform. This helps to refine the security and authorization model.

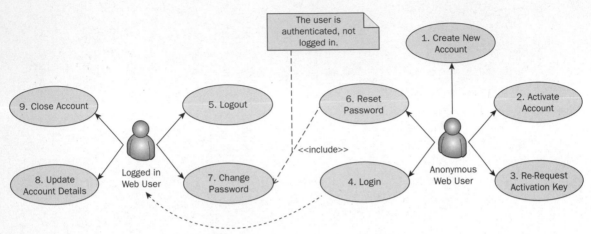

Figures 4-7

It is worth trying to think of all the actors in the system, including account operations and support staff as well as end user groups. Once all the user groups are created, the operations or actions that they perform can be added. The information can be presented in any form, but the key is to build up the information. The following table lists the allowable actions for user groups shown in the completed use-case diagram.

User Group	Allowable Actions
Anonymous Web User	1. Create New Account
	2. Activate Account
	3. Re-Request Activation Key
	4. Log In
	5. Log Out
Logged In Web User	6. Reset Password
	7. Change Password
	8. Update Account Details
	9. Close Account

Although this is a simplistic example, you can use it to start building some of the reference data or configuration, as well as to build some test scenarios and conditions. It also gets you started on the component design.

Use Cases

A use case is a textual representation of an activity that an actor will perform. It includes the individual steps that the actor (and system) will perform and any important alternative flows that might need to be considered. The following table describes the elements of a use case. Chapter 13 discusses all the sample use cases for the case study.

Use Case Identifier:	This is a unique use case identifier — for example, UC-001.
Use Case Name:	This is the name of the use-case — for example, Create New Account.
Description:	This is a brief description of the use case — for example, "The user wishes to create a new account."
Primary Actor:	This is the primary actor involved in the use case — for example, anonymous Web user.
Triggers:	This section describes the actions that trigger the use case — for example, "The user has navigated to the Welcome page and clicked on the 'I am a new customer and I'd like to register' link."
Pre-conditions:	This describes the pre-conditions for the use case — for example, "The user isn't logged in."
Linked Storyboard:	I've included some basic storyboards to present the application and this entry points to the particular storyboard — for example, the storyboard reference for the Create New Account page is SB-001.
Basic Flow:	This section lists all the steps in the use case. For example: 1. The Create New Account page is displayed and all fields are enabled and blank. 2. The user completes the form by entering his or her chosen username, password, confirmation password, e-mail address, confirmation e-mail address, security question, and security question answer, and then clicks Continue. 3. The system checks that all mandatory information has been specified and that each element is valid and correct according to its individual validation rules. 4. The system checks that an account doesn't already exist with the username specified. 5. The system encrypts the information supplied according to the individual encryption rules. 6. The system generates a unique account Activation Key that will be associated with the account.

(continued)

(continued)

Basic Flow:	7. The system creates the account record in the database with a state of "New" and records the date and time the account was created.

Basic Flow:

7. The system creates the account record in the database with a state of "New" and records the date and time the account was created.

8. The system queues a request for an "Activation Key e-mail" to be sent to the user's e-mail address and records the date and time the request was made.

   8a. In the background, the e-mail request will be processed and the system will compose and send the user an e-mail containing his or her account Activation Key and record the date and time the e-mail was sent.

9. The system displays the Activation Key Sent confirmation message and Continue button.

10. On clicking the Continue button, the user is directed to the Activate Account page.

Alternative Flows:

This section describes any alternative flows. In this example, I've linked the alternative flows to the steps in the main flow. For example, 3a (which follows) is linked to Step 3 the basic flow.

3a) If any mandatory information has not been specified, or if any of the elements are invalid, the system will display one of the following validation error messages for each validation error, as appropriate, and allow the user to submit a new request:

- ❏ VEM-001-01 (Username hasn't been specified.)
- ❏ VEM-001-02 (Username specified doesn't meet the validation criteria.)
- ❏ VEM-001-03 (Password hasn't been specified.)
- ❏ VEM-001-04 (Password specified doesn't meet the validation criteria.)
- ❏ VEM-001-05 (Confirmation password hasn't been specified.)
- ❏ VEM-001-06 (Password and confirmation password values don't match.)
- ❏ VEM-001-07 (E-mail address hasn't been specified.)
- ❏ VEM-001-08 (E-mail address specified doesn't meet the validation criteria.)
- ❏ VEM-001-09 (Confirmation e-mail address hasn't been specified.)
- ❏ VEM-001-10 (E-mail address and confirmation e-mail address values don't match.)
- ❏ VEM-001-11 (Security question hasn't been specified.)
- ❏ VEM-001-12 (Security question specified doesn't meet validation criteria.)
- ❏ VEM-001-13 (Security question answer hasn't been specified.)
- ❏ VEM-001-14 (Security question answer specified doesn't meet the validation criteria.)

4a) In the event that an account already exists with the username specified, the system will display the following validation error message and allow the user to submit a new request:

- ❏ VEM-001-15 (Username specified already exists.)

Requirements Map:	This section would list the requirements that are met or linked to the use case. Some use cases might include both functional and non-functional (technical) requirements. Technical requirements are typically included when it is very clear that a particular "quality characteristic" must be met. The following represents some sample functional requirements:

HFR-USAA-001 (User not logged in.)

HFR-DATAFORM-* (Common data entry and form requirements.)

HFR-CREATEACC-001 (Account data element specification.)

HFR-CREATEACC-002 (Paste not allowed in confirmation password.)

HFR-CREATEACC-003 (Paste not allowed in confirmation e-mail address.)

HFR-CREATEACC-004 (Password and confirmation password match.)

HFR-CREATEACC-005 (E-mail address and confirmation e-mail address match.)

HFR-CREATEACC-006 (All fields validated.)

HFR-CREATEACC-007 (Account Activation Key generated.)

HFR-CREATEACC-008 (Date/time created retained.)

HFR-CREATEACC-009 (Activation Key requested date/time.)

HFR-CREATEACC-010 (Activation Key sent date/time.)

HFR-USERNAME-001 (Username must be unique.)

HFR-USERNAME-002 (Username validation rules.)

HFR-PASSWORD-001 (Password validation rules.)

HFR-PASSWORD-002 (Password encryption rules.)

HFR-EMAILADDR-001 (E-mail address validation rules.)

HFR-EMAILADDR-002 (E-mail address encryption rules.)

HFR-SECQUESTION-001 (Security question validation rules.)

HFR-SECQUESTION-002 (Security question encryption rules.)

HFR-SECQANSWER-001 (Answer validation rules.)

HFR-SECQANSWER-002 (Answer encryption rules.)

HFR-EMAILPROC-001 (E-mail sent asynchronously.) |

The VEM prefix is simply short for Validation Error Message, and HFR is short for High-level Functional Requirement.

The use case describes all the steps involved and provides a mapping to the functional requirements. The "system" processing also helps to draw out the high-level components and their high-level functionality. The use cases also provide the basis for determining and refining requirements, defining the test cases and test scenarios as well as the logging and diagnostic mockups. It is very important to determine the level of detail you are going to include in your use cases. This can sometimes depend on the level of information you have at the point you are writing your use cases. It also depends on the activities that follow use case specification. If the use cases are for development purposes, they will need to contain more detailed information, such as "The system updates the record in the database including updating the Created Date and Time (which is obtained at the start of the flow.)" This supposes there is either a requirement or desire to record the date and time or the logical data model includes one. While this information may not be relevant to the end user, it is relevant to the system processing and the test cases. If the use cases are being used for further detailed design activities, they may not need to include such detailed steps. In either case, it is important that use cases document "what" is happening rather than "how" it is being done or implemented.

Walking through the high-level flow helps to flesh out more requirements, design, and test characteristics. It highlights key functional areas and can be used to determine more test conditions and validate them to identify gaps. The more detailed the steps are, the more you can flesh out from them. The flow helps to flesh out:

❑ **Inputs and outputs** — The flow can be used to define the expected inputs to the processing and the subsequent outputs. Inputs and outputs are also used in other processes and batch processing, and modeling these helps to flesh out the details.

❑ **Validation** — What constitutes a valid entry? How are the entries going to be validated? Will the invalid fields be cleared? The flow can be used to model page layouts and page transitions. Validation will also need to be done for certain batch activities. For example, a bulk upload file may contain thousands of records that will need to be validated. Does this validation use the same components? How long will it take to validate all these records? What outputs are expected? Another important thing to remember is that validation rules are likely to change as the project progresses. Making it easier to change them will greatly reduce the impact.

❑ **Local and/or remote processing** — Where is the processing going to take place? Is the validation going to be done at the client, at the server, or both?

❑ **Security** — Who can perform this activity? How often can it be attempted in a single session? What validation error information is going to be displayed?

❑ **Performance** — How long should this transaction take? How many people are likely to be performing it concurrently? What times of the day are these transactions likely to be executed? Estimating the number and volume of transactions can greatly help to refine the testing effort so that components are tested early and performance considerations can be highlighted.

❑ **Errors and diagnostics** — What information is going to be logged during the activity? What performance counters need to be updated? What happens when it goes wrong? What information is displayed to the user? What alerts need to be raised?

❑ **Processing and components** — The flows help to draw out processing and components, such as data components, validation components, and processing components. The processing components can highlight special processing, such as wait-retry. For example, how many times will a user be allowed to attempt to create a new account before failing? Other special processing includes encrypting or decrypting values. You can see from the Create New Account flow that the system needs to encrypt certain information entered by the user.

❑ **Functional gaps** — Walking through the flows very often helps to identify any processing gaps or missing areas of functionality. Dead-ends and unexpected processing can be easily identified by walking through the flow step-by-step and drawing out the expected results. For example, if-else decisions are made often in the flow. Everything that doesn't match the if branch will follow the else branch. Is this really expected?

❑ **Noteworthy scenarios** — You'll see this in Chapter 13 when I walk through the sample use cases for the case study. However, the flow can often highlight areas of concern or noteworthy scenarios. For example, the system looking up the same record twice because of specific "pre- and post-validation requirements." Drawing these scenarios out of the flow can help to ratify the requirements and design.

❑ **Test conditions and complexity** — The flow helps to add more test conditions and can help to determine the complexity of the component based on the number of different conditions and variations of inputs.

Navigation Maps

A navigation map is a handy visual that shows the individual pages and how they flow into each other. Figure 4-8 shows the navigation map for the case study used in this book.

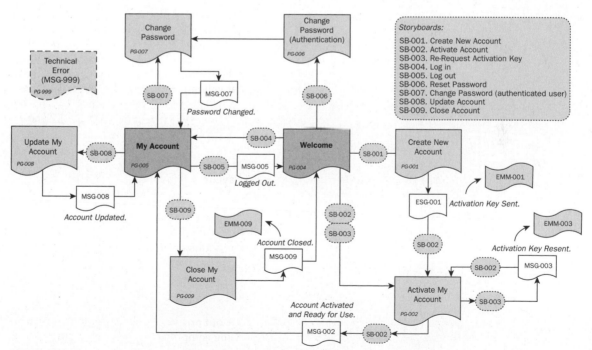

Figures 4-8

The navigation map helps to draw out the pages and any "functional" messages that will be displayed to the user. I always choose to uniquely identify everything so that they can be easily catalogued. The actual messages that get displayed or output should be configurable. However, the identifiers could also be used by the application and form the basis of some enumerators. You can use the elements on the navigation map as a starting point for your solution inventory and list all the items.

The following table contains the starting point for the solution inventory based on the navigation map:

Abbreviation	Description
SB – Storyboard	Each storyboard is uniquely identified. There are nine storyboards in the case study that relate to the use-case diagram.
PG – Page	Each logical page in the solution is uniquely identified.
MSG – Message (Display)	Each functional confirmation message that is displayed to the user is uniquely identified.
EMM – Email Message	Each e-mail message sent from the system is uniquely identified.

The solution inventory would continue to be built up as the project progresses through the various activities.

Storyboards

I always try to work through a simple set of "concept art" and user stories. I find that they really help to validate the solution and highlight potential gaps. The storyboards that I've produced in this instance aren't actually working versions. They have all been hand-drawn. I often find that this approach "keeps the fingers out of the code," allowing me to walk through the application without getting tied up in too many of the technical details (although it is not usually long before the code or detailed design needs to be approached, especially to flesh out the exemplars). The user interface is very much tied to the user interface architecture. In some cases it really helps to understand the architecture to ensure that pages and flows will align with the underlying architecture.

The high-level storyboards that I've produced for the case study don't go into the low-level technical details or full activity breakdowns, nor do they discuss the actual pages and elements. It is fairly easy to do things by hand in this instance because the application isn't too excessive. Storyboards help you to visualize the application by showing the entire flow from the primary actor's perspective. In Chapter 13, you'll see the complete set of sample storyboards for the case study.

Figure 4-9 shows the storyboard for the Create New Account functionality.

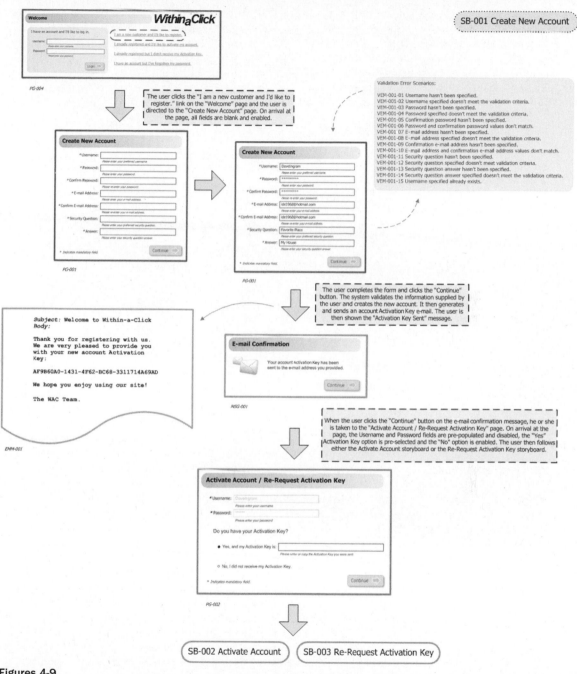

Figures 4-9

Storyboards show all the pages and interactions involved. They also help to shape up the requirements and page specifications. A simple prototype can also help to get the usage right. The size and scale of the application will determine whether a prototype can be developed. Furthermore, detailed storyboards such as the one shown can take a while to produce by hand. Using a simple tool, such as Microsoft Expression to model the pages, flows, and outputs can really help. Storyboards don't need to show detailed page layouts; in some cases simple textual representations are good enough to document the page contents and the flow. For example:

❑ The user navigates to the Welcome page.

❑ The Welcome page contains a link allowing the user to create a new account.

❑ The user clicks the "Create New Account" link.

❑ The system directs them to the "Create New Account" page.

❑ The "Create New Account" page is displayed and contains the following controls:

  ❑ Username entry field

  ❑ Password entry field

  ❑ Confirmation password entry field

  ❑ E-mail address entry field

  ❑ Confirmation e-mail address entry field

  ❑ Security question entry field

  ❑ Security question answer entry field

  ❑ Continue button

❑ The user completes the form and clicks the continue button.

❑ The system validates the user inputs, proceeds to create the new account, e-mails the user their unique account Activation Key and directs the user to the "Activate Account" page.

To keep things simple, I'm not going to list all the detailed steps and processing. However, you can see that this type of textual storyboard representation is rather like the steps in a use case.

As soon as you start to produce storyboards and include page transitions, it becomes necessary to start thinking about state and state management. State management is the process of maintaining information between multiple requests, whether these requests are for the same page or a different page. The HTTP protocol by nature is stateless. No information is retained between requests and responses. In the preceding example, when an error occurs, the user is directed to the error page. You want to retain the information and the context so that all is not lost if the user needs to resubmit the request. The user may be able to simply press the Back button on the browser and resubmit the request. When you get to some of the more complex functionality, such as ordering, you will need to manage state across multiple pages during the process. You can maintain state in many ways, both on the server side and the client side. The following are some typical client-side and server-side options:

❑ **Cookies** — A cookie is a file that is placed on the user's computer and managed by the browser's settings. A cookie is usually used to store a small amount of data. and due to their limitations, most browsers support only a 4KB limit on the size of a cookie, although 8KB cookies are becoming common. Cookies typically are used for "remember-me" functionality because the cookie is located on the client machine and can be read when the page loads. Cookies can be disabled by the client and therefore are not guaranteed to be usable. Cookies can also expire when the user's session ends, but this depends on the user's browser settings. A cookie can also be interfered with by the user, which could cause security issues.

❑ **Query string parameters** — Query string parameters, which are appended to a web page's URL, are name-value pairs. Each name-value pair is separated by the ampersand character (&). The parameters are separated from the URL by a question mark (?). An example query string is `http://www.withinaclick.co.uk/homepage.aspx?username=Dave`. Query strings are sometimes useful for passing small amounts of data between pages. Unless the data is encrypted, it is transmitted in the clear. This can lead to what is called *URL hacking*, in which a person can handcraft a URL and query string based on what he or she has received and seen before. For instance, I may have a directory component that looks up a particular individual based on first name and last name. The query string may look something like `.../directory.aspx?firstname=David&lastname=Ingram`. Based on this information, I would be able to compose a URL and query string containing anybody's first and last names and submit my request. If only authenticated users are allowed access to the directory and state is not being managed correctly, it is possible that URL hacking can cause security issues. Query strings are often limited to 255 characters, which again means that only small amounts of data can be passed.

❑ **Hidden fields** — Most browsers support the use of hidden fields on forms. Hidden fields are in the HTML source, thus on the client side, but not displayed in the browser window. Hidden fields are used to store small amounts of data that can be transferred between page requests. Each field contains a discrete piece of information that users can see by viewing the HTML source, and this information potentially can be modified, which can cause security issues. Hidden fields are a very simple implementation if you are not concerned about the data being stored in the field. The more information that is stored in hidden fields, the greater the effect on page load times, because there is a lot more data to transfer.

❑ **Database** — The database is another place to store state between requests. The database allows long-term storage and provides a level of fault tolerance in the event of a restart. The database allows much larger data sets to be stored and in a richer format. One challenge with storing state information in the database is separating the transient data from the long-term data. For example, assume that state is stored in the database for every user session. One storage set would be the user's shopping cart, which would be maintained throughout the duration of the session. When the session ends, the data should be removed, unless you want to retain the information for the next time the user comes in. This poses a further question regarding anonymous usage. You might not be able to identify the customer, and, in any case, he or she could have two browser windows opened simultaneously. The shopping cart is typically session-specific state that should be removed when the session ends or thereafter. Another challenge with storing state in the database is matching the state information with a specific browser session, retaining a session identifier, and passing it around requests.

There are many platform- and technology-specific methods of storing state. Microsoft's ASP.NET provides a number of features, including application- and session-specific objects.

Page Layouts and Specifications

Page layout diagrams and low-resolution mockups help you to visualize the application and flesh out more detail in the requirements. I mentioned earlier that designing page layouts sometimes requires a good understanding of the user interface architecture. It is not uncommon for the actual final pages to look different to those drawn in the early days of a project. Textual representations can often be used to prioritize page controls and actions instead of using actual page layouts or mockups.

Figures 4-2 and 4-4 showed mockups of typical pages or screens. The simple mockups showed typical labels, fields, controls, and other elements that can help to refine many lower-level requirements as well as to help shape the design and test characteristics, such as:

❑ **Styles** — Each of the label types, fields, and controls will have a defined style, including font, color, and border style.

❑ **Standard usage indicators** — The indicators include the asterisk character (*), to indicate mandatory entries, and the wheelchair icon, to indicate alternative features. They also include "confirmation fields." It is not uncommon for pages to ask for double entry of critical information, such as a user's e-mail address and password, so that it can be validated and matched. In such cases, copy-and-paste functionality is usually disabled so that the user is forced into typing the information into both fields. Other fields may also have specific usage requirements. The conceptual design should indicate where specific functionality must be considered so that it is not forgotten during development and testing.

❑ **Entities and the data dictionary** — The entity definition is drawn out from the text fields and includes the following: logical data types, minimum and maximum lengths, precision, display characteristics, case sensitivity, format, allowable or disallowable values and characters, as well as any other special processing. Allowable characters and escaping are especially important between interfaces and other processing. For example, it might be valid to have a comma in an entry; however, if this entry is extracted into a comma-separated file, problems will result. Lengths and formats are also important. If the lengths or formats differ, truncating and reformatting will need to be done.

❑ **Logical data model** — The logical data model can be derived and verified against the logical page designs to highlight any gaps.

❑ **Reference data** — The reference data gets built up from the pages — for example, the drop-down list of security questions. What are they? Where are they going to be stored? Examining the reference data also helps you to determine maintenance requirements (see next point). It is paramount that you also consider the potential number of reference data records that need to be displayed. It is not uncommon for a page mockup to include a drop-down list (or similar control) only to find that there could be hundreds of entries making selection difficult and impacting the user experience.

❑ **Maintenance screens** — Are additional screens required to maintain the reference data? Who can update or change it? What workflow process is required for this? Are changes reflected immediately or do they need some form of start date and validity period? What happens to the existing transactional data when these are changed or deleted?

❑ **Test conditions and test data** — You can start to produce the test conditions and test data based on the entities and reference data.

❑ **Processing and progress** — The flow also highlights the system processing that will be performed. It is worth thinking about what information is displayed after a user presses the Continue button. It might be worth using a progress meter, an "egg timer," or even text to indicate that the system is processing the request. It is equally worth documenting what processing is actually going to be performed and where it will be performed — for example, entry-field validation is being performed on the client side, on the server side, or both. In addition, you might consider whether the Continue button should be disabled after it is pressed to avoid multiple hits and orphaned processes.

Some of the information and questions can equally be derived from a logical table or database design. It depends on the approach taken. That is, designing from the bottom up would start with the logical data model, which would determine the field values that would be stored in the database. Using the Create New Account example, the page layouts that contain the "confirmation" fields would not be stored in the database; hence, some of the more subtle design features are derived from page layouts or flows, such as the Confirm Password and Confirm E-mail Address fields. The page specifications should ideally include the following items, as well:

❑ **Default selections** — It is important to specify which elements will be defaulted on the page and why the default has been chosen. There may be a number of ways of getting to the page, and a single default value may not be appropriate in all cases.

❑ **Field-level validation** — The requirements may not stipulate any specific acceptable values for fields. Field-level validation is almost always implemented and even more so highlighted to the user when invalid information is submitted. Validation errors need to be considered. Some sites display a series of validation errors at the top of the page, and others simply indicate fields that have invalid entries. Some fields will have a certain number of selectable values, in this case the country and phone number type fields indicate drop-down lists to restrict the possible values. Acceptable values may also change over time, which will have an impact on existing data and information.

❑ **Tab order** — It is vitally important to ensure that the tab order is correct and not frustrate users by having a misaligned tab order when moving from field to field or entry to entry.

❑ **Validation error messages** — When users input invalid information, the system should display an error message. You need to think carefully about what is displayed to the user and how the information could be used for malicious intent as well as in normal usage. For example, if the user tries to register with a username or an e-mail address that already exists on the system, it would be easy to display an error message such as "The e-mail address you have entered already exists." I always find this an interesting one. On the one hand, it is very useful to users if they are registering their own e-mail address, as it would be a shock to find that their e-mail address had already been registered, unless, of course, they had forgotten about registering. On the other hand, this information is potentially useful to other people for malicious purposes. It categorically tells the person that the e-mail address is registered with the system. Validation error messages are likely to change, so a generic solution should be incorporated to make them easy to change. The generic solution also helps to limit the impact of internationalization and localization.

❑ **System error messages** — The system will need to display error messages to the user. These messages can be technical in nature or be based on functional rules. The likelihood is that these messages will change as the project progresses. As with validation error messages, a generic solution should be employed.

❏ **Security and access requirements** — Some pages will be available only to certain users or roles. The conceptual design should list the security and access rights for the page — for example, specifying that only Administrators are allowed access to the reference data pages.

❏ **Actions, states, and functions** — The page will typically have different actions depending on the state of record. For instance, an account record will generally have different states — for example, New, Active, Closed, and so on. Ideally, the page should list all the actions and the states they can be applied to. For example, it might not be possible to "Close" a "New" account. This type of activity can also be controlled through the menu access, but it is important to determine the actions that can be applied to the various states.

❏ **Actions and responses** — The design should consider each of the appropriate dynamic controls on the page and specify the appropriate action and response. For example, a Continue button might state, "Check that all fields are valid. If there are invalid fields, show the validation errors; otherwise, the system saves the record." This information should also be included in the use cases to ensure that it is captured appropriately.

❏ **Data access requirements and mapping** — The page will typically contain information from the database. The page should list the relevant data access requirements, along with the appropriate transaction isolation — for example, "This page will use Read Uncommitted for product data." The specificity of the requirement will depend on how far along the logical data model is. For example, if the data model contains a set of stored procedures, the page could state which stored procedures are used and the actions they are associated with.

❏ **Multi-purpose forms** — Pages can be used for multiple purposes. For example, in addition to being used to create new accounts, the Create New Account page might be used to edit account details. Having multi-purpose forms can dramatically reduce the number of forms in the application. This also helps with internationalization and localization, as well as to reduce development effort. When things change, it is often easier to update one form than many forms, although this needs to be balanced against how the actions the form is supporting differ. The walkthrough helps to identify similar pages where re-use and multi-purpose actions can be incorporated. The form shown could very well be re-used to edit a user's account by pre-populating the fields from the existing data and changing the title and button caption. The code behind the form will control the actions that are being performed based on a "function" or "action" value. It is best to restrict the number of uses of the form to very similar actions and values. For example, it would be possible to re-use the Create New Account for the login page, but this would complicate the issue. The walkthrough also helps to identify discrete controls that can isolate specific functionality and be used on other forms. This also helps to reduce the number of moving parts in the solution.

❏ **Online help** — Most sites also provide help pages to provide the user with helpful hints and tips.

The preceding list provides some high-level outputs that can be drawn from a simple page. The following section takes a look at some additional functional considerations.

The Data Dictionary

The data dictionary is essentially meta-data about the data elements within the solution. The data elements are captured from the page specifications, component specifications, and other design elements. A good data dictionary can really help to progress development and testing quickly. The conceptual design should capture as much information as possible for the data dictionary, including:

❑ **Entity names** — The fields on the page will typically indicate the associated data dictionary entity. Common entities should be re-used across the board to provide consistency. It is very useful to compile all the entity names and cross-check them against the data dictionary to ensure that no duplicates or inconsistencies exist — for example, one person adding an entity called Account Name and another listing it as User Name when they could be the same thing.

❑ **Entity types** — The field types on the pages will need to be determined. For instance, which fields are ALPHA, ALPHA-NUMERIC, NUMERIC, DATE and TIME, and so forth? It is important to specify the field type in its lowest form. For instance, generically using a field type of DATETIME when the time portion may not be used can cause issues and is confusing; instead, it is much better to state DATE, TIME, or DATETIME. The element types are not only for the simple data types; the data element type should be specified clearly — for example, BINARY, GUID, and so on. The conceptual design will generally use simple types like these rather than database-specific types such as VCHAR(50). The basic element types are then mapped to the physical database types.

❑ **Minimum and maximum field lengths** — I've mentioned this before, but it bears repeating: minimum and maximum field lengths should be included and checked in the data dictionary. A lot of issues can be caused by them being misaligned — for example, when one form allows a user to enter 11 characters for a username, whereas another form allows only 10 characters. Referring to common entities reduces the chances of error.

❑ **Fixed-width fields** — Although this could be considered a part of the minimum and maximum field lengths, I've kept it separate. Fixed-width fields imply padding, which often causes issues during comparison. For example, comparing the value "David" (no trailing spaces) with the value "David   " (which contains trailing spaces) will typically return false. It is always a good idea to know when data elements are padded.

❑ **Formats** — The entries on the page may have a specific format — for instance, that of a telephone number. The format could be for display purposes only, or it could indicate that the data is stored in the database in native format. The format should be understood and consistently applied across the solution.

❑ **Case sensitivity** — The entities should state whether they are case-sensitive, as case sensitivity can cause issues during comparison.

❑ **Allowable characters** — It is not uncommon to restrict the characters that can be entered into fields. For example, many sites and applications do not allow certain characters, such as single quotes (' '), double quotes (" "), commas (,), periods (.), pound signs (#), greater than signs (>), lesser than signs (<), colons (:), and semicolons (;). There are many reasons for not allowing certain characters in fields — some have to do with functionality and others are more technical in nature, for example, characters that other systems or databases might interpret as being "escape" or special reserved characters. Sometimes data is extracted from the database, placed is comma-separated files, and transferred to other systems. Allowing data to contain commas can cause issues down the line if the information is not properly formatted or escaped. Escape characters are used by text processors to treat a sequence of characters differently. For instance, using the double quote (" ") characters signifies that the text in between the quotes should not be modified or interpreted. Allowing only certain characters to be typed in fields and entries greatly reduces problems later. Furthermore, it can help with security by not allowing malicious use of text entries. The conceptual design should state which special characters are and are not allowed. You should keep in mind that there may be many different sets of allowable character validation rules.

181

❑ **Allowable values** — Allowable values would typically be reference data. It is important to specify the allowable values for a data element and where the allowable values are stored and obtained from.

❑ **Auto-generated and calculated values** — The data element might be generated automatically. It is important to list elements that are auto-generated, such as ID fields and GUIDs. Another form of auto-generated values is calculated fields, in which the field value is calculated based on the values in other fields.

❑ **Default values** — Default values can apply to the pages as well as to the data elements. It is important to specify whether a field has a default value.

❑ **Null values** — Null values typically cause huge sets of problems during development and testing. The application needs to be coded to support Null values properly. All too often the code just blindly accesses a column value and starts generating Null value exceptions. It is important that entities that support Null values be clearly specified.

❑ **Composite fields** — Often forms and pages contain composite fields. A composite field comprises one or more elements put together. For example, Full Name is a composite of "First Name," a "SPACE" and "Last Name." It is important to specify computed fields and how they are formed to ensure they are properly and consistently composed throughout the application.

❑ **Special considerations** — There may be other considerations that need to be mentioned. I always design maintenance pages so that they have a search facility. The entry criteria fields allow the user to specify criteria that is used in a SQL LIKE clause — for instance, specifying David%. Generic validation rules could conflict and cause issues.

Architecture and Application Component Specifications

Defining the high-level architecture helps to flesh out components. It also helps to define the end-to-end transaction flow and reusable components.

Figure 4-10 shows a number of component layers.

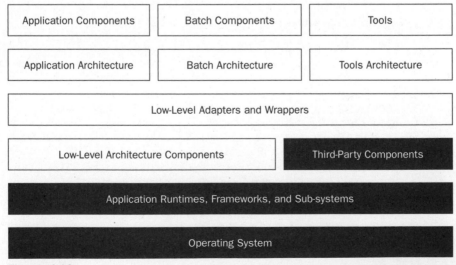

Figures 4-10

The items in black are created externally, whereas the items in white are created internally. Defining them helps to keep them in mind and also draw out further requirements or technical details. For instance, should the batch components be able to make use of the tools architecture? The stack also helps in defining the build process and build order once components have been defined in each layer. As you progress through the stack, the components become more specialized, whereas the lower-level components are more generic. This helps to shape the libraries and packaging structure of the application, and identifies reusable components.

❑ **Low-level architecture components** — Includes, components for logging and tracing, performance counters, events, database access, configuration setting access, and other generic components. This layer is also hierarchical in that the data access components should make use of the logging components. The performance counter components will also make use of the logging components, and so on. It is worth modeling these interactions to flesh out more detail in the design. It also helps to define the build order.

❑ **Low-level adapters and wrappers** — These components wrap third-party interfaces and provide a richer interface that ideally isolates the semantics of communication and processing. For instance, a typical third-party component is the database, and the data access wrappers isolate connection, disconnection, and stored procedure execution from the developer. Similarly, File Transfer Protocol is often used in systems, and the components can be isolated in the same way to provide an easier-to-use set of components.

Breaking down the layers into components and interfaces helps to shape the design, but also to define the interfaces, which can be compared side-by-side to drive out further details. Flows can also be used to refine the design and highlight potential cyclic relationships between components. For example, the logging component will probably need a `LogFilePath` parameter. This may be stored in the database or in a configuration file. However, the configuration access component will also make use of the logging component. This often leads to default parameters being included within the components or no logging taking place until the component is initialized. Modeling these flows highlights these nuances and shapes the design, which can be agreed up front. Initialization should be modeled and flowed as early as possible to ensure that these nuances are captured.

Modeling the architecture also helps to draw out more configuration settings and test conditions, as well as to shape the security and access model.

Figure 4-11 shows a typical high-level, three-tier architecture and some of the components that could reside on each tier for the "Create New Account" example used earlier.

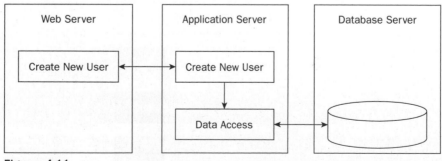

Figures 4-11

The simple picture can be used to define or highlight:

❑ **The components that reside on each server** — This information can be fed into the packaging and deployment process as well as help to separate configuration. In this instance, the figure doesn't show any database components such as stored procedures. Does this mean the application is using dynamic SQL or is it just missing?

❑ **The security contexts the components will execute within** — The security flow is very important and often something that causes problems. For example, a web user runs in a different security context from the application component. Therefore, the stored procedures and database elements need to be configured for the application component, not for the user. This is also true in the development environment, where all components generally run under the same user and these issues are not usually highlighted until multiple server environments are used.

❑ **The information flow between the components** — The inputs and outputs of the transaction are important for testing. They can also highlight the bandwidth requirements based on the amount of data being transferred, which has a bearing on performance.

These issues will come up as the project progresses, so you should address them early or have them on the design query list to avoid forgetting them further down the line. Keeping the components simple and modular helps to reduce the complexity and promotes reuse and parallel development.

Component Lists and Specifications

It is often handy to have high-level component specifications that list the members of a class or component. Many of you are likely to be familiar with component specifications from reading MSDN articles. The component specification can simply be a set of tables that describe the individual members. On the other hand, if the component is architectural in nature, it may describe some usage scenarios and how-to information. I mentioned using high-level flow diagrams earlier, but classes, methods and properties can equally be described in simple tables. The components can generally be determined from the use cases and processing. The following table provides an example of a simple class list:

Class	Layer	Description
RegistrationManager	Business	Used to validate create new account, activate account and resend Activation Keys requests.
RegistrationProcessor	Business	Used to orchestrate the processing of create new account, activate account and resend Activation Keys requests.
AccountProvider	Business Framework	Provides methods for account processing, such as creating a new account and activating an account.
AccountDataAccess	Data Access	Provides methods for accessing account data from the database.
AccountData	Data Entity	Contains properties for accessing account data.

The following table provides an example list of properties for the `AccountData` class:

Property	Type	Description
Id	ulong	Contains the unique identifier for the account.
State	byte	Contains the account state (1) New, (2) Active and (3) Closed
Username	String	Contains the unique username.
Password	String	Contains the user's password.
EmailAddress	String	Contains the user's e-mail address.
SecurityQuestion	String	Contains the user's security question.
SecurityQuestionAnswer	String	Contains the user's security question answer.
DateTimeCreate	DateTime	Contains the date and time the account was created.
ActivationKey	String	Contains the string representation of the user's unique account Activation Key.
DateTimeActivated	DateTime	Contains the date and time the account was activated.

An important aspect of the component specification is to provide some high-level information regarding the business exceptions that it could potentially raise. This really does help when "tightening the screws" for development. The following table lists some example exceptions:

Error	Description
AccountNotFound	Generated when system can't find the username entered.
AccountNotOpen	Generated when the user's account is not in an open state.
AuthenticationFailure	Generated when the authentication component returns false.

This information should map back to the use case and again use the same identifiers. It also helps to start fleshing out the exception-handling strategy and whether these will be implemented as true exceptions in the business layer.

With a solid list of components, you can start to flesh out the processing and build up to a detailed component specification, including public and private members.

Message and Interface Mappings

Defining and creating mockup messages and interfaces draws out more entities and their characteristics. The mockup messages also provide useful test data. When it comes to integration testing, the interfaces and messages between components will play a crucial part. If two components are being designed independently, it is worth performing a joint review to ensure that what comes out of one component is valid as an input for the next. There can also be many permutations, and, depending on the number of elements and variations, this can be quite an undertaking but well worth doing early.

The inputs, outputs, and internal or calculated values, as well as their types and characteristics, are used to provide the information and close the loop. This is done by performing a side-by-side comparison, similar to that described in the following table.

Create New Account Inputs	Logical Account Table	Observations
	UserId (Unique)	The UserId should be generated by the database and passed back to the component to enable suitable logging and diagnostics.
UserName	UserName	The username needs to be unique.
Password	Password	The password field needs to be encrypted.
ConfirmedPassword		Not stored in the database.
EmailAddress	EmailAddress	The e-mail address needs to be encrypted.
ConfirmedEmailAddress		Not stored in the database.
SecurityQuestion	SecurityQuestion	The security question needs to be encrypted.
SecurityQuestionAnswer	SecurityQuestionAnswer	The security question answer needs to be encrypted.
Not entered by user	DateTimeCreated	When will this date and time be populated?
Not entered by user	ActivationKey	How will this be generated and stored?
Not entered by user	DateTimeActivated	When will this date and time be populated?

Although this is a very simple example, it highlights areas that need to be fleshed out in more detail. For instance, the DateTimeCreated needs to be populated, which could be done by the web server, the application server, or even at the database. A decision like this can be made only by walking through the transaction and determining the best place to allocate the date and time. Chapter 15 discusses this subject in more detail. In addition, modeling interfaces in this way highlights possible mismatches in length, format, and variation. These outputs provide invaluable information for integration testing and end-to-end testing.

Logging and Diagnostics

Walking through the flow helps to flesh out logging and diagnostics. A logging and diagnostics mockup helps to flesh out other design considerations and characteristics. It is best to split the mockups into functional and technical categories to avoid potential re-work. For example, the following shows a basic verbose functional log mockup for the Create New Account flow:

```
Create New Account - Processing Start
Create New Account - Inputs:
Create New Account -    UserName = 'user name'
Create New Account -    Password = 'password'
Create New Account -    ConfirmedPassword = 'confirmedpassword'
Create New Account -    EmailAddress = 'emailaddress'
Create New Account -    ConfirmedEmailAddress = 'confirmedemailaddress'
Create New Account -    SecurityQuestion = 'securityquestion'
Create New Account -    SecurityQuestionAnswer = 'securityquestionanswer'
Create New Account - Inputs End
Create New Account - Validating Inputs
Create New Account -    Username
Create New Account -    Username Valid
Create New Account -    Password
Create New Account -    Password Valid
Create New Account -    ConfirmPassword
Create New Account -    ConfirmPassword Valid
Create New Account -    Checking Password and ConfirmPassword Match
Create New Account -    Password and ConfirmPassword Match
Create New Account -    EmailAddress
Create New Account -    EmailAddress Valid
Create New Account -    ConfirmEmailAddress
Create New Account -    ConfirmEmailAddress Valid
Create New Account -    Checking EmailAddress and ConfirmEmailAddress Match
Create New Account -    EmailAddress and ConfirmEmailAddress Match
Create New Account -    SecurityQuestionAnswer
Create New Account -    SecurityQuestionAnswer Valid
Create New Account - Checking If Account Already Exists
Create New Account - Account Does Not Already Exist
Create New Account - Creating New Account
Create New Account - New Account Created with UserId = 'userid'
Create New Account - Returning "Account Created"
Create New Account - Processing End
```

Even though this log is quite basic, it is a very verbose log that could probably be reduced. If all components were logging such verbose information, it would probably have a big impact on performance. There are typically four high-level logging levels: Information, Warning, Error, and Debug. Walking through the verbose log helps to identify the entries and their appropriate level. For example, all the entries below the "Validating Inputs" might be better as debug-level entries. Early identification of the different levels of log entry helps during development.

The basic mockup shown highlights other important points, including:

❑ Which information should be shown in the log? Do you really want to show passwords and e-mail addresses? Furthermore, the log does not show encrypting entries. Has this functionality been missed somewhere along the line? The use case mentions that certain entries should be encrypted, so the steps should be included in the logging mockup.

❑ If you don't show the passwords or the e-mail addresses, and the validity or matching fails, how can you determine what the values were? If the encrypted values were shown in the log, how do you decrypt them for verification?

❑ The log does not show the validation rules that the inputs are being validated against. It might be worth including them to ensure that the values are expected.

❑ The log does not map back to the use case steps and solution inventory. The logs should map back to the solution inventory and the use cases, and wherever possible the identifiers should be used within the application — for example, including the use-case identifier and the step number.

❑ If you are going to surround the input values with quotation marks, what do you do if the input value contains the same characters? This is also true for processing and validation, which could be used in batch processes.

❑ Which log entry categories can be included to reduce the log for different environments and purposes?

❑ Which contextual information needs to be included to provide a comprehensive understanding of what is going on?

The mockup can be used to determine an overall approach to logging as well as the components required. Producing sample logs can also help to flesh out support and operability requirements. The sample logs can take into account the different conditions and processing. For instance, the following sample shows an error being encountered:

```
Create New Account - Creating New Account
Create New Account - Error Encountered during Create New
      Account - 'Error Message'
Create New Account - Processing End
```

Taking a step back and looking at the sample log will enable you to determine whether there is enough information to diagnose the issue. This is best achieved by assuming that you only had the log and the event. Could you determine what went wrong and would you have enough information to re-create the issue?

Creating a mockup of the technical elements of the log entries also helps to further refine the requirements and design. For example, consider the following technical sample log:

```
[Timestamp][ComponentName][MethodName] Entry
```

This sample log highlights a number of questions:

❑ What if components can run on multiple servers? Do you want to include the machine name in the log? Would it serve any purpose?

❑ What if multiples of the same components can run on the same computer? Do you want to include the process ID?

❑ What if you have multiple threads? Do you want to include thread ID?

❑ Which tools are going to parse the logs, and how are they going to find/extract the information they require?

Another good thing about log mockups is that they help to determine whether logging should be session-based, transaction-based, or component-based. For example, an end-to-end transaction may go through many different components, which could reside on multiple servers. How can each of these logs and entries be threaded together to get a complete, end-to-end picture? In a case like this, you would need some form of unique transaction ID that is included in the different entries to isolate all entries for a particular transaction, which may help to piece together a timeline for incident investigation. Incident investigation and logging are discussed in more detail in Chapters 11 and 21.

Event mockups flesh out the details required for events, such as their level, source, and description. They also help to determine how the event log will be used, as well as whether separate event logs are created for different categories of components or everything is placed in the Application event log. This often highlights a number of configuration values, such as the different event log names, event categories, sources, and so forth. You will also need components that are used to create event logs and raise events within the application.

Other mockups include performance counters. For example, which performance counters need to be updated by the component? Are these counters aggregated? How frequently is the counter updated? What purpose does the counter have?

It is worth thinking about tools to extract information from logs, events, and performance counters for testing, verification, and live support to help diagnose and resolve issues.

All the information that can be drawn out of simple mockups can be fed back into the requirements and included in the design documentation.

Interactions and Exceptions

I'd like to introduce a diagram that you're probably not familiar with. I refer to it as *fluml* — a cross between a flow chart and a UML sequence diagram. In case it takes off, it is pronounced *flu-em-el*.

Figure 4-12 uses typical UML symbols and, as far as I'm concerned, captures a serious amount of information for a developer to use.

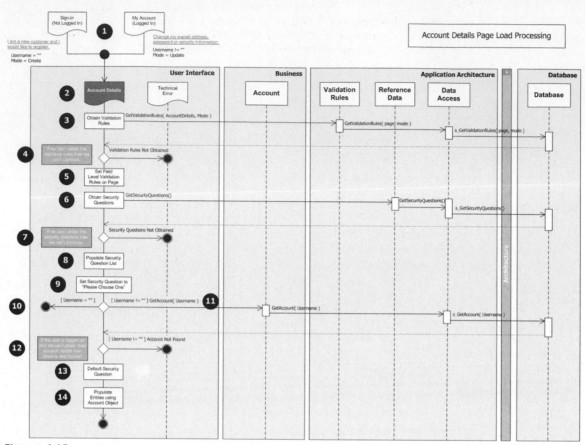

Figures 4-12

It shows every component used and the high-level steps for the process. It is the sort of diagram that gets drawn on a whiteboard when brainstorming the solution — in this case, an example Account Details Page Load processing. The picture reads from the top down to the bottom and left to right. It starts at the top with the pages that can trigger the process. The following points correspond to the figures in the diagram:

1. This shows the starting point for the process. In this example, it is either the Sign-In page or the My Account page. The different triggers show the key *state* information, such as whether the username is populated or not and what mode the page is in. In this example, a single page is being used for more than one purpose.

2. The Account Details page is being called from either of the two pages mentioned in item 1. The sequence represents the Account Details page load logical functionality.

3. The account details page first attempts to obtain the validation rules for the page. In this case, it is calling the Validation Rules component that resides in the Application Architecture layer. This component is then using the Data Access layer, which, in turn, is calling a stored procedure in the database. The arguments in this instance are for illustration purposes but could equally be the actual parameters required.

4. The sequence then makes a decision based on whether the rules were obtained. If not, the user is directed to the Technical Error page, where a suitable message would be displayed. The annotation provides some notational text.

5. If the validation rules have been obtained successfully, the page proceeds to populate the field-level validation controls. The page is dynamically setting the validation controls when the page is loaded.

6. The processing then continues to obtain the security questions. In this instance, the page is using the Reference Data component. The Reference Data component is then using the Data Access layer again to call a stored procedure to obtain the questions from the database.

7. The processing then makes a decision again based on whether the security questions were obtained. If not, the user is redirected to the Technical Error page.

8. If the questions were obtained, the page proceeds to populate the drop-down list with the questions. If this were a real example, this step would also add the Please Choose One option. Additional annotation could be provided to highlight this additional step.

9. This step defaults the selection to the Please Choose One option.

10. The processing is now making a decision based on whether the username state value is populated. If the username is not populated, there is no more processing to be done, so the page can be rendered and served to the user.

11. If the username is populated, the processing continues to obtain the user's account details, passing in the username to the Business layer Account component. The Account component then uses the Data Access layer to call a stored procedure to obtain the account details from the database.

12. The processing now makes a very critical decision as to whether the user details were obtained. In this instance, if the user details aren't obtained, this would be a very serious situation. A user is logged on because the username field is populated, but the system is unable to locate their account details! The chances of this situation actually happening are slim, which opens up an entire debate on defensive programming. This condition would need to be tested, which could increase development and test timescales. This needs to be balanced against the effects of continuing without the account details if they can't be obtained.

13. If the account details were found, the processing then proceeds to default the security question drop-down to the user's chosen security question. This also raises the question of reference data maintenance. If the question had been removed from the database list and stored in the user's account data as text, the question would not be in the list, so this step would cause an exception.

14. Finally, the entries on the page are populated with the information obtained from the database, and the page can be rendered and served to the user.

Walking through flows like this can really help to flesh out some details. Clearly, this is a book, so the diagram needs to be neat; however, in reality the diagram could be drawn on a whiteboard. It just depends on how many people need to see it and understand it.

The flow also highlights an interesting consideration for the exception-handling strategy. It is important to determine the exception strategy early on. Deciding whether components should return Boolean values or throw exceptions can be difficult. The act of throwing an exception can impact performance, but this needs to be balanced with its likelihood. I'm not a fan of using exceptions to control execution flow unnecessarily.

An example pattern that is often used occurs when the application is determining whether to update a record in the database or to insert a new one. The application first attempts to insert the record, and only when a `Unique Constraint Violation` exception occurs does the application perform an update or other processing instead. This type of pattern is typically used when the chances of the record actually existing are very slim. If a check was made prior to every insertion, this would impact performance. I must admit that I am not a fan of this type of pattern and feel that it just causes problems further down the line. However, exceptions are not reserved for solely technical reasons. If you expect something to exist and it doesn't, or vice versa, it is an exception, and therefore the application should throw an exception and it should be dealt with in the most appropriate way. For example, consider the "File Not Found" exception. This error occurs when you attempt to open a file for read access that doesn't exist. Let's say you have a stored procedure that gets an account by name for update purposes. If you applied the same logic, the procedure should really throw an Account Not Found exception, or at least the data access component should. It all comes down to what the component expects. If the outcome is expected, it is not an exception; otherwise, it is an exception. There are pros and cons for each approach, and they should be considered early to ensure that everyone follows the same patterns and guidelines.

Depending on the chosen strategy, the decision points on the diagram could be treated as exception points rather than actual decisions in the code. The diagrams should also map back to the use case and flow to ensure that everything is captured accordingly. I've used this type of diagram only as an example and to highlight the preceding messages. Of course, you could equally specify the component interactions and processing using standard UML (Unified Modeling Language) diagrams, such as activity diagrams, sequence diagrams and so forth.

Summary

In this chapter you've seen a number of analysis and design considerations and the potential array of outputs that can come out of them. It is important to consider as many aspects as possible prior to full scale development to ensure that the appropriate foundations can be put in place. You've seen that all these inputs ultimately have their place in the "out-of-the-box" contents. This chapter has highlighted some of the inputs and how they can be improved to ensure quality. The case study that it used in this book is described later, and I'll use a number of these inputs to describe its functionality and technical behaviors.

This chapter has also provided a high-level overview of the types of design considerations and the inputs to further design and development activities. Throughout this book we'll build on these, which can then be folded back into the analysis and design activities to provide a more robust scope and design. This information can then be used for effective estimating and planning.

As you have seen, walking through the design of two very simple pages has outlined a myriad of considerations and design outputs. The more that you can do up front, the more scope you can flesh out. And you'll also have a much better understanding of how long it will realistically take to implement. You should try to cover as much as possible. The best way I find to do this is to assume that I'm on the receiving end. You shouldn't assume that the person you're giving the information to knows as much as you regarding the solution. You should really test each activity as much as possible and thoroughly review each element. Furthermore, playing the "what if" game will flesh out as much additional detail (or areas for consideration) as possible.

You should reference the solution inventory consistently throughout the application. It can be used to ensure that all requirements are captured and implemented accordingly. Keeping the components simple will maximize the number of developers that can potentially work on them. In addition, the simpler the component, the more likely it is to be developed correctly and the easier it should be to document properly.

The following are the key points to take away from this chapter:

❑ **Think "Out-of-the-Box"** — The key contents of the virtual software box can essentially help to shape your overall project roadmap. The contents discussed included:

  ❑ The "Back of the Box," which shows the key features of the software, the business benefits, and other high-level sales collateral.

  ❑ The "media," which is the DVDs or CDs that contain the actual software, help files, and installation files.

  ❑ The "User Guide," which provides all the instructions for using the software effectively and performing the day-to-day tasks. The Developer's Guide essentially mirrors the technical or detailed design and would be used by the development team and application maintenance team.

  ❑ The "Operations Manual," which provides all the instructions and information for planning deployment, installation, and configuration, and monitoring and operating the software. The operations manual is discussed in further detail in Chapter 7.

By thinking about what would come "out-of-the-box," you can shape the high-level roadmap of the project and its ultimate development and implementation.

❑ **Consider the Design** — Design considerations and decisions clearly have a domino effect on the remainder of the project. The high-level categories of considerations discussed included:

  ❑ Accessibility

  ❑ Implementation

  ❑ Support and maintenance

  ❑ Custom built vs. off-the-shelf

In addition to the preceding categories, this section also listed some high-level general design considerations, including:

  ❑ Auditing

  ❑ Housekeeping and cleanup

  ❑ Security and access

  ❑ Transactions and transaction boundaries

  ❑ Reference data validity

  ❑ Immediate and pending updates

- ❏ Workflow

- ❏ Concurrency and transaction isolation (read committed, read uncommitted)

In addition to the preceding considerations, the following high-level items were also discussed:

- ❏ The technical requirements can, and often do, apply to both the online application and the administration application.

- ❏ Sensitive information should be stored securely, but this is not without its own implications.

- ❏ Misuse should be considered and gaps should be plugged.

- ❏ Where necessary, supporting browser controls such as Forward, Back, F5, and Ctrl+F5 will greatly improve usability of the site.

❏ **Define the Analysis and Design Outputs** — If the analysis and design outputs are good, they can provide the basis for some realistic estimates. You should ensure that each output has the necessary level of information to take forward. The outputs discussed in this chapter included:

- ❏ Scope (the items that are in or out of scope)

- ❏ Requirements (both functional and technical)

- ❏ Use-case diagrams and use cases

- ❏ Navigation maps

- ❏ Storyboards

- ❏ Page layouts and specifications

- ❏ The data dictionary

- ❏ Architecture and application component specifications

This chapter completes our high-level walkthrough of the production-readiness landscape. The chapters that follow look at a hypothetical production-running landscape for your applications and examine some more of the key areas for software development and implementation consideration.

Part II

The Production Landscape

5

The Production Environment

The production environment is the foundation of the production system. It encompasses both the solution architecture and the operations architecture. It can also involve multiple data centers for fault tolerance and disaster recovery. This chapter examines a hypothetical, medium-scale, highly resilient, and scalable production environment. It also re-enforces the importance of and the techniques for designing a production architecture (and solution) that is fit for purpose and meets all the necessary quality characteristics from both a hardware and software perspective.

This chapter is organized into the following sections:

❑ **The Big Picture** — Examines the architecture hardware diagram, including the solutions architecture and the operations architecture environments. The architecture hardware diagram is a snapshot view of the overall production environment showing the different hardware (servers and network components) it encompasses.

❑ **The Hardware Topology** — Examines the usage and resiliency of individual server groups. It also looks at the high availability and fault-tolerant features of the architecture, along with some items that should be considered. It examines shared storage for use by the application by making use of the SAN. And, finally, it takes a quick look at network segmentation which can be employed for improved security and performance.

❑ **The Software Topology** — Describes how the software topology is put together, examining each of the server groups and the applications being used. It looks at how the applications are mapped to the servers and what sort of information should be captured and documented.

❑ **The Primary and Secondary Data Centers** — Describes the primary and secondary data centers organizations use to provide failover capabilities. It also describes how data centers can be either active-passive or active-active in their configuration, and the benefits and drawbacks of each.

The Big Picture

Mission-critical systems are fundamental to the business, so failures or outages in these systems can be disastrous. The primary goal of enterprise architectures is to have no single points of failure. The system should be tolerant to a single component failure. A component can be an entire server or an internal component of a server, such as a power supply, a fan, or a network card.

The actual size, scale, and characteristics of the production environment are determined largely by the key technical requirements, the applications being deployed, and their usage. The key technical requirements that you should take into account include, but are not limited to, the following:

- ❑ Number of users
- ❑ Transaction profiles
- ❑ Performance
- ❑ Availability
- ❑ Scalability
- ❑ Operability
- ❑ Backup and recovery
- ❑ Disaster recovery

A typical production hardware environment is a multi-server topology in which the application components are distributed across different physical servers (web servers, application servers, databases servers, and so forth). The production architecture is highly robust and fault tolerant in order to meet all the quality requirements. In many cases, the production environment also has a disaster recovery counterpart, which is usually hosted in a completely separate data center.

One of the most widely used diagrams throughout the project lifecycle is the production architecture (or deployment) diagram. The objective of the diagram is to show in a single picture, a high-to-medium level view of all the key physical sites, environments, servers, storage components, networks components, and other devices that form the production environment. In addition, the diagram typically includes important information regarding the base operating system, the size and scale (CPU and memory), and the fault tolerance or scalability features of each server or device group. Depending on the size and scale of the overall solution, the diagram can, in fact, be a very big picture.

Figure 5-1 shows a typical medium-scale architecture diagram.

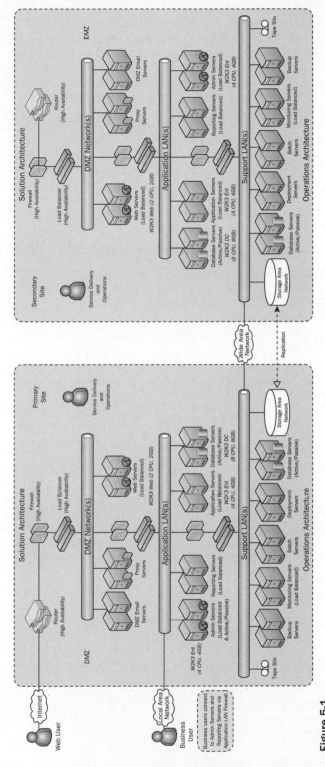

Figure 5-1

The production environment depicted is hypothetical and is used to demonstrate the different types of servers and their usage. The diagram is also used to highlight some of the fault-tolerant features of the production architecture.

The production architecture contains many different servers, and one important aspect to mention right now is date and time synchronization. If the dates and times of the individual servers are not synchronized, it can cause issues with transaction traceability. For example, as a transaction flows through each server (or group of servers), it passes through different timestamps. If the date and time of the database server is one minute behind that of the web servers, it may appear that the transaction hit the database one minute before it actually arrived at the web server. It's important to consider how the dates and times of all the production servers are synchronized. If they're not synchronized, what are the implications to transaction traceability? It depends entirely on the way in which the solution is implemented. However, the most likely impact is that all the logging and diagnostic information will have different timestamps, making it harder to thread all the trace entries together into a consistent timeline across all the servers.

The production architecture diagram evolves as the project progresses. Initially, it's similar to that shown in Figure 5-1, which shows the high-level components and resiliency features. The initial diagram is then used to further design and enhance many other areas of the production environment, including the detailed network design, the security design, the application design, and the deployment design. The hardware and software architecture topologies typically go hand-in-hand, although I've split them into two separate sections for discussion later in this chapter. Figure 5-1 contains a few specific abbreviations, which are clarified in the following table.

Abbreviation	Description
W2K3 Web	Microsoft Windows Server 2003 Web Edition
W2K3 Ent	Microsoft Windows Server 2003 Enterprise Edition
W2K3 DC	Microsoft Windows Server 2003 Data Center Edition

The choice of base operating system and specific version depends on its usage and the hardware it resides on. It is important to understand the various families, features, and versions of the operating system to ensure that the system requirements are met and that the architecture is scaleable, both horizontally and vertically. For example, Microsoft Windows Server 2003 Web Edition (at the time of this writing) supports up to a maximum of 2GB of RAM and a maximum of 2 CPUs. Therefore, scaling up (adding more memory and CPUs) is not possible beyond 2GB and 2 CPUs. However, web servers are load balanced, so they can be scaled out (by adding additional servers). You should also consider and document the licensing costs of the operating system to ensure that the architecture is cost effective and makes the best use of the operating system's licensing models.

The following sections provide an overview of the production architecture shown in Figure 5-1.

The Demilitarized Zone

Services that are provided to the outside world (usually the Internet) are generally placed in the Demilitarized Zone (DMZ). The purpose of the DMZ is to reduce the risk of attack to the back-end systems by placing it between two tiers of firewalls. The two firewalls are referred to as *front-end* and *back-end*, respectively. The servers and components in the DMZ can communicate with one another (although it's not advised), but they can't communicate directly with other servers and components on the internal networks. Limiting the level of communications between components in the DMZ will also limit the degree of attack penetration. Many companies specialize in offering penetration testing to see how far they can get through the system and what potential damage could be caused. These companies also provide invaluable advice on how to properly lock-down networks, servers, and components.

The most common services that are placed in the DMZ include the following:

❑ **Web servers** — Although the web servers are associated with the solution, they are typically placed in the DMZ. The web servers host the web pages and related items, such as configuration, web framework components, and so on. Because the web servers will need to communicate with the other servers in the solution, all traffic goes through the internal network's firewall. In some systems the web servers communicate with the database (via the firewalls), although again this is not advised. The web servers should really communicate with an application server, which acts as a bridge between the web server and the database. Although this is more complex, it adds an additional layer of security and protection.

❑ **E-mail servers** — As their name implies, e-mail servers are used to send, receive, and filter e-mail. The servers placed in the DMZ really should not be used to store e-mail; they act simply as a relay between the internal and external mail servers. In some systems they are even termed *e-mail relays*. The organization's internal e-mail servers would actually store and manage e-mail. The case study application, that is used in this book and discussed later, would need to send solicited e-mails to customers, so it's an important aspect to note on the production architecture diagram.

❑ **Proxy servers** — Proxy servers are typically used by organizations to monitor and control access to the Internet. They also offer the benefit of being able to cache certain content, such as images and static pages, thereby saving on bandwidth. Proxy servers can perform the same functions for both incoming and outgoing traffic. Images, pages, and content can be cached so that both incoming and outgoing requests can be served quicker.

As you can see from Figure 5-1, everything is "doubled up," including the network components, to provide high availability and fault tolerance. When designing the architecture, it's a good idea to document servers and components as either "new" or "existing." For example, you might be using existing e-mail servers, so the project wouldn't be purchasing any new hardware. This is a very important point to note. The existing servers (and services) would typically need to meet the requirements; if they do not, this would need to be fully understood and agreed to. Furthermore, it's well worth noting the operating system and components to ensure compatibility with the core application being implemented.

The Solution Architecture Hardware Components

In this hypothetical example, the solution architecture consists of a number of different servers and devices, which are briefly described here:

❑ **Web servers** — Multiple web servers are used to support performance, and to provide horizontal scalability and fault tolerance. The web servers (as discussed previously) are placed in the DMZ.

❑ **Application servers** — Application servers are placed on the internal network, where access can be restricted. Multiple application servers can be load balanced depending on the applications installed. The application servers host the application software components, which provide the core application functionality. The application components may manifest themselves as XML web services as well as traditional application components. The application components process the incoming requests and act as an interface between the web servers and the database.

❑ **Administration servers** — The administration servers are similar to the application servers in that they are typically connected to the internal network, they host application components, and web services, and they can be load balanced, clustered, or even both. Business users can connect to the administration servers to perform routine administrative tasks. The administration servers can also be used to host other processes and components of the system.

❑ **Reporting servers** — The reporting servers are usually load balanced and are used to execute reports against the database. I'll discuss reporting in more detail in Chapter 9. However, business (and some technical) reports are often executed against a replicated database to reduce the load and impact on the primary database servers.

❑ **Database servers** — The database servers are usually configured in an active/passive cluster to provide fault tolerance to the back-end data storage, which is typically a database stored on the storage area network (SAN).

The Operations Architecture Hardware Components

The operations architecture supports the solution architecture by providing vital monitoring, maintenance, and support management. The operations architecture, which is controlled and managed by the service delivery and operations team, is critical to the successful running and operation of the production solution, so it's important to capture and incorporate all the necessary operational aspects in the solution. Note that I've drawn each server "doubled up" to indicate that the operations architecture is also highly available and fault tolerant. There may be many other physical servers that form part of these operational groups.

The operations architecture comprises many components, as follows:

❑ **Backup servers and tape silos** — The backup servers manage and control the backup schedules. Servers that create only transient data are not usually backed up because they can be re-imaged by the deployment servers in the event of a failure. Specific batch processes may archive the logs, events, and any other information on the individual server to the storage area network (SAN). The backup solution is used to back up the databases and the SAN to offline storage, such as DVD or tape. The backup solution will typically back up to a disk array before going to tape to limit the impact of the backup to the online service. Tape backups are sometimes configured so that the primary site uses the secondary site's tapes, and vice versa. This cross-site backup strategy prevents you from having to send tapes offsite, although tapes are periodically sent offsite anyway for safety.

❑ **Monitoring servers** — The monitoring servers host the applications that provide all the environment monitoring capabilities. Monitoring is critical in a production environment to ensure that the system is functioning and performing correctly. The monitoring applications typically provide performance monitoring, end-to-end transaction monitoring, system monitoring (CPU and memory usage, and so on), network monitoring, and event monitoring.

Most monitoring packages support configuration and development of custom rules and packs to enhance the out-of-the-box monitoring capabilities.

❑ **Batch servers** — The batch servers run the batch scheduler and associated programs. The batch scheduler is responsible for executing and controlling the various batch schedules. Batch is an integral part of the operations architecture. The batch schedules contain custom jobs that perform routine maintenance tasks as well as other functional background processing that is not included in the Online Transaction Processing System (OLTP).

❑ **Deployment servers** — The deployment servers provide remote server deployment capabilities. Server images or installation scripts are remotely deployed to any server in the environment. The deployment software stores all the server configurations and images. It provides a user interface that can literally allow one-click deployment of an entire server installation from the ground up, not including the hardware, of course. Obviously, this sort of power needs to be carefully managed and secured. This approach to deployment has removed the need to backup servers individually using the backup solution because re-imaging is far faster than restoring backups. The deployment applications also support customization for the individual project's needs.

❑ **Database servers** — The database servers host the databases for the operations applications. The database servers are connected to the SAN and can be used to provide network shares on the SAN that can be used by other applications, if necessary.

❑ **Storage area network (SAN)** — The SAN is a high availability, highly fault-tolerant data storage system consisting of multiple mirrored disk arrays.

Many other applications and servers form part of the operations architecture. The ones shown in Figure 5-1 provide some background for the discussions later in this book.

The operations architecture depicted in Figure 5-1 highlights the key operations services that need to be included in a production-ready system. The number, size and scale, and configuration of the operations architecture depends entirely on the existing infrastructure and the system being deployed. The operations architecture (and requirements) should be captured, documented, and included in the estimates and scope. The vendor's documentation should provide deployment guidelines that can be used (and enhanced) to provide a robust, fault-tolerant, and scalable operations architecture. Although the physical operations architecture is not covered anywhere else in this book, service delivery and operations, monitoring, and batch are discussed in more detail in Chapters 7, 8, and 10, respectively.

The Hardware Topology

This section takes a look at the hardware architecture — specifically, the typical server configuration, high availability and fault-tolerant features, shared storage and the storage area network (SAN), and, finally, network segmentation.

Individual Server Configuration

In keeping with the fault-tolerant theme, every "enterprise-level" server usually has internal fault-tolerant and redundancy characteristics to provide a robust environment and to reduce single points of failure. These include:

- ❑ **Dual power supplies** — Protects against hardware failure in one of the power supplies.

- ❑ **Dual fans** — Protects against hardware failure in one of the cooling fans.

- ❑ **Dual network interface cards (NICs)** — Protects against hardware failure in one network card. Depending on the number of network connections required, the server will have dual network cards for each connection — one acting as the primary and the other acting as the backup. This is generally referred to as *teaming*.

- ❑ **Dual fiber cards** — This is usually required only for the database servers that are connected to the SAN or other fiber channel resources. Doubling up the network cards protects against a failure in one. However, four network cards and slots are required to support both dual NICs and dual fiber cards.

Fault tolerance is paramount in a production system; however, memory and local disk still remain problematic. These issues can cause an outage with an individual server, which may require you to replace it. Many vendors offer, and support, "hot-swappable" components, such as memory and PCI cards, which you can replace without having to take the server down or out of live service. The move toward non-stop commodity hardware is very much on its way.

Irrespective of the amount of internal redundancy and fault tolerance, servers can still fail and need to be taken out of service for routine maintenance and upgrades. Load balancing and clustering techniques can be used to maintain a level of service while maintenance activities are carried out. Performance degradation can also be caused by software and memory leaks. Regular re-boots, maintenance, optimization, and de-fragmentation can help to reduce the number of these issues and also improve performance.

The type, size, and number of servers will depend entirely on the system being implemented. Where horizontal scaling is implemented, additional servers are added as and when more server capacity is required. If third-party applications are being implemented, the vendor's documentation often contains deployment guidelines that can be used to determine the number of servers required. The deployment guidelines should be well-documented to ensure that future scalability options are fully understood. This information would usually be included within the Operations Manual.

Web Servers

The web servers are usually the lowest specification of all the server groups. Figure 5-1 shows these as having 2GB of RAM and two CPUs. This is actually the maximum for the operating system chosen in the example. The web servers are on the front line and they service the incoming client requests. The web servers host the website and related items. They are load-balanced to provide fault tolerance, and also for performance and scalability. When more capacity is required, more servers are added to the group. The amount of processing power required is generally minimal, as the web servers communicate with the application servers, which perform the heavier transaction processing. That said, web servers can be configured with larger amounts of memory depending on the size and number of websites being hosted and the information being cached in memory. The amount of memory and CPU included in a web server is also dependent on the operating system and whether it can support the additional memory and/or CPUs.

Application Servers

The application servers are part of the middle tier. These servers typically have more memory and CPU than the web servers, and there are usually fewer of them. The application servers isolate the web servers from direct access to the database, which adds an additional layer of processing as well as an additional layer of protection. Whether the middle tier servers support load balancing and horizontal scalability depends entirely on the applications being hosted. In a typical Web environment, the application servers host web services, which can be easily load balanced. The size and number of application servers is again dependent on the system being implemented.

Administration Servers

The administration servers shown in Figure 5-1 would typically host administrative pages and administrative functionality. Keeping this functionality off the front-end web servers can greatly reduce the vulnerability of the application. In some cases they can be somewhat of a hodgepodge, in that they could be used to host a variety of components required by the production system. To save space and money, applications often are co-hosted on the same server. In this example, I'm referring to these as *administration servers*, although they could be called anything at all. For example, the administration servers can also be referred to as *job servers*, *shared information servers*, or anything else. As the project progresses, there's normally a need to host a particular type of component that doesn't really fit into any of the other groups or categories. These components are generally hosted on the "best fit" server, which in most cases would be something like an administration server.

You can see from Figure 5-1 that I've indicated that the administration servers can be load-balanced and clustered, which is generally dictated by the nature of the components hosted. The requirements (and the design) will generally determine which servers will be required. However, including these types of servers up-front will provide a platform for administrative functionality, such as authentication, thick-client upgrade capabilities, shared storage access, FTP, and batch processing. These types of functions generally don't warrant separate server groups because of their timing and infrequent usage. For example, most housekeeping batch processes run out-of-hours, and software upgrades are not part of a daily routine. Which servers are required really depends on the nature of the solution. The servers required to host these functions are usually medium-sized and somewhere between the application servers and the database servers. The administration servers can provide shared storage capabilities, in which case they require access to the SAN, and accessing the SAN requires fiber-channel cards. If everything is being "doubled up," the servers will require at least four network slots — two for standard network connectivity and another two for fiber-channel access. In addition, the servers may also need another one or two slots for remote administrative access. This keeps the server administration activity separate from the main network traffic.

Database Servers

The database servers are usually the most powerful servers because they can't be scaled horizontally. Multiple databases and multiple database servers can provide additional performance and scalability, although ultimately a single database server is still processing requests on behalf of numerous clients. To this end, database servers are typically clustered in an active passive configuration to provide resilience. Because the database itself is typically stored on the SAN, the database servers both connect to the network and require fiber-channel connections to the SAN.

High Availability and Fault Tolerance

This section walks you through some of the high availability and fault-tolerant features of the production architecture, specifically load balancing and clustering.

Load Balancing

A *server farm* is a collection of servers that all perform the same functions. Having more than one server to perform the work improves performance, scalability, and availability. The server farm is resilient to one or more server failures. A *load balancer* is a physical hardware device used to spread requests between physical servers in a group.

The following list describes the information flow between the client and the server (see Figure 5-2).

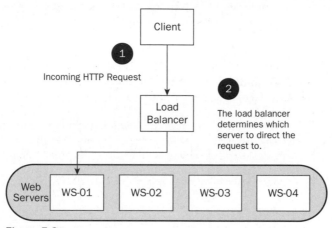

Figure 5-2

1. The client sends an incoming HTTP request, which hits the load balancer. The request can come from a web browser or any program that has the capability to send/receive HTTP requests and responses.

2. The load balancer determines which server to direct the request to, and forwards the request. There are various algorithms that a modern load balancer uses to determine which server to forward the request to, including:

    ❑   **Round robin** — Round robin is usually the default and most basic and popular of load-balancing algorithms. Each server is sent a request in-turn irrespective of its current load or number of connections. For example, assuming there are only three servers and four incoming requests, the load balancer sends the first request it receives to Server A, the second request to Server B, the third request to Server C, and then the forth request to Server A. Although this may not be the most sophisticated algorithm, it is widely used and serves its purpose very well, with each server getting the next request, especially when all servers are of the same or similar specification and all performing the same tasks.

    ❑   **Least number of connections** — This algorithm determines which server to forward the request to based on how many connections the load balancer has to each server. The server with the least amount of connections is forwarded the request. This can be thought of as sending the least busy server the request. However, this algorithm does not take into account CPU or memory usage; it simply works on the number of current connections from the load balancer to the server. A server could have only one connection but be working on a particularly heavy transaction and may not be the most appropriate server to deal with the request.

❏ **Weighted** — Weighting is a technique that can be employed to apply a weight to each server in the farm. The weight of each server determines the number of connections that will be forwarded to it. Servers with a higher weighting are forwarded a larger percentage of connections. This algorithm can be useful when the server specifications are not the same or similar. For instance, the application server farm might contain five servers, all of which are different in specification (e.g., number of CPUs and amount of memory). The higher specification servers can be given a higher weighting to receive more connections. In general, it is best to keep all servers in a group consistent.

❏ **Quickest response time** — The requests to and from the servers in the farm are recorded and aggregated. This algorithm forwards the request to the server that is currently considered to have the fastest or quickest response time.

❏ **Source IP address and/or destination IP address** — The source IP address is mapped to a specific server or range of servers in the farm. This algorithm is useful when servers are divided by clients — for example, when all requests from particular clients are forwarded to a specific server or range of servers. The destination IP address load-balancing algorithm works in a similar way by mapping the incoming request (based on its contents) to the specific destination IP address.

❏ **URL hashing** — All or part of the URL is mapped to a specific server or range of servers in the farm. This algorithm can be useful if the servers are divided into different functional areas. For example, all administration requests can be forwarded to administration servers, whereas all other requests can be directed to the standard web servers.

Most load balancers can also be configured for *sticky sessions* or persistence. In sticky sessions, all subsequent requests from a specific client are directed to the same server that was chosen for the original request. A sticky session generally is required if a process retains state that is used in subsequent requests. HTTP is a stateless protocol and all data is discarded after the request has been processed. No state is maintained between requests or even from the same client. Sticky sessions are often useful in Web-based applications to ensure that subsequent requests (from the same client) arrive at the same server. This makes managing state much easier. However, where required, the application should be tolerant to a server failure. Where it's not, the impact of a server failure should be fully documented and understood.

When a server fails, it is taken out of the list of available servers and not used in the load-balancing algorithm until it is deemed to be online. The load balancers use a number of different techniques to determine whether a server is alive or online. This usually involves sending a request to the specific server and determining whether a response is received. The request is retried a configurable number of times before the server is deemed to be out of service. The time taken to determine a server is unavailable and the time taken to determine a server is back online needs to be taken into account in the technical characteristics and technical testing.

As shown in Figure 5-3, to achieve high availability, two load balancers are often used and configured to remove any single points of failure (SPOF). A hot-standby is configured to take over when the live or primary load balancer fails.

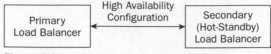

Figure 5-3

Although load balancing is performed primarily at the network level, it's important to understand the basic concepts in order to develop software and systems that support load balancing for performance and scalability. It's also important to understand the characteristics of the load-balancing technology to increase the effectiveness of performance testing. Modeling the requests and responses end-to-end will help to uncover more design considerations and test conditions. The following are some important concerns:

❏ **How long does it take to determine whether a server is up or down?** It is important to test this condition and obtain a real-world figure rather than going according to a manufacturer's documentation. Although this can be used as a starting point, it invariably relies on other performance configuration settings and profiles.

❏ **How long does it take to fail-over from the primary load balancer to the secondary load balancer?** This figure may be different from the one above and should be considered during performance and technical testing.

❏ **What happens to connections that are already established when the server or load balancer fails?** In almost all cases, the connections will be lost and the client will need to re-establish a connection with another server. When the solution is truly stateless, this is unnoticeable by the user. When he or she clicks a link or a button, a new HTTP request is sent to the load balancer, which will be directed to a different web server and processed.

❏ **What happens to the transactions that were in-flight or completed in the event of a failure?** This is probably the most concerning question and opens the discussion on state management, transaction control, and transaction boundaries. In the majority of cases, a server failure results in an error message being presented to the user. As for what happens next, it is highly dependent on what the transaction was and when the failure occurred. These types of failures should be modeled in order to flesh out more design considerations and test conditions.

It's important to understand and be prepared for these scenarios, even though they are exceptions to the rule. Monitoring the network and servers will give an indication of what has happened prior to any further calls from clients and users.

A single load balancer (irrespective of high availability configuration) can manage multiple groups of servers or farms, although there is a finite capacity. This is useful because it enables you to re-use existing hardware, assuming it's available and has sufficient capacity. Figure 5-4 shows a single load balancer forwarding requests to two server groups.

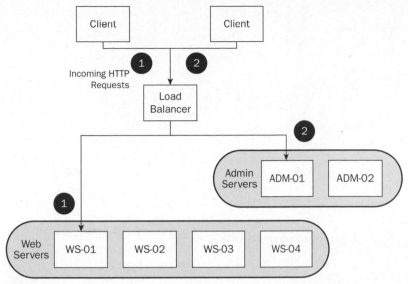

Figure 5-4

There are other practical approaches to distributing HTTP requests that do not require specific hardware devices, including Network Load Balancing (NLB) and DNS load balancing, although these are not discussed in this book. It is important to understand and agree on the "load balancing" architecture, as it can impact further design decisions.

The low-level network and infrastructure components are often expensive and have a finite capacity. If new hardware isn't included in the budget, it is wise to ensure that the existing hardware has the required capacity for the proposed architecture and growth; otherwise, it could be a rather expensive business to buy more hardware. Similarly, when purchasing new hardware, it's advisable to ensure that its capacity meets the needs of the architecture and growth.

High Availability Cluster

A cluster is a group of servers that appear as a single server. Each server in the cluster is referred to as a *node*. Clusters are used to improve performance and reliability that would otherwise not be available through the use of a single machine. The most typical cluster implementation is a high availability (HA) cluster. An HA cluster comprises two nodes — one active and one passive. The active node performs all the processing, and the passive node acts as a hot-standby in the event of a failure in the primary node and, under normal circumstances, does not perform any processing. An HA cluster reduces single points of failure within the architecture. In the architecture presented in Figure 5-1, the database servers are clustered, which is a very typical use of an HA cluster, shown again in Figure 5-5.

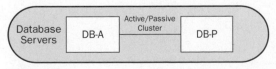

Figure 5-5

The clustering software manages the nodes in the cluster and determines whether a node is available. If the node is not available, the cluster controller will failover to the passive node. The cluster manager is hosted on the nodes in the group, rather than being separate. The nodes communicate with each other and share state information to determine which server is the active node.

The difference between load balancing and HA or failover clustering is that only one server is doing the work in an HA cluster, whereas in a load balanced group all the servers are performing work. As only one server is performing the work in an HA cluster, the servers are generally vertically scaled, in that they have more memory and more processors to cope with the workload.

When very large numbers of transactions are being processed, often a single database is not sufficient. Multiple databases are deployed to reduce the amount of work being carried out by each cluster. It is worth bearing this in mind during design and separating the databases where it makes most sense. That way, if multiple databases are required, it should be a deployment and configuration exercise rather than a coding exercise.

Furthermore, it is not just the database servers that are clustered, although this is the most typical usage given the nature of databases and data stores. Applications that are not web-based are typically clustered. For example, the operations architecture has many HA clustered applications, such as the batch job controller and monitoring servers.

It is important to understand the characteristics of the applications being deployed and whether they need to be clustered, load balanced, or both. Figure 5-1 shows the administration servers being both load balanced and clustered. The system requirements of these applications can also affect where components are hosted. In addition, when developing software, you should take into account whether the software needs to support clustering.

As with load balancing, an HA cluster has similar concerns with respect to failover and recovery:

❑　How long does it take to determine if a server is up/down?

❑　How long does it take to failover from the primary server to the secondary server?

❑　What happens to connections that are already established when the server or load balancer fails? The connections are almost always lost and need to be re-established.

❑　What happens to the transactions that were in-flight or completed in the event of a failure? This should be transparent at the database layer. Assuming the application also has some fault tolerance built in, such as reconnect and retry logic, subsequent database transactions will be directed to the promoted live node, which is looking at the same database.

There are other clustering techniques that can be used to provide fault tolerance, such as majority node set clusters (not discussed in this book). Again, it's important to understand the clustering approach, as this may also affect further decisions and choices. Many third-party applications don't support clustering.

Dual- or Multi-Site Configuration

As shown in Figure 5-1, dual-site or even multi-site environments are used to provide a highly resilient and fault-tolerant production architecture. Most medium- to large-scale companies have a secondary data center (SDC) or disaster recovery (DR) site that is in a completely different location and acts as a backup should the primary site become unavailable. In most circumstances, the DR environment is an exact mirror of the architecture at the primary site. If the disaster recovery site is not an exact mirror, not all the quality characteristics will be met, which should be noted and understood. Data centers and dual-site environments are discussed later in this chapter.

Using a Shared Storage Area

A shared storage area can be used for anything that is not stored in the database. For example, it could be used to store documents, pictures, and binaries for instance. The shared storage area is typically located on the SAN, which means it is generally easier to integrate it within the backup strategy. It is also typically exposed to the other servers in the solution via network shares.

To provide a shared storage capability, assume your administration servers expose a "network share" that the other servers could use to place items on the SAN. Given that only one of the servers can expose this share at any one point, the administration server group is clustered in order to remove this as a single point of failure (see Figure 5-6).

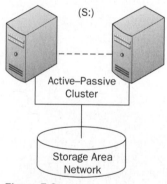

Figure 5-6

Furthermore, it's possible that the passive server could also be used to expose a different network share (if required). For example, you could place all documents on the S: drive and all binaries on the T: drive. This would spread the load between both servers; if either server failed, the other would take over and expose both network shares. Figure 5-7 shows a primary server failure. It would impact performance and capacity, of course, but the system would remain up and running.

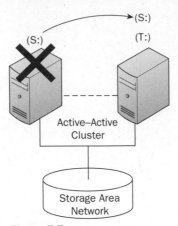

Figure 5-7

This configuration is usually termed "active-active" because each server is providing "live" services. It's a good idea to look at areas where an otherwise truly "passive" server can be used to make use of all the available hardware in the estate. It depends on the circumstances, but the benefits and drawbacks need to be clearly noted. For example, when a server fails, the single server will be performing both tasks. Both tasks running on the same server would need to be tested for performance as well as the individual failover scenarios.

The major benefit of a shared storage area is recoverability. If all dynamic content that is not stored in the database is stored in a shared storage area, when a server completely fails, it should be possible to rebuild it from the ground up without requiring the restoration of a backup. A new server can be built and all the components and static content are deployed to it. There should be nothing on the server that needs to be backed up individually via the formal backup strategy. Anything on the server, such as log files, event logs, and other locally generated matter, can be copied to the shared storage area via batch processes (if required), where it can be included in the formal backup process at regular intervals.

You must consider shared storage requirements early on to ensure that they're incorporated in the design (where necessary). Shared storage can greatly simplify other areas of the overall solution design. For example, batch processes often are required to generate files from database content, which requires transfer or collection to or from other systems. Batch is discussed later, but I'll use this job as an example for promoting shared storage capabilities. You could have a single job that performs both operations mentioned (it generates the file and then FTPs it somewhere). If the job failed during the FTP stage and was restarted, it would either have to have check-pointing logic so that it didn't go through the whole business of regenerating the file, or it would, in fact, regenerate the entire file. It would be better (and simpler) to have two separate jobs — one to generate the file and one to transfer it. If the generate job stored the file on local disk, then the transfer job would need to run on the same machine to pick it up. This is not often supported by batch schedulers, so the transfer job more often than not runs on a different server. When it fails to transfer the files, it's typically re-run and again it could execute on a different server. In this situation, it is better for the files to be generated locally to take advantage of local disk speed and then move the files to the shared storage area, which provides a single point of access. This actually helps to improve the design of the batch components and makes them much easier to maintain and support. It doesn't matter which server the jobs are executed on because the share will be available to all servers. The shared storage area is highly fault tolerant, so it's almost guaranteed that the file(s) will be there and ready to transfer elsewhere. Furthermore, because the SAN is replicated between sites and backed up, the files would also be available in the event of a disaster.

I'll discuss the reporting and analytics solutions in Chapter 9. However, web analytics solutions often require access to the web server logs, which could be regularly transferred to the shared storage area for analysis and backup. This again simplifies the overall solution and improves recoverability.

Network Segmentation

Network segments are used to improve performance by reducing the amount of network traffic within a single collision domain. A collision domain is simply an area of the network where data packets can collide. Collisions cause network inefficiency whereby each device needs to retransmit the data following a collision. This is a precise example of where the wait-retry pattern is implemented. When packets collide, the network components wait for a configured amount of time and then retransmit the data. Network segmentation reduces the number of servers and devices per network segment thus reducing the number of potential collisions. Network segments can also provide increased security within a specific domain.

Clustered servers are often included in their own segment to improve the performance of communication between them and thus improve up/down detection time. This is also true of the load-balanced groups and the load balancers themselves.

Switches (or other network components) can be used to connect multiple network segments, as shown in Figure 5-8.

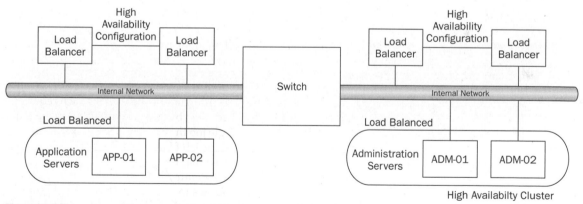

Figure 5-8

The figure shows a simplified example of two application servers on their own network segment along with a set of high availability load balancers, as well as two administration servers and a set of high availability load balancers on their own network segment. A network switch is used to connect the two network segments together to allow cross-segment communication, although other network components might be used instead, such as a router or hub.

Network segmentation is designed and performed by networking experts and specialists, although it is useful to understand the basic concept. The performance of the production system will be improved by low-level networking implementations that are not generally implemented in test environments except where it may prove critical because of load.

The Software Topology

The software topology maps the applications and components from the solution onto the hardware topology. The idea is to get as much information as possible regarding the software components themselves, where they will be hosted, and their baseline configuration. The software topology has the following benefits:

- ❏ It defines the applications and components that are going to be used and their baseline configuration.

- ❏ It feeds into the installation and deployment process by highlighting the different components, layers, and servers.

- ❏ It feeds into the development, test, and other environments used throughout the project.

- ❏ It assists with identifying key batch, maintenance, and operational aspects of the system.

- ❏ It identifies key security considerations and communications between the software applications.

The software topology covers all the applications and can be grouped into the following:

- ❏ Base operating system (including specific service packs, security patches, and hot fixes)

- ❏ Runtime and framework components (including specific service packs, security patches, and hot fixes)

- ❏ Third-party applications

- ❏ Custom applications and components

The simplest way to start building up the software topology is to list out the applications at a high level using the preceding groups. Most of the high-level information should be available from the requirements and the technology constraints. A typical starting list would look something like the following for this book's case study application:

- ❏ Base operating system

  - ❏ Microsoft Windows Server 2003

- ❏ Runtime and framework components

- ❏ Microsoft Internet Information Services
- ❏ Microsoft .NET Framework
- ❏ Microsoft SQL Server
- ❏ Microsoft Exchange
- ❏ Third-party applications and components
  - ❏ Batch agents
  - ❏ Deployment agents
  - ❏ Monitoring and operational agents
- ❏ Custom applications and components

  - ❏ ASP pages
  - ❏ Application components
  - ❏ Architecture or framework components
  - ❏ Batch components
  - ❏ Reporting components

The preceding list contains some sample third-party applications and components, which will be discussed briefly, later. If you've done your homework on all these products and applications, it should be a lot easier to define the software topology. To take the list to the next level of detail, you must ask the following questions:

- ❏ Which version?
- ❏ Which service packs, security patches, hot fixes, or other extensions?
- ❏ Do any of these cause any issues regarding requirements and constraints?
- ❏ Can all of them be co-hosted?
- ❏ Is anything missing?

The answers to these questions may already be documented or available, but the important message is to try and answer them as early as possible. Although this section focuses on the production architecture, this information applies equally to the development, test, and operational environments. For example, if you were to look quickly at the third-party applications for the development environment, you could draw out the following:

- ❏ Development environment
- ❏ Unit-testing tools
- ❏ Code-coverage tools
- ❏ Documentation-generation tools

Each server group should be documented with as much detail as possible. The starting point for the baseline installation and configuration is taken from the vendor documentation, which is then complemented with the system-specific configuration.

The hardware and software topologies are very closely related. As mentioned previously, some applications dictate the required hardware topology. For example, the vendor's documentation will almost certainly recommend a specific hardware (and software) configuration which helps to answer the third question in the preceding list. Furthermore, the vendor's documentation might stipulate that clustering is not supported. In this instance, you would need to understand what other resilience characteristics the software offered in order to meet the requirements. You should read the vendor's documentation thoroughly and draw out all the system and deployment requirements so that you can map them to the software topology correctly. Gathering all the various hardware and software requirements, you can start to draw up a list of components or applications that could potentially be co-hosted, which helps to answer the fourth question, although co-hosting would need to be thoroughly assessed.

There are many tools to lock down environments for security purposes. These tools could lock down account privileges and access rights, specific internal configuration, and anything else. Running these tools after the site has been deployed is too late and could cause horrendous issues. Furthermore, running these tools in the technical test environment is also quite late. Something fundamental could be highlighted, which could mean re-factoring components and going back to build. This is just an example of why these types of tools should be considered early, executed early, and used in all environments to avoid issues later in the lifecycle. It is very important that you understand and document these additional requirements to ensure that every environment is using a near-production configuration. In general, only the environment-specific values should differ between environments, although this is sometimes not possible because of cost and budget constraints. Where it's not possible, the differences (and impacts) should be noted and understood.

I encouraged you earlier to ask the question "Is anything missing?" For example, is antivirus (AV) software deployed to the production environment? AV software often causes issues, especially when file checking is enabled. Every time a file is created or written to, the AV software scans it. Most applications create log files, so performance could be seriously impacted when AV software is deployed and running in the production environment. You should carefully consider when, and if, AV software is going to be executed. In some cases, AV software in a production environment is executed at strictly periodic intervals (via an ad-hoc batch schedule), which are outside of normal operational hours. The rationale for this is that all the servers should be locked down and behind the firewall, so an attack would have to come from within the organization. Having said that, some organizations enforce AV software scans, so it's worth making sure you understand the frequency, timing, and configuration. You can address this by canvassing the operations team and understanding their requirements and existing configurations.

Another troublesome piece of software is "automatic updates." Although it's great to have a home computer up-to-date, it's not so good in a production environment. For example, imagine if a new security patch were deployed to the production environment overnight. There's no telling the impact it could have on the production system. It really is worth capturing as much information as possible about what should and shouldn't be running in the production environment and ensuring that everything is understood clearly. Although this not in the realm of development, it's certainly in the realm of architecture. A new version of a runtime engine would need to be fully regression tested prior to its deployment, irrespective of the manufacturer's "100 percent backward compatible" statements.

Licenses will be required for all purchased applications, and understanding the vendor's licensing model will help you to plan the software architecture. Development shouldn't really start on an evaluation license unless it's absolutely necessary. There's the danger that products could be deployed to the production environment on an evaluation license, which would cause major issues when the license expires. All licenses and expiries should be fully documented along with the procedures for obtaining new licenses.

Knowing which components reside on which servers and how they are hosted also provides valuable input into the batch design, maintenance activities, and operability criteria. This includes the services and processes that need to be monitored, the services that need to be started and stopped, and the logs and files that need to be cleared out. The software topology should describe in detail the components, their specific configuration, and configuration requirements, as well as any other useful information. Reiterating what I mentioned in the hardware topology section, the production environment should be locked down completely and only the features that are absolutely necessary should be enabled. The software topology needs to stipulate what these features are, why they are necessary, and how they are used.

Figure 5-9 shows a high-level outline for a web server's software topology diagram.

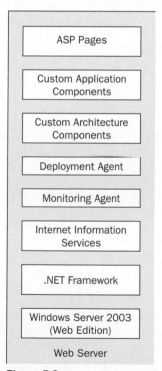

Figure 5-9

The high-level outline should be expanded into further detail that describes the configuration of each application in question. For example, the IIS configuration would need to state the proposed websites, applications, virtual directories, application pools, and the identities that each of these would execute under. You won't know all the information at this time, however, so you will have to define some of it later. At a high level, the diagram should show the components that will reside on the server, as well as describe the third-party agents. Third-party applications often use the master-agent architecture, which is described later. Finally, the custom components need to be described. In this case, there will be custom architecture components that provide common services to ASP pages. If you were so inclined, you could produce a software topology for the case study application used in this book and map all the components to the individual servers.

Figure 5-10 shows an example of an expanded version of the software topology. In this example, the figure shows the exact versions and service packs that would be installed. It shows some of the high-level component types (and groups) that would be installed, as well as some of the additional placeholders, such as the websites, virtual directories, application pools, and identities for IIS. As the project progresses and more detailed information is available, the diagram (and documentation) would become even more informative and include the specific websites, virtual directories, application pools, and identities that would be configured, as well as the components that would be installed and configured. The diagram simply evolves as the project progresses, becoming more and more detailed.

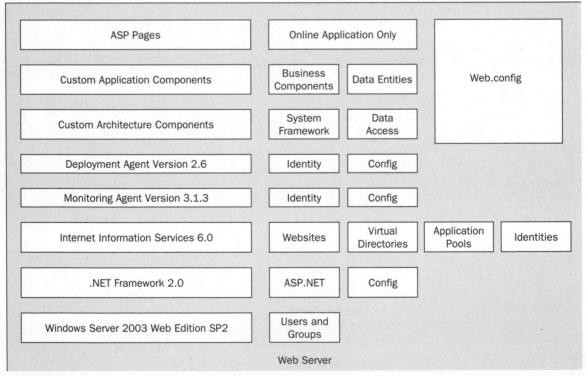

Figure 5-10

All the information in the software topology feeds into the deployment process. As illustrated in Figure 5-1, there could be lots of servers in the production environment that would need to be included in the software topology. Each server type (or group) would show the components that would be installed and configured on them. The software topology helps to design the software packaging structure so that not everything is included in a single library; otherwise, everything would be installed on every server. Breaking the components into discrete libraries enables you to deploy them to only the servers that require them.

The software topology also provides the foundation for the security architecture. By listing all the applications, you can start to determine the identities they will run as. This information is used to lock down the environment. Local System account or administrator accounts should not really be used in the production environments, so specific application domains and users should also be taken into account in development and test environments. This helps to ensure that the application is developed in the same way that it will execute in production. It also avoids late-breaking issues with security and access.

In addition to the components that reside on the server side of the architecture, the client side also features heavily in the software topology and includes the following groups of software:

❑ Supported client browsers (such as Internet Explorer and Safari) and specific versions (such as IE 6, IE 7, and so forth.)

❑ Documentation viewers (such as Office and PDF files)

❑ Flash, Silverlight and so forth.

There may also be internal clients that need to have specific software installed, such as performance-monitoring software for capturing true end-to-end latency figures.

Master-Agent Architecture

Figure 5-10 showed a sample web server software topology that included a "Deployment Agent" and a "Monitoring Agent." A number of third-party applications are implemented using the master-agent architecture. The master application resides on a server, and its agents are deployed to the individual servers that they need to reside on. The master sends commands to the agent, and the agent actions these commands, as shown in Figure 5-11.

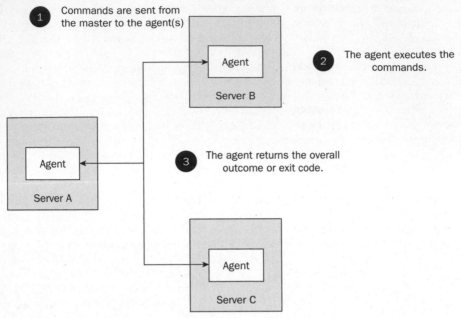

Figure 5-11

The agents can perform any processing on behalf of the master and return whatever they need to. In many cases, the master is responsible for monitoring the agent, although in practice it is worth including the agent within the monitoring solution to be doubly sure it's up and running. A lot of operations software uses the master-agent architecture. Agents typically manifest themselves as services or background tasks. It's important to identify what applications will require an agent to be installed on a server as this will need to be incorporated in the software topology diagram. Furthermore the identity (for example, the security context under which the agent will run) will also need to be determined to ensure that the appropriate access rights and privileges are granted. It is also important to understand the high availability capabilities of the agents and whether they support clustering and failure, automatic recovery, and so on.

An increasing number of vendors are producing agent-less software that makes use of technologies such as Window Management Instrumentation (WMI). This subject is somewhat of a misnomer because the vendor's software is actually making use of an agent, in this case the WMI service agent, to perform commands on its behalf. The WMI agent would still need to be installed and configured on the relevant servers. However, the WMI agent can service commands from many applications, which avoids specific vendor or application agents to be deployed to the servers. If an application was using the WMI service agent, this would be noted on the software topology diagram.

The Primary and Secondary Data Centers

A data center is a highly fault-tolerant facility where an organization houses all its servers, networking components, and infrastructure. It has redundant power supplies and power sources, as well as redundant communications equipment. The facility uses air conditioning to keep the equipment at an optimum temperature. Data centers are totally secure and have strict security policies regarding anyone entering. Under normal circumstances, only operations staff is permitted entry. In addition, as you might expect, data centers contain special fire and emergency control equipment.

Data centers are critical to the organization. Because mission-critical systems are used to run the business, assist in the decision-making process, and form the basis of growth and revenue generation, a failure in the data center could be disastrous. Therefore, most organizations have two data centers — a primary data center (PDC) and a secondary data center (SDC), which in some cases is also referred to as the disaster recovery (DR) site or the alternative site.

Data centers can be of any size — a single room, multiple rooms, a floor, multiple floors, or an entire building. They are very carefully designed and constructed, with detailed standards, guidelines, and regulations. The floor is often raised to allow for better air flow and room for cabling. A raised floor can also alleviate interference caused by ground movement, and it's typically covered with specially perforated tiles that reduce static.

The servers are stored in racks, cabinets, or cages. Cabinets and other low-level infrastructure components that provide routing, switching, SAN, and fiber-channel access are also highly available and fault tolerant. A common technique to protect against a single cabinet failure, which would render all servers in the enclosure out of service, is to separate components between cabinets. This is possible because of the multi-server nature of the production environment. The cabinets would be connected to different electrical circuits. In some cases, the cabinets are at opposite ends of the server room or even in different rooms, depending on the requirements, to provide further protection against cabinet failure. Figure 5-12 shows a hypothetical separation.

Although Figure 5-12 shows only the core architecture servers, the other network and infrastructure components would also be separated for fault tolerance.

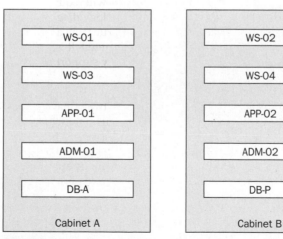

Figure 5-12

The racks are placed in rows that allow access to both the front and the back of the cabinet. The racks are standard 19-inch width, as is the equipment housed in them. The equipment height is specified in "rack units." A single rack unit is 1.75 inches in height, although the equipment is generally slightly smaller to leave a gap between components, making them easier to install and remove. Each rack typically houses 42 rack units (written as 42U).

In addition to housing the power and communication equipment, each rack or group of racks houses a slim-line pull-out pop-up monitor. Traditionally, software was installed on the servers manually. This is still the case in some situations, although access to the servers can be achieved via Remote Desktop software and packages that can be installed using application deployment tools without ever having to see the server. Access to the servers is still very tightly controlled even via remote desktops and is again usually reserved for operations staff once the system is live. There's often a need to reboot or shutdown the server from the machine itself.

Figure 5-13, courtesy of Wikipedia, shows a very typical server rack with pop-up monitor.

Figure 5-13

Not counting infrastructure and networking components, Figure 5-1 showed ten solution architecture servers. If each server is 1U, almost a quarter of a rack is already taken up, although the servers could be separated across different racks. This is important because in most data centers rack space is at a premium. If the space is not available, it can take a long time to install new cabinets, wiring, and other components, not to mention the additional costs. All this can have a dramatic impact on the budget and schedule. So, it's a good idea to have an understanding of the environments and the total amount of equipment required by the project.

To alleviate the need for multiple servers, a virtual server could be used. A virtual server allows multiple operating systems and applications to be installed on it. Essentially, a single server acts as multiple servers that can be assessed for development and test environments. The use of virtual servers should be carefully considered because it is not without its own challenges.

The Primary Data Center

The PDC houses all the primary production equipment. The PDC can also be used to host all the development and test equipment. Many companies choose to house development and test kit (hardware) in the PDC to control access and reduce security risks. Developers and testers access the servers through remote desktops to conduct their work. This is increasingly true with the advent of offshore development. It is therefore paramount to ensure that stable, fault-tolerant, and speedy communications are in place to avoid unnecessary delays and downtime. The larger test phases will most definitely have dedicated environments in the PDC.

The Secondary Data Center

The SDC houses the disaster-recovery equipment. The disaster-recovery environment is typically an exact mirror of the primary production environment. In cases where the applications are not mission critical, the disaster-recovery environment can be scaled down to reduce costs, but this also reduces its performance and capacity. This is not necessarily an issue because there will probably be greater things to worry about in the event of a disaster, although all critical systems will need to be cut-over to the secondary data center and maintained in the event of a complete failure at the primary site. The key technical requirements should stipulate the cut-over time and data loss tolerances — for example, in the event of a major disaster, the full system must be recoverable to a disaster recovery site within a target time of 2 hours with no more than 10 minutes data loss. This requirement represents that of an active-passive configuration in that the DR site is essentially a hot standby. A fully mission-critical system would not normally be able to tolerate such an outage and so would normally be configured in an active-active configuration.

The following sections look at the different data center configurations.

Active-Passive Primary and Secondary

In an active-passive configuration, the SDC houses a dormant version of the entire production environment. The servers are in a hot standby mode, in that core services are running on the servers but not actually performing any operations until they are cut-over from the primary site.

To meet the disaster-recovery requirements, all required data needs to be replicated between the two sites. You can probably see why I mentioned previously that you should keep all necessary files and information on the SAN. The SAN is highly fault tolerant and is typically replicated between sites. SAN replication typically makes use of dedicated bandwidth on the WAN between the two sites. This avoids the impact to local area traffic.

The databases also need to be replicated between sites. In an active-passive scenario, the passive database can either be a complete copy or a subset of the primary, as shown in Figure 5-14.

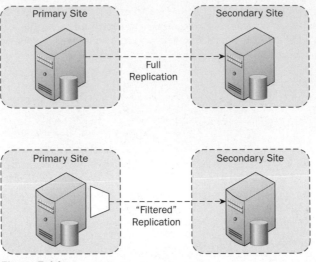

Figure 5-14

Most database systems support replication features to keep databases and tables in-sync. These cover a wide variety of options, so it's well worth understanding the features and benefits of each replication scenario. Where replication features are not used, the passive database will probably need to be restored from the last consistent backup, and "redo" logs will need to be applied for all "new" transactions. Reducing the amount of manual effort and time it takes to failover should be considered carefully.

It's also important to consider environment-specific values that are stored in the database. For example, a table that contains server names, IP addresses, or port numbers most likely needs records for each environment (such as production, disaster recovery, and so on) If the table simply contains a single value for the "current" environment, this would need to be changed during replication or not included as part of the replication strategy. This is shown in Figure 5-15.

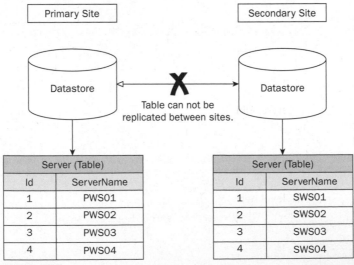

Figure 5-15

The figure shows that a single table is used to store server names. The table might be used by a batch process to gather logs from each of the servers and store them in the shared storage area. The server table shown can't be replicated across sites, as the record values are actually different, which stands to reason given that the server names are going to be different across sites and environments. However, if the table is extended to include an environment identifier, the table could be replicated back and forth without issue. This is shown in Figure 5-16.

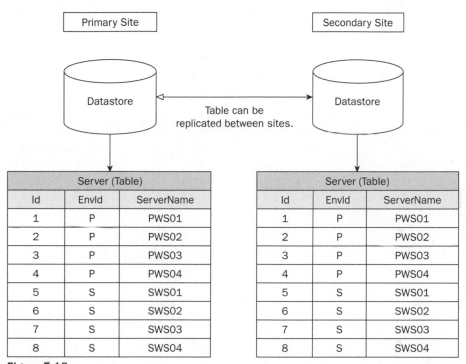

Figure 5-16

The table contains all the records for the specific environments (in this case, the primary site and the secondary site), and is not impacted by the replication strategy. It also means that a backup of the database table could be restored in either environment without requiring any post-restoration procedures. However, this does mean that any processes that use the records in this table would need to be configured to select only records for a particular environment (or environments.)

Restoring a database can be very troublesome. Time has passed since the backup was taken, and it's possible that some sequence numbers and other identification data need to be updated before the database can be brought fully online. It's well worth noting in the application if there are any specific procedures required when a database restore needs to be performed, such as incrementing sequence numbers and so forth.

In the event of a disaster, low-level networking components will typically need to be reconfigured to route all requests to the secondary site instead of the primary site. Although the SAN is shared between sites, each site is configured to point at a specific location. Low-level configuration is often required to switch to the production site replica. Additionally, the application may need to be reconfigured, which might involve running or executing scripts that update any environment-specific information in the database and configuration files with the correct information. Typical examples of this are again updating server names and IP addresses. It is important to try to limit the amount of environment-specific information in the database and configuration files to reduce the re-configuration overhead. Where a subset of the database can be replicated, it will ensure that only "transactional" tables are actually replicated. This reduces the overhead of re-configuration. If re-configuration is required, application services may also require restarting to bring the environment into a ready for action state.

A disaster poses interesting questions around data loss. For example, if the user were right in the middle of completing an order, what state will that order be in when the DR site is invoked? It could be completely lost. Does this matter? There will be business procedures in place that will deal with announcements surrounding disasters. However, it is important to take these considerations into account when designing and implementing the application. A lot can happen in 10 minutes using the preceding example. So, the cut-over scripts also need to deal with the subtleties of orphaned or incomplete transactions and sessions. For example, let's say there's a flag in the database indicating the user is logged on. Let's assume for the moment that this is to protect against the same user logging on again. In the event of a disaster or even a regular connection failure, this flag would need to be reset before the user could log on again. Where possible, the application itself should be capable of dealing with these exception scenarios, limiting the amount of manual intervention required. Furthermore, these kinds of considerations may result in design changes to avoid the situation completely, which is another reason for thinking about them up front.

Take a step back and think about what would need to be done in a disaster at various stages in the application and see how this maps to the design. Play the "what-if" game. If it is unavoidable, it needs to be included in the disaster recovery procedures. Of course, you also need to ensure the procedures meet the disaster recovery requirements.

An active-passive configuration is usually easier to manage, although the disaster recovery steps need to be clearly documented and the actions and scripts need to be executed in a very strict order. Opening the front door before the backend is ready can cause major problems. Disaster recovery batch schedules are often put in place to manage the automation along with the manual tasks to provide this level of sequencing.

Technical and/or acceptance testing will need also to exercise the disaster recovery procedures, usually over a weekend, to ensure that everything works according to plan. It will generally involve a few iterations to get it right and update the necessary steps and scripts. It's worth bearing in mind that even if the disaster recovery plans and timings for your application can meet their own target Service Level Agreements (SLAs), it's not necessarily the "total time to recover." For example, if the entire data center were lost, every single (critical) application would need to be failed over to the secondary site. This is a much larger planning exercise and normally comes down to application priority and staffing issues. Wherever possible, you should look for ways to reduce the manual effort and the time it takes to fail over to the secondary site.

It's also very important to remember that once the site or application has been failed over to the secondary site, it will need to be brought back to the primary site at some point. Figure 5-1 indicated this by showing a "non-filled" arrowhead between the secondary site and the primary site on SAN replication.

Active-Active Primary and Secondary

In an active-active configuration, the SDC houses a fully live environment that is also processing requests. This poses some interesting challenges, not only in the event of a disaster at either site but also during normal running.

During normal running, the application is updating a particular site's database. With both sites running, a replication architecture doesn't really work. As such, all transactional data needs to be stored in both databases. This often involves distributed transactions across the WAN. If storing items in the database can be taken off the critical processing path, database updates don't affect the core transaction processing and latency.

In the event of a disaster, the secondary site continues running. An active-active configuration doesn't alleviate the need for any cut-over activities. Low-level cut-over activities will still need to be performed and scripts will still need to be executed to deal with in-flight transactions and sessions along with any other updates. In an active-active configuration, the same rules apply to environment specific values such as server names, IP addresses and ports, and so on.

An active-active configuration typically doubles the capacity of the system, allowing almost twice as many users and transactions. In the event of a disaster, the capacity would be reduced. In an active-passive configuration, a lot of very costly equipment is doing pretty much nothing, whereas in an active-active configuration, all the equipment is being used. By halving the number of servers at each site, you reach the same capacity as a single site.

The biggest question is this: What is the likelihood or probability of a disaster? It is usually very rare, so an active-active configuration gives you the comfort factor of knowing there are dual sites and both are operating at full capacity. In the rare event of a disaster, the capacity will be reduced but not lost altogether, as it would if only a single site were used. In this scenario, you should have plans in place (where appropriate) to procure and install more equipment to lessen the overall period of reduced performance and capacity.

Although a disaster is rare, it is important to ensure that the steps to recover are in place and tested. As the application changes, the DR procedures may also need to be updated and re-proven.

Summary

The production environment is the most critical environment of all (once the system is actually in live service). It is sized and scaled to meet the requirements and it includes many fault-tolerant and high availability features. The operations architecture is in place to support the production environment and ensure that it is up and running and kept in good working order.

This chapter looked at some of the servers and what they typically perform, as well as how each server provides fault-tolerant internal components.

The following are the key points to take away from this chapter:

❑ **Understand the production environment.** The production environment is critical and it is important to understand it thoroughly. Each application will have its own requirements for fault tolerance and deployment. It is important that the production environment be sized and scaled appropriately and you should consider the following when defining the production architecture and enviroment:

    ❑ **Date and time synchronization** — When the date and time differ from server to server, it's difficult to piece together a real timeline, as the date and times could be different across the estate.

❏ **Third-party components** — You should understand whether agents will need to be deployed to the servers and whether they can support the necessary high availability features.

❏ **Application deployment** — The application components need to be packaged such that they can be easily deployed around the environment.

❏ **Monitoring and operations** — You need to monitor and operate each component. Listing out the components and services, along with their operational characteristics, will help to define the operability criteria and the batch schedule.

❏ **Production configuration** — You must understand and document how the system is configured among all the different applications and document the identities that are being used for each of them.

❏ **Have no single point of failure.** Where possible, the production environment should have no single point of failure. If there are areas of concern, these should be noted and discussed. The high-level, fault-tolerant features discussed included:

❏ Load balancing (round robin, least number, weighted, quickest response, and so on)

❏ Clustering (active-passive and active-active)

❏ Database replication

It's important to note the failover timings and understand the implications of any established connections. It is also important to have all the right procedures in place for failover. The load balancers can provide *sticky sessions,* which can be useful; however, if you lose the web server they're connected to, you need to understand and potentially support this. Where possible, the application should be stateless and tolerate switching between servers.

❏ **Test failover procedures.** It is important that you test all failover procedures fully. Scripts and tools need to be developed to support failover to the disaster recovery site and vice versa.

❏ **Develop and test on a near-production configuration.** Wherever possible, development and testing should be performed on a near-production configuration. You should try to limit the number of environment-specific values, such as server names, IP addresses, and port numbers, if they are not all included in the same database. This helps to turn around environments quickly.

❏ **Rack space is at a premium.** It is important to ensure that there is available space and capacity in the center, as well as in shared infrastructure components. In addition, where possible, split servers across racks to increase fault tolerance.

❏ **Understand the disaster-recovery configuration.** The disaster-recovery configuration affects how you design your solution, so you need to understand the replication and backup implications of the architecture. The configurations discussed included:

❏ Active-passive, primary-secondary

❏ Active-active, primary-secondary

6

Activities and Environments

This chapter takes a quick look at some of the testing and proving activities involved in the development lifecycle, and some potential environments where they can be carried out. You can use this information to flesh out tooling and configuration requirements, as well as to add to the testing and deployment approach, essentially working backwards from the production environment.

Once the system (or a particular release) is in live service, the live production environment is essentially deemed out-of-bounds for any testing activities, unless they are carried out during periods of scheduled down-time. Many different types of testing and proving activities are performed on a project prior to "go-live," and these include functional testing, technical testing, and acceptance testing. Each activity requires a fit-for-purpose environment where it can be carried out without impacting the live service, especially if you are developing multiple releases. To reduce costs, a single environment might even be used to perform multiple activities. However, the various activities would generally require careful planning and scheduling to avoid interfering with each other. Furthermore, each activity will have its own specific environment requirements that are driven by the individual scenarios being tested and proven. For example, to test the cluster failover, a clustered environment is required. To effectively test and gauge the overall performance characteristics of the system, a suitably sized environment needs to be used, preferably the production environment itself or an equally sized environment. To ensure the disaster recovery procedures are adequate, they also need to be fully executed and verified, preferably in the secondary site environment or another equally sized environment. Once all the pre-live testing and proving has been performed and the system (or a particular release) is in live service, the post-live activities begin. These include fixing live service issues, minor enhancements, and future releases, all of which will need to be developed, tested, and proven prior to being deployed into production.

This chapter is organized into the following sections:

❑ **The Types of Testing** — Examines the types of tests that need to be performed to ensure that the system is fit for purpose. The types of testing discussed in this section include:

  ❑ **Acceptance testing**

  ❑ **Technical testing**

❑   **Functional testing**

❑   **Regression** testing

❑   **Testing in the "Production" Environments** — This section discusses the different types of production environments where some of the preceding tests can be carried out. The "production" environments discussed in this section include:

   ❑   **The primary site environment**

   ❑   **The secondary site environment**

   ❑   **The pre-production environment**

Given that there are so many options, I've decided to concentrate on the core activities and their environment requirements. Out in the field, you'll need to perform a similar exercise to determine which activities will be performed and the most appropriate environments to perform them in.

The Types of Testing

This section takes a look at the different types of testing activities that are performed to ensure that the system is fit for purpose, including:

❑   **Acceptance testing** — Acceptance testing is performed by business users and is generally referred to as *user acceptance testing* (UAT). UAT primarily focuses on the functional aspects of the system. Acceptance testing, however, can also include *operational acceptance testing* (OAT). OAT typically involves the operations team, the service delivery team, and the application maintenance team. The tests focus on the core operational aspects of the system to ensure that the live service processes and procedures are in place, such as monitoring, backup and restore testing, and disaster recovery testing. OAT also encompasses end user training, routine maintenance, and fix-on-fail. Some issues may simply require process changes; however, when issues require updates to the solution, the system needs to be fully tested prior to releasing a fix into the production environment which can involve a number of different test activities.

❑   **Technical testing** — Technical testing typically encompasses performance tests, failure and recovery tests, and operability tests. There's a clear overlap between technical testing and OAT when it comes to operability testing. It depends on how the project and organization is structured as to who is responsible for the various testing activities. However, it is not unusual for a project team to test all the technical aspects of the system prior to entering formal OAT activities.

❑   **Functional testing** — Functional testing is typically carried out by the project team prior to entering formal UAT activities that involve the actual end users. However, again, this depends on how the project team and organization are structured. There is also a clear overlap between the tests carried out as part of functional testing and those carried out in UAT.

❑   **Regression testing** — Regression testing is typically automated and executed against a software release prior to it (the software) being used for any other testing or proving activities.

Acceptance Testing

Acceptance testing is performed as part of the overall system testing activities, which also include functional testing and technical testing. Acceptance testing is performed by the business, and for the purposes of this book, acceptance testing includes user acceptance testing (UAT) and operability acceptance testing (OAT). The UAT and OAT activities overlap with functional testing and technical testing and contain many of the same tests and scenarios. Functional testing and technical testing are typically performed by the project team prior to formal acceptance testing involving the business. However, it depends entirely on how the project team and organization are structured. For example, in an agile project, members of the business form part of the overall project team. Furthermore, it is not uncommon for members of the service delivery team to be involved in technical testing. It is also possible that functional and technical testing is simply absorbed into a single set of acceptance testing activities and not performed in isolation. Alternatively, some rudimentary functional and technical tests could be incorporated during developer testing, such as unit and integration testing. This section simply focuses on the types of tests that are carried out and the environment requirements for them.

The following provides an overview of the testing carried out during acceptance testing:

❑ **User acceptance testing (UAT)** — User acceptance testing by its very name implies that it is performed by the end users. Irrespective of whether the project team tests the actual functionality of the software, it needs to be tested by the people that will be using it as part of their daily routine. The UAT environment should really be identical to the production environment, or at least as close as possible. Testing the system's functionality on a smaller environment or perhaps even a local workstation doesn't really give end users a feel for how the system will perform in live service. The short story I mentioned at the start of Chapter 2, whereby the representative's computer hung during a support call, is a typical example of what could be missed if UAT isn't performed in a live-like environment. The more realistic the testing environment is, the better chance you have of capturing (and rectifying) issues that might occur during live service.

❑ **Operational acceptance testing (OAT)** — The majority of operational acceptance testing (OAT) should also be conducted in a live-like environment to ensure the scenarios are realistic to live service situations, which includes both the primary site and the secondary site (if there is one). However, there are certain areas, such as user training, where additional environments could be used to allow the users to "play around" with the system to get a feel for its functionality and streamline their own processes. The tests carried out as part of OAT cover a variety of different scenarios, including:

  ❑ **Monitoring procedures** — Monitoring scenarios focus on ensuring that the operations team can monitor the system effectively. It is during these tests that the monitoring rules are typically adjusted to reduce unnecessary "noise," to ensure the right alerts are in place, and to simulate the alert procedures.

  ❑ **Operational procedures** — The operational procedure tests focus on the core procedures that will be carried out by the operations team (for example, responding to alerts). Each alert will have an associated set of actions that need to be carried out (for example, restarting a service or re-executing a batch process). The procedures should be documented in the Operations Manual, and the individual scenarios should be tested to ensure that the procedures are streamlined and provide the right result.

❑ **Recovery procedures** — The recovery procedures test and practice various recovery scenarios, such as restoring a full backup and applying the partial backups to a known position. The recovery procedures would also include disaster recovery, which would almost certainly involve practicing (and streamlining) a single site failure and "cutting-over" to the secondary site (or an alternative). There could also be specific procedures for moving part of the live service to another environment within the primary data center, such as a pre-production environment (discussed shortly). In some cases, it is far quicker to resume live-service on machines that are within the same datacenter than it is to move everything to the secondary site.

❑ **Maintenance procedures** — The maintenance procedures typically cover release deployment and verification as well as other routine maintenance tasks, such as re-configuration. It is important to ensure that new releases can be deployed quickly and efficiently, especially following a live-service incident. As part of the live service, it may also be necessary to adjust certain configuration settings, and these scenarios should also be proven and streamlined.

❑ **User training** — User training is probably one of the most important areas of testing. It is important for users to be properly trained, and providing training environments allows them to learn how to use the system effectively. It is equally important to note that user training covers operational staff as well as end users. Training in a realistic and live-like environment generally provides the best result, and the OAT scenarios outlined previously are a prime example. However, it is also possible to provide end users (or groups of end users) with "sandboxes" where they can play around with the system without affecting anyone else. These types of user training environments would be similar to the functional test environments, as discussed in the "Functional Testing" section, and might utilize certain stubs and simulators instead of real components, unless it's necessary to connect to other systems.

The preceding points give you an idea of the types of tests carried out as part of acceptance testing. It is important that the individual scenarios be tested in an environment that's fit for purpose.

Technical Testing

Technical testing focuses on ensuring that the system meets all the technical quality characteristics. The types of tests that will be carried out are as follows:

❑ **Atomic component tests** — This type of testing puts each component (or assembly) through its paces in isolation to the rest of the application. An assembly isn't necessarily an individual library; it's simply a logical grouping of modules or classes that would be tested in isolation. For example, the data access layer, which could comprise many libraries, could be tested atomically to ensure it meets the technical requirements. Atomic tests are typically used to highlight (and remove) potential bottlenecks before the solution is tested end-to-end. The tests carried out would be very similar to the following tests, which are conducted for the entire solution.

❑ **Load tests** — Load tests are used to measure the technical characteristics (such as performance and resource utilization) by subjecting the system (or assembly) to an expected transaction or usage load. For example, if the system needs to support 30,000 concurrent users, load tests would be used to ensure that the solution is capable of doing so. The load tests are typically phased, starting with a smaller number of users and transactions and building up to the anticipated number of users and transactions required for live service. The load tests are often executed in blocks of time appropriate to the requirements. For example, a load test may be executed for 20 minutes. The first 5 minutes allow for the tools and tests to "ramp up" the number of users and transactions to the appropriate load point. The last 5 minutes allows for the tools and tests to "ramp down" and disconnect. The 10 minutes in between is where the system was under the load point. The transaction timings and diagnostics are taken from that load point. These timings and performance figures will give a minimum value, maximum, and peak value (an average value). During load tests, CPU, memory, hop timings, and end-to-end timings are monitored and recorded. Hop timings are the times taken during each layer of the architecture (for example, time taken at the web server or application server), whereas the end-to-end time is measured from the time the request hits the Web server to the time the response is sent back to the browser or client. Other information specific to the layers is also recorded during the load tests — for example, database activity and transaction times.

❑ **Soak tests** — Soak tests are executed over a longer period than load tests, with the anticipated production load. Designed to prove that the system is capable of handling a sustained load, soak tests can uncover memory leaks or issues that manifest themselves over a greater period of time — issues that would not be seen during shorter load tests. The information monitored and recorded during soak tests is typically the same as the load tests, although there is a lot more information to analyze. The analysis often reveals peaks and troughs where certain events occur, such as garbage collection and other background tasks that kick in unexpectedly. Garbage collection often leads to the implementation of pooling and caching strategies so that objects are re-used instead of being re-created and disposed of. It is worth thinking about pooling and caching during design to avoid late-breaking activities when performance issues are identified.

❑ **Stress tests** — Stress tests are similar to load tests, but stress tests put even more load on the system. This enables you to gauge where the system's breaking point is. The analysis will show when the system is completely maxed out. This information can be used to calibrate certain configuration values that will throttle the load on the system during production to avoid it being taken to the breaking point. It is worth thinking about the key throttle configurations at design time — such as connections, transactions, and throughput — so that the application is resilient to being maxed out. During stress testing, it is important that the throttles be set high or support being disabled or turned off to ensure that the system can be truly maxed out.

❑ **Third-party integration tests** — The separate integration tests focus on testing all the third-party components that are not included elsewhere. Third-party components and applications are good candidates for atomic testing to ensure that they do not present any bottlenecks in the overall solution. Third-party components might also be used during batch and other offline processing. For example, the batch solution might compile files containing transaction data that are transferred throughout the day to the third-party for additional processing. It may also involve the receipt and processing of information from a third-party system. Regardless of whether the third-party components or applications are used during online processing or offline processing, it is important that these integration points be thoroughly load tested, soak tested, and stress tested.

❑ **Acceptance tests** — The acceptance tests cover a wide range of scenarios, including failure and recovery, backup and restore, disaster recovery, and batch scheduling. Driven from the operability criteria and requirements, these tests ensure that the system meets the stipulated requirements. The tests will often prove the scripts and operability documentation that is put in place. This will involve the operator carrying a specific procedure and ensuring that it works correctly. The project team should typically carry out rudimentary acceptance test scenarios prior to involving real operators and service delivery staff. However, it will greatly depend on how the project team is structured.

Technical testing involves a variety of different tests. The tools and hardware required to support this level of testing are equally varied. There are tools that can be used to generate a sufficient user and transaction load, although this could also be done manually. Furthermore, tools are also used to inject the generated transactions into the system automatically and these "load injection" tools would typically be installed on separate hardware, commonly referred to as *load injectors*. Hosting the load injection tools on separate hardware ensures that they don't impact the performance characteristics of the actual solution during testing.

Figure 6-1 shows a single load injector that would be used to inject transactions into the online system via the load balancer, although additional load injectors could be used to increase the number of transactions. It is important that the tools (and hardware) are up to the job; otherwise, this can impact the testing greatly. Furthermore, the test data required for a technical test is of production scale, often involving thousands if not millions of records. Test data generation tools can be used or developed to generate this test data from standard templates. Technical test data is often a superset of data that can be trimmed down for other test environments, such as functional tests, unit tests, integration tests and smoke tests.

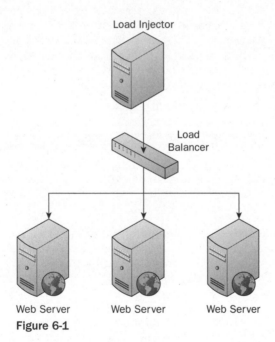

Figure 6-1

As defects are uncovered, various scripts and productivity tools could be developed to analyze the root cause. When scripts and tools are developed, they should be retained so that they can be used by live service during incident investigation or alternatively as part of the overall monitoring solution.

It is not always possible to include the technical tests in the regression framework due to the manual nature of some of the scenarios and the environment requirements. However, where it's possible to do so, technical tests should be included in the regression test suite.

Finally, it is worth thinking about a technical user interface (UI) where all technical elements and configuration of the system can be performed. Messing around in the database or configuration files can often cause problems. For example, a group of related values may need to be changed; if only one value is changed, the entire configuration profile could be altered. The technical UI would need to ensure that all the values in the group are calibrated correctly. It is equally important that the operational documentation includes all the configuration values and thorough instructions for setting them.

Functional Testing

Functional testing primarily focuses on the functional aspects of the system. The tests that are carried out are based on the functional requirements and functional designs. The project team would typically carry out functional testing activities prior to moving into formal UAT activities. The size and scale of the functional test environments will depend entirely on the project and the testing being carried out, although it's advisable to use a tiered architecture so that the testing is performed in a realistic environment with realistic data.

Figure 6-2 shows a functional test environment using a three-tiered approach. In this example, the environment has a single web server, a single application server, and a single database server. Although an environment like this is useful for testing the functionality, it has its limitations. For example, all test data would be shared between the testers. Alternatively, the testers' workstations could have everything installed locally or a single shared server could be used. The advantages of a tiered approach is that at every stage the product is tested using a realistic environment. It also ensures that the deployment and configuration are consistently maintained. Testing in a realistic environment should reduce the number of issues that are highlighted during formal UAT.

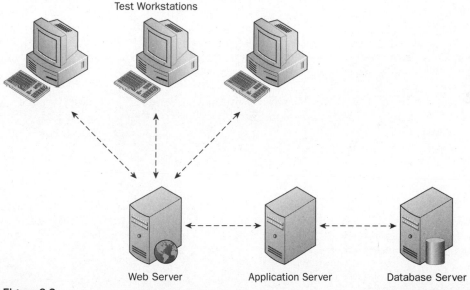

Figure 6-2

Functional test environments are not usually monitored by the operations architecture, nor are they generally connected to any integration environments, either, unless there is a specific requirement to do so. Where the environments are not connected to the integration environment, they will use stubs or simulators. This is another reason for ensuring that the stubs are suitably configurable and mimic the real system as much as possible. The functional tests generally don't involve exception testing; instead, they concentrate on the core functionality. An integration test environment can be used to test third-party applications and their integration, although this will still test only the core functionality.

Functional tests often involve lifecycle testing, which means testing on day 0, day 1, day 2, day 3, and so forth. One example of this type of testing is daily transaction processing. On day 1, a record is entered on the system. Under normal circumstances, the record should be processed on day 1. However, the application (on day 2, for instance) may support processing of the previous day's records if they were not processed, in this example on day 1. This means that the system needs to be put into a scenario where it doesn't process the record on the day it is entered. It also means that the system needs to be put into day 2 (such as moving the date forward) so that the processing of "previous day's records" can be verified. It would be unreasonable in a functional test scenario to expect a tester to enter the records on day 1 and then wait until the next day to see if the test worked. However, during acceptance testing and formal UAT, this could very well be the case.

In today's locked-down and managed environments, it is often not possible to change the system date, and in any case this is not the right approach. This is another example of where the Custom Calendar component can come in handy. The component can use the configuration value if it's set; otherwise, it will get the actual system date. If the application is using the system date, all the servers would need to be kept in sync.

Furthermore, certain test scenarios will require the system to be put into a particular state. The state will depend on the functional scenario being tested. This could involve updates to test data, configuration values, and potentially configuration of various stubs and simulators. It is important to try and reduce the amount of manual effort involved by providing productivity scripts that can be executed to put the environment into the specific state. Finally, once the tests are complete, it is equally important to have scripts that can reset the environment back to its original state.

The test data for functional tests is often reduced due to the size and scale of the environment; thus, functional testing does not stress the system. The test data needs to be managed and based on production-like data.

Functional testing is often conducted through the front-end user interface. Tools that capture these inputs can be used to record the scripts for automated playback.

Once successful, the functional tests (where possible) should be included in the automated regression test suite. This means that the functional test tools need to be capable of integrating with the regression test framework. If this is not possible, the tests will need to be executed outside the managed regression test framework.

Regression Testing

The regression test suite is added to at various stages throughout the lifecycle. In the early days, a single server is often viable to execute all the tests sequentially. However, as the project progresses, the end-to-end time will extend, so additional servers may be required to execute tests at the same time.

When there are lots of regression tests, it is important to be able to execute the regression tests on multiple servers in parallel. That additional servers are required shouldn't be too much bother. The use of additional servers will reduce the overall execution time of the regression testing. This can be quite complex with all the different tools, scripts, and configurations, so it is worth trying this out up-front, along with the other readiness activities (as required).

The regression test capability is part of the overall build cycle and provides a level of confidence in the system prior to it being deployed elsewhere. It is therefore prudent that the tests are developed and executed using real-world scenarios and data as the project progresses.

Just because the unit tests pass, or even the integration tests pass, doesn't necessarily mean the application does what it should. Having a series of different tests all running in parallel will help to gauge the overall quality of the build and reduce the overall time it takes to execute the tests end-to-end.

Figure 6-3 shows a sample overall build quality table. The build and regression tools could fill in this table (or something similar) with the statistics after each build and test run. This means the tools would need to extract information from other tooling outputs; therefore, if this is desired, it should be tried out up front.

Build Statistics				
	Total	Executed	Passed	CC%
Unit Tests				
Integration Tests				
Smoke Tests				
	Errors	Warnings		
Static Code Profiling				
Dynamic Code Profiling				
Documentation Generation				

Figure 6-3

Most modern software build applications support collation and generation of this type of information. The rows and columns in the table are as follows:

❑ **Unit Tests** — This row contains the total number of unit tests included in the unit test suite. It shows the number of tests that are executed as part of *this* execution and the number of tests that have passed. The CC% column would contain the total amount of "code coverage" achieved.

❑ **Integration Tests** — This row includes the same information as the Unit Tests row, except it is for the integration tests. I am a firm believer that code coverage should also be captured for integration tests, as it provides a good basis for investigation, further testing and can also highlight areas of redundant code.

❑ **Smoke Tests** — I've mentioned that the regression test suite would be added to as the project progresses. In this example, the Smoke Tests row can be used to encompass all the functional and technical tests that are included in the regression test suite. It is also possible to break out the additional tests into separate rows. However, the information would be the same as the other rows for unit and integration tests.

❑ **Static Code Profiling** — This row simply indicates the total number of errors and warnings raised by the static code profiler(s).

❑ **Dynamic Code Profiling** — This row contains the number of errors and warnings raised by the dynamic code profiler(s).

❑ **Documentation Generation** — This row contains the number of errors and warnings raised during the automatic generation of the documentation.

All the results and reports should be collated so that they can be easily viewed. However, the single table provides an overview of the quality for *this* build. It shows at a glance the number of tests that have passed, the amount of code covered, the profiling results, and any errors or warnings encountered during documentation generation.

Testing in the "Production" Environments

This section discusses some of the production environments and the types of testing that could be carried out in them. In addition, it discusses some of the challenges once the system is in live service; some of these environments are no longer available for testing activities. The production environments discussed in this section include:

❑ **The primary site environment** — The primary production environment is where the live service will be hosted. In the run-up to go-live, the production environment can be used to perform various testing and proving activities. However, as mentioned earlier, once the system is in live service, this environment is out-of-bounds for any testing activities. This section lists the types of activities that can be performed in the primary production environment.

❑ **The secondary site environment** — In an active/passive primary and secondary site configuration, the secondary production environment is essentially a "hot standby" environment where various tests can be carried out. However, in the event of a primary site disaster, the secondary site would be running the live service and no testing could be performed. In an active/active primary and secondary site configuration, both sites are being used for the live service, so no testing can be performed in either environment once the system is in live service. This section lists the types of activities that can be performed in the secondary site production environment when it's "passive".

❑ **The pre-production environment** — A dedicated pre-production environment can be used to perform many different types of testing prior to deploying a release into the live-service production environment. Furthermore, the pre-production environment can also be used in the event of a live-service issue. This section looks at a dedicated pre-production environment and the activities that could be performed within it.

The Primary Site Environment

The previous chapter introduced a typical, medium-scale production environment. The activities you can perform in this environment depend on where you are in the project. They also depend on whether the environment is specific to this system and not shared with any other systems. The following list looks at some of the activities the production environment *could* be used for if it were solely for the system being implemented:

❑ **Live service system** — The primary purpose of the production environment is to host the live service system. When the system is in live service, you can't perform any activities in the environment, other than investigating live service incidents, where allowed.

❑ **Technical and acceptance testing** — Prior to the system going live, you could use the environment (if it's built and available) to perform technical and acceptance testing. But one thing to bear in mind is that additional servers are often required to host "injection" tools and other applications. However, once the system has gone live, where are you going to perform technical and acceptance testing for future releases? The following presents a couple of options:

  ❑ **If the secondary site is "passive," you could use the secondary site environment** — This is possible because the code-base and configuration are the same. However, this requires careful scheduling and roll-back procedures. It would also require "dual" SANs to ensure that the technical testing doesn't impact live service replication. If the secondary site is active, then one option is to perform thorough testing in a dedicated pre-production environment.

  ❑ **A specific pre-production environment** — Most architects and systems developers recommend that the pre-production environment be sized and scaled exactly the same as the primary site production environment. This will increase costs, although it is possible that it could be scaled down but this would need to be considered carefully and the limitations would need to be well understood.

  ❑ **Incident investigation** — Issues that occur in live service need to be re-created and investigated, and you could use this environment to perform these activities. This needs to be carefully balanced with production to remove any chance of impacting live service.

  ❑ **Fix-on-fail testing** — This needs to be treated very carefully and performed during periods of scheduled down-time. Although incident investigation doesn't actually change the code-base, once a fix has been identified, it will need to be tested and accepted. If performing fix-on-fail testing in this environment is deemed to be too high of a risk, the secondary site or pre-production environment is another option.

The Secondary Site Environment

The secondary site environment typically is identical to the primary site environment. However, some organizations choose to scale it down based on risk assessments. It is important to understand whether this is the case, as it can have an impact on failover and testing. Testing is this environment also depends on whether the secondary site is "active" or "passive." If it's active, all testing needs to be carried out prior to the system entering live service. Once this environment is being used for live service, it's no longer possible to perform any testing in it. However, if it's passive, there are a couple of ways in which it can be used:

❑ **For technical and acceptance testing** — It is not uncommon for new releases to be tested in the secondary site environment prior to deployment in the primary site. However, this needs to be considered carefully and roll-back plans need to be in place to ensure that the environment can be returned to its original state (if and when required.) The pre-production environment is another option for performing new release testing.

❑ **For incident investigation** — You could also use the secondary site to perform these activities.

❑ **For fix-on-fail testing** — When an updated release is deployed into the secondary site for final testing, the primary site and the secondary site are out of-sync at a code level. If there's a failure in live service, you need to redeploy the production release to the secondary site. This could take time and re-enforces the use of rapid deployment tools. The pre-production environment is another option for performing fix-on-fail testing.

The Pre-Production Environment

The pre-production environment should essentially mirror the production environment, albeit without a secondary site counterpart, as shown in Figure 6-4.

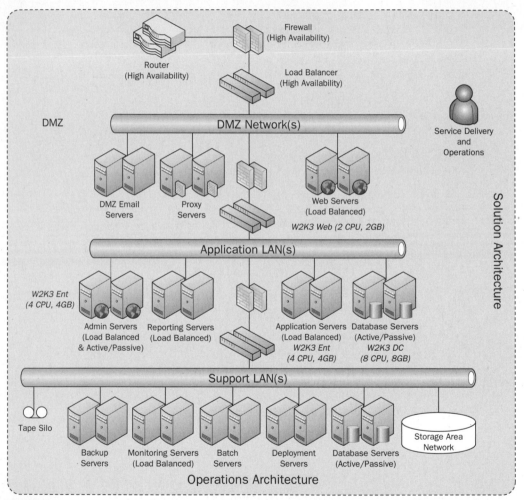

Figure 6-4

The size and scale of the pre-production environment is recommended to be the same as the primary site production environment. Given the number of servers in the production environment, this is often costly, so the pre-production environment may not be a full-scale replica. In these situations, there are subtleties that can only be realized in the production environment or secondary site. However, this will greatly depend on how the environment is trimmed down.

The pre-production environment can also be used as a fallback in the event of a failure in the production system. It is sometimes quicker to fall back on pre-production than to fail over to another site. Again, however, this needs to be balanced against risks. If you're using the pre-production environment for fix-on-fail testing, then production and pre-production could be out-of-sync. Depending on the configuration, the pre-production environment could be connected to development or test instances of the operations architecture software, as well as other integrated components and solutions. This provides a platform for testing the operational elements prior to their promotion to the live operations environment.

The pre-production environment is often shared when used for testing. It can be used to perform any pre-production testing, including technical testing and acceptance testing. The pre-production environment needs to be turned around quickly in the event that it needs to be used for production during a failure. Therefore, it is vital to take a rapid deployment and configuration approach rather than having to install the software on a server-by-server basis.

The pre-production environment should be configured in exactly the same way as the production environment to ensure that a near-production test is conducted. I've mentioned previously that credentials often differ between environments, and that is for a very good security reason. It is therefore important that even though the usernames may be different, the privileges (access rights) are exactly the same.

Unless it is absolutely necessary, the pre-production environment generally shouldn't have a disaster recovery option. In the event of a disaster, the pre-production environment, along with everything else at the primary data center, is lost. Organizations may choose to place a pre-production environment at the secondary data center to counter this.

Summary

This chapter looked at the different types of testing and where they can be performed. We've also looked at some of the other activities that can be performed in the production environments and their considerations.

The following are the key points to take away from this chapter:

❑ **Acceptance testing covers two primary areas of testing**:

  ❑ User acceptance testing (UAT), which focuses on the functional aspects of the system.

  ❑ Operational acceptance testing (OAT), which focuses on the operational aspects of the system.

Where possible, acceptance testing should be performed in a live-like environment.

❑ **OAT includes a variety of different test scenarios, including**:

  ❑ Monitoring procedures

  ❑ Operational procedures

  ❑ Recovery procedures

- ❏ Maintenance procedures
- ❏ User training
- ❏ **Technical testing includes a variety of test scenarios, including:**
  - ❏ Atomic assembly tests
  - ❏ Load tests
  - ❏ Soak tests
  - ❏ Stress tests
  - ❏ Third-party integration tests
  - ❏ Acceptance tests
- ❏ **Functional testing focuses on the functional aspects of the system**. Functional testing can be performed in a local environment prior to entering formal UAT activities.
- ❏ **Regression testing focuses on automatically testing the system**. Where possible, the regression suite should cover as much as possible and execute on a number of servers to reduce the end-to-end time. The build outputs should include the following information:
  - ❏ Unit tests executed and code coverage achieved
  - ❏ Assembly tests executed and code coverage achieved
  - ❏ Smoke tests executed and code coverage achieved
  - ❏ Static code profiling results
  - ❏ Dynamic code profiling results
  - ❏ Errors and warnings during documentation generation
- ❏ **The "production" environments can be used for testing**. To ensure that your system meets all its requirements and readiness criteria, technical and acceptance testing needs to be performed in a live-like environment. The environment options include:
  - ❏ The production environment (where there is no live service as yet)
  - ❏ The secondary site environment (where it's passive)
  - ❏ The pre-production environment (if there is one)

You need to understand the different types of testing that needs to be performed and the most suitable environment to test the various scenarios.

- ❏ **Additional hardware and software may be required**. It is important to remember that additional hardware and software may be required during testing, such as load injectors and load injection software.

7

Service Delivery and Operations

The service delivery and operations teams, which typically are based out of the data centers, take care of all the environments, servers, and systems. These are the folks you should work closely with to understand how the system should operate and be operated in live service. Because the teams have looked after many systems and learned many lessons over the years, they can provide great guidance and advice. Supporting the system should be as straightforward as possible. Manual procedures take time and are also prone to human error. The service delivery and operations teams can help you to define the operability criteria for the system. However, this needs to be considered and included in the scope appropriately. One of the most important documents pertaining to the system and its operation is the Operations Manual and you've already seen a number of the items that would typically be included it.

In addition to discussing the roles of the service delivery and operations teams, this chapter looks at the contents of a typical Operations Manual in more detail. You can use the Operations Manual as a roadmap for designing the overall solution. As you progress through the next few chapters, you'll see the various activities in more detail.

This chapter is organized into the following sections:

❑ **The Three Levels of Live Service Support** — This section provides an overview of the three different levels of support and how the individual teams interact. It also provides some high-level activities that the different teams will perform in the event of a live service incident. It then takes a more detailed look at the roles and responsibilities of the operations and service delivery teams and provides insights into the routine day-to-day tasks that are performed. Chapter 12 discusses the roles and responsibilities of the application maintenance team, which also could be assumed by the service delivery team. In short, the three levels of support are as follows:

    ❑   Level 1 — Operations

    ❑   Level 2 — Service Delivery

    ❑   Level 3 — Application Maintenance

❏ **The Operations Manual** — Takes a look at some of the reasons why you should understand the Service Delivery and Operations organizations and what you can do to make your life and theirs a lot easier. This is typically achieved through the Operations Manual, which is one of the most important documents produced for the system. The Operations Manual would typically cover the following high-level subject areas:

❏ Solution overview

❏ Planning the architecture

❏ Installation and configuration

❏ Maintenance and administration

❏ Monitoring and alerts

❏ Reporting

❏ Batch

❏ Incident investigation (which is linked to monitoring and alerts)

The Three Levels of Live Service Support

In most organizations there are three different levels of support, generally referred to as Level 1, Level 2, and Level 3, respectively. It really depends on the organization as to which tasks are performed at each level and who actually performs them. This section uses a typical scenario.

Under normal circumstances, the three levels of support are formally introduced once the system is in live service. Throughout the project, "live-service readiness" will assess and ensure that all the processes and procedures are in place.

Figure 7-1 shows a typical support model.

Figure 7-1

I discuss each role in more detail later in the chapter, but for now the following scenario will highlight some of the key roles and actions that take place.

Assume that a Windows Service called the Batch Agent Service has stopped. A Critical alert is raised on the operations console, and the following transpires:

1. The operator logs the live service incident (the "ticket") in the incident-tracking tool.

2. He or she checks the Operations Manual for something along the lines of "Batch Agent Service Alert: Stopped."

3. The Operations Manual says to restart the service and wait for it to indicate that is has started. In this instance, restarting the service is achieved by right-clicking on the service and selecting Start. The service itself would enter a Starting state and subsequently transition to Started.

4. The operator restarts the service.

5. The service stops immediately and raises the same alert ("Batch Agent Service Alert: Stopped").

6. The operator checks the procedures in the manual. The manual contains no further remedial steps and says the issue should be "escalated."

7. The operator updates the incident in the tracking tool and escalates it to Level 2 support.

Before continuing, it's worth noting that this is a very simplified scenario and there could be many other factors and tasks that could be performed. I discuss this in more detail shortly.

The incident has now been escalated to Level 2 support. The service delivery team is primarily responsible for Level 2 support, although there are many other roles it can and does perform, as you'll see shortly.

The support lead or primary contact will assign the ticket to an individual for further analysis. The assigned individual will then progress the incident further. This generally involves the following high-level actions:

1. Understanding the incident from the ticket and discussions with the operations team

2. Getting "temporary" access to the servers and environments

3. Checking the logs, events, and so on to try to work out why the service is stopping

4. Resolving the issue (where possible) and closing the ticket

5. Updating the ticket and escalating it to Level 3 support (in the event it can't be resolved)

Once the ticket is returned from the application maintenance team, the solution is verified and deployed into live service (at an appropriate point), and the ticket is updated and closed.

In this sample scenario, assume that the service delivery team has done everything it can to resolve the issue, so it needs to be escalated further. The incident has been raised to Level 3 support, which is typically handled by the application maintenance team. The application maintenance team will investigate the issue further, which will generally involve the following:

1. Getting the background on the issue, obtaining the logs, events, and steps already taken, as well as any other associated materials (which should be attached to the ticket)

2. Re-creating the incident in a fix-on-fail (or other equivalent) environment

3. Proposing a workaround (where possible)

4. Implementing (and testing) a full or temporary solution

5. Passing the ticket back to the service delivery team for final verification and deployment

I've simplified the scenario and the steps greatly, but this shows how the ticket generally progresses through the different levels of support and the high-level activities performed.

In some organizations, the service delivery and application maintenance teams can be one and the same. Furthermore, the application maintenance team can also be the development team. It all depends on the structure of the organization, so it's important to understand who the different contacts are and the roles and responsibilities of each group involved.

The Scope of Support

Figure 7-2 shows a typical scope of support for the operations, service delivery, and maintenance teams. Bear in mind, of course, that this can differ from organization to organization.

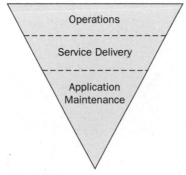

Figure 7-2

The *operations team* is responsible for operating and monitoring *all* the systems that are in live service. As you can imagine, in a large organization, this could involve potentially operating and monitoring a very large number of different systems. This is typically why the operations team doesn't perform detailed incident investigation. The shear number of systems and the knowledge required would be enormous. Instead, the operations team performs routine steps according to the Operations Manual. The Operations Manual typically dictates strict, step-by-step procedures to follow in the event of a failure.

The *service delivery team* can be split into different groups and sub-teams. For example, there may be one team solely responsible for the Online Store and another responsible for the Order Processing System. In addition, SD contains a number of "pockets" of resources whereby certain resources have very specific skills and perform specialized tasks. For instance, there may be a team that specializes in backups and the backup solution. Another could specialize in the batch solution. These activities would encompass many, if not all, of the systems in live service. Although in the case of batch, the solution might be broken up according to system or application.

The *application maintenance team* is typically responsible for a single application or system. The application maintenance team is similar to the development team and could be organized in the same way. For instance, there may be resources that specialize in the User Interface or the Framework Components. Application maintenance is discussed later in this book. However, as you can see the scope of the activities is very much aligned with Defect Management and Fix as well as Change Control. The "ticketing" or "Incident Management" system used in live service could also be very different to that used during development.

The Role of the Operations Team

The operations bridge (also known as the control room) is part of the data center from where the organization's systems are primarily monitored and operated. The operations bridge usually contains many displays, each showing the state of one or more of the live service systems. There's usually one huge display to show the state of the *latest* system alerts.

Figure 7-3, courtesy of Wikipedia, shows an operator sitting in front of a network monitoring display.

Figure 7-3

The operations team is charged with monitoring all the production systems. The team typically works in shifts to cover the system around the clock. As one person leaves, another joins and gets the low-down on the current state of affairs and events.

The operations team usually has a set of procedures for everything it does, to protect against unnecessary mistakes and human error. It is a detailed, step-by-step guide to performing a particular task. For many routine tasks, these procedures would traditionally be printed out, laminated, and posted in the operations room. This led to the term *"laminates"* to describe the key operational procedures for the systems being monitored and operated. They're very much like other signs and instructions you would expect to find in buildings, such as "In Case of Fire," although the steps would be more detailed.

Operations procedures need to be very clear and contain *all* the necessary steps to complete a task. If a step is missing in the procedures, it's likely it will be missed in the process. For instance, by assuming that the system will be restarted after a corrective action and not actually stating this action in the procedures is not helpful and might not be performed by the operators. The operations team has many systems to look after and many actions to perform. Ensuring that each action is fully documented and easy to follow is critical to effective operations. The other benefit of the laminates is that each step can be ticked off with a marker, and when all steps have been completed, the marks can be wiped off. The procedures also need to contain all the alternative flows that might need to be followed. In the scenario presented earlier, the operator looked in the Operations Manual for a particular alert and what to do with it. It is important that the Operations Manual captures all the alerts that will require operator attention. (The next chapter looks at monitoring and alerts.)

As the system progresses throughout its live service, incidents will occur and be resolved. As this happens, the Operations Manual will be updated to include workarounds and updated operational procedures. The operations team will use these procedures to better operate and monitor the system in live service. Furthermore, the service delivery and application maintenance teams will also use the updated Operations Manual.

I'm a firm believer that as part of any developer's growth, he or she should spend time on the operations (and service delivery) teams, as it really provides some invaluable insights into developing production-ready solutions. One gets to see all the operations and activities that need to be performed as part of live service support. Furthermore, it really helps to understand the importance of good procedures and diagnostics. This can often happen naturally during the run-up to implementation and during post-implementation support by sitting in the Ops Bridge and providing support and guidance to the operations team. In the run-up to actual live service, the operations (and service delivery) team will be involved in monitoring the system and ensuring that everything runs correctly. If there are a lot of issues with monitoring — for example, the system raises too many alerts or batch jobs keep falling over — it will cause an overhead for the operations teams. This often involves members of the project team working with the operations and service delivery teams and babysitting the system to work through the issues.

The Role of the Service Delivery Team

The service delivery team also monitors the system, but in a more peripheral fashion, especially when the system is fully operational. In the early days, all the teams will be watching the system and ready to deal with any issues that might occur. Service Delivery is typically responsible for all the installation, configuration, support, and maintenance for all the servers, databases, networks, and network components.

The service delivery team also performs additional systems administration–related tasks, including installation, configuration, maintenance, support, and incident investigation. The team usually includes specialists from all disciplines, including:

❑ Infrastructure (cabinets, hardware installation, cabling, power, and cooling). The infrastructure role is very specialized and some organizations use external vendor's to provide this.

❑ Networking and communications, including all low-level network components as well as high-level components such as routers and load balancers for both the wide area network (WAN) and the local area networks (LAN).

❑ System administration, commonly referred to as *sysadmins*. Sysadmins typically understand the following areas:

❑ Base operating systems and settings

❑ Runtimes and frameworks (such as ASP and IIS)

❑ Security and roles (including user maintenance)

❑ Group Policy or other managed environments

❑ Database administration, which would include DBAs who would have strong knowledge of:

❑ General database administration tasks

❑ Database planning and implementation

- ❏ Performance tuning techniques
- ❏ Database replication techniques

❏ Security administration, the members of which would typically understand the following:

- ❏ Secure Sockets Layer (SSL) and certificates
- ❏ The security solution (such as Active Directory)
- ❏ Encryption techniques

❏ Backup and recovery functions, although this could be included in system administration I've pulled it out separately. The team members would typically understand:

- ❏ Full or partial backups
- ❏ Tape and silo management
- ❏ Restoration activities and techniques

❏ Batch administration, including the following specific areas of expertise and knowledge:

- ❏ The batch architecture and solution
- ❏ Implementing batch schedules and dependencies
- ❏ Executing and monitoring the batch schedules

❏ Reporting, which requires specific knowledge of the following areas:

- ❏ The reporting architecture and solution
- ❏ Developing and customizing reports
- ❏ Executing reports

❏ Deployment, which covers the following areas and activities:

- ❏ Developing (automated) deployment solutions.
- ❏ Disk imaging.
- ❏ Installing and configuring the software.
- ❏ Performing upgrades and software rollouts across all environments. In the event that an update or new version of the software needs to be deployed, this will usually be undertaken by the service delivery team. It is vital that installation and configuration be fully understood and streamlined to support rapid deployment. It is also important that release notes be well documented.

❏ Application development and application maintenance. It is generally not the purpose of the service delivery team to develop new software systems or applications, although the team does develop productivity tools and automation scripts and provide enhancements to existing systems (especially if its members are also part the application maintenance team). The team may also develop applications for its own internal use. As such, the team has a good understanding of programming languages and technologies, which also assists with issue resolution.

The preceding list is not exhaustive, but it provides an overview of the kinds of knowledge and expertise offered by the service delivery team. In addition to the preceding specific areas, the service delivery team is also knowledgeable in the following areas:

❑ Load balancing and resilience techniques

❑ Antivirus techniques

❑ Logs and event analysis

❑ Change control and version control procedures

❑ Documentation production (especially operational procedures)

The role of Service Delivery changes throughout the project lifecycle. In the very early days, the team would help to shape the operability requirements and criteria. There is usually a baseline set of criteria based on previous systems that provide an initial input.

During the project, the team provides reviews and feedback, and prepares the organization for the system's implementation into live service. Typically the team is also involved in both operability testing and acceptance testing. The service delivery team can provide valuable input into the operations procedures while they are being developed. In some cases, the team can also be engaged to write the operations documentation by working with the project team to ensure that everything is covered off appropriately.

It is always a good idea to have the service delivery team involved from the start. The operability and maintenance criteria are crucial to any implementation. During acceptance testing, the service delivery team typically provides feedback on whether they believe the system is ready to go-live. This testing is carried out toward the latter end of the lifecycle, and having major operability issues cropping up at this late stage could cause delays and impact the project.

Service Delivery wants to ensure that the system is operable during live service and that the number of manual procedures is reduced. The team will be interested in any defects that could potentially affect the operability of the live service. This is especially true of failure and recovery — for example, if the system were to encounter an exception and simply stop. Operationally, someone would need to manually re-start the service. The service delivery (and operations) team is very keen that this sort of thing doesn't go on in the application unless it is absolutely necessary. Where manual steps are required, clear step-by-step procedures need to be put in place for either the service delivery or operations teams to follow.

Service Delivery is usually heavily involved in the cut-over to live service and the post go-live support. Key members of the project team are on support standby, too. During the post go-live support period, the operations team will monitor the system, but Service Delivery and the project team will also monitor the system and provide incident investigation. It is in this period that you get a true feel for the production system — how it operates and what needs to be done to support it.

Although the system has been fully tested, it is often too early to determine which alerts should be switched off, whether the logging level is optimal, or whether the batch schedule works entirely as it should. During the post go-live support period, Service Delivery will be looking to do a number of different activities, including:

❑ Investigating issues raised. This will involve reviewing the logs, checking the database, running reports, and trying to determine what caused the issue, as well as ascertaining what needs to be done to resolve it.

- ❏ Calibrating the alerts so that only the key alerts or events are raised. The term "noise" refers to a situation in which the system is raising many alerts when they are not really necessary. The Service Delivery folks are generally a fun bunch and the monitoring solution is sometimes hooked up to different WAV files or sound files. So, when the system generates an alert or specific event, you'll hear this bellowed throughout the office floor. The more that can be done to reduce unnecessary alerts and "noise" the better.

- ❏ Calibrating the logging and tracing so that the optimum information is present to help with incident investigation.

- ❏ Identifying and implementing additional monitoring features, such as monitoring more services and processes, tuning the monitoring thresholds, and monitoring more counters.

- ❏ Tweaking the batch schedule and dependencies to streamline the end-to-end batch.

- ❏ Adding blackout windows to the monitoring solution to avoid alerts being raised for known issues or within known periods.

- ❏ Identifying known issues and implementing interim manual or scripted workarounds until they are included in a release.

- ❏ Creating reports and data extracts to help with management reporting and incident investigation.

- ❏ Creating productivity tools and scripts to help better support the system.

- ❏ Updating the operations procedures with newly identified or refined information and steps.

These activities refine the operation and monitoring of the system. It wouldn't be in live service if it didn't work properly, so these issues are not generally mission critical to the system, although some workarounds might need to be put in place to plug a particular gap while a full solution is being worked on.

Once the system is out of post go-live support, the operations team will take full responsibility for monitoring the system and escalating alerts. (Monitoring and alerting are discussed in the next chapter).

With the system in full production mode, Service Delivery will take on the second line support role, which will involve some or all of the following activities:

- ❏ **Peripheral monitoring** — Service Delivery will continue to monitor the system, albeit in the background, and provide enhancements and continuous improvement to streamline monitoring and alerts.

- ❏ **Incident investigation** — Service Delivery becomes the primary incident investigator for all issues that arise during production running. Incidents that can't be resolved directly by Service Delivery can be passed to the application maintenance team. In any case, Service Delivery should liaise with Application Maintenance to ensure that updates are captured, understood, and implemented correctly.

- ❏ **Batch** — The batch schedule(s) will generally be continuously improved and streamlined as the database grows and system is used more. New batch jobs may be identified for specific enhancements by the service delivery team.

❏ **Reporting** — The service delivery team will be responsible for running reports and ensuring that all the relevant information is collated. Reports will be refined to provide additional information and new reports will be identified. The service delivery (or application maintenance) team will be responsible for updates to the reports and reporting solution.

❏ **Tuning** — The DBAs and other technical staff will be looking at ways of tuning and improving the performance of the system throughout its lifetime. As additional users are introduced, the system may require further tuning and calibration to support them.

❏ **Tooling** — Service Delivery will continuously look for tools and scripts to improve maintenance and support activities. This will also include developing their own. The less manually intense support and maintenance tasks are, the more Service Delivery will be streamlined.

As mentioned previously, the service delivery team could also perform application maintenance functions, which are discussed in Chapter 12.

The Operations Manual

It is important to be ready for a lot of the activities discussed early on in the development lifecycle. You need to make sure the system can support the level of tuning and calibration required by post go-live support and live service. You also need to make sure that the system is well understood by all the teams.

The service delivery team will initially install and configure the system for production use. This will involve understanding all the installation and configuration settings and procedures. Operations will monitor the system 24/7 to ensure that it's up-and-running. When it fails, especially in the early days, it's the developers who get the call at 3 A.M. to look into the issue. The quicker you can resolve the issue, the quicker you can get back to sleep. If the logs or the alerts don't have the right level of information, it's going to take a while to locate and resolve the issue. The better the diagnostics, the easier your life will be. Similarly, the more you can configure and tune your alerts and logging, the easier it will be to put effective monitoring in place. You can also make your life so much easier (and that of the service delivery and operations teams) by adding as much contextual information as possible to errors, events, and logs. This information can be included in the operational procedures, along with the steps to ensure effective operations. This ultimately means you shouldn't need to get a call at all. Chapter 11 covers this subject in more detail.

The more you can do up-front, the more you can include in the scope to ensure that the project is successful and not delayed because of operational or monitoring issues. This includes all third-party applications and runtime environments. These must be fully understood so that common operations scenarios can be documented in the Operations Manual. This could involve starting, stopping, failover, and other common operational scenarios.

The Operations Manual is probably one of the most important "documents" in the entire solution. It will be used (and reviewed) by both the service delivery and operations teams, as well as by the application maintenance team. Although it might not be the responsibility of the project team to produce it (depending on the scope), everything about the system needs to be captured in it. It almost becomes a single point of reference when the system is in live service. It essentially captures all the production environments, hardware and software topologies, configuration settings, deployment concepts, and operational procedures. Although the information could be split across multiple documents, it is a single collection of all information relating to the entire system.

The Operations Manual is usually born out of many documents produced early in the lifecycle, including the technical requirements. One such document is known as the Solution Architecture Design, which is typically built up from the function and technical requirements. This document would typically describe the proposed architecture and follow a very similar pattern to the Operations Manual, albeit without quite as much fully fleshed out content. The Solution Architecture Design usually starts out with what is known about the system. The Operations Manual is a great place to start planning the Solution Architecture Design, by fleshing out a high-level outline or table of contents for the Operations Manual and then essentially filling in the gaps with the solution design. This approach helps to identify areas that need to be completed and understood. Again, this promotes my vision of being on the receiving end of the information that we as developers produce. For instance, if you were looking to use a third-party product, simply obtaining an executable wouldn't help you to understand how it should be deployed, installed, supported, maintained, and so on. The Operations Manual outline can help to provide a high-level roadmap for the solution design, gap analysis, and scope definition.

Figure 7-4 shows the Operations Manual and its table of contents feeding back into the Solution Architecture Design, as well as the Operations Manual helping to shape the technical requirements through question and answer sessions. By starting at the end, you actually save yourself a lot of time and effort; you can simply start by shaping the Operations Manual, which will grow as the project continues. It doesn't matter what the actual documents are called along the way; the fact is that they cover all the necessary elements of the Operations Manual. As the project progresses, the documents become more specifically defined.

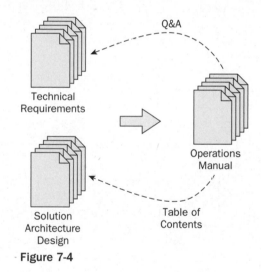

Figure 7-4

Figure 7-5 shows the high-level categories or subject areas that would form part of the Operations Manual.

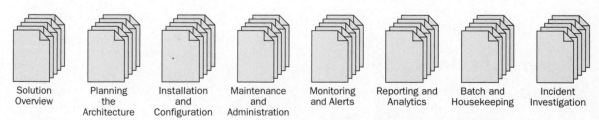

Figure 7-5

The following provides an overview of the different documents or sections shown in Figure 7-5:

- **Solution Overview** — This section or document would describe the overall solution architecture and the individual components. It includes the logical architecture including client software, base operating systems, foundation software (such as IIS and ASP.NET), database solution, and security solution, as well as the high-level application components and the low-level networking components. The solution overview would typically contain the hardware and software topology diagrams and supporting information previously discussed in Chapter 5.

- **Planning the Architecture** — Covers topics such as sizing and scaling the system, fault tolerance, automatic failure and recovery, security, caching, and shared services (such as shared storage).

- **Installation and Configuration** — Walks through the installation and configuration of each application, including its prerequisites. Each configuration setting is fully documented, including ranges and optimum values based on the deployment model selected.

- **Maintenance and Administration** — Covers the core maintenance activities, such as starting and stopping, backup and recovery, tuning and calibration, and other administrative functions.

- **Monitoring and Alerts** — Provides information on how the system should be monitored effectively, including what should be monitored (for example, specific counters and events). It also provides a breakdown of the events and alerts produced by the system and how they can be configured and tuned. The alerts would map to incident investigation, where detailed procedures would be in place for dealing with incidents. Monitoring and alerts are discussed in more detail in Chapter 8.

- **Reporting and Analytics** — Discusses the reporting solution and how it should be deployed and used. It also provides a breakdown of the operational reports, as well as the analytics solution. Reporting and analytics are discussed in Chapter 9.

- **Batch and Housekeeping** — Covers all the batch jobs, schedules, and dependencies required to keep the solution in good working order. Batch is discussed in more detail in Chapter 10.

- **Incident Investigation** — Covers the specific alerts and the detailed procedures for correcting them. It also covers the logging mechanisms and where to look for information regarding specific errors and alerts. In a typical Operations Manual, this would be referred to as *troubleshooting*. Incident Investigation is discussed further in Chapter 11.

Chapter 4 also touched on the Developer's Guide, and that discussion continues in Chapter 12. The following sections provide more information on the following subjects:

- Planning the architecture
- Installation and configuration
- Maintenance and administration

Planning the Architecture

Among the documentation in the Operations Manual is the Deployment Guide. The Deployment Guide documents the stages and activities involved in planning the overall deployment of the solution. It depicts the architecture for the solution, the types of servers involved and their placement (DMZ or internal network), and information on which servers the application components would typically reside, along with their respective communications protocols. The majority of this was previously discussed in Chapter 5, which provided an overview of the production environment, the servers, and the overall architecture from a hardware and software perspective. Chapter 5 also discussed the various scaling and fault tolerance techniques that can be employed.

The Deployment Guide also discusses the benefits and drawbacks of the different deployment options — for example, how shared storage can be configured and used, and so on. It would include the solution's high-availability and scalability options, such as load balancing options, clustering, and so forth. The Deployment Guide solidifies all of this information and captures all the relevant "touch points" and areas for further consideration. The following sections provide additional information on these subjects.

Sizing and Scaling the System

This section of the Deployment Guide discusses each of the individual server types and components in the solution and how to arrive at the optimal deployment pattern. To complete this, you need to understand the different usage patterns and transaction flows. It's possible to start with questions such as "What is the expected number of concurrent users?" "What are the expected transaction patterns?" and "What is the anticipated response time?" — all of which should be documented in the requirements. This information is mapped to a deployment model, which shows how the system should be scaled according to changes in these values. The usage patterns also draw out the high ranking percentage page (and functionality) hits, as well as the timings — for example, a login page being used primarily between 8:30 and 9:30 in the morning. The usage patterns capture the transaction volume at peak and normal load. The high volume and high-transaction areas help to identify areas where caching may need to be introduced, as well as how often it needs to be refreshed.

Capturing this information and using it to provide a deployment model helps to solidify the solution design as well as to provide the basis for future scalability. For instance, the initial version of the solution may support up to 10,000 concurrent users; however, the deployment model could be used in the future to determine which additional servers and enhancements would be required to increase this to 30,000.

Part of planning the system also involves understanding the existing enterprise network capabilities and capacity (including low-level network components). This also helps to draw out potentially new hardware requirements. You can start to draw up and shape a basic "planning questionnaire" with questions such as:

- ❑ What is the anticipated number of concurrent users?

- ❑ What is the geographic spread of the user population?

- ❑ What are the expected load and associated usage patterns?

    - ❑ When looking at the expected load and usage patterns, you should rank each transaction (and flow) in terms of its usage and frequency.

- ❑ What is the anticipated response time (or completion time) per transaction?

    - ❑ When looking at the anticipated response time, you should list all online transactions as well as all the batch or background transactions.

- ❑ Which networking infrastructure is already in place?

- ❏ Which firewalls are already in place?
- ❏ Which proxy servers and caching are already in place?
- ❏ Which load balancers are in place and what is their "free" capacity?
- ❏ What network bandwidth and capacity are in place?

❏ Which other required infrastructure is already in place?

- ❏ Security servers (Active Directory, and so on), capacity, existing load, and existing interfaces
- ❏ E-mail servers, capacity, existing load, and so on

❏ What availability is required for the system?

- ❏ Proposed up-time
- ❏ Maintenance windows and schedules
- ❏ Failure and recovery timings

❏ Which resource usage restrictions are in place? These can be expressed in terms of both "normal" and "peak" usage.

- ❏ Maximum CPU usage (e.g., up to 60 percent for normal utilization or 80 percent peak)
- ❏ Maximum memory usage (e.g., up to 70 percent normal utilization or 90 percent peak)

The preceding list provides a few sample questions that would form the basis of the planning questionnaire (as well as the requirements). The questionnaire would then be extended and enhanced for different scenarios and purposes. Based on the answers to the questionnaire, the deployment model would be used to come up with a reasonable deployment approach, such as:

- ❏ The number of web servers required and their CPU and memory capacities
- ❏ The number of application servers required and their CPU and memory capacities
- ❏ The number of administration servers required and their CPU and memory capacities
- ❏ The size and scale of the database servers
- ❏ The number, size, and scale of additional hardware, such as e-mail servers.

Using this approach not only helps in the first instance, but provides a basis for all ongoing upgrades and how the system should be sized and scaled appropriately. The topics covered would include sections such as:

- ❏ Scaling the web servers
- ❏ Scaling the application servers
- ❏ Scaling the administration servers
- ❏ Scaling the database servers

Each server group could have its own individual nuances with respect to sizing and scaling; therefore, each section would discuss these in detail along with the calculations used to arrive at the optimum values. This provides a thorough understanding of how the system can be scaled for future capacity and, more important, what is involved in doing so — for example, listing the existing (or proposed) load balancers and their current and future capacity. Would scaling the servers require additional hardware? What's the current maximum that they could be scaled to within the existing infrastructure?

The initial amount of hardware should be based on peak usage to ensure the system is capable of handling the peak load. Normal load would then be adequately handled. The production environment's size and scale can then be used to determine the size and scale of other environments, such as the disaster-recovery environment (which, as you've already seen, would typically mirror the production environment).

Every system is different, so the deployment model would vary according to each system. However, it's possible to use some simple formulas for calculating the number of hits per second (hits/sec) by examining the number of users and the transaction patterns. For example, let's assume that the system needs to support 10,000 users. It is difficult with Internet-based applications to determine exactly when transactions will be performed. Therefore, you can use uptime to provide the basis of the deployment model. Let's assume the uptime for the system is 24 hours per day. In short, if the load were spread equally throughout the day, you could express this as (10,000 ÷ 86,400 = 0.11). This very simple calculation indicates that the system must support (at least) 0.11 hits/sec. However, 10,000 users may not be a realistic figure for an Internet application. Let's increase this number to 2,000,000 users. In this scenario, the system would need to support at least 23.14 hits/sec. Furthermore, transactions are not generally equally spread throughout the day; there are generally usage peaks throughout the day. For example, multiple users logging on in the morning will create a peak load within a certain period of time. The number of concurrent users (or transactions) then starts to have an effect. A figure of 10,000 concurrent users all using the system at the same time would mean the system (at its very peak) would need to support 166 hits/sec. This is based on the calculation 10,000 ÷ 60. That's 10,000 users all hitting the system within the same minute. Of course, you could go to the very maximum and show 10,000 hits/sec, although this is not typical. It depends on the site or application and that's why it's important to understand the usage patterns and the transaction mix. If the user community is spread across the globe, peaks would also occur at regular intervals throughout the online day as each country came online.

Once you understand the usage patterns (or put some indicative figures in place), you can start to look at how this translates to the size and scale of each server and group. Again, this depends greatly on the applications being hosted and the variety of transactions. However, assuming a single web server could cope with 25 hits/sec (varied across transactions), you'd need at least six web servers to support the anticipated load in the last scenario. Calculating the performance of each server and group typically involves thorough research and/or testing based on number of CPUs, memory, and configuration. The figure used here is simply for illustration purposes. The more servers and groups there are in the architecture, the better the overall performance. Where commodity hardware is used, it is typically cost effective to add more servers.

Security and Communications Model

The security section of the Deployment Guide describes the overall security model as well as the individual security contexts for the various application components. It also discusses the use of Secure Sockets Layer (SSL) and other security-related features, such as Active Directory and encryption/decryption. It shows the end-to-end flow of information and the different communication protocols and ports used, as well as the security contexts used.

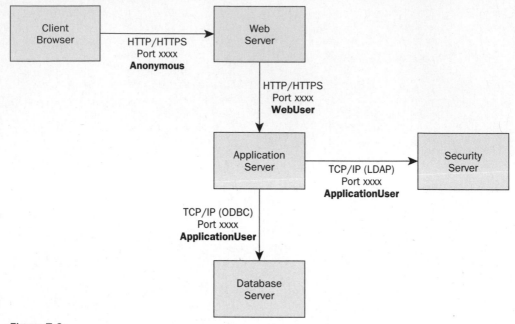

Figure 7-6

Figure 7-6 shows a simplified communication protocol diagram. It shows the protocol, port, and security context (user) for communication between each of the servers.

The figure is only an example of the information that should be captured for the end-to-end flow. In Figure 7-6, the client browser is making an HTTP or HTTPS request to the web server on a specified port, typically port 80 (HTTP) and port 443 (HTTPS), respectively, although these could be changed. The website typically runs under a specific security context or "identity." By default this is usually some form of local account user. However, this should be changed to a domain account that can be given all the appropriate security and access rights. In this example, the web server is using the WebUser identity to communicate with the application servers, again over HTTP or HTTPS. The figure shows that the application server is communicating with some form of external "security server" over TCP/IP using the ApplicationUser identity. The TCP/IP communication also needs a specific port to be assigned. Similarly, the application server is communicating with the database over TCP/IP using the ApplicationUser identity.

It's important to capture this type of information because it helps to ensure that all the relevant ports are opened and the security and access rights are properly assigned. For instance, the database, stored procedures, and tables (in this example) would need to allow the ApplicationUser identity to perform the required actions. The information also helps to ensure that testing is performed using similar accounts and privileges.

Fault Tolerance and Automatic Failure and Recovery

This section of the Deployment Guide discusses all the fault tolerant features of the solution as well as the automatic failure and recovery mechanisms and how to achieve them. Using a similar approach to the previous section, you can build up a simple questionnaire to provide the basis for the requirements and features of the solution.

- ❑ Which servers and groups need to be (or should be) load balanced?

    - ❑ Which load balancing algorithm should they use?

    - ❑ Do these (or will these) require sticky sessions?

- ❑ Which servers and groups need to be (or should be) clustered?

    - ❑ Which clustering mechanism should they use (active/passive or active/active)?

- ❑ What is the minimum time allowed (or supported) for failover?

- ❑ Which databases need to be replicated and/or backed up?

- ❑ Is there a dedicated disaster-recovery site?

- ❑ Which application components need to support automatic recovery?

You can also use the information presented in the previous chapters to complete the basic questionnaire to arrive at a suitable set of questions for preparing the various deployment considerations.

Installation and Configuration

The Installation and Configuration Guide would list all the individual components, and information on how they should be installed, and how they should be configured. Each configuration setting would be fully documented so that it can be set appropriately according to the size and scale of the deployment. The installation and configuration would start from a base server and build up through all the different applications and layers. In addition, the installation and configuration would cover the network and networking components where necessary. The following provides a very high-level set of sample areas that would be covered in a web application:

- ❑ Installing and configuring the web servers, including:

    - ❑ IIS configuration (ports, users and permissions, websites, applications, and so on)

    - ❑ ASP.NET configuration

    - ❑ Web application configuration

    - ❑ Load balancer configuration

- ❑ Installing and configuring the Application servers, including:

    - ❑ Custom application configuration

    - ❑ Third-party application or agent configuration

- ❑ Installing and configuring the Administration servers, including:

    - ❑ Administration application configuration

    - ❑ Batch job configuration

    - ❑ Shared storage configuration

    - ❑ Cluster configuration

❏   Third-party application or agent configuration

❏   Installing and configuring the Database servers

❏   File system and storage configuration

❏   Security configuration

The Installation and Configuration Guide walks the user through each of the steps (and options), including all the prerequisites for the installation as well as any required post installation procedures and checks. The information can be used to build automated deployment scripts as well as disk images and automated verification scripts to support rapid installation. The verification scripts can also be included as part of the batch solution. The organization may already use existing tools for automated deployment, so it is worth finding out what these are and any specifics that may need to be noted.

Maintenance and Administration

The maintenance and administration procedures cover a number of different tasks and activities, including but not limited to:

❏   General administration functions, including the following:

❏   Starting and stopping the system

❏   Creating/changing security contexts (and passwords)

❏   Performance tuning and calibration tasks, including the following:

❏   Web server tuning

❏   Application server tuning

❏   Administration server tuning

❏   Database server tuning

❏   Network tuning

❏   Backup and recovery tasks, including:

❏   The databases and file systems that are backed up

❏   The frequency of backups and whether they are full or partial

❏   How long the backups/tapes should be kept for

❏   Recovery procedures, including any post-recovery updates and/or configuration

❏   Disaster recovery and failover tasks, including:

❏   Failing over to the alternative site

❏   Failing over to an alternative environment

❏   Recovering the primary site

Each section should discuss the topic in detail and provide all the necessary information to make an informed decision. In the early days, the information should be used to "sign-off" on the approach. As the project progresses, the information solidifies and is used as the formal procedures.

Summary

In this chapter, you learned a little bit about who is going to support your system once it's live, and you've seen some of the routine functions they perform as well as those leading up to go-live. The chapter also discussed the Operations Manual, which forms a large part of the system, and you saw a high-level outline that would need to be completed throughout the project. Using the high-level outline, you can start to shape a useful roadmap for moving forward. This will save time and effort later and promotes thinking out-of-the-box by using the end goals as a good starting point.

The following are the key points to take away from this chapter:

- **There are typically three levels of live service support.** The levels of support and the groups we discussed in this chapter included:

  - Level 1 (Operations)
  - Level 2 (Service Delivery)
  - Level 3 (Application Maintenance)

These levels can differ from organization to organization.

- **Understand each support group's requirements and gather their insights.** The easier it is to support the system, the easier everyone's life is. Think about the levels of support and what can be done to ensure that everyone has the right information to perform their job.

- **Develop the Operations Manual and Operational Procedures**. Start developing the operations procedures early and identify key operations procedures for third-party software. It's a good idea to have an outline of the Operations Manual and what it should contain. This really helps to flesh out areas of the design and incorporate features that could otherwise be missed early on. The very high-level subject areas include the following:

  - Solution Overview
  - Planning the Architecture
  - Installation and Configuration
  - Maintenance and Administration
  - Monitoring and Alerts
  - Reporting and Analytics
  - Batch
  - Incident Investigation (Troubleshooting)

- **Reduce manual effort.** When designing your solution, especially for operability, you should look for areas where you can reduce manual effort during live service support. Think about how the system is supported and what can be incorporated in the application as well as the tooling, reports, and scripts that can make supporting the system more efficient.

8

Monitoring and Alerts

The environments of many organizations are complex entities consisting of many different servers and applications. You've already seen what a typical production environment can look like, and that's just for one system. Monitoring is an integral part of the organization's effectiveness. Knowing when something is or isn't functioning correctly or requires manual intervention is critical to the operation of the business and its customers. Effective monitoring will help to ensure this. As mentioned in Chapter 7, the operations team is primarily responsible for monitoring all the systems in live service. This chapter looks at monitoring the different environments, servers, and applications.

This chapter is organized into the following sections:

❑ **What Is Monitoring?** Examines the monitoring architecture and the various rules that can be put in place to filter and escalate information. It also discusses monitoring blackout windows, which are used to filter out alerts at certain periods of time.

❑ **What Is Monitored?** Examines the various monitoring sources as well as some typical application and server monitoring. It also discusses the types of events that are captured, Windows and other third-party application performance counters, and custom performance counters updated by the application.

❑ **What Are Alerts?** Examines how alerts are the trigger for incident investigation.

What Is Monitoring?

Monitoring provides an end-to-end view of the organization's production environments. There are two primary purposes of monitoring a system. The first is to provide the operations team with a complete picture of the current state of the live systems, from both a hardware and software perspective. This can range from the amount of available disk space on a server or disk array to a full-scale shutdown of a system or component. The second purpose is to provide effective information and tools that the operations team can use to rapidly respond to incidents and alerts.

Monitoring software keeps track of what's happening on the numerous servers and devices within the organization as well as the diverse range of applications and software that runs on them. Many monitoring solutions are available, including BMC Patrol and Microsoft Operations Manager (MOM). The software is mainly used to monitor all the systems and applications in the production environment. Some organizations also monitor other key environments, such as the disaster recovery environment and the pre-production environment (if there is one) to ensure that these environments are ready to serve when necessary. However, the pre-production environment may be integrated with development or test versions of the monitoring tools.

Monitoring software is typically implemented using the master/agent paradigm, as discussed in Chapter 5, in which the agents capture and send events and performance data back to the master. The monitoring master usually records this information in a central database. Figure 8-1 shows a typical architectural scenario.

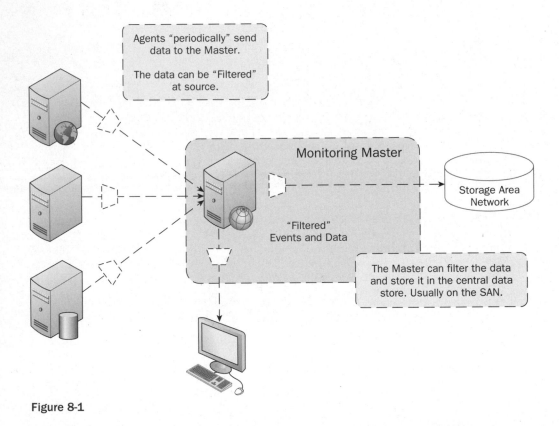

Figure 8-1

The monitoring agents periodically send information to the monitoring master. This is known as the *sampling period*. Effective monitoring typically relies quite heavily on the sampling period. Too much sampling can have an effect on performance, whereas too little can have an effect on the visibility of performance.

There are typically four high-level categories of data that the agents send to the master:

- ❏ Performance data
- ❏ Event data
- ❏ Process and service data
- ❏ Configuration data

In Windows environments, performance data is generally obtained from Windows performance counters. In other environments, the agent may be collecting the data directly or forwarding from another source. Figure 8-2 shows the Reliability and Performance Monitor in Windows Vista.

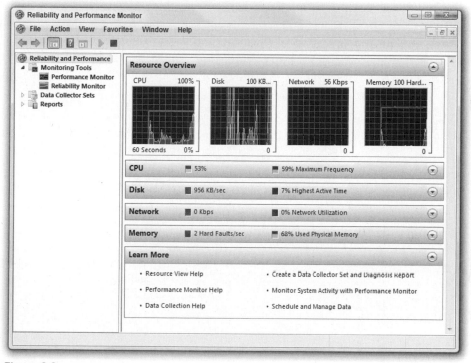

Figure 8-2

Performance counters are grouped into categories (also referred to as *performance objects*). The category can contain one or more actual performance counters. For instance, the Processor performance object contains a number of different counters. The following list shows just a few of the processor object counters:

- ❏ % Idle Time
- ❏ % Processor Time
- ❏ Interrupts/sec

Furthermore, each performance counter category can be either a single instance category or a multiple instance category:

❑ A single instance category is used when there is only one instance of the category required — for example, the memory category. Because memory is treated as an entirety, it makes no sense to have multiple instances of the memory category.

❑ A multiple instance category is used when there is more than one instance — for example, the processor category. There would be an instance for each physical processor within the computer and an instance for the overall total.

The monitoring solution would typically obtain the counters from the configured servers. However, the Reliability and Performance Monitor application shown previously can also be used to view and trace performance counters. The Performance Monitor is simply a lightweight application that displays performance counters selected by the user in a rolling graph. Lightweight applications like this are useful during testing to obtain performance information.

Events indicate something that has occurred within the application or on a server or device. In a Windows environment, events are obtained from the Windows Event Logs. In other systems, events can be obtained from log files and other sources. Figure 8-3 shows the Windows Event Viewer, which allows you to browse events in the Windows Event Logs.

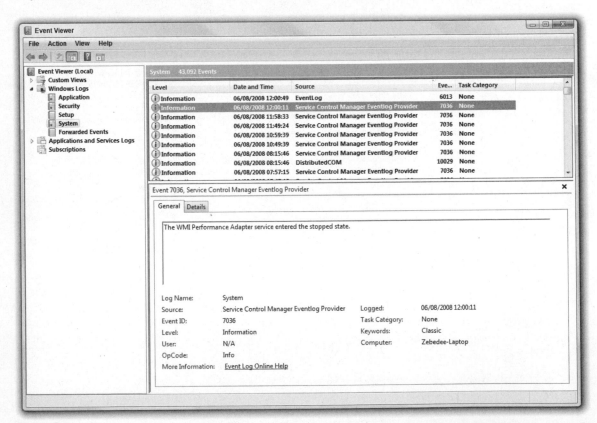

Figure 8-3

An event has a number of key properties, including the following:

❑ **Level** — Specifies the event level for the entry. The event type can be one of the following:

  ❑ **Error** — Indicates an error event. The error event type should be used to indicate a significant issue to the operational team. An error event will typically trigger an incident investigation. An error event is typically raised when the application can't continue processing with this issue.

  ❑ **Warning** — Indicates a warning event. The warning event type should be used to draw attention to something that could potentially lead to a problem. A warning event is typically raised when the application can continue processing, but should the problem persist, the application may escalate to an error state.

  ❑ **Information** — Indicates an informational type event. The information event type should be used to indicate a significant functional or processing milestone. Information events, or more important, the lack of informational events, can also be used to trigger alerts.

  ❑ **Success audit** — Indicates a successful security-related event. The success audit event type should be used to indicate that a significant security-related function has completed successfully. For instance, an event could be raised each time a user successfully logs into his or her account or is authenticated accordingly.

  ❑ **Failure audit** — Indicates an unsuccessful security-related event. This event type should be used to indicate a failure has occurred in a security-related function—for example, when an unsuccessful login is attempted.

❑ **Date and time** — Specifies the date and time the event occurred (or was recorded).

❑ **Source** — Specifies the name of the component or application raising the event.

❑ **Description** — Contains the full text of the event raised. This is the most important value and should really contain all the relevant information about the event. The description is particularly important in error cases because the event will lead to an incident investigation.

Processes and services that are running on the server are also monitored. In a Windows environment the processes that are running can be viewed using the Windows Task Manager (see Figure 8-4).

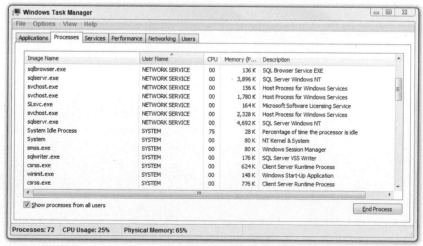

Figure 8-4

Configuration data is usually obtained from the system configuration such as the System Registry or by examining the hardware and/or software. It provides the monitoring master a detailed view of the server being monitored.

In the production environment, the application could be running on Windows Server; however, the screenshots are from Windows Vista, which I use on my home computer. It is important to understand that there can (and probably will) be differences between the tools and technologies used in development compared to those used in production. It is equally important to identify where this can cause issues and goes some way to re-enforcing the previous messages that wherever possible the tools and technologies that will be used in production should be used in development, although costs may be prohibitive.

The operating system and applications raise events and update performance counters, which are then used to monitor the system's performance. Operating system performance counters include CPU usage, memory usage, disk usage, and so on. There are literally hundreds of events and performance counters included in the base operating system and third-party applications, not to mention those created and raised by other installed applications.

As you can probably imagine, capturing and recording all these performance counters and events results in a huge amount of data. To reduce the amount of information, the monitoring software supports rules that are customized and determine the information that is collected by the agent. This is typically referred to as *downstream filtering*. The information collected by the agents is used for immediate display and for historical and trend reporting. The master may also apply further "upstream" filtering to the data prior to display and/or storage.

Figure 8-5 shows the operations team's monitoring master obtaining information from other monitoring masters and filtering it for display on "the big screen" in the control room.

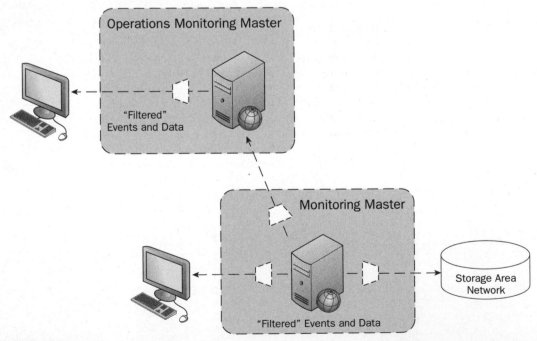

Figure 8-5

Monitoring Requirements and Rules

The technical requirements, which stipulate performance-related behavior, are a great starting point for defining specific monitoring rules. Consider, for example, the following performance-related technical requirements:

❑ All database servers will have processor utilization, measured over any 5 minute period, of less than 80 percent for 95 percent of the time.

❑ All database servers will have fixed memory utilization, measured over any 5 minute period, of less than 60 percent for 95 percent of the time.

❑ All Web, application, and administration servers will have processor utilization, measured over any 5 minute period, of less than 70 percent for 95 percent of the time.

❑ All Web, application, and administration servers will have fixed memory utilization, measured over any 5 minute period, of less than 90 percent for 95 percent of the time.

Each of these requirements can be measured and monitored during testing and live service to ensure that the system is performing according to its requirements and design goals.

Custom performance counters can be monitored in exactly the same way. The rules allow these kinds of models to be implemented so that an alert is raised when the condition has been reached.

Performance counters can also be used as a heartbeat to indicate that a process is actually up-and-running. Just because the process appears to be "running" on the machine doesn't necessarily mean that it is actually executing. A performance counter could be updated periodically (even during idle time) to indicate that the process is alive. The rules could be implemented in such as way that if the counter doesn't increase (or change) within a specified period of time, an alert is raised.

Rules can also be implemented on the basis of events. An event's criticality can be changed according to the rule when multiple events occur at the same time. For instance, during live service, transactions may be retried for robustness. The system may raise a warning each time it retries the transaction. However, if there are multiple processes, on multiple machines, all retrying at the same time, this may be escalated to an alert. For example, "10 of *these* warnings within a 1 second interval really means an alert."

It is important to understand monitoring and rules. The monitoring packages are often very sophisticated and remove the need to include custom code within the application. The application can concentrate on what it does and let the monitoring software deal with filtering the information. The application should be instrumented and configurable to support effective monitoring.

Monitoring solutions tend to provide a series of out-of-the-box rules and packs that can serve as a starting point to monitoring the production hardware and applications.

Blackout Windows

A *blackout window* is a period of time when certain rules and monitoring are switched off to avoid an influx of unnecessary alerts being raised. For example, a blackout window may be used during periods of batch processing when services and applications are taken off-line. Under normal operation, an application stopping would constitute a critical alert, whereas during routine batch it is expected.

Blackout windows can usually be manual or automated. A manual blackout window is simply a documented and well-established period when certain events should be recognized by the operations team. This is part of the operations documentation as well as part of the handover to the operations team. An automated blackout window is incorporated into the rules of the monitoring software so that certain events are not raised during the blackout period. Blackout periods can also be used during routine maintenance periods.

What Is Monitored?

Under normal circumstances every server in the production architecture (including the operations architecture) is monitored. At a high level, the monitoring agent will:

❑ Access performance counters or other performance indicators.

❑ Extract information from logs and events.

❑ Check services and processes.

❑ Obtain configuration information from the underlying system.

It is also possible for the monitoring agent to execute custom scripts that gather information specific to a particular application or service. This can be very useful during post go-live support when additional monitoring capabilities might be required. A simple script can be developed to check certain records in the databases for consistency, and to raise an alert on inconsistent records. This could be very useful, especially if there are distributed transactions across multiple databases.

During testing (whether unit, integration, functional, or technical), numerous scripts and database extracts are used to verify expected results and check values. These scripts should be catalogued because they may prove very useful in live service. This is also true during incident investigation.

Each server and application will have its own monitoring requirements. For example, a SQL Server database server will be monitored for specific purposes, including but not limited to the following:

❑ The state of its services (SQL Server, SQL Agent, and so on)

❑ The state of the databases

❑ Available space

❑ Connections

❑ Blocked processes

❑ Events

A base server would typically be monitored for the following performance characteristics:

❑ **Processor performance** — This information is used to determine the preceding rules and to determine whether a server is running "hot." A spike in the processor can occur when an application starts or a heavy transaction is in progress. The important thing to remember is that spikes don't last long. This is why the processor is measured over a period of time to indicate that it is running high for an extended duration. If the monitoring system raised an alert on the value of a single processor sample, it would create a lot of noise.

❑ **Memory utilization** — Memory utilization is measured in the same way as the processor. Memory will experience peaks and troughs, so memory is measured over time. The information can be used to detect memory leaks. For example, if memory is constantly increasing and not decreasing it could indicate a memory leak somewhere or that garbage collection hasn't initiated.

❑ **Logical and physical disk space and performance** — The amount of logical and physical disk space available is monitored. Alerts are usually raised when the amount of available space drops below 20 percent, although warnings may also be raised at pertinent thresholds, such as 40 percent available.

❑ **Network utilization** — The network utilization and activity is also monitored. This shows the processes that are sending/receiving data and the amount.

There are many other performance counters that can be (and are) monitored, although these give an indication of the types of performance counters monitored.

In addition to performance counters, the following types of events are also monitored:

❑ **Events indicating services have started, are stopping, or have stopped** — A service starting is a good thing, especially when it is supposed to — for example, during batch execution or when the service has been started manually following an incident. A service stopping can be a good thing and a bad thing. That is, it's a good thing when a service stops during batch execution so that routine maintenance can be performed. During normal execution, however, a service stopping would be considered an alert and would require investigation.

❑ **Events indicating a cluster has been brought online or offline** — Clusters starting and stopping are similar to services starting and stopping.

❑ **Events indicating an exception occurred** — Exceptions can be both technical exceptions and business exceptions. An example of a technical exception would be that the database is down, whereas a business exception might be someone sending in an order over a particular threshold. The important thing with exceptions is to understand what can be or will be done about it. A downed database is obvious, but there are other exceptions that the application might raise.

❑ **Events indicating a warning** — Warnings are often interesting because you need to know what to do about them. For instance, if the application raises a warning that the cache is 80 percent full, it doesn't really indicate a problem unless it can be complemented with other data, such as how quickly it is filling up. At what point is it anticipated that it will be full? This kind of information provides a better basis for decision-making about whether action is required. Warning thresholds also should be configurable.

❑ **Informational events** — Informational events can be very useful at specific times during the day. For example, during batch, when a long process is running, an informational event at key processing points helps to show that the process is still running. A transaction being successfully processed would also be an informational event, although there are likely to be thousands of such events raised throughout the day.

Again, this is just a sampling; there are other events that can be (and are) monitored.

The rules help to filter the events that are captured to alleviate noise. The application should support configurability so that event severities can be changed without have to change the code.

Custom Performance Counters

In addition to monitoring standard and third-party performance counters, the system should include custom performance counters that can be monitored. The custom performance counters can also be used during testing to gauge the system's performance. Some typical performance counter types could include the following, but are not limited to:

❑ **Counters that are updated on a per-transaction basis** — These types of counters can be used to determine the component's transaction throughput.

❑ **Counters that are updated on a per-connection basis** — These types of counters can be used to determine the number of connections a component has.

❑ **Counters that indicate in-memory list/queue counts** — These can be used to determine how many items are in the queue or list. This can be used for queues, in-memory reference data caches, pooled objects, and so on.

Chapter 20 looks at custom performance counters in more detail to provide improved monitoring of the applications you develop.

Custom Events

The application should include custom events to support improved monitoring and operability. The events raised by the application should include the categories listed previously. The application will also write information to log files and trace files. The events raised by the system should really indicate information that is useful from an operational point of view. Tracing is typically used to trace the flow of processing through the system. If the application used the event log as a trace file it would "spam" the event log with unnecessary information. The events raised by the application are raised with an associated event type Error, Warning, Information, and so on. The application should include events for all occasions; good events such as processing milestones reached (especially in batch), bad events such as transaction timeout (although the wait-retry pattern can help with these), and ugly events such as a complete database failure. You should look at the solution, its functional and technical processing, and the individual components to identify events that can be categorized into the groups discussed.

It is easier to identify error events because even when the application isn't specifically raising its own errors or events, there are still system exceptions that can occur and stop further processing, irrespective of whether they are truly handled by the code. If the application is going to stop further processing and/ or exit for any reason, this would typically constitute an Error Event.

Custom Processes

The application may contain custom processes and services and these should be included within the monitoring configuration. For example, the solution may implement a custom service that manages various components and processing. The service state should be monitored as well as its specific performance counters and events.

What Are Alerts?

Alerts are typically displayed on the operations bridge for immediate attention, whereas other, less critical events and information are captured for future use. The operations team may be using a specific monitoring or alerting package that you need to understand. There may be some specifics that you can include within the application or configuration for improved monitoring or alerting. There's also the possibility that the solution uses multiple monitoring and filtering packages. The operations team will be monitoring everything, including low-level network components such as routers and load balancers. There can also be many different systems covering a wide variety of technologies. Certain information gathered by the monitoring master may need to be passed on or obtained by another monitoring solution.

An alert can be raised verbatim based on an event captured, or it can be based on a series of events or performance data. For example, CPU usage is a performance statistic. Based on technical requirements it might be necessary to raise an alert when the CPU usage is running above 90 percent for an extended period of time. This would indicate that a server is "running hot." Another example would be a number of warning events being escalated to a critical event or alert. For example, a system may have a process that is passing transactions to another system and the processing backlog is monitored at regular intervals. As throughput decreases and the backlog increases, a warning is raised; if the backlog has increased at the point of the next sample, another warning is raised; and, finally, if the backlog is still increasing at the point of the next sample, a critical alert is raised.

Alerts are usually raised to get an operator's attention, and sometimes to provide manual intervention or escalation. In most cases when an alert is displayed, it is also accompanied by a sound — a ping or perhaps even the sound of a siren for very critical alerts. This allows operators to hear critical alerts where they're not actively looking at the monitoring console.

It is also important to note that monitoring captures both positive and negative information. Long-running tasks or significant "good" events can be raised to allow operators to see that the system is running as expected. For example, a job processing millions of records might raise an event at specific percentage complete points, such as 25, 50, 75, and 100 percent.

Monitoring software systems generally allow custom scripts and helpful information to be associated with alerts. The scripts and jobs can be executed by operators at the click of a button when an alert has been raised. For instance, a script may be executed to restart a particular service or gather information from the database. Although this functionality and information is very useful, it needs to be incorporated as part of the monitoring solution and scope.

Alerts are raised off of all the information you've seen so far. The rules examine the information gathered and determine whether an alert should be raised. Alerts are monitored by the operations team for immediate action or escalation. Alerts should not be raised for anything that doesn't require some form of investigation or action. When alerts are raised that do not require investigation or escalation, they are unnecessary noise that operators will need to deal with. This usually means that they have to mark the alert in the console as having been dealt with. Implementing the correct rules to only raise alerts at the correct time means that when everything is working according to plan there is simply silence or positive noise.

Alerts are generally the trigger for incident investigation. The operations team will not investigate; they will check the operations procedures to see if this has happened before and whether there are procedures for dealing with it. If so, they will perform them. If not, or the procedures didn't work, the alert will be escalated and a full-on investigation will begin. This is just another reason to ensure that events contain all the necessary information they can about the issue and its resolution.

Summary

In this chapter you looked at monitoring and the sources of monitoring information. You also learned which events and performance counters can be monitored, and received some food for thought regarding an application's custom performance counters.

The following are the key points to take away from this chapter:

❑ **Monitoring is critical to live service.** All production systems should be monitored effectively and the operations team is primarily responsible for all monitoring.

❑ **Alerts are used to draw attention to the system.** Alerts can be raised by the application itself or raised based on monitoring configuration and rules.

❑ **Events can be positive and negative.** You should think about both positive and negative events that might be required by operators.

❑ **Reduce "noise."** Monitoring rules should be implemented to reduce unnecessary alerts and noise. In addition, the application should ideally support monitoring configuration for the severity of its events. This allows tuning during testing as well as live service.

❑ **Implement custom events.** The application should include custom events. The high-level categories of events discussed included:

    ❑ Informational

    ❑ Warning

    ❑ Error

    ❑ Success and failure audit

❑ **Implement custom performance counters.** The application should include custom performance counters to improve monitoring in live service. The following types of performance counters were discussed:

    ❑ Counters that are updated on a per-transaction basis

    ❑ Counters that are updated on a per-connection basis

    ❑ Counters that indicate in-memory list/queue counts

❑ **Capture monitoring requirements early.** Monitoring requirements cover the entire solution, including hardware and software. You should capture your monitoring requirements early to ensure they are addressed.

Reporting and Analytics

There's often a tendency to think of reporting and analytics as simply providing business users and stakeholders with data gathered from around the system, typically from within the database — for example, a report showing sales figures for a particular period or region. Reporting and analytics are sometimes referred to as *business intelligence*. However, reports are not just developed for business users; they can be developed for technical staff as well. As you've already seen, monitoring solutions can capture potentially thousands of events and performance data, all of which can be packaged into very useful reports. For example, a report could show the number of alerts, grouped by type, that were raised on a specific day. A report such as this might be used to better configure the monitoring rules to remove unnecessary noise. Another report might show end-to-end transaction and throughput figures. A report such as this would be useful to both business and technical staff. Good reports can provide the necessary information to make business decisions as well as technical decisions.

This chapter is organized into the following sections:

❑ **Reporting Overview** — Provides an overview of the reporting function and the categories of reports, as well as some specifics on capturing report criteria and requirements. It also shows some typical reports and output styles. The key elements to any report include:

    ❑ The selection criteria

    ❑ The output results

    Reports can generally be categorized into the following high-level headings:

    ❑ Business reports

    ❑ Technical reports

❑ **The Reporting Architecture** — Takes a look at the overall reporting architecture and how report data can be gathered from multiple sources and replicated databases.

❏ **Technical Reporting** — Looks at some of the basic technical reports and how they can be used in various ways, such as:

❏ For monitoring

❏ For trend analysis

❏ For incident investigation

❏ **Analytics Overview** — Provides an overview of the various web analytics software that can be used to analyze web server logs and provide reports and analysis. It also discusses the importance of understanding the analytics architecture, as it could have other implications on the solution architecture and design. Web analytics typically provide reports that show:

❏ Pages visited

❏ Path taken to particular pages

❏ Time spent on each page

❏ Page performance

❏ Pages not visited

❏ Internal/external visits

❏ The pages visitors arrived from

Reporting Overview

Traditionally reports have been thought of as something businesses use to make financial decisions. The fact is that reports are used by many different people for many different purposes. Reports can be thought of as data extracts, although not all reports are generated from the data in the database; some reports are generated from log files and other sources. For example, website analysis systems often run through collections of log files and analyze page hits and user movements.

Reports can be generally categorized into two main categories, although some reports can fit into either category:

❏ **Business reports** — Business reports are used by the organization to make various decisions. The business reports are usually stipulated in the requirements. An example of a business report may be the orders placed on a particular date or range of dates broken down by product category.

❏ **Technical reports** — Technical reports are used by the service delivery team and other technical staff for a variety of reasons — for example, to determine transactions and throughput over time, or to analyze CPU usage. Ad-hoc reports may be run during an incident investigation to pull out an end-to-end transaction view, which will help to pull together the overall timeline.

An organization can use reporting solutions to produce a wide variety of reports, some very simple and others quite complex, including lists, grouped items, charts and graphs, and so on.

Figure 9-1 shows an example report of new accounts created, in a column chart. Although this is a simple report, it could very well be used in the early days of live service to see how many accounts are being created on a daily basis. This information also could be trended over longer periods of time and rolled up at the end of the month for stakeholder meetings. The report shown would typically be generated from the data in the database.

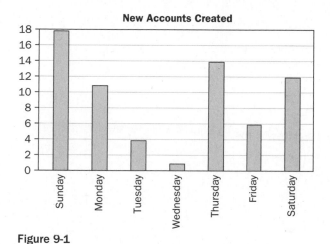

Figure 9-1

Figure 9-2 shows another example, a Transaction Retries report in a nicer looking bar chart. This report shows that transactions are being retried, which means there could be something to investigate. The data would typically be gathered from performance counters or events raised by the application.

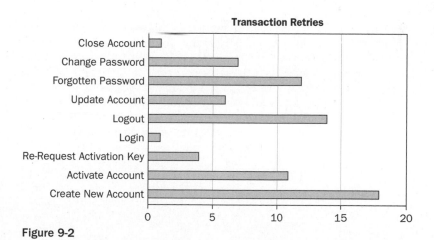

Figure 9-2

While the first report would be of more interest to the business and the second would be of more interest to the technical staff, there are many reports that are of interest to both. A primary example is the end-to-end performance report, as shown in Figure 9-3.

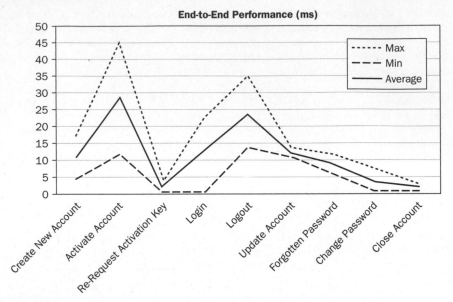

Figure 9-3

End-to-end performance is typically the time taken to complete a transaction. For example, the difference between the time the transaction was submitted from the browser and the time at which the response was received would provide the end-to-end performance figure for the transaction. The report in Figure 9-3 shows the maximum, minimum, and average time, in milliseconds, for each transaction. Technical staff could use this information to ensure the system meets its technical requirements and to possibly identify bottlenecks in the solution. The business might use the information for marketing purposes, especially if the performance figures are better than competing products and services.

Where transactions involve multiple pages and round trips, the complete transaction end-to-end performance would generally be the sum of all the individual requests. For instance, the case study discussed later, has a "forgotten password" flow that links into the "change password" flow. The end-to-end performance in this scenario is actually the processing time taken to perform both transactions. The individual round-trip timings would still need to be captured in isolation. This poses an interesting challenge for calculating the cumulative value, because the flows are actually independent of one another and the change password flow can be used by logged in users. In the case of a forgotten password, the user first would hit the Forgotten Password page, where he or she would enter and submit alternative authentication information. This would cause a round-trip whereby the user would be authenticated and then directed to the Change Password page. This would complete this part of the overall transaction, the end-to-end latency can be recorded as "FP." The user would now change his or her password and submit the request, which would cause another round-trip whereby the system would change the password in the database and display a confirmation message. This would complete the overall transaction. This end-to-end performance of this portion of the transaction can be recorded as "CP." The total end-to-end performance of the entire transaction is essentially FP + CP. However, because the change password flow can also be used by logged-in users, the processing somehow needs to distinguish between the two transactions and add CP to the appropriate performance figures for forgotten password transactions to ensure they are calculated properly.

The data in this report would typically come from performance counters raised by the application, while some technical reports scan application log files for certain events and entries.

There are really only two key aspects when considering a report:

❏ **The selection criteria** — The selection criteria are used to filter or specify the information that will be included in the report. Too much (mandatory) selection criteria can cause a report to become unwieldy, and too little criteria can cause a report to produce too much data. A report that has only a single selection criterion could potentially produce hundreds and thousands of records. A report that has 20 different selections could be difficult to use. However, default values could be provided to support easier execution. The following are some common report selection criteria:

   ❏ Specific field values

   ❏ Value ranges (e.g., between two values)

   ❏ Value masks (e.g., using wildcard characters)

   ❏ Date and time ranges

❏ **The output (content)** — The output (content) of the report should contain all the information the user needs to use the report effectively. Too much information can make the report difficult to read, and too little information can render the report useless. You need to understand what the report is being used for and the information it should contain.

Understanding the reports, what they are used for, and by whom can often help to refine the selection criteria and the output. When designing reports, it is wise to model this information to see if it really does provide what it should. This will avoid late-breaking changes. Reports can obviously contain sensitive information, so security and access control need to be carefully considered. The report author needs to understand the security requirements of the report to ensure that no unauthorized personnel can use it. Security must be considered at all times to protect the information in the system. For instance, consider the abridged table listing shown in Figure 9-4.

Account Listing

Username	DateTimeCreated	DateTimeActivated	ActivationKey	Password	EmailAddress	SecurityQuestion	SecurityQuestionAnswer
ide1968	10/01/2008 11:52:00	10/01/2008 11:53:00	{0000-1111-2222-3333}	*******	*************************	*************************	*************************
SLamps	11/01/2008 10:30:05	11/01/2008 11:20:05	{0000-2222-3333-4444}	*******	*************************	*************************	*************************
BarneyBoo	10/01/2008 12:42:00	10/01/2008 12:43:50	{0000-3333-4444-5555}	*******	*************************	*************************	*************************
Zebedee	11/01/2008 09:15:15	11/01/2008 14:45:28	{0000-4444-5555-6666}	*******	*************************	*************************	*************************

Figure 9-4

Some reports are simply listings from tables and potentially filtered for specific values or ranges. The report shown in Figure 9-4 is pretty useless on its own (unless some analysis into usernames was being performed), but it highlights some important areas for consideration:

❑ **Reports might need to display sensitive information.** For example, encrypted information may need to be decrypted. This typically poses a major problem for the reporting solution. Unless the reporting solution can integrate with application components, the data will need to be stored in clear text for reporting purposes, which is not very secure. However, the encrypted values could be decrypted during replication or data transfer using a custom script or job. The decryption algorithms need to be kept synchronized if the job or script doesn't make use of the core application components.

❑ **There may be other value-added calculations or transformations that are specific to the report output.** These again might be performed during data transfer. For example, an incoming message may be stored in a single database column for the purposes of non-repudiation. However, a single column is not necessarily searchable or easy to read. During transformation the message could be broken out into a more column-based format for reporting purposes.

Understanding and modeling the reports helps to identify areas where certain information would need to be decoded, decrypted, calculated, or even dissected because it is not stored in a way that can be readily used for the report. The development implications can be quite far-reaching and require a lot of time and effort. Finding this out late in the lifecycle could have a dramatic effect on costs and timescales.

Reports can also contain a huge amount of information. In the preceding example, the report could contain millions of users and span multiple pages. Each report should be justified and have a valid reason for inclusion with the solution. Reports may also be accessed by large numbers of people, so the reporting solution needs to support the number of users and the frequencies at which reports will be executed.

Modern reporting solutions contain report authoring tools that can be very comprehensive. The use of report authoring tools can require specialized training, which should be considered early to maximize the usage of the reporting infrastructure. The level of sophistication varies from tool to tool, of course.

Designing and developing reports can be a fairly lengthy process. It depends entirely on the number of reports and their nature. Starting these activities early helps to avoid delays, although reporting often goes beyond the end of development. Reports are often identified late in the process. The use cases, the data model, events, and performance counters alone offer a huge number of possibilities for reports. Reports can also become redundant, so it's worth confirming with the users to avoid working on reports that are no longer required.

You should follow the same principles and due diligence when developing reports that you follow developing other areas of the application. Performance testing a report is generally a good idea, as waiting for large reports to compile can be a pain for an end user. Retrieving the absolute minimum amount of information required for the report is often a good idea, as is keeping the report simple. Some reports may even require some form of custom code. The custom code needs to follow similar best practices and standards so that it can be supported appropriately.

Reports should be modeled in a similar fashion to screen mockups to ensure that the relevant selection criteria and output is captured. Figure 9-5 shows a very simple report mockup for the New Accounts Weekly report.

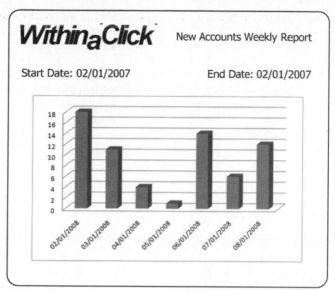

Figure 9-5

While it might not be the most compelling report, it serves the purpose of defining the selection criteria and the output. It shows that the report can be executed across a data range, which means the system needs to store the date and time the account was created. Mocking up reports helps to ensure that the application can support them (it has the right events or data). Mocking up the reports also helps to flesh out the information they contain and the data sources for the information. For example, in terms of the case study, does the business really want to see "new accounts" or does it want to see accounts that have been fully activated? There's a difference between the two. Understanding the underlying criteria of the report will help to ensure that the report fulfills its purpose and that the application supports it. It will also help to define the underlying data model.

Reporting is often one of the tasks left right until the last moment. At the start of the project there's typically a feeling or view that there won't be many reports. This is generally not the case. There's usually a long list of reports that need to be produced — for both the business and the support staff.

If you keep reporting in mind along the way, a huge amount of what will be put in place can be reused for reporting. Test scripts that extract and compare data from two databases can be used not only during unit testing, but during batch and for reporting as well. Obviously some tweaks might need to be done, but the foundation is in place, and it gets people talking (and thinking) about additional reporting capabilities.

The Reporting Architecture

One of the key challenges with reporting is deciding the database that the reports will be executed against. For example, reports could be executed against the secondary site's databases and storage area network (SAN). In this case, the report data would be traveling across the wide area network (WAN). This would need to be balanced against bandwidth availability and the reporting performance. The monitoring master database also records performance and event data into a central database (located on the SAN), although this information wouldn't necessarily be replicated to the secondary site. Furthermore, certain technical reports may need to be executed against the production database, especially during live incident investigation. The replication timings may not support live reporting.

Figure 9-6 shows the reporting solution obtaining data and information from a number of sources and providing it to both business users and technical users.

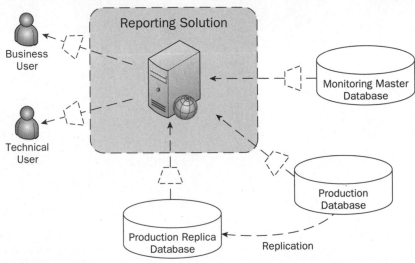

Figure 9-6

Having a reporting solution that executes against a replicated database will reduce the amount of direct access to the production database. The reporting solution will often execute stored procedures or queries that will return the data. If the stored procedures are being executed against the live database, they must ensure that the transaction isolation level is `read-uncommitted` to prevent locking problems. All queries for reporting purposes should use this approach to avoid any issues. However, the information returned may not be the complete picture due to the database reading un-committed data. The timing of replication between the live database and the replicated database also means that the reports are not the complete picture, so it will depend on the reports being executed and how timely the information needs to be.

It is important to have an idea of the timing and frequency of the reports, as well as how up-to-date the information needs to be. The replication architecture needs to be considered to ensure that data is replicated from the primary data sources to the reporting sources at the appropriate frequency.

Some monitoring solutions also include reporting capabilities that execute against the monitoring database. The reporting solution could be made up of different reporting products, and, you'll see, analytics can further increase the architecture. The reporting solution will probably also have its own batch and housekeeping requirements as well, which must be taken into account.

Technical Reporting

This section provides a quick overview of some of the technical reports that can be used to assist in system monitoring, trend analysis, and incident investigation:

❏ **Monitoring** — Monitoring the system was discussed previously. However, scripts can often execute stored procedures or queries, analyze the results, and determine whether an alert is raised. For example, the application can be storing some processing state in the database. A script can execute periodically to check the processing state and raise an event. The reports can also be executed manually at regular intervals to check the processing state. These tend to be quite subtle reports required by the service delivery team.

❏ **Trend analysis** — You saw in the monitoring section that a large amount of data is being captured from the various servers around the estate. The technical reports can be executed against the collected data to provide a huge range of analysis and trending reports, including:

  ❏ CPU utilization over time

  ❏ Memory utilization

  ❏ Disk utilization

  ❏ Availability analysis (uptime/downtime)

  ❏ Failure analysis

  When capturing the data for the monitoring requirements and rules, it is often a good idea to start thinking about how that data can be reported.

  Analysis and trending reports can also be executed against the transactional data to provide application trending analysis, including:

  ❏ Transactions over time

  ❏ Transaction timings

  ❏ Auditing and security

❏ **Incident investigation** — When there is a fault with the system, reports can be executed to piece together a transaction timeline. This will involve extracting information from key tables and pulling it together so that it can be easily viewed — for example, extracting information from the audit tables and transaction tables to see who made updates to the system and when. The stored procedures and scripts used during the testing phases to analyze expected results can very often prove useful for these reporting purposes. If you are running an extract for any reason, it is worth keeping in mind whether the extract can be used elsewhere.

Some of these reports can be provided out-of-the-box by the monitoring solution. It is important to understand whether these out-of-the-box reports can be used as-is, which will avoid any development effort. For example, the monitoring solution might already include a report that shows CPU usage over time. The development effort should focus on the specific application events and counters that require inclusion in the application code and the custom reports required for them — for instance, an application-specific end-to-end transaction latency report, such as that shown in Figure 9-3.

Analytics Overview

Various products (for example, WebTrends) analyze web server logs and provide reports and analysis. The packages essentially trawl the logs and capture a wide variety of information, including but not limited to:

- ❑ Pages visited
- ❑ Path taken to particular pages
- ❑ Time spent on each page
- ❑ Page performance
- ❑ Pages not visited
- ❑ Internal/external visits
- ❑ The pages visitors arrived from

Because these tools are analyzing the web logs, they may require specific logging configuration on the web server. For instance, the analytics software may require the logs to be in a specific format and/or contain specific information not included by default. It is important to understand the configuration requirements of the tools. In Internet Information Services, many different properties can be recorded in the logs (if logging is switched on). The following lists just a handful of the properties that can be output:

- ❑ Date and time
- ❑ Client IP address
- ❑ Website name
- ❑ Page name
- ❑ Query string
- ❑ Bytes sent
- ❑ Bytes received

Turning on additional logging could affect the performance characteristics of the online application and should therefore be understood prior to technical testing.

Some web analytics solutions are implemented using the master/agent paradigm. The agents gather data from the web server logs, analyze them, and then send data to the master for storage and display. It is important to understand the implications on performance and network traffic.

In addition, some web analytics software packages also offer offline analysis. This can often mean getting the files from the various web servers and placing them somewhere to be analyzed and imported into the analytics solution, as shown in Figure 9-7.

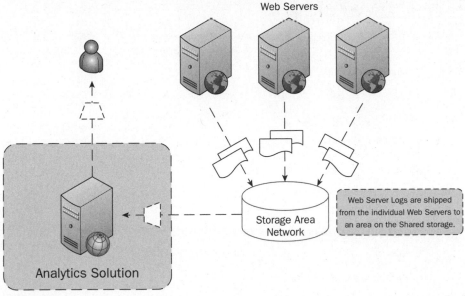

Figure 9-7

If the analytics solution doesn't provide the functionality to obtain the web server logs, you may need to provide jobs and/or scripts that move the files to a shared location for subsequent analysis. Alternatively, you could move the files directly to the analytics server. It is important to understand the timing and frequency of any potential log shipping to ensure that the logs are transferred at the appropriate times and to determine where the transfer jobs would fit into the batch schedule. In addition, the web server configuration may also need to take the frequency into account. For example, starting a new log file every hour could also have performance implications. If the logs are shipped at multiple times throughout the day, the batch process to ship them would need to be included in an intraday schedule.

It is worth understanding the analytics solution architecture to determine whether any custom jobs are required. The analytics solution will probably use a database of some description, which may also have its own batch and housekeeping requirements, such as re-indexing tables, clearing out log files, and so forth. You should read the software's Operations Manual or administrator's guide to ensure that all operational procedures are captured as well as the optimum configuration.

Summary

In this chapter, you have seen that reporting is used to assist the business decision-making process. You have seen that reports can be used to assist in supporting and maintaining the system as well as helping with issue investigation. Report design and construction can help define the database, but more important, they can take time, so it's worth starting early.

The following are the key points to take away from this chapter:

- ❑ **Reports are not just for the business.** Reports can also be used by technical staff, including operations and service delivery for a variety of different purposes, including:

    - ❑ Monitoring

    - ❑ Trend analysis (performance, events, and alerts)

    - ❑ Incident investigation

- ❑ **Keep reports simple and easy to use.** The reports you design and develop should include the most relevant information for its purpose. There are two primary elements to any report — the selection criteria and the output.

- ❑ **Report selection criteria should be limited to the most appropriate values.** Some typical report criteria include the following:

    - ❑ Specific field values

    - ❑ Value ranges (e.g., between two values)

    - ❑ Value masks (such as like clauses)

    - ❑ Date and time ranges

    Where possible default values should be included.

- ❑ **Report output should be limited to the most appropriate information.** The output of the report should be easy to read and only contain the most appropriate information. The report output can include the following:

    - ❑ Images

    - ❑ Lists or groups or records

    - ❑ Individual fields

    - ❑ Charts and graphs

- ❑ **Gather the reporting requirements early.** The reports, including the selection criteria and the outputs will ensure that the reports are fit for purpose and that the application can support them. This information will also help to shape the data model as well as replication and transformation requirements. The output results in some cases may need to show computed (or calculated) information, for example encoded or encrypted data will need to be decrypted for display. Reports executed against a replicated database may not contain the latest view of the data. The analytics solution may require specific web server configuration so the web servers output specific information in the logs. It could also require log shipping from the web servers to an alternative location for analysis.

❏ **Reuse existing scripts and data extracts.** Where possible, scripts and extracts should be reused to save development time and effort. More often than not, scripts written during development and testing can also be used in live service.

❏ **The reporting and analytics solutions need to be robust and secure.** The reporting and analytics solutions need to support the necessary users and usage criteria. Reports can contain sensitive information and as such should only be available to the relevant users.

❏ **Reporting must not impact live service.** Reports that run against the live database should execute using `read-uncommitted` (or equivalent) to avoid any locking issues with the live application. The analytics should also be performed off-line to avoid impacting live service.

10

Batch

This chapter examines batch and batch processing. Batch processing has its roots in the mainframe era with the earliest batch or job schedulers. Batch jobs run in the background without operator interaction. Batch jobs do not have a user interface; all inputs to a batch job are either through command parameters, scripts, configuration files, or configuration data. Traditionally batch was an overnight activity, with jobs processing millions of records and taking hours to execute — the theory being that there was a very large batch execution window between the end of one business day and the start of another. This is still very true today for some organizations and financial institutions, which enter transactions on the system during the business day and process them at the end of the day. Printing is another batch-related task in which letters, bills, and other documents are printed in the background. Today the batch window is ever decreasing with 24/7 availability requirements.

This chapter is organized into the following sections:

- ❑ **Batch Processing** — Discusses the batch processing required in today's software systems and the different batch processing groups. It looks at the batch window and some techniques for reducing the batch window.

- ❑ **The Batch Scheduler** — Examines the batch scheduler, batch jobs, and schedules. It also looks at the dependencies between jobs and groups, as well as at the batch nodes and node groups.

- ❑ **The Batch Run Date** — Highlights the importance of including a batch run date in the architecture to ensure that batch jobs process the appropriate information.

Batch Processing

Although batch is traditionally associated with large transaction-processing systems and conjures up visions of overnight processing, batch is very much an integral part of modern systems. Batch can also be referred to as *scheduled processing*, but essentially it is a process or function that executes in the background. It is important to differentiate batch processes from other processes, such as

Web services, that also execute in the background and don't have a user interface. Typically a Web service provides functionality based on a single transaction (known as *event-based processing*), whereas batch typically operates on larger sets of transactions (known as *scheduled tasks*).

Batch jobs perform a variety of different tasks in modern computer systems. Some perform a single function, whereas others perform more traditional functions, such as processing large numbers of records, performing intense calculations, and compiling statistical information. There is no real distinction between what each batch job performs; it is merely a process or function that is not included as part of the Online Transaction Processing (OLTP) System.

Figure 10-1 shows a hypothetical high-level "daily lifecycle" which will help when looking at some of the jobs listed shortly. Batch jobs can be divided into two main categories:

❑ **Functional jobs** — Functional batch jobs perform business-related actions. For example, a functional batch job might cycle through a set of orders, bundle them up into pick lists, and send them to the warehouse. A "pick list" is a list of items that a warehouse resource ("a picker") would use to gather the items from the warehouse shelves for packing and distribution. Another functional job might cycle through the order history and archive and purge (or delete) orders older than a certain date.

❑ **Technical jobs** — Technical jobs perform system-related actions. For instance, a technical batch job might start or stop the World Wide Web Publishing service on a web server. Another technical job might re-align a cluster onto its preferred node in the event of failover. Technical jobs are mainly used to keep the system in a healthy and operable state.

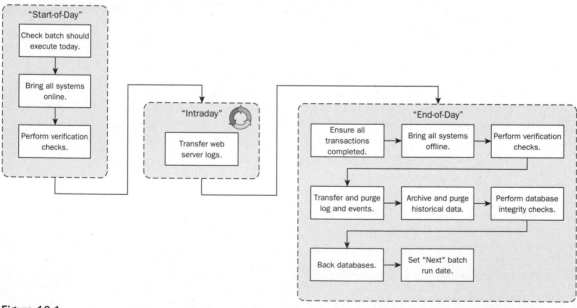

Figure 10-1

Whether a job is functional or technical doesn't really matter, as it is only a high-level grouping, although it can help when organizing the batch schedule. A simple rule of thumb when categorizing a job is to determine whether it is intended to meet a functional requirement or a technical requirement. Identifying batch jobs early will save time and effort later in the development cycle.

Individual batch jobs are part of an overall batch schedule. Batch schedules are usually organized into calendar periods daily, weekly, and monthly, and so on indicating their execution frequency. Ad-hoc schedules are also defined and are executed when required.

The following are examples of some of the common batch schedules and some of the jobs that would typically be executed:

❏ **Daily batch** — The daily batch schedules are often sub-categorized into Start of Day, Intraday, and End of Day. Some systems, especially those with 24/7 availability, perform batch processing and recycling at the system's quietest times to avoid interruption to users. The jobs are typically staggered to ensure the minimum amount of disruption. The system's quietest times are usually during the night. The following jobs are typically executed on a daily basis:

  ❏ **Starting and stopping processes and services** — Routine recycling of processes helps to improve performance and reduces the risk of high-impact memory leaks. Processes often cache information, and recycling the process gives it the opportunity to load updated or new data if it doesn't load this information periodically throughout the day. Stopping processes also removes any locks that may be open on database transactions or log files, allowing them to be archived and purged.

  ❏ **Transferring log files** — It may be necessary to transfer certain log files to another server or storage area for analysis. For example, you can use web analytics software to scan the IIS log files and produce analysis reports.

  ❏ **Archiving and purging of logs and events** — Over the course of the day the log files grow and need to be archived and cleared out. Archiving log files is typically achieved using file system commands such as move or copy to place the files in a separate archive location. Purging log files typically deletes historical files from the archive location. Archiving the log files also retains a backup, which can prove invaluable in an incident investigation. This is also true for the events in the Event Log. Although the Event Log is overwritten (depending on its settings), it is good to have a backup of the day's events for analysis.

  ❏ **Archiving and purging of historical database records** — Historical records take up space and degrade performance. Only the records that are required for transaction processing need to be kept online and older records should be archived and purged, where appropriate. The archived records do not necessarily need to be archived to a separate database; they can be archived into another table in the same database. However, if the records are not required after a period of time, they should be purged completely. However, this entirely depends on the system being implemented. There are often regulatory requirements whereby records must be kept accessible for long periods of time.

  ❏ **Abridged data integrity checks across multiple databases** — Data integrity checking is primarily used when multiple databases or instances are in play. Multiple databases can greatly improve performance across application tiers and allow database backups to be staggered, although the databases need to be kept in-sync. The abridged data integrity checks perform row-by-row comparisons of key tables to ensure that the databases are aligned.

❏ **Data processing, extraction, and transfer** — The data processing, extraction, and transfer jobs are usually dictated by the requirements. Any triggers used in the database will probably need to be disabled and re-enabled, which leads to additional jobs and complexity. It is for this reason that use of triggers should be very carefully considered. There is usually a requirement to extract data into a file and transfer it somewhere else, or, reversely, to take a file or extract from somewhere else and import it into the database.

❏ **Daily database backups** — Backing up the database on a daily basis is good practice and ensures a recoverable position in the event of complete failure. The database backups are also used for incident investigation and testing. A daily database backup is typically a partial backup, in that only the changes are backed up, which makes it much faster to perform. Restoring a daily backup requires restoration of the last full backup and then restoring the daily backups to a known point. However, it depends on the criticality of the system as to whether a full or partial database backup is taken on a daily (or perhaps more frequent) basis.

❏ **Truncating and shrinking database transaction logs and files** — Database transaction log files grow throughout the course of the day, sometimes very significantly. Truncating and shrinking the database logs greatly reduces their size, improves performance, and speeds up the backup time. Truncating database transaction logs is usually done by issuing commands to the database engine. This differs from normal log file archiving and purging, where standard file system commands are typically used.

❏ **Validating and setting the batch run date** — The batch run date is discussed later in this chapter. These jobs are in place to validate that batch is running on the correct date and setting the batch run date for the next batch run.

❏ **Weekly batch** — Although the weekly batch schedule can be split into multiple schedules, depending on the requirements, the following list is representative of jobs that would typically be executed on a weekly basis:

❏ **Weekly database backups** — A weekly backup is another safeguard against potential data loss. A weekly backup is typically a full backup of the entire database. Performing full backups on a regular basis helps to reduce the time and effort required to restore the database in the event of a failure. Restoring the database involves restoring the last full backup and then restoring any additional partial backups. Therefore, reducing the number of partial backups that need to be restored will reduce the overall database restoration time.

❏ **Database re-indexing and statistics updates** — The query optimizer uses statistics to determine the most efficient plan for retrieving or updating data. Ensuring that the statistics are up-to-date greatly improves database performance. Statistics can be updated automatically, although this needs to be balanced against performance.

❏ **Recompilation of stored procedures** — It may be necessary to recompile stored procedures and other database items. Over time, as the data changes, stored procedures can become inefficient, so recompiling them would take into account new and updated query optimizations.

❏ **Full database integrity checks** — The full data integrity checks are an extension of the abridged checks. In this instance, all tables that are common to multiple databases should be checked for integrity.

❑ **Disk defragmentation** — Disks become fragmented with the creation and deletion of files and storage space. Local disks and SAN disks should be regularly defragmented to improve performance. Defragmentation takes a long time, as you know if you've run it on your own machine, which is why it is a weekly or monthly activity.

❑ **Ad-hoc batch** — The ad-hoc schedules are executed as and when required. A schedule is put in place in order to control the execution rather than control it manually. The following lists some high-level ad-hoc schedule categories:

❑ **Database backup restore** — While the system is in live service, many backups are taken to protect against data loss. It is often prudent to restore these backups in an alternative environment where the data can be analyzed and used online. This activity proves that the backups can be restored correctly and that they contain all the necessary data. In the event of a real issue and a backup needs to be restored, it is not worth finding out at that point that the restore doesn't work or the backup is incomplete.

❑ **Cut-over and migration** — There are many steps involved in cut-over and migration, whether it is cutting over to production or just into a test environment. A batch schedule can be used to control the automated migration activities and provide a robust and managed process. Data migration and data cleansing tasks are typical examples of migration activities.

❑ **Testing** — Batch schedules can be implemented for both test environments and production environments. A test schedule can be used to control the test environment and manage the execution of multiple test scripts. When the test schedules make use of real jobs that would be used in the production schedule, this essentially verifies that the production jobs work correctly. However, it is also important to test all the batch schedules in an appropriate environment to ensure they execute correctly in the specific environment.

❑ **Recycling environments** — Similar to the testing and pipe-cleaning schedules, the recycling schedules can be used to shut down environments, clear the database, insert canned data, and restart the environment with a different configuration.

❑ **Antivirus (AV) scanning** — AV scanning is a prudent activity, even though all the servers are behind firewalls, and should be conducted at regular intervals to ensure that no viruses exist across the estate.

❑ **Disaster recovery** — This is probably the most ad-hoc schedule of them all. In the event of a disaster, the disaster recovery schedule is used to manage and control the recovery steps (both automatic and manual).

The schedules, jobs, and frequencies depend entirely on the system being implemented. The following lists a few hints and tips about where you will find a requirement for a batch job:

❑ **Vendor documentation** — The documentation from vendors will generally contain routine maintenance tasks. However, in most cases the documentation needs to be scrutinized intensely to uncover some of the more advanced tasks. If you have a chance to go to a reference site where the technology is already being used, be sure to ask about which batch and maintenance tasks are in place.

❑ **Existing systems and implementations** — Unless you are dealing with brand new technologies, chances are that a lot of these tasks have already been identified by other companies. If the company has used the technologies in previous implementations, try to find out which tasks are already performed and whether there are any gaps.

❑ **System administrators** — Assuming the technologies aren't brand new, the system administrators will have worked with the technologies for a while and will generally know which batch processes and maintenance tasks should be in place.

❑ **Application and environment architecture** — Review the application and environment architectures and topologies. These diagrams contain the tell-tale signs for batch jobs. Any server in the diagrams (and the processes running on them) will need to be kept well maintained using the jobs identified earlier. The database will most definitely require routine maintenance.

❑ **Functional, technical, and database designs** — The design documents for the system should highlight specific batch requirements. The functional and technical design documents that you produce should include as much information as possible regarding the functionality of the batch jobs required; their dependencies; and when the job should be executed, start of day, end of day, or intraday for instance. Batch job properties, as discussed later in this chapter, provide a good starting point for documenting batch jobs.

❑ **Testing and live service** — Finally, new and updated batch jobs are always identified during testing and live service. Batch evolves over the lifetime of the system.

In short, many batch jobs are required to keep the system in a healthy and operable state. Whether the system is a simple website or a complex transaction processing system, there is a need to perform routine, automated maintenance tasks. These jobs need to be organized into schedules that execute at the appropriate intervals.

The Batch Window

Many organizations stipulate that batch must complete within one hour, during which the system must still be partially available. In more severe cases, the batch window is removed completely and all processing carried out while the system is up and running. This is especially true in these days of 24/7 availability.

Performing jobs in parallel wherever possible is a key factor for reducing batch execution time. The jobs need to be distributed across a number of servers to make use of all the processing power and to avoid overloading one or two servers, which has a negative impact. Running jobs in parallel and distributing jobs requires in-depth knowledge into their functionality to ensure that they can truly be executed in parallel and not cause issues between themselves.

You should ensure that any processes outside of your control are either exempt from the batch window you are signing up to or at least noted for exemption. Third-party applications such as backup technologies that are used across the enterprise are a prime example. The batch job will submit only the backup request to the backup application. Once the backup request has been submitted, the batch job typically loses visibility of what's actually happening. The backup application will almost certainly have its own priorities for backup execution, and the batch job will not actually know when the backup is going to be taken. The batch job has to simply wait until the backup application returns, which could be a long while. For example, many other systems may be backed up as part of the overall enterprise backup solution. Submitting a backup request simply adds it to the backup queue, and the request could be quite far down the list based on its priority. You need to understand these priorities early and ensure that measures are in place to increase the backup priorities when the system goes live.

Large transaction-processing jobs and integrity checks are other potentially long-running jobs. Identify potential long-running jobs early and split them up into manageable chunks that can be executed in parallel. These types of jobs are usually record count–based, so it is generally easier to play the "what if" game and test against thousands, tens of thousands, or even millions of rows.

Staggering batch schedules helps to keep a proportion of the system up and running while other activities are performed. For example, taking down one server in a group at a time leaves the others available to process requests while jobs are executed on the downed server. This reduces capacity but it should only be for a short time while the server is turned around.

In a 24/7 environment the database becomes the primary concern. Although historical records can be archived, some of the more subtle jobs may require the database to be taken offline or not used, although again this should only be done for a short period of time. For example, jobs running against the database while the database is being backed up could impact the overall backup of the database.

The Batch Scheduler

The batch scheduler is the application that executes batch schedules and jobs. Most batch schedulers support multiple operating systems and platforms. Batch schedulers, also known as job schedulers, support the following high-level functions:

- ❑ Defining batch jobs and batch schedules
- ❑ Defining batch calendars
- ❑ Defining batch nodes and node groups (servers)
- ❑ Executing and controlling batch schedules and batch jobs
- ❑ Monitoring schedules and job execution (including alerts and re-submission)
- ❑ Recycling batch schedules for the next run date

The batch scheduler is normally installed on a dedicated server, whereas agents are installed on individual servers that execute batch processes. This follows the master-agent architecture previously discussed.

Most schedulers show a diagram view of the batch schedule, using a colored, "traffic light" system:

- ❑ Red typically indicates a job has failed.
- ❑ Green means the job has completed successfully.
- ❑ Amber means the job is running or executing.
- ❑ Blue or some other color is often used to indicate a communication error with a node or server to distinguish the failure.

Jobs waiting for scheduling typically are not colored. Figure 10-2 shows a mockup of the batch scheduler execution display where all jobs are essentially waiting to be scheduled, as they are not colored. As the schedule starts executing, the jobs would be colored according to their state.

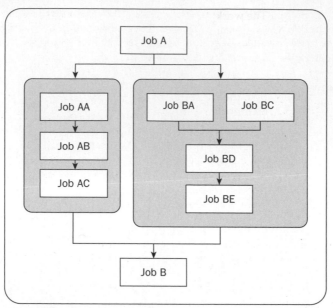

Figure 10-2

In the early days of testing and deployment for batch, this is the most watched screen. Once the system is live and the batch schedule has been proven, operators generally don't sit and watch this screen. It is used only in the event of a failure, and that is generally to re-submit the job. *Information* and *alerts* should be raised and displayed on the bridge to inform operators of the batch schedule's progress and status.

Batch Jobs

Batch jobs are usually executables or scripts initiated from the command line. I personally put a thin wrapper framework in place that allows development and execution of batch processes without having to understand all the mechanics of their instantiation and execution from the scheduler. (Chapter 16 discusses the batch framework in more detail.) Furthermore, as mentioned previously, batch jobs execute without operator interaction and all inputs to batch jobs are either through parameters or configuration.

Basic Batch Job Properties

The following describes a few properties that are common to all batch jobs and batch schedulers:

- ❑ **Name** — Specifies the name of the batch job or process. It is worth having a batch job naming convention to standardize the names of batch jobs and batch processes.

- ❑ **Type** — In most cases the batch job type is *"job."* Some batch schedulers support a *"dummy"* job type, which is used to define a placeholder in the schedule for a job that has not yet been developed. When you have a large batch schedule with a lot of parallel executions, a dummy job can be used simply to indicate the dependencies and bring everything into a single point again, without an actual job executing. Batch schedules are discussed later in this chapter.

- ❑ **Command** — Most batch schedulers support execution of jobs via the command shell. The command property is used to specify the command and parameters. For instance, the command line to stop the World Wide Web Publishing Service is
  `net stop "World Wide Web Publishing Service"`.

❑ **Working directory** — The working directory or folder identifies the directory in which the job will be executed. This is especially handy when other artifacts are stored in the working folder (such as configuration files, resource files, and so on) that the job needs to access without specifying full paths.

❑ **Start time** — Some jobs must not start before a certain time in the day. For example, you do not want to start tearing down the environment while users are still using it. The start time for the job protects against a job executing out of time.

❑ **Dependencies** — Almost all jobs will have dependencies — that is, other jobs that must execute successfully prior to the job running. For example, in order for a job to archive and purge log files, there mustn't be any processes using them. To this end, the archive and purge job would have a dependency on the stop process job or jobs. Dependencies are discussed later in this chapter.

❑ **Node or node group** — The node or node group stipulates the nodes or servers that the job will execute on. It is important to ensure that jobs execute only on the servers they need to in order to avoid unnecessary failures or complications. For instance, the database backup job should only run on the database servers; therefore, the database servers would be defined as a node or node group. Node groups are discussed later in this chapter.

You should consider these properties when defining batch jobs and schedules. Each batch scheduler has its own unique settings and properties, so you should read the documentation thoroughly to understand and make use of any other features.

Execution and Output

A batch job is treated as an individual unit of work. The job executes, performs its function(s), and terminates with an exit code indicating its success or failure. If the batch job throws an exception, the batch schedule treats it as a failure.

As mentioned previously, batch jobs are typically command line–based, and all output is usually directed to the console. With batch processes executing in the background, no visible console window is displayed to the operator, although most batch schedulers allow the operator to view the output.

The following shows an example of the console output from the previous `net stop` command:

```
C:\>net stop "World Wide Web Publishing Service"
System error 5 has occurred.

Access is denied.

C:\>
```

When you are outputting to the console using statements such as `Console.WriteLine`, the output is actually being written to the standard output stream *StdOut*. The .NET `Process` class has a `StandardOutput` property that can be used to read the output from a process that would otherwise be displayed to the console. Batch schedulers use this kind of functionality to read (and store) the output from the process, allowing operators to view it while the job is executing and when it has completed.

Identity and Security

Batch jobs execute within the security context of the batch agent service. Therefore, any specific access required by the batch process must be granted to the user the batch agent is executing as. This is important because a lot of security issues are encountered when hooking jobs up to the scheduler. When testing batch jobs, it is best to test with the security context of the batch agent.

The batch agents should not be executed using the LocalSystem account. Instead, you should use a specific account whose privileges and access you can control and manage within the environment. This really applies to any third-party applications as well as other base framework components.

Batch Schedules

Individual batch jobs are executed as part of an overall batch schedule. The schedule dictates the execution flow of the individual jobs through dependencies. A batch schedule can really be thought of as a workflow, in that each job is executed in a particular order. When jobs are executed in parallel, there is often a point where the jobs come back together into the main flow.

Figure 10-3 shows a representation of a basic batch schedule. Job A executes individually, after which Jobs B, C, and D execute in parallel, and, finally, Job E executes individually.

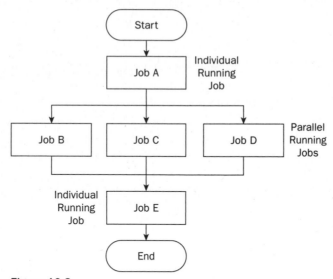

Figure 10-3

Jobs are executed according to their dependencies. In the majority of cases, batch schedulers treat a dependency as the successful execution of a previous job, a set of previous jobs, or an entire scheduling group. In Figure 10-3, jobs B, C, and D will not execute until Job A has completed successfully, and Job E will not execute until Jobs B, C, and D have *all* completed successfully. If any one of the jobs fails, the dependency will not be met and the dependent jobs will not execute.

Jobs B, C, and D will all start to execute once Job A has completed successfully. Job B might only take a couple of seconds to execute, whereas Jobs C and D might take considerably longer. In any case, Job E will not execute until they have all successfully completed. It is important to take this into account when defining the batch schedule to ensure that all the dependencies are absolutely necessary. When possible, long-running jobs should start as early as possible in the batch schedule to avoid extending the batch window.

Some more sophisticated batch schedulers support other types of dependencies, such as success, failure, or even dependencies based on the return code of a job. This can be useful when a job fails to have another job execute and perform some rudimentary analysis or even remedial action that the operator would otherwise have to perform manually. This type of operation is quite advanced and needs to be planned carefully.

Jobs that perform related functionality are generally grouped together into a *scheduling group*. The jobs in a scheduling group can still execute individually, in parallel, or a combination of both, as shown in Figure 10-4.

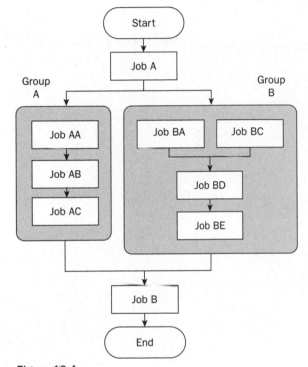

Figure 10-4

The figure shows two scheduling groups, A and B. Group A has sequential execution of Jobs AA, AB, and AC, whereas scheduling Group B has Jobs BA and BC executing in parallel, followed by Jobs BD and BE executing sequentially.

A scheduling group makes it easier to define and manage the overall schedule and dependencies. A job can be added or removed to a scheduling group without affecting the rest of the schedule. For example, in Figure 10-3 Job B is dependent on Groups A and B and will not execute until those groups have executed successfully. This continues to remain true when jobs are added or removed from either group. For instance, Group B doesn't contain a job BB which could have been removed at some point without affecting the dependencies for Job B. However, the removal of job BB would certainly affect the dependencies of Job BD, so it is definitely worth thinking about scheduling groups when multiple dependencies need to be managed.

Nodes and Node Groups

Nodes and node groups determine the server or servers the batch job will run on. A *node* is an individual server, and a *node group* is a group of servers. Most batch schedulers support running a job either on a single server in the node group or on all servers in the group (referred to as a *multi-node job*). Node groups are very powerful and can also be used to add resiliency to the batch architecture.

Figure 10-5 shows a sample node group comprised of two administration servers at the primary site.

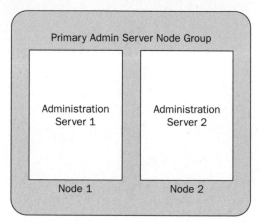

Primary Site

Figure 10-5

The following table lists the different nodes and groups and where a job would run based on its node configuration.

Node/Group	Servers	Explanation
Node 1	Administration Server 1	A job configured to execute on Node 1 will execute only on Administration Server 1.
Node 2	Administration Server 2	A job configured to execute on Node 2 will execute only on Administration Server 2.
Primary Admin Server Node Group	Either Administration Server 1 or Administration Server 2	A job configured to execute on the Primary Admin Server Node Group will execute on either Administration Server 1 or Administration Server 2. If both servers are up and running, the scheduler will typically round-robin through the nodes with each job. If a server is down, the scheduler will execute on one of the available nodes in the group. This provides a layer of resiliency.
Primary Admin Server Node Group (multi-node)	Both Administration Server 1 and Administration Server 2	A job configured to execute on the group node will execute on all the servers in the group.

When defining batch jobs and schedules, it is important to think about which nodes and groups they should run on as well as to define the different node groups by looking at the production architecture diagram and picking out the nodes and groups.

The nodes and node groups are the servers that contain batch agents, although some vendors offer an agentless architecture. Node groups and job execution should be carefully planned for both the primary site and the secondary site. The preceding examples would equally apply to the standalone secondary site. However, when you consider that a node group could contain servers that span the primary site and the secondary site, a single job could execute on all the servers configured in the node group. This is shown in Figure 10-6.

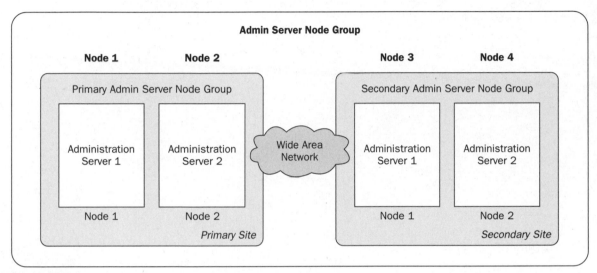

Figure 10-6

Figure 10-6 shows an "Admin Server Node Group" that contains all the administration servers in the production environment. Nodes 1 and 2 are located in the primary site, and nodes 3 and 4 are located in the secondary site. This configuration can be very useful, but it needs to be considered carefully. First, there is cross-site communication, which could be subject to delays. Second, the individual job could take a long while to execute, depending on the number of servers in the group. Finally, a failure on either site would interrupt the overall schedule. That said, in an active-active primary and secondary site configuration this functionality may very well be required.

Node groups should be distinguished between the primary site and the secondary site.

Batch for Batch Sake

Batch schedulers often need to execute a series of jobs to turn the batch environment around for the next day's scheduling. For example, after a daily schedule has executed on "day 1," it needs to be rescheduled for "day 2." The batch scheduler generally provides processes or commands that perform this functionality. However, these typically need to be included in separate "new day" batch schedules.

It is well worth understanding the specific intricacies of the batch scheduler and turning around the batch schedules, as this can be quite tricky to get right.

The Batch Run Date

I mentioned previously that the application should have a date and time component that can be configured for testing. The batch components must have a date and time component that contains the current batch run date. The reason for this is that batch scheduling can often be delayed and cross the midnight boundary of the current day into the next day, especially when batch is executed in the evening.

To explain, there are usually batch jobs that use the current date (and possibly time) for processing purposes. Assume a job archives and purges records that are older than three days (including today). If the batch schedule executes on time, the job will delete all the correct records. However, if the schedule runs after midnight, it will archive and purge one day less (see Figure 10-7).

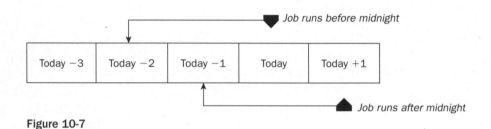

Figure 10-7

Figure 10-7 shows that if the job runs before midnight, it will archive and purge records older than Today-2, whereas if it runs after midnight, it will delete records older than Today-1. This could cause a variety of issues when the data isn't present during the online day.

It is therefore paramount that batch components have a common batch date/time component and do not rely on the system clock. The batch run date needs to be updated as part of the batch schedule — usually as one of the last jobs in the schedule to set the next batch run date based on the business calendar.

Obviously, this introduces a separation between the batch scheduler's calendar and the application's batch calendar. The alternative is to execute the batch schedule earlier in the day, although this still poses the question of what happens if it doesn't run for some reason. Having an independently controllable batch framework alleviates any issues because it can be put into an assumed date and executed manually.

If there has been a catastrophic failure, the batch date also allows multiple days of batch to be run to catch up to the current date.

Summary

Batch is still an important part of keeping your system healthy and in a good state to meet your requirements. This chapter looked at the types of jobs that need to be executed and how the jobs fit in to the overall batch schedule. You also saw the importance of having an application-specific batch run date.

The following are the key points to take away from this chapter:

- ❑ **Batch is not dead.** There are a number of jobs that need to be executed to keep the system in a healthy state. In addition, there could be many functional jobs required for the system.

- ❑ **The batch window is ever decreasing.** In today's 24/7 operations, batch processes need to be fast. In addition, some or all of the system may need to be available whilst batch jobs are executing. You need to ensure that all batch jobs can be executed within the required time. Where possible, jobs should be executed in parallel to reduce the end-to-end execution time. In addition, you should include all third-party applications, such as backups and anti-virus (where appropriate), to ensure that these jobs are captured appropriately.

- ❑ **Capture batch requirements early.** You should capture batch requirements early in the lifecycle and there should be a significant amount of time in the plan to develop and test batch jobs thoroughly as a standalone component. Batch testing should not rely on other test activities.

- ❑ **Understand the batch architecture.** You should understand the batch architecture to ensure that it supports the batch requirements and processes you need to put in place. In addition, you should understand the necessary jobs that the batch architecture itself may require, such as new day jobs and schedules.

- ❑ **Batch jobs have no user interface.** Batch jobs run in the background and have no user interface. The batch jobs are visible to the outside world via their performance counters, events and logs, and usually their console output (which is captured by the scheduler). It's important that batch jobs can be monitored and operated effectively.

- ❑ **Think about when and where jobs need to run.** Batch is usually organized into periods: daily, weekly, ad-hoc, and so on. It is worth noting each of the jobs and when they should run. The job dependencies should also be noted. Batch jobs are scheduled via the batch scheduler, in batch schedules with various dependencies. Batch jobs should run only on the nodes that they are required to run on.

- ❑ **Implement a custom batch run date.** The application should support a custom batch run date to ensure that jobs process the correct date.

11

Incident Investigation

Incident investigation can be one of the most stressful and difficult areas of software development. The stress is compounded by how critical the situation is, how difficult the problem is, and how quickly it needs to be resolved. Some of the most critical situations include production outages and issues that endanger deadlines and milestones. Incidents can occur for many different reasons. Some are caused by defective software (both internal and third-party) or hardware failures. Others can be caused by external influences such as users, transactions, operators, and other situations. For example, a website may suffer performance degradation on occasion because the number of users or transactions exceed tolerances at the time. It can also occur because of backups running in the background or for a number of other reasons. Incidents can range from simple misunderstandings with software usage, configuration, or functionality to complex functional and technical issues. Incident investigation is concerned with understanding what the issue is, when it happened or happens, what caused it, and, finally, what, if any, corrective actions should be put in place to ensure that it doesn't happen again or what should be done if it does happen again. Not all incidents are resolved with software or hardware modification or configuration; some incidents can be resolved by further user and/or operating training, education, and procedures. Incidents will happen, so understanding and preparing for them are vital parts of software development.

This chapter is organized into the following sections:

❑   **The Investigation Roadmap** — Looks at the steps involved in incident investigation and resolution.

❑   **Typical Incidents** — Lists some of the typical functional and technical incidents that occur in the everyday environments.

The Investigation Roadmap

Not all issues are the same, of course, so each incident will take on its own unique investigation. However, in almost all cases each incident will follow the roadmap shown in Figure 11-1 and in the list that follows:

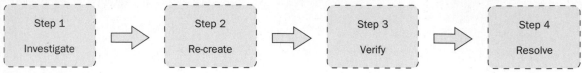

Figure 11-1

1. **Investigate** — To understand the issue, you must obtain as much information as possible. Each incident will differ, so the amount of information required will depend entirely on the complexity and criticality of the problem. Ultimately, you want to have enough information to be able to re-create the conditions and situation, preferably in an isolated environment so that you can fully exercise and approve the proposed resolution.

2. **Re-create** — Once there is enough information, you can re-create the issue so that you can repeatedly and accurately reproduce the incident in isolation and perform the appropriate analysis. It is sometimes difficult to re-create an incident in isolation because of its nature, environmental scale, data, configuration, and many other reasons. In my personal experience issues that can't be reproduced are notoriously difficult to resolve and generally involve a large amount of trial and error. Conversely, issues that can be reproduced allow a more scientific or analytical approach to be taken to resolve them.

3. **Verify** — This is a very important step in the process. You need to ensure that the incident is really something that needs to be addressed and resolved. This can often be achieved in Step 1, although you still need to verify the proposed resolution. In some cases the issue is easily identifiable and a resolution is often immediately apparent. However, all too often a fix or process is put in place without being fully understood and verified. This can lead to further issues down the line. Verifying the incident, and testing and validating the resolution are paramount to a successfully resolved incident.

4. **Resolve** — Once a resolution has been agreed on and verified, it can be implemented according to the formal process and rolled out to all the necessary environments and resources. Remember that issues or incidents can be resolved simply by putting processes in place.

An interesting example of a critical incident I had to investigate was what I refer to as *screen locking*. The system was a typical web-based solution. The main page contained a list of articles like those shown in Figure 11-2.

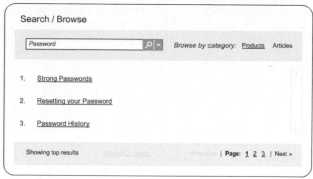

Figure 11-2

Clicking on an article hyperlink would display a pop-up dialog box with the article's content, like the one shown in Figure 11-3.

Figure 11-3

At the bottom of the pop-up dialog box was a "Click here to close this window" hyperlink that would close the window. Users complained that when they clicked the hyperlink, the dialog box would close and, on occasion, the system would lock or freeze. The article content window closed but the mouse cursor remained as a pointing finger and nothing happened when they tried to click on any other links or controls in the main browser. Over time, the users were getting increasingly frustrated as the situation got worse. The only way they could get going again was to close the main browser window, open a new browser, log back in to the system, and continue their work. As you can imagine, this took valuable time away from their day-to-day routine and caused a lot of frustration, especially when it happened when they were on the phone to customers.

The system was being tested for go-live readiness, but the intermittent nature of the issue made it difficult to catch at the time it occurred or obtain a concrete set of steps to reproduce it — until I managed to re-create it myself, that is. Because the situation was critical to the go-live nature of the system, it had to be resolved quickly. The issue hadn't been seen in any of the other development or test environments and only surfaced during this phase. Hours could elapse without the incident occurring and some days it wouldn't happen at all. All in all, this added up to a most perplexing incident.

The issue had been raised with all the third-party vendors, and many steps had already been taken to try and resolve it, including un-installing and re-installing various software packages, installing patches and upgrades, trying different browsers, and hours of additional ad-hoc testing in an attempt to re-create the problem. This was a lengthy and tedious business primarily because the issue couldn't accurately be re-created at the time, so any potential resolution couldn't be verified in isolation beforehand. Unfortunately in this instance, nothing that was done resolved the issue.

It was only after I managed to re-create the issue and provide simple step-by-step instructions on how to re-create the problem that it was possible to come up with a resolution. Curiously enough it actually only took me a couple of hours to re-create and understand the issue. I use this instance to reiterate how important it is to try to reproduce and fully understand the issue to ensure that a structured and analytical approach to its resolution can be taken and documented.

In the interest of finishing this story, I'll tell you how I managed to re-create the issue but not how it was eventually resolved. I started the same way as everybody else — by simply clicking randomly on article links and closing the window. I started clicking faster and faster, trying to open another article while the window was still closing. Nothing happened. Everything worked as expected. I opened one article and closed the window. The window closed and bingo, the system locked and the mouse pointer remained the same. The cursor was still a "hand" floating over a hyperlink, and clicking on hyperlinks did nothing. I tried the same article again after opening a new browser window and this time it worked fine. Things went on like this for a while. I kept thinking about the mouse cursor and why it was a "hand." To cut a long story short, I thought it must be something to do with hyperlinks. I opened an article and placed the pop-up window so that the "Click here to close this window" link was directly over another link on the main page, as shown in Figure 11-4.

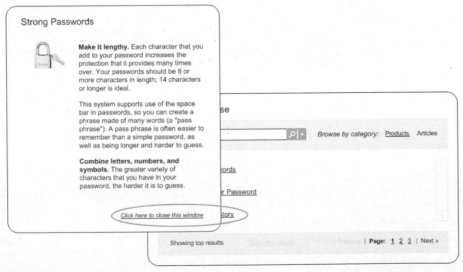

Figure 11-4

I clicked on the link where it overlapped with the link below and presto — it locked every single time. As it turns out, this was an issue with one of the underlying third-party framework components. Although a resolution was investigated by the third-party, a remedial fix was also implemented in the application to stop the issue from occurring. It is now obvious why the issue was so intermittent. It was totally dependent on whether the Close link was over another link and whether the user clicked on the overlapping region.

An issue like this would never have been considered during design, build, or testing unless it was previously known. Only by understanding the issue and re-creating it was it possible to ultimately identify the definitive resolution. In this instance, software upgrades didn't harm the system; however, they were not necessary to resolve this particular incident. This is often the case in instances like this where critical issues arise and understanding them and reproducing them prove difficult. The more critical the situation becomes, the more trial and error is attempted to resolve it.

In my experience, issues do not just go away all by themselves. Something happens to either resolve them or the conditions to cause them are not encountered. An unresolved issue is an incident waiting to happen. I don't mean to say that every issue is critical; it simply means that it is likely that it will occur again unless it is fully understood and definitively resolved.

Aside from the importance of trying to understand and re-create the issue, this example demonstrates a couple of other important factors. Imagine if this incident occurred while users were filling in a large form with data and clicked a link that displayed a pop-up help window. As soon as the incident occurred, they would lose everything they had typed in. It would be incredibly frustrating for them to have to start over again, even more so if they were taking the information from somebody over the phone. You can imagine the response when having to tell the person on the other end of the phone that you need all the information again after you get back to a working system. Data loss such as this is very problematic, so managing sessions and transaction data effectively will help to ensure that users can return to where they left off in the event of an incident. However, this type of management and recovery needs to be considered during design and built into the system. Another important factor is obtaining the exact information necessary to understand the incident in full.

Investigating the Incident

The simple brief I wrote earlier about this particular incident could have easily been entered into a defect-tracking system or even mentioned over the phone during a support call. Although it's very obvious, the more specific and detailed the information, the more chance you have of getting to the bottom of the incident and ultimately understanding and resolving it. In some situations, the description of the incident may be more than enough to pin-point the root cause of the issue and even highlight its resolution. More often than not, however, the description or overview is simply the starting point and further investigation is required to fully understand the situation and move on through the other steps.

In production, an incident investigation typically follows from an alert being raised. In some cases it can be raised by users or customers. The first port of call for the incident investigation is usually the help desk or the operations team. Unless the incident has previously been seen, the operations team will generally pass it on to the service delivery or support team. If the service delivery or support teams are unable to understand and resolve the issue, it is generally passed on the third line of support, usually subject matter experts for the system or the application maintenance team. It is important that all the information gathered and what has already been done are passed on accurately to avoid any unnecessary duplication of effort.

The alert is clearly the first indicator and needs to contain enough information to allow an investigation to follow. If the alert contains a comprehensive amount of detail, it is often possible to diagnose the issue almost immediately. Sadly, this is often not the case, and the alert contains not much more than the fact that an issue has been encountered. It is important to note that not all alerts are generated from exceptions. You saw earlier in this book that alerts can be raised based on monitoring rules and thresholds. Event logging and tracing are discussed in more detail in Chapter 21.

Understanding an incident can be very challenging if the right level of information isn't available. For instance, I often refer to the 3 a.m. call. An alert is raised in production and the first port of call is to phone the relevant support individual. The call could go something like this:

> *[Support] "Hello." (Said very tiredly due to the timing of the call)*
>
> *[Operations] "Hi. It's John from Operations. There's a problem with the system."*
>
> *[Support] "Hi, John. What's the problem?"*
>
> *[Operations] "Not sure, mate. It just says 'An Error Has Occurred.'"*
>
> *[Support] "What does it say in the logs?"*
>
> *[Operations] "There aren't any logs. I checked and I can't find anything."*
>
> *[Support] "I'll dial-in and have a look."*

More often than not, the first thing to do when a production system is impacted is to understand the incident and get the system back up and running as soon as possible to minimize the impact. This can sometimes involve applying temporary fixes to the data, database, or configuration that don't require the application to be recompiled. However, the first challenge in an incident investigation is piecing together a timeline or profile to understand exactly what happened, when it happened, and why it happened. One of my favorite questions in this area is "If you only had the alert to go on, would you know what the problem is?" This would clearly be the best starting point, followed by what caused it and how to resolve it. However, producing a timeline usually involves much more than just the alert. It invariably requires the analysis of:

❑ Event logs and events

❑ Trace logs and trace files

❑ Database extracts and reports

❑ Instrumentation and performance counters

For example, an alert could be raised because the CPU on a server is running hot — that is, running at more than 95 percent utilization for more than 10 minutes. The alert itself doesn't tell why it's running hot; however, it should at least tell the particular server and the sample start/end times. With these two pieces of information, you can at least start an incident investigation. The important thing here is that the times are based on the actual server times rather than the sampling server's time. Otherwise, you could get into all sorts of trouble trying to convert times for different servers, assuming they are not synchronized. This could also be an issue across the estate if the database server time differs from that of the application servers.

Incident investigation is often sped up by the use of tools to gather this type of information quickly so that it can be analyzed in a single place and threaded together to provide a complete picture. This is one area where incident investigation needs to be considered during design, as well as designed into the application. For example, when a process is updating a record in the database you should consider capturing the following items in the database table:

- ❑ Some form of "updated date and time"
- ❑ The name of the server the process that updated the record is running on
- ❑ The name of the process that updates the record
- ❑ The name of the user who instigated the update (where necessary)

The information listed above would need to be captured in the database design as well as included in the transaction processing which would affect the development timescales and costs. However, the information would enable you to run a report of all transactions created by a particular process on a particular server within a specific time period, which could dramatically reduce the effort required in an investigation.

I mentioned earlier that the investigation is often a joint effort or relay, and clearly the objective is for the system (and tools) to provide as much information as possible to assist the investigation. Furthermore, the information and analysis that the operations and service delivery teams can provide and perform up-front will greatly reduce the impact on the development team and other resources. In production, tracing is generally reduced to optimize performance, so one of the most common challenges is obtaining event logs and traces for incidents. Later in this book, Part IV, "Patterns and Practices," looks at designing for incident investigation and at some of the patterns you can implement when trying to piece together an incident timeline. Having to turn on tracing and wait for something to happen again is not an ideal situation, although it is somewhat of an occupational hazard. By thinking about incident investigation and incident timelines during design and development, you can dramatically reduce the amount of effort spent investigating issues.

In the "screen locking" example mentioned previously, the application logs wouldn't and didn't help, primarily because the issue wasn't transactional. The third-party logs also offered nothing concrete. The key to the resolution was simply repeating what the users were doing and using the existing information to try ad-hoc scenarios in an attempt to re-create the issue. In piecing together a timeline, you ultimately want to obtain enough information to provide detailed step-by-step instructions, data, and configuration to repeatedly reproduce the issue. If you can quickly analyze the inputs, logs, events, and data to pull out all the relevant information, you stand a good chance of being able to quickly and efficiently re-create the issue and start looking at a resolution.

Formal test phases usually follow a test script that has detailed environment set-up, data, inputs, and expected results, which can be used to re-create the issue in an isolated environment. However, that's not to say that even with all this information you can still reproduce the issue in an isolated environment, but it's a good starting point. The issue could be specific to the machine (or the environment) where the test is being executed. When you're unable to re-create the issue in a separate environment, you need to start looking at the environment specifics where the tests are being executed to try and work out what's happening. This is where the events, logs, and the scripts used to extract actual results can be useful. The scripts used to extract and compare actual results against expected results during testing can also help when investigating live service issues. However, the extract scripts often require some environment-specific re-factoring, such as changing the database name to the production database or changing file names and locations, and so on. In some complicated test scenarios, data extract scripts are developed to verify that a number of different updates (potentially across multiple databases and sites) are completed correctly and that all the updates are consistent. Scripts such as this can also be re-used in the production environment as part of the monitoring solution, as well as to help piece together the overall timeline for an incident. In production, you are reacting to what users are doing, so you need to understand exactly what they were doing as part of the overall timeline or profile.

Re-Creating the Incident

Ultimately, your goal is to reproduce the issue so that you can perform a detailed analysis and provide a resolution. Everything that you log, persist, and output needs to help you understand and re-create the issue. This even goes as far as the comments in the code and other artifacts to help re-create conditions. Re-creating the issue in an isolated environment affords you the luxury of being able to try out and validate the various resolutions prior to implementing the preferred solution. It's not entirely possible to re-create some issues because of restrictions on the environment, data, and scale. For example, a complex issue encountered with clustering would need to be re-created in an environment that was clustered or at least simulated clustering effectively. For some of the most intricate and complex production issues, an environment that mirrors the production environment is very beneficial. That said, the more that the issue is understood, the more chance there is of re-creating the same conditions in a "lab." In these instances, performing a detailed analysis often boils down to the amount of time and effort required to re-create the exact conditions.

Not all incidents are straightforward to reproduce, so a lot of effort can be required to create the exact conditions, data, and transactions. Complicated issues often require a lot of analysis just to gather the information to understand what is going on, let alone to re-create the exact conditions. Striving to reproduce the issue needs to be balanced against the current understanding. In some cases a best-guess is often the only way forward in absolutely critical situations. For example, if the production system is down, quick thinking and analysis are required. There are often many people involved in trying to resolve the incident, and keeping control of their efforts can be difficult given the pace at which actions are being performed. Furthermore, if an outage is suffered in production, bringing the system back online is paramount; therefore, the formal incident investigation will either be performed in parallel or follow stabilizing the production environment. Ensuring that each action is recorded will help to further refine operational procedures, in the event they need to be performed again. Furthermore, any scripts or automated tasks can also be reused at a later date.

All issues should be re-created in order to verify that the resolution is definitive. This is even true for the times when you know exactly what the problem is and why it is happening. In such cases, it should be easy to re-create the issue, and being able to present the evidence before and after will help to validate the resolution and move forward.

Verifying the Incident and the Proposed Resolution

Many times when an issue occurs, a resolution is thought of almost immediately. The resolution might not be wrong, but it hasn't gone through the appropriate channels and controls to be validated. A classic example of this is an incorrect test script. So many times the code is modified to meet the test script without validating whether the test script is actually correct. Another example is when users believe that something is wrong when, in fact, the system is functioning correctly. Whether it's a production issue, a test issue, or even a design decision, the incident should be verified to ensure that it is really an issue with the system and, where necessary, the proposed resolution should also be validated so that everything is in sync and you avoid wasted effort.

In production, an alert can be raised for something that happens by design — for example, two database tables being out of sync. There may be plausible reasons for this to occur, so the alert simply informs the operational staff that an ad-hoc procedure will need to be carried out later to realign the tables. This is an example of where the application isn't modified but additional procedures and/or checks are put in place. Sometimes solving basic issues with complicated technology solutions introduces even more issues or complexities, whereas simple manual or semi-automated tasks and/or corrective actions could be far easier.

When looking at resolving issues and validating solutions, you need to look at the complete picture and be pragmatic about the resolution. The solution will be dictated by the criticality and impact of the issue, as well as how long it will take to implement the resolution, manually or otherwise. Everyone involved in the project will have his or her own view. In my experience, the simplest solution is often the best solution. Overly complex solutions can often introduce further issues and complications, so it's best to keep it simple and not to over-engineer the solution.

Implementing the Resolution

After a resolution has been identified, validated, and agreed to, it needs to be implemented throughout all the required environments. If a code change forms all or part of the resolution, it may also involve changes to test data and scripts, as well as require additional test cases. Where possible, the specific test cases should be added to the regression test suite to ensure that all future releases are tested for the exact issue and to ensure that it is not regressed. This is particularly important for highly visible or critical issues to ease concerns of the issue arising again. The resolution may also require that you update support and operational documentation, as well as rules and procedures — all of which needs to be verified by the operations and service delivery teams.

Typical Incidents

Many functional and technical incidents can occur in the daily running of a system. Some are due to faulty or defective software, while others are simply due to quirks and environmental conditions. For example, when a user attempts to start a particular service, it fails, but when the user tries again, it starts perfectly. A review of logs and events might not highlight the actual reason why the service stopped in the first instance, although my firm belief is that there is a legitimate reason for the incident. Computer systems have become so complicated that it's nearly impossible to understand everything that's going on under the covers all the time. That doesn't mean to say that there's not a legitimate reason for a crash; it simply means that it could be difficult to determine the reason if the logs and events don't highlight any clues. This reinforces my message that logs and events should contain as much information as possible to enable you to understand and re-create the incident. Furthermore, using the wait-retry pattern can help to alleviate a complete stop to the processing. That doesn't mean you shouldn't log the issue and/or gather as much information as possible; it simply means that some issues are accepted or anticipated, and as long as the action is retried and successful, the system will continue to function.

Part II: The Production Landscape

Some common technical issues and incidents that can occur during the day-to-day running of the system include but are not limited to the following:

- ❑ Processes and services not starting or stopping as required
- ❑ Processes and services hanging or terminating unexpectedly
- ❑ Database transactions deadlocking and/or timing out
- ❑ Performance degradation (transactions taking longer than anticipated)
- ❑ CPU and other resource utilization increases and spikes
- ❑ Out-of-memory and stack overflow exceptions
- ❑ Null reference exceptions
- ❑ Unhandled exceptions
- ❑ Access denied and "file not found" issues
- ❑ Network and connectivity issues
- ❑ Third-party component issues
- ❑ Event and trace logs spamming and rolling over
- ❑ Monitoring noise (alerts that are not really issues)
- ❑ Incomplete and incorrect logging of status and events
- ❑ Incorrect configuration and post deployment issues
- ❑ License and certificate expiry
- ❑ Inconsistent, out-of-sync, and non-integral data and/or configuration
- ❑ Disk full/insufficient disk space exceptions
- ❑ Fragmented disks
- ❑ Backup and/or restore failures

Although functional issues depend on the system being implemented, some common design and implementation issues can hinder incident investigation, as well as cause issues themselves. These include but are not limited to the following:

- ❑ Date and time conversion issues
- ❑ Insufficient transaction and data validation
- ❑ Little or no security and audit information (non-repudiation and history)
- ❑ Concurrency issues and user profiling
- ❑ Opening and closing connections, files, and transactions
- ❑ Character set and code page conversion, validation, and storage issues
- ❑ Not enough or incorrect information reported in traces, errors, and exceptions

❏   Insufficient request/response checking and validation

❏   Insufficient transaction traceability and history

❏   Reference data management and validity

Not all systems are the same, but there is a lot of commonality between systems and the functions they perform and the way you should perform them. The industry strives to standardize and implement solutions with proven patterns and practices to help to reduce the number of incidents and outages. Taking a step back during design and development to think about the kinds of incidents that might occur and build in the appropriate information, controls, and processes will dramatically reduce the time and effort spent when an incident occurs. Wherever possible, the system should be designed and implemented so that it is resilient to typical incidents. The Operations Manual should cover as many known failures and outages as possible and provide detailed guidance for investigation and rectification.

Summary

In this chapter you saw that incident investigation is a key part of the project lifecycle and is often very difficult. Issues and incidents need to be resolved quickly and efficiently. By taking a step back and looking at some of the common incidents, you can design your systems to help piece together a timeline to support incident investigation.

The following are the key points to take away from this chapter:

❏   **Incidents will happen.** It is important to remember that incidents will happen and they need to be resolved. Not all incidents will require changes to the application code, configuration, and so forth. Some incidents can be resolved through process changes.

❏   **Understand the incident.** Gathering as much information as possible will greatly help as you identify the root cause of the problem. Incorporating the right amount of diagnostics in the application will help you understand the incident without having an effect on performance or functionality.

❏   **Re-create the incident.** Incidents should be re-created in an isolated environment so that you can take a structured and analytical approach to resolve the issue as well as try out various options.

❏   **Verify the incident and the proposed solution.** It is vital that issues be formally verified. You don't want to waste time trying to resolve things that actually aren't issues. It is equally important to verify the proposed resolution to ensure that it will in fact resolve the issue.

❏   **Implement the solution.** Once the issue has been verified and the proposed solution has been agreed to, it can be implemented, tested, and deployed.

❏   **Cater for typical incidents.** Common incidents provide a basis for improved design and implementation. The Operations Manual should also include all known incidents and the step-by-step procedures for dealing with them.

12

Application Maintenance

The application maintenance team is responsible for maintaining the application while it is in live service. Application maintenance functions generally include third-line support, issue resolution, bug fixing, application enhancements, testing, and release management. In some cases, application maintenance can be provided by the service delivery team. Irrespective of who does it, application maintenance is a vital part of the project lifecycle, drawing on everything put in place during design, development, testing, and deployment. Application maintenance is essentially a mirror of change control and defect management in construction. When you're providing support during testing and early live service, you're doing nothing more than application maintenance activities.

This chapter is organized into the following sections:

❑ **The Application Maintenance Team** — Provides a brief overview of the application maintenance team and its services. It also reinforces the message that while the system is still under construction, the development team essentially performs all the same activities and functions as the maintenance team.

❑ **Application Maintenance Functions** — Examines the types of activities the application maintenance team carries out as part of its day-to-day operations, including:

  ❑ Defect analysis and fix-on-fail

  ❑ Application enhancements and changes

  ❑ Release and configuration management

❑ **The Developer's Guide** — The Developer's Guide provides a good basis for the application maintenance activities. It includes the following high-level areas:

  ❑ Solution Overview

  ❑ Standards and Guidelines

  ❑ Testing Approach and Guidelines

❏   Code Profiling and Analysis

❏   Configuration Management

❏   Submission to Release

The Developer's Guide also documents key areas of enhancement where frameworks or placeholders have been put in place during the initial development.

The Application Maintenance Team

Once the system is in production and the initial post go-live support is completed, the project team hands over the system to the application maintenance team, which takes on the management and maintenance of all the source code and other project artifacts throughout the system's lifetime, including configuration, data, test scripts, builds, and regression. The application maintenance team utilizes development environments, test environments, configuration management, and build and regression environments. The environments, tools, and processes are no different from those used throughout the project.

The application maintenance team, which is typically smaller than the project team, comprises people who have a full understanding of the system's functional and technical aspects. The structure of the application maintenance team depends entirely on the organization. However, the application maintenance team is very similar to the service delivery team, and sometimes the two functions are combined. The team is made up of functional designers, developers, database administrators, build and release personnel, testers, and so on. In some cases, the individuals perform multiple roles to reduce the size of the team and reduce costs. The application maintenance team may also look after multiple systems within the organization. In many cases, resources from the application maintenance team are involved early in the project to ease the handover process and share their knowledge. It is also not uncommon for some members of a large project team to transfer to the application maintenance team following implementation.

As you can imagine, handing over the system is no minor task. All the knowledge that has been built up during the project needs to be captured and handed over appropriately — for example, ensuring that the standards and guidelines are adhered to when updates are made to the applications, and ensuring that all the tools and environments are understood and used appropriately. All known issues must be fully understood, and any outstanding development items must be logged. The application maintenance team should operate in the same way as the project team and, where necessary, enhance the processes and practices to streamline the maintenance operation.

Thinking about application maintenance early in the lifecycle will help to ensure that the system is handed over efficiently and will allow the application maintenance team to perform its functions appropriately. As you will see later in this chapter, the Developer's Guide provides a great foundation for achieving this. There's nothing worse than trying to update an application when you have no idea what it's doing. It is important that the documentation and comments be in good shape so that people with less experience with the application can follow it properly.

Maintenance activities are further hindered when the tests don't work or don't produce the right results. Application maintenance is no easy task and you must do everything you can to ensure that the team has a full understanding of the system and its inner workings.

While the system is still under construction, the development team is essentially the application maintenance team and therefore all the scenarios and activities apply to you, too.

Application Maintenance Functions

The application maintenance team performs similar functions to the design, development, test, and configuration management teams. The application maintenance team will usually provide the following types of services:

❑ **Defect analysis and fix-on-fail** — In the previous chapter, we looked at incident investigation and some of the typical incidents that can occur. The application maintenance team is responsible for analyzing issues and providing fixes for the system. This could involve putting workarounds in place as well as root cause analysis and resolution.

❑ **Application enhancements and changes** — Throughout the lifetime of the system there will be updates and enhancements that need to be made. In some cases, there are minor issues or enhancements that were not completed during development that are handed over to the application maintenance team providing a small pipeline of work. The scope of the project will be restricted at the start and there may be features that have been deemed low priority that the application maintenance team will implement through minor updates. The operations and service delivery teams are always looking at ways to improve stability and performance of the application, which typically results in enhancements being made to the application by the application maintenance team.

❑ **Release and configuration management** — As fixes and enhancements are provided, they need to be packaged into releases and tested appropriately. This process is exactly the same as it is during the construction phases of the project. The application maintenance team will perform this function and provide the service delivery team with the appropriate release for deployment into the relevant environments.

The application maintenance team is usually bound by Service Level Agreements (SLAs) that stipulate the turnaround time for its activities. For example:

❑ Severity 1 defects must be turned around in less than 4 hours.

❑ Severity 2 defects must be turned around in less than 12 hours.

❑ Severity 3 defects must be turned around in less than 24 hours.

These times are only samples, of course; the SLAs will depend on the organization and the severity definitions. The application maintenance team is measured according to their SLAs, and penalties may be levied if it fails to meet them.

Incident Investigation and Fix-On-Fail

The previous chapter discussed the activities involved in incident investigation: investigate, re-create, verify, and resolve. Again, it will depend on how the organization is structured as to how much investigation into a live-service incident has been performed prior to it being raised to the application maintenance team. However, the activities involved in incident investigation and fix-on-fail are all just a part of a live-service support function. Live-service incidents need to be resolved and this is commonly referred to as "fix-on-fail," which involves some or all of the following activities:

❑ Understanding the incident

❑ Re-creating the incident in an isolated environment

❑ Verifying the problem

❑ Proposing and validating a fix

❑ Implementing a fix and thoroughly testing it

❑ Submitting the fix into a release for deployment

These activities are the same functions the fix team provides during the project's test activities and phases. The application maintenance team would follow the defined defect-management approach (as discussed in Chapter 3) so that all the lessons learned and processes are consistent. It is very important to take a step back and think about these functions. The functions will be re-used throughout the lifecycle, so ensuring that the tools and processes are streamlined and fit for purpose will benefit the system throughout its entire lifetime. Ensuring that the system includes all the appropriate diagnostics will also dramatically reduce the amount of time and effort spent analyzing defects.

The Different Types of Updates

There are many different scenarios, but resolving an issue will almost always involve one or more of the following types of updates:

❑ **Code updates** — Code changes are very common. In many situations, the infamous "one liner" comes into play — that is, a simple one-line fix is required. However, code changes invariably affect the test scripts and expected results. This means that these need to be updated as well. When you make a code change, chances are that the documentation and comments will also need to be updated. There is no difference to a code change being made during development, fix, or application maintenance; the same standards and guidelines need to be followed, as well as the same process. The easier the code is to understand and maintain, the easier it is to fix. Having the right processes and practices in place from the start makes it so much easier throughout the entire lifecycle. Complex fixes may require completely new classes or overloaded methods to reduce the impact to other areas, and your templates and tools will greatly help in this area.

❑ **Data and database updates** — Data changes are often scripted into a live environment to minimize the impact to the production system and preserve existing data and integrity. Very rarely would a new database be installed from scratch into a live environment. Data and database changes need to be managed carefully to ensure the right data is deployed to the right environment. For example, the database often contains hostnames or IP addresses as well as other environment-specific entries. A fix may involve different scripts for different environments. Deploying the wrong data to the production environment can be disastrous. Scripts need to be checked and double-checked, as they are often a one-off because the data can't be tested in any other environment. The scripts need to be deployed along with the other artifacts, so ensuring they can be included within a properly packaged release with help.

❑ **Configuration updates** — Configuration changes can be tricky to manage, as every environment will have both common and specific configurations. Values that are tweaked in one environment need to be carefully tested before tweaking them in another environment. For example, dropping a "queue warning threshold" in the pre-production environment may be perfectly viable, whereas deploying the same change to the production environment could have a dramatic impact. Configuration changes are highly environment-specific, so ensuring that your configuration management and tools support the different environments will make configuration changes easier. Again, the configuration, whether through scripts or fully deployed files, needs to be included in the release to reduce the risk of impact.

❑ **Process updates** — Some incidents require a change to a process. It could be an operational, business, user, or even a development process. Ensuring that the relevant documentation and procedures are updated and rolled out to everyone concerned is very important. I am a firm believer that documentation should be included in a release so that everything is consistent across the board.

❑ **Environment updates** — This category includes hardware upgrades, network upgrades, and foundation software upgrades. In fact, it includes anything that is not directly implemented by the application or system.

Fix Implementation, Testing, and Release

After identifying and proposing a fix, validating it, and determining what needs to be updated, it is time to actually implement and test it. Again, it will depend on what updates are required for the fix; however, the following provides an example of some of the tasks that could be performed:

1. Scripting the data and database updates

2. Updating the configuration

3. Updating the source code (for instance, updating architecture components, updating application components, and/or updating tools developed in-house)

4. Updating the tests (unit, integration, functional, technical, and regression)

5. Updating the documentation

With the fixes in place, you will need to perform some or all of the following, depending on the development approach that has been implemented:

1. Execute the tests (unit, integration, functional, technical, and regression).

2. Profile the code (static and performance).

3. Generate the documentation as well as updating manually produced documentation.

4. Compile the completion results.

5. Submit all the updated artifacts to a release.

Chapter 2 showed all these activities as part of the build process, and there's nothing different when it comes to application maintenance. The key is to ensure that all these activities don't create a bottleneck in the process. More important, you need to ensure that these activities maintain the quality bar that has been set. Updating the code and ensuring that it compiles is not good enough to say the fix works. You've seen how the system can become unmanageable when certain activities are skipped or left behind. Having streamlined procedures, practices, and tools in place will ensure that quality is maintained and reduce the cost of poor quality.

The level of testing will depend on the circumstances, but the unit, integration, and regression tests should be updated and executed as a matter of course prior to submission into a formal release to reduce the likelihood of a failed build or release.

Application Enhancements and Changes

Some enhancements and minor updates — such as changes to validation rules or minor updates to batch jobs — can be thought of as fixes and therefore will follow the same pattern. In other cases, enhancements will involve a more formal design approach, such as adding new functionality or changes to existing functionality, which should follow the same or similar pattern as the original design activities, especially if there are specific tools and technologies used for design and perhaps even code generation or enhancement. A major new release will probably involve a new project team, which is why the application maintenance team generally only works on fixes and minor enhancements. However, it's entirely dependent on the organization and project.

Many ideas will be raised during the project's lifecycle, some of which will be implemented and others deemed "nice to have." Often the items that were not delivered during the formal project stages will be taken on by the application maintenance team (assuming, of course, there is a valid business case for the enhancement or change). For instance, the following list could represent areas deemed out-of-scope for Release 1:

❑ Internationalization and localization

❑ Accessibility support

❑ Specific multi-channel processing

❑ Secure Sockets Layer (SSL)

❑ Online help

❑ Remember-me functionality

❑ Picture verification

❑ Password strength indicator

❑ Password history

If the project is split into multiple releases, some of these items might be carried over into a future release. It is also possible that the application maintenance team is working in parallel with future release development teams. Some or all of the items not being delivered in the formal releases could be carried over into the application maintenance activities for ongoing implementation. This means the application maintenance team needs to understand the system and the processes to ensure that the enhancement is implemented correctly and doesn't adversely affect existing functionality. As the system is used in live service, there will always be areas of improvement and enhancement that would typically be implemented by the application maintenance team.

The tools, patterns, and practices that were put in place during design and development will help the application maintenance team implement enhancements correctly. For example, an enhancement may involve the introduction of a new database table and associated reference data tables. The application maintenance team should not do anything different to implement the new functionality and it should adhere to all the existing standards and guidelines. The templates and tools provide a solid foundation for further development.

It is important to note that the application maintenance team will also take ownership of all the tools associated with the development and testing of the system and, as such, may also need to make fixes and enhancements to them as well as to the core application. Ensuring that everything follows the same patterns and practices will help ease the transition.

Release and Configuration Management

The application maintenance team will probably be working on both enhancements and fixes at the same time. Some enhancements may take a while to implement, which means that the application maintenance team will be managing multiple releases. Not all enhancements and fixes will be included in a single release, so the source code and artifacts need to be managed appropriately. A change destined for a later release could be catastrophic if deployed incorrectly. Common files are often the root cause of this issue. Furthermore, working on fixes or enhancements to the code-set that is in production can cause serious headaches. For example, a developer may be part way through implementing a low-priority fix or enhancement when a major production issue occurs. A fix for the production issue needs to be deployed into the production environment rapidly. The developers and the release management team usually need to work together to back out what they have implemented so far so that the production fix can be included on its own and deployed without taking anything else along with it. This can be a costly exercise and can waste valuable time and effort.

Managing the source code and artifacts throughout the project and post-implementation is vital to ensuring that fixes and enhancements do not affect production and/or get muddled up in releases. In source control applications, branching helps with this, although branching is not without its own challenges and intricacies. I discussed branching and merging in Chapter 3 as part of getting ready for production. In short, code branches need to be maintained for each of the different releases. Fixes (and possibly even enhancements) might need to be analyzed as to their impact and implemented (or merged) across a number of different releases. In addition, the build and test projects may also change as new components are added to future releases. This means that there is a Release 1 build project and possibly a Release 2 build project. Thinking about multiple releases up-front will not only save time during application maintenance, it will also save time when another formal release is being introduced. That said, supporting multiple releases has many other impacts throughout development, testing, and release management. The project team uses many tools and scripts, all of which could contain folder locations, database names, and other specific commands and information that must be considered and incorporated across each release.

Dealing with multiple releases can be especially difficult once the system is live and multiple teams are working on different releases, which also affects testing and issue reproduction. Everyone needs to be working on the right release. A classic example is when a defect is found in the production system that is no longer an issue (in a later release) because of changes or enhancements. However, the later release may not be scheduled to be deployed until a much later date and a decision needs to be made about whether to patch or update the previous release. A patch would mean that the current production release needs to be updated and re-built with the fix. If the code has subsequently changed for Release 2, this could be a complete nightmare to deal with. Once a version of the system is deployed to production, all the source code and artifacts should be locked down so that a fix-on-fail capability can always get to the right version of the software. There may also be incidents that require multiple source code streams to be updated — for example, if the fix identified in production is also required in Release 2. Let's say a patch must be provided for production because the business can't wait for Release 2. In this situation a change needs to be made in the production code stream, tested, and deployed. The changes then need to be folded into the Release 2 stream, which could have a domino effect on Release 2's schedule.

The release notes that are produced need to be very well documented to ensure that the release contains only what it should for deployment to the production system.

The Developer's Guide

The Developer's Guide is used both by the core development team and the application maintenance team. Figure 12-1 shows the high-level table of contents for a typical Developer's Guide.

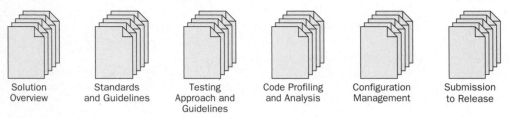

| Solution Overview | Standards and Guidelines | Testing Approach and Guidelines | Code Profiling and Analysis | Configuration Management | Submission to Release |

Figure 12-1

Although I've discussed the majority of these subjects earlier in this book, the following provides a quick overview of the sections that would be included in the Developer's Guide:

- ❑ **Solution Overview** — The Solution Overview is the outline of the code solution as well as the tools and technologies involved. It also includes overviews of hardware architecture and components, such as the individual servers, load balancers, and networking components, as well as software components such as batch job overviews, report overviews, and component overviews, including information on how they will be implemented — for example, adding new batch jobs or adding new reports, and so on. The Solution Overview documents the configuration of the development environment as a starting point for further enhancement. The Solution Overview also covers areas such as development environment tools and their installation and set-up.

- ❑ **Standards and Guidelines** — The Standards and Guidelines section collates and documents all the various standards and practices that should be incorporated in the solution, including coding standards, commenting standards, logging and events, and architectural patterns and principles.

- ❑ **Testing Approach and Guidelines** — The Testing Approach and Guidelines section documents the various approaches and techniques of all the various testing activities, including unit, integration and regression. Specific areas discuss each stub and simulator and how they should be used for effective testing.

- ❑ **Code Profiling and Analysis** — The Code Profiling and Analysis section discusses how to perform all the profiling and analysis functions, as well as the tools and technologies involved.

❑ **Configuration Management** — The Configuration Management section documents the configuration management solution and layout. It also documents the routine tasks that need to be performed, such as checking in, checking out, labeling, and so forth.

❑ **Submission to Release** — The Submission to Release section documents the various steps involved in submitting artifacts to a release, along with all the evidentiary documentation and checks.

Again, by thinking about these areas upfront, you can save yourself from spending unnecessary time and effort producing multiple sets of documentation for different purposes.

The Developer's Guide also provides information on typical areas for solution enhancement — for example, if the development team adds placeholders for the application maintenance team to implement features the development team did not implement in the initial version. Let's use the scope list from Chapter 4 as a basis for discussion:

❑ Internationalization and localization

❑ Accessibility support

❑ Specific multi-channel processing

❑ Secure Sockets Layer (SSL)

❑ Online help

❑ Remember-me functionality

❑ Picture verification

❑ Password strength indicator

❑ Password history

The Developer's Guide discusses how these features should be implemented (or enhanced) according to the existing framework and placeholders. For instance, the initial version might support only the default culture or language. The internationalization and localization documentation would show how additional languages should be implemented in the overall solution. The Developer's Guide would cover only areas where placeholders or frameworks had been put in place for future enhancements.

It is also useful to collate any and all analysis that has been performed on out-of-scope features to ensure that the handover captures them appropriately. For instance, when you've examined a particular feature in the early days of the project and discounted it for any reason, the information and decision should be captured for future use. A number of external products, such as picture verification, may have been reviewed and it would be a good idea to ensure that all this information is handed over, too. This will save the application maintenance team from wasting time and effort covering the same ground.

As you can see, the Developer's Guide is nothing more than a collection of what's already discussed in this book. Bringing it all together in this way helps to define a single document that can be updated as the project progresses. In the early days, the Developer's Guide is used to sign off on the proposed approach and scope. As more detail is added, it is used as the formal guide for all teams.

Summary

The application maintenance functions are very similar to the development functions. Members of the application maintenance team may or may not have been involved in the project; therefore, it is vitally important that the application maintenance team fully understand the application and the processes required to update it, fully test it, and include everything in a release. The Developer's Guide is a useful tool to ensure the application maintenance team operates smoothly and efficiently. If it's good enough for the core development team to follow, it should be good enough for the application maintenance team. The recommended approach is to think "out-of-the-box," starting with the end goal and working backwards.

The following are the key points to take away from this chapter:

❑ **Application maintenance is software development.** While the system is still under construction, the development team essentially performs the same activities and functions as the application maintenance team. The key activities discussed included:

   ❑ Defect analysis and fix

   ❑ Application enhancements and changes

   ❑ Release and configuration management

❑ **The application maintenance team is usually responsible for third-line support.** Once the application is in production the application, tools, and processes will have been handed over to the application maintenance team for its own use. You need to ensure that your processes and practices are fully documented so that they can be handed over accordingly.

❑ **The application maintenance team is usually bound by Service Level Agreements (SLAs).** You must do what you can to ensure that changes and updates can be made to the application quickly and efficiently. This means documenting code properly, ensuring that the tests run correctly and that the processes you employ are stable and efficient to ensure that turnaround times for repairing defects or implementing changes are minimized.

❑ **Start preparing the developer's guide early** — The Developer's Guide can be used not only early in the project, but also handed over to the application maintenance team. The high-level contents discussed included:

   ❑ Solution overview

   ❑ Standards and guidelines

   ❑ Testing approach and guidelines

   ❑ Code profiling and analysis

   ❑ Configuration management

   ❑ Submission to release

The Developer's Guide should document key areas of enhancement where frameworks or placeholders have been added during the initial development. The Developer's Guide should include instructions and guidelines for implementing additional functionality.

Part III
Case Study

13

Conceptual Design

This chapter presents a high-level overview and conceptual design for the case study associated with this book, Within-a-Click. I've already touched on some of the basic aspects and functionality in previous chapters. The case study is an end-to-end membership sub-system that should allow users to perform the following basic operations:

❑   Create a new account by specifying typical account information, such as username, password, e-mail address, and other security-related information.

❑   Activate their account by specifying a system-generated account Activation Key, which will have been e-mailed to them after they created their new account.

❑   Log in and log out of the website.

❑   Update their account details, change their password, and close their account.

Although there are many third-party products and framework components to help you implement some or all of this functionality (for example, the ASP.NET Membership system), this book concentrates on designing a custom solution.

This chapter first takes a holistic view of the overall functionality, and then defines some fundamental guiding principles, requirements, and constraints. Chapter 14 looks at planning the architecture and Chapter 15 looks at modeling the application components according to the conceptual architecture. The patterns and practices discussed in Chapters 16 through 24 then use the case study's conceptual design as the basis for further discussion.

This book is not intended to teach you how to implement a good membership system. The book simply uses the case study to promote and discuss some of the production-readiness challenges. A membership sub-system provides a good basis for these discussions because it encompasses a number of different functional and technical challenges. The system needs to support logged in users as well as non-logged in users. Certain user information must be encrypted and stored securely, which presents challenges for testing. The functionality needs to be fully tested, which also provides some challenges for test data preparation and management. The site and application must also be capable of supporting a potentially large number of different users, so it needs to be tested rigorously for performance and resilience. Finally, there are also some basic processes running in the background that need to be fast, resilient, and operable.

This chapter is organized into the following sections:

❑ **The Guiding Principles** — Reintroduces the guiding principles that were outlined in Chapter 4. The guiding principles will help to shape the design and will underpin the solution.

❑ **Online Application Walkthrough** — Provides a walkthrough of the user stories and functionality specific to the Within-a-Click online application. The user stories provide the end-to-end view of the overall functionality from the end user's perspective. The walkthrough covers the following user stories:

    ❑ Creating a new account

    ❑ Activating a new account

    ❑ Re-requesting an account Activation Key

    ❑ Logging in

    ❑ Logging out

    ❑ Resetting a password

    ❑ Changing a password

    ❑ Updating account details

    ❑ Closing an account

❑ **Defining the Requirements** — Takes the user stories outlined in the application walkthrough section and builds a set of high-level requirements for each area of functionality. It discusses some of the design choices and the comparisons between similar features and functionality that can be found on most modern websites today. These discussions are used to set the scope of the project. The requirements outlined include:

    ❑ Basic account data elements

    ❑ Web pages and processing

    ❑ Batch and reporting requirements

    ❑ Technical requirements

❑ **Documenting the Use Cases** — Pulls together all the information from the previous sections into a set of detailed use cases that will complete the functional picture and the overall processing. In this instance, the use cases and activities break down the user stories into a set of individual processing steps and flows. Use cases are typically used to confirm existing requirements, derive additional requirements, and to highlight various system components and processing. It is therefore important that the use-cases contain as much detail as possible and map back to the functional requirements to ensure that they are documented and incorporated appropriately.

The Guiding Principles

Chapter 4 looked at some of the inputs and outputs of the software "construction" activities, which for the purposes of this book include design, build, unit, and integration testing. I have listed the guiding principles here (albeit abridged) as a reminder before embarking on the journey through the conceptual design:

- ❑ **Positive user experience** — Positively impact the user experience and satisfaction of the system while retaining and satisfying the business goals and requirements. The design needs to come up with an easy-to-use interface while providing all the relevant functionality.

- ❑ **Flexible** — Support for a growing, changing, and adapting marketplace by adding new functionality quickly and easily. The solution should be flexible enough without dramatically affecting costs and timescales when it comes to adding new functionality.

- ❑ **High performance** — Support for global transaction levels and volumes. The site could be accessed by millions of users, so performance is a key principle that should underpin the design. The end-to-end transaction time is crucial to end users.

- ❑ **Cost effective** — Efficient and cost effective to operate, support, maintain, and enhance. The system shouldn't introduce an unnecessary burden on the support organization. The solution needs to be generally easy to operate. The system needs to be relatively easy to maintain.

- ❑ **Highly secure** — Implement highly secure protocols for capturing, viewing, extracting, and amending data. The system must maintain and protect customer and user privacy.

- ❑ **New technologies** — The system should be built and tested using the latest generation of technologies.

- ❑ **Custom built** — The system should be custom built to demonstrate the production-ready challenges and patterns and practices that can be employed.

Although this is not an exhaustive list of guiding principles, it provides a reasonable basis for the discussions in this chapter and the chapters that follow. I've added an additional guiding principle, "custom built," to capture the fact that this chapter concentrates on a custom solution.

The conceptual design is used solely to promote and discuss the patterns and practices in this book and not necessarily for verbatim implementation. You should apply the concepts and practices to the work you do in the field.

Online Application Walkthrough

Figure 13-1 shows the use-case diagram for the Within-a-Click online application. The points that follow provide an overview of each of the functions shown in the figure:

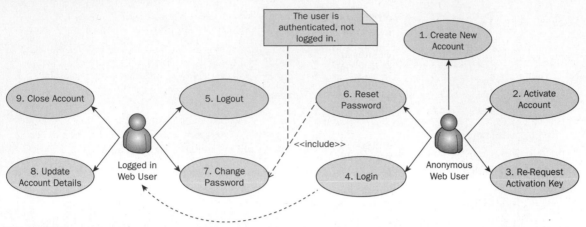

Figure 13-1

1. **Create New Account** — Users first create a new account by specifying their account details. The key user account information will include username, password, e-mail address, security question, and security question answer.

2. **Activate Account** — After users have created a new account, they will be sent a unique account Activation Key via e-mail, which they will use to activate their account. This is a pretty common pattern for validating a user's identity. Once their new accounts have been successfully activated, users will be automatically logged in to the system so that they can make use of the basic account management functionality.

3. **Re-Request Activation Key** — E-mail isn't guaranteed; I've personally had many occasions where I haven't received an e-mail for one reason or another. In some cases, e-mail can take a long time to arrive. Taking these situations into account and the fact that there's a real possibility that the Activation Key e-mail could be "lost in the ether," the system will provide users with the ability to directly re-request their account Activation Key.

4. **Login** — When users have an active account (it has been successfully activated), they are free to log in and use the relevant functionality whenever they choose.

5. **Logout** — This functionality enables logged in users to directly log off the system when they're finished using it.

6. **Reset Password** — Users can often forget their password to a system. It is not very surprising when you consider that there are so many systems and websites that require passwords. The sheer number of passwords each person has to remember can be huge. Furthermore, users can often forget their password when they haven't used a site or system for a while. Users will have the ability to change their password. In the case of a "forgotten" password, users aren't actually logged in, so it is a two-step process whereby they will first need to be authenticated using alternative information — in this example, their username and e-mail address — and then the user can change his or her password via the change password functionality.

7. **Change Password** — This functionality enables authenticated users to change their existing password. To be protected against unauthorized password changes, users will need to provide their security question answer before they are allowed to change their existing password.

8. **Update Account Details** — Provides logged in users with the ability to change their existing account details, including their username, e-mail address, security question, and security

question answer. The update account functionality does not allow users to change their password, as this is achieved via the change password functionality.

9. **Close Account** — A lot of sites and systems make it difficult for users to close or remove their account. I've experienced this and I eventually had to contact Customer Services to have an account removed. The application will allow logged in users to close their account completely. It will allow them to specify comments for why they are closing their account and to request e-mail confirmation that the account has been closed.

The preceding features and functions will be organized across a series of different pages and flows on the site. Each web page will be responsible for gathering user input and passing it on for back-end processing. Figure 13-2 shows the high-level navigation map for the site and the associated user stories.

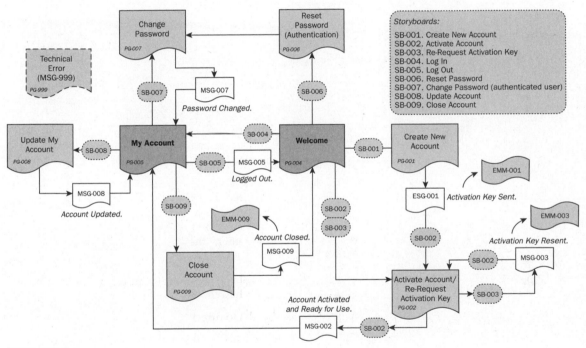

Figure 13-2

As you can see from the diagram, all the user stories start from either the Welcome page or the My Account page. The user stories can also flow from one into another — for example, Create New Account flows into Activate Account, which can also flow into Re-Request Activation Key. The navigation map doesn't show all the possible scenarios; it just shows the "normal" flows, the "confirmation" messages that are displayed to the user, and the e-mail messages that are sent to them.

In the diagram, each of the pages, display messages, e-mail messages, and flows is uniquely identified to help with compiling the overall solution inventory and mapping to requirements. The individual element identifiers are not necessarily sequential. I've mapped them to the storyboard identifiers to keep things synchronized as much as possible. If you are concerned about gaps in the numbering you could always keep the references sequential.

The following table explains the elements in the navigation map.

Abbreviation	Description
SB – Storyboard	There are nine storyboards in the case study that relate to the use-case diagram. They are identified as follows: ❑ SB-001 Create New Account ❑ SB-002 Activate Account ❑ SB-003 Re-request Activation Key ❑ SB-004 Login ❑ SB-005 Logout ❑ SB-006 Reset Password ❑ SB-007 Change Password (authenticated user) ❑ SB-008 Update Account ❑ SB-009 Close Account
PG – Page	Each logical page in the solution is uniquely identified as follows: ❑ PG-001 Create New Account ❑ PG-002 Activate Account / Re-Request Activation Key ❑ PG-004 Welcome (and Login) ❑ PG-005 My Account (and Logout) ❑ PG-006 Reset Password (Authentication) ❑ PG-007 Change Password ❑ PG-008 Update Account ❑ PG-009 Close Account ❑ PG-999 Technical Error
MSG – Message (Display)	Each functional "confirmation" message that is displayed to the user is uniquely identified: ❑ MSG-001 Activation Key Sent ❑ MSG-002 Account Activated and Ready for Use ❑ MSG-003 Activation Key Resent ❑ MSG-005 Logged Out ❑ MSG-007 Password Changed ❑ MSG-008 Account Updated ❑ MSG-009 Account Closed ❑ MSG-999 Technical Error
EMM – E-mail Message	Each e-mail message sent from the system is uniquely identified: ❑ EMM-001 Account Activation Key ❑ EMM-003 Account Activation Key Re-Request ❑ EMM-009 Account Closed

Although all these numbers and identifiers might seem confusing at first, they help to ensure that as you progress through the project, you can account for all the items in the solution inventory. As you continue, you'll identify additional items that will be added to the inventory along with the actual solution components. I guess it is my background, but I do tend to catalog and index things. I've chosen to map the item identifiers to the storyboards to make them slightly easier to remember. For instance, SB-004 is the Login storyboard, PG-004 is actually the Welcome page (although it contains the login controls), and UC-004 is the Login use case. There is no "confirmation" message or e-mail message associated with login; hence, no MSG-004 or EMM-004. Similarly, there isn't a confirmation message after the user is authenticated for reset password, so there is no MSG-006

The Welcome Page

The Welcome page (PG-004) is the primary starting point for all the user stories within the case study. It is the page that users will see when they first navigate to the site.

Figure 13-3 shows the conceptual page layout. I've chosen to use a medium resolution at this point to help visualize (and define) the pages, styles, and graphics. All the page layouts in this chapter use this approach rather than low-resolution wire-frames.

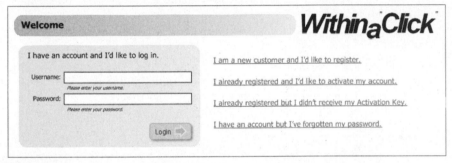

Figure 13-3

The Welcome page is accessible only to non-logged in users. The page has a set of controls that allow registered users to log in, as well as a set of useful links for accessing the additional "non-authenticated" functionality. In this example, the login controls do not show the mandatory field indicators. This is pretty standard for login pages, as users are generally familiar with having to provide both their username and password to login. Many sites adopt this approach, and as users become more familiar with the applications and functionality, they don't need to be reminded of the mandatory fields all the time. This provides users with a standard user experience, although it is not necessarily a formal requirement to not include them — it is just good practice on occasion.

The following outlines the controls and links, along with the user stories they relate to:

❑ The login controls (in the shaded area) allow registered users to log in. The login storyboard is identified as SB-004 Login. On successful authentication and login, users are directed to the My Account page (PG-005), where they can make use of the account management functionality.

❑ Users who do not have an account can create a new one by clicking on the "I am a new customer and I'd like to register." link. The storyboard associated with this functionality is referred to as SB-001 Create New Account. This storyboard links to the SB-002 Activate Account and SB-003 Re-Request Activation Key storyboards, where users can either activate their account using their supplied account activation key or re-request their key if they didn't receive it. The SB-003 Re-Request Activation Key storyboard links back to the SB-002 Activate Account storyboard.

❑ Although the SB-001 Create New Account storyboard flows into the SB-002 Activate Account functionality, there's a possibility that users didn't complete the action for some reason. For example, they could have simply closed the browser or the session could have timed out. In any case, the Welcome page contains the link "I already registered and I'd like to activate my account," to allow users to activate their account without having to go through all the business of creating a new one. The account activation is still achieved through the SB-002 Activate Account storyboard.

❑ In the event that users have not received their account Activation Key, the Welcome page also contains the link "I already registered but I didn't receive my Activation Key. This allows the user to re-request their Activation Key through the SB-003 Re-Request Activation Key storyboard.

❑ Users may have forgotten their password. The link "I have an account but I've forgotten my password." can be used to change their password through the SB-006 Reset Password storyboard, where they will be authenticated via their username and e-mail address. This storyboard then links into the SB-007 Change Password storyboard, which can also be used by logged in users.

All of the preceding user stories and features will be described in more detail shortly.

The My Account Page

The other primary page in the case study is the My Account page, which is accessible only to logged in users. Logged in users have the ability to manage their account from this page. Although the functionality of the application isn't the most extensive, it provides a solid foundation for the discussions in this book.

Figure 13-4 shows the conceptual layout for the My Account page.

Figure 13-4

The simple page is just a set of basic menu options and functions that logged in users can perform:

❑ Users can change their password via the SB-007 Change Password storyboard by clicking the link "I would like to change my password."

❑ Users can update their account details by clicking the link "I would like to update my account details." The storyboard associated with this functionality is SB-008 Update Account.

❑ Log off functionality is provided via the Logout button, which follows the SB-005 Logout storyboard. This page owes its identifier to serving this storyboard.

❑ If users want to close their account, they can click the "I would like to close my account." link, which will take them through the SB-009 Close Account storyboard.

On both pages (Welcome and My Account) I've chosen to use links that describe the functions from a user's perspective — for instance, "I am a new customer and I'd like to register." This is a somewhat friendly approach, although it is equally viable to use links such as "Create New Account" and so forth.

The storyboards associated with the case study are discussed individually in the following sections.

SB-001 Create New Account

Before users can really make use of any of the site's functionality, they first must create a new account. The first real user journey in the Within-a-Click website is creating a new account. This is realized through the SB-001 Create New Account storyboard, as shown in Figure 13-5.

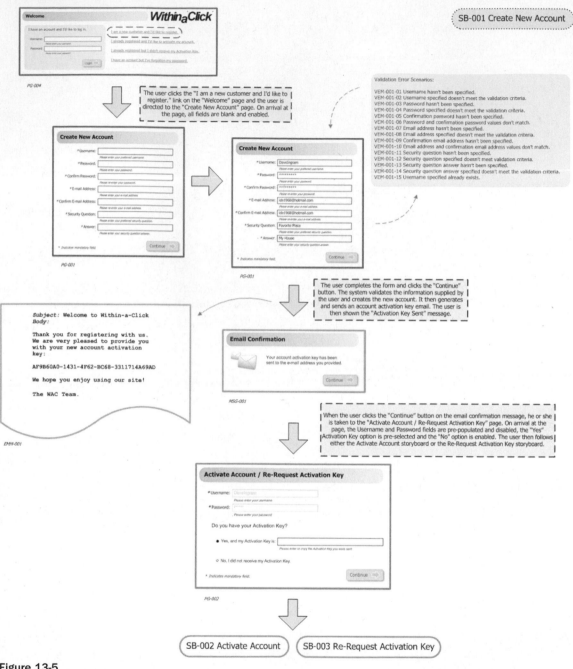

Figure 13-5

This is a fairly simple journey. It starts at the Welcome page, where users click the link "I am a new customer and I'd like to register," and it ends on the Activate Account / Re-Request Activation Key page. The journey flows through the Create New Account page, where users specify their chosen account details. The Create New Account page is pretty simple, too, and I'll discuss the individual page elements later. However, in this instance, all the inputs are text boxes and mandatory. There are no drop-down lists, combo boxes, or other entry controls. Users simply fill out the complete form and then click the Continue button to submit their request.

The users' submissions are validated, and there are a number of validation error scenarios listed in the storyboard. The validation errors are again uniquely identified to help with compiling the solution's inventory and requirements. The identifier is split into three portions separated by a dash (-). The first "VEM" is simply an abbreviation of "Validation Error Message." The second portion is the "Storyboard Identification Number" — in this instance, "001" for SB-001 Create New Account. The final portion is simply an incrementing scenario number. The scenario description is not necessarily the text that will be displayed to the user; it just identifies the particular validation error scenario. Validation and validation errors and messages are discussed in more detail later. If there are any validation errors with the submission, the page will display these errors and clear the appropriate entries, and users will need to correct or re-enter them and re-submit their request.

On successful validation of the submission, the system will create a new account in the database. The system will also compose and send users an account Activation Key via e-mail (EMM-001). A mockup of the e-mail that users will receive is also included on the storyboard. Once the new account has been created and the account Activation Key has been sent, users will be shown the Activation Key Sent confirmation message (MSG-001). On clicking the Continue button, users then flow into the SB-002 Activate Account storyboard, which can also be used to re-request their Activation Key (via the SB-003 Re-Request Activation Key storyboard.)

When users arrive at the Activate Account / Re-Request Activation Key page from this storyboard, the Username and Password fields are pre-populated and disabled. This stops users from changing these values and simplifies entry for users when following the standard path. The Activation Key Received option is defaulted to Yes and the No option is enabled, just in case users don't receive their Key. All users have to do is to wait for the e-mail to arrive, copy and paste the Activation Key from the e-mail they received into the entry field, and then click Continue. In the event that users didn't receive the Activation Key in a suitable timeframe, they can simply select the No option and click Continue. These storyboards are coded SB-002 Activate Account and SB-003 Re-Request Activation Key, respectively, and are discussed in the next sections.

SB-002 Activate Account

Once users have created their new account, they will need to activate it using their account Activation Key, which they should receive via e-mail. This form of account activation is used on many popular sites and is seen as a fairly good way of validating a user via their e-mail address. The Activate Account / Re-Request Activation Key page is dual-purpose in that it supports both the SB-002 Activate Account storyboard and the SB-003 Re-Request Activation Key storyboard. This section concentrates on the SB-002 Activate Account storyboard.

Figure 13-6 shows the overall flow either from the Welcome page, from the SB-001 Create New Account storyboard, or via the SB-003 Re-Request Activation Key storyboard (which will be discussed in the next section).

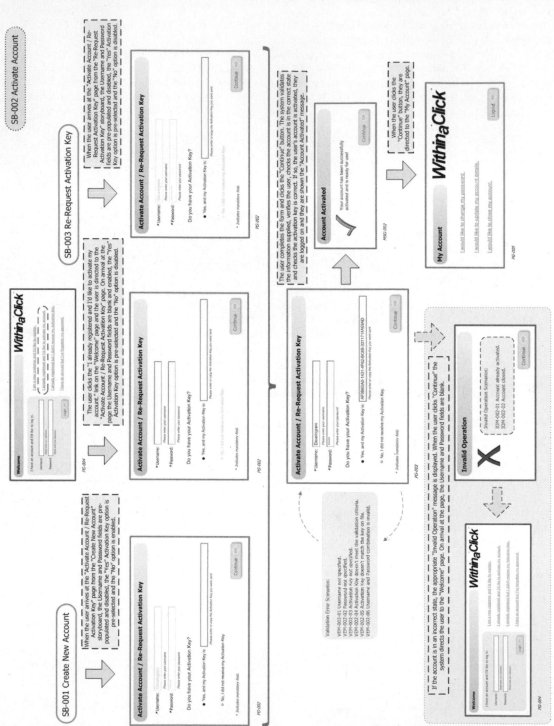

Figure 13-6

There are three routes into this storyboard:

❑ The first (and most normal or expected) route is via the SB-001 Create New Account storyboard. In this instance, the Activate Account / Re-Request Activation Key page is pre-populated with the most appropriate information. The Username and Password fields are pre-populated and disabled, the "Yes" Activation Key Received option is selected, and the "No" option is enabled.

❑ The second route into this storyboard is via the Welcome page, where users click the link "I already registered and I'd like to activate my account." In this instance, the page is pre-populated with the "Yes" Activation Key Received option and the "No" option is disabled. This makes pretty good sense, given that users have indicated they've received their Activation Key by clicking this link. It is a fair point that the e-mail mockup shown in the SB-001 Create New Account storyboard doesn't actually give users explicit and step-by-step instructions for activating their account for each of the different scenarios. This just plays into the "configurability" of the solution. A configurable solution should be employed because the e-mail could change as the project progresses. Anyway, on the page the Username and Password fields are blank and enabled, allowing users to enter them. In this case, users simply need to enter their username and password, copy and paste the Activation Key from the e-mail, and then click Continue.

❑ The final route into this storyboard is from the SB-003 Re-Request Activation Key storyboard. In short, after users have re-requested their Key, the system composes and sends an e-mail containing their account Activation Key. Users are shown a confirmation message that the e-mail has been sent. When they click Continue, they are taken into this flow. In this instance, the Username and Password fields are pre-populated and disabled. This again stops users from re-entering them and makes the form easier to complete. The "Yes" Activation Key Received option is pre-selected, but the "No" option is disabled. Having "No" disabled essentially blocks users from re-requesting their Activation Key again and again from this route.

The validation error scenarios depend entirely on the route into this page and flow and the fields that are enabled for user entry. For instance, in some cases the Username and Password fields are enabled, which could lead to validation and authentication errors. However, the most probable validation errors are that the Activation Key isn't supplied, the supplied value does not meet the required validation criteria, or it may not actually match the Key stored with the account.

The system will validate all the entries. In this instance, the Username and Password fields are only validated for being specified, because they are mandatory fields. They are not, however, validated against their field-level specifications. This avoids validation failures where the rules may have changed since the account was created. Users are authenticated via their username and password. The system also checks that the account is in the correct state for activation. If it is not, an "Invalid

Operation" error could result. The system then checks that the Activation Key matches the Key held against the account. If the Activation Key specified doesn't match the value on file, the user is presented with a validation failure message, the field is cleared out and they can resubmit a new request. If the Activation Key does match, the system proceeds to activate the account, log the user on automatically, and display the "Account Activated" message (MSG-002). When the user clicks Continue, they are taken to the My Account page, where they can make use of the authenticated and logged in user functionality.

In addition to the validation error scenarios, this storyboard also highlights some invalid operations. The first invalid operation message is IOM-001-01 Account Already Activated. Because the page is accessible through a number of routes, it would be perfectly reasonable to assume that the account has already been activated. The application needs to deal with the situation whereby an attempt is made to activate an account that is already active. It could be a mistake or it could be someone messing around and seeing what the system does. The second invalid operation message is IOM-001-02 Account Closed. Again, the system needs to deal with the situation whereby an attempt is made to activate a closed account. In both situations, the system will display a message similar to the confirmation messages. When users click the Continue button, they are taken back to the Welcome page. In any case, the scenarios will need to be tested.

SB-003 Re-Request Activation Key

This storyboard deals with sending users their account Activation Key in the event that they didn't receive it. This storyboard can also be reached from the SB-001 Create New Account storyboard or directly from the Welcome page.

Figure 13-7 shows the storyboard associated with this functionality. This storyboard is similar to the SB-002 Activate Account storyboard, so the commentary will be limited to the specifics for re-requesting an account Activation Key.

There are only two routes into this storyboard:

❑   The first route is via the SB-001 Create New Account storyboard. On arrival at the page, the Username and Password fields are pre-populated and disabled. The Yes option is pre-selected and the No option is enabled.

❑   The second route is directly from the Welcome page. On arrival, the Username and Password fields are blank and enabled. The Yes Activation Key Received option is disabled and the No option is pre-selected.

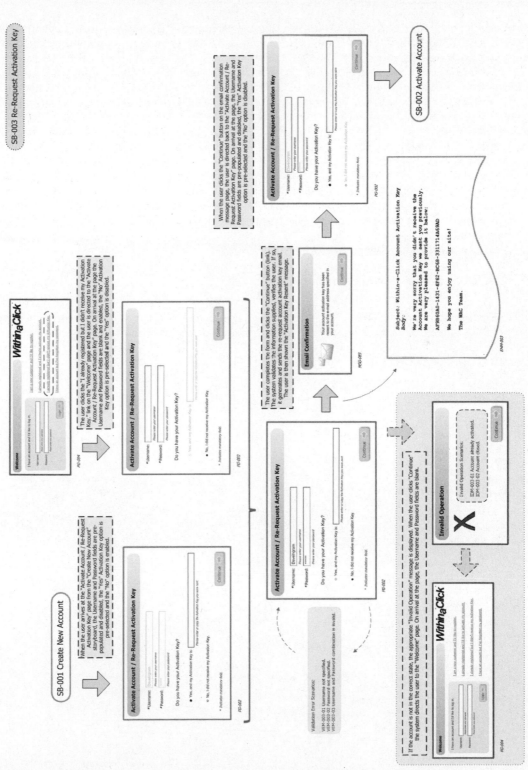

Figure 13-7

343

On successful validation of the user's entries (again, the username and password are only validated for being specified), the system authenticates the user, checks that the account is in the correct state, and proceeds to send the Activation Key. The system composes and sends the Activation Key Re-Request e-mail (EMM-002). A mockup of the mail is also shown in the storyboard. Users are shown the e-mail confirmation message — in this case, the Activation Key Resent message (MSG-003). When users click Continue, they are directed to the Activate Account / Re-Request Activation Key page. On arrival at the page, the Username and Password are pre-populated and disabled, the Yes Activation Key Received option is pre-selected and the No option is disabled, which, as mentioned, simply stops users from re-requesting it again and again in this flow.

Walking through the storyboards helps to refine the way in which the user interacts with the page and which controls are enabled or disabled. This is especially true for multi-purpose pages. Furthermore, you can decide later whether you want to keep the controls visible on the page and disable them or make them invisible. You could also change the page title to give a more appropriate heading for the function being performed.

SB-004 Login

Once users have created and activated a new account, they are free to log in at any time and use the site's functionality. However, the functionality available to them is pretty basic in this instance.

Figure 13-8 shows the SB-004 Login storyboard.

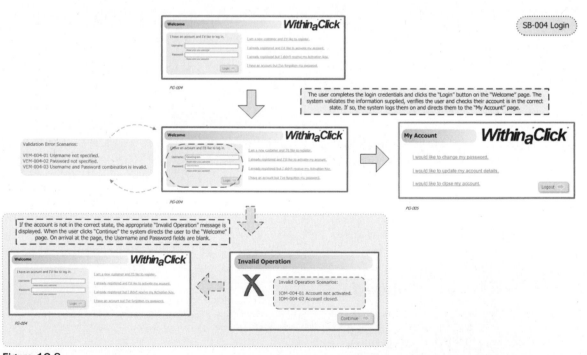

Figure 13-8

Users are authenticated using their username and password, as specified on the Welcome page. The username and password are not validated against their field-level specifications for the reasons previously mentioned. When users click the Login button, the system proceeds to validate that the entries have been specified, authenticate the users, check that the account is in the correct state, and log in the users. After users have been successfully logged in, they are directed to the My Account page.

SB-005 Logout

Users who are logged in to the system have the ability to directly log off using the SB-005 Logout storyboard, as shown in Figure 13-9.

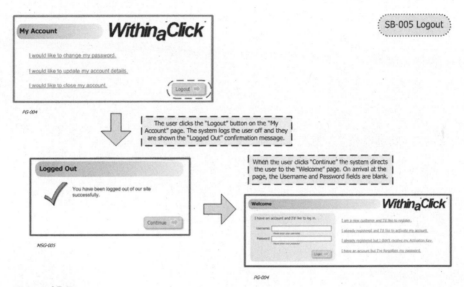

Figure 13-9

Once users are logged off, they are shown a confirmation message stating that they've been logged out successfully. When they click Continue, they are directed to the Welcome page, where the Username and Password fields are blank. I've chosen to display a confirmation message during logout because users are becoming increasingly conscious that they are actually logged out of a system to ensure that they are protected against any unauthorized use. It is possible that the system could close the browser window when users click Continue, but taking them back to the Welcome page leaves the system open for future enhancements without dramatically affecting the current user experience. It also follows a similar pattern to the other pages and flows.

SB-006 Reset Password

If users forget their password, they can change it using the Reset Password flow. A lot of websites choose to e-mail users their password, although I personally feel this is somewhat insecure. I don't think it is a good idea to e-mail passwords in the clear, especially in these days where identity theft is rife.

Figure 13-10 shows the SB-006 Reset Password storyboard, which leads into the SB-007 Change Password storyboard.

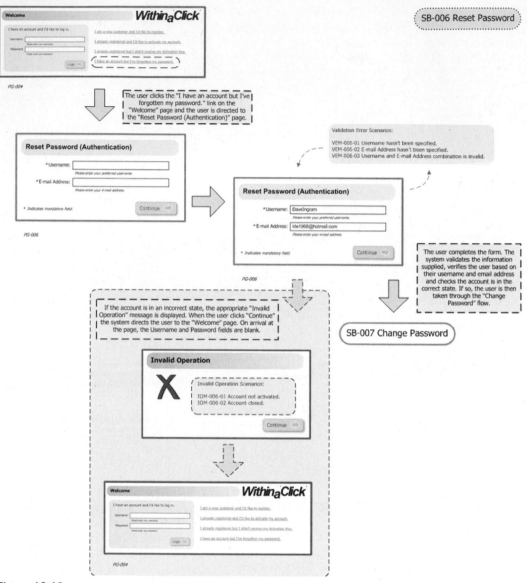

Figure 13-10

The Reset Password flow starts with authenticating users via an alternative means to username and password authentication. In this instance, users will be authenticated using their username and e-mail address. On successful authentication, users then flow into the SB-007 Change Password storyboard. The system does not support password changes when an account hasn't been activated or when the account is closed. Any attempt to do so will result in the display of an Invalid Operation message.

SB-007 Change Password

Users can change their password either by joining from the SB-006 Reset Password flow or by directly choosing to do so from the My Account page by clicking the "I would like to change my password" link.

Figure 13-11 shows the SB-007 Change Password storyboard.

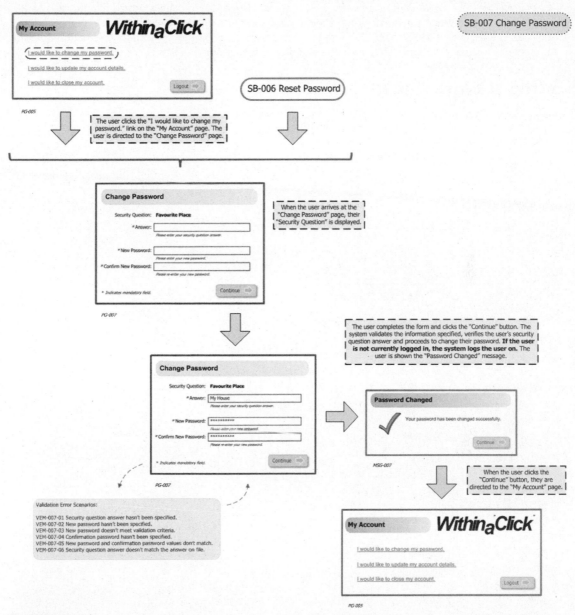

Figure 13-11

To prevent unauthorized password changes, users must supply their security question answer along with their new password (which also needs to be confirmed). This provides an additional layer of protection. Once the password has been successfully changed, users are directed to the MSG-007 Password Changed message page.

If users have joined from the Reset Password flow, they are automatically logged in. On clicking Continue on the confirmation page, users are directed to the My Account page. This automatic login streamlines the functionality. If users were taken back to the Welcome page and had to enter their username and password again, it would be somewhat annoying and unnecessary. It is worth thinking about these little details, which the storyboards help to highlight. Logging on users and taking them to the My Account page not only simplifies the diagram, but also improves the user experience.

SB-008 Update Account

Users can update their account using the SB-008 Update Account functionality (see Figure 13-12).

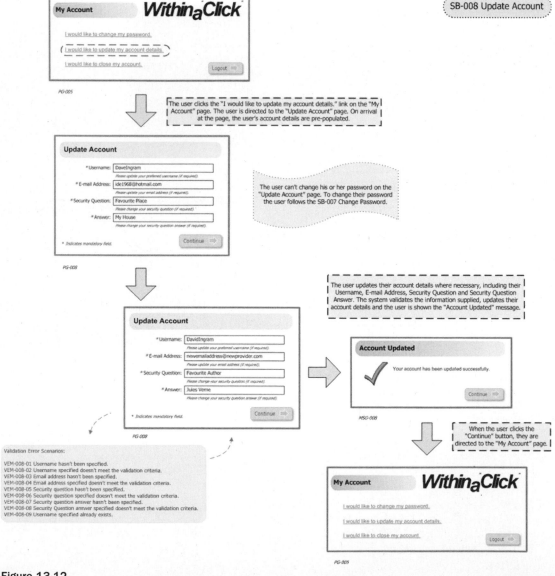

Figure 13-12

Note that the SB-008 Update Account storyboard does *not* enable users to change their password; this functionality is achieved via the SB-007 Change Password storyboard. The SB-008 Update Account storyboard allows users to change their username, e-mail address, security question, and security question answer. After updating their account details, users are directed to the Account Updated confirmation message page. On clicking Continue, they are directed to the My Account page. The validation error scenarios in this instance are pretty much the same as those for the SB-001 Create New Account storyboard. Given that users can actually change their username, it is possible that the username they try to use already exists. This poses a real challenge for displaying a "generic" message, so the system will need to display a more informative message. That said, because the message should be configurable, it can be changed without too much effort.

SB-009 Close Account

The final storyboard is SB-009 Close Account, which is shown in Figure 13-13.

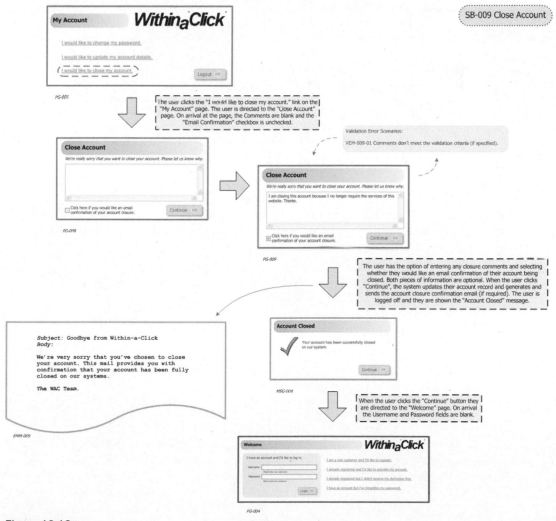

Figure 13-13

Users have the option of specifying some comments and whether they would like an e-mail confirmation of their account closure. A mockup of the confirmation e-mail (EMM-009) is included in the storyboard. When the account has been successfully closed by the system, the user is automatically logged off the system and shown the Account Closed confirmation message. On clicking Continue, they are directed to the Welcome page, where the username and password are blank.

This storyboard completes the walkthrough of the online features and functionality. The next section takes a closer look at the application and defines some high-level requirements that are not necessarily or explicitly captured in the storyboards shown.

Defining the Requirements

The storyboards are only a part of the overall solution design, so you shouldn't be jumping for the keyboard just yet. However, they have provided a solid way forward. You've seen the application from a complete end-to-end flow and how it should work successfully from a user's perspective. The storyboards and walkthrough have also helped to flesh out some messages and alternative flows.

This section fleshes out the high-level functional and technical requirements, which can be used to build up the detailed use cases and processing. Requirements are often derived from use-case specifications. In reality, I find that the two are somewhat interrelated because detailed use cases help to define requirements. The case study's functionality is a pretty well known subject, so I chose to start by fleshing out a series of storyboards, which helps to define the requirements and the detailed use cases. In the field, analysis and design will include a number of these activities which can be performed simultaneously.

The requirements are not going to be an exhaustive list, but they will capture some of the core business and processing rules. A full set of detailed low-level requirements would be a rather long list, even for such a relatively small application. I'll also take a look at some of the features and functions that are offered by similar systems to help define the scope and, more important, determine what's out of scope for this release.

Functional Requirements

This section builds up the functional requirements, including batch and reporting requirements. The use-case diagram, storyboards, and application walkthrough have already outlined the following high-level business rules:

1. The Welcome page and/or any of its functionality and storyboards can be accessed and executed only by non-logged in users.

2. The My Account page and/or its functionality and storyboards can be accessed and executed only by logged in users.

3. Users can "use" their account only after it has been activated and while it isn't closed. The purpose of activating an account is to ensure that users have been sufficiently verified before they can use the features of the system. "Use" refers to all the storyboards except SB-001 Create New Account, SB-002 Activate Account, and SB-003 Re-Request Activation Key, because these are the only storyboards that do not require an activated account.

Given these fundamental business rules, it is easy to draw up a simple table of the allowable actions based on the state of a user and the state of an account.

The following table lists the allowable actions for the first two business rules. The HFR abbreviation stands for High-Level Functional Requirement, and the USAA abbreviation stands for User State Allowable Action.

Requirement	User State	Allowable Actions	Business Rule
HFR-USAA-001	Non-Logged In	SB-001 Create New Account SB-002 Activate Account SB-003 Re-Request Activation Key SB-004 Login SB-006 Reset Password	BR-001: The Welcome page and/or any of its functionality and storyboards can be accessed and executed only by non-logged in users.
HFR-USAA-002	Logged In	SB-005 Logout SB-007 Change Password SB-008 Update Account SB-009 Close Account	BR-002: The My Account page and/or its functionality and storyboards can be accessed and executed only by logged in users. *Note: In the case of Change Password transitioning from Reset Password, users aren't actually logged in. They are simply "authenticated" until completion.*

While the mapping table provides some concrete business rules, it also highlights possible areas of enhancement or refinement. For example, assume some users didn't receive their account Activation Key after several failed attempts. It is possible that they might wish to close their account or remove their registration altogether, without ever activating their account. It is also possible that they might wish to change the e-mail address associated with their account to an alternative address, although there's nothing stopping them from creating another account. In this instance, you could proceed on the basis of the business rules outlined above and the allowable actions listed in the table. When defining the scope, it is often a good idea to identify and agree on the scenarios that are not supported. These could become candidates for a future release. Although you might not be incorporating this functionality, you might choose to design the system in such a way that makes this functionality easier to implement in the future — for example, by using a rule-based approach to security and access.

Given the third fundamental business rule, you can define the logical account state transitions and the allowable actions for each logical state. Figure 13-14 shows the logical account state transitions.

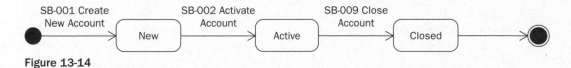

Figure 13-14

You can map the allowable actions to the logical account states as listed in the following table. The ASAA abbreviation stands for Account State Allowable Action.

Requirement	Account State	Allowable Actions
HFR-ASAA-001	New	SB-002 Activate Account
		SB-003 Re-request Activation Key
HFR-ASAA-002	Active	SB-004 Login
		SB-005 Logout
		SB-006 Reset Password
		SB-007 Change Password
		SB-008 Update Account
		SB-009 Close Account
HFR-ASAA-003	Closed	No user actions can be performed on closed accounts.

Again, this simple table solidifies the allowable actions and can be used to highlight further areas of improvement.

The remainder of this functional requirements section will discuss the following areas:

❑ The account's data element requirements

❑ The user interface and processing requirements

❑ The e-mail requirements

❑ The batch requirements

❑ The reporting requirements

The Account's Data Element Requirements

In its simplest form, an account consists of the following functional data elements:

❑ Username

❑ Password

❑ E-mail address

❑ Security question

❑ Security question answer

You can log this as the first high-level requirement:

❑ **HFR-ACCOUNT-001** — The basic account elements must consist of: username, password, e-mail address, security question, and security question answer.

Each of these account elements is further discussed and refined in the following sub-sections.

Username

The username will uniquely identify users in the membership repository. I've chosen this approach rather than using an e-mail address to allow a degree of flexibility in the system. It is really a personal choice, but using a username allows e-mails and greetings to be addressed using the user's preferred username rather than their e-mail address. The username will need to be validated according to a set of specified validation rules. The validation rules will determine what a username can contain and how it can be specified — for example, whether it can contain spaces, full stops, and other special characters. I've mentioned previously that validation rules are likely to change throughout a project and releases, so a flexible approach should be taken to validation (discussed later).

For the moment, you simply want to list the high-level functional requirements that apply to the Username element. The following table lists two such high-level requirements:

Requirement	Description
HFR-USERNAME-001	The username must be unique.
HFR-USERNAME-002	The username must conform to a specified set of username validation rules.

Password

Passwords should not be stored in clear text. They should be encrypted to protect user account details from theft and misuse. The encryption strategy would entirely depend on whether the system actually needed to decrypt the password for any reason. For instance, if you were to be mailing users their password in the event that they'd forgotten it, you would definitely need to decrypt it first. However, in this instance, you're not. When comparing passwords either for authentication or validation purposes, the original password should never be decrypted. The password supplied by users should be encrypted and the subsequent encrypted passwords compared. The most secure mechanism is not to actually store the encrypted password at all, but to store only a *hash* value of it. Hashing is a one-way encryption technique. You can always encrypt a value, but you can never decrypt it afterwards, and comparison is done by first encrypting and hashing the user-supplied information and then comparing it to the hash values stored.

The following table lists the high-level password requirements:

Requirement	Description
HFR-PASSWORD-001	The password must conform to a specified set of password validation rules.
HFR-PASSWORD-002	The system must use one-way encryption techniques (hashing) for password storage and comparison.

E-mail Address

Field-level validation rules ensure that the e-mail address is syntactically correct. There are many published rules for e-mail address validation, which can be very intensive to read and follow. For instance, some domains will allow an e-mail address of "_@example.com". Others will allow "123@somewhere.co.uk".

Syntactically validating a user's e-mail address can range from a very simple "has it got a single '@' symbol and at least one dot somewhere after the '@' symbol" to a fully qualified Internet-compliant e-mail address validation expression. Rather than define these validation rules right now, I'll simply state that the e-mail address must be validated according to a defined set of validation rules.

Some sites choose to identify users by their e-mail address, which would clearly mean that they would need to be unique. However, the case study identifies users by their username. Therefore, the user's e-mail address invites the following two questions:

❑ **Should the e-mail address be unique?** The e-mail address must be validated using the Activation Key pattern previously mentioned. This already reduces the vulnerability of a malicious attack on a user's e-mail address, so the chances of a user's e-mail address already existing on the system are very slim — unless, of course, they've been sloppy controlling access to their e-mail account. So the question really comes down to whether the system should allow the same e-mail address to be associated with multiple accounts and this is clearly a design choice. However, you should consider all the associated flows and functionality when making decisions like this. For example, when a user updates their account, they have the ability to change their e-mail address. The e-mail address entered during update account is not subject to further verification via the Activation Key pattern. The system isn't sending any unsolicited mail so there is reduced risk of the user actually using the system and e-mail account maliciously. In this instance, you can allow multiple accounts to be specified using the same e-mail address, as this reduces the amount of validation required when creating and updating accounts, although it could be considered for a future release.

❑ **Should the e-mail address be encrypted in the repository?** E-mail addresses are personal information, and I personally think that they should be considered private. If there were a security breach, it is possible that thousands of users' e-mail addresses could be disclosed and used inappropriately. To avoid this situation and increase the protection of private information, their e-mail address will be encrypted. You could apply the one-way hashing technique here, but it would mean asking users for their e-mail address every time the system required it. To keep the system simple, you can encrypt the e-mail address using a two-way encryption algorithm. As the system progresses, it may send "unsolicited" e-mails, which would not be possible if one-way encryption were used. Furthermore, if the application were to grow into a full-blown website with subscription features, the system would be sending updates to users via e-mail and other means. In this case, it is easier to move forward with a two-way encryption algorithm that supports future enhancements to the system.

The following table lists the high-level e-mail address requirements:

Requirement	Description
HFR-EMAILADDR-001	The e-mail address must conform to a standard set of e-mail address validation rules.
HFR-EMAILADDR-002	E-mail addresses must be stored in a two-way encrypted form.
HFR-EMAILADDR-003	The system must ensure that when e-mail addresses need to be compared to those on file, comparison is done using an encrypted form (for example, using two-way encryption on the e-mail address entered and comparing it to the encrypted e-mail address stored on file).

Security Question and Security Question Answer

The security question and answer will be used when users need to change their password. This is a pretty standard and acceptable approach to forgotten passwords and password changes. The following are typical security questions:

- ❏ Mother's maiden name?
- ❏ First school?
- ❏ First pet's name?
- ❏ Favorite color?

Whether to use a list of questions or allow users to specify a question (or even a combination of both) is entirely a design choice. It is much easier to allow users to specify the question because it doesn't involve any reference data maintenance and associated functionality. In addition, the security questions are likely to change throughout the project and releases. From a security point of view, it is possible that another person could know the answer to an individual's security question. If the mechanism isn't implemented effectively, it could allow them to change a user's password and use the account inappropriately. This is a situation where the implementation needs to be considered carefully as well as the purpose of the function.

In this example, the objective ultimately is to provide users with the ability to change their password securely. Providing a list of questions would make it somewhat easier for users, but to really ensure total security, the selected question should never really be revealed when the answer is required. To explain, if users chose "Mother's maiden name?" from the list of questions, when they came to change their password, the original list of questions should be displayed again so that users are forced to pick the right question again, as well as enter the correct answer. This would mean that someone else would have to know which question the person had used for their account. If the system displayed the question, it would be easier for someone else to guess or obtain the answer. If the list of questions has changed throughout the lifecycle of the project, the original question that the user selected would also need to be added to the list if it didn't exist. For this reason, the actual security question is typically stored in the main user table rather than as a foreign key identifier. So, you're not really saving any database space and using related tables. In my opinion, it is generally more secure to allow users to specify a question of their choosing. It also avoids additional development and testing effort using a list of questions for very little gain.

Chapter 4 showed a typical mockup of a create account page with a drop-down list of security questions to highlight that reference data is a key consideration in systems development. Many sites use a standard list of questions and allow users to specify their own. These are ultimately design choices and the development and test effort is only one area of consideration.

The security question definitely needs to be stored using two-way encryption so that it can be displayed to users when required. The SB-007 Change Password storyboard highlights this. I think it would cause a lot of confusion if users had to type the question exactly as they did when creating or updating the account, and this could lead to further problems. The user's security question answer should also be encrypted to protect the user's personal data and provide additional security, although some systems choose not to do this. The security question answer needs to be encrypted using two-way encryption so that it can be displayed to the user in the Update Account page. Furthermore, when the security question and answer are created or updated, they should be validated according to a set of validation rules.

The following table lists the high-level security question and security question answer requirements:

Requirement	Description
HFR-SECQUESTION-001	The security question must conform to a standard set of security question validation rules.
HFR-SECQUESTION-002	The security question must be stored using a two-way encryption form.
HFR-SECQANSWER-001	The security question answer must conform to a standard set of security question answer validation rules.
HFR-SECQANSWER-002	The security question answer must be stored using a two-way encryption form.
HFR-SECQANSWER-003	The system must ensure that when security question answers need to be compared to those on file, comparison is done using an encrypted form (for example, using two-way encryption on the answer entered and comparing it to the encrypted answer stored on file).

The Online User Interface and Processing Requirements

The requirements are starting to shape up. The storyboards and some data element requirements are in place. You can now start to define some additional high-level functional requirements based on the storyboards and the pages involved in them. Figure 13-2 showed the high-level navigation map; you can map the requirements to each of the stories and the pages.

To start with, there are a number of forms, so it is a good idea to group common requirements into a single set. The requirements ensure that the design follows a consistent pattern and provides a standard user experience.

The following table lists some common data entry and form requirements:

Requirement	Description
HFR-DATAFORM-001	The data entry forms and pages should consistently indicate to the user which data entry fields are mandatory — for example, by using the asterisk (*) symbol in each field label. Exceptions to this requirement must be noted.
HFR-DATAFORM-002	Field labels should be consistently aligned (for example, right-justified or left-justified) and end with a colon.
HFR-DATAFORM-003	The "tab order" for data entry should be logically organized to allow consistent data entry.
HFR-DATAFORM-004	The data entry fields should be sized appropriately and aligned with their validation rules (for example, by setting minimum and maximum field lengths and data entry formats).

Requirement	Description
HFR-DATAFORM-005	Checkboxes should not create "double negatives" or be confusing (for example, "Click here if you don't want e-mail confirmation" should be "Click here if you want e-mail confirmation").
HFR-DATAFORM-006	The system must validate the entire form data on submission and display all the validation errors consistently. Validation consists of the following rules: 1) Mandatory fields are specified. 2) Values conform to the relevant field-level specification criteria (length, format, type, and so on). 3) Where necessary, the actual values submitted are valid (dates, times, list items, ranges, and so forth).
HFR-DATAFORM-007	Validation errors should be meaningful and state what needs to be specified (for example, "The Username should be between 5 and 10 characters long (inclusive) and contain at least 1 uppercase character."
HFR-DATAFORM-008	Information such as "passwords" should not be displayed in plain text (for example, "Password" fields should be used which will display asterisks instead of the real characters).
HFR-DATAFORM-009	Entry fields that are not displayed to the user (for example, "Password" fields) which have validation errors should be cleared out to reduce the possibility of re-submission of invalid data.
HFR-DATAFORM-010	The system should support "copy & paste" and other common controls where appropriate. Exceptions should be noted.
HFR-DATAFORM-011	The system should protect the user from duplicate or multiple submissions from the same form (for example, disabling the "submit" button after the initial form submit or by other means)
HFR-DATAFORM-012	The system must be tolerant of and support the standard browser navigation actions (idempotent): 1) Refresh / Previous Form Re-submission (F5) 2) Back 3) Forward

This is not a particularly long list of high-level data entry and form requirements, but it highlights some of the basics you need to take into account. Although most of them are pretty straightforward, a few will require some thought and discussion — for example, supporting the browser navigation actions.

Now let's go around to each page, starting with PG-001 Create New Account, and define some individual requirements for the pages and processing.

PG-001 Create New Account

Figure 13-15 shows the conceptual layout for the Create New Account page (PG-001).

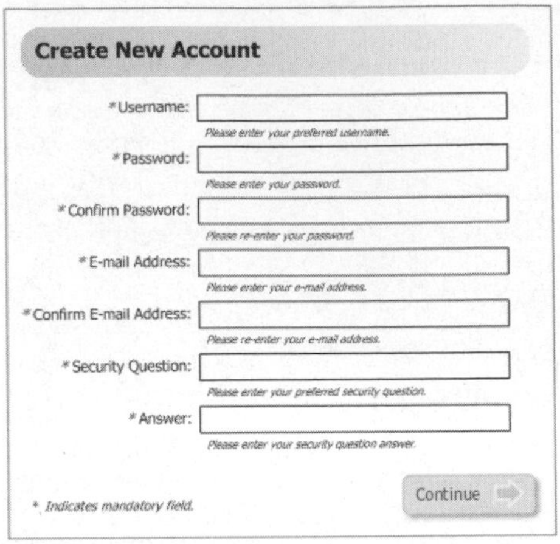

Figure 13-15

It is pretty standard for registration pages such as this to ask for double-entry of key information such as password and e-mail address to avoid typing mistakes. Typically, the "confirmation" entry doesn't allow "copy & paste" to force the user into re-typing the information. I find this terribly annoying at times, but it does allow the system to ensure that the information matches and is not subject to any copy & paste errors. The page also indicates which fields are mandatory, but again, you should ensure that these are properly captured in the requirements. I've mentioned before that mandatory fields often change, and it is somewhat debatable whether the high-level requirements actually stipulate each mandatory field. In this instance, I'll list each field for the purposes of clarity, given that the basic account elements are pretty stable.

The following table lists the high-level requirements for the Create New Account page and functionality:

Requirement	Description
HFR-CREATEACC-001	When creating a new account, users must specify at least the following information, which the system must validate is present and correct: ❑ Username ❑ Password ❑ Confirmation password (not stored) ❑ E-mail address ❑ Confirmation e-mail address (not stored) ❑ Security question ❑ Security question answer
HFR-CREATEACC-002	The system must not allow the user to paste a value into the Confirm Password field.
HFR-CREATEACC-003	The system must not allow the user to paste a value into the Confirm Email Address field.
HFR-CREATEACC-004	The system must ensure that the password and confirmation password entries match.

Requirement	Description
HFR-CREATEACC-005	The system must ensure that the e-mail address and confirmation e-mail address entries match.
HFR-CREATEACC-006	The system must ensure that all the account data element entries are validated according to their individual validation rule sets.
HFR-CREATEACC-007	When a new account is created, the system must generate a unique "account Activation Key" (for example, GUID) and send it to the user's specified e-mail address (according to the solicited e-mail processing requirements).
HFR-CREATEACC-008	The system must retain the Activation Key in the database for later comparison.
HFR-CREATEACC-009	The system must retain the date and time the account was created.
HFR-CREATEACC-010	The system must retain the date and time the account Activation Key e-mail was requested.
HFR-CREATEACC-011	The system must retain the date and time the account Activation Key e-mail was sent.

PG-002 Activate Account / Re-Request Activation Key

The Activate Account / Re-Request Activation Key page (PG-002) is a dual-purpose page in that it allows users to either activate their account or re-request their Activation Key. The page can be arrived at from the Welcome page, via the Create New Account flow, or from itself. The page will behave slightly differently depending on how it was arrived at. For instance, if users come from the Create New Account flow, the Username and Password fields will be pre-populated and disabled, whereas if users come from the Welcome page, the Username and Password fields would be blank and enabled.

Figure 13-16 shows the conceptual layout of the Activate Account page. Note that in this instance none of the fields are populated or disabled, as they would be from the individual flows.

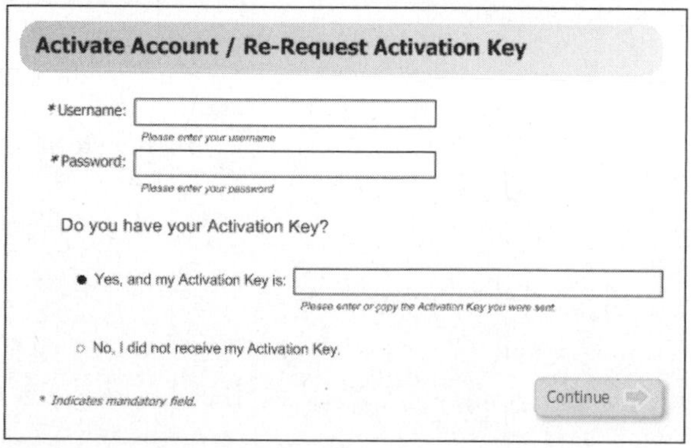

Figure 13-16

359

It is pretty clear that users will need to specify their account Activation Key during the activation process. However, this page could become a never-ending cycle if you consider validation failures. Users could continually attempt to activate an account with an incorrect key. This type of activity could be used maliciously to slow the system down and cause problems for other users. The biggest question is how many times do you allow users to perform this action? You do need to be careful in this situation because the system could have a fault whereby it is actually sending out incorrect Activation Keys, and when users come to activate their account, the Keys don't match and it is not their fault. This is a less likely situation but it is still worth considering. Allowing only a certain number of attempts at account activation would protect the system against any misuse; however, the necessary features to stop this would need to be implemented and tested accordingly. It is worth discussing features like this with the stakeholders. If the features aren't necessary in the first release, you could always note them for potential inclusion in a future release of the application, should they become absolutely necessary at some point.

The account Activation Keys are typically long strings such as Globally Unique Identifiers (GUID) and as such would require careful typing in. The page could contain a number of individual entry fields for each portion of the Key. However, I've chosen to include a single field. Users can copy the Key from the e-mail they receive and paste it into the field. To this end, the Activation Key field must support "paste" functionality; therefore, it is prudent to include this in the requirements. You should also include some basic requirements for Activation Key field-level validation.

Another major part of the account activation and re-activation processes deals with authentication and authentication failures. This is somewhat addressed by the flows disabling the Username and Password fields. However, when users initiate either of these activities from the Welcome page, they will need to be properly authenticated, but not logged in, until their account is fully activated. The application should use a similar, if not the same, mechanism to the Login flow to ensure consistent authentication across the application.

The following table lists the high-level requirements for both the Activate Account flow and the Re-Request Activation Key flow:

Requirement	Description
HFR-ACTIVATE-RR-001	Users must be authenticated via their specified username and password.
HFR-ACTIVATE-RR-002	When authenticating the username and password, the data element validation rules should not be checked.
HFR-ACTIVATE-RR-003	The system must allow "paste" functionality in the Activation Key field to reduce the possibility of validation errors.
HFR-ACTIVATE-RR-004	On activating an account, users must specify their account Activation Key.
HFR-ACTIVATE-RR-005	The system must ensure that the Activation Key specified conforms to a basic set of Activation Key validation rules.
HFR-ACTIVATE-RR-006	The system must ensure that the account Activation Key entered matches the initial key generated and sent by the system.
HFR-ACTIVATE-RR-007	The system must retain the date and time the user successfully activated their account.

Requirement	Description
HFR-ACTIVATE-RR-008	The system must retain the date and time users re-requested their Activation Key.
HFR-ACTIVATE-RR-009	The system must retain the date and time the re-requested Activation Key was sent.

PG-004 Login

The Welcome page provides the controls to allow users to log in, in this instance requiring only their username and password. During login, these entries should not be validated. The reason for this is that validation rules typically change throughout the project and the application lifetime. Users who previously created accounts may not be able to log in if the validation rules have changed. I like to stipulate things like this in the requirements to ensure that it is covered and not implemented incorrectly. I've also included this requirement previously to ensure consistent authentication throughout the application.

A lot of applications implement account locking. After a certain number of invalid login attempts, users are locked out of their account. Typically, if account locking is implemented, an unlocking mechanism must also be provided. Many sites and applications implement an overnight unlocking policy in which accounts are automatically unlocked by an overnight process. I had a lot of trouble when I locked my account on one particularly popular e-mail site. For some reason, there was no way I could unlock it or even reset my password. I eventually had to get in touch with customer service to have the account unlocked. Each feature or function of the system should be thoroughly reviewed and discussed when building up the requirements. In terms of the case study, the first version of the requirements will neither state account locking nor will they specify retaining the number of unsuccessful login attempts. These items are essentially out of scope and should again be noted for potential inclusion in a future release.

The following table lists the basic login and authentication requirements:

Requirement	Description
HFR-LOGIN-001	Users must log in to the application using their specified username and password.
HFR-LOGIN-002	During login or authentication the data element validation rules should not be checked.
HFR-LOGIN-003	The system should retain the date and time the user last successfully logged in.

PG-005 Logout

There isn't really much to say about logout apart from the fact that you're retaining the dates and times of other user actions. Although it is a simple piece of functionality, it is best not forgotten. So, note it in the high-level requirements for completeness and regularity. It is possible that users don't specifically log off the system, but instead, their session times out or is terminated. A session time-out should really be treated as a direct logout to protect users.

The following table lists the basic logout requirements.

Requirement	Description
HFR-LOGOUT-001	The system must retain the date and time users last logged off the system.
HFR-LOGOUT-002	A session timeout or termination should be treated as a full user logout.
HFR-LOGOUT-003	The system must display a confirmation message when users have successfully logged out of the system.

PG-006 Reset Password (Authentication)

When users forget their password or want to change it, an alternative mechanism will be required to authenticate them. The user is not logged in so authenticating a user in the first instance will involve them specifying their username and their e-mail address. On successful authentication the user will be directed to the Change Password functionality.

Figure 13-17 shows the Reset Password (Authentication) page (PG-006).

Figure 13-17

Similar questions arise with this page regarding constant requests and endless looping due to validation errors. However, again it should be noted so that if you need to address this, it can be impacted and assessed accordingly.

The following table lists requirements for the Reset Password (Authentication) page:

Requirement	Description
HFR-RPAUTH-001	Users must be authenticated via their specified username and e-mail address.
HFR-RPAUTH-002	During authentication the data element validation rules should not be checked.

PG-007 Change Password

It is becoming more popular for systems to force users to change their password regularly for security purposes. This type of feature is typically known as *password expiry*. Users are forced to change their password every *n* days. Some sites (and applications) also retain a "password history" so that a new password can't be the same as the last ten or so. Furthermore, it is not uncommon for security systems to apply a minimum password age policy. This stops users from changing their password immediately after it was just changed. This is typically referred to as *minimum password age* functionality. You can see already that even with a simple application the scope could start to increase by including more and more functionality as each feature is discussed. Examining each of the features and functions helps to clearly define the scope of the project (for example, what will actually be implemented) and provides the basis for realistic estimates.

Figure 13-18 shows the conceptual layout of the Change Password page (PG-007).

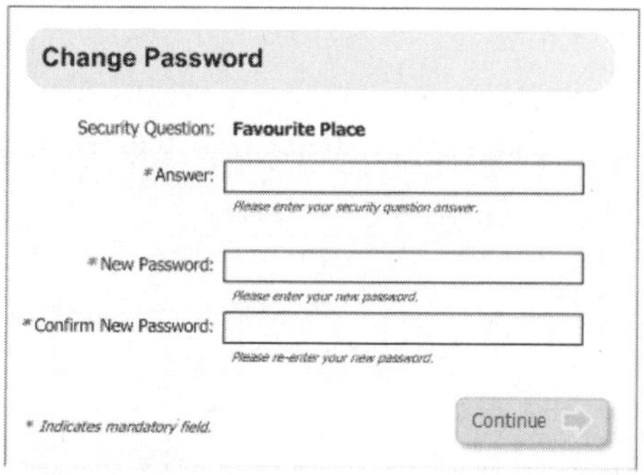

Change Password

Security Question:	**Favourite Place**	
* Answer:		
	Please enter your security question answer.	
* New Password:		
	Please enter your new password.	
* Confirm New Password:		
	Please re-enter your new password.	
* *Indicates mandatory field.*		Continue ➡

Figure 13-18

The page shows the user their security question and the user must supply the answer. As shown in the storyboards earlier, the answer is in clear text. However, like the other authentication checks, the answer should not be validated against the validation rules. It should simply be compared against the value held on file. The value held on file is actually one-way encrypted, so the answer typed in by the user must be compared using this technique.

In this instance, the system is not retaining any password history or expiry information, so users can change their password to something meaningful, regardless of whether they have previously used it.

The following table lists the high-level requirements for the Change Password page:

Requirement	Description
HFR-CHANGEPASSWORD-001	The user's security question answer should not be validated against the data element validation rules.
HFR-CHANGEPASSWORD-002	The system must not allow users to paste a value into the Confirm New Password field.
HFR-CHANGEPASSWORD-003	The system must ensure that the New Password and Confirm New Password fields match.
HFR-CHANGEPASSWORD-004	The system should retain the date and time users last changed their password.

PG-008 Update Account

In this example application, an account doesn't contain any more information than it did when it was created. Most sites allow users to update their account details and, more often than not, allow users to store additional information along with their account. For instance, online stores allow users to create and maintain delivery addresses and payment details, and so on. It is possible that the validation rules for the elements have changed since the user last logged in or updated their account. You want to ensure that the updated information conforms to all the latest validation rules. This actually makes the implementation simpler because it means you don't need to retain multiple versions of the validation rules for the data elements.

Figure 13-19 shows the conceptual layout of the Update Account page (PG-008).

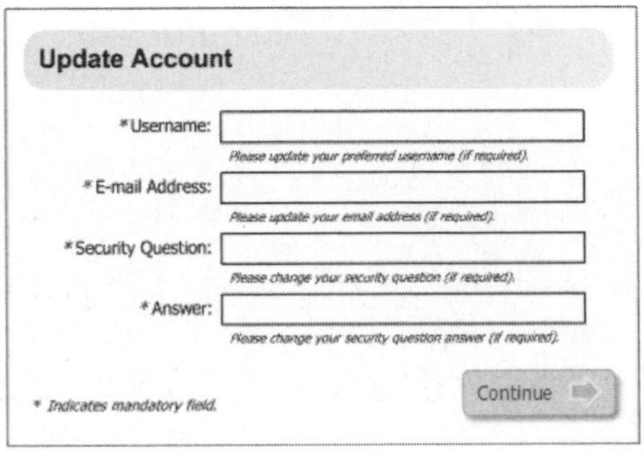

Figure 13-19

The page allows users to change any of their account details (except their password). To change their password the Change Password functionality can be used. The question arises as to whether the updated e-mail address should be validated in the same way as Create New Account. Typically, sites allow registered users to change their e-mail address without having to re-activate it. The initial activation is really intended to prove that a genuine user is registering. Once they have activated their account, they are usually considered a "genuine source." Note that the Update Account page does not require users to confirm their e-mail address, although this could easily be included in a future version if necessary.

The following table lists the high-level requirements for the Update Account page:

Requirement	Description
HFR-UPDATEACC-001	The system must allow users to change or update their account information, including: 1) Username 2) E-mail address 3) Security question 4) Security question answer
HFR-UPDATEACC-002	The system must ensure that all the updated account data element entries are validated according to their individual validation rule sets.
HFR-UPDATEACC-003	The system should retain the date and time the user last updated their account details.

PG-009 Close Account

Figure 13-20 shows the conceptual layout of the Close Account page (PG-009).

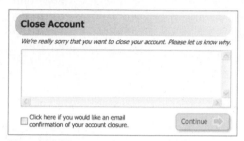

Figure 13-20

The close account functionality is very straightforward. The system allows users to close their account at any point after it has been activated. After the account has been closed, it will be removed to ensure that the system is kept neat and tidy and in good shape for other users. When closing an account, most systems will ask for some form of reason or comments for the account closure. The business can use this information to make changes to their services, assuming that they report and review these comments. It is customary for systems to e-mail users when their account has been closed. However, in this instance, users have the option to request this functionality, rather than it being provided by default. (I don't like sending e-mails unless the user requests one.) Default values were discussed earlier in this book, and in this instance the default selection should be set to "no" (that is, an e-mail confirmation message is *not* required).

Some systems make it easy for users to re-activate their account after it has been closed. For example, keeping the user's account on file for a certain period of time after it has been closed. This allows the user to return to the site and reactivate their account rather than creating a new one. The user is sometimes given a re-Activation Key or, when they simply attempt to log in to a closed account (that's still on file), they are given the opportunity to re-activate it. This is usually the case when the account has been paid for and the payment is based on some form of annual renewal. Users really shouldn't have to pay another subscription fee when simply re-activating their account. Of course, this assumes the payment period hasn't expired. The system will keep closed accounts on file for a period of time, but simply for reporting purposes, not re-activation.

The following table lists the high-level requirements for the Close Account page:

Requirement	Description
HFR-CLOSEACC-001	When closing an account, the user should be given the option to specify a reason why they are closing their account.
HFR-CLOSEACC-002	Closure comments should be validated against a set of closure comment validation rules.
HFR-CLOSEACC-003	The default value for e-mail confirmation should be set to "no" (an e-mail confirmation message is not required).
HFR-CLOSEACC-004	The system should retain the closure comments.
HFR-CLOSEACC-005	The system should retain the date and time the account was closed.
HFR-CLOSEACC-006	If the user requested e-mail confirmation, the system should retain the date and time the closure e-mail was requested.
HFR-CLOSEACC-007	If the user requested e-mail confirmation, the system should retain the date and time the closure e-mail was sent.

The E-mail Processing Requirements

I've mentioned in previous chapters that e-mail sub-systems can suffer from instability, so the system will need to send e-mails asynchronously. Users don't have to wait when there are problems with the e-mail server or sub-system. You also avoid waiting for connections to the e-mail server and dealing with timeouts in the online application. If the e-mail system is down for some reason or there are network issues, the user experience would be impacted. E-mails will be queued and sent in the background. After the e-mail request has been queued, users are shown a message confirming that the e-mail has been sent, although in this case it really means that the e-mail message has been queued. This reduces the number of external system dependencies the online application has. However, assuming everything is working as it should be, the e-mail will be picked up and sent very shortly after it was queued. It is worth capturing requirements like this so that they are not forgotten when it comes to the actual implementation.

The following table lists the high-level requirement for e-mail processing:

Requirement	Description
HFR-EMAILPROC-001	The system must ensure that e-mail messages are sent to users asynchronously to avoid the user experience being impacted by failures and other issues relating to the e-mail subsystem.

The Batch Requirements

At first glance, it might seem as though the application doesn't actually require any functional batch processes. However, this is how most applications start out and the batch requirements are not typically specified or even identified. In keeping with the messages in this book, capturing as much information as possible up front, let's define some high-level batch requirements that you can carry through the project. As you progress through the project, you'll probably find that there will be more batch jobs than initially thought or identified. The following provides a brief overview of the functional housekeeping jobs required by the system:

❑ **Aged Account Removal** — There are a number of areas within the application where accounts can age. That is, they are either not activated or not used frequently enough. For example, the Create New Account storyboard takes users through the Create New Account page and joins the SB-002 Activate Account and SB-003 Re-request Activation Key storyboards. However, it is possible that users never actually activate their account. You have options for users to re-request their Activation Key if they didn't receive it, so that shouldn't be the problem. However, users might still not continue with the registration process and could essentially break out of the flow. A new account exists in the database but doesn't actually get activated. These records will take up valuable space and impact performance. Furthermore, users can create and activate an account but thereafter never actually use it. A set of jobs is required to remove aged accounts, in this instance, accounts that have not been activated, although this could be extended in future releases. It is possible that there could be potentially thousands if not millions of records lingering in the database, and cleaning out these records will keep the system in good working order and generally improve performance.

❑ **Closed Account Removal** — A set of jobs is required to remove closed accounts. Closed accounts can't be used and therefore should be removed. It is also possible that the system could actually delete the account record during closure processing. However, you would still need to retain closure comments for reporting purposes.

In these "housekeeping" situations, the batch processes can physically delete the records after a certain period of time. However, the jobs do not normally delete the records physically in the first instance; they typically "flag" or mark aged records for deletion. This is a simple scenario of essentially "archiving" followed by deletion. The system retains the records for reporting purposes, allowing the business to run reports against the system showing the current "flagged" accounts. It would be wise to inform users that their account has been flagged for removal, although this would introduce "unsolicited" e-mail. The system would need to e-mail users to inform them that their account was going to be removed on a certain date if they didn't activate it. The user experience would be quite poor if they returned to the site after a while only to be confronted with an authentication failure. Closed accounts are not a problem, but "New" accounts are. As you can see the scope begins to creep and there are many routes you can take. It is also possible that the accounts are not removed at all. In this instance, new accounts will be flagged and removed at a later date but the system will not send an e-mail. This functionality could be included in a future release. Similarly, closed accounts will be removed after a certain period of time but no e-mail will be sent. The accounts will remain on the system for reporting purposes. The "flagging" and "removal" periods will be configurable; so, for argument's sake, the timeframe could range from 1 day to 100 years. Typically, the removal period would be something like 7 days after the account was flagged.

I mentioned that "closed" accounts are not a problem. This is because they are automatically "flagged" due to their Closed status. "Aged" accounts, on the other hand, can only really be flagged by another process.

These types of requirements keep the database and the system neat and tidy. However, they also add to the complexity of the application and the normal processing. For example, it is very possible that an account has been flagged for removal and the user attempts to activate it. What should the system do in this situation? It is precisely these kinds of requirements that are often missed or left until the last minute. Although you don't want to get into the technical details of the implementation, you need to be sure one way or the other. In this instance, although an account is "flagged" for removal, it will not stop users from performing any normal allowable action. However, it does mean that the processing needs to remove the "flag" when users actually activate their account. This should be an extremely simple exercise, which will also ensure that the reports that are executed will always contain the most up-to-date information.

The following table lists some high-level requirements for flagging and removing new accounts:

Requirement	Description
HFR-AGEDACCFR-001	Accounts that have aged should be flagged for removal after a specified period of time in days (for example, "aged account expiry period in days"). Aged refers to new accounts that have not been activated within the specified aging period.
HFR-AGEDACCFR-002	The New Account Expiry Period in Days configuration value must be greater than or equal to 0.
HFR-AGEDACCFR-003	A value of 0 for New Account Expiry Period in Days indicates that account expiry is not performed.
HFR-AGEDACCFR-004	The system must ensure that the flagging of aged accounts does not impact the users' ability to perform any normal allowable actions.
HFR-AGEDACCFR-005	When users perform a normal action on a flagged account, the account should no longer be flagged for removal.
HFR-AGEDACCFR-006	Accounts that have been flagged for removal should be physically removed after a specified period of time (according to the New Account Removal Period in Days value). This period of time is in addition to the New Account Expiry Period in Days value.
HFR-AGEDACCFR-007	The New Account Removal Period in Days configuration value must be greater than or equal to 0.
HFR-AGEDACCFR-008	A value of 0 for New Account Removal Period in Days indicates that removal expiry is not performed.

And the following table lists a set of requirements for the removal of closed accounts:

Requirement	Description
HFR-CLOSEDACCR-001	Accounts that have been closed should be removed after a specified period of time (based on the Closed Account Removal Period in Days configuration value).
HFR-CLOSEDACCR-002	The Closed Account Removal Period in Days configuration value must be greater than or equal to 0.
HFR-CLOSEDACCR-003	A value of 0 for Closed Account Removal Period in days indicates that account removal is not performed.

The preceding requirements focus only on the functional aspects of the system; however, additional batch jobs are often identified throughout the project. It is a good idea to list the batch jobs to ensure they are captured and included in the scope. You've already seen in previous chapters some of the technical jobs that can form part of an overall solution. The batch requirements help to shape the batch design (which is discussed in Chapter 16).

The Reporting Requirements

During the definition of the core functional requirements, a few batch requirements have been added to keep the system in good shape. These include removing accounts that are closed or not activated. The removal of these records takes place after a certain period of time. The reason for this is to provide a window of opportunity for functional reporting. It is likely that the business would want to know how many accounts are being created, how many are not being activated, how many are closed, and so on. These would be pretty straightforward requests. Reports are sometimes left to the last minute and can have a big impact on a project's budget and timescales. It is a good idea to have a basic set of reporting requirements, even if they simply list a set of required reports.

Reports are often identified throughout the project and in many cases additional reports are developed after the system has been implemented in live service.

The following table lists some high-level reporting requirements:

Requirement	Description
HFR-REPORT-001	The system should provide a report showing the number of new accounts created over a specified period of time.
HFR-REPORT-002	The system should provide a report showing the number of accounts activated over a specified period of time.
HFR-REPORT-003	The system should provide a report showing the average time between creating and activating an account over a specified period of time.
HFR-REPORT-004	The system should provide a report showing the number of aged accounts that have been flagged for removal.
HFR-REPORT-005	The system should provide a report showing the number of accounts closed over a specified period of time.

The preceding list represents a very simple set of reports.

Technical Requirements

Now that a fairly reasonable set of functional requirements is in place, things start to get a little more interesting with the technical requirements. I've discussed technical requirements previously, and having a baseline set in place is a good idea. For the purposes of time and space, I'll define a very high-level set of technical requirements for the case study. A large project can have hundreds if not thousands of technical requirements. You've already seen how a simple application such as this could grow and have many functional requirements.

The following table lists the high-level technical requirements:

ID	Description
HTR-GEN-1	The system must not use any hard-coded values or "magic numbers" — for example, validation rules, messages, configuration values or settings, filenames, pathnames, or host names.
HTR-GEN-2	The system must be designed so that internationalization, localization and accessibility features can be added or enhanced without significant rework.
HTR-GEN-3	Executable files should return a defined exit code. A value of 0 indicates success and non-zero indicates a failure.
HTR-GEN-4	Each executable exit code greater than zero must be clearly identified and fully tested.
HTR-GEN-5	Executables and processes must not exit until all tasks or threads have been completed, successfully or unsuccessfully.
HTR-GEN-6	The system must use the appropriate level and techniques for data locking during updates to ensure consistency.
HTR-GEN-7	All data input to the system, via any means, must be validated accordingly.
HTR-GEN-8	The system must be designed so that changes to moving parts, such as validation rules, configuration values, and other functionality, can be added or changed without significant rework of the application code.
HTR-ACC-1	The system should support all the major web browsers (with exceptions and major/minor versions defined and documented). An initial list of browsers would include Microsoft Internet Explorer, Apple Safari, and Mozilla Firefox.
HTR-OPA-1	The system must incorporate diagnostics (event logging, tracing, performance counters, and other associated techniques) to ensure that the system can be monitored and operated effectively.
HTR-OPA-2	The diagnostics should be implemented in such a way that they can be tuned and refined (turned up, down, on, or off) without requiring an application restart or loss of connectivity (exceptions to be fully documented).
HTR-OPA-3	All known exceptions (system errors) must be documented and procedures put in place to ensure their resolution.

ID	Description
HTR-OPA-4	All configuration values and settings should be documented and include the optimum tolerances and ranges as well as detailed instructions to their use and setting.
HTR-OPA-5	The system must be designed in such a way that manual intervention and "hands-on" operation is significantly reduced (e.g. starting, stopping, monitoring, and so forth).
HTR-RES-1	The system must be tolerant and resilient to typical exception scenarios and re-try transactions where appropriate. In the event that the exception is fatal or processing can't continue, the system must handle the scenario gracefully.
HTR-PER-1	The system must perform an average screen response for each minor operation of better than 2 seconds, with no transaction taking more than 15 seconds, assuming no reported network problems. An example of a minor operation is viewing the Welcome page.
HFR-PER-2	The system must perform an average screen response for each complex operation of better than 5 seconds, with no transaction taking more than 15 seconds, assuming no reported network problems. An example of a complex operation is creating a new account.
HFR-PER-3	The system must support a minimum number of concurrent users equal to at least 5,000 users.
HTR-EFF-1	All database servers will have their processor utilization, measured over any 5-minute period, of less than 80 percent for 95 percent of the measured period.
HTR-EFF-2	All database servers will have their fixed memory utilization, measured over any 5-minute period, of less than 60 percent for 95 percent of the measured period.
HTR-EFF-3	All web, application, and administration servers will have their processor utilization, measured over any 5-minute period, of less than 70 percent for 95 percent of the measured period.
HTR-EFF-4	All web, application, and administration servers will have their fixed memory utilization, measured over any 5-minute period, of less than 90 percent for 95 percent of the measured period.
HTR-AVA-1	The system must provide 24 hour, 7 day a week access to all functionality and facilities (*exceptions to be confirmed*). The system must be available for a minimum of 99.5 percent of each calendar month, excluding planned outages.
HTR-AVA-2	All batch processes must be completed within a 1-hour batch window (timing to be defined).
HTR-AVA-3	All batch processes must execute in such a way that the entire system does not need to be taken offline to perform batch operations.
HTR-SCA-1	The system must be designed in such a way that is can be scaled both horizontally (additional processors, memory, and processes) and vertically (additional servers and instances) without requiring any code changes.

The technical requirements listed are not exhaustive, but they do provide a reasonable basis for some rudimentary performance testing, availability testing, and benchmarking during build, unit testing, and integration testing. You should be able to gauge whether the application will meet these requirements early on. Any performance issues or concerns identified during the build activities can be highlighted and taken forward rather than finding out during a performance test cycle or soak test.

As previously mentioned, testing environments need to be fit for purpose. However, only so much can be tested on a single developer machine, so the results will only be indicative until the system is tested fully on a live-like environment in the lab. Technical and performance testing should be based on the system's performance in the server room, not necessarily on response times and performance over the Internet, as these can fluctuate based on a user's connection speed, although in some cases user testing can be used to obtain a true end-to-end performance figure.

Documenting the Use Cases

This section wraps up this chapter by specifying the detailed use cases. The storyboards capture the application from the end user's perspective, and the requirements stipulate some processing rules. Now it is time to pull all this information together to give a more complete picture to continue with. The storyboards, requirements, and use cases will be used to further design, build, and test the application. The use cases capture as much information and detail as possible to refine the system and processing. They focus primarily on the main flow, although they do include the primary alternative flows. The use cases documented in this section also contain a "requirements map" section that lists the functional requirements associated with the use case. This really helps when defining the test cases and also ensures that the developer is fully aware of them. It is a good idea to have a set of agreed upon use cases to help with the furtherance of the project. Although the use cases might seem repetitive, they only help to ensure a common understanding of the functionality.

Once again, I'll start at the first storyboard and work around to each one. The commentary will be restricted to only where necessary, as the use cases should be fairly straightforward.

UC-001 Create New Account

The first use case in the series is the Create New Account use case (UC-001). This use case documents the functionality and processing required when users want to create a new account on the system.

Use-Case Identifier:	UC-001
Use-Case Name:	Create New Account
Description:	An online user wishes to create a new account.
Primary Actor:	Anonymous web user
Triggers:	A user has navigated to the Welcome page and clicked on the link "I am a new customer and I'd like to register."
Pre-Conditions:	The user isn't logged in.

Linked Storyboard:	SB-001

Basic Flow:

1) The Create New Account page is displayed and all fields are enabled and blank.

2) The user completes the form by entering their username, password, confirmation password, e-mail address, confirmation e-mail address, security question, and security question answer, and then clicks Continue.

3) The system checks that all mandatory information has been specified and that each element is valid and correct according to its individual validation rules

4) The system checks that an account doesn't already exist with the username specified.

5) The system encrypts the information supplied according to the individual encryption rules.

6) The system generates a unique account Activation Key that will be associated with the account.

7) The system creates the account record in the database with a state of "New" and records the date and time the account was created.

8) The system queues a request for an Activation Key e-mail to be sent to the user's e-mail address and records the date and time the request was made.

    8a) The e-mail request will be processed in the background and the system will compose and send the user an e-mail containing their account Activation Key and record the date and time the e-mail was sent.

9) The system displays the Activation Key Sent confirmation message and the Continue button.

10) On clicking the Continue button, the user is directed to the Activate Account page.

Alternative Flows:

3a) If any mandatory information has not been specified, or if any of the elements are invalid, the system will display one of the following validation error messages for each validation error, as appropriate, and allow the user to submit a new request:

❑ VEM-001-01 (Username hasn't been specified.)

❑ VEM-001-02 (Username specified doesn't meet the validation criteria.)

❑ VEM-001-03 (Password hasn't been specified.)

❑ VEM-001-04 (Password specified doesn't meet the validation criteria.)

❑ VEM-001-05 (Confirmation password hasn't been specified.)

❑ VEM-001-06 (Password and confirmation password values don't match.)

❑ VEM-001-07 (E-mail address hasn't been specified.)

(continued)

(continued)

Alternative Flows:	❏ VEM-001-08 (E-mail address specified doesn't meet the validation criteria.)
	❏ VEM-001-09 (Confirmation e-mail address hasn't been specified.)
	❏ VEM-001-10 (E-mail address and confirmation e-mail address values don't match.)
	❏ VEM-001-11 (Security question hasn't been specified.)
	❏ VEM-001-12 (Security question specified doesn't meet validation criteria.)
	❏ VEM-001-13 (Security question answer hasn't been specified.)
	❏ VEM-001-14 (Security question answer specified doesn't meet the validation criteria.)

4a) In the event that an account already exists with the username specified, the system will display the following validation error message and allow the user to submit a new request:

❏ VEM-001-15 (Username specified already exists.)

Requirements Map:

HFR-USAA-001 (User not logged in.)

HFR-DATAFORM-* (Common data entry and form requirements.)

HFR-CREATEACC-001 (Account data element specification.)

HFR-CREATEACC-002 (Paste functionality not allowed in confirmation password.)

HFR-CREATEACC-003 (Paste functionality not allowed in confirmation e-mail.)

HFR-CREATEACC-004 (Password and confirmation password match.)

HFR-CREATEACC-005 (E-mail and confirmation e-mail match.)

HFR-CREATEACC-006 (All fields validated.)

HFR-CREATEACC-007 (Account Activation Key generation.)

HFR-CREATEACC-008 (Date/time created retained.)

HFR-CREATEACC-009 (Activation Key requested date/time.)

HFR-CREATEACC-010 (Activation Key sent date/time.)

HFR-USERNAME-001 (Username must be unique.)

HFR-USERNAME-002 (Username validation rules.)

HFR-PASSWORD-001 (Password validation rules.)

HFR-PASSWORD-002 (Password encryption rules.)

HFR-EMAILADDR-001 (E-mail address validation rules.)

HFR-EMAILADDR-002 (E-mail address encryption rules.)

HFR-SECQUESTION-001 (Security question validation rules.)

HFR-SECQUESTION-002 (Security question encryption rules.)

HFR-SECQANSWER-001 (Answer validation rules.)

HFR-SECQANSWER-002 (Answer encryption rules.)

HFR-EMAILPROC-001 (E-mail sent asynchronously.)

UC-002 Activate Account

The Activate Account use case (UC-002) covers all the functionality and processing steps involved when users want to activate their account. The use case can be entered from either the Welcome page, the UC-001 Create New Account use case, or the UC-003 Re-Request Activation Key use case.

Use-Case Identifier:	UC-002
Use-Case Name:	Activate Account
Description:	An online user wishes to activate their account.
Primary Actor:	Anonymous web user.
Triggers:	❑ The user has been directed from UC-001 Create New Account.
	❑ The user has navigated to the Welcome page and clicked on the link "I already registered and I'd like to activate my account."
	❑ The user has been directed from UC-003 Re-Request Activation Key.
Pre-Conditions:	The user isn't logged in.
Linked Storyboard:	SB-002
Basic Flow:	1) The Activate Account / Re-Request Activation Key page is displayed and the blank/pre-populated fields are enabled/disabled according to the route from which users arrived:
	1a) From UC-001 Create New Account — The Username and Password fields are pre-populated and disabled. The Yes Activation Key option is pre-selected, and the No option is enabled.
	1b) From the Welcome page — The Username and Password fields are blank and enabled. The Yes Activation Key option is pre-selected, and the No option is disabled.
	1c) From UC-003 Re-Request Activation Key — The Username and Password fields are pre-populated and disabled. The Yes Activation Key option is pre-selected, and the No option is disabled.
	2) The user completes the form by entering their Username and Password (where necessary), selecting the Yes Activation Key option (where necessary) and specifying their "Account Activation Key," and clicks Continue.
	3) The system checks that all mandatory information has been specified and that each element is valid and correct according to its individual validation rules (where required).
	4) The system checks that an account exists with the username specified.
	5) The system authenticates the user by comparing the password entered with that stored on file.
	6) The system checks that the account is in a state of New.
	7) The system checks that the supplied account Activation Key matches the Key stored on file.

(continued)

(continued)

Basic Flow:	8)	The system proceeds to activate the user's account by setting the account state to Active and recording the date and time the account was activated.
	9)	The system logs the user in to the system and records the date and time the user was logged in.
	10)	The system removes any "flagged for removal" mark that may be present on the account.
	11)	The system displays the Account Activated confirmation message and the Continue button.
	12)	On clicking the Continue button, the user is directed to the My Account page.
Alternative Flows:	3a)	If any mandatory information has not been specified, or if any of the elements are invalid, the system will display one of the following validation error messages for each validation error, as appropriate, and allow the user to submit a new request:

❑ VEM-002-01 (Username not specified.)

❑ VEM-002-02 (Password not specified.)

❑ VEM-002-03 (Activation Key not specified.)

❑ VEM-002-04 (Activation Key doesn't meet the validation criteria.)

4a) In the event that an account doesn't exist with the username specified, the system will display the following validation error message and allow the user to submit a new request.

❑ VEM-002-06 (Username and password combination is invalid.)

5a) In the event of an authentication error, the system will display the following message and allow the user to submit a new request.

❑ VEM-002-06 (Username and password combination is invalid.)

6a) In the event that the account is not in the correct state, the system will display the appropriate Invalid Operation error. On clicking Continue, the user will be directed back to the Welcome page. The invalid operations are as follows:

❑ IOM-002-01 (Account already activated.)

❑ IOM-002-02 (Account closed.)

7a) In the event that the supplied account Activation Key doesn't match the Key on file, the system will display the following validation error message, clear the field, and allow the user to submit a new request.

❑ VEM-002-05 (Activation Key doesn't match the Key on file.)

Requirements Map:	HFR-USAA-001 (User not logged in.)
	HFR-ASAA-001 (Activation allowed only on new accounts.)
	HFR-ASAA-002 (Activation not allowed on active accounts.)
	HFR-ASAA-003 (Activation not allowed on closed accounts.)
	HFR-DATAFORM-* (Common data entry and form requirements.)
	HFR-ACTIVATE-RR-001 (Authentication — username & password.)
	HFR-ACTIVATE-RR-002 (No username and password validation.)
	HFR-ACTIVATE-RR-003 (Paste functionality must be allowed for the Activation Key.)
	HFR-ACTIVATE-RR-004 (Activation Key must be specified.)
	HFR-ACTIVATE-RR-005 (Activation Key validation rules.)
	HFR-ACTIVATE-RR-006 (Activation Key comparison.)
	HFR-ACTIVATE-RR-007 (Activation date and time recorded.)
	HFR-PASSWORD-002 (Hashing password comparison.)
	HFR-AGEDACCFR-004 (Flagged account not impacting user.)
	HFR-AGEDACCFR-005 (Removal of flag.)

UC-003 Re-Request Activation Key

The Re-Request Activation Key use case (UC-003) is very similar to the Activate Account use case but I've documented it separately because of the main differences and for clarity. The use case covers all the high-level requirements and processing steps involved when users re-request their account Activation Key.

Use-Case Identifier:	UC-003
Use-Case Name:	Re-Request Activation Key
Description:	An online user wishes to re-request their account Activation Key.
Primary Actor:	Anonymous web user

Triggers:

1) The user has been directed from UC-001 Create New Account.

2) The user has navigated to the Welcome page and clicked on the link "I already registered but I didn't receive my Activation Key."

Pre-Conditions:	The user isn't logged in.
Linked Storyboard:	SB-003

Basic Flow:

1) The Activate Account / Re-Request Activation Key page is displayed and the blank/pre-populated fields are enabled/disabled according to the route from which users arrived:

    1a) From UC-001 Create New Account — The Username and Password fields are pre-populated and disabled. The Yes Activation Key option is pre-selected and the No option is enabled.

    1b) From the Welcome page — The Username and Password fields are blank and enabled. The No Activation Key option is pre-selected and the Yes option is disabled.

2) The user completes the form by entering their Username and Password (where necessary) and selecting the No Activation Key option (where necessary), and then clicks Continue.

3) The system checks that all mandatory information has been specified.

4) The system checks that an account exists with the username specified.

5) The system authenticates the user by comparing the password entered with that stored on file.

6) The system checks that the account is in a state of New.

7) The system queues a request for an Activation Key re-request e-mail to be sent to the user's e-mail address and records the date and time the re-request was made.

    7a) In the background, the e-mail request will be processed and the system will compose and send the user an e-mail containing their account Activation Key and record the date and time the re-request e-mail was sent.

8) The system removes any "flagged for removal" mark that may be present on the account.

9) The system displays the Activation Key Resent confirmation message and then Continue button.

10) On clicking the Continue button, the user is directed to the Activate Account / Re-Request Activation Key page (*entry point 3 on UC-002 Activate Account.*)

Alternative Flows:	3a)	If any mandatory information has not been specified, or if any of the elements are invalid, the system will display one of the following validation error messages for each validation error, as appropriate, and allow the user to submit a new request:

❑   VEM-003-01 (Username not specified.)

❑   VEM-003-02 (Password not specified.)

4a)   In the event that an account already doesn't exist with the username specified, the system will display the following validation error and allow the user to submit a new request.

❑   VEM-003-03 (Username and password combination is invalid.)

5a)   In the event of an authentication error, the system will display the following validation error and allow the user to submit a new request.

❑   VEM-003-03 (Username and password combination is invalid.)

6a)   In the event that the account is not in the correct state, the system will display the appropriate Invalid Operation error and the Continue button. On clicking Continue, the user will be directed back to the Welcome page.

❑   IOM-003-01 (Account already activated.)

❑   IOM-003-02 (Account closed.)

Requirements Map: HFR-USAA-001 (User not logged in.)

HFR-ASAA-001 (Re-request only allowed on new accounts.)

HFR-ASAA-002 (Re-request not allowed on active accounts.)

HFR-ASAA-003 (Re-request not allowed on closed accounts.)

HFR-DATAFORM-* (Common data entry and form requirements.)

HFR-ACTIVATE-RR-001 (Authentication — username & password.)

HFR-ACTIVATE-RR-002 (No username and password validation.)

HFR-ACTIVATE-RR-008 (Re-request date and time recorded.)

HFR-ACTIVATE-RR-009 (Re-request sent date/time recorded.)

HFR-PASSWORD-002 (Hashing password comparison.)

HFR-AGEDACCFR-004 (Flagged account not impacting user.)

HFR-AGEDACCFR-005 (Removal of flag.)

HFR-EMAILPROC-001 (E-mail sent asynchronously.)

UC-004 Login

The Login use case (UC-004) covers all the functionality and processing steps required when users want to log in to the system.

Use-Case Identifier:	UC-004
Use-Case Name:	Login
Description:	An online user wishes to log in to their account.
Primary Actor:	Anonymous web user
Triggers:	The user has navigated to the Welcome page, which contains the login controls.
Pre-Conditions:	The user isn't logged in.
Linked Storyboard:	SB-004

Basic Flow:

1) The Welcome page is displayed and the Username and Password fields are blank and enabled.

2) The user completes the form by entering their Username and Password, and then clicking the Login button.

3) The system checks that all mandatory information has been specified.

4) The system checks that an account exists with the username specified.

5) The system authenticates the user by comparing the password entered with the password stored on file.

6) The system checks that the account is in a state of Active.

7) The system logs the user in and records the date and time the user was logged in.

8) The system removes any "flagged for removal" mark that may be present on the account.

9) The system directs the user to the My Account page.

Alternative Flows:

3a) If any mandatory information has not been specified, or if any of the elements are invalid, the system will display one of the following validation error messages for each validation error, as appropriate, and allow the user to submit a new request:

- ❑ VEM-004-01 (Username not specified.)
- ❑ VEM-004-02 (Password not specified.)

4a) In the event that an account already doesn't exist with the username specified, the system will display the following validation error and allow the user to submit a new request.

- ❑ VEM-004-03 (Username and password combination is invalid.)

5a) In the event that there is an authentication error, the system will display the following validation error and allow the user to submit a new request.

- ❑ VEM-004-03 (Username and Password combination is invalid.)

6a) In the event that the account is not in the correct state, the system will display the appropriate "invalid operation" error. On clicking Continue, the user will be directed back to the Welcome page.

- ❑ IOM-004-01 (Account not activated.)
- ❑ IOM-004-02 (Account closed.)

Requirements Map:	HFR-USAA-001 (User not logged in.)
	HFR-ASAA-001 (Login not allowed on new accounts.)
	HFR-ASAA-002 (Login only allowed on active accounts.)
	HFR-ASAA-003 (Login not allowed on closed accounts.)
	HFR-DATAFORM-* (Common data entry and form requirements.)
	HFR-LOGIN-001 (Login using username and password.)
	HFR-LOGIN-002 (Validation rules not checked.)
	HFR-LOGIN-003 (Login date and time recorded.)
	HFR-PASSWORD-002 (Password comparison.)
	HFR-AGEDACCFR-004 (Flagged account not impacting user.)
	HFR-AGEDACCFR-005 (Removal of flag.)

UC-005 Logout

The Logout use case (UC-005) is fairly straightforward. It simply documents the high-level processing steps required when users want to log out of the system.

Use-Case Identifier:	UC-005
Use-Case Name:	Logout
Description:	An online user wishes to log out of their account.
Primary Actor:	Authenticated and logged in web user
Triggers:	The user clicks the Logout button on the My Account page.
Pre-Conditions:	The user is logged in.
Linked Storyboard:	SB-005
Basic Flow:	1) The user clicks the Logout button on the My Account page.
	2) The system logs the user off the system and records the date and time the user was logged off.
	3) The system removes any "flagged for removal" mark that may be present on the account.
	4) The system displays the Logged Out confirmation message and the Continue button.
	5) On clicking the Continue button, the user is directed to the Welcome page.

(continued)

(continued)

Alternative Flows:	1a) A session timeout will be treated as a full user logoff.
Requirements Map:	HFR-USAA-002 (User logged in.)
	HFR-LOGOUT-001 (Logged out date and time recorded.)
	HFR-LOGOUT-002 (Session timeout treated as full logout.)
	HFR-LOGOUT-003 (Logout confirmation message displayed.)
	HFR-AGEDACCFR-004 (Flagged account not impacting user.)
	HFR-AGEDACCFR-005 (Removal of flag.)

I've chosen not to list the Account State requirements here primarily because the account must be active in order for the user to log in. In addition, if the state were to change for some reason, it would require an Invalid Operation error, which in turn would log the user off and return him or her to the Welcome page. So, in this instance, it makes sense to simply log off the user as normal and not over-complicate the implementation.

UC-006 Reset Password

The Reset Password use case (UC-006) covers the functionality and processing steps when users have forgotten their password. The flow is transient in that it joins to UC-007 Change Password once users have been authenticated. If users pop out of the flow prior to completing the transaction, their account will not be updated.

Use-Case Identifier:	UC-006
Use-Case Name:	Reset Password
Description:	An online user has forgotten their password and wishes to change it.
Primary Actor:	Anonymous web user
Triggers:	The user has navigated to the Welcome page and clicked on the link "I have an account but I've forgotten my password."
Pre-Conditions:	The user is not logged in.
Linked Storyboard:	SB-006
Basic Flow:	1) The Reset Password (Authentication) page is displayed and the fields are blank and enabled.
	2) The user completes the form by entering their Username and E-mail address, and then clicks Continue.
	3) The system checks that all mandatory information has been specified.
	4) The system checks that an account exists with the username specified.
	5) The system authenticates the user by comparing the e-mail address entered with that stored on file.

	6)	The system checks that the account is in a state of Active.
	7)	The system directs the user to the Change Password page, where they join the UC-007 Change Password flow.

Alternative Flows:

3a) If any mandatory information has not been specified, or if any of the elements are invalid, the system will display one of the following validation error messages for each validation error, as appropriate, and allow the user to submit a new request:

❑ VEM-006-01 (Username not specified.)

❑ VEM-006-02 (E-mail address not specified.)

4a) In the event that an account already doesn't exist with the username specified, the system will display the following validation error and allow the user to submit a new request.

❑ VEM-006-03 (Username and e-mail combination is invalid.)

5a) In the event of an authentication error, the system will display the following validation error and allow the user to submit a new request.

❑ VEM-006-03 (Username and e-mail combination is invalid.)

6a) In the event that the account is not in the correct state, the system will display the appropriate Invalid Operation error and the Continue button. On clicking Continue, the user will be directed back to the Welcome page.

❑ IOM-006-01 (Account not activated.)

❑ IOM-006-02 (Account closed.)

Requirements Map:

HFR-USAA-001 (User not logged in.)

HFR-ASAA-002 (Change password authentication only allowed on active accounts.)

HFR-DATAFORM-* (Common data entry and form requirements.)

HFR-RPAUTH-001 (Authentication via username and e-mail.)

HFR-RPAUTH-002 (Validation rules should not be checked.)

HFR-EMAILADDR-003 (E-mail address comparison rules.)

HFR-AGEDACCFR-004 (Flagged account not impacting user.)

You'll note in this use case that the "flagged for removal" mark isn't specifically removed as part of the processing. This is primarily based on the fact that this is a transient page and the user hasn't actually completed a transaction that requires a write to the database. They have simply indicated that they have forgotten their password. It also saves you from having to write to the database during this use case. It is very subtle but walking through the processing like this can help to refine these areas of functionality. Depending on how the application is finally implemented, the database update could be included or made easier for a later date if necessary.

UC-007 Change Password

The Change Password use case (UC-007) contains the high-level processing steps when users want to change their password. The flow can be initiated from either the My Account page or joined from the UC-006 Reset Password flow.

Use-Case Identifier:	UC-007
Use-Case Name:	Change Password
Description:	An online user wishes to change their password.
Primary Actor:	Authenticated or logged in web user
Triggers:	1) The user has clicked on the link "I would like to change my password" on the My Account page.
	2) The user has joined from the "UC-006 Forgotten Password" use case.
Pre-Conditions:	The user is authenticated or logged in.
Linked Storyboard:	SB-007
Basic Flow:	1) The system obtains the user's account information.
	2) The system decrypts the security question.
	3) The Change Password page is displayed, the user's security question" is displayed, and the entry fields are blank and enabled.
	4) The user completes the form by entering the security question answer, a new password, and the confirmation password, and then clicks Continue.
	5) The system checks that all mandatory information has been specified and that each element is valid and correct according to its individual validation rules (where required).
	6) The system authenticates the user by comparing the security question answer entered with that stored on file.
	7) The system encrypts the user's new password according to the encryption rules.
	8) The system updates the user's account and records the date and time of the password change.
	9) The system removes any "flagged for removal" mark that may be present on the account.
	10) If the user isn't logged in, the system logs the user in to the system and records the date and time the user was logged in.
	11) The system displays the Password Changed confirmation message and the Continue button.
	12) On clicking the Continue button, the user is directed to the My Account page.

Alternative Flows: 5a) If any mandatory information has not been specified, or if any of the elements are invalid, the system will display one of the following validation error messages for each validation error, as appropriate, and allow the user to submit a new request:

    ❑   VEM-007-01 (Security question answer hasn't been specified.)

    ❑   VEM-007-02 (New password hasn't been specified.)

    ❑   VEM-007-03 (New password doesn't meet validation criteria.)

    ❑   VEM-007-04 (Confirmation password hasn't been specified.)

    ❑   VEM-007-05 (New password and confirmation password values don't match.)

    6a) In the event of an authentication error, the system will display the following validation error and allow the user to submit a new request.

    ❑   VEM-007-06 (Security question answer doesn't match the answer on file.)

Requirements Map: HFR-USAA-002 (User logged in or authenticated.)

HFR-ASAA-002 (Change password only allowed on active accounts.)

HFR-DATAFORM-* (Common data entry and form requirements.)

HFR-CHANGEPASSWORD-001 (Answer validation rules not checked.)

HFR-CHANGEPASSWORD-002 (Paste functionality not allowed when confirming new password.)

HFR-CHANGEPASSWORD-004 (New password and confirmation password match.)

HFR-CHANGEPASSWORD-005 (Password change date and time recorded.)

HFR-SECQANSWER-003 (Answer comparison rules.)

HFR-PASSWORD-001 (Password validation rules.)

HFR-PASSWORD-002 (Password encryption rules.)

HFR-AGEDACCFR-004 (Flagged account not impacting user.)

HFR-AGEDACCFR-005 (Removal of flag.)

You've probably noticed that, similar to the Logout functionality, the Change Password functionality listed doesn't include a check for the account state. In this example, it is actually implied that the account is in an active state, given that the user must be logged in to use this functionality. If the account state had changed for some reason, you'd need to direct the user somewhere else; in fact, it would almost certainly invalidate their logged on status, so they would need to be logged off and directed to the Welcome page. Once users are logged in, they are free to perform all the allowable actions. In this instance, there would need to be a valid case for why the account state could change (while the user was logged in) to incorporate this functionality. The impact of including a check against the account state in this and the remaining use cases could be looked into at the time it was determined necessary. However, this is a very subtle choice based on the usage of the system through the user interface. It is a classic example of the business rules essentially being implemented via the user interface. Given that only logged in users can access the My Account page, all functionality pertaining to their account automatically implies it is in an Active state.

If the solution were being used by external systems, you might well want to check the account state in the business logic to ensure that everything is processed according to a common set of business rules. An external system could be using the repository for its own purposes. If an external system were using the underlying business components and these didn't actually check the account state for the operation, it would be possible to breach the business rules set out earlier. Again, it is worth thinking about these subtle usage scenarios to determine what should happen under the covers and whether functionality like this needs to be included in the first instance. You have a set of requirements and allowable actions, and although the "current" design supports them, future enhancements may need to change more than anticipated. Furthermore, if you include this functionality now, it could also have an effect on the performance of the system.

It is definitely worth weighing the pros and cons of these choices. For instance, if you proceed with implementing this check, you'd need to devise a test scenario whereby the state was changed while the user was logged on and then attempt to perform an operation on the account. The system would need to behave in such a way that was consistent for all other operations (that is, logging the user off and returning them to the Welcome page). This is essentially an area of "defensive" design. There is no valid business reason (in this instance) for the situation to occur given the current design and usage. The development and test effort is solely for future usage and consistency. Although this might not be the most difficult implementation, it does have an effect on the budgets and timescales. More important, if it were deemed necessary part way through development, it could have an even bigger impact on what was already in place. This is one area of where "fit for purpose" becomes a matter of discussion and what should be included to meet the current requirements versus future enhancements. As the design progresses, you'll find other areas like this that would need to be discussed and agreed to.

In terms of the case study, let's proceed on the basis that these checks will be performed for consistency in the underlying processing. You'll see the effect of this decision and how it opens a number of areas that would need to be clarified and discussed. I won't update the storyboards because this is not a truly valid scenario from the web front end. You will need to update the use-case steps to capture this appropriately, as well as the alternative flows.

Basic Flow:	1)	The system obtains the user's account information.
	2)	The system checks that the account is in a state of Active.
	3)	The system decrypts the security question.
	4)	The Change Password page is displayed, the user's security question is displayed, and the entry fields are blank and enabled.
	5)	The user completes the form by entering their security question answer, new password, and confirmation password, and then clicks Continue.
	6)	The system checks that all mandatory information has been specified and that each element is valid and correct according to its individual validation rules (where required).

Basic Flow:	7)	The system authenticates the user by comparing the security question answer entered with that stored on file.
	8)	The system checks that the account is in a state of Active.
	9)	The system encrypts the user's new password according to the encryption rules.
	10)	The system updates the user's account and records the date and time of the password change.
	11)	The system removes any "flagged for removal" mark that may be present on the account.
	12)	If the user isn't logged in, the system logs the user in to the system and records the date and time the user was logged in.
	13)	The system displays the Password Changed confirmation message and the Continue button.
	14)	On clicking the Continue button, the user is directed to the My Account page.
Alternative Flows:	2a)	In the event that the account is not in the correct state, the system will display the appropriate Invalid Operation error and the Continue button. On clicking Continue, the user will be logged off and directed back to the Welcome page.
		❑ IOM-007-01 (Account not activated.)
		❑ IOM-007-02 (Account closed.)
	6a)	If any mandatory information has not been specified, or if any of the elements are invalid, the system will display one of the following validation error messages for each validation error, as appropriate, and allow the user to submit a new request:
		❑ VEM-007-01 (Security question answer hasn't been specified.)
		❑ VEM-007-02 (New password hasn't been specified.)
		❑ VEM-007-03 (New password doesn't meet validation criteria.)
		❑ VEM-007-04 (Confirmation password hasn't been specified.)
		❑ VEM-007-05 (New password and confirmation password values don't match.)
	7a)	In the event of an authentication error, the system will display the following validation error and allow the user to submit a new request.
		❑ VEM-007-06 (Security question answer doesn't match the answer on file.)
	8a)	In the event that the account is not in the correct state, the system will display the appropriate Invalid Operation error and the Continue button. On clicking Continue, the user will be directed back to the Welcome page.
		❑ IOM-007-01 (Account not activated.)
		❑ IOM-007-02 (Account closed.)

The remaining use cases will also include this check, along with the alternative flows to demonstrate the domino affect and draw out further discussion points.

UC-008 Update Account

The Update Account use case (UC-008) incorporates the high-level processing steps required when users want to update their account details. As previously mentioned, users can't change their password as part of this flow. To change their password, they must use the UC-007 Change Password use case.

Use-Case Identifier:	UC-008
Use-Case Name:	Update Account
Description:	An online user wishes to update their account details.
Primary Actor:	Logged in web user
Triggers:	The user has clicked the link "I would like to update my account details" on the My Account page.
Pre-Conditions:	The user is logged in.
Linked Storyboard:	SB-008
Basic Flow:	1) The system obtains the user's account information.
	2) The system checks that the account is in a state of Active.
	3) The system decrypts the e-mail address, security question, and security question answer data elements.
	4) The Update Account page is displayed, and the username, e-mail address, security question, and security question answer fields are pre-populated with the user's account details, and enabled.
	5) The user completes the form by entering/updating their username, e-mail address, security question, and security question answer, and then clicks Continue.
	6) The system checks that all mandatory information has been specified and that each element is valid and correct according to its individual validation rules.
	7) The system checks that the account is in a state of Active.
	8) The system checks that an account doesn't already exist with the username specified.
	9) The system encrypts the information supplied according to the individual encryption rules.
	10) The system updates the account record in the database and records the date and time the account was updated.
	11) The system removes any "flagged for removal" mark that may be present on the account.
	12) The system displays the "Account Updated" confirmation message and the Continue button.
	13) On clicking the Continue button, the user is directed to the Activate Account page.

Alternative Flows:	2a)	In the event that the account is not in the correct state, the system will display the appropriate Invalid Operation error and the Continue button. On clicking Continue, the user will be directed back to the Welcome page.

       ❑   IOM-008-01 (Account not activated.)

       ❑   IOM-008-02 (Account closed.)

6a) If any mandatory information has not been specified, or if any of the elements are invalid, the system will display one of the following validation error messages for each validation error, as appropriate, and allow the user to submit a new request:

       ❑   VEM-008-01 (Username hasn't been specified.)

       ❑   VEM-008-02 (Username specified doesn't meet the validation criteria.)

       ❑   VEM-008-03 (E-mail address hasn't been specified.)

       ❑   VEM-008-04 (E-mail address specified doesn't meet the validation criteria.)

       ❑   VEM-008-05 (Security question hasn't been specified.)

       ❑   VEM-008-06 (Security question specified doesn't meet validation criteria.)

       ❑   VEM-008-07 (Security question answer hasn't been specified.)

       ❑   VEM-008-08 (Security question answer specified doesn't meet the validation criteria.)

7a) In the event that the account is not in the correct state, the system will display the appropriate Invalid Operation error and the Continue button. On clicking Continue, the user will be logged off and directed back to the Welcome page.

       ❑   IOM-008-01 (Account not activated.)

       ❑   IOM-008-02 (Account closed.)

8a) In the event that an account already exists with the username specified, the system will display the following validation error and allow the user to submit a new request:

       ❑   VEM-008-09 (Username specified already exists.)

Requirements Map: HFR-USAA-002 (User logged in.)

HFR-ASAA-002 (Update account only allowed on active accounts.)

HFR-DATAFORM-* (Common data entry and form requirements.)

HFR-UPDATEACC-001 (Account data element specification.)

HFR-UPDATEACC-002 (All fields validated.)

HFR-UPDATEACC-003 (Date/time updated retained.)

HFR-USERNAME-001 (Username must be unique.)

(continued)

(continued)

Requirements Map:	HFR-USERNAME-002 (Username validation rules.)
	HFR-EMAILADDR-001 (E-mail address validation rules.)
	HFR-EMAILADDR-002 (E-mail address encryption rules.)
	HFR-SECQUESTION-001 (Security question validation rules.)
	HFR-SECQUESTION-002 (Security question encryption rules.)
	HFR-SECQANSWER-001 (Answer validation rules.)
	HFR-SECQANSWER-002 (Answer encryption rules.)
	HFR-AGEDACCFR-004 (Flagged account not impacting user.)
	HFR-AGEDACCFR-005 (Removal of flag.)

Based on the earlier decision point regarding checking the account state, the Update Account use case now includes two checks for the account state. The first is in Step 2, after the account has been obtained, and the second is prior to the account being updated in Step 7. This further increases the scope of testing and the complexity of the testing scenarios. You can see quite clearly that one subtle decision can have bigger consequences in the long run. The system would also need to obtain the account from the database twice, once at the start of the use case and again prior to updating the account, which will impact performance. This is a classic example of where walking through the use cases can really help to draw out design decisions.

UC-009 Close Account

The Close Account use case (UC-009) — the final use case in the Within-a-Click series — documents the steps involved with users closing their account. When completed, users are returned to the Welcome page.

Use-Case Identifier:	UC-009
Use-Case Name:	Close Account
Description:	An online user wishes to close their account.
Primary Actor:	Logged in web user
Triggers:	The user has clicked the link "I would like to close my account." on the My Account page.
Pre-Conditions:	The user is logged in.
Linked Storyboard:	SB-009

Basic Flow:	1)	The system obtains the user's account information.
	2)	The system checks that the account is in a state of Active.
	3)	The Close Account page is displayed and the fields are blank and enabled. The Email Confirmation checkbox is enabled and not pre-selected.
	4)	The user completes the form by entering their comments (if required) and selecting whether they would like e-mail confirmation (if required), and then clicks Continue.
	5)	The system checks that the closure comments are valid and correct according to the individual validation rules (if specified).
	6)	The system checks that the account is in a state of "Active."
	7)	The system updates the account record in the database, saving the closure comments and e-mail request. It sets the account state to Closed and records the date and time the account was closed.
	8)	If the user requested e-mail confirmation, the system proceeds to queue an Account Closed e-mail request recording the date and time the request was made.
	8a)	In the background the e-mail request will be processed and the system will compose and send the user an e-mail containing confirmation that their account has been closed, and will record the date and time the e-mail was sent.
	9)	The system logs the user off and records the date and time the user was logged off.
	10)	The system removes any "flagged for removal" mark that may be present on the account.
	11)	The system displays the Account Closed confirmation message and the Continue button.
	12)	On clicking the Continue button, the user is directed to the Welcome page.
Alternative Flows:	2a)	In the event that the account is not in the correct state, the system will display the appropriate Invalid Operation error and the Continue button. On clicking Continue, the user will be directed back to the Welcome page.
		❑ IOM-009-01 (Account not activated.)
		❑ IOM-009-02 (Account closed.)

(continued)

(continued)

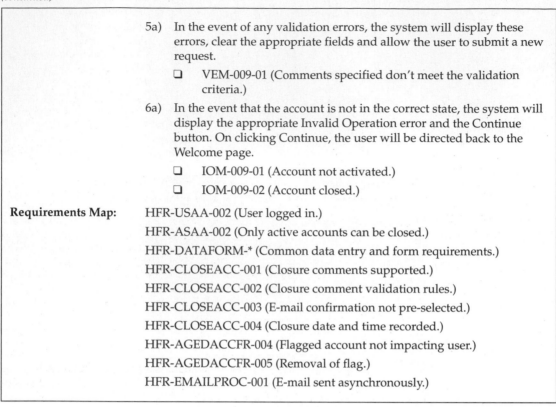

5a) In the event of any validation errors, the system will display these errors, clear the appropriate fields and allow the user to submit a new request.

❏ VEM-009-01 (Comments specified don't meet the validation criteria.)

6a) In the event that the account is not in the correct state, the system will display the appropriate Invalid Operation error and the Continue button. On clicking Continue, the user will be directed back to the Welcome page.

❏ IOM-009-01 (Account not activated.)

❏ IOM-009-02 (Account closed.)

Requirements Map: HFR-USAA-002 (User logged in.)

HFR-ASAA-002 (Only active accounts can be closed.)

HFR-DATAFORM-* (Common data entry and form requirements.)

HFR-CLOSEACC-001 (Closure comments supported.)

HFR-CLOSEACC-002 (Closure comment validation rules.)

HFR-CLOSEACC-003 (E-mail confirmation not pre-selected.)

HFR-CLOSEACC-004 (Closure date and time recorded.)

HFR-AGEDACCFR-004 (Flagged account not impacting user.)

HFR-AGEDACCFR-005 (Removal of flag.)

HFR-EMAILPROC-001 (E-mail sent asynchronously.)

This use case is another example whereby the system would be checking the account state twice, once at the start of the operation and then again prior to completing the operation. If this account state check is absolutely necessary for these later use cases, it should be encapsulated within a single component to ensure the application code uses a standard approach. However, this will not address the fact that the application would need to access the account twice in each flow.

Summary

A little effort can go a very long way in ensuring that the project team has everything it needs to implement the system. This chapter started with a fairly straightforward application. However, you saw that even a simple system offers many functional and technical design choices and decision points. A simple design choice can have far reaching affects. You should model the suggested processing to get a true picture of what it really means. You saw this in the later use cases and the effect it can have on the overall system. It is important to know where to draw the line to ensure that the scope of the application is set appropriately. The design elements discussed in this chapter help to set a very clear scope. The case study doesn't include all the features that you might expect to find on a full-blown membership system. However, as I mentioned at the start, the book is not about teaching you how to implement a good membership system. It is about implementing a good solution to any given problem. Ensuring that you have a very clear vision for moving forward is paramount to this objective.

The material in this chapter offers a great starting point for the User Manual. The high-level actions and the system processing steps are in place. Of course, there are still some areas to complete, such as defining the detailed validation rules for each data element. The next chapter builds on the elements discussed in this chapter and starts to outline the foundations for the overall solution architecture.

The key messages from this chapter are as follows:

❏ **Identify the use cases.** The use-case diagram is a good place to start because it shows the high-level functions that users can perform. It also helps to define the different types of users and the security model.

❏ **Storyboard the flow.** The storyboards help to flesh out the system from the user's perspective and provide a reasonably solid walkthrough of the application. They also provide the basis for further refining the requirements, both functional and technical. Storyboards don't need to be high-resolution, they just need to capture the key inputs, outputs, and flow.

❏ **Document the decision points.** Walking through the overall design helps to flesh out the requirements. At the same time, it is worth documenting all the various decision points and their rationale. Although this chapter didn't do that formally (for the purposes of time and space), it is a good idea to do so. Documenting the decisions makes it easier to justify the out-of-scope items and functionality.

❏ **Track the solution inventory.** The solution inventory helps to list and document the individual elements in the solution. I've chosen to uniquely identify each element of the solution, some of which will be used in the actual sub-system design. Even walking through simple use cases will help to highlight additional items for the solution inventory.

❏ **Document the requirements.** The requirements help to shape the solution and provide more detail regarding the user interface and expected user experience. They also help to define the underlying data elements and their storage and processing. The technical requirements need to be documented and capture the key quality characteristics.

❏ **Document the use cases**. The use cases pull everything together into a clear picture of both the user interactions and the high-level system processing requirements. The use cases help to flesh out the processing components, highlight areas of concern, as well as helping to define the functional test cases for the application. If you were so inclined, you could revisit the sample use cases presented in this chapter and complete them according to you own decisions and ideas.

14

Planning the Architecture

This chapter looks at planning and modeling the conceptual architecture for the case study. The storyboards, requirements, and use cases presented in the previous chapter provided a good starting point for this activity. You have a good overview of the application functionality and if you've incorporated all the decision points in the inputs then it should be pretty well defined. Even with the limited information presented previously, I'm sure you're already thinking about how you would go about planning the architecture. It is a delicate situation at this point because you're armed with a reasonable amount of information and might be tempted to dive into the code and work it out as it goes along. In Chapter 25 we'll see some of the impacts of this approach. It is best to take a step back and think about how things will fit together into an overall picture. There'll still be much to do, but this chapter builds up a reasonable starting point for additional discussion and detailed design. The architecture (and the components) will provide a basis to start looking at how the patterns and practices can be applied to them. This chapter doesn't go into enormous detail; it simply examines how the architectural layers fit together and where the high-level components reside within them. The placement of components and their functionality will probably change as the design progresses and this is to be expected. Design is an iterative process and this chapter provides the first pass for the conceptual architecture design.

Furthermore, note that this chapter, as well as Part IV, "Patterns and Practices" (Chapters 16–24), works through a conceptual design, not a completed solution. This underpins the basic premise of this book, which is to think about the design before diving into the code, and provides the foundations for further refinement and improvement.

This chapter is organized into the following sections:

❑ **The Conceptual Architecture** — Discusses the high-level conceptual architecture, including the deployment concept and the transaction flow.

❑ **The Presentation Tier** — Shows the conceptual web page layout and the high-level processing pattern.

❑ **The Web Service Façade** — Looks at the web services that provide a conduit between the web pages and the business-processing components. The following four web services are split by functionality:

> ❑ The Registration service
>
> ❑ The Activation service
>
> ❑ The Authentication service
>
> ❑ The Account Management service

❑ **The Business-Processing Components** — Discusses each of the different component groups in the architecture and their responsibilities. The business-processing components are split into the following high-level layers:

> ❑ The business managers
>
> ❑ The business processes
>
> ❑ The business framework
>
> ❑ The batch processes

❑ **The Logical Data Model and Data Access** — Presents the conceptual data model based on the information in the previous chapter. It looks at the data access layer and the individual data entities that are used for communication between the architectural layers.

❑ **The Reporting Components** — Takes a look at the reporting requirements outlined previously and the basic components that would need to be in place to support them.

❑ **Logical Component Model** — Rounds off the chapter by presenting all the high-level components outlined in the previous sections in the first pass conceptual component model.

The Conceptual Architecture

It is a good idea to set out some high-level guiding principles for the architecture's design. The high-level architecture outlines the layers and component groups and how they shape the overall component model. As I did for the application, I've listed three primary guiding principles for the case study's conceptual architecture:

❑ **Multi-tier model** — The application should employ a multi-tier model. In principle, the user interface, business processing, and data access should be separated. This is a pretty standard model for an application's architecture. The model also fits very well with the production environment shown in Chapter 5.

❑ **Incorporate web services** — A lot of companies are moving to service-orientated architectures (SOA), so I thought it would be a good idea to include some web services in the overall architecture. It also fits rather well with the production architecture and allows future scaling opportunities for the application components. The application components could also be exposed to other applications as services.

❑ **Modular approach** — The architecture should be modular to promote reuse, ease of maintenance, and logically separate discrete processing and functionality. This guiding principle is in keeping with all the messages in this book. It also helps to promote the patterns and practices discussed in the later chapters.

It is not an exhaustive list of guiding principles, but it captures the key elements that are right at the heart of the architecture and sets the scene for moving forward.

The Logical Layers

The case study follows a very similar pattern to a three-tier architecture, consisting of the user interface layer, the business-processing layer and the data access layer. I've also introduced some other layers that you may not be familiar with. Figure 14-1 shows the core conceptual architecture outline.

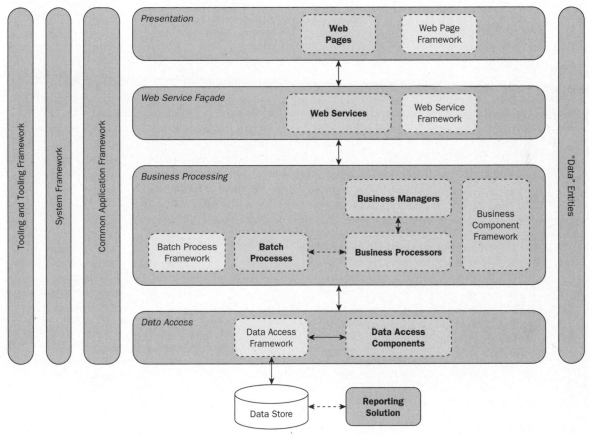

Figure 14-1

By breaking up the architecture into discrete areas, you can start to fill in the blanks with some high-level components. It also helps to model the application and pull together conceptual component overviews. The following provides an initial overview of each of the core component groups and layers shown in the conceptual solution architecture outline:

❑ **Presentation** — The web pages are responsible for displaying the pages, capturing the user's input, passing it to a web service for processing, and displaying the outcome of the transaction. As per the previous chapter, the outcome could be a successful transaction Confirmation message, an Invalid Operation message, or a series of Validation Error messages. I've also included a placeholder for a web page framework that will contain components that provide common services to all the web pages in the solution. It could be something as simple as a Base class that all pages inherit from, but this would reside in the web page framework. I touched on state management and page transitions previously. The web page framework is an ideal place to put these types of components to avoid duplication across all the pages. It enables you to wrap services so that they can be changed more easily in the future. For instance, the first iteration of the application could store state in the State object provided by the ASP.NET framework. If all interactions with the State object are done through a single conduit, it makes changes and enhancements a lot easier. It also forces you to think about what additional information may be required to ensure that future enhancements can be implemented without too much trouble. It is always a good idea to put these placeholders in place, as it helps you to shape the solution and understand where components best fit.

❑ **Web services façade** — The web services façade provides a series of web services that act as a simple conduit between the web pages and the business processing. They are not responsible for any formal functional processing; they simply pass the requests from the web pages to the business components and pass the results back. In the future it would be possible for external applications to use the web service façade to access the application's functionality. These external applications would also allow you to support multiple channels into the application back-end. There's a web service framework placeholder for components that provide common services to all the web services in the solution. Again, this could be as simple as a base class, or it could include a much richer set of components.

❑ **The business processing components** — The business-processing tier is broken into a number of different component groups. This approach fits with the guiding principles set out earlier and it also allows you to model a much larger scale solution within the confines of the basic case study.

  ❑ The *business managers* are responsible for validating the request prior to passing it on for business processing. The validation includes mandatory-field specification, "double-entry" validation, field-level validation, as well as business-level validation. For example, one business-level validation would be ensuring that an account with the same name doesn't already exist for a new account request. In this instance, the business managers are acting as a simple "firewall" for request validation.

  ❑ The *business processors* are responsible for performing the functional processing and returning the outcome. The business processors "orchestrate" the transaction and make use of the business framework components. The business processors could also be used by the batch jobs. This is especially useful at times and helps to ensure that the business processors are "tuned" and implemented effectively.

  ❑ The *business component framework* contains components that provide common services to all business components, including business managers and business processors, as well as a large number of components used during processing.

  ❑ The *batch processes* are responsible for sending solicited e-mails and performing routine maintenance tasks, including account flagging and removal. The case study doesn't contain a large amount of functional batch. As I've mentioned before, batch typically grows over time. A *batch process framework* will provide common services and execution control for all batch processes.

❏ **The data access layer** — The data access components act as a conduit between the business-processing tier and the physical databases. The data access components would typically model the database — for example, tables, views, and stored procedures. Modeling these components against the database provides opportunities for code generation. For example, using a common template, rules, and a custom generator, it would be possible to generate all data access classes from the data model. There are also off-the-shelf applications that can perform this for you — LINQ, for example. Although code generation is out-of-scope for the case study, planning the architecture in this way allows you to identify areas where code generation could be used and adopted for reduced timescales and improved quality. In this instance, the case study continues with our "custom built" guiding principle. A *data access framework* will provide common services to all data access components.

❏ **"Data" entities** — The data entities are lightweight, data-only (model) classes that are used to communicate information among the architectural layers. You can think of these as data structures simply consisting of properties. The data entities cross all layers. Thus, they are not a true layer, which is why they're drawn to the side. The data entities usually model the database as well as any data structure. They're typically *serializable* so that they can be easily transported across the individual layers. They are also good candidates for being generated from the data model where appropriate.

Modeling a single or even a couple of "vertical slices" of the application and architecture highlights the patterns that all components in the group should follow. This allows you to standardize the patterns and spot similar functionality which you can combine into a discrete set of components which reside in the appropriate *framework* layer. The patterns provide the basis of the templates and the exemplars. They also allow you to determine whether you can consolidate functionality into data-driven or even data-generated components. When planning the architecture, it is often best to model it in stages so that these opportunities are highlighted and can be assessed and incorporated where necessary.

I find that it is generally best to start with a series of placeholders for "framework" components to try and ensure that the application is sufficiently broken up and provides hooks for consistent processing and functionality. The following sections provide an overview of the following:

❏ The common application framework

❏ The system framework

❏ The tooling framework

The Common Application Framework

The common application framework will provide services that are common to all web pages, web services, business components, batch components, and data access components. Chapter 4 discussed the custom calendar component, which is one such component that would reside in this layer. It would be used by the various application components to obtain the application's current date and time. In the case of batch, some batch processes (as discussed previously) would need to use a specific batch calendar component to obtain the current batch date and time. As you've seen, this could actually be different from the system and application date and time due to the potential midnight crossover. The batch calendar component would actually reside in the batch framework. Some batch processes may also need to use the application's date and time. This can be exposed via the batch calendar component, or the jobs can use the application's calendar component directly when required.

The common application framework isolates components and functionality into a single group and provides consistent processing across the application. Another good example of the common application framework's usage continues with the discussion on tracing. The web pages, web services, batch processes, and business logic all need to trace their processing flow. The .NET Framework has many classes that support outputting of debug and trace information. The common application framework can contain a single class that all application components use for a consistent approach. For instance, consider the following methods:

```
TraceError( string message )
TraceError( string message, params object[] args )
TraceInformation( string message )
TraceInformation( string message, params object[] args )
TraceWarning( string message )
TraceWarning( string message, params object[] args )
```

These methods allow the application to pass a string or a string for formatting to be output. The custom calendar component could contain tracing, such as:

```
TraceInformation( "Obtaining system date and time using DateTime.Now" )
TraceInformation( "System date and time = '{0}'", DateTime.Now )
```

The output of these statements would look similar to the following:

```
Obtaining system date and time using 'DateTime.Now'
System date and time = '15/02/2007 12:53:02'
```

Chapter 4 discussed trace modeling and examined some typical trace prefixes for nicely formatted output, such as:

```
[15/02/2007 12:53:02][CalendarProvider][Now] Obtaining system date and time using
    'DateTime.Now'
[15/02/2007 12:53:02][CalendarProvider][Now] System date and time = '15/02/2007
    12:53:02'
```

In this example, the tracing output contains a basic timestamp, the component or class name, and the method name. Chapter 4 also concluded that all tracing timestamps would use the actual system date and time to avoid any confusion throughout the application trace when using a Custom Calendar component. Therefore, the system framework trace provider, the lowest in the architecture stack, doesn't necessarily need to expose a specific date and time parameter. It could simply expose parameters for the *class name* and *method name*, such as:

```
TraceProvider.TraceInformation( string className, string methodName, string
    message )
TraceProvider.TraceInformation( string className, string methodName, string
    message, params object[] args )
```

This provides a very basic low-level wrapper for consistent tracing across all the applications within the solution. In addition to adding the *timestamp*, the system framework trace provider also adds other information to the output, such as the *computer name*, *process ID*, *thread ID*, and so forth. Instead of every method call needing to change, you can simply add this functionality in a single place, and all tracing output will include it.

You'd want the same level of output in the tracing included in your tools. The tooling framework can also make use of the system framework components, as shown in Figure 14-2.

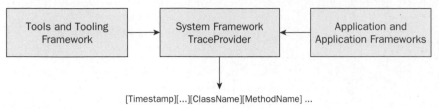

Figure 14-2

In this instance the system framework trace provider is providing the lowest level of acceptable trace for the entire solution, including the tools.

Moving up the stack, the additional frameworks are simply layers of abstraction that provide value added functionality for each of the respective layers. For example, the common application framework, the subject of this section, could include a trace provider that adds application-specific information to the output prior to passing it on to the system framework. For example, let's assume that all application trace needs to also include the application's date and time for traceability purposes. The common application framework trace provider could expose methods similar to those previously mentioned, but the component would add the application's date and time (obtained from the custom calendar) to the tracing output before passing it on to the system framework. The figure now looks something like Figure 14-3.

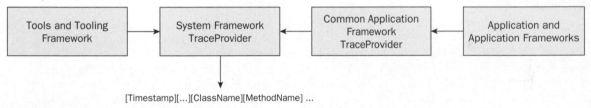

Figure 14-3

The output might look something like the following which now contains the system date and time, the class name, the method name, and the application specific date and time:

```
[15/02/2007 12:53:02][ClassName][MethodName][31/12/1999 11:59:59] message
```

This approach can then be extended and built up into a full hierarchy in which each framework layer adds specific value to the output, without every component in the group having to specify it explicitly. This is shown in Figure 14-4.

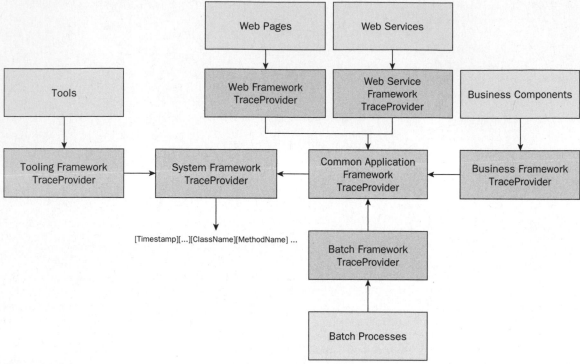

Figure 14-4

Figure 14-4 shows seven independent trace providers, each of which would be responsible for adding its own value to the output. Although this may seem somewhat excessive, there's another key benefit to this approach, which has to do with the components themselves and the method signatures. Each trace provider can be specifically designed for the consumer group, and the interface can provide verbose and meaningful methods and parameters. For instance, in the case of web pages, although className and methodName could be used as parameter names, the methods could actually use something more meaningful, such as *pageName* and *eventName*. It also means that the XML comments associated with these methods can be specific to the purpose they should be used for and describe the added value they offer. For example, "The pageName argument should be specified without the *.aspx* extension, as this will be added by the framework." This approach solidifies the standards and guidelines within the code itself and also supports documentation generation for the Developer's Guide.

You can extend this approach further and apply it to many other components and groups, such as event logging and performance counter updates. It is simply a question of starting at the bottom (the lowest acceptable common denominator) and adding value at each layer up the chain. The individual frameworks provide an ideal opportunity for this, and even if they don't add a huge amount of value in the first instance, they provide useful hooks for future enhancement.

For the purposes of the case study, let's place the following components in the common application framework:

- **Custom Calendar** — Used to obtain the application specific date and time.
- **Diagnostics Provider** — Used to "wrap" the system framework's diagnostic features (discussed next).

The System Framework

The system framework provides low-level services (such as logging and diagnostics) to all components in the solution, as well as the tooling framework layer. Part IV, "Patterns and Practices," fleshes out some of the components that reside in this layer. The components in this layer typically include access to configuration settings, event logging, tracing, performance counter updates and so forth, all of which will be required by the tools and all the applications.

The components are very much like those provided by the low-level runtime. The system framework components essentially wrap these features so that the solution has a consistent approach across all layers and processes. This architecture layer is typically thought of as being right at the bottom of the solution stack. However, I tend to draw it (as I have) to the side because it is used by all the different layers (or frameworks.)

The system framework components can be thought of as *adapters*. For example, the .NET Framework's System.Diagnostics namespace contains a number of classes, including the EventLog, Trace, Debug, and PerformanceCounter. These classes are totally generic and reusable across all applications and solutions. The system framework's wrapped versions of these classes would provide a more value-added service to the entire solution, as you've already seen.

The runtime's framework components provide a good starting point for the system framework's extension services, such as:

❑ Access to configuration settings

❑ Tracing (error, information, warning, and debug)

❑ Event logging (e.g., Windows Event Log)

❑ Performance counter utilization

❑ Database connectivity and interaction

❑ Exceptions

You can split the system framework into different *namespaces*, similar to the runtime's namespaces. It is a good idea not to use the same names to avoid confusion and conflicts. Furthermore, you can provide application (or tool) specific wrappers of these components in the appropriate frameworks.

In the case of the system framework (where components are adding specific value), it can also make use of its own services. This would provide solution-wide consistency. For example, the Configuration component can make use of the low-level Tracing and Event Logging features. This is an interesting situation and worthy of a brief discussion because there are some key considerations to take into account.

When an application starts up, it typically obtains some configuration values that will be used during processing. You would expect these actions to follow the standards and guidelines. For instance, you'd expect tracing, exception handling, and event logging to be incorporated in the system framework. Let's assume the configuration provider is going to use our trace provider for consistent tracing. Let's also assume that the trace provider is configurable (for example, allowing specification of where the output files reside and a file name mask). In this instance, a cyclic-relationship is created whereby both components are dependent on each other. For consistency, the trace provider needs to use the configuration provider to obtain the log location, and the configuration provider also needs to trace. We can further complicate the issue by assuming that in the event that a configuration parameter can't be found, an event needs to be raised. The event log provider typically also needs to obtain configuration values, such as the name of the event log to use, as well as to incorporate tracing and exception handling.

Assume the `ConfigurationProvider` has a method, such as `Get`, which takes a configuration value name and returns a `string` value:

```
string Get( string name )
```

Also assume that this method uses the low-level runtime framework components, as well as the System framework's `TraceProvider` and `EventLogProvider` components. The following pseudo code represents the `Get` method processing (albeit extremely simplified):

```
string ConfigurationProvider.Get( string name )
{
    traceProvider.TraceInformation("ConfigurationProvider", "Get",
    "Attempting to obtain configuration values for setting {0}", name );

    try
    {
        configValue = AppSettings.Get( name );
    }
    catch( Exception e )
    {
        throw eventLogProvider.RaiseEvent( ConfigValueNotFoundException, name, e );
    }

    traceProvider.TraceInformation("ConfigurationProvider", "Get",
    "Obtained configuration values for {0} which equal {1}", name, configValue );

    return configValue;
}
```

The example contains a number of hard-coded values and doesn't conform to best practices, but it provides the basis for this example and discussion.

You can instantly see that the first line of code calls the trace provider. The question is "where will the output go?" If the trace provider isn't initialized, it is going to need to obtain its configuration settings (using the `ConfigurationProvider`) before it can actually output anything at all. The following shows a simplified example of this:

```
void TraceProvider.TraceInformation( string className, string methodName, string
    message, params object[] args )
{
    if( !initialized )
    {
        logFileLocation = configurationProvider.Get("LogFileLocation");
        ...
        initialized = true;
    }
    ...
}
```

As you can probably see, this type of implementation can lead to recursive calling and ultimately result in a `Stack Overflow` exception. This situation can equally apply to other components and relationships within the overall solution and framework components.

Although these are only examples, you can see that re-using the components consistently presents some challenges for the low-level system framework design. This is generally why the system framework components are very often lightweight providers of specific functionality and do not rely too heavily on other framework components. Another good example of this situation (cyclic-relationships) is with database access. The database components ultimately require configuration settings, such as the database connection string. In addition, the components also need to trace their processing steps and raise events.

The system framework is one area where default behaviors can be implemented. For example, all uninitialized trace output goes to a specific file or location. All uninitialized events are raised in the standard Application event log (or equivalent). This helps to alleviate some of these problems while providing a consistent approach to reuse. It is equally important to document any default behaviors so that the Operations Manual captures them appropriately. If the default values were embedded in the code (for example, hard-coded), the values would need to be clearly understood and very well-documented.

This is a classic "chicken-and-egg" situation and there's clearly another balance here, one that is well worth thinking about to ensure that the underlying foundations of the system are solid and consistent. Walking through the various initialization procedures highlights these subtle characteristics. Making use of the underlying runtime's features can also help to alleviate some of these problems. In addition, encapsulating initialization logic and related components and processing can also help. Problems typically occur during startup and initialization, so it is a good idea to trace these activities and log the appropriate events so that they can be investigated (and resolved) effectively. The Operations Manual is the place to document these startup procedures and where the relevant outputs and events are logged.

For the purposes of the case study, let's just place the following low-level components in the system framework:

- **Configuration Provider** — Provides consistent low-level access to configuration settings.
- **Trace Provider** — Provides consistent low-level tracing capabilities.
- **Event Logging Provider** — Provides consistent low-level event logging capabilities.
- **Performance Counter Provider** — Provides consistent low-level access to performance counters.
- **Exception** — Provides a common base for all exceptions within the solution.

It is important to remember that wrapping functionality higher up in the framework stack helps to keep the low-level system framework components reusable across all applications and tools in the solution. If every application in the solution requires its own low-level framework then this will increase costs and timescales.

The Tooling Framework

The tooling framework layer provides services to external tools, including unit tests, integration tests, stubs, and simulators. The tooling framework can make use of the low-level common services offered by the system framework, resulting in a consistent approach and further reuse.

The tooling framework is one of my personal favorites. There are so many situations where tools are developed for a specific purpose. In most cases, the tools also need to include diagnostics and will often need to make use of a variety of other components. The tooling framework provides a consistent way for tools to reuse these specific elements. Tools will undoubtedly use the system framework components. The tooling framework is yet another layer that can drill down into further sub-sections for test tools, construction tools (code generators, and so on), build tools, and so forth. Development environments are becoming more and more sophisticated, which can sometimes reduce the number of specific tools that are required on a project.

The previous chapter discussed the case study and how it (or its underlying components) can be used by other external applications. The tools are a classic example of this. It is very possible that a test tool (or even an administration interface) also requires some form of user repository and authentication functionality.

In this example, it is possible that the tools could reuse the application components. However, there may be some specific orchestration required to reuse them effectively. This is where you start to see the case study potentially providing services to other parts of the solution. The underlying components start to form an overall framework, and different business rules will apply, depending on whom the consumer is and how the components need to be used. For instance, I discussed checking the account state during updates. Having this functionality embedded in the business logic provides consistent business rules across the application. But are these rules also appropriate for the tools?

This is another area where the hierarchy of the framework layers comes into play. The low-level components can provide the basic services — for example, creating a new account in a database. The physical database and its location will be configurable. The business components perform the validation and orchestration, according to the business rules for the application. The tooling framework orchestrates the validation and creation of a new account, according to its own business rules.

Designing in this loosely coupled way invites and promotes reuse, but it also means that you need to carefully assess the impact of a change. For example, a change to a commonly used component can affect the core application, the administration interface, and the test tools. The impact will depend entirely on what the change is and how it is tied to a specific set of business rules.

The case study is essentially a user repository, and I chose it specifically because it highlights these areas of consideration and reuse. While the front-end application provides a user interface for web users and "the site," the back-end can be reused by many applications that require a user repository. I've seen many occasions where this functionality is necessary, and a set of good foundations will provide consistency and security across the board. It is very easy to develop a test tool that requires user login and maintenance that doesn't incorporate all the encryption and decryption features. It can store passwords in the clear, which wouldn't be very secure. Reusing the foundations of the case study provides all these features.

Although the focus of this book isn't about developing an administration front-end or test tools that require these features, it is worth thinking about them for the underlying design. Incorporating frameworks and layers like this really helps to provide the necessary hooks for future enhancement and reuse. It is very easy to develop very specific components because you have total control of what the component needs to do. When you start to think about reuse, you open up a series of challenges around the design, governance, and development of the components. For example, you may need to consult various teams to understand the different uses of the component. There could be different and potentially conflicting delivery timescales and priorities for the component. You need to make sure that all the relevant development teams have everything they need to reuse the component effectively, including documentation, test stubs, and simulators for example. The primary purpose of reuse is to reduce effort, so you need to ensure that the component is supported and managed appropriately. You don't want individual teams making changes to the same component without consultation.

The Production Deployment Concept

It is important to distinguish between logic layers and physical tiers (for example, servers and hardware). The high-level deployment concept determines which components reside on the physical servers. Figure 14-5 shows the deployment concept for the case study based on the conceptual architecture outlined in the previous section.

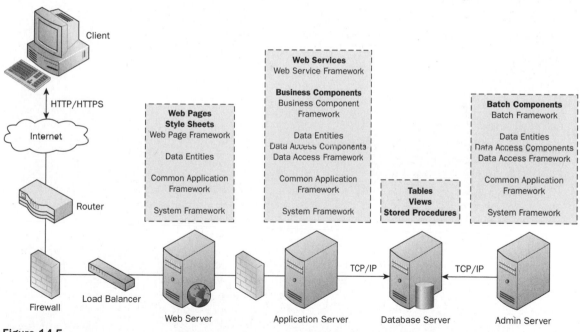

Figure 14-5

The figure doesn't show the tooling framework because these components would be installed on the development and test servers and not deployed to the production servers. The pre-production environment can contain servers that run these components, if the environment is being used for testing purposes. In this instance, I've shown only the core components in the architecture and the hypothetical deployment concept.

The figure shows the various component groups in the solution and the types of servers they would be deployed to. You can design the physical architecture in many different ways. I chose the preceding approach to illustrate and demonstrate natural separation of the components across the physical architecture.

The diagram, which is quite simple, helps to solidify some of the high-level packaging and deployment requirements. Although you probably wouldn't be installing the solution in the production environment manually, you would certainly be installing the solution in development and test environments. You can use the diagram to start shaping out the high-level packages, which Chapter 24 discusses in more detail.

High-Level Transaction Flow

Figure 14-5 showed the conceptual deployment concept. In short, users make an HTTP (or HTTPS) request from their web browser. The request goes over the Internet and through the organization's routers, externally facing firewalls and through the load balancers to arrive at a particular front-end web server. From there, the application processing takes place. The web servers communicate with the application servers using HTTP (or HTTPS), and the application servers communicate with the database using TCP/IP. Figure 14-5 also showed the administration servers, which communicate with the database via TCP/IP.

Figure 14-6 shows the high-level transaction flow through the core components. It also shows the high-level responsibilities of each component/group in the solution. The figure doesn't show the frameworks or data access layers; it simply captures the high-level flow that will be used to define some additional classes and details for the architecture.

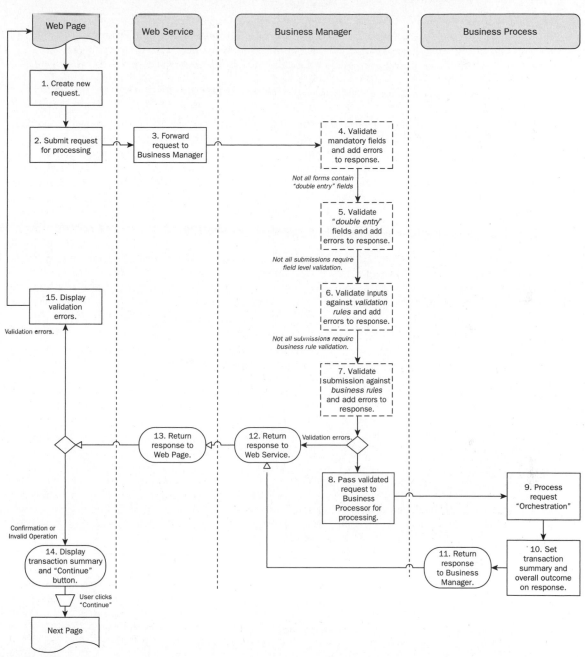

Figure 14-6

The end-to-end transaction flow is pretty straightforward and easy to follow. It shows the primary responsibilities for each core component in the architecture. Although this is a fairly simple diagram, it provides another series of placeholders that need to be completed. Using these placeholders, you can develop high-level processing patterns that each component would follow. The patterns provide a consistent approach to the architecture and also help you to shape the framework layers, as well as the templates and exemplars.

You can see from Figure 14-6 that the web page creates a new request in Step 1, which is passed through all the layers, and a response is returned to it (via a web service) in Step 13. Based on the response, the web page determines whether to display the validation errors or the overall transaction outcome, which as you know by now can be either a confirmation message or an invalid operation message. In the event that the response contains an overall transaction outcome, on clicking the Continue button, the user is directed to the next page in the flow. If the response contains validation errors, they are displayed to the user for correction and re-submission of the request. This communication protocol, which is very similar to the HTTP request / response protocol, provides a good starting point to model some conceptual transaction data classes.

The .NET Framework provides an `HttpRequest` class, the summary of which simply states "enables ASP.NET to read the HTTP values sent by a client during a Web request." It is pretty clear that you're going to need something similar to allow the components in the application to get the values entered by the user on the page. For the moment, let's call this conceptual class `TransactionRequest` and say that it "enables components to get the values sent by a client during a Web request." Similarly, the .NET Framework provides an `HttpResponse` class, which "encapsulates HTTP-response information from an ASP.NET operation." Again, you can reuse this concept and include a conceptual `TransactionResponse` in the design to "encapsulate transaction response information from an application operation." Finally, the .NET Framework's `HttpContext` class "encapsulates all HTTP-specific information about an individual HTTP request." As with the other two classes, you can earmark a conceptual `TransactionContext` class that, for the purposes of the case study, "encapsulates all transaction-specific information about an individual transaction request." This provides you with a handy placeholder to include additional information, such as the date and time the request was created, the date and time the response was delivered, and so forth.

Looking for similarities with other technologies and concepts is a very good thing. You've now got three high-level placeholder classes for all communications within the system. At this point, don't distract yourself by working out exactly what information these classes will contain. As you walk through the individual transactions, you'll see what inputs and outputs are required. That said, you can see that you will require an overall transaction context, which wraps the request and response. You can also add to this during the patterns and practices sections.

For the time being, I'll put a stake in the ground and highlight some information that these classes need to contain:

❑ **TransactionResponse** — The transaction response needs to contain the following information so that the web pages can perform the appropriate processing:

❑ **The overall status or success indicator of the transaction** — The web page uses this information to determine the next action to take (for example, to display validation errors or to display the overall transaction outcome).

❑ **The transaction summary message identifier** — This would be the identifier of either the Confirmation Message, such as MSG-002, or the Invalid Operation message, such as IOM-002-01.

❑ **The transaction summary message itself** — This is the actual Confirmation message — for example, "Your account has been successfully activated and is ready for use." Or it would be the Invalid Operation message, such as "Account Already Activated."

❑ **In the event that there are validation errors, the transaction response also needs to contain these** — Each validation error needs to contain the name of the field that failed validation. This is required so that the web page can display the validation error in the appropriate place. It should also contain the validation error message identifier, such as VEM-001-01, as well as the validation error message, such as "Username hasn't been specified." This allows the web page to identify the field that has been incorrectly entered and display the appropriate validation error message.

❑ **Some transactions will also need the account information entered into or extracted from the database** — For instance, some transactions need to display account information to the user, such as in Update Account. In order to display the information correctly, it will also need to be in plain text (i.e., decrypted), where necessary. There are certain fields that can't be decrypted, as they only contain a hash value for comparison purposes. However, these are not used during update account.

❑ **TransactionRequest** — The transaction request will clearly need to contain all the fields entered by the user. There are many transactions within the system and some of them are multiple-step processes. The next chapter goes through the individual transactions in more detail to flesh out some of the finer details and specifics.

❑ **TransactionContext** — The transaction context wraps the request and response classes into a single transaction envelope. As mentioned previously, it provides you with a placeholder for other types of information, including but not limited to:

❑ The transaction being performed, such as CreateNewAccount, ActivateAccount, and so forth, although this information can equally be stored in the `TransactionRequest` class.

❑ The date and time the request was created, submitted, processed, and so on. As the transaction flows through the system, it can be stamped by each component.

You'll find that you need more information, so it is best not to define these things too rigidly right now. Plus, you don't want to get too bogged down in the detail when you're focusing on the conceptual level. The detail will come later. For now, you know you need this type of information, so it is good enough to continue on this basis. As these classes are seemingly "data-only," they typically reside in the "data entities" layer.

The Presentation Tier

The web pages are responsible for capturing the user's input and calling a web service to initiate the business processing chain. Let's look first at the conceptual web page layout, the starting point for all user journeys through the user interface.

Figure 14-7 shows the conceptual layout of the Create New Account page, with various annotations.

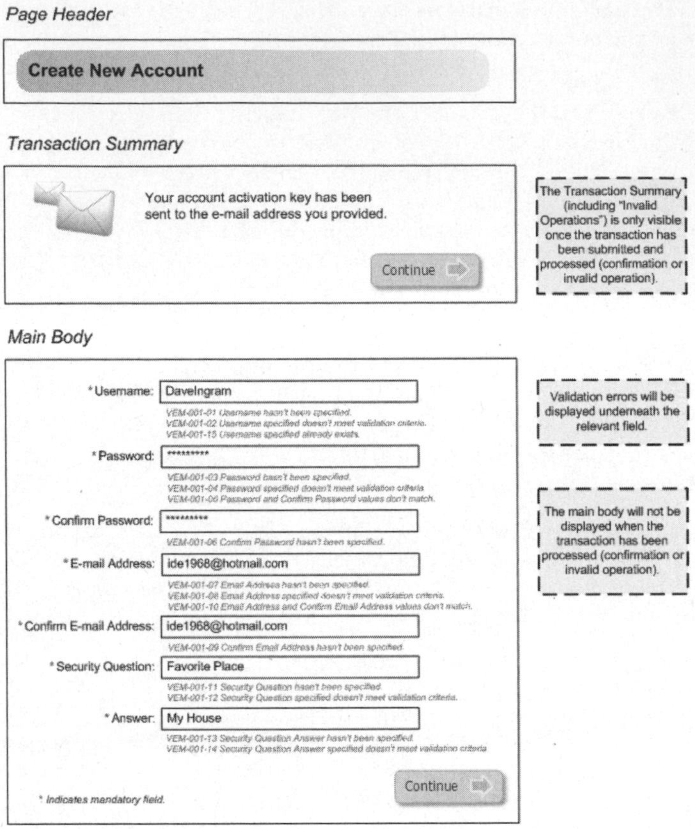

Page Header

Create New Account

Transaction Summary

Your account activation key has been
sent to the e-mail address you provided.

Continue ➡

The Transaction Summary
(including "Invalid
Operations") is only visible
once the transaction has
been submitted and
processed (confirmation or
invalid operation).

Main Body

* Username: DaveIngram

VEM-001-01 Username hasn't been specified.
VEM-001-02 Username specified doesn't meet validation criteria.
VEM-001-15 Username specified already exists.

* Password: ⁕⁕⁕⁕⁕⁕⁕⁕⁕

VEM-001-03 Password hasn't been specified.
VEM-001-04 Password specified doesn't meet validation criteria
VEM-001-05 Password and Confirm Password values don't match.

* Confirm Password: ⁕⁕⁕⁕⁕⁕⁕⁕⁕

VEM-001-06 Confirm Password hasn't been specified.

* E-mail Address: ide1968@hotmail.com

VEM-001-07 Email Address hasn't been specified.
VEM-001-08 Email Address specified doesn't meet validation criteria.
VEM-001-10 Email Address and Confirm Email Address values don't match.

* Confirm E-mail Address: ide1968@hotmail.com

VEM-001-09 Confirm Email Address hasn't been specified.

* Security Question: Favorite Place

VEM-001-11 Security Question hasn't been specified.
VEM-001-12 Security Question specified doesn't meet validation criteria.

* Answer: My House

VEM-001-13 Security Question Answer hasn't been specified.
VEM-001-14 Security Question Answer specified doesn't meet validation criteria

* Indicates mandatory field.

Continue ➡

Validation errors will be
displayed underneath the
relevant field.

The main body will not be
displayed when the
transaction has been
processed (confirmation or
invalid operation).

Figure 14-7

The page is split into three individual panes: Page Header, Transaction Summary, and Main Body. The main reason for this approach is that it is going to be easier to control the flow and avoids redirecting the browser to a separate message page. You can use common controls to avoid each page duplicating the Page Header and Transaction Summary panes. Furthermore, you can also use base classes, which every web page would inherit from. These base classes would encapsulate common functionality, which is also in keeping with the modular approach, and they would reside in the web framework layer. At this point, let's simply earmark a single `PageBase` class.

Figure 14-8 shows the web page's call down to the web services and the conceptual processing pattern. All the web pages in the solution will follow a similar pattern.

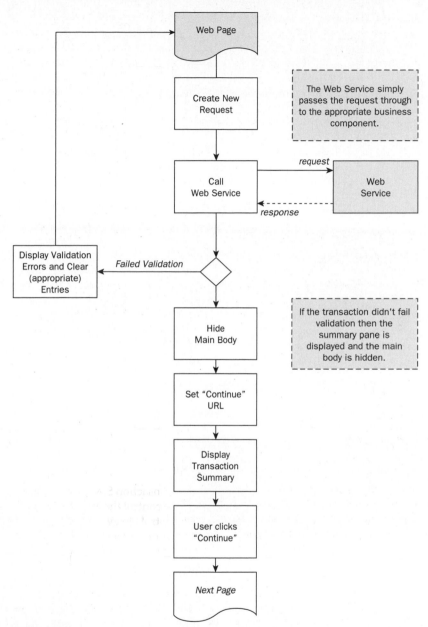

Figure 14-8

Again, these simple steps provide some useful placeholders to fill in while moving forward. Although I'm not discussing the details, I'm providing you with a series of discrete tasks that you can flesh out later. As you progress through the patterns and practices you'll see more information regarding the flow of events from the browser when the user requests a page. You'll recall from earlier chapters that defining the scope is clearly an important part of the project. In the same way that the underlying architecture is layered, so is the overall design process. At this point, you're not attempting to resolve everything. You're simply trying to gain a holistic view of the conceptual architecture that you can build on. For instance, the actual parameters passed to the web service and the return values/output can be fine-tuned at a later stage in the design process. For the moment, you know that you need to pass in a request and get a response back. You've already looked at some of the classes that you need to support this.

One of the most interesting steps in this overall flow is the Set Continue URL step. This is one area where the user interface processing blurs with the business processing. The use cases and storyboards show which pages come next. It is possible that this information is included within the `TransactionResponse`. However, it would need to be populated by the business-processing components. A change in the User Interface flow then impacts business components, as well as their potential reuse. In this instance, it is usually better to separate this logic and delegate the functionality to a web framework component, rather than tying user interface movements into the business-processing layer, which fits with the *Model-View-Controller* (MVC) pattern. The business rules, in this instance, determine the next possible business process (or processes) based on the outcome of the overall transaction. The controller then maps these possible processes to individual web flows or pages. Therefore, it is important that the outcome (from the business-processing layer) can be distinguished appropriately to support the necessary page transitions. This is yet another area where rule-based processing can be employed, rather than embedding the decision within the code.

The Web Service Façade

Traditionally, the application servers host application components, which are invoked via some form of *remoting* or *remote procedure* calls from the web servers. More and more organizations are moving over to web service-based application components to adopt a more service orientated architecture (SOA). Web services can be used to "wrap" existing application components and expose them to the outside world via HTTP (or HTTPS).

The web servers have no direct access to either the application servers or the database servers for security purposes. Communication between the web servers, application servers, and database servers can be locked down at the network level to protect the system from being breached. These restrictions need to be born in mind when designing the application foundations.

The web services will act as a conduit through to the business components. In this scenario, they will not actually be performing any formal business processing. I've chosen this approach to keep all the business processing within the actual business components themselves. This model has the benefit of supporting both web services and the traditional *connection* to the business-processing components. For example, the business components can be deployed to any server and other components, such as batch, or even an Admin user interface can make use of them without having to go through the web service layer. This retains the business logic and business processing consistently across the application, irrespective of the communication protocol.

You can use a single web service to act as a conduit to all the business components. In keeping with the modular guiding principle, I've broken them up into discrete processing groups. The following provides an overview of the individual web services:

❑ **The Registration service** — The Registration service will be used for creating new accounts. It will be called by the Create New Account page.

❑ **The Activation service** — The Activation service will be used for account activation and account Activation Key re-request processing. It will be called from the Activate My Account page.

❑ **The Authentication service** — The Authentication service will be used for authentication, login, and logout processing. It will be called from the Welcome Page (Login), the Change Password (Authentication) page, and the My Account page (Logout).

❑ **The Account Management service** — The Account Management service will be used for account updates, password changes, and account closure. It will be called from the Update My Account page, the Change Password page, and the Close My Account page.

I've chosen this approach simply to break up the architecture and because it also models a much larger application, which is good for demonstrating the basic concepts.

Figure 14-9 shows how the web pages map to the web services and how the web services map to the business managers.

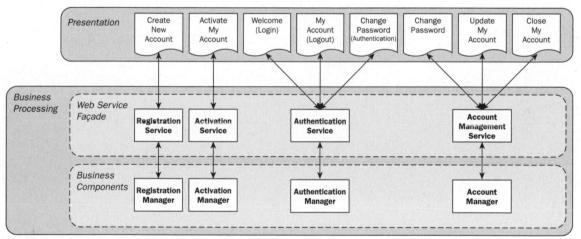

Figure 14-9

The web services and web pages are somewhat aligned according to their functionality. It is really quite an easy way to break it up. Of course, there are many ways this could be done, but this way just seems a reasonable approach for the purposes of this book. The principle is to look for patterns and try to break things up in a modular way. Figure 14-10 shows the web service conceptual processing.

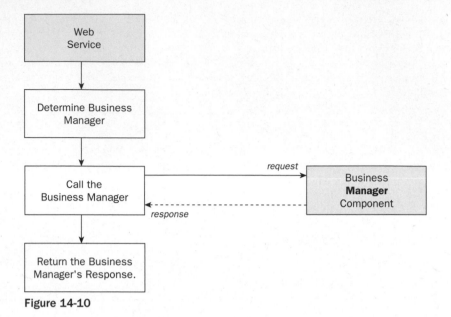

Figure 14-10

You can see from Figure 14-10 that the web service processing is very lightweight. The first step in the processing is to determine the appropriate business manager component to call. The web services are mapped directly to the business managers, as shown in Figure 14-9. In a one-to-one mapping, this step is simply instantiating the business manager component. The web service then simply passes the original request to the business manager and returns its response back to the web page. Simple patterns like this can highlight areas where you can use rule-based processing, instead of having multiple classes all performing similar functionality. If the code-base isn't really changing and only the values are different, this is a good indication for consolidation and rule-based processing through configuration. This actually highlights the possibility of a single web service code-base and using configuration to provide the mapping. Using an approach like this allows you to map the web services to business managers in many different ways. Again, you don't need to determine how this will work right now. There's a placeholder for the "determine business manager" step, which you can flesh out later. For the moment, stick with the current one-to-one mapping as an initial starting position.

The Business Processing Components

The business-processing components encapsulate all the business logic and functional components (including batch). The business-processing layer is used by the web services, batch processes, and possibly other external consumers (as required). This section takes a closer look at the components within the business-processing tier.

The Business Components

The web services call down to the core business-logic components that actually perform the required functionality. You've seen how the web pages relate to the web services and how the web services relate to the business managers. This section looks at the business managers and the business processes.

I prefer the methods in the business-logic layer to mirror actual functional scenarios and actions rather than a straight object-orientated design. I tend to design business components so that they mirror the user or functional journeys, rather than having a single component perform every task. For example, in this application, it would be possible to have a single Membership or Account component that encapsulated all the relevant functionality for creating new accounts, activating accounts, updating account details, and so forth. This would make for a fairly large component and, in most cases, restrict its development and testing to a single individual. In a very large system this functionality could simply form part of the overall solution. With respect to the case study, it is the main part of the solution, so it has been broken up according to the guiding principles. I am simply not a fan of overly large objects. From a logical design point of view, large objects can make sense. From a practical implementation point of view they don't.

Splitting the functionality across a variety of components allows development parallelism within a project, which typically results in shorter delivery timescales. The business logic components can also be used by batch components. If the batch components were making HTTP/HTTPS requests to web services, it would have a dramatic effect on their overall performance and, in some cases, affect their functionality. For example, a batch process can be making a web service call that can be directed to any application server, and the batch functionality can be specific to the server that the job resides on. To avoid this situation, the batch processes (and any other components) can make use of the base business-logic components.

The user interface and the batch jobs are typically the trigger for the business process to happen. In my opinion, the business logic should encapsulate the end-to-end functionality and perform all the necessary tasks. The business components can use the business framework components to provide additional processing, but the business component controls the overall flow of execution. The business logic can be thought of as "orchestration," which is why I tend to call the core business-processing components *business processors*. In front of the core processing components is a thin layer of business managers. These are responsible for validating a request prior to passing it to a processing component. Splitting the functionality like this is quite useful for batch processes or other "trusted" components and systems. The "trusted" sources can use the business processes and bypass validation, which improves their performance, although this needs to be managed carefully. The core field-level validation and functional validation can be performed by the business-processing components to ensure consistency across the application, if required. You could simply collapse everything into a single component but this would also need to be considered carefully. It is important to remember that this is a conceptual design and nothing is really cast in stone.

The business-processing logic will be broken up in a similar way to that of the web services, as shown in Figure 14-11.

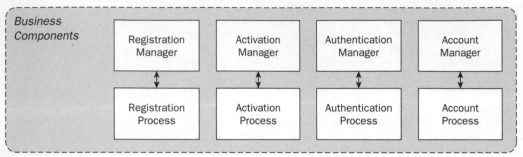

Figure 14-11

The figure shows a series of four business manager components aligned with the business processing components–registration manager, activation manager, authentication manager, and account manager. It is these components that are responsible for validating the request. Underneath each business manager there's an associated business process component that is responsible for processing the actual request.

The Business Manager Components

The business managers are solely responsible for validating a request before passing it on to a business-processing component. If there are any validation failures they will pass these back to the web service, which in turn will pass them back to the web page for display. I've already mentioned that the web pages require a populated `TransactionContext` object, so I won't cover this ground again. And the previous chapter discussed the validation error messages, so I won't list those again, either. Figure 14-12 shows the business manager's conceptual main processing pattern.

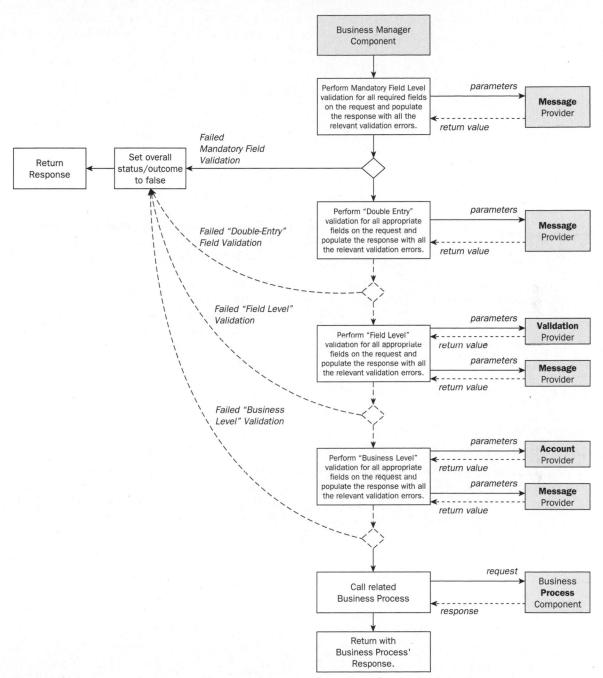

Figure 14-12

It depends on the actual business manager as to exactly what validation is performed. Almost all business managers will need to perform mandatory field validation. In keeping with the modular design principle, the business manager will check if the field has been specified and if not, it will obtain the relevant validation error message via a `MessageProvider` business framework component. At this point, you needn't be concerned with where the messages are kept or even how `MessageProvider` will obtain them; you just know that you need a component to perform this functionality.

Some business managers will need to validate "double entry" fields. These include Create New Account and Change Password. This is very simple processing and can be performed directly by the business manager itself by comparing the values and again, obtaining the validation error message from the `MessageProvider` when required.

Field-level validation, on the other hand, is better delegated to another framework component — in this instance, the `ValidationProvider` which will reside in the business framework. It will be the responsibility of this component to validate a given field against its appropriate field level validation rules. The business manager will use the `ValidationProvider` to validate the necessary fields. In the event that the validation fails, the business manager will obtain the appropriate validation error message using the `MessageProvider`.

Finally, some business managers are required to perform "business-level" validation, such as ensuring that an account doesn't already exist with the same name. I've specified an `AccountProvider` component in Figure 14-12 which the business manager can use to determine whether an account exists or not. The business manager will obtain the appropriate validation error message using the `MessageProvider` in the event of a validation failure.

It is important to remember that these patterns are high-level and conceptual. The blanks will be filled in as the project progresses. You do know that you'll need components such as those highlighted, and you want to try to build up a high-level component model that you can then take down to the next level later.

The Business-Processing Components

You can probably see from my personal design approach that I have a tendency to push processing down as far as it can go. I like the term "orchestration" because the business processing components are rather like a conductor in an orchestra. The musicians actually play the instruments, while the conductor controls the overall piece. To this end, I design business-processing components that are somewhat lightweight and follow a similar pattern to the following:

```
Call a framework component to do some processing
If the outcome is a failure
  Update Response
  Exit accordingly (cleaning up objects and state)
End If

Call a framework component to do some processing
If the outcome is a failure
  Update Response
  Exit accordingly (cleaning up objects and state)
End If
```

```
[Repeat above cycle until complete]

Cleanup objects and state

Update Response and return
```

I much prefer more manageable components that group related functionality. Some of the business components in the case study provide a variety of functionality, although the process components are really nothing more than the conductor. The business framework components are the musicians; the infrastructure, the instruments.

I like this approach because it provides a totally reusable base and avoids all the tedious situations where a different process needs to perform some similar functionality but the code is all tied up in one place and needs to be split out or worse surrounded by lots of `if...else` statements. That is not to say that the business logic is a direct one-to-one mapping, but separating the functionality makes for discrete processing components that can often be reused more readily. Of course, this clearly depends on the situation at hand.

The core difference between business-processing components and framework components is that the business-processing components include additional business-level processing and diagnostics. For instance, although the framework component can record in the database the number of authentication failures, which might not be a bad thing, it would mean that the framework component couldn't be reused without taking everything else with it. If all the business functionality is required, the business component should be reused instead. If straight authentication is required, the framework component should be reused.

This approach increases the number of components in the overall solution, which should be considered carefully. Each layer simply becomes a higher level "wrapper" of the overall processing functionality. That said, my personal rule of thumb is the smaller the unit, the quicker and easier it is to develop, implement, and signoff. Grouping the functionality also means that the developer responsible for the component is also aware of other areas of functionality and can incorporate reuse within the component itself, such as defining base classes and common functionality. This helps to reduce the overall complexity of the solution and benefits application maintenance.

Given the variety of processing, it is not possible to "patternize" the business processor's conceptual processing (apart from the pseudo code example). Although each business process will differ, there will be areas of commonality between their processing and functionality. For instance, the use cases outline a number of situations where the business processes are required to "update the database and enqueue an e-mail request" (for example, Create New Account, Re-Request Activation Key, and Close Account). These actions should be conducted under a single transaction to ensure consistency. Figure 14-13 shows this, using Create New Account as an example.

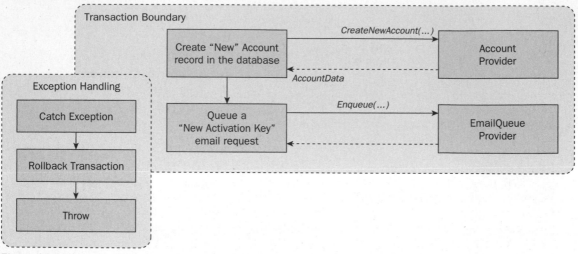

Figure 14-13

This is an interesting situation. You know that both providers are storing the information in the database, in this example, although, this may not always be the case. In the future, the e-mail queue could use a real messaging and queuing system. Or perhaps the records could be stored in a completely separate database. Supporting this functionality involves using a "distributed transaction" and a two-phase commit mechanism. This is just another part of the overall transaction orchestration; so again, you don't need to overly concern yourself with the final semantics of transaction co-ordination at this point. You are simply highlighting these areas for further discussion and clarification.

The Business Framework Components

By scanning the use cases, you'll instantly identify a number of framework components that are required by the business processes. This is a good way to start, as the use cases often provide good indications of high-level components and component groups. Most object-oriented methods look for verbs and nouns within the use cases to highlight the various classes and methods. The following table maps the use-case statements to their required framework components:

Use-Case Statements	Framework Object Required
The system checks that all mandatory information has been specified and that each element is valid and correct according to its individual validation rules.	The business manager components are performing all the validation, as discussed. The `ValidationProvider` framework component will be used to validate the individual fields according to their validation rules.

Use-Case Statements	Framework Object Required
The system checks that an account doesn't already exist with the username specified.	The account data will be stored in the `Account` table in the database. All data access is clearly going to go through the data access layer. Given the nature of the system, it is a good idea to put a bridge between the business components and the data access layer to provide value-added services, such as encrypting values on the way in and decrypting them on the way out. This component will be referred to as the `AccountProvider`, as already highlighted. The primary data entity in this case will be `AccountData`, and the data access component will be `AccountDataAccess`.
The system encrypts the information supplied according to the individual encryption rules. The system decrypts the e-mail address, security question, and security question answer data elements.	This requires a `CryptographyProvider` to encrypt the data elements. You know from the requirements that this needs to encrypt one-way and two-way values, and decrypt two-way encrypted values. Cryptography is quite a low-level function and this component might be best placed in the system framework. There's no reason why higher level framework components can't add additional value.
The system generates a unique account Activation Key that will be associated with the account.	This will require some form of `ActivationKeyProvider`. You know from the requirements that this needs to generate a GUID or equivalent value.
The system "queues" a request for an "Ativation Key e-mail" to be sent to the user's e-mail address, and records the date and time the request was made.	This is going to need an `EmailQueueProvider` to enqueue e-mail requests. The e-mail queue will reside in the database and will need a data entity as well as a data access component. These will be `EmailQueueData` and `EmailQueueDataAccess`, respectively,
The system creates the account record in the database with a state of "New" and records the date and time the account was created.	The data access has already been captured. The common application framework will include the `CalendarProvider` component.

This quick and simple approach really helps to identify key components. As you progress, you can flush these out in more detail. The more detailed your use cases are, the more components that you can identify from them.

The Batch Processes

The requirements essentially specified the following six functional batch processes for the solution:

1. Sending new account Activation Key e-mails.

2. Re-sending existing account Activation Key e-mails.

3. Sending account closure confirmation e-mails.

4. Flagging new accounts that haven't been activated within a specified period of time ("aged").

5. Removing aged or flagged accounts after a specified period of time.

6. Removing closed accounts after a specified period of time.

It is pretty clear from the preceding list that the functional batch processes naturally break down into two separate groups of similar functionality.

One set of jobs is required to compose and send e-mails. These jobs will essentially process messages in the e-mail queue, mentioned previously. They will need to dequeue e-mail requests using the `EmailQueueProvider`. The `SolicitedEmailProvider` framework component will be responsible for actually composing and sending the e-mails.

The other group of jobs is concerned with specific account clean-up and additional maintenance activities. These jobs will essentially process records in the `Account` table and use the `AccountProvider` framework component for various operations.

In both cases, the jobs need to select a series of records from the database that meet a specified set of criteria and perform a specific set of actions on each record. The case study will split the functionality between the manager components and the processing components in the following way:

❑ The manager components will be responsible for obtaining the appropriate work items and delegating the processing of an individual work item (or batch of work items) to a processing component. The manager will also be responsible for maintaining the overall status of the job so that it can be reported to the outside world.

❑ The processing components will perform the actual functional batch processing on the individual work item or batch of work items (using framework components where necessary).

We'll talk about bulk processing in Chapter 16 which is very often employed in batch processing for performance purposes. It is important that batch processes are quick and efficient. This grouping means that similar patterns and base classes can be used for each of the jobs and groups to limit the amount of specific code required in any single job. For instance, Figure 14-14 shows the conceptual processing for a `SolicitedEmail` batch manager.

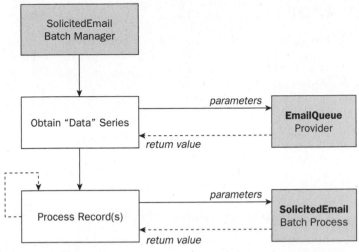

Figure 14-14

Although the figure doesn't show all the detailed steps, it again highlights an area where rule-based processing can be employed to reduce the overall batch code-base. Similarly, the conceptual processing for a SolicitedEmail batch process would look something like that shown in Figure 14-15.

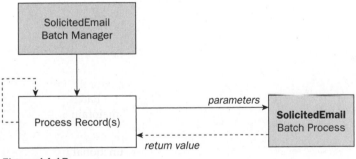

Figure 14-15

Again, this looks like a good candidate for consolidation. However, before attempting to consolidate the functionality of the different types of components, it is best to look at each of the individual jobs and groups to map their specific functionality to the different components and layers. Chapters 15 and 20 look at the batch jobs in more detail.

At this point, you are not going to concern yourself too much with how the batch processes are triggered and controlled — for example, whether they are triggered by a batch scheduler or executed as services, and so on. Ideally, how the batch processes are actually triggered and executed shouldn't really matter. Layering the batch classes and processes should allow for "execution wrappers" to trigger them in the most appropriate fashion, control the overall execution, and report the status and final outcome. The most important thing right now is to understand what the jobs need to do and how they will do it from a conceptual perspective. You'll look at the triggering and control mechanisms a bit later.

The Logical Data Model and Data Access

Most applications use a database or some type of data store. Maybe one day you will not need to continue to send information to a database or data store, and everything will be held in memory. In the meantime, there is a need to store the data somewhere, and the database is generally the place for it. In physical terms, this architectural layer contains the actual tables, views, and stored procedures, along with any other database-specific elements, such as triggers, functions, configuration files, and security settings that belong to the physical database or databases.

Figure 14-16 shows the sample logical data model.

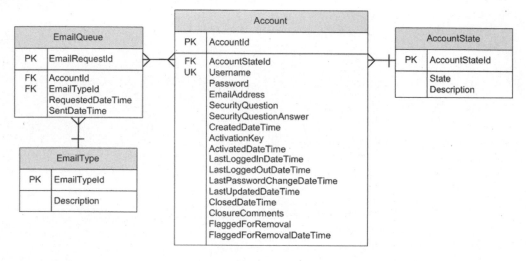

Figure 14-16

I've chosen not to use a prefix or naming convention for the logical data model. This can be applied later, if necessary. The logical data model contains the main Account table and associated tables. At this point it would be a very good idea to compare the logical data model against the requirements outlined in Chapter 13 to ensure that everything has been captured appropriately. While this may seem long-winded, it really does help to ensure that all the requirements have been captured appropriately and corrected where necessary. For the purposes of space and time in the book, we'll not go over all the requirements again. If we were to have done this throughout the chapter then this would be quite a long read. Suffice it to say that you should regularly checkpoint to ensure that all the necessary requirements have been captured and no inconsistencies exist.

The Account table contains two additional columns: `FlaggedForRemoval` and `FlaggedForRemovalDateTime`. These two columns have been added to support the following batch requirement:

❏ **HFR-AGEDACCFR-001** — Accounts that have "aged" should be flagged for removal after a specified period of time in days (for example, "aged account expiry period in days"). "Aged accounts" refers to new accounts that have not been activated within the specified period.

The data model also contains the `EmailQueue` and `EmailType` tables, which were added to support the following high-level requirements:

❏ **HFR-EMAILPROC-001** — The system must ensure that e-mail messages are sent to the user asynchronously to prevent them from being impacted by failures and other issues.

❏ **HFR-CREATEACC-010** — The system must retain the date and time the account Activation Key e-mail was requested.

❏ **HFR-CREATEACC-011** — The system must retain the date and time the account Activation Key e-mail was sent.

❏ **HFR-ACTIVATE-RR-008** — The system must retain the date and time users re-requested their Activation Key.

❏ **HFR-ACTIVATE-RR-009** — The system must retain the date and time the re-requested Activation Key was sent.

There can be many records in this table for a single account. You can use this table to determine the date and time the user re-requested their Activation Key, simply by selecting the last "Re-request Activation Key" record for the account. You can also obtain the number of times they have re-requested their Key. It is important to ensure that the design meets the requirements, but it is also important to ensure that it is understood how the design meets the requirements.

Data Entities

The data entity "layer" encapsulates the pure data-only classes that resemble entities within the database. The data entity components do not implement any business logic at all, including validation. These are sometimes referred to as *model classes*.

The data entity classes simply expose a set of *getter* and *setter* properties that resemble a logical entity — for example, an account or an e-mail message. The application uses the data entity classes to get or set the appropriate property values. As you can see, data entities are not just modeled on the database content.

The data entity classes provide a consistent way of transporting the raw data through the application layers, without having to worry about their physical storage or layout. The data entities are serialized for lightweight transport across the network. They are a logical representation of an entity, and keeping the business logic separate from the entity itself typically simplifies the solution. For example, if you were to assume that the "username" property was validated every time it was set on the data entity, the data entity class would need to use a business logic component to perform the validation, or it would need to do it itself. This could cause dramatic performance overheads, or even functional issues for the application if the data entity didn't cache or pool data and other components in a completely consistent fashion.

I prefer to control the system's behavior consistently by using business and framework components that operate on simple data entity classes, although this is clearly another design choice. This design pattern also means that the data entity classes can be generated easily from the database or any other structure.

A data entity based on the data model doesn't have to be a single table, either. It could, and often does, resemble any structure that is commonly used in the application. A lot of applications use *model* components for data entry screens. The model class allows for easy manipulation. As long as the application components can manipulate the object successfully, it doesn't really matter what they store.

Strictly speaking, the data entity layer is not a layer because the components are often shared across the architecture layers, whereas the term *layering* implies that each layer can access layers below it.

Data Access

The data access layer encapsulates all data access components that manage the interactions and communications between the application framework layers and the physical database or data store. The data access layer simply acts as a *"transport* and *transform"* mechanism between the physical database and the business-processing components. It translates raw information to and from the database using the associated data entities. The data access layer also leverages the value-added features of the system framework layer.

The case study will initially require two data access components based on the tables in the data model:

❑ **Account Data Access** — This component will be responsible for managing interactions between the components and the Account table.

❑ **Email Queue Data Access** — This component will be responsible for managing interactions between the components and the EmailQueue table.

Access to the database will be provided through a `DataAccessProvider` component to ensure a consistent interface and approach to data access. This component is also placed in the data access framework.

The Reporting Components

The reporting system typically accesses the database directly through views, stored procedures, and dynamic queries. Under a custom reporting solution, it would be a good idea to use the components in the other layers in the architecture. Most implementations these days use an off-the-shelf reporting product of some description because of the advances in reporting applications and the sophisticated features they offer. These reporting applications introduce an additional layer of complexity and learning curve, but the costs of using them typically outweigh the costs of developing a custom solution.

I also mentioned previously that reports are sometimes executed against a replicated version of the data store. The reporting components (stored procedures, views, and queries) can also be used for incident investigation, which in most cases would be executed against the live database in the event of a live priority issue. I'll discuss these in more detail in the next chapter.

The requirements specified that the solution should use the following business reports:

❑ New Accounts

❑ Activated Accounts

❑ Average Activation Time

❑ Aged Accounts

❑ Closed Accounts

The reporting components in this instance are nothing more than a set of stored procedures with queries that will be executed against the database. The stored procedures will provide the basic selection of information for the reports to be produced.

Logical Component Model

Figure 14-17 shows the first pass of the component model based on the information discussed in this chapter.

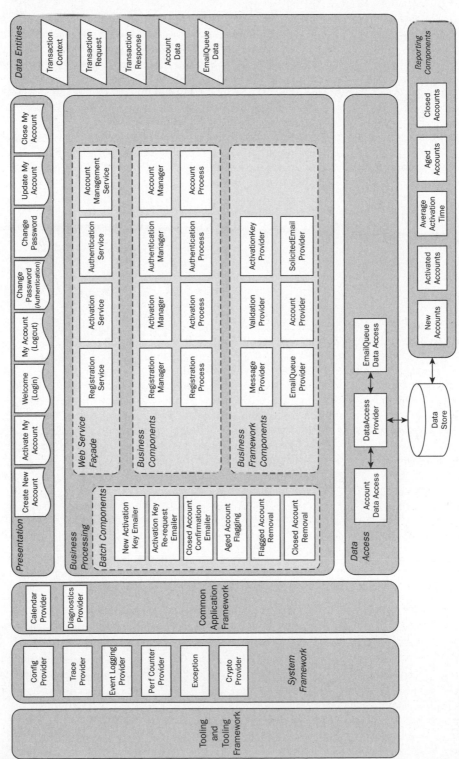

Figure 14-17

The figure doesn't show all the framework components, such as the web framework or the batch framework, but it captures all the high-level components discussed so far. You have a fair idea of what these need to do and which parameters and return values they should support. Ideally, you'd list out all the components and pull together the high-level component specifications for each of them. The high-level specifications actually provide the basis of the XML comments for the components. Once you're in a position to generate the documentation from the code, you could drop the original specs in favor of the generated documents. For the purposes of space and time, this will not be performed here.

As you can see from the logical component model, the architecture has been broken up considerably and has introduced a wide variety of different components and types. Although this might seem over-the-top for such a simple application, it demonstrates the *method* rather than the *result*. Only by performing these types of exercises can you gauge the true scope of the project.

The logical component model is another diagram that will be frequently referred to throughout the project, so it should contain as many components as possible. This can create a very large diagram, so breaking it up can help readability.

Summary

This chapter looked at how the architecture from such a simple application can be broken down into multiple layers and moving parts. It also identified a whole host of potential components for the solution. I can't reiterate enough the messages in the earlier chapters regarding scope, budgets, and timescales. The previous chapter started off with a simple statement membership system. Through the process of extrapolation and extension, the component model has grown considerably (and it doesn't include base classes, web controls, stored procedures, tables, or views). The number of components gets even bigger if you start to add in unit tests, integration tests, stubs and simulators, configuration, and batch-execution frameworks. As the book progresses, you'll see that applying the patterns and practices to the solution will extend the scope even further. You started with some simple guiding principles, which have truly expanded, and created a good number of components.

The following are the key points to take away from this chapter:

❑ **Have an architecture.** You should always ensure that you have a solid architecture to build upon. Producing a conceptual architecture design helps to layer the solution appropriately.

❑ **Keep the architecture modular.** You should separate components into discrete layers and include frameworks that can add value. Although this increases the number of components, it simplifies the design of each layer and promotes reuse across the solution components.

❑ **Capture the components.** The purpose of the conceptual architecture is to capture the components. What may seem like a simple solution can actually involve a lot more components than you first think. The more components that you can identify, the more you have to carry forward.

❑ **Highlight the processing patterns.** Walking through the design and the architecture will help you to draw out processing patterns which can be used as templates and frameworks. The patterns can also be used to include data-driven approaches to reduce the number of physical components.

❑ **Design is iterative.** If you were thinking that this chapter has raised as many questions as it has answered (or possibly even more), you'd be right. The true purpose of design is to flush out all these questions so that you can capture and deal with them appropriately. Starting with a conceptual design helps to define the next set of activities.

❑ **Question the design.** Design by its very nature invites debate and a collective vision. Better to have design discussions up front than to find yourself potentially re-factoring many components at great cost. Although you might disagree with certain elements of the conceptual design presented, as previously mentioned, this is for the purpose of the studying the process and demonstrating the method, not the result.

❑ **Log your design queries.** Again, if you were truly going by the book, you would have logged all your queries and questions along the way. This would form the basis of your design log, which you could take forward to the next set of activities.

❑ **Check the requirements.** It is important that you regularly check that the requirements have been captured in the design and the design shows how it meets the requirements.

The next chapter takes some of these conceptual components further to draw out additional high-level processing steps, inputs, outputs, and transaction boundaries.

15

Modeling the Application

The previous chapter laid down some of the foundations for the case study. It also discussed the overall conceptual architecture and high-level components. This chapter examines application-specific processing and the responsibilities of each component. The storyboards and the use cases in Chapter 13 provided the low-resolution page layouts and the overall flow. This chapter uses this information, especially the use-case steps, the requirements, and the logical component model, to essentially connect the dots. The previous chapter also highlighted some conceptual processing patterns for web pages, web services, and the manager components.

This chapter focuses on the underlying processing and orchestration. However, in doing so, I'll highlight areas that need to be considered higher up in the processing stack and, of course, lower down. The objective is to solidify some of the methods, inputs, outputs, transaction boundaries, and any other items that will provide additional placeholders for further design and discussion. As you progress through the processing, you'll see how the processing components interact with the provider components, which will help to flesh out some of their methods, too. Conversely, the methods on the processors will provide the methods for the managers and the web services. You know that the `TransactionContext` entity class will be initially populated by the web pages and passed down through the components to the processors, and that it contains the `TransactionRequest` and `TransactionResponse` entity classes. So, you just need to identify the individual methods on the components and document the processing. Although you may already have a pretty good idea from what you've already seen, it is best to put some of it down "on paper" before diving into the code.

This chapter is organized into the following sections:

❑ **Component Responsibility Modeling** — This section presents the *responsibility diagram*, which maps the steps documented in the use cases to high-level components in the logical component model. The diagram (or process) enables you to visualize the processing steps before formally applying them to classes and methods. It helps to solidify the component responsibilities and their inputs and outputs. It also provides a good basis for further design, review, and agreement prior to heading into full component design. This section walks through the core transactions in the case study and pulls out areas for discussion and interest.

❏ **Web Page Processing** — This section uses the information (inputs and outputs) gathered in the previous section to capture and highlight the key web page processing areas. These primarily include state management, page transitions, and access control.

❏ **Business Processing** — The basic responsibility models identify the key methods, inputs, outputs, and processing steps that the components will perform.

❏ **Batch Processing** — This section looks at the individual batch jobs and batch processing.

❏ **Reports** — This section looks at the individual reporting components.

Component Responsibility Modeling

The previous chapter looked at the high-level transaction flow, showing the web page, web service, business-processing manager, and the business processor. It included placeholders for the specific functionality that each component performs. Before starting to define classes, methods, parameters, and return values, it is a good idea to go through a very basic modeling exercise to highlight any gaps and/or potential inconsistencies. It will also help to solidify some architectural decisions and further patterns.

I quite like things to be simple. Before diving into a full-on modeling tool, it is amazing what you can do with a simple table and a set of use-case steps. The idea is to draw a simple table that contains each of the component types in a row, as shown in Figure 15-1

Web Page	Manager	Process	Provider...	Provider...

Figure 15-1

Note that Figure 15-1 omits the web services, as they are simply pass-through components and take up unnecessary space. If they were performing activities and processing, they would be listed in the table. The web services determine the appropriate business manager to forward the request to and do not need to be included in the tables at this point.

The next task is simply to place the steps listed in the use cases under the components that are going to be responsible for the step. Figure 15-2 shows a sample of this for the Create New Account flow. In this example I've also included the additional processing that would be performed by the components.

Create New Account Page	Registration Manager	Registration Process	AccountProvider	EmailQueueProvider
1) The "Creat New Account" page is diplayed and all fields are enabled and blank.				
2) The user completes the form by entering their Username, Password, Confirm Password, E-mail Address, Confirm E-mail Address, Security Question and Security Question Answer and clicks "Continue".				
The Web Page creates the TransactionContext and populates the TransactionRequest.				
CreateNewAccount →	3) The system checks that all mandatory information has been specified and that each element is valid and correct according to its individual validation rules.			
	4) The system checks that an account doesn't already exist with the Username specified.			
	CreateNewAccount →	5) The system generates a unique "Account Activation Key" which will be associated with the account.		
		BeginTransaction		
		Create →	6) The system encrypts the information supplied according to the individual encryption rules.	
			7) The system creates the account record in the database with a state of "New" and records the date and time the account was created.	
		Enqueue →		8) The system "queues" a request for an "Activation Key Email" to be sent to the user's email address and records the date and time the request was made.
		EndTransaction		
		Populate and Return Response		
	Populate and Return Response			
9) The system displays the "Activation Key Sent" confirmation message and "Continue" button.				
10) On clicking the "Continue" button the user is directed to the "Activate Account" Page.				

Figure 15-2

The diagram looks somewhat like an abridged wire-frame sequence diagram, which in fact it is. You can see in an instant which components are responsible for implementing the individual processing steps. I've dotted the use-case steps into the cells and included some sample method names for discussion. The figure shows some activities that are not explicitly listed in the use case, such as populating the request, and populating and returning the response. It also shows the transaction boundaries that need to be considered.

You can finalize the exact technical processing behind each step later, when you're happy with what each component type is going to perform. For instance, in Step 4 the registration manager is responsible for checking that an account doesn't already exist. It is highly likely that this step will make use of the `AccountProvider` framework component. It may also make use of other components in the architecture, and perhaps even highlight additional components.

Although Figure 15-2 is a very simple diagram, it provides the basis for further design and decision-making. It is also very straightforward to read, so it can be discussed with non-technical people on the business team. One of the challenges in the industry is presenting ideas and concepts to non-technical folks. Simple drawings and tables help to present the information more clearly which helps a great deal. While not everyone is technical, they can usually see when something doesn't look or flow as expected.

The previous chapter determined the processing that the web pages and the business managers will perform. The web pages would compile the request, and the managers would be responsible for validation, including business-level validation, as shown in Figure 15-2. The diagram highlights some further queries which are listed here:

❏ For Step 5, the registration process is generating the account Activation Key. However, should the `AccountProvider` generate the account Activation Key instead for encapsulation purposes?

❏ For Step 7, the `AccountProvider` is noted as setting the created date and time on the account record. Should the date and time really be obtained and set by the `AccountProvider`?

❏ Also for Step 7, should the `AccountProvider` set the account's state to new?

The first question looks at whether certain processing should be pushed further down the architecture for encapsulation and isolation purposes. The remaining two questions ask whether processing should be pulled further up the processing chain. This is precisely the purpose of the diagram and modeling the application. It should be used to determine where the best place to perform the processing actually is.

In the first instance, the business processor is providing the transaction orchestration and returning the overall transaction outcome. It generates the account Activation Key and passes it down to the layer below. If the `AccountProvider` was going to be reused by another component (or even application), would the Activation Key functionality be required? Although this application is activating accounts via the Activation Key pattern, another may not. That said, does it really matter that much? The previous chapter explained that the `AccountProvider` should provide encryption and decryption. This avoids all the components and classes having to do it themselves and is a common piece of functionality. It also defines clear boundaries of responsibility and avoids unnecessary complication in the provider. Its job is to encrypt the information and pass it on to the data access layer, and vice versa. If another application (or consumer) wanted to reuse the Activation functionality, it could use the business process instead. Otherwise, it would have to generate its own key. In this instance, it could always make use of the ActivationKeyProvider, as well. These types of decisions depend entirely on the application and situation. However, it is good to model the application in an easy-to-see way and make a decision about how things should work rather than arriving at a solution that hasn't been thought about. The cost of rework would be much greater further down the line.

The second question is quite interesting. Again, this is really a processing question, so it depends on the application. The allocation and specification of the date and time is quite low down in the system. Let's assume that there was a reasonably large delay between when the user clicked the Continue button and the time at which the account was actually created. An investigation wouldn't highlight this, unless, of course, the transaction was stamped with the date and time it passed through each component. In actual fact, this is a business versus a technical decision. Is the date and time the account was created based upon the user's perspective or the system's? If it is from the user's perspective, it is better to use the date and time that the request hit the web server. If it is from the system, it is fine as it is. However, what would be the impact of changing it later? The web page would need to allocate the date and time and pass this down as part of the request. It also means that the processor needs to be aware of it and that the AccountProvider accepts it. This is in addition to updating all the documentation and diagrams, of course. Under normal operating circumstances, there wouldn't be a big difference between the times. Almost all transactions in the system are recording the date and time at which they occurred, so it makes sense to do this from the user's perspective. If you also consider the reuse angle, it is better to allow the processing to specify the date and time for consistency. Another application or consumer might want to specify the date and time. In this instance, you would change this so that the web page actually allocates the date and time (using the CalendarProvider) and passes it down in the request. So, you would simply move the date and time allocation up a few layers.

Finally, there's the third question of where to set the account state. In this instance, the data access is being "wrapped" with the AccountProvider for two important reasons. The first reason is that it will enable you in the future to generate the data access layer, such as the AccountDataAccess and EmailQueueDataAccess, or perhaps even use something else, such as LINQ. The second reason is so that you have a guaranteed place to perform encryption and decryption in an isolated fashion. The Create method on the AccountProvider would typically encapsulate business related functionality. Whereas the data access components would typically include CRUD (create, read, update, and delete) actions. This decision can be revisited, but the business process should actually set the account state to what's appropriate for the given transaction. There are a number of places in the application where the use-case steps dictate what the account state should be set to. This is a good example of where the steps don't always map to the diagram but need to be split up. For traceability, you need to ensure that all the steps are actually covered off and included.

Walking through this first example solidified some processing rules and areas of responsibility for the individual components. Figure 15-3 shows the updated table based on the decision points discussed.

Create New Account Page	Registration Manager	Registration Process	AccountProvider	EmailQueueProvider
1) The "Create New Account" page is diplayed and all fields are enabled and blank.				
2) The user completes the form by entering their Username, Password, Confirm Password, E-mail Address, Confirm E-mail Address, Security Question and Security Question Answer and clicks "Continue".				
7) The system obtains the current date and time using the CalendarProvider and adds it to the request as Created Date and Time.				
CreateNewAccount	3) The system checks that all mandatory information has been specified and that each element is valid and correct according to its individual validation rules.			
	4) The system checks that an account doesn't already exist with the Username specified.			
	CreateNewAccount	5) The system generates a unique "Account Activation Key" which will be associated with the account.		
		7) The system sets the Account State to "New".		
		BeginTransaction		
		Create	6) The system encrypts the information supplied according to the individual encryption rules.	
			7) The system creates the account record in the database with a state of "New" and records the date and time the account was created.	
		Enqueue		8) The system "queues" a request for an "Activation Key Email" to be sent to the user's email address and records the date and time the request was made.
		EndTransaction		
		Populate and Return Response		
	Populate and Return Response			
9) The system displays the "Activation Key Sent" confirmation message and "Continue" button.				
10) On clicking the "Continue" button the user is directed to the "Activate Account" Page.				

Figure 15-3

As you can see from the diagram, there are now lots of step number 7s. This is because the original use-case statement included a number of processing elements—7. *The system creates the account record in the database with a state of "New" and records the date and time the account was created.* This single statement has been broken up into discrete areas of processing that the individual components would perform. You could label these steps in the diagram with a, b, c, and so forth. However, I've chosen to leave them as-is. The key point is to determine which components will perform what processing. The more discrete the use-case steps are, the easier they align to individual components.

Adding the Inputs and Outputs

Before proceeding it is worth going through a couple of more areas where the table can be used and to help flesh out more design areas and considerations. The first area deals with inputs to the steps, and the second deals with the outputs from them. This involves modeling both the inputs and the outputs through the system components, finishing with the database (albeit without encryption). We looked at this process earlier in this book and we'll do it again here for the Create New Account page. The following table lists some sample inputs for each of the entry fields on the page:

Field	Value
Username	DavidIngram
Password	HelloWorld
Confirm Password	HelloWorld
Email Address	ide1968@hotmail.com
Confirmation Email Address	ide1968@hotmail.com
Security Question	Favorite Place
Security Question Answer	My House

The table contains the information that would be entered on the page. You know that the web page will now allocate the date and time that will also be passed down in the request. You now also know that the business process will allocate the Activation Key and set the state to "New." The purpose of this exercise is to determine whether there is anything else that needs to be taken into account. The following table shows the final version persisted to the database for the preceding transaction.

Field	Value
AccountId	Unique Account Identifier (allocated at the database level)
AccountStateId	Integer value representing the Account State ("New")
Username	DavidIngram
Password	HelloWorld (hash value)
Email Address	ide1968@hotmail.com (encrypted)
Security Question	Favorite Place (encrypted)
Security Question Answer	My House (encrypted)
Created Date Time	DateTime (allocated by the Web page)
Activation Key	GUID (allocated by the business process)

All other fields will be null unless at some stage default values are introduced. In addition to the main Account table, the EmailQueue table is also worth scanning. The following table shows the EmailQueue table's entries:

Field	Value
EmailRequestId	Unique Account Identifier (allocated at the database level).
AccountId	This will need to be passed in when queuing an e-mail request. It also means that it will need to be returned when the account is created.
EmailTypeId	Integer value representing the e-mail type.
RequestedDateTime	This could be allocated by the EmailQueueProvider when the request is queued. Alternatively it could be the same date and time used for the created date and time.
SentDateTime	Null.

This table highlights the fact that the EmailQueue requires the AccountId, which you will need to have returned by the AccountProvider when a new account is created. It is simply worth noting this because it is a critical piece of information that needs to be returned during the creation of a new account. The table also poses another question as to what the requested date and time should be. This is discussed later. These tables can also be used to model the test data and test scenarios end-to-end.

Figure 15-4 shows the table partially completed with inputs and outputs.

Create New Account Page	Registration Manager	Registration Process	AccountProvider	EmailQueueProvider
1) The "Create New Account" page is diplayed and all fields are enabled and blank.				
2) The user completes the form by entering their Username, Password, Confirm Password, E-mail Address, Confirm E-mail Address, Security Question and Security Question Answer and clicks "Continue".				
7) The system obtains the current date and time using the CalendarProvider and adds it to the request as Created Date and Time.				
CreateNewAccount - Username, Password, Confirm Password, E-mail Address, Confirm E-mail Address, Security Question, Security Question Answer, Created Date and Time	3) The system checks that all mandatory information has been specified and that each element is valid and correct according to its individual validation rules.			
	4) The system checks that an account doesn't already exist with the Username specified.			
	CreateNewAccount - Username, Password, E-mail Address, Security Question, Security Question Answer, Created Date and Time	5) The system generates a unique "Account Activation Key" which will be associated with the account.		
		7) The system sets the Account State to "New".		
		BeginTransaction		
		Create - Username, Password, E-mail Address, Security Question, Security Question Answer, Activation Key, Created Date and Time	6) The system encrypts the information supplied according to the individual encryption rules.	
			7) The system creates the account record in the database with a state of "New" and records the date and time the account was created.	
		AccountData		
		Enqueue - Accoutld, EmailType		8) The system "queues" a request for an "Activation Key Email" to be sent to the user's e-mail address and records the date and time the request was made.
		EndTransaction		
		Populate and Return Response		
	Populate and Return Response			
The system caches the Username, Password and Previous Transaction for use by the Activate Account page.				
9) The system displays the "Activation Key Sent" confirmation message and "Continue" button.				
10) On clicking the "Continue" button the user is directed to the "Activate Account" Page.				

Figure 15-4

At this point you're not really looking at the specifics and/or semantics of each of the parameters. You're simply looking at what the components require as inputs and what's required as an output. Of course, if you know them, there is no harm in actually including them. In the previous decision points, you've added to the inputs coming from the Web page, so it was a worthwhile exercise to capture them. You'll also notice that once the transaction has passed through the manager, the Confirm Password and Confirmation Email Address inputs are no longer required. As transactions pass through the layers, it is expected that certain information will not be required for lower-level processing and that additional information may be added for the components being called — for example, the Activation Key.

You can produce input and output tables for each component and layer, which again provides a good basis for test conditions and scenarios.

I've included an AccountData class being returned from the AccountProvider component. The previous chapter explained that the data entity classes typically model the database structure. The AccountData class would model the Account table (and possibly the AccountState table).

The AccountProvider is providing encryption and decryption processing (although this will be achieved by using the CryptographyProvider), as per the discussion in the previous chapter. Therefore, it is reasonable to say that the AccountData class returned can be populated as follows:

- AccountId contains the unique account identifier.

- AccountStateId contains the account state identifier (for example, 1, 2, 3, and so on).

- AccountState (optional) contains the textual representation of the state id (e.g., New, Active, Closed).

- AccountStateDescription (optional) contains the associated description for the account state.

- Username contains the same value as the input.

- Password contains a hash value of the password input. The password is being one-way encrypted and as such can't be returned in any other form.

- EmailAddress contains the same value as the input. While the e-mail address in encrypted for the database, the AccountProvider is providing usable account information to the outside world. It is perfectly possible that this could be done on a case-by-case basis—for instance, when creating a new account the output e-mail address remains encrypted. These diagrams help to flesh out these details and can easily include these annotations.

- SecurityQuestion contains the same value as the input, although the previous discussion would also apply.

- SecurityQuestionAnswer again contains the same value as the input, although the previous discussion would also apply.

❑   CreatedDateTime contains the date and time obtained by the web page and passed through the system to the AccountProvider. The web page obtains the value from the CalendarProvider component (which resides in the common application framework).

❑   ActivationKey contains the account Activation Key generated via the ActivationKeyProvider.

❑   All other fields would typically be null (or possibly default values).

If you follow the flows (and the requirements), there is the requirement—HFR-SECQANSWER-003: The system must ensure that when security question answers need to be compared to those on file, comparison is done using an encrypted form (for example, using two-way encryption on the answer entered and comparing it to the encrypted answer stored on file). In the example above, the value is being returned in decrypted form. Therefore, the application would need to re-encrypt it to meet the comparison requirement. You can see that what seems like a logical choice can affect other areas of the design. In this instance, it would be a good idea to leave the values encrypted (e.g. as they are in the database) and only decrypt them when required.

The use cases are pretty well-defined in this instance. You can see that a lot of the account information isn't actually required for the processing steps, which will become more apparent as we go through the individual flows. Decrypting the information will have an impact on performance, especially when it is not necessary to do so. It might be a good idea to expand on the methods in the AccountProvider to cater for this situation, for example, by including a method such as Get, which would simply return an exact representation of the data in the database. You could add other methods that return only partial account data required for the transaction. In addition, you could include a GetForUpdate method that would return the decrypted information required for the account update process. By encapsulating this functionality into the AccountProvider business framework component, you have the ability to provide a verbose interface to the business processing while encapsulating the encryption and decryption semantics in a single place.

This leads into the next area to consider: where the business process and the business manager simply state "populate and return response." While they will undoubtedly use the MessageProvider to obtain the various messages they require, you need to determine whether these components should populate anything else in the response. The AccountProvider returns an Account data class that can be used to determine what information you want to pass back up the chain in the TransactionResponse (in addition to the overall outcome). You can again do this on a transaction-by-transaction basis (as discussed) to ensure that each transaction has all the information it requires.

When the AccountProvider returns, the system needs to queue an e-mail request. It will do this using the EmailQueueProvider. As per the logical data model, this component requires the AccountId and EmailType fields. Figure 15-4 also captures this important information.

From a user's perspective, the Create New Account process flows into the Activate Account process. The initial use-case steps in the Activate Account process are as follows:

1. The Activate My Account page is displayed and the fields are blank/pre-populated and enabled/disabled according to the route from which they arrived:

   a. **From UC-001 Create New Account** — The Username and Password fields are pre-populated and disabled. The "Yes" Activation Key option is pre-selected and the "No" option is enabled.

   b. **From the Welcome page** — The Username and Password fields and blank and enabled. The "Yes" Activation Key option is pre-selected and the "No" option is disabled.

   c. **From UC-003 Re-Request Activation Key** — The Username and Password fields are pre-populated and disabled. The "Yes" Activation Key option is pre-selected and the "No" option is disabled.

The Create New Account page appears to have everything it needs to cache for the transition to the Activate Account page. Before actually looking at how these transitions will take place, you just need to ensure that you've captured all the information. In this instance we'll use a conceptual transition placeholder that will need to include the following information to support the functionality just mentioned:

❑ Username

❑ Password

❑ Previous Transaction — Including the previous transaction, such as "Create New Account," will allow the Activate Account page to make an informed decision (based on where the user has arrived from) and populate and enable/disable the fields accordingly.

These have been noted on Figure 15-4 to ensure that they are captured appropriately. As you progress, you can build up this placeholder or property bag. Once it is complete, you can look at the different ways of implementing it technically.

Finally, in rounding off this review of the responsibility diagram, the web pages, the business managers, and the processor components would all use other framework components and classes, such as the message provider, cryptography provider, and so forth to help with their processing. The modeling diagram could also include these components to show their interactions. In this instance, I've simplified the diagrams to show the basic concept. Although most seasoned developers and architects might find this exercise quite simplistic, I personally find that it is the way I think (placing high-level processing in boxes and seeing how it fits together). As I mentioned in the previous chapter, the early stages are all about trying to capture as much information as possible. In this example, you've already saved yourself a certain amount of time and effort by examining the initial diagram and changing things around to avoid inconsistencies, improve reusability, and follow the overall business processing. Moving things around in a table is much easier than rippling through the code, unit tests, integration tests, functional tests, and so on. Once you've settled on the component responsibilities, you can start drawing more high-definition diagrams, including classes, methods, parameters, return values, and so on. Of course, it would be possible to model the entire solution using interface definitions. However, you need to arrive at these somehow. When all the models are complete, you can use them to look for more inconsistencies and perhaps even to change the conceptual design.

Looking for Repeating Patterns

Before modeling the remaining responsibilities, you need to determine the best place to start. This can be achieved by looking at the use cases and/or architecture to identify core dependency patterns. This essentially involves scanning the use cases to determine whether there are any reusable functional areas or processing. There are many repeating patterns such as "The system checks that the account is in a state of New," or "The system checks that an account exists with the Username specified," and so forth. These help to identify areas where you can potentially implement reusable functionality. However, these are lightweight, single-step functions. The use cases often contain other areas of much larger reuse, which may need to be considered carefully beforehand.

In the case study, there is one such functional area that is reused: the Login functionality. There are a few places in the use cases where the steps state, "The system logs the user in to the system and records the date and time the user was logged in," or "If the user isn't logged in, the system logs the user in to the system and records the date and time the user was logged in." This type of repeating pattern has wider consequences because it is probably a much bigger block of functionality being reused.

Modeling the Flows

The following sections concentrate on drawing out additional information from the flows:

❏ Login

❏ Logout

❏ Activate Account

❏ Re-Request Activation Key

❏ Reset Password

❏ Change Password

❏ Update Account

❏ Close Account

You could continue to populate all the tables for each of the flows. However, the previous discussions indicated some high-level responsibility guidelines that the remaining models would need to take into account. For the purposes of time and space, I'm not going to produce all of them. I'll produce them for the Login, Logout, and Activate Account flows so that you can understand the reuse implications and patterns. The remaining flows will concentrate on the use-case steps instead.

Login

Figure 15-5 shows the Login model.

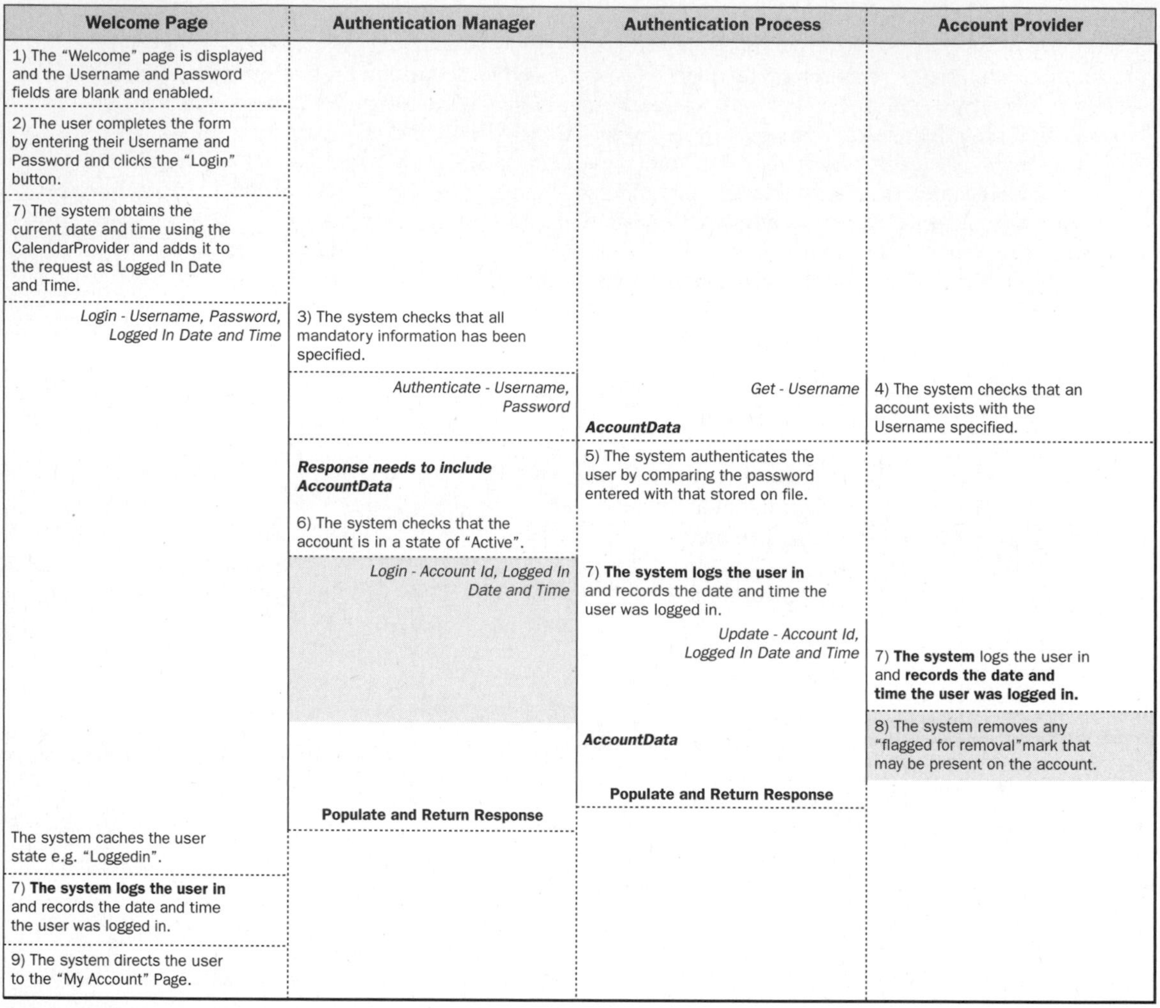

Welcome Page	Authentication Manager	Authentication Process	Account Provider
1) The "Welcome" page is displayed and the Username and Password fields are blank and enabled.			
2) The user completes the form by entering their Username and Password and clicks the "Login" button.			
7) The system obtains the current date and time using the CalendarProvider and adds it to the request as Logged In Date and Time.			
Login - Username, Password, Logged In Date and Time	3) The system checks that all mandatory information has been specified.		
	Authenticate - Username, Password	*Get - Username* ***AccountData***	4) The system checks that an account exists with the Username specified.
	Response needs to include AccountData 6) The system checks that the account is in a state of "Active".	5) The system authenticates the user by comparing the password entered with that stored on file.	
	Login - Account Id, Logged In Date and Time	**7) The system logs the user in** and records the date and time the user was logged in. *Update - Account Id, Logged In Date and Time*	**7) The system** logs the user in and **records the date and time the user was logged in.**
		AccountData	8) The system removes any "flagged for removal" mark that may be present on the account.
	Populate and Return Response	**Populate and Return Response**	
The system caches the user state e.g. "Loggedin".			
7) The system logs the user in and records the date and time the user was logged in.			
9) The system directs the user to the "My Account" Page.			

Figure 15-5

This figure highlights an interesting situation. In the case of login, the only formal processing is to update the database with the last logged in date and time, although this process could perform a lot more in the future. For example, you might actually store some application (middle-tier) level state. You could also update the database with a `LoggedInIndicator` or something similar, although this tends to have further consequences. For example:

❑ Would you want to check this flag when the user logged in? If so, where would you direct them if they were already logged in?

❑ Is it possible that the user isn't actually logged in but the flag indicates that they are? If so, this would stop them from logging in. It may then require other processes and functionality to remove or reset the flag.

It is useful to think about these things, and the diagrams can actually highlight these types of considerations. I've had to draw these diagrams and figures in detail to put these messages across; however, you don't need to draw the figures, you need to go through the exercise and ask the questions. Just because the application isn't making that much use of the Login method on the Authentication process, it doesn't mean that it won't in the future.

The Authentication process's Authenticate method would also provide the basis of being reused by the Activate Account and Re-Request Activation Key flows during their use-case processing steps:

- ❑   4) The system checks that an account exists with the Username specified.
- ❑   5) The system authenticates the user by comparing the password entered with that stored on file.

This kind of reuse is possible because the method itself is passive. That is, it doesn't write to the database, it simply obtains the account from it. Given that this method obtains the account from the database, then performs the authentication step, and then returns the Account Data in the response, it would be a good idea to ensure that all the other processing flows (where necessary) make use of this component in the first instance. The method encapsulates this functionality quite nicely and can be overloaded to support the other authentication scenarios, even if only the username is specified. It simply provides a good opportunity to obtain an account from the database before proceeding.

The second problem is slightly more involved. You saw the Login flow and the Authentication process's Login method, which is shown again in Figure 15-6.

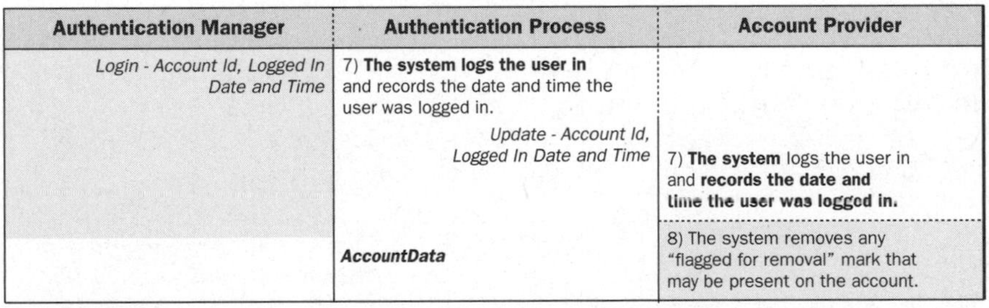

Authentication Manager	Authentication Process	Account Provider
Login - Account Id, Logged In Date and Time	7) **The system logs the user in** and records the date and time the user was logged in.	
	Update - Account Id, Logged In Date and Time	7) **The system** logs the user in and **records the date and time the user was logged in.**
		8) The system removes any "flagged for removal" mark that may be present on the account.
	AccountData	

Figure 15-6

The Login method uses the Update method on the AccountProvider. You can see that this updates the logged in date and time, and removes any removal flag. You can also see from the use-case steps that during the Activate Account and Change Password flows, there are other updates to the database. Reusing the Authentication provider's Login method (as-is) results in a double database hit, whereby the Activate Account and Change Password processes first update the account with the necessary information. The Login method will then subsequently update the account again. Although you know in this instance that the Login method isn't performing anything special in the application layer, you can't afford to not reuse its functionality. If the functionality changes in the future, you need to retain consistency throughout the application. This is a common situation whereby reusing a method introduces double-hits or duplicate processing. There are many ways of dealing with this, including:

1. Simply leave it as it is and accept the fact that there will be a double hit on the database for this transaction.

2. Implement a new method on the Authentication provider that performs both operations, although the Authentication provider's job is to provide authentication as well as login and logout functionality.

3. Revisit the architecture, responsibilities, and layers to move things around so that the processing flows in a different way (which should always be an option because you're in the design stage, not the build stage).

As I mentioned previously, it is only by examining the holistic processing that you really get a feel for these situations. In Chapter 13 you saw double database hits during use-case definition. It's lucky that you're working only on a conceptual level, because nothing is really cast in stone. You took some high-level storyboards and requirements and put together some building blocks and conceptual components, and now you're drilling these down into more detail and finding areas that need to be considered.

It is equally important to understand the transactional boundaries just in case reusing the method could cause blocking—for example, trying to update the same record in the database under a single transaction.

In this situation, it is really the classic question of functionality and extensibility over performance, an often much discussed subject. There's often a tendency to leave these areas behind only to find that they do come back and require revisiting. Although the case study is being used as a sample, it highlights situations common across systems development and implementation.

In the case of the Activate Account flow, the user is definitely logged in, whereas in the Change Password flow, it is optional, as the user may already be logged in. You could, if you wanted, pass the Login method on the AuthenticationProvider an AccountData class in the TransactionRequest. Remember, these are business processors, which are passed a TransactionContext as their input. The AccountData class would be pre-populated with the ActivatedDateTime and the Active account state, which would support the following use-case steps:

❑   5) The system proceeds to activate the user's account by setting the account state to Active and recording the date and time the account was activated.

❑   7) The system logs the user in to the system and records the date and time the user was logged in.

Passing a pre-populated `AccountData` class to the `Login` method would remove the database double-hit. The `ActivationProcessor` wouldn't update the database and then call login. It would simply update the `AccountData` and then call `Login`, which would update the database with the updated account information.

This would work equally well for the Change Password flow. If the user is logged in, Change Password would use the `AccountProvider` to update the database with the updated account information; otherwise, it would use the `AuthenticationProcess` to ensure that the updates to the account were saved and reuse the login functionality.

If you follow this through, the `AccountData` is simply being passed around many different components, acted upon, and then finally saved in the database. This type of implementation ties the updates to each other, and a failure will cause the entire transaction to fail. However, this is not a bad thing in this instance. It would be better to display a technical error to users during the Activate Account flow (meaning they have to go through the process again) than to not know the actual state of their account. To explain, if the Activate Account process updated the database (e.g. activated the users account), and then reused the login functionality which we know will update the database again, but for some reason the Login update failed, the user would be directed to a technical error page but wouldn't know if the account had been activated. This applies equally to Change Password, although some users are coming from the Reset Password flow. Either way you need to ensure that both actions are completed in a single instance and this can't be done under a single database transaction for the reasons already mentioned. Therefore, you're essentially forced down one route or the other — either keep the individual database updates or pass an AccountData class between components so that it is updated accordingly and only save it at the very end.

Logging the user in at the web layer simply involves updating the user state in the cache (session) to indicate that a user is logged in. It could also store other properties.

The important thing is to think about these situations and highlight them wherever possible. Looking at the use cases and a simple diagram has already done that. The question now is what are we going to do about it? A decision like this will have an effect on how the rest of the application is modeled, so it is best that we have a going in position. In this example, let's say we'll extend the Authentication Process and pass it a pre-populated `AccountData` object, which it can use to perform the login and update functionality on behalf of the consumer.

Logout

Logout essentially continues the discussion on extensibility and consistency. The initial flow is shown in Figure 15-7.

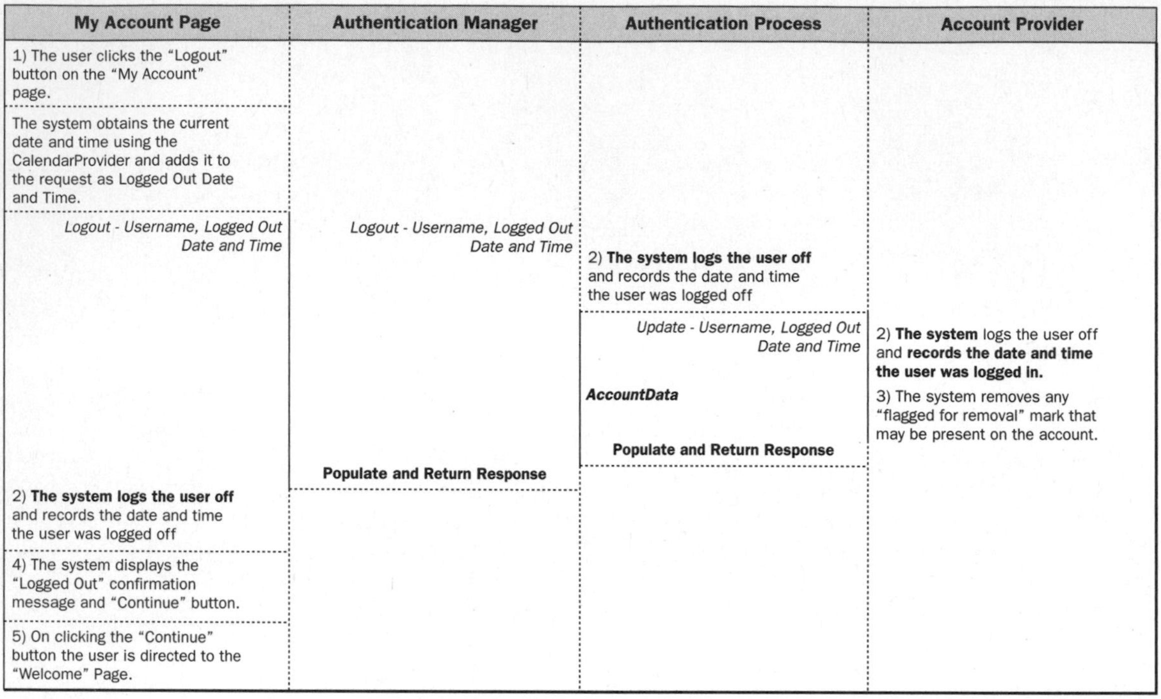

My Account Page	Authentication Manager	Authentication Process	Account Provider
1) The user clicks the "Logout" button on the "My Account" page.			
The system obtains the current date and time using the CalendarProvider and adds it to the request as Logged Out Date and Time.			
Logout - Username, Logged Out Date and Time	*Logout - Username, Logged Out Date and Time*	**2) The system logs the user off** and records the date and time the user was logged off	
		Update - Username, Logged Out Date and Time	**2) The system** logs the user off and **records the date and time the user was logged in.**
		AccountData	3) The system removes any "flagged for removal" mark that may be present on the account.
		Populate and Return Response	
	Populate and Return Response		
2) The system logs the user off and records the date and time the user was logged off			
4) The system displays the "Logged Out" confirmation message and "Continue" button.			
5) On clicking the "Continue" button the user is directed to the "Welcome" Page.			

Figure 15-7

In this instance, the business manager and the business process components are actually not doing very much. They simply provide consistency across the architecture. They do populate the response which may require some specific processing. In addition, the process has a place holder for logging the user off although there is nothing to do because the web page actually logs the user off and this step involves clearing the cache. However, we haven't yet determined all our monitoring and diagnostics so we don't want to start collapsing layers and removing components just because it appears that they aren't adding any functional value right now.

The Close Account flow also needs to log the user off and the same approach to Login will be taken for Logout. The process will accept a pre-populated `AccountData` object which it will update and save in the database. This is essentially an internal hand-over of processing.

Finally, the addition of the account state checking meant that if an account wasn't in the correct state, the system would log the user off. This would definitely mean reusing the logout functionality just in case it does something meaningful in the future.

Activate Account

The Activate Account flow can be initiated either from the Create New Account flow, or from the Welcome page. We saw earlier that this transaction has some specific inputs that it would need in-order to perform this. Figure 15-8 shows the flow including the use of the Login functionality provided by the authentication process.

Activate Account Page	Activation Manager	Activation Process	AuthenticationProcess	AccountProvider
Inputs - Username, Password, Previous Transaction 1) The "Activate My Account" page is diplayed and the fields bank/pre-populated are enabled/disabled according to the route from which they arrived.				
2) The user completes the form by entering their Username and Password (Where necessary), selecting the "Yes" Activation Key option (Where necessary) and specifying their "Account Activation Key" and clicks "Continue".				
The system obtains the current date and time using the CalendarProvider and adds it to the request as Activated Date and Time				
ActivatedAccount - Username, Password, Activation Key, Activated Date and Time	3) The system checks that all mandatory information has been specified and that each element is valid and correct according to its individual validation rules (where required).			
	Authenticate - Username, Password		*GetAccount - Username* **AccountData**	4) The system checks that an account exists with the Username specified.
	Response will include AccountData		5) The system authenticates the user by comparing the password entered with that stored on file.	
	6) The system checks that the account is in a state of "New".			
	7) The system checks that the supplied "Account Activation Key" matches that stored on file.			
	ActivateAccount - AccountData	8) The system sets the account state to "Active" 8) The system sets the Account Activated Date and Time		
		Login - AccountData	9) **The system logs the user in** to the system and records the date and time the user was logged in.	
			Update - Account Data	9) **The system** logs the user in to the system and **records the date and time the user was logged in.**
			Response will include Account Data	10) The system removes any "flagged for removal" mark that may be present on the account.
		Populate and Return Response		
	Populate and Return Response			
9) **The system logs the user in** to the system and records the date and time the user was logged in.				
Populate cache.				
11) The system displays the "Account Activated" confirmation message and "continue" button.				
12) On clicking the "Continue" button the user is directed to the "My Account" page.				

Figure 15-8

The completed diagram can be used as a pattern for the remaining flows. It shows the inputs that are required and it reuses the Authentication process as discussed earlier. The process avoids the double-hit at the same time as providing a single transaction without a formal database transaction. Should an exception occur at any point during the flow, the database state would be consistently maintained without any special processing.

However, there is one point to note. Now that you've set a pattern whereby the Activate Account process is reusing the Authentication process, the Activate Account process can't be reused without taking this Login functionality along with it. It is clear from the Login discussion that there are likely to be overloaded methods that perform different actions and this is one such area where additional method overloads can be implemented. It is possible to have one Activate Account method to simply deal with the semantics of updating the `AccountData` and another to log the user in as well. How much of this is implemented is entirely dependent on whether or not it is required. In the case of login, you have a clear requirement to log the user in so it makes good sense to reuse the existing functionality.

Re-Request Activation Key

The use-case steps for this flow are listed below and annotated where necessary.

1. The Activate My Account page is displayed and the fields are blank/pre-populated and enabled/disabled according to the route from which they arrived:

    a. **From UC-001 Create New Account** — The Username and Password fields are pre-popu-lated and disabled. The "Yes" Activation Key option is pre-selected and the "No" option is enabled.

    b. **From the Welcome page** — The Username and Password fields are blank and enabled. The "No" Activation Key option is pre-selected and the "Yes" option is disabled.

    Both of these tasks can be performed using the "Previous Transaction." However, it does mean that the Welcome page must either clear this value out or store a specific value in it when it is first requested. It would be much better to store a specific value than rely on blanks or null values.

2. The user completes the form by entering their Username and Password (where necessary) and selecting the "No" Activation Key option (where necessary) and clicks the Continue button.

3. The system checks that all mandatory information has been specified.

4. The system checks that an account exists with the Username specified — as with Activate Account.

5. The system authenticates the user by comparing the password entered with that stored on file — as with Activate Account.

6. The system checks that the account is in a state of "New" — as with Activate Account.

7. The system queues a request for an "Activation Key Re-Request Email" to be sent to the user's e-mail address and records the date and time the re-request was made. This processing would follow the same principle as that shown for Create New Account whereby the date and time is passed from the web page and the e-mail is queued under a formal database transaction.

    a. In the background the e-mail request will be processed and the system will compose and send the user an e-mail containing their account Activation Key and record the date and time the re-request e-mail was sent. This will be performed by the Activation Key E-mailer batch process.

8. The system sets the account state to Active. They system sets the Account Activated Date and Time.

9. The system displays the Activation Key Resent confirmation message and the Continue button. The business process would use the Message Provider to obtain the relevant message and return it through the `TransactionResponse`.

10. The system removes any "flagged for removal" mark that may be present on the account. This would be performed by the AccountProvider as part of updating the account in the database.

There's nothing really special about this flow; everything discussed so far fits in with its processing steps. It is also worthwhile to cross-check against the requirements to capture additional steps. In the remaining sections, I'll list only the use-case steps of interest to avoid duplication.

Reset Password

The Reset Password flow is actually a two-stage process. The first step is simply to obtain users' account information and authenticate them so that they can change their password. The second step allows users to change their password using the Change Password page and functionality.

In this case, the `AccountProvider` could include a method `GetForChangePassword`. The name indicates that it is getting an account for a specific reason.

In this instance, specific processing is required to ensure that this action can be performed. For instance, the manager needs to ensure that the account's state is correct. The security question will be displayed to the user in the next flow, so you need to capture the security question in the "transition." If not, you incur another lookup on the database because the Change Password flow will also obtain the user's account, according to the use-case steps. The user isn't actually logged in at this point but is simply authenticated. You can capture this information too in the user state. You can map these actions to the components in the diagram to provide processing placeholders.

The Authentication process already has a method for authenticating the user via their username and password, and this flow would simply introduce another method whereby the user is authenticated using their username and e-mail address. This would serve the purpose of obtaining the account from the database in the first instance.

Change Password

Both logged-in users and authenticated users can change their password. You've already seen in Activate Account that the Change Password flow also needs to follow the same pattern for login. In the case of Change Password, it depends on whether the user is logged in. To support this decision, the Change Password flow requires either the user state as an input or an indicator to perform login functionality.

The most interesting use-case step is actually Step 1:

1. The Change Password page is displayed, the user's security question is displayed, and the entry fields blank and enabled.

Where is the security question going to come from? This flow can be accessed from either the My Account page, if the user is already logged in, or via the Reset Password flow. In the case of Reset Password, it was noted that you needed this piece of information for the transition. However, once a user is logged in, you either need to keep this information in state or obtain it from the database.

Caching is good for performance, but its implications need to be understood properly, as discussed later. The user is logged in and you've already gone down to the database once to authenticate them, so you have all the information you need to cache in the transition placeholder. If the information wasn't cached, you would need to obtain it from the database. If you were to model this "logged in" flow, you would find the following:

1. The user's account details would be obtained during login for authentication purposes.

2. The user's account would be obtained in the first part of the Change Password flow.

3. The user's account would be obtained when checking the account state.

4. The user's account information would be updated as part of the Change Password flow.

There's a lot of database lookups going on here, but before you start looking at performance improvements, you need to understand how often Change Password transactions are performed and the resulting load on the system. However, you have identified an area where performance could be improved if necessary. The Update Account flow is similar, so let's look at it, too.

Update Account

The Update Account flow's use-case steps are also worth paying attention to. The first three steps are as follows:

1. The system obtains the user's account information.

2. The system checks that the account is in a state of "Active."

3. The system decrypts the e-mail address, security question, and security question answer data elements.

In this instance the use-case steps are pretty clear, although they do not explicitly state where the information is obtained from. The user is logged in and therefore the account is assumed to be active. (I discussed the implications of changes to the underlying account state previously.) The third step shows the information being decrypted. If the information were cached, you would also need to determine whether it was cached in encrypted or decrypted form.

At the moment, Update Account is pretty lightweight in terms of functionality. The information that would require caching is quite small. However, if you extended the account information to include address books, payment information, and so forth, you probably wouldn't want to cache all this information when the user logged in.

For the moment, we'll work on the basis that this flow follows a similar pattern to those previously discussed, whereby the first part is essentially obtaining an account for the purpose of updating it. Following the current method naming convention, a method such as `GetForUpdate` would perform this action.

The remaining use-case steps are very similar to those already discussed. However, the following use-case step is of interest:

❑   8) The system checks that an account doesn't already exist with the username specified.

The user can change their username as part of their updates, so you need to ensure that this is captured and handled appropriately. The current `AccountProvider` has the `GetAccount` method, which looks up the account based on the username. You need to ensure that this use-case processing step checks the `AccountId`. If you reuse this method, it could very well return the same account, so you can't just base a decision on it returning a record. You need to examine the `AccountId`.

It is good practice to key tables on nonfunctional elements, and this is one place where it comes to light. If you keyed the Account table on the username, you'd either need to stop users from changing it or implement alternative logic.

Close Account

This is the last use case in the series, and there's not much more to draw out. I've already mentioned that it will reuse the logout functionality, so it will need to implement the same patterns previously outlined. It also needs to queue an e-mail request, where required. This is optional from the user's perspective, although, when requested, the e-mail request will need to be queued under a transaction for consistency. This is the main difference between the Close Account flow and the other flows that send e-mail. The "Begin Transaction" and "End Transaction" are required only if users specified that they want an e-mail confirmation of their account closure.

Modeling the Batch Jobs

This section covers the batch components identified in the requirements and the previous chapters. The conceptual design is still very much a hybrid between a functional design and a technical design document; it is certainly not as detailed as a full technical design document would be. However, as you progress through the patterns and practices, you'll build on what you have so far and uncover more of the framework components and how best to implement them to meet the quality characteristics. What you have so far would not be "client-ready," but it is good enough for further design and planning meetings. You are looking to get a complete view of the application and its functionality so that you can really start to apply the patterns and practices and concentrate on the key areas. The diagrams and flows help to walk through the conceptual solution. The requirements specified in Chapter 13 identified a number of batch jobs, and this chapter provides an overall view of the functionality and requirements. The following subsections go through the solicited e-mail batch jobs and the account clean-up jobs.

The Solicited E-mail Batch Jobs

This group of batch processes will concentrate on sending out solicited e-mails to the customer. With all data processing involved in batch processes, I generally find the best way to start is to model some of the underlying data. The solicited e-mail group is centered on the EmailQueue table, which is also related to the Account table via the AccountId column. The following table lists some sample records for the Email Queue table:

Id	RequestTypeId	AccId	RequestedDateTime	SentDateTime
1	1 = NewActivationKey	1	10-09-2008 06:00:00.000	Null
2	2 = KeyRerequest	2	10-09-2008 07:10:00.000	Null
3	3 = ClosedConfirmation	3	10-09-2008 08:10:10.000	Null

Modeling the table in this way also enables you to flesh out the related tables and reference data values, such as request types. It also helps you to define and think about the necessary precision of the values, such as the date/time column.

You will recall that the initial requests were placed on the queue using the EmailQueueProvider component. This component will be extended so that it can be used to obtain records from the e-mail queue table. Layering the components in this way allows you to replace the actual functionality without having to change any of the upper layers. For instance, in the future, the e-mail queue table might be replaced by a real queue or series of queues provided by a formal messaging and queuing system. In this example, a new method, Dequeue, will be added to the provider component. This method (or series of methods) needs to return records based on a set of specific criteria. The selection criteria matches with the actual type of job, as listed in the following table:

Job Type	Dequeue Criteria
New Activation Key	RequestType = "New", SentDateTime = Null
Re-Request Activation Key	RequestType = "Rerequest", SentDateTime = Null
Closed Account Confirmation	RequestType = "Closed", SentDateTime = Null

Behind the scenes, the Dequeue method will use the data access layer to obtain the actual request records to be processed from the database. Specifically, it would use the EmailQueue data access component. This functionality can be replaced at a later date to work with a message queue, although this is sometimes easier said than done. Under normal circumstances a *dequeuing* operation would obtain only a single item (in priority or another specified order) and physically remove it from the queue for processing. This stops multiple processes from obtaining the same item from the queue. In fact, as you progress, you will need to support multiple instances of the same job type for performance and resilience purposes. In this example, you'll apply some *artistic license* and this Dequeue method will return a set of records based on the input criteria, and the records will not be removed from the underlying physical storage. It is rather like performing the dequeue action under transaction control, without the overhead.

The EmailQueue table is related to the Account table, for which you also need to provide some "model data." The Account table is quite large, so I'll simply look at some of the key fields that you need as inputs to the processes. The following table lists the key fields and data records for these walkthroughs:

Id	AccountStateId	E-mailAddress	ActivationKey
1	1 = "New"	{ide@abc.com}	AF9B60A0-1431-4F62-BC68-3311714A69AD
2	2 = "Active"	{sarah@abc.com}	AF9B60A1-1431-4F62-BC68-3311714A69AD
3	3 = "Closed"	{john@abc.com}	AF9B60A2-1431-4F62-BC68-3311714A69AD

You're not designing a totally generic messaging and queuing object model, so the Dequeue method could also return the account information associated with the e-mail request. This will help to improve performance and reduce the overall complexity by saving you from having to look up each account as each request is processed.

If this were a real queuing system, the Enqueue method would typically pass all the information required to process the e-mail request. However, in this instance, the Enqueue method simply creates a record in the database that is used by the Dequeue method, but it is worth noting for future enhancements.

Looking at the data model, you can see that the table layout would allow an entry in the EmailQueue table to point to any account record. Therefore, it's possible, although unlikely, that a "NewKey" Activation Key request could somehow relate to an "Active" account or a "Closed" account. I raise this issue now, first because the business and technical processes need to be examined and, second, because the e-mail is actually customer-facing. The impact analysis is simply based on the fact that a customer could receive an e-mail that is totally incorrect — for example, receiving a new account Activation Key when the customer's account is already active, or even closed. The customer could receive a closure confirmation e-mail when his or her account is actually active or new. I must admit that I am always very wary when it comes to customer-facing output, although situations should be analyzed on a case-by-case basis. As with all things in life, it is simply not a case of "one size fits all."

These are essentially "potential gaps" that need to be filled in and are really subject to probability analysis. The best way to describe the individual scenarios is with a permutation table, as shown in the following table. The process is to determine how the situation (incorrect records) could be arrived at. It is a given at this point that you haven't seen the entire functionality end-to-end, so it will be somewhat difficult to answer all the questions right now.

RequestType	AccountStateId	Comment
1 = "NewKey"	1 = "New"	Required State/Correct Functionality
1 = "NewKey"	2 = "Active"	Not Applicable/Mismatch
1 = "NewKey"	3 = "Closed"	Not Applicable/Mismatch
2 = "RerequestKey"	1 = "New"	Not Applicable/Mismatch
2 = "RerequestKey"	2 = "Active"	Required State/Correct Functionality
2 = "RerequestKey"	3 = "Closed"	Not Applicable/Mismatch
3 = "ClosedConfirmation"	1 = "New"	Not Applicable/Mismatch
3 = "ClosedConfirmation"	2 = "Active"	Not Applicable/Mismatch
3 = "ClosedConfirmation"	3 = "Closed"	Required State/Correct Functionality

It is really quite simple to produce the table, as the number of individual permutations is very low. However, in a more complex situation, these permutations could be in the hundreds if not thousands. Furthermore, there may be other conditions that the job needs to take into account across the different values — for example, ensuring that the `ActivationKey` field is not null, and so on. You can discount some of these conditions and variations by examining and implementing the appropriate database constraints and rules. The business logic and processes may also make certain situations unlikely — for example, if the business logic and processes are analyzed and the conclusion is that there should be no valid business reason why the incorrect state could be arrived at. The next place to look is for technical or other reasons that could cause the situation to arise. There is the possibility that a data import has somehow corrupted the records.

In this specific situation, my personal preference is to ensure that the jobs send e-mails only for valid records. I think it would cause perception issues if customers received incorrect e-mails. It wouldn't look very good for the company if their system was sending out incorrect e-mails. There are two ways in which the account state check can be achieved:

❑ **Check it (and potentially other conditions) in the code.** If the checks are in the code, they will need to be developed and unit tested.

❑ **Embed the logic in the provider and pass it to the database queries.** This would remove the need to check the state in the code, as it's essentially being checked in the query. The provider would be passing the values to the data access layer, so it is not technically embedding business logic in the data layer. This approach simplifies the functionality of the jobs but clearly leads to a potential gap in the database. For instance, records in the database could be out-of-sync and need to be dealt with.

Again, it is worth examining these cases because they highlight areas that could be missed. It is unlikely that the records would somehow become invalid or out-of-sync, so the second approach, to select only valid or synchronized records from the database, is probably best. In this case, the jobs can focus on the primary functionality, which will reduce the development and testing effort and also ensure that the customer-facing issues are avoided completely. It also means that the jobs are not performing any unnecessary steps, which will improve their overall performance and throughput. However, it does mean that the database queries need to be tested thoroughly and deployed correctly.

With respect to the potential gaps in the database, these should be noted. Where it is deemed necessary, a very simple report or job can be developed to select invalid or out-of-sync records that can be executed periodically with reduced priority. This is essentially a "consistency check" report or job. If records are identified, the situation needs to be investigated and resolved appropriately. These consistency checks would be performed during testing and post-go-live support, and, assuming everything was okay, they would be relegated to an end-of-day or less regularly performed activity. Based on the analysis, they might not even be necessary at all.

You can accept that the Dequeue method will return a set of complete records for processing based on the RequestType and AccountState parameters passed to it. Each record that needs to be processed will need to contain at least the following information:

❑ EmailQueue.RequestId

❑ Account.AccountId

❑ Account.EmailAddress (decrypted)

❑ Account.ActivationKey (not required in the closed account confirmation)

Now that you've seen the initial selection criteria and the records that will be returned, you can start to look at the functional processing and interactions involved in each job.

The SolicitedEmailProvider component will be responsible for actually composing and sending the e-mails. At a conceptual level, this component will implement the following methods:

❑ Initialize — Responsible for creating objects, opening connections, and general initialization processing for repetitive calling. This allows the component to cache objects and initialize them in memory to improve the overall performance of the job.

❑ ComposeAndSend — Responsible for actually composing the e-mail and sending it based on the template and the parameters supplied. Composition is really nothing more than replacing the placeholders in the template with the relevant parameters/information. Chapter 14 discussed the MessageProvider, which can be extended and passed a MessagesEnum parameter and a series of arguments that would replace the individual placeholders. In a batch process, you need to ensure that these messages are cached appropriately so that they are not reloaded for each transaction. The MessageProvider component must therefore also cache messages while it is alive so that the SolicitedEmailProvider component can use it to improve reuse and reduce the amount of duplicated code. This is a situation where both the online application and the batch components are using the same object; therefore, it is important that this reuse is noted and understood so that it is not missed during the implementation. You don't want the e-mail message template to be reloaded on every single transaction, as this could impact performance.

❑ Terminate — Responsible for closing connections, destroying objects, and general termination processing.

The batch jobs could be processing hundreds, if not thousands or millions, of records, so they need to be fast. Creating objects, accessing the database, and other time-consuming processing need to be limited on a per-transaction basis. The methods described previously will help to reduce the processing required and will improve the overall execution for each transaction.

Chapter 16, "Designing for Batch," looks at the execution and control of the jobs, as well as how the managers and processor are further defined to support the batch solution. For the moment, let's look at the functional processing to further refine the business components. Once you have a complete picture of the functional elements, you can start to look at the technical implications and solutions.

New Activation Key Batch Processing

This job is responsible for sending new Activation Key e-mails, which follow this template:

```
Subject: Welcome to Within a Click
Body:

Thank you for registering with us. We are very pleased to provide you with your new
account activation key:

{0}

We hope you enjoy using our site!

The WAC Team.
```

The high-level individual record processing is as follows:

1. Call the `ComposeAndSend` method on the `SolicitedEmailProvider`, passing in the `MessageType`, `EmailAddress`, and `ActivationKey`.

2. Update the `EmailQueue` with the date and time the Activation Key was sent.

The record processing is relatively straightforward in that only two key steps are involved. The last step in the process is to update the EmailQueue table with the date and time the Activation Key was sent. Now you have to decide whether to embed this functionality in the SolicitedEmailProvider or pass the date and time from the batch process.

Re-Request Activation Key Batch Processing

This job is responsible for sending Activation Key re-request e-mails, which follow this template:

```
Subject: Your Within-a-Click Account Activation Key
Body:

We're sorry that you didn't receive your account activation key. We are very
pleased to provide it below:

{0}

We hope you enjoy using our site!

The WAC Team.
```

The high-level individual record processing is as follows:

1. Call the `ComposeAndSend` method on the SolicitedEmailProvider, passing in the `MessageType`, `EmailAddress`, and `ActivationKey`.

2. Update the EmailQueue with the date and time the Activation Key was resent.

In this instance, the record processing is exactly the same as the new Activation Key processing. You're simply selecting records (which is not shown), sending out the e-mail for each of them, and updating the date and time the e-mail was sent.

Closed Account Confirmation E-mail Batch Processing

This job is responsible for sending closed account confirmation e-mails, which follow this template:

```
Subject: Your Within-a-Click Account has been closed
Body:

We're sorry that you have chosen to close your account. This email confirms that
your account has been closed and removed from our system.

The WAC Team.
```

Once again, the individual record processing is exactly the same as the previous jobs:

1. Call the ComposeAndSend method on the SolicitedEmailProvider, passing in the MessageType and EmailAddress.

2. Update the EmailQueue with the date and time the closed account e-mail confirmation was sent.

Having seen three identical processing steps, it is fair to say that the solicited e-mail jobs could be a single, configurable code-base. The only moving parts are the selection criteria and what is passed to the SolicitedEmailProvider. This provides a solid foundation for consolidation, as is often the case in batch processes. The individual jobs themselves are essentially "logical," mapping to a single "physical" implementation and configuration.

The Account Cleanup Jobs

This group of jobs is concerned with flagging "new" accounts that haven't been activated and cleaning up the account data table. All these jobs process records that are within the core Account table. These jobs, which typically would form part of an end-of-day activity, have a date/time component in their selection criteria. The following sections look at the high-level processing for each job.

Aged Account Flagging

This job is responsible for flagging accounts that have not been activated for a configurable period of time. The job selects records from the account table that meet the "aged account" criteria and that are that not already flagged for removal. The "aged account" criterion is as follows:

```
Account in State "New"
CreatedDateTime < BatchRunDate - NewAccountExpiryInDays
FlaggedForRemoval = Null
```

Based on this selection criterion, it would be pretty easy to model some sample data as input into the process. The job doesn't actually need to perform any formal validation processing; it simply needs to update the account's FlaggedForRemoval column. This is a typical example of where the functionality could actually be performed in a single stored procedure (assuming the BatchRunDate and NewAccountExpiryInDays configuration values were stored in the database), rather than a formal code job.

There are often jobs like this that don't actually require any functional processing but can be performed directly at the database level. It is really a question of traceability. If the job is written in code, it can log and trace its output accordingly. It can also update specific performance counters. In the event of a failure, it can be investigated. In the case of the account cleanup, the function is performed so that the database is kept up-to-date and unnecessary data is removed. The job doesn't need to run under a transaction, and its selection criteria ensures that it would not revisit records it had already processed. In pseudo SQL terms, the job would be nothing more than the following:

```
Update Account

Set FlaggedForRemoval = True

Where

Account in State "New"
CreatedDateTime < BatchRunDate - NewAccountExpiryInDays
FlaggedForRemoval = Null
```

However, as I said previously, for this to be stored and run at the database level, it does mean that the `BatchRunDate` needs to be stored in the database and kept up-to-date as part of the overall batch framework. It also means that the `NewAccountExpiryInDays` needs to be stored in the database, not in an external configuration file.

The chances of the stored procedure failing are very limited. However, the stored procedure would also need to be further configured. Although this looks okay right now, there could be millions of records that require flagging, and a single process would not be efficient. So, you'd probably want to split this up further. This is also true for the remaining jobs.

Removal of Flagged Accounts

This job is responsible for physically removing the accounts that have been flagged. There's a time period between the account being flagged and actually being removed. This can be considered a "grace" period for the customer because the account state isn't actually changed by the previous job — it is only marked. If you follow on from the previous job, the pseudo SQL for this job would be something like the following:

```
Delete from Account
Where
AccountState = "New"
FlaggedForRemoval = True
FlaggedForRemovalDateTime < BatchRunDate - NewAccountRemovalPeriodInDays
```

This job is more interesting because it is possible that the customer is actually in the process of activating an account at the same time this job is running and about to remove the account.

This situation needs to be given a bit of consideration to assess the impact to the rest of the system and the user experience. The Activate Account flow is using the `AuthenticationProcess` to obtain the record in the first instance, which is in turn using the `AccountProvider`. This reuse essentially "hides" the fact that the account doesn't actually exist. The user would essentially be presented with an Authentication Failure message and not the fact that his or her account had been removed. The user wouldn't actually know that the account had been removed. I discussed this in Chapter 13 and concluded that the system wouldn't send the user "unsolicited" e-mail. However, rather than using a blanket Authentication Failure message, you can display an Account Does Not Exist error.

This example is very much a "first come, first served" situation. If the user got in first and activated the account before the job ran, the account wouldn't be removed. Again, this is very much an exception case and should be assessed accordingly to ensure that the right approach is put in place. On this occasion, and because this is a case study let's simply accept that this could potentially happen, although the window of opportunity is pretty slim and the probability of it occurring is minimal. However, the situation should be noted and the impact analysis should determine the effort required to plug the gap.

Closed Account Removal

This job is responsible for physically removing closed accounts. The job is fairly straightforward, with the pseudo SQL as follows:

```
Delete from Account
Where
Account in State "Closed"
ClosedDateTime < BatchRunDate - ClosedAccountRemovalPeriodInDays
```

This job is very simple and follows the same pattern as those before. At this point in time there are no functional situations where this job could run into trouble. Furthermore, it is also working on the series of records that do not conflict with the other jobs, so it is possible that it could be executed in parallel to improve the performance of the overall batch suite.

The Close Account Removal job and the Flagged Account Removal job are physically removing data from the database — in some cases, large amounts of data. In addition to splitting up the jobs into multiple processes, it is important to understand the implications these jobs might have on re-indexing, recompiling stored procedures, and the query optimizer.

The Reporting Components

The requirements specified the following business reports required by the solution:

❑　New Accounts

❑　Activated Accounts

❑　Average Activation Time

❑　Aged Accounts

❑　Closed Accounts

The reporting components in this instance are nothing more than a set of stored procedures with simple queries that will be executed against the database. The stored procedures will provide the basic selection of information for the reports to be produced.

In almost all of the cases, the reports are simply used for trend analysis (for example, the number of accounts created, activated, and closed over time). The data in the database is actually encrypted, so "list" reports would not be possible without additional processing. This is a very common problem and it is one of the reasons that reports should be considered early. The earlier the reports can be identified, the easier it is to address both functional and technical issues. However, in this example, the reports essentially return a data series showing the individual counts per day over the time period. So, to support this basic type of reporting, the criteria would initially require:

- ❏ The start date for the report
- ❏ The end date for the report

The data series would typically be used to create a graph like the one shown in Figure 15-9

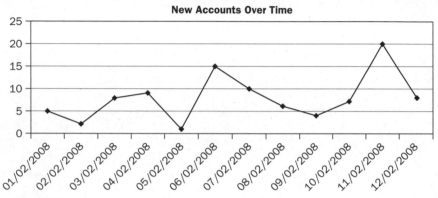

Figure 15-9

The following table provides the very basic selection criteria and comments for each of the reports required:

Report Name	Selection Criteria	Comments
New Accounts	CreatedDateTime >= StartDate CreatedDateTime <= EndDate	I mentioned in Chapter 9 that the business might only want to see "Active" accounts rather than a total count of accounts created per day for each day in the date range.
Activated Accounts	ActivatedDateTime >= StartDate ActivatedDateTime <= EndDate	Returns the count of accounts activated per day for each day in the date range.
Average Activation Time	CreatedDateTime >= StartDate CreatedDateTime <= EndDate	Returns the average amount of time between the total CreatedDateTime and the ActivatedDateTime per day for each day in the date range. That is, for all accounts created on a specific day, the report would show the average time between their creation date and their activation date.

Report Name	Selection Criteria	Comments
Aged Accounts	FlaggedForRemovalDateTime >= StartDate FlaggedForRemovalDateTime <= EndDate	Returns the count of aged accounts flagged for removal per day for each day in the date range.
Closed Accounts	ClosedDateTime >= StartDate ClosedDateTime <= EndDate	Returns the count of closed accounts per day for each day in the date range.

Most of the preceding reports are quite simple, although the first report requires clarification. The Average Activation Time report is the most complex of the set, but even it is quite simple, as reports go. It is important to remember that these are only the initial "functional" reports. As the system grows, additional reports will be required, including technical reports, as well as extracts that will be used for many different purposes.

Summary

This chapter completes the conceptual overview of the case study. The overview started with a high-level outline of the overall functionality from the user's perspective; then it solidified some requirements and defined a set of high-level use cases; finally, it used this information to pull together the conceptual architecture based on some guiding principles.

The conceptual architecture provides a means for modeling the application and drawing out more concerns and areas for improvement. The design process is about asking questions and plugging gaps. You've seen with such a simple application that there are many situations that need to be considered and dealt with. These situations apply to many real-world projects. You've seen that decisions are interrelated and that having a holistic view enables you to understand these relationships and their consequences. Having a clear vision helps to define the scope, which in turn helps you to plan and finance the project appropriately.

Not all the questions have been answered, as is often the case in software design and development. Remember that we're dealing at a conceptual level at this point; the next stage would typically be to take everything done so far and compile a complete solution design. The solution design would map all the decision points and the solution together, as well as formally list the areas for further discussion in the Design Query Log. The case study is also intended to model a much bigger solution (or problem) and provide the basis for these discussions. The case study has been used to highlight processes and practices that you can apply in the real world when looking at your own solutions. If you were so inclined, you could take all the discussions and decision points, along with your own and produce a full solution design. However, this will not be performed in this book. As you build your own solution, it is up to you to flesh out the details and make decisions along the way. As I have mentioned previously, it is not the actual case study's solution; it is the method for arriving at it you should consider.

The modeling techniques shown in this chapter help to define test data and test scenarios, as well as identify gaps in the conceptual solution. You've also seen how modeling the application can help to consolidate and highlight reusable components.

The following are the key points to take away from this chapter:

- ❑ **Model the complete solution.** Modeling the application provides a solid foundation for further design and discussion. A simple modeling technique, such as the one outlined, helps to determine where functionality is best performed. Modeling the application also covers all the batch processes and reporting components, as well as the application.

- ❑ **Look for areas of inconsistency.** When you start modeling you'll find areas of inconsistency between flows. It is important to highlight these and work through the solution.

- ❑ **Look for repeating patterns.** Repeating patterns provide the basis of consistent processing and re-use across the entire solution.

- ❑ **Understand the implications of reuse.** It is important to understand where components and functionality are reused and whether reusing functionality has any implications, such as double-hits on the database or double-processing.

- ❑ **Capture the exception scenarios.** Modeling the application doesn't just focus on normal processing. It also covers the "exception scenarios" and assessing whether the application can get into an inconsistent state.

The chapters that follow look at some patterns and practices that can be applied to the conceptual solution for the case study to provide a better understanding of their use and implications.

Part IV
Patterns and Practices

16

Designing for Batch

Chapter 15 expanded the high-level functionality of the batch jobs identified in Chapter 13. This chapter looks at some of the more technical details and the patterns and practices that could be applied to the batch jobs and the overall batch solution. These concepts can be applied on real-world projects to ensure that the batch solution is fit for purpose and supports all the necessary operability criteria. Although the case study has identified only a handful of functional jobs, the batch framework would provide a solid foundation for executing batch processes that perform a wide variety of tasks and functions. This chapter builds on the previous chapters that discussed batch processing at a high-level and identified various batch components. Earlier in this book you looked at the multitude of different kinds of jobs that form a complete batch solution. Some jobs perform functional processing, whereas others perform more technical processing, such as starting and stopping services, cleaning up logs, and so forth. The batch jobs identified for the case study are fairly lightweight when it comes to their functional processing. However, they provide the basis for the foundation patterns and practices. You also saw previously how the reporting and analytics solution could require additional batch processes to move files from one location to another. It is important that the batch framework and batch solution be extensible to allow for future enhancements and reuse.

This chapter is organized into the following sections:

❑ **The Batch Architecture** — Takes a brief look at a couple of different batch architectures and the differences between using a formal batch scheduler over other approaches and technologies.

❑ **Batch Job Control and Execution** — Walks through batch job execution and control as well as providing a generic framework. It examines the different components and how they can provide consistent interfaces so that they can be executed in the most appropriate way.

❑ **Multiple Threads and Multiple Jobs** — Discusses the key differences of multiple jobs versus multiple threads, as well as some of the challenges and configuration required.

❑ **Generic Jobs and Generic Functionality** — Looks at some typical jobs that are required in today's applications and how certain processes can provide generic and re-usable functionality to reduce the overall development effort. This section also touches on scripting as an alternative to developing processes in code.

The Batch Architecture

In the previous chapters you saw that many different jobs could form part of the overall batch solution. Chapter 13 defined the functional batch jobs specifically required by the case study. You've also seen the high-level mechanics of using a formal batch scheduler.

Figure 16-1 depicts a "batch" architecture that doesn't make use of a formal batch scheduler.

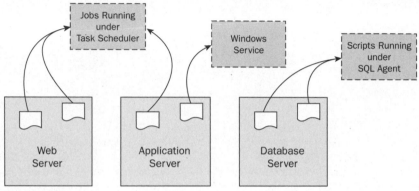

Figure 16-1

In this architecture style, the jobs are executed via different methods and technologies. The actual jobs (or processes) also manifest themselves in different ways, including:

❑   As scripts running under the SQL Server Agent on the database server

❑   As Windows services running on the application server

❑   As a combination of scripts and executables running on the web servers and application servers under the Task Scheduler

This approach works, and can work well, but there are many moving parts that need to be administered and controlled. Furthermore, the individual jobs execute according to their own schedules, as there is no centrally coordinated execution orchestration. When jobs are running in this fashion they can overlap in their execution. For example, a job could be running on the database server that is backing up the database at the same time the Windows service is updating it. In this distributed architecture, it is difficult to manage dependencies. For example, if a job running on the database server fails, and a job running on the application server is dependent on it, this could introduce complexities. The execution schedules need to be managed, maintained, and monitored across multiple servers and via multiple technologies.

A formal batch scheduler consolidates all the scheduling and execution of the jobs into a dependency-based schedule, which is centrally managed, maintained, and monitored. The scheduler executes the jobs according to the schedule and provides feedback to the operator through the user interface.

Figure 16-2 depicts the batch architecture using a formal batch scheduler.

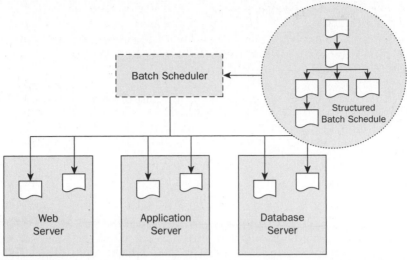

Figure 16-2

The individual batch jobs are triggered from the batch scheduler via the command line. However, there may be some cases where jobs or processes are still run continuously in the background as Windows services (or an equivalent).

Batch processes execute periodically, with the approach to "periodic" execution split into the following two categories:

❑ **Jobs that execute once or twice per day** — In this instance, the actual jobs themselves could be executed as part of a start-of-day or end-of-day schedule. It is unlikely that these types of jobs would run as Windows services, as the frequency of execution doesn't warrant it.

❑ **Jobs that are executed at regular intervals throughout the day (intraday)** — The jobs could be executed every 15 minutes, 30 minutes, and so on. It is primarily these types of jobs that are sometimes implemented as Windows services because the periodic pattern and continuous execution fits very well. The process performs some actions, sleeps for a while, and then continues again, and so forth. This pattern is essentially mirrored by the batch scheduler, in that the job is executed, the scheduler then reschedules the job for the next run, and then it is executed again.

The primary difference between the two styles is that jobs implemented as Windows services can take advantage of initialization and caching mechanisms. For instance, components and configuration can be held in memory for the lifetime of the process. The processing doesn't need to reload or perform heavy initialization logic for each processing cycle. When jobs are triggered by the batch scheduler, they are completely new instances that require initialization, execution, and termination.

Another key difference between the two styles is the way the jobs are controlled. A Windows service can be started, paused, restarted, and stopped using the Services Control panel (depending on the controls supported by the service), whereas jobs that are executed from the batch scheduler (or command line) are typically terminated (killed) by the scheduler when the operator stops or aborts the job.

The final difference between the two types is that jobs implemented as Windows services would report their status through events, log files, and performance counters, whereas jobs executed from the scheduler would typically report their status through the StdOut and StdErr streams along with an appropriate exit code. However, the jobs themselves can still output events, logs, and performance counter updates. Furthermore, it is also highly likely that the batch scheduler would also raise events when jobs start and stop.

The following lists some of the different types of core processing performed by batch processes:

❑ **Jobs that perform only a single action or operation per processing iteration** — An example of such a job is one that simply FTPs a single file (or multiple files) from one location to another throughout the day. Another is a job that executes a single stored procedure or query. The query could affect multiple records, but as far as the core processing is concerned, it is just a single operation.

❑ **Jobs that perform multiple operations per processing cycle** — The solicited e-mail batch jobs outlined in Chapter 15 are typical of this style of processing. In each execution cycle, the job is processing multiple records (or work items). This is an important distinction because the jobs that fall into this category need to make use of better initialization, caching, and reuse logic for performance purposes.

The actual execution style shouldn't matter to the core processing. And in fact, the internals shouldn't even be aware of how they've been triggered. This de-couples the processing from the triggering mechanism. However, given the different triggering methods, the batch execution and control framework needs to be flexible enough to support them as well as future enhancements.

One very important point within batch processing is where the actual processing is performed. You'll see this later when looking at some example jobs. However, it is important to determine whether a batch process should run locally (on the actual server it needs to) or remotely (accessing the server from another machine.) Because batch jobs process lots of data and records, it is important to limit the amount of data transferred over the network. Running jobs locally can definitely help to reduce the network load and improve performance.

An Execution and Control Framework

This section examines the second style of jobs discussed previously — jobs that perform multiple actions per processing iteration. Batch processing by its very nature is "iterative" (and the word itself indicates "multiples"). Chapter 14 stated the following about the case study's batch processes:

❑ The manager components will be responsible for selecting the appropriate records from the database and delegating the processing of an individual record (or batch of records) to a processing component. The manager will also be responsible for maintaining the overall status of the job so that it can be reported to the outside world.

❑ The processing components will perform the actual functional batch processing on the individual record or batch of records (using framework components, where necessary).

This separation is shown again in Figure 16-3.

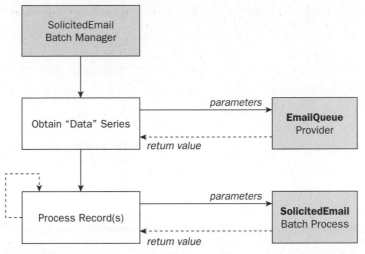

Figure 16-3

This section builds on this simplistic figure to flesh out some of the methods and interfaces that the batch processes (managers and processors) would need to implement to support fast and reliable processing that can be triggered via multiple channels.

In the online application, a web page calls the managers via web services. The managers accept a `TransactionContext` object, which they use, populate, and return to the page. In the case of batch, the manager component needs to be called from the outside world. Given that the components are contained within class libraries, it stands to reason that they will require instantiation and invocation by another process that can be called from the outside world — for example, the batch scheduler.

Figure 16-4 depicts the conceptual batch execution flow where the individual jobs would be scheduled via the batch scheduler.

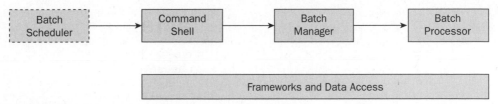

Figure 16-4

The batch scheduler would trigger the job through a lightweight command shell. The command shell would invoke the manager, which would in turn invoke the processor, and the job would start to execute and process. Continuing with this basic concept, you could, if necessary, introduce a "thin" service shell, which would run as a Windows service, and invoke the batch manager in the same way. This is shown in Figure 16-5.

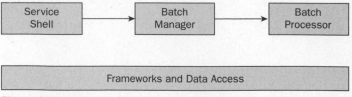

Figure 16-5

Given these two invocation methods, and the possibility of additional ones, you need to introduce a framework component that encapsulates the mechanics of invoking the specific batch manager component. Otherwise, you would need a shell for each and every job in the solution, and there should really be only one per invocation style. The framework component would act as a factory object and provide the consumer (the calling component) with a batch job object that it can call. This immediately introduces the following into the solution:

❑ The `BatchJobFactory` class, which would be responsible for instantiating the appropriate batch job based on some form of input value or type

❑ The `IBatchManager` interface, which the batch manager components would need to implement to support external communication

With these two new requirements you can set about figuring out exactly how the actual implementation would work and what else may be required. The following sections discuss these topics.

The BatchJobFactory Class

The `BatchJobFactory` class needs to provide the execution shell (either the service shell or command shell) with a batch job object that implements the `IBatchManager` interface. To do this, it first needs some kind of value or type to determine which batch manager object to instantiate and return.

The batch scheduler supports the passing of parameters on the command line, as does a Windows service. In fact, it would be hard to believe that any future invocation method wouldn't support passing parameters. So, you can continue on the basis that parameters can be passed from the outside world. The shell will pass in a value (which has been passed to it from either the batch scheduler or the Service Control panel), and you simply need to determine what this value would actually "mean." Command-line parameters are actually strings, and although you haven't decided what the value would mean, you can use a suitably abstract term, such as `BatchJobIdentifier`. You now have enough information to specify the initial public interface for the `BatchJobFactory` class:

```
interface BatchJobFactory
{
    IBatchManager CreateBatchManager( string batchJobIdentifier );
}
```

In this example code, the `BatchJobFactory` interface simply specifies a single method that would create a new batch manager class (which would implement the `IBatchManager` interface) based on the `batchJobIdentifier` parameter, and returns a reference to it. The interface provides a reasonable starting point for determining how to implement the `CreateBatchManager` method's functionality.

One way to determine the appropriate manager to instantiate is to have a `switch...case` statement in the `CreateBatchManager` method and, based on the `BatchJobIdentifier`, instantiate the appropriate manager and return it to the caller. However, as new jobs are added (which is likely in the real world), this requires that the factory's source code be updated and tested accordingly. Furthermore, it is not a typically elegant or extensible solution.

A more extensible solution is to implement "late binding" techniques. In this instance, the factory instantiates the appropriate batch manager class using configuration settings according to the value passed in. It doesn't matter at this point where these configuration settings are actually stored or how they are obtained. You know that you'll use a framework component to obtain them, so you simply need to determine what would be returned. The following is an XML example that could easily be translated into actual configuration settings, a database table, and so on:

```xml
<batchJob batchJobIdentifier="" assemblyName="" className="">
    <parameters>
        <parameter name="" value="" />
    </parameters>
</batchJob>
```

The basic structure supports the specification of the assembly name and class name that the factory would require to instantiate the class. In addition, the structure supports the specification of some custom parameters that could be passed to the batch manager's constructor. It's always a good idea when implementing generic or extensible solutions to support custom parameter specification and passing.

You will recall from the earlier discussion and the conceptual design that the web pages pass the batch manager a `TransactionContext` object. You can follow exactly the same pattern here. The factory can compile a `TransactionContext` object based on the information contained in the configuration and pass it to the manager during instantiation. In this instance, the "request" would contain the individual parameters in the configuration. The factory could also add additional information to the transaction context, such as the job identifier. However, you don't need to focus on this right now. The manager would simply retain the context in readiness for being called by the shell. The manager shouldn't really perform any high-level processing in its constructor.

Figure 16-6 depicts the conceptual processing pattern for the `CreateBatchManager` method and captures all the information discussed so far.

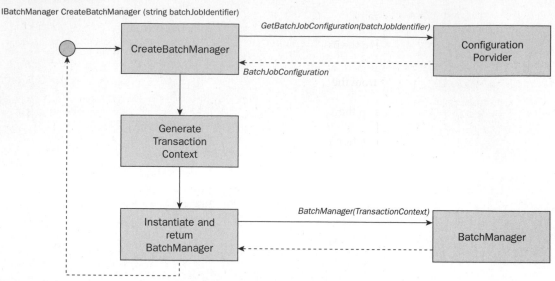

Figure 16-6

Note that the figure contains some placeholders for the outstanding design elements and areas for further refinement, such as the Configuration Provider's GetBatchJobConfiguration method, the IBatchManager interface, and the individual batch manager classes (which implement the IBatchManager interface), all of which can be plugged along the way.

The execution shell will obtain a reference to the appropriate batch manager using the BatchJobFactory object. The next section concentrates on the batch job execution flow and the specific methods on the IBatchManager interface.

Batch Job Execution Flow

This section follows on from the previous discussions, in which an instance of the appropriate batch manager component would be created and returned to the appropriate execution shell by the factory.

The command shell needs to provide progress reporting (for the batch process) to the operators through the StdOut and StdErr streams while the manager (and processor) is processing. To achieve this, the command shell needs to create the manager (via the factory) and invoke it under a separate processing thread. The shell then needs to periodically "probe" the batch manager for its processing progress (or status) and write this out to the appropriate stream.

In the case of the Windows service execution shell, the shell would (by default) invoke the manager under a separate processing thread, as its main thread would be listening for commands such as stop, pause, and so forth issued via the Service Control panel or other means, such as net stop commands or any other specific service control programs.

The manager components need to remain constant, regardless of whether they are called via the command shell, the service shell, or any others for that matter. This is where you need to start defining the IBatchManager interface.

To recap the current "state" of affairs:

❑   The shell has a reference to the batch manager component.

❑   The batch manager component has a populated `TransactionContext` object that contains various items passed in from the batch configuration, including any custom request parameters.

In order to flesh out the methods on the `IBatchManager` interface, it is worth looking at what a typical "resident-and-stay-permanent" processing pattern would look like. This is because batch processes can make use of this type of implementation pattern very well, especially when they are implemented as constantly running background processes such as Windows services. Figure 16-7 shows the basic processing pattern.

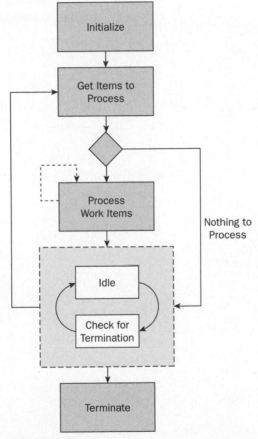

Figure 16-7

First, the process initializes itself. This involves obtaining configuration, creating objects, and so forth. The process would then get some items to process. If there was nothing to do, it would simply go into an "idle" state. If there were work items to process, then it would process them. The process would then idle. Within the idle state it would typically sleep and check whether it should terminate.

The figure provides the basis for the `IBatchManager` interface and actually shows the steps the service shell would typically perform (albeit abridged). The batch manager would implement the methods, and the shell would control the flow.

In the case of the command shell, if the manager returned the fact that there were no items to process, the shell would simply terminate everything. In these circumstances, it is important to reduce the amount of pre-processing that's performed for no reason. For example, the manager's `Initialize` method could instantiate and initialize the batch process, which in turn could perform a number of actions before returning. However, once the entire chain was complete (i.e. all processes had initialized themselves), all the initialization processing would have been for nothing because there would be no actual records to process and the termination would ripple through each the components. Given this scenario, it would be better for the manager to perform only enough initialization for the subsequent `GetItemsToProcess` functionality. Only when there are actual items to process should the manager fully initialize itself for processing. This would improve the overall performance and avoid any unnecessary objects from being created and processed. Figure 16-8 captures all this information diagrammatically.

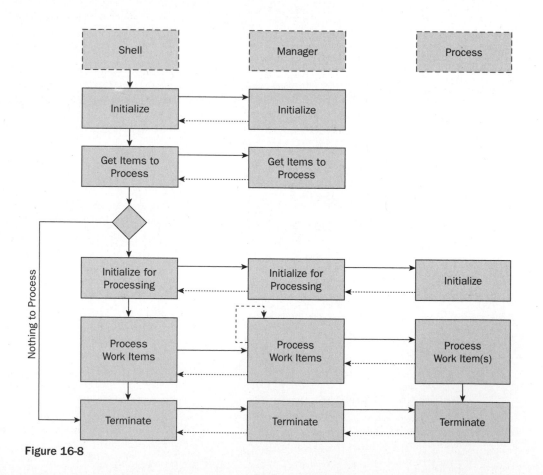

Figure 16-8

You can see from the figure that the batch processors will implement the classic *Initialize-Process-Terminate* pattern. However, these actions should be captured in a formal interface for consistency. In this instance, this would be the IBatchProcessor interface.

The following provides a more detailed overview of the interactions and methods in the diagram:

❑ The shell starts by simply initializing the manager by calling its Initialize method.

❑ The shell then calls the batch manager's GetItemsToProcess method. The GetItemsToProcess method would use a framework component, such as the EmailQueueProvider, to obtain the actual work items. The work items would be loaded into memory in their natural form (DataSet, Array, and so on) and the manager would return an overall count of items to the execution shell.

❑ The execution shell makes a decision based on whether there are any items to process. If there are no items to process, the shell simply calls the Terminate method on the manager (discussed below). If there are items to process, the shell calls the InitializeForProcessing method on the manager.

❑ The manager's InitializeForProcessing method instantiates the appropriate batch process and calls its Initialize method, again passing down the TransactionContext object (which is based on the batch job configuration). The batch processor then performs the remaining initialization tasks and actions required to actually start processing work items.

❑ After the initialization for processing has completed, the shell calls the Process method on the manager. This method call is actually a blocking call. That is, control will not return to the shell until the processing is complete. The shell's "process work item(s)" step (as shown in Figure 16-8) is discussed in more detail in the next section. The manager begins a main processing loop and simply calls the processor's Process method for each of the work items. The manager compiles a TransactionContext object with all the relevant information for *this* transaction, which the processor would use, update, and return.

❑ After the processing completes, the final step in the process is to clean up and exit. The shell calls the manager's Terminate method, which performs all the termination activities, including calling the processor's Terminate method.

It is worth having a discussion on the batch processor's Process method. The online application's processors are typically dealing with a single transaction. However, in the world of batch, performance can often be improved by using bulk processing. For example, performing "bulk" inserts into the database rather than individual inserts can often improve performance. Bulk operations should be used where the technologies support them. The batch processor in this instance would be performing a larger workload in a blocking call. The number of work items should be configurable when bulk processing is implemented so that it can be refined and tuned throughout the testing phases.

If you're going to implement bulk processing, you need to implement the logic appropriately to ensure the correct logging and tracing is in place in the event that anything goes wrong. The manager is simply going to call the `Process` method each time around its main processing loop. The manager isn't performing any functional processing, so it is the job of the processor to ensure that everything is processed fully and correctly. The processor may also need to implement check-pointing logic to ensure this.

In the event that a batch process needed to be re-started it is far better to restart from where it left off rather than going through a series of unnecessary records. Check-pointing can sometimes be avoided simply by the selection criteria of work items although this is usually only when the job is processing and updating as it goes. For example, if a process selected all "New" accounts where the `ActivationKeySentDateTime` was `null`, the process could cycle through each record, process it and update the database field accordingly. This would mean that each record is updated as it is processed. The next time the job executed it wouldn't pick-up records that had already been dealt with because they wouldn't meet the selection criteria. Similarly, a job selecting and archiving files based on a filename mask, such as *.log*, would archive each file to an alternative folder. When the job was re-executed, the files that had already been archived wouldn't exist in the original folder.

A good example of where "real" check-pointing logic is used is when a job is not performing any "updates" on the originally selected work items. In this instance the selection criteria needs to be adjusted depending on where the job was last up to. The original work items would not contain any indication of whether they had already been processed or not. The check-point would provide the starting point for the next run of the job. Check-pointing is often used when reading records from files (or other sources) and inserting them into the database (or vise-versa). This is also a classic example of where bulk operations can also be used very effectively too. Note that if you are going to implement bulk processing, there are other areas in the batch design you'll need to consider. I'll discuss these as and when required. For the moment, let's just say the batch processors *could* be processing more than one work item in any processing cycle.

Because the processing is essentially iterative in both the manager and the processor (irrespective of whether bulk operations are being performed in each iteration), it is important that object creation/destruction is limited. Object creation should ideally be completely removed during iterative processing, and all components used in the processing should implement pooling or caching, where fast recycling can be achieved to avoid overheads in object creation and garbage collection. This subject is discussed in Chapter 18.

Before looking into execution control, processing, and status reporting, I'll just close off on the service shell. If the batch process was being executed as a service, the calling pattern would differ slightly from that described previously. However, the difference would be encapsulated in the shell. There would be no changes to the manager.

Figure 16-9 shows the high-level flow being triggered from a service.

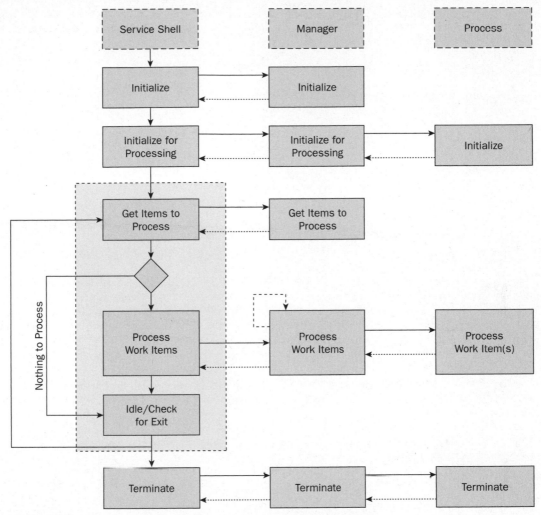

Figure 16-9

The following describes the key steps in the flow as well as the main differences between the flow shown in Figure 16-9 and that shown in Figure 16-8:

❑ In contrast to Figure 16-8, the service shell (shown in Figure 16-9) can take advantage of completing all the initialization of the components up front because they will be held in memory for the duration that the service is running. The service can simply call `Initialize` and then immediately call the `InitializeForProcessing` method to complete all initialization activities. Because the processing is periodic, it is important that these methods are not tied to the contents of the processing data set.

❑ The area surrounded by a dotted line shows the individual iteration processing. The processing iteration first determines if there are items to process. If so, it processes them in the same way as before. If there are no items to process, the service simply waits the specified (configurable) amount of time before entering the next processing cycle. This is essentially dead time (or down time) for the service. This is in contrast to Figure 16-8, where the process would terminate.

❑ If the service is stopped or the processing logic requires an exit, the shell simply calls the `Terminate` method prior to exiting, which ripples down to the processor.

Implementing this type of pattern in the managers and processors allows support for both periodic execution from the batch scheduler or running them as Windows services. The execution shells simply wrap the managers and call them in the most appropriate way. In turn, the managers call the batch processors to perform the actual processing. It is important to remember that this pattern works not only for single record processing, but also for bulk processing. Very often, bulk processing is performed in blocks. A single process wouldn't typically load 1,000,000 records into memory and then perform a bulk operation. It would typically load the records in blocks, say 1,000 at a time. Therefore, the process could still be called iteratively by the manager, in this case 1,000 times, with each individual processing cycle processing 1,000 records.

Progress Reporting

In addition to invoking the appropriate functional (or technical) processing, the shells and managers need to provide the relevant progress (or status) to the operators. The jobs are running in the background, so it is very important that they can be monitored and operated effectively. The manager components should not need to concern themselves with how and when the execution shell specifically reports status and progress. The managers should provide a consistent mechanism whereby the execution shell can obtain the current status or progress and report it in the most appropriate way.

In order to probe the manager for its progress or status, the shells need to call the `Process` method on the manager using a separate worker thread. The following activities are performed while the worker thread is executing:

❑ The execution shell obtains status and progress information from the manager component and reports it accordingly.

❑ The execution shell listens to and acts on operational commands, such as stop and pause.

This section discusses the first set of actions. The manager (and other components) will be raising events, updating performance counters, and logging and tracing, where appropriate. When the job is running as a service, there is really nothing more that the service shell can add to this reporting. From an operational point of view, the events and performance counters are the real measure of what is going on within the processing.

When the job is executed via the batch scheduler through the command shell, the status can be reported via the `StdOut` and `StdErr` streams, as well as via an overall exit code that the batch scheduler uses to control the overall schedule.

The manager has in its possession a `TransactionContext` object. The manager simply needs to update this with its current status and expose it to the shell, which would then have everything it needs to report the job's status as and when required. There are many ways in which this could be technically implemented — for example, using an event, a public property, and so on. The pros and cons of each should be weighed and the appropriate mechanism put in place. If a public property is used, it is important to ensure locking is put in place. However, we have a placeholder for this and can proceed on the basis that the manager will update and expose the `TransactionContext`, which will be used for effective status reporting.

By reusing the `TransactionContext` in this way, the solution is being kept consistent across both the online application and the batch processing. You just need to remember to ensure that the context object is "flexible" enough to support the different situations.

Figure 16-10 shows the end-to-end processing using the command shell example. You can easily map this to the service shell implementation, so I won't revisit this.

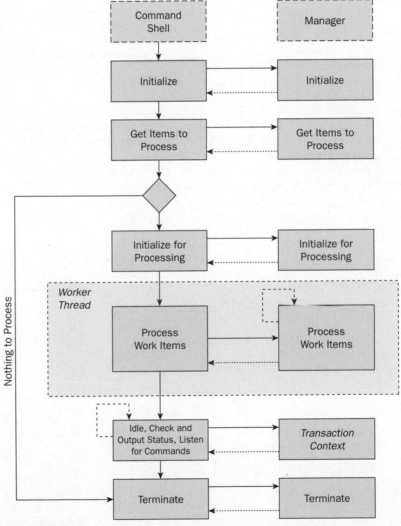

Figure 16-10

The figure shows the shell obtaining the status periodically while the processing is being performed in a separate worker thread.

To improve the overall performance and resource usage, the shell shouldn't enter a tight loop; instead, it should idle for a configurable amount of time, in which period it can perform other "control"-related operations, such as listening for commands (as discussed shortly).

To conserve space, the diagram doesn't show the shell obtaining the status after each method call to the manager. However the shell would actually do this, and the manager should update the status during each and every method. In turn, the processors should do the same so that the manager can obtain any additional information it may require.

It is important to use `TransactionContext` effectively to provide a "real" summary rather than an exhaustive amount of detail that essentially amounts to "information overload." You can use trace files and other mechanisms to provide more detailed information. The key is for the summary to provide clear information that can be used by the necessary personnel, such as the operations team once the system is in live operation.

Now that an approach is in place, let's look at each of the methods on the manager in turn to determine some initial output status information. The outputs discussed are only examples. Each method should be examined in detail, and the best output should be determined for operational readiness. The messages should also be obtained and formatted consistently (for example, using the `MessageProvider` object, discussed in Chapter 14, to maintain consistency and support change). Again, this keeps both the online application and batch in line and provides reuse opportunities. Finally, the messages should not display any information deemed confidential or secure.

The following shows some sample output from the individual methods:

❑   `Initialize` — This method is a blocking call, so the status would not be checked while the method is actually executing. The status would be picked up when the method completes. The summary should contain the component name, method name, process information, parameters, and the final initialization status, a lot of which is available in the `TransactionContext` that was passed in from the factory when the job was created. The output could also include the time it took to complete. For example:

```
[BatchJobIdentifier].Initialize

Parameters:
 [Parameter Name] = [Parameter Value]
 ...

Process Information:
[ThreadingModel = Single | Multiple]
 ...

Execution Time: [Execution Time]
```

❑   `GetItemsToProcess` — This method is also a blocking call, so, again, the status is not checked while the method is executing. Therefore, the output is again a final state summary, as shown in the following output snippet. And as mentioned previously, the status should be a summary. The manager wouldn't necessarily list all the items to be processed, as this would be very detrimental for performance. Instead, a simple message containing the total number of items to process would be more appropriate. That said, there could be occasions where a short list of items to be processed could be useful, but this would need to be determined on a case-by-case basis.

```
[BatchJobIdentifier].GetItemsToProcess
Total Number of Items to Process: [TotalItems]
Execution Time: [Execution Time]
```

❑ `InitializeForProcessing` — This method simply expands on the initial `Initialize` method by adding additional initialization information, such as:

```
[BatchJobIdentifier].InitializeForProcessing
Processors Initialized:
...
Execution Time: [Execution Time]
```

❑ `Process` — This method is executed in a separate thread by the shell, and the shell will need to obtain the processing status periodically. It is clear with the shell only reading the status periodically that it will not necessarily obtain every update. For example, the `Process` method could update the status for every transaction, such as `Processing Item 1 of 100`, `Processing Item 2 of 100`, and so forth. When the shell obtains and examines the status, it could have increased to `Processing Item 11 of 100`. The sample output from the manager could be as follows:

```
[BatchJobIdentifier].Process Processing Item [ItemNo] of [TotalItems]
```

Once the `Process` method returns from the processor, it will have updated its transaction context with the overall outcome of the processing iteration. The manager could obtain this information and append it to its own status to provide additional information. For example:

```
[BatchJobIdentifier].Process Removed Account Id 1
[BatchJobIdentifier].Process Execution Time: [Execution Time]
```

This additional level of item summary may be helpful, although the processing progress is typically the most helpful. At the very least, it shows how many items in the series have been processed and how many are left to process. The manager's `Process` method should also maintain the overall status of the entire job so that it can be reported by the `Terminate` method.

❑ `Terminate` — The last method called, `Terminate`, is another blocking method. The manager should use this to communicate the final status of the job prior to termination (rather than the specific actions being performed in the method). For example:

```
[BatchJobIdentifier].Terminate

Termination Status: [Normal | Aborted/Stopped By User]

Exit Code: [ExitCode] - [ExitCodeMessage]

  Total Items Processed: [TotalItemsProcessed]
Total Items with Errors: [TotalErrorItems]
```

This output shows whether the job terminated normally or whether a user or operator aborted it. It shows the overall processing status, including items processed and items skipped due to errors or inconsistencies. The manager maintains the error count by examining the Success flag of the provider after the processing iteration. The items with errors can then be investigated accordingly. The command shell could add to the final outcome status (or any other for that matter) with additional information, such as:

```
Start Time: [StartTime]
  End Time: [EndTime]


Overall Execution Time: [TotalExecutionTime]
```

In addition to the preceding points, the final piece of status that needs to be reported is whether the job actually succeeded functionally. The manager needs to provide this information to the execution shell so that it can return an appropriate exit code to the batch scheduler.

In this instance, all the information is in the TransactionContext. The Success flag would be set to either true or false by the batch manager, depending on the overall outcome of the job (it either succeeded in its processing or it failed for some reason), and the overall output text would be specified from the message. For example:

```
Exit Status: [Success | Failure] : ([MessageId])- [MessageText]
```

The shell simply obtains these status messages and sends them to the appropriate output streams. In general, the output is always sent to the StdOut stream. However, if the Success flag is false, the shell sends the status output to the StdErr stream as well. The batch scheduler typically provides operators with the ability to examine these streams.

Although this is a fairly quick overview, you can again see how the batch processes can make use of the existing online components. It is important to understand where the components are being used so that the various uses can be considered during their design and implementation.

Controlling Processes

This section examines the final part in batch execution and control — controlling the jobs from an operational point of view, specifically stopping (or aborting) the processes.

When the process executes as a Windows service, the Service Control panel (and underlying frameworks) allows the process to be stopped. The service shell needs to communicate this action to the manager so that it stops processing and returns control to the shell. The service shell or the manager could simply call the Terminate method to shut down the processes properly. It is actually quite easy to implement this functionality in the shell and the manager because the Process method is executed in a separate thread in both instances. While the processing is being executed, the shell can listen for the stop command and simply call a Stop method on the manager.

The manager's Stop method would simply set an internal flag, which would be picked up during the manager's iteration processing. It would also update the TransactionContext with the appropriate status message such as:

```
[BatchJobIdentifier].Terminate Stopped by user (Stopping)
```

The manager would check this internal flag during its main loop. The natural place for it to be picked up would be after the processor returned from its Process method. However, if bulk processing is implemented, the manager's main loop wouldn't pick up the flag the processor had completed and returned. It is sometimes completely acceptable to allow the process to finish what it is doing before exiting gracefully, especially if the work items need to be performed under a transaction or with check-pointing control.

In the case of stopping a batch process, it would be a very good idea to execute the processor in a separate thread so that the manager could also issue a stop command to the processor. The pattern would be the same as the processing loop on the shell. The processor would implement the same functionality as the manager and it would need to stop processing. As you can see, this is another repeating pattern whose implementation could be aided by base classes and reusable components. Once the stop chain had returned control to the shell, it would simply call the Terminate method. This ensures that everything is exited cleanly.

Figure 16-11 shows the threading-and-control mechanism. To reduce its complexity, the diagram doesn't show the steps prior to processing, such as initialization and obtaining the items to process.

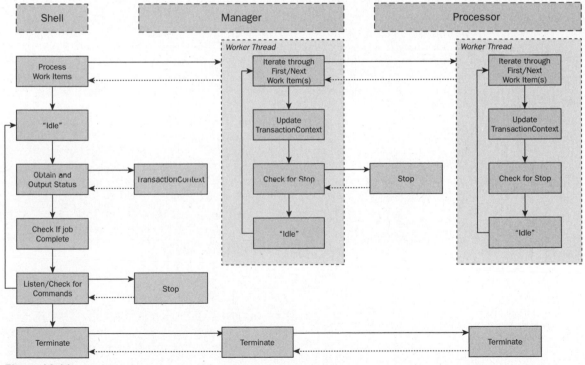

Figure 16-11

As you can see, the manager's processing is executed in a separate thread so that the shell can listen for commands. In turn, the manager executes the processor in a separate thread so that it too can listen for commands.

Additional service-control functionality could include pausing jobs and then resuming them. Of course, this means that the manager and processors must retain the overall processing state (current item number) in instance-level variables or static variables in the Process method. An operator could then simply *pause* the job via the Service Control panel, go under the hood and perform some rectifying actions, and then simply resume the process from where it left off. This kind of functionality can be useful during testing and live support, although it will have an impact on development effort and timescales. Pausing multi-threaded jobs requires all but the main thread to stop executing. Once the job is resumed, the main thread would need to instantiate all the worker threads again.

Controlling the process when it's executed from the batch scheduler is slightly more difficult. Under normal circumstances, issuing a stop from a batch scheduler typically terminates the process. This could render the environment unstable and is an untidy way of stopping processes, as it doesn't allow the process to clean up properly prior to terminating.

Again, there are many ways in which this functionality *could* be technically implemented. The solution could use semaphore (flag) files, or the control commands could be stored in the database, for example. The operator could execute a script that adds or updates a value in a table; the execution shell would read the table, act on the commands, and then reset them. Furthermore, the table could also be used to store other information, such as the current processing status and the final outcome. Storing this kind of data in the database would certainly allow additional technical and management reports to be developed. Alternatively, some inter-process communication mechanism could be used. The important thing is to understand whether the functionality is required and how to implement it effectively.

Regardless of how the control is implemented, the manager exposes the relevant methods and implements the functionality. The execution shells need to implement the appropriate levels of control to allow controlled operational procedures. In my experience, there's always a need to stop a process cleanly, and more often than not there's always a time when you say "I wish I could just pause this job, do what I need to do, and the resume it." Building the appropriate controls and batch architecture will help during production and, more important, during production support and incident investigation.

Multiple Threads and Multiple Jobs

The preceding section touched on the possibility of the batch processor executing its processing in a separate thread to support stop and possibly other commands issued by the manager. This section takes the concept of multi-threading further and examines the benefits of multi-threaded processing in the batch components, specifically in the processing.

There are many situations in batch where multi-threading can improve the overall end-to-end transaction processing time by performing multiple operations in parallel. However, there is generally a limit where multi-threaded processing on a single machine becomes counter-productive and it is far better to perform processing across a number of machines. The sections that follow discuss:

❑ Multi-threaded jobs

❑ Multiple jobs

❑ Batch job parameters

Multi-Threaded Jobs

Getting the most out of multi-threaded processing is really about examining the individual process and ascertaining where separate worker threads or processing threads would generally improve the end-to-end performance. The first and most important thing to take into account when multi-threading is to ensure that each worker thread doesn't impact any of the others. Each thread needs to be working on distinct and separate items as well as using resources effectively.

Assume that you have a batch job that is archiving and/or removing log files and other transient files from a number of different servers around the estate. The manager's GetItemsToProcess could obtain the list of servers that required clearing down. In the "iterative" model, and in this example, the manager would iterate through each of the servers, calling the processor for each one. This is quite a heavy-duty piece of work item processing (and will be discussed shortly). For the moment, in the case of multi-threading, and this example, the manager would invoke a separate batch processor worker thread to process each server, as shown in Figure 16-12.

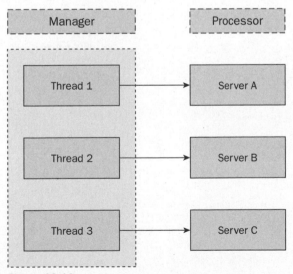

Figure 16-12

The figure shows each thread working on a distinct server. The individual threads would clear out the files and folders on the individual machine. As I mentioned, this could be a pretty large work item. There could be an enormous number of files and folders on each server that needed clearing down. It also introduces the possibility of multiple failures. For example, there could be a problem communicating with servers B and C, in which case the threads would fail.

The model would also have a detrimental effect on status reporting and execution time. The job would essentially enter a "black hole" and take who knows how long to clear down each server, although it does mean that each server is cleared down completely in the processing iteration and any issues are reported for an individual directory and server combination.

To improve the performance and gain through parallel processing, the batch processor could also implement multi-threading. For instance, each individual thread could work on a separate folder, as shown in Figure 16-13.

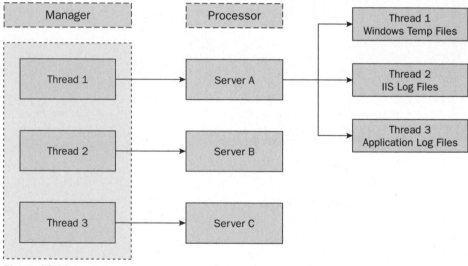

Figure 16-13

In this example, each processing thread is working on clearing down a single server, and each processing thread is using a separate thread to clear down each directory. Even with this level of parallelism, the job could still take a while to execute. It would really depend on how many servers, folders, and files there are in each and their respective sizes.

You can have an "instance" of the job per server, where each job is responsible only for clearing down a single server. The GetItemsToProcess would obtain the folders that required clearing down and can use a separate thread for each folder, as shown in Figure 16-14.

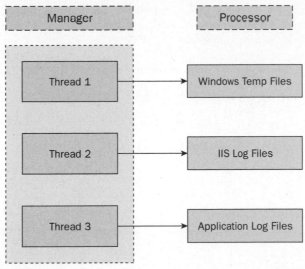

Figure 16-14

There's no absolute right or wrong answer to designing multi-threaded jobs like these examples. It is really a question of what is best for the application and the situation. You need to ensure that the jobs make the appropriate use of system resources, report their status and errors appropriately, and, more important, can be restarted or re-submitted with limited or no re-processing. For instance, assume that the jobs failed to clear down Server C. Without the appropriate check-pointing logic, they would actually need to cycle around each server again to continue where they left off.

There are many ways to slice and dice the work items to optimize the jobs and configuration. It is important to understand the implications of multi-threaded jobs, how long they will take to execute, and how often their status will be updated. The processor returns its status when the `Process` method returns. However, the same model the shell and manager use could be extended into the processor to provide more frequent status updates.

Furthermore, if there's a failure in one of the threads, what will the job do? Will it issue stop commands to all the other threads? Will it wait until they complete and compile a single status? What happens when the job is rerun? Each job in the solution needs to meet the individual quality characteristics so that it performs accordingly.

Effective logging must also be considered with multi-threaded jobs. If all the threads are writing to the same log file, the entries may be written randomly. The log prefix would need to indicate the unique thread so that the logs are readable and can be followed. The real benefit of multi-threading a process needs to be assessed on a per-job basis. When a job executes as a service and is running constantly, there can be performance benefits to multi-threading as opposed to sequential processing.

I much prefer to limit the use of multi-threading to only the jobs that really do benefit from it. Multiple jobs (discussed next), which can be scheduled accordingly in the batch scheduler, for instance, executing either sequentially or in parallel, can often achieve the same result. Clearly, this applies only to jobs scheduled by the batch scheduler (or equivalent mechanism). The smaller the work items, the better and easier they are to manage. Multi-threaded jobs should be used only when there's a real necessity and performance gain. The work item selection is key to batch job performance and processing.

When using multiple threads it is very important to ensure that each thread is controlled and managed properly. The number of threads should also be configurable so that the job can be tuned during testing and production to get the most out of the job.

Finally, each thread should exit correctly and perform all the necessary clean-up operations before returning control to the manager (or other controlling process). This ensures that everything is neat and tidy for the next processing iteration.

Multiple Jobs

Running multiple batch jobs at the same time can also improve the overall performance of the batch schedule. Again, the jobs need to perform discrete functions so that they do not interfere with the other jobs that are also running. You can then configure the batch scheduler to execute jobs at the same time or sequentially. This allows a greater degree of flexibility in the overall schedule. It also means that you can test different schedules without necessarily having to modify any code. The batch scheduler can then execute the jobs in the appropriate way to get the most out of the overall schedule to fit in the batch window.

In terms of the previous example, you could have a single job that archives and clears out the log files in a specified directory. This job could be scheduled by the batch scheduler to execute on each server required. For example, the "Clear Down Windows Temp Files" job could be run on all servers either in parallel or sequentially. There could be another job, "Clear Down IIS Log Files," which again could be executed on the relevant servers either sequentially or in parallel. Having multiple jobs does allow for better control over the schedule, but it also introduces an additional operational overhead for configuration and control. It can also introduce additional costs because many organizations producing batch schedulers charge on a "per production job" basis. There is a balance between multiple jobs, multi-threading, and configuration.

To get a real benefit out of multiple jobs running in parallel, you really should execute them on multiple machines at the same time. There comes a point where executing jobs in parallel from a single machine becomes counter-productive due to the available resources of the machine.

Figure 16-15 shows three jobs running in parallel from the same node. Irrespective of whether the jobs clear out multiple directories, they would all run from the same server and clear down a specific server in the estate. Performance would be greatly improved if each job were executed on the appropriate server. In some cases, this would require a batch agent to be installed on each server that job was going to be executed on. This could also introduce additional cost, deployment, and configuration overheads.

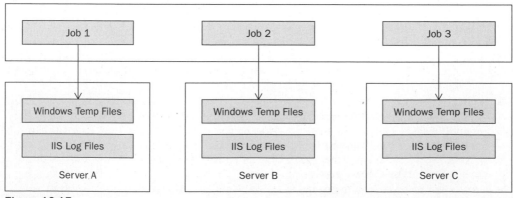

Figure 16-15

The functional batch jobs in the case study are all very similar in their processing functionality. Because each single job potentially could be processing thousands if not millions of records, you could improve the end-to-end performance by executing multiple jobs in parallel, with each job processing a different set of records and work items. It is a bit harder to carve up the jobs into separate processing units because their work items are simply records in the database, so there needs to be some kind of "formula" for separating them into groups that could be distributed across multiple jobs.

This is a very common challenge. It doesn't really matter if the jobs are executed at the end of the day or intraday, although it is likely that there will be more records or data to process if the job runs at the end of the day. However, the challenges remain the same. The jobs need to process all the records in a series and in such a way that they do not interfere with each other. The most interference between the jobs would be caused by potential deadlocks and timeouts due to record locks. Carving up the jobs also depends on how the data is stored in the database. For example, when the data to be processed is stored in a single table, the jobs might naturally be split by date ranges or perhaps even status columns. Where data is stored in multiple tables, a job per table could be used. Further, additional jobs could even be used on this basis, splitting the records by date range or status columns.

Database performance also is often improved by partitioning the database tables so that not all the records are stored in the same partition. Partitioned tables and indexes allow for greater scalability, manageability, and performance. When partitioning tables, the first step is to identify the partitioning key and the number of partitions required. Partitioning is discussed in more detail in Chapter 18, where you'll see that "partitioning" is good for both batch and online performance. When attempting to carve up batch jobs it is exactly the same first step. If the database table were partitioned, the jobs would naturally split on a per-partition basis. The physical partitions help with alleviating record locking and other similar issues.

If the table isn't partitioned, the job needs to define a "logical" partition to select unique records. The logical selection could then help to define physical partitions in the database (if required).

Let's consider an example that concentrates on the most important functional job in the case study, the New Activation Key Emailer. If customers do not get their Activation Keys, they can't activate their account and use the site. The job needs to run periodically throughout the day. The timing interval and processing time will play a crucial role in defining the number of jobs required and ultimately the selection criteria. New e-mail requests are placed in the queue throughout the day.

Assume that 100 records are being placed in the queue every minute (which is not a very large number). A single job would probably be able to process all these records in under a minute. In fact, a single job could probably handle thousands of records in a minute. The problem is that this information can really be determined only during performance testing, and if the job isn't sufficiently configurable, you could have a major problem on your hands.

We'll start by looking at a couple of selection criteria examples that would benefit multi-threaded jobs:

❑ **Date and/or time selection** — It is possible that you could use simple date and/or time selection criteria to increase the number of jobs and limit the number of rows returned to each job — for example, if you just deal with two versions of the same job. Depending on how frequently the job is executed, you could have one thread selecting records that were created within the past five minutes and another that selected records that were older. Of course, the records would also need to meet the existing processing criteria. You could increase the number of jobs, but the last job would always need to process all the remaining records so that there are no gaps.

❑   **ID selection** — An alternative to processing based on date and time is to use ID-based ranges. The range would be based on the "Maximum ID" so far (for example, Max(RequestId). Using this approach, the threads could be separated as follows (again, more jobs could be added and each would process a different set of records):

   ❑   Maximum minus 1000 to Maximum

   ❑   Maximum minus 1001 to Minimum

The first and most important consideration is that the timing of when the criterion is obtained can cause problems. The second consideration is to try to ensure that obtaining the selection criteria doesn't require a lot of processing.

When applied to jobs running at the same time, both of the preceding examples could overlap with each other, for example, when more records are being added to the database and there are delays in scheduling between the two jobs. To help explain, Figure 16-16 shows the jobs being kicked off with different start times.

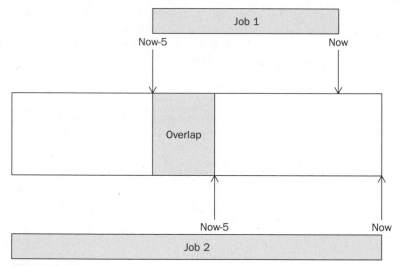

Figure 16-16

When Job 1 starts, it would obtain the records created as of "Now." If you assume this to be 09:00, the job would be selecting records created between 08:55 and 09:00.

Assuming that Job 2 starts at 09:01 and, based on the criteria, it would then be selecting records that were created earlier than 08:56.

This causes Job 2 to overlap Job 1 on records created at 08:55. Although it is reasonable to assume that Job 1 would have already processed these records by the time Job 2 got to them, the fact remains that there's an overlap that might cause problems or require additional processing. The same would be true using the ID criteria.

This selection criteria pattern can be used in multi-threaded jobs because the criteria can be obtained once at the start of the job and then distributed across the individual threads. Therefore, the jobs are always going to be working on distinct records. However, it is not very useful to apply the pattern to multiple jobs because they can be scheduled at different times. Both of these selection scenarios would also cause issues when jobs fail and need to be re-executed because time will have moved on.

You need to execute multiple versions of the same job in parallel without them overlapping, and the records should meet some form of static and non-overlapping selection criteria. To accomplish this, you could go right back to the start of the process and include a unique queue identifier when the item is added to the e-mail queue. The sample architecture would contain one queue provider per application server. This would allow a single job to process records placed on a particular queue.

To take this further and add even more jobs, each queue provider could implement a simple round-robin approach to allocation. You could have each individual queue provider manage a configurable number of queues — for example, 1–5, 6–10, 11–15, and 16–20. This would then support up to 20 individual jobs. Each time the provider placed an item on the queue, it would increment the queue number and start at the lowest number when the max had been reached.

You can even extend this approach further by implementing an algorithm that calculates a queue ID based on the values in the data. By changing some simple configuration values, you can add more queues and, subsequently, more jobs.

All these options allow you to add additional jobs, but they all still allow for a single job to process all the queues, as necessary.

Alternative approaches include selecting records based on pattern matching. Pattern matching is typically a good approach if it doesn't adversely affect the record-selection performance. Using a like clause almost certainly incurs a full scan. It is certainly an easier approach and affects only the batch jobs themselves. However, thinking about the batch processing early means the right controls can be built in up front. Whichever approach you take, you should base it on a formal rationale.

Batch Job Parameters

Offering the level of flexibility discussed previously requires each job to be configurable. The individual job instance can be passed specific parameters, which are used during work item selection and processing.

The level of configuration depends entirely on the job, although a completely generic approach could be taken. For example, you could pass each job an entire WHERE clause for its record selection. Passing an entire WHERE clause would assume that the job (and application) was using dynamic SQL statements. If the job were using stored procedures, it could be passed parameters, which it would use in a WHERE clause. For example, assume a stored procedure selects records based on a QueueId parameter, like so:

```
CREATE PROCEDURE GetEmailRequestsForQueue
    @QueueId int
AS
    SELECT ...
    FROM ...
    WHERE EmailQueueId = @QueueId
```

The batch process parameter specification might look something like the following:

```
<parameter name = "QueueId" value = "1" />
```

In this example, the batch process would use this parameter when executing the stored procedure so that the rows returned were associated with a QueueId of 1.

If the job was going to support the processing for multiple queues, it could be passed ranges, such as:

```
<parameter name = "MinQueueId" value = "1" />
<parameter name = "MaxQueueId" value = "4" />
```

These parameters could be used in a WHERE clause like the following:

```
CREATE PROCEDURE GetEmailRequestsForQueueRange
    @MinQueueId int,
    @MaxQueueId int
AS
    SELECT ...
    FROM ...
    WHERE EmailQueueId BETWEEN MinQueueId AND MaxQueueId
```

The parameters offer a completely flexible approach to configuring the individual jobs and their internal processing rules. The parameters can specify any name/value pair.

So far, this section has concentrated on the configuration of batch manager components. However, the configuration of the batch processor is also important. You know that the batch processor is instantiated by the manager and used accordingly. You also know that the processor will be passed the TransactionContext (which contains the batch manager configuration) during initialization. It is important that the TransactionContext be flexible and extensible, and also support specific configuration parameters that the batch provider can obtain.

To include this functionality, and much more, you can simply add to the abstract configuration model specified previously, as follows:

```
<batchJob batchJobIdentifier="" assemblyName="" className="">
    <parameters>
        <parameter name="" value="" />
    </parameters>
    <Processor assemblyName="" className="">
        <parameters>
            <parameter name="" value="" />
        </parameters>
    </parameters>
</batchJob>
```

As you can see, there is a separate configuration for the batch processor included in the overall batch job configuration. This prevents the processor from having to obtain its configuration from somewhere else, which will also improve performance. The factory, the managers, and the processors simply need to know how to "transform" and "interpret" this information within the confines of a TransactionContext class. But don't forget that this is still at the conceptual level; you don't need to figure all this out right now. At this point, all the batch requirements have an extensible and reusable architecture.

The configuration enables you to specify an assembly and class name for the batch manager, as well as to then specify the actual assembly and class name for the processor it should use. This allows you to "mix and match" managers and processors, which is quite useful, especially when looking at generic batch processes (the subject of the next section).

Generic Jobs and Generic Functionality

Generic and reusable functionality is pretty much a key feature of an extensible design. You can see from the patterns already discussed that you need only a single execution shell per invocation method. As it stands right now, you need a batch manager for each "type" of job. This is because the manager is responsible for the specific "work item selection." You could even make this functionality totally generic and simply delegate this task down to the batch processor, as shown in Figure 16-17.

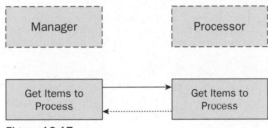

Figure 16-17

The processor would have already been called during initialization with all the parameters, and so forth, so it would already have everything it needed to obtain the records. It could either return the number of items back to the manager, or perhaps even a collection of items. It really depends on the threading model chosen and what information each processing thread required. Of course, the manager would then need to pass the items to process to the processor thread, which could require a certain level of interpretation.

Using this type of approach helps to implement a completely generic manager and there's no reason why we couldn't implement this. It would reduce the overhead in introducing new jobs, reduce development timescales, and reduce the number of moving parts in the solution. Given all the implementation details discussed so far, the manager would be a reasonably sized component, so it is a good idea to try to reduce the number of them that require development. That said, the use of base classes and inheritance would reduce the development timescales because most of the core code would be in the base class, allowing the manager to perform job-specific, value-added functionality. The choice again comes down to what fits best. However, a single "generic" batch manager and base class would be a good starting point and would provide the basis of an exemplar. You should design batch processes in such a way that they can be re-used wherever possible without impacting performance or functionality.

Batch is often extended throughout the project as more jobs and processes are identified, which is why it is a good idea to reuse and build generic processes and components. The following provides a brief overview of some categories of generic technical batch processing that form a major part of an overall batch solution:

❑ **SQL execution** — This can take on many forms, but in essence the processing would support the execution of SQL statements or stored procedures against a particular database. The batch process (or processes) would require some form of a connection string and a statement or stored procedure to execute, along with the appropriate parameters.

❑ **Data extraction** — There's generally always a time when records and data need to be extracted from the database and placed in text files (and other formats, database included). The processing would execute queries or stored procedures to return rows and output the information to a text file. The process (or processes) would probably need more configuration information, such as the format of the file to be outputted. This might introduce more database tables that contain the file format information, but the process could be passed a parameter containing the configuration ID for the output file. Alternatively, the process could use a specific configuration file instead.

❑ **Data importation** — In addition to getting data out of a database, you're often required to put data into it — for example, test data or migration data. The processing would essentially be the reverse of "data extraction" in that it would take records and data from flat files (and other formats, database included) and put them in the database according to a specific set of rules. The rules would stipulate whether the records (or certain types of records) are inserted into the database or updated if they already exist.

❑ **Data comparison** — This processing provides comparison of data extracted from the database or flat files, and so on. It can be used for reconciliation jobs where tables in different databases should be kept in-sync. It can report differences between the individual records, record counts, and so on. It can also be used during testing to compare expected results with actual results.

❑ **File archiving** — Archiving files and logs is always required in a solution. The processing would be configured to archive various files and folders. Archiving is typically done prior to purging to ensure that a certain number of log files are retained for incident investigation. The archiving process can compress the files and place them in a single location for later use and purging. The processing can use a list of servers and a list of folders that need archiving.

❑ **File purging (or deletion)** — This processing deletes the old archive files to keep the amount of storage to a minimum. The configuration would be similar to the "file archiving."

❑ **Controlling Windows services** — This processing supports controlling Windows services — for example, starting and stopping them, although you could use the `net start` and `net stop` commands, respectively. However, the custom processing can also check that the particular service has, in fact, started or stopped, thereby providing an additional level of robustness.

❑ **Controlling clusters** — This processing supports controlling clusters — for example, bringing them online, taking them offline, and resetting nodes. Cleaning up machines and resetting the environment on a daily basis could require the clusters to be taken offline.

❑ **Controlling processes** — This processing supports controlling processes (executables), specifically stopping processes or killing rogue processes where required. However, the processing can also be used to start processes. Rogue processes can sometimes be running when they shouldn't, especially when using third-party components that haven't been written correctly.

❑ **Transferring files** — This processing supports file transfer. File transfer is something that always seems to come up late, whether it is copying log files from one folder to another or transferring files to a remote location using FTP. Log files are often scanned by the analytics solution and need to be moved into a particular location so that they are not scanned in place. The processing could form a group of batch processes that offered various file transfer options.

This list of jobs and processors is for example purposes only. All of them could be executed from a single generic manager.

Using generic processing allows the batch jobs to make use of the existing application framework and configuration. Clearly, it would be possible to call other components and command-line executables from the batch scheduler. However, implementing generic jobs allows them to report status and be monitored and investigated in a consistent manner. When designing the batch schedule, it is always good to look at what other offerings are available as alternatives and weigh the pros and cons.

In many cases, passing configuration parameters and making jobs configurable and extensible require greater control over the parameters being passed. For example, a job may need to calculate or obtain a date and time. This is especially true when archiving older records. In this instance the processor can make use of the calendar component to calculate the date and keep the entire application consistent. It is important that the jobs be kept simple and that the parameters do not become a formal and unwieldy scripting language. Name/value pairs are simple and generally meaningful. They can also be specified in any order.

Summary

Using the approaches outlined in this chapter, you can come up with a generic and extensible batch architecture and framework. You can reduce the number of moving parts to support the functional batch processes by re-using common components and various configuration settings. You can also use generic processes during development and testing, as well as in the production environment.

The following are the key points to take away from this chapter:

❑ **Have a batch framework.** Implementing a reusable framework will reduce development and test effort, as well as reduce the number of moving parts in the solution. The framework should encapsulate the execution and control to avoid all jobs having to implement this functionality.

❑ **Keep each job simple and discrete.** This is the first rule of thumb for batch. The scheduler is designed for managing dependencies, ordering, and job execution, so the jobs themselves shouldn't include logic for checking or determining whether other jobs have executed (either correctly or incorrectly). The job wouldn't be executed by the scheduler if the relevant dependencies hadn't been met, so the job should simply focus on the discrete processing it needs to perform.

❑ **Ensure batch processing is as quick as possible.** The batch window is ever decreasing, so each batch process should perform its processing as quickly and efficiently as possible. Where possible (and appropriate) the batch jobs should make use of bulk processing to improve performance.

❑ **Report batch job progress regularly.** All jobs should report their processing progress regularly. This is especially important for long-running jobs so that operators can determine how much processing is outstanding and estimate how long the job has left to run.

❏ **Implement check-pointing "logic".** This is the second rule of thumb for batch: to ensure that each batch process can be re-run and preferably continue from where it left off to avoid unnecessary delays in the batch window by including some form of check-pointing logic. Jobs that process millions of records need to be quick. And when they fail, they should not process the same records again. Where jobs are updating the records they are selecting, the selection criteria can naturally reduce the number of records returned. However, when this is not possible, specific check-point logic will need to be implemented.

❏ **Use multi-threading and multiple jobs where necessary.** Where possible, batch should make use of multiple threads and multiple jobs to improve performance and shorten the batch window, although this needs to be balanced with deadlocks and timeouts. When batch processes are working on discrete servers or work items, they can make maximum use of multi-threading and multiple instance patterns.

❏ **Determine remote vs. local execution.** Where possible, batch processes should execute on the server they are working on to avoid network latency and transferring large amounts of data over the network.

❏ **Consider generic batch processes.** Generic services and providers should be used wherever possible to reduce the amount of code and moving parts in the solution. This can often save development time, assuming they are tested correctly.

17

Designing for Reporting

This chapter looks at some patterns and practices you can employ to improve the overall reporting within the solution. Reports can be used by the business team and the technical team, and during incident investigation. Reporting is not just database reporting; it also includes the log file analytics. However, this chapter concentrates on the database side of things. Thinking beyond the initial reporting requirements and capturing information in the database right from the start will help to ensure that the low-level data is in place and will help to support future reporting requirements.

This chapter is organized into the following sections:

❑ **Maintaining Meaningful Data** — This section looks at some of the specific data elements that can improve the overall reporting capabilities, including:

  ❑ Using lookup tables

  ❑ Recording dates and times

  ❑ Maintaining transaction counts

  ❑ Defining the master data set

❑ **Providing an Audit Trail** — This section looks at providing an audit trail at the database level. An audit trail can help during incident investigation because it contains all the changes that have been made to database records and, more importantly, who (or what) changed them. Reports of this nature can also be very useful for Service Delivery.

Maintaining Meaningful Data

Chapter 13 defined the high-level requirements for the case study's reporting, processing, and data elements. This section discusses some of the data elements and tables you can use to improve the solution's overall output and reporting capabilities. The focus will be on the application itself, and what the application should record and maintain in the database. The reporting solution (and other external sources) can then make use of this data to provide meaningful reports.

The following represent the four primary principles for maintaining meaningful data:

- ❑ Use lookup tables.

- ❑ Record dates and times.

- ❑ Maintain transaction counts.

- ❑ Define the master data set.

Using Lookup Tables

It is exceptionally useful for the database to be self-referencing — that is, the data should essentially describe itself so that it is easily understood. This is equally important for reports and the information they contain. For example, consider the following abridged data sample from the EmailQueue table, which could be used as the basis for a report listing items in the queue:

```
EmailRequestId    AccountId    AccountStateId    EmailTypeId
-----------------------------------------------------------
1                 1            1                 1
2                 2            2                 2
3                 3            3                 3
```

The EmailRequestId value is simply a unique identifier for each record in the table; the AccountId field is the unique account identifier associated with the e-mail request; the AccountStateId is an identifier on the account record that indicates the account state; and the EmailTypeId is an identifier for the type of e-mail to be sent out.

The report (or extract) is pretty meaningless unless you know what the values themselves actually mean and what the report is meant to show. In this example, the information would be more meaningful if it contained textual descriptions for the AccountStateId table and the EmailTypeId, not just the numerical value. Including this information is easy enough because the logical data model already includes lookup tables for all referenced values, such as the EmailType table, as shown in Figure 17-1.

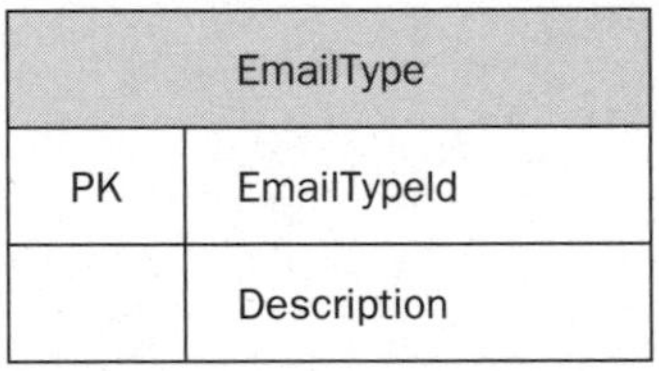

EmailType	
PK	EmailTypeId
	Description

Figure 17-1

The following table contains a list of records that the EmailType table would contain:

EmailTypeId	Description
1	New Activation Key Email
2	Activation Key Re-Request Email
3	Closed Account Confirmation Email

The preceding list contains the different types of e-mails that the case study would be sending out. The data model also contains the `AccountState` table, which would contain values similar to those in the table that follows.

AccountStateId	State	Description
1	New	New accounts awaiting activation
2	Active	Activated accounts
3	Closed	Closed accounts

Although this is quite basic, the database should always include lookup tables to ensure that the information it contains is easily understandable. Reports can contain more meaningful information. It is much easier for developers and operators to decipher the data in the database when codes in tables have an associated decode or lookup table.

Reports are typically executed at the database level, so they don't usually have access to the application components to convert the values into meaningful information. The following shows the extract containing some additional information from the `AccountState` and `EmailType` tables:

```
EmailRequestId AccountId AccountState EmailTypeId EmailTypeDescription
--------------------------------------------------------------------
1              1         New          1           New Activation Key Email
2              2         Active       2           Activation Key Re-Request Email
3              3         Closed       3           Closed Account Confirmation Email
```

Although it is not the most compelling report, the information is now far more meaningful in that you can see the actual account state and the e-mail type description. The overhead of including lookup tables is minimal, but the benefits are substantial. The following sections look at a couple of the additional benefits of lookup tables that are not directly related to reports or data extraction.

Using Enumerators in the Code

In addition to making the database, the data, and the reports more readable and understandable, lookup tables also provide the values for enumerations that the application source code can use, such as:

```
public enum AccountStates
{
    New = 1,
    Active = 2,
    Closed = 3
}
```

The preceding enumeration is based on the values contained in the `AccountState` table. Instead of the code containing expressions and statements like those shown in the following code snippet:

```
switch (thisAccount.AccountState)
{
    case 1:
        // new account
        break;
    case 2:
        // active account
        break;
    case 3:
        // closed account
        break;
    default:
        // unsupported account state!
        break;
}
```

The code is much easier to read and maintain when an enumeration is used, as shown here:

```
switch (thisAccount.AccountState)
{
    case AccountStates.New:
        // new account
        break;
    case AccountStates.Active:
        // active account
        break;
    case AccountStates.Closed:
        // closed account
        break;
    default:
        // unsupported account state!
        break;
}
```

If the actual value of the account state changes, it needs to be changed only in the enumeration and not everywhere else in the code. Wherever lookup tables are included in the database, you should also consider their values for enumerations in the code.

Including Information for Generating Enumerations

Finally, it would even be possible to generate the enumerators from the lookup tables using some form of code generator. However, as with most programming languages, variables and enumerations can't contain spaces or special characters. The descriptions in the `EmailType` table would need to be pre-processed in some way in order for them to be used as enumerations. One way would be to remove the spaces and any other special characters so that the enumeration would look as follows:

```
public enum EmailTypes
{
    NewActivationKeyEmail = 1,
    ActivationKeyRerequestEmail = 2,
    ClosedAccountEmail = 3
}
```

In fact, the preceding enumeration is pretty much how you would create it manually from the values in the table. Only developers see the code, so the enumerations just need to be meaningful enough to match with the functionality. When using code-generation techniques, it is often prudent to ensure that the descriptions can be used as enumerations or, alternatively, to include an additional column in the table that is used for the enumerations. The following EmailType table contains an example whereby the EmailType column could be used when generating enumerations instead of pre-processing the description.

EmailTypeId	EmailType	Description
1	NewActivationKeyEmail	New Activation Key e-mail
2	ActivationKeyRerequestEmail	Activation Key Re-Request e-mail
3	ClosedAccountConfirmationEmail	Closed account confirmation e-mail

Having the additional EmailType column separates the functional descriptions, which can be used on reports and extracts from the values that would be used for code-generation purposes. Of course, there are many other ways of achieving the same result, such as using a configuration file that simply maps the enumeration descriptions to the EmailTypeId to separate the code-generation configuration from the database. It is really a question of determining what is best for your own code-generation solutions.

Recording Dates and Times

Because a large proportion of reports are based "over time," wherever possible the application should record dates and times against operations. The case study has a date and time for each of the key actions that takes place on an account. Although not all these are used for the reports right now, that's not to say they won't be in the future. For example, you could generate reports that calculate the user's average session time based on the difference between LastLoggedInDateTime and LastLoggedOutDateTime. In addition, the number of users logging in per hour or day can form the basis of a very common report that is often required but not always specified up front. The latter report is often used to highlight key times of the day when most users log in, and the first report allows you to determine how much time the user stays logged in. The following shows a very simplified example of an extract that could be based on LastLoggedInDateTime and LastLoggedOutDateTime:

```
Thursday 29th June 2008

LoggedInTime    AverageSessionTime   UniqueUsers
------------    ------------------   -----------
09:00 - 09:29   0:15:00              689
09:30 - 09:59   0:20:00              1067
10:00 - 10:29   0:30:00              2178
10:30 - 10:59   0:40:00              4109
...
```

The preceding hypothetical example shows the number of users and how long they are spending on the site at 30 minute intervals for a particular day. The raw data would be presented on the report in the most appropriate format. The example shows that most users are logging in between 10:30 and 10:59 and spend 40 minutes on average on the site. Although there are no specific requirements for a report like this right now, simply recording the LastLoggedInDateTime and LastLoggedOutDateTime makes it entirely possible to produce the report in the future. Furthermore, recording the dates and times a transaction takes place will allow this information to be enhanced by showing the types of transactions being carried out at these times. For example:

```
Thursday 29th June 2008

LoggedInTime    AverageSessionTime    UniqueUsers    Transactions    Count
-----------     ------------------    -----------    ------------    -----
09:00 - 09:29   0:15:00               689
                                                     UpdateAccount   235
                                                     CloseAccount    306
...
```

Again, this is a very simplified example, but it shows the transactions being performed during the time span. The case study has limited functionality right now, so the information is somewhat limited. However, as it grows, the transactions would become richer, so the reports would contain more information. The daily data could be consolidated with other days to provide a complete trend analysis. By simply recording dates and times in the database, you can support a magnitude of different reports. If you're not recording the date and time of a transaction, you should be.

This type of reporting would typically be included in the analytics solution. You can generally extract the information required to generate the reports from the web server log files by analyzing the pages visited. However, in the absence of an analytics solution, recording the dates and times of when transactions take place, as well as which transactions were performed, allows you to generate these types of reports from the data in the database.

You already have requirements for an "aged" account report, which currently refers to "new" accounts that haven't been activated. In order to support this reporting requirement, the application must record the date and time a new account was created because the report can't be solely based on the account state (for example, "New"). Additional reporting requirements could include reports showing accounts that haven't been logged into for a certain period of time. The requirements that were put in place in Chapter 13 to record various dates and times will support some of these future requirements. As I've mentioned many times, new reports are always identified throughout the project lifecycle and throughout the software's production lifetime. Again, this is quite simple but recording dates and times is well worth remembering when validating the application's requirements, design, and processing.

It is equally important to ensure that the precision of the date and time is suitable for the potential reporting purposes. The preceding examples were based on 30-minute intervals; however, during incident investigation, the precision might need to go down to a sub-millisecond value, especially when dealing with high volumes and throughput. Trying to work out which transactions took place at a particular point in time is often helped by having highly precise dates and times that include milliseconds or even sub-milliseconds. Without the dates and times, there's no telling when an operation took place, so finding a particular transaction could be difficult.

Maintaining Transaction Counts

As with recording dates and times, maintaining transaction counts can help bolster the reports — for instance, recording the number of times users re-request their Activation Key, the number of times users change their password, and so on. This is an interesting subject and one that's often debated because of performance concerns. For instance, the `AuthenticationProcess` class could very well record the number of authentication failures against an account, for instance by recording `FailedLoginAttempts`. The debate stems from the fact that it is a "passive" process. That is, `AuthenticationProcess` has already been down to the database to obtain the account record, so if it is going to record the failures, it needs to write back to the database each time the authentication comparison fails. If the information isn't going to be used for any purpose, this is considered a waste of processing. "Active" processing components, on the other hand, can generally increment the counts while they are writing to the database anyway, which will not impact performance unduly. When information needs to be recorded by "passive" components, the processing and performance overheads need to be fully understood and included in the requirements.

There are a couple of challenges with maintaining transaction counts in the database. Let's assume that the `AuthenticationProcess` class does, in fact, need to record the number of authentication failures. The following lists the high-level flow and the various considerations:

❏ The `AuthenticationProcess` class needs to obtain the specified account, either via the username or the e-mail address, depending on the page the user is being authenticated on. It will do this using the `AccountProvider` class.

❏ The `AuthenticationProcess` class then needs to compare the account details obtained to those specified by the user, and the following concerns need to be addressed:

    ❏ What happens when the account specified by the user doesn't actually exist? The process can't update an account that doesn't exist. A new database table could be introduced to record any and all anonymous authentication failures. However, this would need to be factored into the requirements and it would also require periodic clearing out, which, in turn, would add to the batch requirements. This is another example of the domino effect.

    ❏ When the account exists and the authentication comparison fails, the `AuthenticationProcess` would update a `FailedLoginAttempts` column on the table. If an audit trail is being maintained on this table (discussed later in this chapter), this update could constitute a new audit record being created for every single failed login attempt. This could have a dramatic effect on performance. In addition, the user could constantly enter incorrect authentication details, which would create even more records and updates. The application would probably need to include functionality to reduce this — yet another example of the domino effect. Furthermore, the `FailedLoginAttempts` column would need to be reset at some point, which would again require additional processing. However, this could easily be done when the user successfully logs in — and this is a prime example of an "active" process. When the user logs in, the system records the date and time, so it is already writing to the database; therefore, it can easily reset the `FailedLoginAttempts` count as well as clear any flags marked for removal.

You need to carefully consider when transaction counts are actually maintained. Based on the preceding discussions, it is clear that recording transaction counts for "active" processing is the simplest. For example, in terms of the case study, you could easily record the number of times a user updates his or her account or changes his or her password, because the process is already writing to the database. These values would provide the basis for reports showing the average number of times users change their password or update their account, as well as the average frequency of changes. The transaction counts provide the basis for reporting minimums, maximums, and averages. Where possible you should record transaction counts to support these types of reporting requirements, especially if the information can't be obtained from elsewhere in the data model or via other means.

Another example for recording transaction counts is a report showing the average number of times Activation Keys are being re-requested. Couple this with the dates and times, and you have the basis for a trend report. The report could highlight some interesting values. For instance, it might show a particularly high number of re-requests on a certain day. Tying this to the `EmailQueue` table and comparing the differences between the `RequestedDateTime` and `SentDateTime` columns could indicate an underlying issue with the application or the e-mail sub-system. However, a simple extract of the data in the `EmailQueue` table would also provide the basis for this type of report.

Transaction counts can also be recorded using performance counters, although they are not tied to a particular account or database record. Where record-specific counts are not required, performance counters should be considered. Performance counters are really useful for "passive" processes and also in situations where you can't record the count against a specific record, such as the authentication failure example shown earlier in this chapter where the account record doesn't exist.

It is important to think about where, when, and how the transaction counts need to be maintained to ensure effective reporting. Unfortunately, it is not a one-size-fits-all situation. Transaction counts can be directly maintained in the database or via performance counters, and they can sometimes be indirectly gathered from the web server log files or application log files. By listing all the transactions and/or actions, you can determine the pros and cons of each approach. The following table shows an example of this:

Transaction/Action	Count Available Via	Pros and Cons
Anonymous authentication failure	"AnonymousAuthenticationFailure" performance counter	Recorded in master monitoring database and can be used for trend reporting. Easy to implement and test.
	"AnonymousAuthenticationFailure" table	Requires additional tables and stored procedures.
User specific authentication failure	"FailedLoginAttempts" column in User table	Would allow a report showing the "unique" number of users that actually fail to authenticate and the number of authentication failures. However, requires a write to the database for each failure and reset on successful authentication.
	"UserAuthenticationFailure" performance counter	Recorded in master monitoring database and can be used for trend reporting. Easy to implement and test but wouldn't show "unique" number of users.

Defining the Master Data Set

The master data set specifies where the data for each report will be obtained from. It needs to be defined clearly to avoid potentially conflicting information and reports. In many cases, it is possible to obtain the "same" information from multiple sources. However, the data is all too often not exactly the same. There are often inconsistencies in the data or reports. Sometimes the inconsistencies can be glaringly obvious, and on other occasions they can be very subtle, which can lead to problems. When thinking about reporting and maintaining meaningful data, you should think about the master data set and where the data is actually maintained and obtained from. This will ensure that the data is at least consistent every time a report is executed.

Listing the reports, the information they contain, and where the data is/or will be obtained from will help to define the master data set. In addition, it will help to define where and how the application should maintain the master data. For example, if the Failed Login Attempts report is going to be based on performance counter data, the data should be obtained from the master monitoring database. There shouldn't be another report that uses the application's database to obtain similar information because it could differ in some way. Similarly, the application shouldn't record this information in its own database unless it is actually going to do something with it.

Providing an Audit Trail

An audit trail can provide valuable information for reporting purposes. Remember, reports are not just for business people. Incident investigation, for example, can involve looking further into the database and transaction activity. Pulling the timeline together may require looking at a particular transaction and how the data has changed from end-to-end. A report showing changes to records, especially reference data, might be very useful for Service Delivery. A complete audit trail can often help with this by identifying which records have changed and who or what changed them. Knowing who or what changed (or created) a record generally means adding columns to the database tables, such as:

❑ CreatedDateTime

❑ CreatedBy

❑ LastModifiedDateTime

❑ LastModifiedBy

❑ LastAccessedDateTime

❑ LastAccessedBy

The columns act much like a "file explorer" in that you can see when a file was last modified and by whom. The drawback is that the application needs to update the columns, which presents a couple of challenges:

❑ **What should the "By" columns contain?** When a user triggers an action, the "By" column would normally contain that user's username or unique identifier. However, other processes and people are operating on the database records as well, such as batch processes and the operational staff. Ideally, the values should represent exactly who or what updated (or created) the record. In the case of a system-generated update, the value really should be a unique process identifier, such as the batch process name or the process ID. If members of the operational staff make the update, the value should be their system username.

❑ **What was the record before the change?** Typically, to see the contents of a record in its previous state, you must create audit tables that store every change to the record. This can dramatically increase the size of the database and sometimes involves storing the audit tables in a separate database, which has its own challenges. It also means that the audit tables need to be cleared out appropriately to retain performance. The audit table contains a copy of the record "before" the action, and the main table simply contains the current view (i.e., the view after the action has been performed). The audit table's columns are a complete replica of the main table columns, plus the following additional columns:

> ❑ **AuditId** — Contains the unique audit record identifier.

> ❑ **AuditDateTime** — Contains the date and time the audit record was created.

> ❑ **Action** — An optional column that can contain a specific action that was performed on the record, such as an "update" or "delete." In the case of deletion, this would be the last record in the audit table and the primary record would have been deleted.

❑ **Do you really want to update the record every time it is read?** Recording `LastAccessedDateTime` and `LastAccessedBy` would require that these column values every time the record was read from the database. This would have a pretty substantial performance impact that you would need to consider very carefully. Furthermore, if the audit tables were being updated via triggers, this could also mean that an audit record was being written every time a record was read or accessed. Retaining last-accessed information would typically be reserved for very sensitive and highly confidential data records. In a typical application this would be unnecessary.

Having the additional information as well as audit records can really help when trying to piece together the timeline for an incident because the information is easily available to extract from the database. It allows you to see everything that's happened to a record and, more important, who (or what) performed the action (create, update, delete, and so forth).

The following provides an example of the `AccountState` table containing `LastModifiedDateTime` and `LastModifiedBy`:

```
AccountStateId    State     Description                     LastModifiedDateTime
LastModifiedBy
-------------------------------------------------------------------------------
1                 New       New accounts awaiting activation  10/09/2008 10:10:51
DINGRAM
2                 Active    Activated accounts                10/09/2008 10:10:51
DINGRAM
3                 Closed    Closed accounts                   10/09/2008 10:10:51
DINGRAM
```

The following shows an example of the `AccountState` table where one of the reference data states has been changed:

```
AccountStateId   State    Description                      LastModifiedDateTime
LastModifiedBy
-----------------------------------------------------------------------------
1                New      New accounts awaiting activation  10/09/2008 10:10:51
DINGRAM
2                Open     Fully activated accounts          01/12/2008 08:50:00
JMASTERS
3                Closed   Closed accounts                   10/09/2008 10:10:51
DINGRAM
```

The preceding example shows that what was previously the Active state has been changed to Open. You can only really tell that the record has changed because you have the "before" view in the first example. If this information weren't present, you wouldn't know what information had changed, which is where the audit tables provide their true value. They enable you to see all the changes that have been made to a record by recording the "before" view, as shown in the following example:

```
AuditId AuditDateTime        Action  AccountStateId State  Description
        LastModifiedDateTime LastModifiedBy
-----------------------------------------------------------------------------
1       10/09/2008 10:10:51 UPDATED 2              Active Activated accounts
        10/09/2008 10:10:51  DINGRAM
```

Using the information in the primary table and the audit table, it is possible to determine exactly what has changed in the record. If the change caused issues in production, the audit table would contain all the information to reconstruct and put back the original record as it was prior to the change.

Under normal circumstances, there's no need to record the "after" view in the audit — first, because it's the same as the record in the primary table and, second, because it doubles the number of records in the audit table. For example:

```
AuditId AuditDateTime         Action    AccountStateId State  Description
        LastModifiedDateTime LastModifiedBy
-----------------------------------------------------------------------------
1       10/09/2008 10:10:51 ORIGINAL 2               Active Activated accounts
        10/09/2008 10:10:51  DINGRAM
2       01/12/2008 08:50:00 UPDATED  2               Open   Fully activated accounts
        01/12/2008 08:50:00  JMASTERS
```

The first record in this example shows the before view, and the second record shows the after view. When using this approach, it would be a good idea to include another column to distinguish the before and after records. As the record is updated, it would cause two updates to be made and the before view would typically be identical to the previously changed after view, as in the example that follows:

```
AuditId AuditDateTime        Action   AccountStateId State  Description
        LastModifiedDateTime LastModifiedBy
-------------------------------------------------------------------------------
1       10/09/2008 10:10:51 ORIGINAL 2               Active Activated accounts
        10/09/2008 10:10:51  DINGRAM
2       01/12/2008 08:50:00 UPDATED  2               Open   Fully activated accounts
        01/12/2008 08:50:00  JMASTERS
3       01/12/2008 08:55:00 ORIGINAL 2               Open   Fully activated accounts
        01/12/2008 08:50:00  JMASTERS
4       01/12/2008 08:55:00 UPDATED  2               Active Activated accounts
        01/12/2008 08:55:00  DINGRAM
```

The preceding example shows that records (2 and 3) are pretty much identical, apart from the actual audit trail-specific information (`AuditId` and `Action`). You'll remember from the earlier discussion regarding the recording of failed login attempts that updating a database value could cause additional audit records to be created. Using this "before and after" approach could cause two records to be created, which would be identical apart from the count increasing. When considering an audit trail, it is worth thinking about all the transactions that cause updates to the records and whether an audit of the action is actually required. Furthermore, where audit records are kept, it is vitally important that all actions be performed consistently. There should be no manual updates to the data, as this could result in audit records not being maintained.

When a record is deleted, there is no after view because the record no longer resides in the primary table. Only the audit record remains, as shown in the following example:

```
AuditId AuditDateTime        Action   AccountStateId State  Description
        LastModifiedDateTime LastModifiedBy
-------------------------------------------------------------------------------
1       10/09/2008 10:10:51 UPDATED  2               Active Activated accounts
        10/09/2008 10:10:51  DINGRAM
2       02/01/2009 12:18:00 DELETED  2               Open   Fully activated accounts
        01/12/2008 08:50:00  JMASTERS
```

You can see from the preceding example that the before view for a delete action is actually the last view of the record from the primary table.

In most of the preceding examples, the audit dates and times are the same as the last modified dates and times. This would actually depend on how the dates and times were obtained and whether they are from the "user" perspective or the "system" perspective. The audit records could be from the "system" perspective (for example, the date and time the audit record was created, not the date and time the user action was actually performed). Recording the dates and times from the "user" perspective helps in the case of a delete action because the audit record's date and time is the date and time the user performed the delete action, and the last modified date for the original record remains unchanged.

There's one more subject I'd like to cover, and that's batch processing. There are a number of batch processes that are operating on records, such as flagging them for removal and actually removing them. If these actions are going to be audited, you need to determine what will be recorded in the

LastModifiedBy column. Under normal circumstances, this would be the unique batch process ID. The following shows an abridged example of the primary record and the before audit record:

```
AccountId FlaggedForRemoval LastModifiedDateTime      LastModifiedBy
--------------------------------------------------------------------
1         Y                 21/12/2008 23:00:00       AAF202

AuditId   Action   AccountId FlaggedForRemoval LastModifiedDateTime  LastModifiedBy
-----------------------------------------------------------------------------------
4         UPDATED 1          N                 10/09/2008 10:10:51   IDE1968
```

The primary record has the "latest" view containing FlaggedForRemoval, the LastModifiedDateTime, and the LastModifiedBy, in this case the batch process that updated the record — in this instance, the AAF202 process. This presents another minor challenge. If LastModifiedBy is the batch process for the delete, it would not be possible to determine what the LastModifiedBy value was prior to the delete. Remember that closed accounts are simply removed and not flagged beforehand. The original LastModifiedBy value will be lost if the batch process is going to use this value when deleting records. For example:

```
AccountId FlaggedForRemoval LastModifiedDateTime      LastModifiedBy
--------------------------------------------------------------------
1         Y                 21/12/2008 23:00:00       AAF202

AuditId   Action   AccountId FlaggedForRemoval LastModifiedDateTime  LastModifiedBy
-----------------------------------------------------------------------------------
5         DELETED 1          Y                 21/12/2008 23:00:00   AAF402
```

The preceding example shows LastModifiedBy in the audit record has overwritten the current value. This is one example of where the before and after view could be recorded to ensure that the views are captured appropriately and the original data can be reconstructed.

Implementing such auditing controls requires very strict practices. Once again, this starts by defining the auditing strategy. Primarily, the strategy needs to determine the following:

❑ **Which database will contain the audit records?** High-volume systems typically keep audit records in a separate database. The additional database is configured accordingly and can have its own configuration, access rights, and disk space, which presents a challenge when it comes to accessing the audit tables. The application can either maintain separate connections (assuming the application code is performing the auditing), or the tables can be configured as "linked" databases so that they are visible to the primary database, and the stored procedures can use tables in them. However, linked databases can sometimes cause problems, and connections can be lost. This approach would need to be reviewed, tested, and understood thoroughly. It is possible that low- and medium-volume systems will have the audit tables in the primary database, although it really depends on the system being implemented. It is well worth making a decision early to avoid late-breaking updates to stored procedures and triggers (if used), and having to redesign your entire physical database layout. That said, if only a handful of tables will incorporate auditing functionality, this isn't too much of a problem.

❑ **How the audit records will be created and maintained** — There are many ways to manage the audit records, including:

❑ **Within the source code** — Updating the audit records from within the code is slightly involved because the code needs to obtain the original record first, write it to the audit table, and then apply the updates/actions to the primary table, all of which needs to be done under a transaction. You can use this option when the application is not performing the audit via stored procedures or triggers for database access.

❑ **Within the database's stored procedures/queries** — Implementing the audit logic from within the stored procedures/queries is relatively straightforward. For example, the stored procedure would perform actions similar to the following during an UPDATE:

```
BEGIN TRANSACTION

INSERT INTO AccountAudit
(
 AuditDateTime,
 Action,
 Username,
 Password,
 LastModifiedDateTime,
 LastModifiedBy
)
VALUES
(
 @DateTime,
 "UPDATE",
( SELECT
    Username,
    Password,
    LastModifiedDateTime,
    LastModifiedBy
  FROM Account
  WHERE AccountId = @AccountId
 )
)

UPDATE Account
SET
 Username = @Username,
 Password = @Password,
 LastModifiedDateTime = @LastModifiedDateTime,
 LastModifiedBy = @LastModifiedBy
WHERE AccountId = @AccountId

END
```

❑ **The preceding snippet isn't a complete stored procedure; however, it shows the SQL first inserting a record into the audit table based on the account being updated.** In this instance, it is inserting based on selecting a record where the AccountId equals the @AccountId parameter (which would need to be passed in). This establishes the before view in the audit table. The SQL then simply updates the original account record with the values passed in.

❏ **The drawback with this approach is that the stored procedure needs to contain the code for auditing.** The stored procedure also needs to be passed the date and time from the application so that it is consistent with the rest of the application. However, this approach keeps the auditing code along with the functional code so that changes to the table aren't missed — which is not a bad thing, really.

❏ **Using database triggers** — The audit records can be created by triggers on the primary table, which is quite similar to the approach using stored procedures. The trigger approach has the benefit of being able to implement auditing "behind-the-scenes." Some updates require that triggers be disabled prior to performing the update and then re-enabled afterwards to avoid additional audit records. Triggers are also fired on a "per-record" basis; therefore, batch processes that update potentially thousands of records can be impacted by the performance of the trigger approach. Furthermore, triggers have access only to the values in the record. They are not passed any parameters, so any additional information, such as the audit date/time, needs to be coded into the trigger. The stored procedure approach would be better all round because you could develop specific stored procedures that didn't include auditing logic or bulk processing for batch purposes.

❏ **The strategy for purging audit records** — Adding the additional audit records also means that they need to be cleared out, although this is slightly easier if you implement generic batch processes, as it should simply be a matter of configuration rather than physical coding. The records could be cleared out by date/time or removed in their entirety, depending on the processing required. For example, when an account is closed and it is time to remove it, all the audit records can be removed completely.

There is no doubt that even basic auditing increases the effort and cost involved in development and testing. As usual, however, this needs to be balanced with the benefits it provides in traceability, reporting, and incident investigation. It is also important to note that only the really key tables need to be audited. You don't need to apply auditing across the board unless it is absolutely necessary and there is a valid case for doing so.

Summary

This has been a fairly short journey. However, we've covered the main points required to provide effective reporting. Reports will be identified throughout the lifecycle and it is therefore good to be prepared for this. Maintaining the right level of information in the application (or the architecture) will help reduce the amount of "additional" work that's required when implementing reports.

The following are the key points to take away from this chapter:

❏ **Include lookup tables in the data model.** The data in the database should be self-describing. Reports are much more meaningful when they contain decode values.

❏ **Record dates and times.** It is important to record dates and times in the database so that reports can be generated based on these values. Reports often include data "over time" for trend reporting.

❏ **Maintain transaction counts.** You should think about how the application can record transaction counts, such as failed login attempts so that reports can be generated against these values.

❑ **Consider "Active" vs. "Passive" processing.** Active processes are good candidates for writing information to the database as they are already writing to it. Passive processes are good candidates for updating performance counters because they are not specifically writing to the database.

❑ **Define the master data set**. It is important that the reports are based on a single set of master data. The master data set needs to be defined clearly to avoid potentially conflicting information.

❑ **Consider implementing an Audit Trail.** An audit trail at the database level can provide useful information to Service Delivery and used during incident investigation. The audit trail shows what records have been modified, when they were modified, and by whom. There are many ways to implement an audit trail, and the options and considerations discussed included:

  ❑ Where the audit data should be kept (in the local database or maintained in a separate database)

  ❑ How (and when) to update audit records (using stored procedures, application code, or triggers)

  ❑ When (and how) audit records will be cleared out (using batch processes and/or during Online Transaction Processing)

18

Designing for Performance

This chapter takes a brief look at some patterns and practices you can employ to improve the solution's overall performance. It is important that performance enhancements do not affect the functionality of the application. Understanding the end-to-end processing helps to identify areas where performance enhancements can be implemented. Most modern code profilers will highlight issues and performance concerns with the source code. Modern database systems also include profilers for ascertaining the database performance. In most cases, they contain huge rule sets that cover a wide variety of functionality. It is important to use these tools wherever possible to ensure that any concerns are highlighted and addressed. This chapter looks at just a few of the most popular performance-tuning techniques. The goal is to ensure that you have a good idea of where you could implement them and ensure that they are captured appropriately. It may not be necessary to actually implement all the techniques, but it helps to understand where they could be implemented.

This chapter is organized into the following sections:

❑ **Tuning the Database Layer** — Examines a few areas within the database where performance can be improved, including:

❑ Indexing tables

❑ Partitioning tables and data

❑ Optimizing queries

❑ Caching database data

❑ **Tuning the Application Layer** — Examines some specific functionality that the application can implement to improve performance, including:

❑ Avoiding unnecessary method calls

❑ Implementing object recycling

❑ Using object pools

❑   Caching frequently used data

❑   Performing bulk operations

❑   Optimizing method processing

Tuning the Database Layer

The database is one of the key areas where tuning can really benefit the application and its overall performance. There are many ways that the database can be tuned effectively, including setting block sizes, setting optimizer options, cursor caching, database parameters, and so forth. A good DBA will be able to provide many tips for performance tuning the database, and the database itself typically will offer a suite of tools for performance analysis and tuning. You should use these tools as early as possible to highlight areas of potential improvement. The execution of these tools should be included in the work plans and their outputs, and details of how to rectify situations should be clearly understood.

For the purposes of this chapter, you should understand the following four key principles and implement them, as appropriate:

❑   Indexing

❑   Partitioning

❑   Optimizing queries

❑   Caching

The following sections do not go into the *n*th level of detail; they simply provide an overview of the particular subject, which should be bolstered by further investigation.

Indexing Tables

The database tables should be properly indexed to improve the performance of database queries. This is one of the most basic principles in database design. Understanding how the data in the database is accessed and used helps to define the right indexes. Some database systems require the indexes on tables to be "re-indexed" periodically to improve query performance. As data is inserted, updated, and deleted, the indexes can become inefficient, so re-indexing will optimize them. It is important to understand these requirements to ensure that the jobs are included in the batch schedules and executed appropriately. For instance, the Remove Flagged Accounts job could be deleting a large number of records, which could affect the database optimizer and also require the tables to be re-indexed.

The logical data model in Chapter 14 showed the `Account` table, which has a primary key on the `AccountId` column and a unique key on the `Username` column. These keys are noted in the data model as PK (indicating primary key) and UK (indicating unique key). Keys on tables are always indexed for performance purposes. A primary key is used to uniquely identify a record within the table. Unique keys are additional keys that can be used to uniquely identify a record in the table. These keys and indexes support the primary functionality in the application — the `AccountId` column is used as a foreign key in the `EmailQueue` table, and the `Username` and `EmailAddress` columns are used to identify the account record. All online operations are being performed using these fields. The `EmailQueue` table showed an index on the `EmailRequestId` column. However, if you extend the batch processing and implement multiple jobs, then this table could contain additional values that would need to be indexed properly. Changes in the functionality should also consider additional indexes.

The basic rule of thumb when considering what to index on a table is to start by looking at how the data will be selected. This involves looking at any and all queries and the WHERE clauses that they will use. The WHERE clause in a query specifies the record selection criteria, and the query will execute much faster if the values in the WHERE clause are indexed. The primary key is always indexed; however, the WHERE clause can also be made up of multiple selection criteria. In the case study, there are a number of queries that would be selecting records based on dates and times and, as such, the following columns would also be good candidates for indexing:

❑   CreatedDateTime

❑   ActivatedDateTime

❑   FlaggedForRemovalDateTime

❑   ClosedDateTime

Furthermore, indexes can be made up of multiple columns. These "composite" indexes can help to improve the performance of queries that contain multiple columns in the WHERE clause. For example, in the case study's Account table, you could include indexes that combined the following columns:

❑   **AccountState + FlaggedForRemoval + CreatedDateTime** — This composite index would benefit the "aged account flagging" process because the process would be selecting records based on the columns in the index. The process would select only "New" account records. It would require only records that were not already flagged for removal, and it would select records created prior to a certain date.

❑   **AccountState + FlaggedForRemoval + FlaggedForRemovalDateTime** — Similarly, this composite index would benefit the "aged account removal" process. It would select only "New" account records that had been flagged for removal prior to a certain date.

It is always worth trying different indexes and running execution plans to ensure that the queries are optimized accordingly. An execution plan shows how the query will be executed against the database and the indexes it will use. It is important to remember that the more indexes there are on a table, the longer it takes to write and update records. The application should be thoroughly tested to ensure that the number of indexes is optimized accordingly.

JOIN statements are used to join one or more tables together. A join is typically based on the primary key of a table. For example:

```
SELECT

Username
State

FROM Account LEFT JOIN AccountState ON
Account.AccountStateId=AccountState.AccountStateId
```

In this example, the query is selecting records from both the Account table and the AccountState table. The two tables are joined by matching the AccountStateId column, which is the primary key in the

`AccountState` table. It is also indexed in the `Account` table. However, it is also possible to join tables using columns other than the primary key. It is important that columns used in `JOIN` statements also be indexed to ensure that the query is optimized. Again, running execution plans will help to identify potentially slow queries.

Partitioning Tables and Data

Partitioning tables, indexes, and databases is another good way to improve performance (and scalability) at the database level. A common approach to partitioning tables is to use "horizontal" partitioning. This approach splits one large table into a number of smaller tables, each table containing a different set of rows. Each table has the same number of columns but will contain fewer rows based on the partitioning criteria. Each partition can reside on a separate file system where the data is spread across multiple disks. This supports parallel I/O operations and improves the overall performance of queries. Partitioning is typically performed by DBAs, although it is a good idea to understand the concepts and where they can be employed to improve performance.

> *"Vertical" partitioning also splits one large table into smaller tables. However, in this approach, each table contains a different set of columns but the same number of rows. This section focuses on "horizontal" partitioning.*

Partitioning is performed primarily on large database tables — that is, tables that contain large amounts of data. It is not just the size of the table that needs to be considered, however; partitioning can also help with tables where the usage patterns and access vary. Partitioning is also useful when it comes to archiving old data.

Tables are partitioned according to value-based criteria. The "partitioning key" is one or more columns from the table that result in an unambiguous value. There are many horizontal partitioning approaches, although *value range* partitioning and *value list* partitioning are most commonly used and are discussed in this section. However, before looking at these approaches, let's first look at determining partition keys.

When considering which columns to use as partitioning keys, you can use similar practices to those previously discussed for indexes. For example, the `WHERE` clauses in the queries determine the columns being selected and provide a good starting point for the partitioning keys. Primary keys typically make for good partitioning keys because they are often used in `WHERE` clauses. In general, the fewer columns in the partitioning key, the better the performance. You need to understand how data is being selected, inserted, updated and deleted to ensure you have the appropriate partitions and partitioning keys.

A *list partition* is based on a list of values from a single column. For example, Figure 18-1 shows the `Account` table partitioned according to the `AccountState` column.

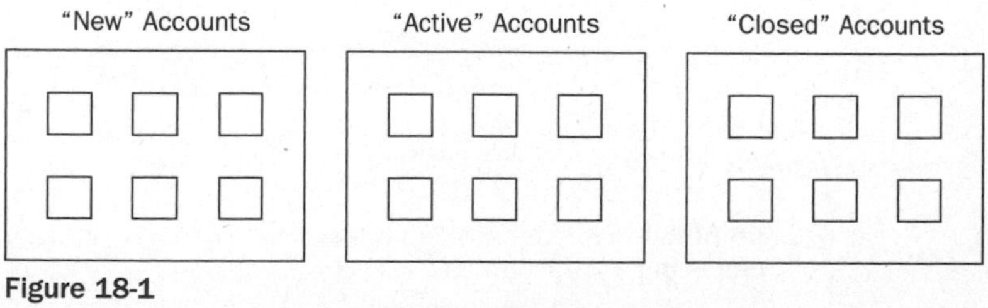

Figure 18-1

Each table partition would contain the accounts for the particular state. This would be good if you were selecting accounts only via their state. For example, selecting "New" accounts would only ever use the partition that included accounts with that state. A single partition could also include multiple states, such as "New" and "Closed." However, in terms of the case study, a lot of the account selection is done using username, and the queries would need to examine multiple partitions (which would be sub-optimal).

Another technique is to partition a table based on a range of values. For example, you could partition the Account table on its Username column so that each partition contained a specific range of usernames. The simplest example range is alphabetical (A–Z) and splits the accounts across 27 tables (including the main table). Figure 18-2 shows an abridged version of this.

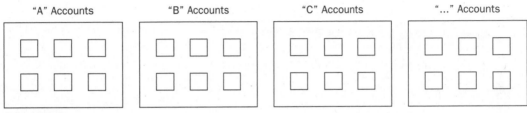

"A" Accounts   "B" Accounts   "C" Accounts   "..." Accounts

Figure 18-2

This partitioning approach would optimize queries based on the Username column. However, the reporting queries and the queries used for batch processes would need to select records from all the partitions, which again would be sub-optimal.

You could alleviate the latter problem of the batch processes selecting from all the partitions by splitting the processes into multiple jobs (as discussed in Chapter 16). Each "instance" of the job could work in a particular partition and thus gain from parallel execution. For example, the Aged Account Flagging job could be split into the same number of instances and would work on records meeting the following criteria:

```
Username < "B"
Account in State "New"
CreatedDateTime < BatchRunDate - NewAccountExpiryInDays
FlaggedForRemoval = Null
```

This would restrict the job to working in the first partition (for example, the "A" table in Figure 18-2). The partitioning strategy for the database is a good way to identify the initial split for batch jobs.

Regardless of whether you use list partitions or range partitions, the queries used for the reports would generally span all the table partitions, which is sub-optimal. Long-running or sub-optimal queries can also adversely impact the online application when they are executed at the same time the online application is performing its normal processing. The database has a finite amount of processing capacity, which should be used efficiently. Extracting the data and replicating it in a separate reporting database can alleviate this issue by turning the reporting database accordingly.

It is worth looking into the different database partitioning options and working with the DBAs to ensure that the right partitioning strategy is in place.

Optimizing Queries

The underlying database typically optimizes queries so that they make use of the best indexes available on the table. However, when developing queries, you should consider the following to ensure that their processing and record selection are optimized:

❑ Do include locking hints.

❑ Do select the minimum amount of data required.

❑ Do understand and use the most efficient SQL statements.

❑ Do use parameterized queries.

❑ Don't perform full table scans.

❑ Don't join tables excessively.

❑ Don't cause unnecessary database locks.

All queries should be executed against a reasonably sized dataset and "semi-production" database instance. I've chosen "semi-production" because the local partitions wouldn't spread across multiple disks. Where possible, the local database should mirror the production configuration so that you have a reasonable idea of query performance.

Later in this chapter I'll briefly discuss the use of bulk operations from the application's perspective to improve performance. Most database engines support bulk operations, such as BULK INSERT and BULK UPDATE. Bulk operations can greatly improve performance, however, their use needs to be balanced against incident investigation as well as the use of triggers. When triggers are used on tables, such as an INSERT trigger. The trigger will "fire" for each and every record inserted. This has the effect of turning a bulk insert into an iterative one, which somewhat cancels out the performance gains of using a bulk command. Speaking of performance, when the application isn't performing as expected, triggers can often mask what is going on "under the covers" and can be very hard to debug and rectify. The use of triggers should be minimized and fully understood.

Caching

Data cached at the database layer can improve performance and avoids the application having to cache it specifically. Most database systems support and implement caching mechanisms and techniques that can be tuned and optimized by administrators. In addition to the database itself, there are a number of third-party caching products. These sit between the application and the database layer and provide the caching. These are typically referred to as *middle-tier caches*.

The database cache itself essentially includes queries results. The database engine will ascertain whether the cached data can be returned instead of going to the physical disk to obtain it. This not only reduces disk I/O, but also processor usage. However, the query typically needs to be an exact match with that stored in the cache. For example:

```
SELECT AccountId, AccountSate, Username FROM Account
```

This query would return all the records in the Account table and they would be cached (depending on space and scavenging algorithms). *Scavenging* is the process whereby if space is not available, the engine will attempt to make space by removing old data from the cache.

Executing a further query, such as

```
SELECT AccountId, AccountSate, Username FROM Account WHERE AccountId=1
```

would *not* use the cached information because the query itself doesn't match with the previous one and would not return the exact same output.

Database caching is useful when the exact same queries are executed and return the exact same output data. For example, executing a query that selects records based on the account state would be cached at the database layer. However, the results of this query would only be returned from the cache if the subsequently executed query (or queries) contained the exact same WHERE clause (for example, selecting the exact same records). Each time the database engine needs to perform "hard parsing", the processing of determining the execution plan for the query, costs valuable processor cycles and can greatly impact performance, especially when there are many processes all running at the same time. Using parameterized queries can greatly improve performance because the database engine doesn't need to evaluate the query each time. It is simply the parameter values that change between executions. The database will cache the compiled code, which will be shared between all the queries.

When designing the data layer, you should understand the database engine's capabilities before diving into a coding what could potentially be a very inefficient model. A lot of applications choose to also implement caching in the application tier, where adding items to the cache and selecting from it is more granular. That's not to say that database caching is not a viable option; understanding the database and its caching strategies and options can really help to improve performance greatly.

Tuning the "Application" Layer

The application processing is essentially a key area where performance gains can be harvested. As you saw in the modeling exercises in Chapter 15, removing unnecessary database calls and combining functionality reduces the number of hits on the database. You can also employ the following techniques to improve the application's performance:

- ❑ Avoid unnecessary method calls.
- ❑ Implement object recycling and pooling.
- ❑ Cache application data.
- ❑ Use bulk operations.
- ❑ Optimize method processing.

Avoiding Unnecessary Method Calls

As developers, we're well used to pushing functionality and decision-making lower down in the application components. However, in some situations, a large amount of processing is performed higher up for no reason. This has a detrimental effect on the application's performance. A classic example of this is during logging and tracing. The argument goes something like this: "The application components shouldn't care if logging or tracing is switched on. All they need to do is call the right method and it will decide whether to output the information." The following pseudo code demonstrates this:

```
Trace( LogType.Information, String.Format( "{0}:{1}:{2} Authenticating {3}, {4}",
    className, methodName, DateTime.Now, username, password) )

Trace( EnumLogType logType, string logEntry )
{
    if( IsLoggingOn )
    {
        // output trace information
    }
}
```

Although this type of pattern has been used widely throughout the industry, it has performance implications. The problem is that the call to the `Trace` method is actually performing a number of operations for no reason:

❑   It is performing quite a bit of string formatting using the `String.Format` method, which involves converting the parameter values to strings, if they aren't already. For instance, `DateTime.Now` has to be converted into a string. The .NET Framework would achieve this by calling the `ToString` method on the `DateTime` object returned by the `DateTime.Now` property.

❑   It is placing a reasonable amount of information on the stack prior to making the call.

❑   It needs to clean up the objects used to make the call.

Chapter 21 discusses tracing in more detail, but as you can see from the preceding example, if the code is "littered" with these types of tracing calls, performance is going to be greatly impacted.

This type of implementation should be avoided wherever possible. Instead, the code should make the fastest check possible to determine whether an operation should be performed prior to actually performing the operation, which might be unnecessary. For example:

```
if( IsLoggingOn )
{
    Trace( LogType.Information, String.Format( "{0}:{1}:{2} Authenticating {3},
    {4}", className, methodName, DateTime.Now, username, password) )

}

Trace( EnumLogType logType, string logEntry )
{
    if( IsLoggingOn )
    {
        // output trace information
    }
}
```

This sample now makes a very quick check to determine whether logging is on prior to actually performing any logging processing and will greatly improve performance. There are many cases where even more up-front processing is done, including the creation of new objects, string formatting, and other method calls, which ultimately ends up in zero output. By surrounding all this processing with the simple `if` condition, the code isn't executed unless the tracing is configured.

It is not just logging and tracing that can cause unnecessary processing and negatively impact performance. Walking through the processing helps you to identify areas where a call could be unnecessary because of a decision lower down in the code. Where this is the case, the decision making should be exposed in such a way that it can be checked higher up to avoid a potentially long chain of unnecessary processing.

Object Recycling and Pooling

Creating and destroying objects can drain available memory. The garbage collector will reclaim this memory once it executes and determines the objects that are no longer used. Garbage collection frees you from having to manage memory manually, helps to reduce memory leaks, and alleviates other memory management issues. In addition to causing memory issues, creating and destroying objects takes time and can impact performance. A common programming mistake is creating objects during loops. For example:

```
While not done

   Create an object
   Use it for some processing
   Determine whether to exit

Wend
```

In this example, memory would grow — and you don't know by how much, either. It is not as though the pseudo code contains a magic number that tells you how many objects would be created. This is actually quite common and should be on any and all code review radars and eradicated. As the processing increases (for example, the number of iterations), so does the number of objects that it creates. If the objects are large and a large number of them are created, the application could suffer an OutOfMemory exception.

In this example, you could employ the recycling pattern. In short, recycling an object involves tearing down its current state and reinitializing itself. The object would implement an interface — for instance, IRecyclable. The interface would simply specify a single method, such as Recycle, which would be responsible for performing the operations previously discussed. The follow represents the preceding pseudo code when the recycling pattern is being used:

```
Create an object
While not done

  Use it for some processing
  Determine whether to exit
  If not exiting
      Recycle object
  End If

Wend
```

The size of the object and the number of initializing steps determine whether the recycling pattern could be used. For example, recycling an object could actually take longer than creating a new one. However, in my personal opinion, recycling is better than the possibility of exceptions and/or excessive memory use. The recycling pattern is useful in situations where iterative processing is required that would otherwise create new objects. Therefore, it can often help to optimize batch processes.

Another useful strategy to improve performance and reduce memory usage in the application layer is to employ the object pooling pattern. An object pool holds a finite number of objects that have been created during initialization or lazy instantiation. The maximum number of objects created would typically be the `MaximumPoolSize`. Consumers *acquire* an object from the pool; when they are finished with it, they *release* the object back into the pool so that it can be reused. It is important that objects are returned to the pool as quickly as possible to avoid the pool becoming a bottleneck in the solution. "Poolable" objects would implement an interface, such as `IPoolable`, that contains the properties and methods required by the object pool. Poolable objects naturally need to implement the recycling pattern unless the object pool is performing this functionality on the poolable object's behalf. In either case, the objects need to be reinitialized and ready for use when required. The `IPoolable` interface could include the `Recycle` method or, alternatively, all poolable objects could also implement the `IRecyclable` interface.

Figure 18-3 shows the pooling pattern diagrammatically.

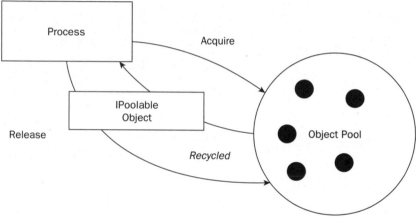

Figure 18-3

This pattern is very useful when you know that objects are going to be reused regularly throughout the application processing. It's also useful during batch processing. The object pool itself could be configurable and include additional processing logic. The pool exposes the `Acquire` and `Release` methods to the outside world. The following shows the `Acquire` method:

```
Object Acquire()

    Check current availability
    If Object available

        Decrement availability
        Return Object

    Else

        Throw Exception

    End If
```

This is the most basic implementation of the `Acquire` method for illustration purposes. The method first checks the current availability in the pool. If an object is available, it decrements the available object count and returns the object reference to the caller. If an object isn't available, the method simply throws an exception. However, advanced implementations could extend the pool by creating more objects. However, at some point the pool could be fully utilized and the consumer could actually use wait-retry logic in the event of an exception indicating a poolable object isn't available to further improve robustness.

The following shows the `Release` method:

```
Void Release( Object )

    Recycle the object
    Add it back into the pool
    Increment current availability
```

Again, this is the most basic implementation. The method would first recycle the object by calling the Recycle method. It would then add the object back to into the pool and increment the number of available objects in the pool.

Pooling objects is useful for long-running and/or multi-threaded processes that would need to make use of many objects. For example, a multi-threaded service that processes requests could make use of an object pool. As each request came in, the service would acquire a new object from the pool, populate it with the information, and pass it on to a processing thread. As each thread terminated, the *poolable* objects would be returned to the pool and be recycled. This would avoid garbage collection and maintain consistent memory use.

The sample processing outlined could be enhanced to support a wider variety of functionality. For example, the objects could be allocated at the start or allocated in chunks until a maximum number is reached.

Application Caching

Maintaining state across transactions is essentially caching data, although this can be thought of as a transient cache — that is, the data is being used only for the particular user session and the specific transaction being performed. The application itself can employ specific caching techniques to improve its overall performance. Caching is usually implemented to avoid hitting the database or other resources unnecessarily.

Caching data depends on the frequency that it changes. If the data is constantly changing, the cache needs to be constantly updated, which negates its purpose. Data that changes infrequently (or never) is a good candidate to cache in memory, for example, reference data, decode values, messages, and so forth. The most important thing to remember is that when the data does change, the cache needs to be updated.

Caching also applies to batch. Long-running, high-volume batch processes are good candidates for making use of cached data for maximum performance.

Performing Bulk Operations

Bulk processing isn't simply reserved for batch or offline processing, online applications can also make use of bulk operations. For example, an online store that allows users to browse and place items in their basket may employ bulk processing when it comes to storing the order in the database. The application could perform a bulk insert to insert all the order items in the appropriate database table. Bulk operations are often far faster than iterative operations. The database engine is often tuned for bulk inserts and bulk updates. However, as mentioned previously, if triggers are being used, this can cancel out the benefits of using a bulk operation.

Where processing is taken off the critical path, for instance, leaving all database updates until a particular point in time, bulk operations can greatly improve performance. Imagine you have a high-volume messaging system. As messages pass through the individual layers, saving the message in the database is a costly business. You may therefore choose to pass the message to an "offline" component which is responsible for saving the message. The message would be free to pass through the entire online system without being affected by database updates. This would greatly reduce the overall latency of the Online Transaction Processing. The "offline" database component would typically stack database updates because performing them one at a time would not really improve performance. When the component had received a certain number of messages, it would perform a single bulk insert into the database of all the messages it had received. This would greatly improve the performance of the "offline" processing.

Bulk operations should be used carefully. While they provide great performance benefits, they can also affect operability and transactionality. For example, if the bulk operation fails, there could be many implications for each record that hasn't been saved or updated. If the component fails (stops running), there could be a large number of unsaved transactions. The component would need to implement check-pointing logic to ensure that it could pick up where it left off. This could further hinder operational procedures, incident investigation, and the time the component took to restart.

Optimizing Method Processing

Optimized processing is another area where performance improvements can be gained. You saw how batch processing can be improved by having multiple jobs all running in parallel. Optimized processing in the application works in a different way. Instead of having multiple processes all processing at the same time, a single method can be optimized by performing its processing in a particular way.

Methods generally contain `if` statements to control the flow of execution. By organizing the condition checks in the appropriate priority order, you can improve performance, especially in negative cases. You need to ask yourself "What is the most likely situation?" and deal with this first. By ranking each condition and implementing them in the method in the appropriate order avoids the method performing unnecessary processing.

Another performance enhancement is organizing methods so that "heavy" processing is started early (or as early as possible) and performed asynchronously. While the asynchronous processing is being performed in the background, the method can continue performing other operations. When the method has completed as much as it can, it needs to wait for the asynchronous processing to complete before returning the final result. This type of implementation can greatly improve performance through parallel processing. Imagine you have a system whereby you are sending messages on a queue to an external system. Instead of immediately waiting for the response, it is likely that the method could perform other operations between the time the message was placed on the queue and the time the response was returned. It clearly depends on what the method is doing, but implementing this type of logic is worth thinking about early. Re-factoring components, as I've mentioned before, can be a costly and time-consuming business.

These are just two ways of improving individual method performance. The first is very simple to implement and the second requires a bit more thought. You need to look at the performance characteristics early and try to improve the individual method's performance. When it comes to performance testing, the faster the individual methods are, the faster the entire solution.

Summary

This chapter provided an overview of some of the techniques you can employ to improve the solution's overall performance. Although there are no "silver bullets," including these patterns and practices in the design (and, of course, in the implementation) will help greatly. It is often the simplest things that provide the greatest result. Including the patterns and practices from this chapter early will alleviate performance tuning and, more important, re-factoring, which could ripple through all the components in the solution, as discussed in Chapter 2.

The following are the key points to take away from this chapter:

❏ **Include indexes on tables.** Indexes improve the performance of database queries. You should review the query's WHERE clauses and JOIN statements to determine the best indexes to include. Remember, the more indexes you have on tables will affect the performance of INSERT, UPDATE, and DELETE operations.

❏ **Partition tables.** Partitioning tables can improve the overall performance of the application. Again, you should review how the database is accessed to determine the most appropriate partitions and partitioning keys. Remember, partitioning should also take into account reporting and batch components.

❏ **Optimize queries.** The database queries you develop should be optimized. You should generate execution plans for queries based on a reasonable set of data. The following lists the do's and don'ts for queries:

❏ Do include locking hints.

❏ Do select the minimum amount of data required.

❏ Do understand and use the most efficient SQL statements.

❏ Do use parameterized queries

❏ Don't perform full table scans.

❏ Don't join tables excessively.

❏ Don't cause unnecessary database locks.

❏ **Understand and employ the database's caching options.** Database performance can be greatly improved through the use of caching mechanisms. You should understand and employ database caching where appropriate.

❑ **Avoid unnecessary method calls.** You should avoid making unnecessary method calls in the application code. Performance can be greatly improved by surrounding diagnostic code with quick `if` statements to determine whether the specific diagnostics are switched on. Remember, this approach can also be applied to other areas of processing within the code.

❑ **Implement object recycling.** Garbage collection and object creation can be greatly reduced by implementing object recycling, especially when objects are reused in iterative processing. Remember, objects should be recycled as quickly as possible.

❑ **Use object pools.** Object pools allow you to manage memory usage more efficiently. A finite number of objects are created and reused, again reducing garbage collection. Remember, object pools mustn't become a bottleneck. Objects should be returned to the pool as quickly as possible.

❑ **Cache frequently used/infrequently updated data.** You should employ caching strategies within the application layer. Good candidates for caching include reference data, decode values, and messages.

❑ **Perform bulk operations.** Bulk operations can often improve the application's performance. However, you should understand the support and operational implications of performing bulk operations. In addition, when using triggers on the database, bulk operations can be turned into iterative operations, canceling out the performance gain.

❑ **Optimize method processing.** You should optimize your methods. The processing should be organized such that the statements are executed in the most appropriate order. In addition, you should consider using parallel processing to improve the method's performance.

19

Designing for Resilience

Although resilience comes in many forms, in the purest terms it refers to an application's ability to deal with adverse conditions and still provide an acceptable level of service. Adverse conditions can be caused by the user — and as you've seen already, many different users could be interacting with the system. System failure, whether software-related or hardware-related, is another area where issues can arise. And then, of course, there's the infrastructure, load balancers, routers, network, connectivity, and so on. This chapter looks at some practices you can employ to provide resilience against typical (and unexpected) incidents in the solution. I'm not going to cover every possible scenario, as that is beyond the scope of the book; rather, I'm going to focus on a couple of key areas where the solution can provide robustness and, as a result, provide a level of service to the consumer. Incidents can occur in all areas of the solution, including the core application, the batch solution, and even in the reporting components. It is important that all components be resilient and robust to reduce down-time and unnecessary outages.

This chapter is organized into the following sections:

❑ **Human Error and User Behavior** — Examines some of the typical failures and scenarios that can be caused by human error. This section also discusses supporting and controlling user behavior.

❑ **Handling System Failure** — Examines the exception-handling techniques you can employ to provide robust processing and to recover from typical failure scenarios.

❑ **Non-Stop Processing** — Examines how planning the architecture, frameworks, and infrastructure configuration can help to provide non-stop resilient processing.

Human Error and User Behavior

As you already know, you can have a variety of different users, including both business users and technical users. In this section we're going to look at a couple of scenarios where the solution can provide both documented and programmatic resiliency to human errors and user behavior. The journey starts with one of the most common causes of system failure due to human error: configuration changes. The second scenario involves supporting and controlling user behavior.

Managing Configuration Changes

An application can't be totally resilient to every possibility. For instance, suppose a member of the service delivery or operations teams changed a configuration value beyond an "acceptable" threshold. What would the application do? Obviously, it depends on which setting was changed, why it was changed it, and what the solution was using it for. If the value was being used to "throttle" incoming requests, fewer requests would be passed in for processing. As a result, the end-to-end processing time should improve, but you'd also see a decrease in throughput because the number of transactions entering the system has been constrained. Is this what's expected? If you're monitoring both end-to-end processing time and throughput, these fluctuations would be highlighted in the monitoring console. However, you need to consider what the most appropriate throttle values and ranges for them should be. For example, the throttle may have an appropriate range of 1,000 to 2,000. I raise this point now because configuration settings are typically strings in a configuration file. The application converts the values into their real data type and uses them. Unless the code has hard-coded acceptable ranges and the value converts correctly, the application has no way of knowing whether the value is right; therefore, it will simply execute according to the way it's been programmed. For instance, if an operator changed a throttle value in the configuration to 0 (zero), you need to understand the impact this would have on your application. Similarly, the operator could change the value to –1 or 2500, both of which are well outside the acceptable range.

To ultimately protect against this, the acceptable ranges would have to be hard-coded. If the range values are outside the code, then they too are "configurable," so you're back to the same problem. What values can the ranges have (and so on)? This is an area where both user behavior and the application processing must be aligned. I'm not suggesting that you have hard-coded values, however. You simply can't perform everything programmatically, unless you are prepared to accept hard-coding and "default behaviors" (as discussed shortly). The procedures need to be well-documented, as do the configuration values and their acceptable ranges. Changes to the configuration values need to be managed very carefully, verified fully, and signed off by at least two people or groups. This ensures that the change must have been done through collective agreement or "collusion." Many high-profile software failures and outages have been attributed to someone changing a configuration value without understanding its full impact. Figure 19-1 shows an example of this.

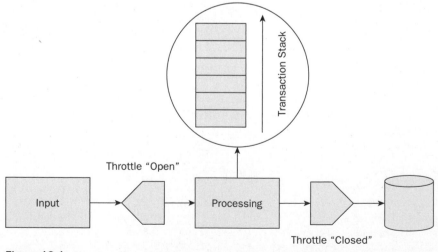

Figure 19-1

The figure shows inputs coming into the system when the throttle is "open." The exact values aren't important, but assume a high number of transactions. However, at the other end of the cycle is a "closed" throttle, which is constraining throughput. As a result, the transactions would start to stack up (queue) over time and could eventually fail due to an OutOfMemory exception (or something similar). It is equally important to consider the impact of the reverse (closing the first gate and opening the second gate). In such a case, the stacking would simply move higher up the end-to-end flow.

There are many different manifestations of transaction stacking, which include but are not limited to:

❑ The load balancer or router directing traffic to fewer servers than anticipated.

❑ The database being configured for fewer connections (or transactions) than the application or external connections require.

❑ An external system not being configured for the same throughput requirements that the application has been configured for.

All these scenarios could contribute to a customer-facing outage, which could be catastrophic for an organization. It is extremely important to think about where "human error" could compromise the system. Each and every "touch-point" needs to be thoroughly worked through, documented, and understood — for example, "changing value x requires a change in value y," and so forth. You might not have programmatic control over all your systems, so the documentation, processes, and tools need to meet the resiliency requirements of the solution.

Supporting and Controlling User Behavior

Users typically navigate through web browsers by typing a web address (or clicking a link) or by clicking either the Forward, Back, or Refresh buttons. It is important that you understand what these actions mean and how they work. You may have noticed that certain sites don't support all these actions and in some cases there's a very valid reason for this. The following walks you through the basics of the browser interactions with the web server.

The browser communicates with the server using HTTP (Hypertext Transfer Protocol). There are two important differences in the way the information is submitted from the browser:

❑ GET — This method passes the input parameters to the server as part of the URL — for example, www.within-a-click.com/login.aspx?username=david.

❑ POST — This method passes the form data within the body of the HTTP message when the user submits a request from the browser.

Figure 19-2 shows the basic flow of events in a browser-based application.

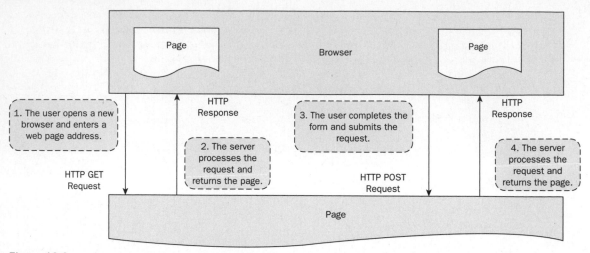

Figure 19-2

1. The user opens a new browser window and requests a page by typing the URL into the browser address bar. The browser sends a GET request to the server. Optionally, the page parameters can be included in the query string.

2. The server processes the request, and then constructs the page and returns it to the browser for display. The most basic page generally contains the static page elements, data entry fields, and a "Submit" button.

3. The user completes the form (which can cause postbacks) and clicks the Submit button. The browser sends a POST request to the server with the form data contained within the message body.

4. The server processes the page and returns the response to the browser. If there is no custom code, this is exactly the same as Step 2; the page is returned to the browser as it came into the server, and the fields are populated with the data the user entered.

A postback is the action of the browser submitting the request to the server for some additional processing. The server processes the request and returns the very same page to the browser for display. A typical use of a postback is when you have a dependency on a value that the user types in or selects. For example, you may have two drop-down lists, one containing countries and one containing cities. When the user selects a value in the country drop-down list, a postback is typically used to populate the cities drop-down list with the cities for the chosen country.

I'm not going to describe in-depth what happens on the server for each of these requests and responses. That depends on the type of runtime platform the solution is executing within. However, the following will generally occur:

❑ The application runtime or host will initialize and create all the necessary objects for handling the requests and responses.

❑ The server will create a new "session" for this browser connection. In .NET, this is the Session object.

A lot more goes on under the covers, so it is worth understanding the flow of events from the browser to the server for the particular runtime engine being used. Most runtime engines offer hooks for custom code to be included when certain events are fired — for example, during application initialization, session initialization, and so on.

This section, however, concentrates on the user and browser behavior. Figure 19-3 highlights the flow of events.

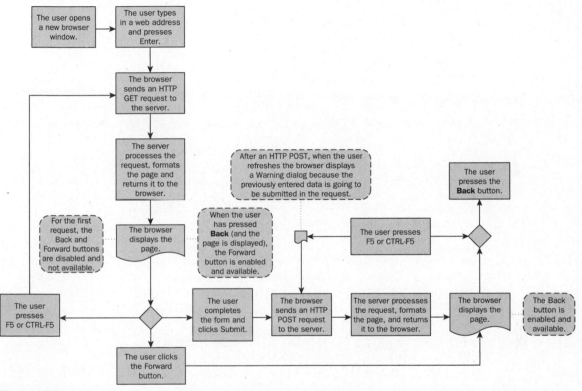

Figure 19-3

When the user opens the browser and requests a page (in this case, `default.aspx`), the browser sends the GET request, which the server processes, and the server returns the page to the browser for display. The browser displays the page, with the Back and Forward buttons disabled (see Figure 19-4).

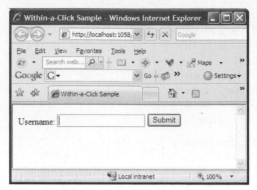

Figure 19-4

This is a very basic page and is used for discussion purposes only. It simply has one label, one text field, and a Submit button. The following describes the flow of events and actions that the user can perform at this point:

1. If the user presses F5 (refresh) or Ctrl+F5 (hard refresh) at this point, the browser will send the exact same GET request to the server, which again isn't a postback. In some cases the browser will cache information and when the user presses F5 (in Internet Explorer) it will not send a request to the server. However, Ctrl+F5 (in Internet Explorer) will always send a request to the server for processing, so this is termed a *hard refresh*.

2. When the user clicks the Submit button, the browser submits the form to the server. The browser sends a POST request that contains all the form data. After the server has processed the request, the page looks like that shown in Figure 19-5. Note that it doesn't matter at this point whether the user entered any text, although you can see that I have.

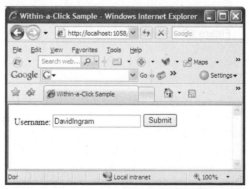

Figure 19-5

In this instance, I chose to enter a username to differentiate between the two flows. However, if I hadn't, the page contents would look exactly the same as that shown in Figure 19-4. The following describes the flow of events and actions from this point:

1. Because this is the second request from the browser, the Back button is enabled. If the user clicks the Back button, it has the exact same effect as the first request. The browser sends the same GET request it did in the first instance. The request is processed and the resulting page looks like that shown in Figure 19-4. However, at this point the Forward button is enabled:

    a. The Forward button is enabled because the user previously performed an action, and the browser saved this action in memory, as well as the resulting page and information from the server. Clicking the Forward button at this point doesn't send a request back to the server. Instead, the browser actually displays the cached page and data. The result is exactly the same as that shown in Figure 19-5.

    b. If the user has clicked on the Forward button and is now on the page shown in Figure 19-5 and then presses F5 or Ctrl+F5, the browser actually sends the previous POST request, which follows the same flow as Step 2, which follows.

2. If the user presses F5 or Ctrl+F5, the browser needs to resubmit the request. In this instance, it needs to submit the last POST request. It depends on the browser, but Internet Explorer shows a warning dialog box similar to that shown in Figure 19-6. The warning is displayed because the information that is going to be submitted in the request is the same data that they previously submitted. If the user clicks the Retry button, the request is sent to the server in the same way as it was in Step 2 from the previous flow (prior to Figure 19-5).

Figure 19-6

This is a somewhat simple example, but it demonstrates the basic browser behavior and the actions the user can perform. The following sections discuss the following important points:

❑ Validating and encoding user input

❑ Protecting against URL hacking

❑ Protecting against the resubmission of data

Validating and Encoding User Input

The user input can be validated — on the client side, on the server side, or both. Validating user input on the client side can improve performance by reducing the number of server-side hits from the browser. However, the validation rules need to be kept in-sync, and I've already mentioned the possibility of validation rules changing and potentially causing issues. It is also important to note where validation actually needs to be performed. For the moment, we're simply concentrating on the server-side validation and protecting the system against malicious attack.

If a user were to enter scripts and/or other "special" characters in a web page's data entry fields, these could inadvertently affect the system processing and be used for malicious purposes.

All user inputs must be validated. Validating the inputs against a set of rules will help to protect the system against attack. Fields that allow "special" characters, such as < (less than), > (greater than), % (percent), and so forth could be used to compromise the system. Where possible, you should reduce the number of fields that accept special characters to the absolute minimum.

Fields that must accept special characters should be HTML-encoded and decoded in the application. This mirrors the encoding that the browser uses on the URL. For example, if the data entry field allows the user to type in the less than character (<), the data in the form field would be passed as-is, such as "<script>". However, if the value were passed on the URL, it would be encoded and the value would be <script> (because the value is subject to HTML encoding).

Where necessary, the application should use and keep data in its encoded form to avoid potentially harmful results from inadvertent execution. This, of course, means understanding where these values are used and ensuring that all consumers of the data use it in the appropriate manner. Framework components can be used to isolate the encoding and decoding functions.

Protecting Against URL Hacking

Chapter 4 touched on the subject of URL hacking. There are two important aspects to the URL. First, it contains the page the user is requesting. Second, it can contain parameters that are passed to the page. When parameters are passed on the URL, it is important to understand:

❑   Which parameters are being passed and how they are being used

❑   Whether the system needs to "protect" itself against any of these parameters

It is not unusual for web pages to contain links to other pages that pass parameters as part of the query string. For example, instead of storing items in state, you could change the Confirm button on the Account Created message to use a link similar to `www.within-a-click/ActivateAccount .aspx?username=DavidIngram&activationkey=796E0-D3B855248-FCA4D88B46FD55659789-ADE644`.

In this example, the link is essentially specifying the username and Activation Key. *URL hacking* is the term used when the user types in the URL directly. In this example, even though the parameters are somewhat meaningful, the user would have a difficult job infiltrating the system and causing any damage. The Activate Account page requires the user to enter their password, so the information on the URL would be used only to pre-populate the fields.

Let's follow this simple pattern through to the Update Account page, assuming that it, too, accepts the username parameter on the URL. There's a possibility that without the right protection in the system, the page could inadvertently load and display the account details. Although the page doesn't contain the user's password, it does contain everything else. For instance, it displays the user's e-mail address, security question, and security question answer, all of which could be used for malicious purposes on this site and potentially others.

The scenario goes something like this:

1. A user could potentially use another page, such as the Create New Account page (or the Update Account page) to ascertain whether an account already existed with a particular username.

2. The user could use this information to compose a URL and send it into the system to cause a problem. The problem doesn't have to be performance-related; it could simply affect another user.

Although this example uses the pages from the case study, the scenario applies to any web-based solution. Parameters passed on the URL should be innocuous and not give away potentially damaging information. If there is a need to pass parameters with potentially damaging information, they should be encrypted so that they cannot be read by humans.

The case study isn't actually passing any parameters on the query string. However, there are a number of pages that should be accessible only to logged-in users or users that aren't logged in. This links back to the user state allowable actions discussed in Chapter 13 and therefore you need to take steps to protect the system from URL hacking.

If a user logs in and enters the URL for the Create New Account page, the page needs to determine whether it should allow the request or direct the user elsewhere. Figure 19-7 shows this conceptually for the Create New Account page.

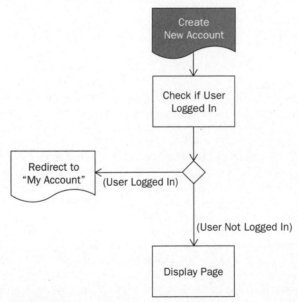

Figure 19-7

The Update Account page would be opposite. The approach needs to be extended throughout all the web pages to ensure that when a user types in a URL the system performs the relevant functional checks. This is another area where base classes and framework classes can help by encapsulating the functionality so that it is not replicated in every page.

In Internet Explorer, when the user presses Ctrl+N, a new browser window is opened. This browser session is in fact attached to the same session as the first browser window, so you now have two browsers using the very same session. This is often referred to as *"session hijacking"*. Depending on how the application is coded, actions in one browser can affect the actions performed in the other. For instance, you could add items to a shopping cart in browser 1. If the application stores this in "state", going to browser 2 and viewing the shopping cart will show the item added. The user could use browser 2 to delete the item in the cart, and then use browser 1 to proceed to checkout. What's going to happen? As I mentioned, it really depends on how the application has been coded. So it is important that you understand and model these situations to ensure that you have everything covered.

Protecting Against the Resubmission of Data

You might have noticed that some online banking sites don't allow you to perform certain browser actions on certain pages. When you attempt to perform a "forbidden" action, you are taken to another page, usually a "start" page of some form. For instance, part way through a multi-step log in, pressing F5 might return you to the login start page again.

In these situations, the websites are invariably implementing some form of token-synchronization pattern. Websites that are totally secure use this pattern to prevent users from resubmitting previously entered form data. The server performs token synchronization as it is processing the requests from the browser. The basic steps are as follows:

1. While processing the first GET request, the server generates a unique token of some form and passes it back in the response, and then stores it locally in state.

2. When the server receives the next request, it checks that the token in the request matches the one stored locally; if not, the request is invalid and the user is directed elsewhere.

At this point (assume the user has clicked F5 and been presented with the resubmission warning), users have the ability to click Retry. If they do, the previously submitted request will be submitted to the server for processing. Without token synchronization, the page will simply process the request, which may be perfectly viable when the processing is *idempotent*. That is, resubmitting the data doesn't change any of the underlying state. When the transaction isn't idempotent, there's the potential for the transaction to be processed multiple times. In general software development terms, idempotence means that calling a method or routine multiple times for the same operation does *not* change the underlying state. For example, you could change the underlying state when the user is performing an online payment, submits his or her request, and then presses F5. Under these circumstances, there is the potential for the transaction to be processed twice and, as such, the user could get charged twice. This is precisely why Internet Explorer displays a warning message when resubmitting data. If the underlying functionality is safely implemented or idempotent, it would recognize the fact that payment had already been taken and payment wouldn't be taken again during subsequent requests. Looking up an account is considered idempotent because this type of transaction wouldn't be updating the database.

Let's assume the user has just created a new account via the Create New Account page and the confirmation message is displayed. At this point they hit F5 (refresh) or Ctrl+F5 (hard refresh); the previous Create New Account request will hit the server for processing. Without some form of check, the request would be processed and the user would be presented with a validation error because the username already exists in the database. In the terms of the case study, the resubmission of a previous request would always result in either a validation error or an Invalid Operation message (IOM). This in itself is something worthy of improving, but that's not the discussion right now.

However, if the site were extended to include an online store, it is possible that the resubmission of a previous request could result in "double-payment" if there were no check on the request. This is an example of where token synchronization is typically employed. A mismatch in the tokens indicates an invalid request, so the request is subsequently rejected.

Figure 19-8 shows a simplified example of the processing pattern for token synchronization.

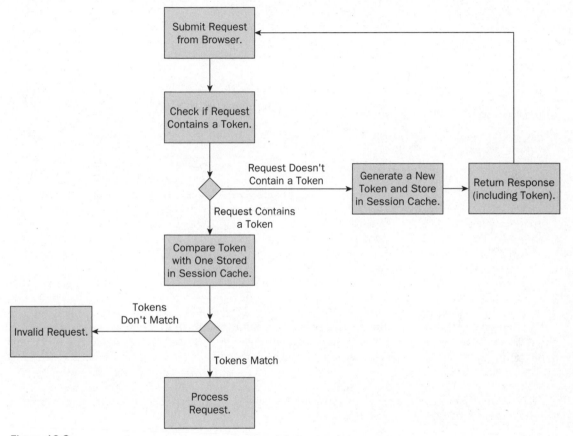

Figure 19-8

This pattern could be extended to support all the different scenarios that could arise, such as during postback processing. It is important to understand where transactions could require some form of token synchronization implementation, and the best way to do that is to walk through the processing. Making it harder for someone to manipulate the data sent from the browser is very important. The application should be coded in such a way to ensure that it only processes what it expects. For example, if the page expects a POST, it should be coded as such. If the page receives a GET, then it should deal with this appropriately.

Before closing this subject, there's one more important item to cover: multiple requests. Suppose a user simply clicks the Submit button continuously, which would fire multiple requests at the server. Only the last request would be connected to the browser; all previous requests would be in the *ether*. You can actually stop the user from doing this by disabling the Submit button after it has been clicked, as shown in the following JavaScript sample code snippet:

```
// The following JavaScript simply disables the Submit
// button to stop duplicate submissions
function submitForm()
{
    // disable the submit button
    frmMain.elements("btnSubmit").disabled = true;

    // submit the form data
    frmMain.submit();
}
```

Obviously, this requires JavaScript to be allowed and supported, which may not be the case, as a lot of organizations don't allow JavaScript.

As a second example of dealing with multiple requests, assume that a user hits F5 (refresh) or Ctrl+F5 (hard refresh) immediately after clicking the Submit button. This, too, has the effect of de-coupling the first request. The information that the response would have displayed to the first request, and that the user needs in order to proceed, could be lost because of the second request. Although you can't stop the user from doing this, you should ensure that the application is designed in such a way that the user can get back to a "known state," as necessary. For example, in the case of the Activate Account page, if the user entered his or her username, password, and Activation Key, clicked the Continue button, and then hit F5, the first request would activate the account (assuming it was in the correct state, and so forth) and the second request, which would be the response to the browser, would contain an IOM.

This is a very interesting scenario. Is the user logged in at this point? You will recall that the Activate Account flow is supposed to log in the user after activating the user's account. However, the first request is now off in the ether and disconnected from the browser. But will it continue end-to-end and log in the user? The answer to this question lies in a true understanding of how individual requests are processed by the underlying runtime and modeling the individual scenarios. If the user is logged in, you now have an IOM being presented to the user but they are actually logged in. Following this through according to the proposed functionality:

1.   When the user clicks the Continue button after being displayed in the IOM, they are directed to the Welcome page.

2.   If the Welcome page implements allowable action checks, such as those shown in Figure 19-7, then the user is re-directed to the My Account page because they are actually logged on — a "known state" and one they would have essentially arrived at if they hadn't hit F5 in the first place.

Of course, it is possible for the IOM processing to perform the necessary checks (where possible) and re-direct the user to the My Account page. I say "where possible" because it depends entirely on where the "user state" is stored and how it is accessed. It is unknown how far the first request got in its processing; to know this would require some "in-flight" transaction state. In any case, the user could just keep pressing F5 or Ctrl+F5 and firing more and more requests. Implementing a simple token-synchronization pattern has the effect of canceling everything out.

It is important to understand these issues even if it is simply to include a "design placeholder" for further discussion and prototyping. Although they are in the realms of more advanced testing and proving, these types of issues should be considered up front to ensure they are captured.

Handling System Failure

Exception handling is one of the core ways to provide resilience within the application code itself. In Chapter 4 you saw that clustering can provide resilience against processes stopping unexpectedly, and that monitoring can help to identify when services and/or processes stop. This section covers what you can do in the application to provide resilience against some of the typical incidents that were listed in Chapter 11, some of which are listed again here:

❑ Database transactions deadlocking and/or timing out

❑ Null reference exceptions

❑ Unhandled exceptions

❑ "Access denied" and "file not found" issues

❑ Network and connectivity issues

❑ Third-party component issues

Resilience to these types of incidents (or exceptions) is typically achieved by including robust exception-handling routines.

Effective exception handing is more than implementing a `try...catch` block of code and raising an event and/or logging an exception when it occurs. This approach should be the minimum amount of acceptable exception handling within an application. Really effective exception handling starts with understanding:

❑ What the code is going to do.

❑ What it is going to be using and executing.

❑ Which exceptions could occur when it executes.

❑ And most important, what could be done to handle the exceptions.

There are five simple rules that I follow when thinking about exception handling:

❑ **Exception handling should never be an afterthought.** Retro-fitting exception handling to an application is an all too common exercise. Production-ready software isn't just about adding exception handling. However, adding exception handing is one of the most common late-breaking activities. It is actually in first place before effective logging and diagnostics. You should think about exception handling right from the very start of design and carry it all the way through build and test.

❑ **Have an exception handling strategy.** A common strategy for handling exceptions will help to ensure that the entire development team follows the same approach. You should ensure that there is a documented and well-known exception-handling strategy in place. Templates and exemplars will help to educate and promote how the exception handling should be implemented and tested.

❑ **Handle exceptions where you can.** There are many situations where exceptions can be handled by the application to ensure continued running and operations. These situations are often not considered thoroughly enough at the start, which often leads to the *try-catch-log-exit* approach. The exception handling strategy should encourage understanding and dealing with "known issues" and other documented exceptions.

❑ **Add value where you can't "handle."** If the application can't resolve exceptions automatically, the application should add value where appropriate. In some severe cases the system may be unstable and it is not worth attempting any further operations. In cases where you can't handle an exception, you should provide as much information as possible regarding the execution and processing to help in the ensuing incident investigation.

❑ **Exceptions lead to operational procedures.** As soon as you start thinking about exception handling, you should put yourself in the shoes of the operators and support staff. What does it really mean if there is an exception at this point? What would need to be done? Think about the implications of the exception to the operator. Does it mean they need to restart the system? Can I document a procedure for them to follow?

There are probably many more rules and sub-rules, but I find that following the preceding five rules promotes better resilience to internal and external factors within the application. The following sections take a closer look at each rule.

Exception Handling Should Never Be an Afterthought

It is easy for developers to get stuck in the code and write for hours on end, compiling and running the solution every so on. Timescales and pressure often lead to thoughts and discussions about filling in the exception handling later, while the main concentration is on getting the actual functionality working. The reality is that there typically isn't enough time to implement effective exception handling, which means that the majority of exception handling becomes really nothing more than catching, logging, and (potentially) re-throwing exceptions. This can be even truer in a retro-fit exercise. An exception handling retro-fit will typically be based on timescales and costs–and the cheapest and quickest option is to catch and log. How long can it really take to add some exception handling to a component? The answer is actually quite astonishing. Adding effective exception handling can sometimes equate to as much as 80 percent, 90 percent, or an even higher percentage of development and test effort *in a single component*.

Assume that you're going to retro-fit exception handling to an application that doesn't have any exception handling already. You'll ensure that you have a diagnostics framework you can use to raise events, log exceptions, and so forth. At every point in every class you'd need to examine the processing and determine what (if any) exceptions could occur and what they mean functionally and operationally. The scale of the problem would depend on the number of classes and the complexity of each class and method. The effort also increases when the person performing the retro-fit didn't write the original code, as there is a much steeper learning curve to understanding the functionality.

You've come across a method that attempts to open a file called config.xml. The example uses the following pseudo code:

```
Open File "config.xml"

...

Exit
```

In this example, the filename is a bit of a giveaway, as it suggests that the file contains some configuration values. Nonetheless, you still need to determine the following:

- What is the file being used for and what does/should it contain?
- Where should the file be located and are there any alternative locations?
- Which access rights does the file/application require?
- What potential reasons could there be for the file not being in the specified location with the correct security settings?
- Which other processes could be using the file at the same time (for example, could it be locked?)
- What should the application do if it can't find/open the file?
- Which operational procedures are required to correct the issue?

Although the questions and the example situation are quite simple, my personal view is that the questions should be asked at the point of design and development. The test cases would then be aligned to the actual functionality. Let's not forget that a retro-fit would also need to be tested thoroughly, which could involve a lot of time and effort. And that's why a typical shortcut retro-fit would end up like the following pseudo code:

```
Try

  Open File "config.xml"

  ...

  Exit

Catch( Exception e )

  Log "The config.xml file could not be found: " + e.Message

  Exit
```

The pseudo code example is a very typical implementation in that it simply catches any and all exceptions. Catching any and all exceptions is actually quite bad practice and not encouraged, unless it is being used to add value or it is at the very highest level in the application and is designed to "handle" any situation in a consistent manner.

A personal bugbear of mine is that a lot of "example" programs and code snippets found on websites and forums often contain very bad practice. Many training courses and associated materials also contain bad practice. It stands to reason that junior developers will follow what they see and learn. If so much bad practice is being presented, that's what will be followed and implemented in the first instance. The information should be presented in a way that is readable but duly noted that it's for discussion purposes only and not for verbatim implementation.

Asking the right questions at the right time will help to ensure that exceptions are handled correctly within the application and, more important, that they will feed into the operational processes. For example:

❑ **What is the file being used for and what does it/should it contain?** The answers to these questions help to define operational touch points. In this example, the file contains configuration values that may need to be adjusted by the operations team. A detailed description of each of the values and their purpose would be required by operations and support staff.

❑ **Where should the file be located and are there any alternative locations?** This determines whether the application needs to check multiple locations for the file. The application would need to check each location in turn until it found the file. This type of deployment approach is usually implemented for local overrides. For example, if the file is in the "working directory," it may override global settings. If not, the application would look higher up and so on. This goes hand-in-hand with the first question, as the operations team would also need to know the best place to modify the configuration. It also feeds in nicely to the deployment process.

❑ **Which access rights does the file/application require?** I have a personal affinity for this question. During development, everything is usually conducted under the same user, but when the system is deployed into other locked-down environments, the application will be using specific accounts and access rights. The application may require only read-only access; on the other hand, it may require write and delete access. The application would also need access to all the locations where the file could reside. The code also needs to ensure that it opens only the file for the specified access. The code may also need to determine what the actual issue is. Does the file actually exist in the location? Are the access rights wrong? These questions could potentially be answered by examining (and testing) the different exceptions thrown by the low-level file access components.

❑ **What potential reasons would there be for the file not being in the specified location with the correct security settings?** The simplest answer to this would be an issue during deployment. Post deployment procedures would need to ensure that all the relevant artifacts were deployed to the right locations with the necessary security settings. This may also require some basic tooling to verify the installation. The file could have been deleted by mistake, which would cause problems. Again, this comes down to who has operational access to the different folders and the files.

❑ **Which other processes could be using the file at the same time — for example, could it be locked?** The application may need to support files being locked. Again, this could be a specific exception thrown by the low-level file access components. Files could potentially be locked by operational staff during incident investigation. It is actually quite typical for files to get locked accidentally by users and support staff, which can cause outages. This again comes down to access rights and whether the application needs to lock the file or worry about whether it is locked or not.

❑ **What should the application do if it can't find/open the file?** The answer obviously depends on what the file is being used for and what it contains. In this example, the application might use some default settings. (Default behaviors are discussed later.) This question also covers all the necessary event logging and associated actions the application should perform under these (or any other) adverse conditions.

❑ **Which operational procedures are required to correct the issue?** This is one of the most important questions that needs to be answered early on. The application may be able to "handle" a situation of defaulting values. However, the fact remains that in this example the file doesn't exist or can't be accessed. This is not expected behavior, so the situation needs to be corrected. The end result is that the file needs to be in the correct location with the correct access rights. It also needs to contain the correct information, but this is another set of exceptions.

This is a simple `FileNotFound` example. Other components and methods could be more complex and require much further analysis. So, not only does thinking about exception handling up front make for a better solution, it also helps to define robust deployment and operational procedures early on. A retro-fit will be far more involved later in the project.

There are many other ways to avoid exceptions or limit their number in the first place. For example, database locking issues and execution timeouts are common in multi-user, multi-process, and long-running transactions. There are a couple of very simple patterns that can be employed to elevate the number of occurrences of these types of issues:

❑ **Use custom timeout values.** Custom timeout values help to limit the number of timeout-related exceptions. A connection timeout value can be specified in the database connection string. The default connection timeout is 15 seconds. The `SqlCommand` class has a `CommandTimeout` property that can be used to set a custom timeout value. The default command timeout value is 30 seconds. Long-running transactions or transactions that are prone to locking issues would benefit greatly from an extended timeout period. Whether the default value is deemed to be enough or not, my personal experience is that timeout exceptions are inherently waiting to happen. It is always a good idea to define configuration values for any and all timeout values. The application will be using other configuration values, so these can be specified and obtained in the usual manner. Timeouts are also used in other I/O arenas such as FTP and other connections and transactions where, again, the use of custom timeouts will protect the application. Reviewing and identifying areas where a custom timeout would provide additional resilience is most definitely encouraged.

❑ **Specify locking hints and/or the transaction isolation level.** Another way to avoid potential locking issues is to specify hints and/or the transaction isolation level. Many timeout issues are actually caused by locking issues and deadlocks. The transaction times out after waiting for a lock for the specified period of time. You can specify locking hints for individual tables in various SQL statements, including `SELECT` and `INSERT`. For example:

```
SELECT [VALUES] FROM [TABLE] WITH (NOLOCK)
```

It is important to note that SQL Server may block a `SELECT` statement under certain conditions even when `NOLOCK` is specified. There are many other locking hints that should be reviewed and considered when designing data access. The transaction isolation level can also be set when reading data from the database — for example:

```
SET TRANSACTION ISOLATION LEVEL READ UNCOMMITTED
```

It is important to review the data access requirements and ensure that the appropriate hints and/or isolation level are specified.

These examples pertain to data access and similar technologies. Wherever possible you should examine which measures and controls you can put in place to limit the number of exceptions that can occur in the application in the first place. It doesn't mean that they won't happen from time to time, but it certainly means that the application will not suffer from unnecessary exceptions.

Layering the application appropriately will help when a late-breaking emergency is identified. For example, if all data access goes through a common application component, it would be possible to update only one component with custom timeout support. However, it would usually mean that all data access would use the same timeout value, which would not necessarily be appropriate for the application. I think that it is always best to understand what the application is doing and to look for ways to improve resilience against exceptions. In some cases this means that additional configuration values are required so that they can be "tweaked" during performance testing and live service. A late-breaking activity of reviewing and updating every stored procedure or SQL statement with the right transaction isolation or hints would be difficult and time-consuming.

Have an Exception Handling Strategy

The exception handling strategy defines the basic approach and framework for exception handling within the application. It also helps to define specific code-review checkpoints and automatic profiling rules. In a large project defining the approach early really does save a lot of time and effort. Instilling the approach into the development team early will avoid a lot of pain later. Working examples, exemplars, and references can help with this. There are really only two groups of exceptions, both of which ultimately derive from the Exception class:

❑ **System exceptions** — These are raised by the underlying system frameworks and operating system. System exceptions can be thrown by an application and set the specific error message — for example:

```
throw new System.InvalidOperationException("The process (xyx) can't be paused.");
```

I am not a fan of using this approach, preferring instead to define specific application exceptions. This allows the exception handling in the application to differentiate between real system exceptions and internal exceptions thrown by the application itself.

❑ **Application exceptions** — These are defined, created, and raised by the application itself. Application exception classes ultimately derive from the ApplicationException class. The number and type of exception classes depends entirely on the application, although there are typically a good number of "standard" exceptions. To keep things extensible, I prefer to define a single "base" application exception class, such as WACException, which derives from the ApplicationException class. All additional application exceptions would derive from this base class.

This simple technique allows additional properties and methods to be included in the WACException class, which can then be accessed and used by all application exceptions and used by the application itself. A fairly reasonable example is to add static methods that can be used during exception handling routines to examine certain system exceptions. For instance, a GetRetryLimit could return the number of retries allowed for a specific exception. The applications and/or application frameworks could use this property to determine whether an operation should be retried. Many situations where an exception isn't actually fatal to execution can be remedied by the wait-retry pattern, as discussed in the following section.

The strategy starts by setting out the basic rules and regulations for good exception definition and handling practices. There are two basic rules to keep in mind when defining an exception-handling strategy:

❑ **Exceptions should be thrown by the application when normal execution can't continue.** For example, a method could throw an (application-specific) InvalidArgumentException when one or more parameters are invalid. It could also throw an InvalidOperationException when it is not in the correct state to perform a particular operation — for instance, attempting to call an ExecuteSql method without first calling an OpenConnection method. The Message property could contain something along the lines of "Connection Not Open."

The preceding examples are interesting because they are generic exceptions. When defining the application exceptions, you should think about when and when not to use generic exceptions versus specific exceptions. Generic exceptions are typically harder to handle and interpret than specific exceptions. You should try to imagine what the exception handling code would need to do to deal with the exception. In both of these cases the handling code would need to examine the Message property (or another property, such as Data or ParamName) to determine the exception context. In my experience, generic exceptions should really be used only when it is not possible or realistic to have a specific exception. It would be silly to start defining an exception for every method argument, so you need to live with a generic exception in this case and ensure that the contextual information contains the actual argument that has been specified incorrectly. However, in the case of the InvalidOperationException containing a message such as "Connection Not Open," it would probably be best to define a specific ConnectionNotOpen exception. The handling code could catch this specific exception and call the OpenConnection method and retry the ExecuteSql. However, one would have to question why the connection wasn't open in the first place.

❑ **Exceptions should not be used to control the flow of normal execution.** Return values and other state type values should be used to control the overall program flow. The term "exception" refers to something that is not expected. Consider the method AreEqual(a, b). A method like this would typically return a boolean value of true or false. It could make for a nasty piece of code if the method was void and threw an exception when the items weren't equal. This, too, is quite interesting because there is another argument. The application may be expecting the values to always be the same, so it is an exception when they aren't.

Assume you have a GetBalance message that passes an account number. The response message should also contain the account number and the associated account balance. In this example, the application would expect the "requested account number" and the "responded account number" to be the same every single time. If they weren't, there would be a serious flaw somewhere in the application. To ensure that they are the same, a defensive step in the code would need to compare them. In the first instance, the application needs to make the AreEqual method call, check the return value, and then make a decision based on it. In the example, this would probably be throwing an exception. To simplify the code, the `AreEqual` method could throw the exception. It all depends on what the method is doing and where it is being used. It also depends somewhat on the name of the method and the object it belongs to. Method names can often imply a return type — for instance, methods starting with `Is` would typically imply a Boolean return type. My basic rule of thumb is to use exceptions where they really are an exception to the rule. I tend to use return values to indicate certain status when it is applicable for the application to do so, such as in the batch providers and batch managers. Throwing an exception for every transaction that can't be processed would be nonsense, in my personal opinion.

❑ `System.Exception` **should not be caught and/or re-thrown by individual application components and methods.** Individual application components and methods should not catch and/or re-throw `System.Exception` unless they can really add some specific value or add contextual information (discussed later) that would be useful in an incident investigation or they are at the top of the component model dealing with the "catch-all" case.

Whatever the strategy and the rules, they should be defined, stated, and have a reason. The strategy should not just happen by chance. Armed with the basic rules, you can define the exemplars, templates, and base classes, and then roll them out for the development team. The remaining subsections build additional rules that should be incorporated into the exception-handling strategy.

Handle Exceptions Where You Can

To me, "handling" implies doing something with the exception that's been caught. I don't see raising an event, logging, and re-throwing it as "handling." I see this as adding value when you can't really handle the exception (which is the subject of the next section).

Given that handling exceptions is a broad subject and there could be potentially hundreds of different exceptions and resolutions, I want to concentrate on one simple resilience pattern: the wait-retry pattern. Although it is one of the simplest patterns, it provides valuable protection against minor issues and outages. In short, the flow is as follows:

1. Try something.
2. It fails.
3. Wait a configurable amount of time.
4. Try it again and continue a configurable number of times before finally throwing an exception.

The wait-retry pattern also highlights the 80/20 rule somewhat in that the majority of the processing is simply to provide resilience within the application. Figure 19-9 shows this diagrammatically.

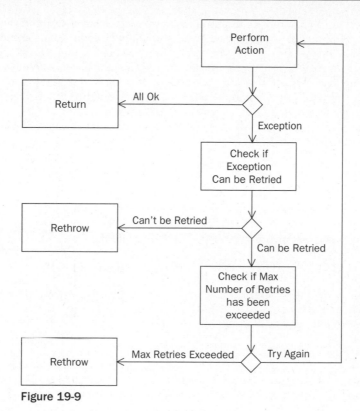

Figure 19-9

The pattern could be applied across-the-board to all exceptions. However, there are some situations and exceptions where retrying is simply a waste of time — for example, OutOfMemory and StackOverflow exceptions, to name but a couple. Furthermore, when the system is starting up, the operations team often wants to know immediately whether there is a problem. If the system is retrying, this could impact the time to react and investigate.

To get the most out of the wait-retry pattern, you should review each potential exception to determine whether retrying it is suitable. The following are a couple of high-level areas where you can employ the wait-retry pattern:

❑ **Timeouts** — A timeout exception can occur for many different reasons. The network could be running slow because of an influx of traffic, or a database query could be blocked while waiting for a lock to be released, or any other reason. In situations like these, the wait-retry pattern can really provide resilience within the application. Without it, the application would simply generate an exception at the very first instance, so it is essentially "game over." Even with custom timeout values, it is still possible for a timeout to occur, although coupling an application with the wait-retry pattern offers even more enhanced resilience.

❑ **Locks** — A typical lock exception can occur when two or more processes are trying to open and write to the same resource at the same time. The "write" transaction may be very short-lived, so waiting and retrying will make the application more robust and resilient to occasional locking exceptions. Although this is a reasonable example, you would also need to fully understand why two or more independent processes were writing to the same file (or record).

The possibilities and uses are too innumerable to go into here, but each exception should be treated on a case-by-case basis. However, it is very important to thoroughly understand the end-to-end operation being performed and the possible exceptions, because the wait-retry pattern can come in handy in the most unexpected places. For instance, assume that you are trying to access a file on a shared drive using a Universal Naming Convention (UNC) path, such as `\\SharedStorageServer\SharedDrive\SomeFile.xml`. You would probably use a `StreamReader` class to open the file. The documented exceptions for the constructor accepting a specified `path` are as follows:

- ❑ `ArgumentException` occurs when the `path` is an empty string.

- ❑ `ArgumentNullException` occurs when the `path` is a null reference.

- ❑ `FileNotFoundException` occurs when the file can't be found.

- ❑ `DirectoryNotFoundException` occurs when the specified `path` is invalid, such as being an unmapped drive.

- ❑ `IOException` occurs when the `path` includes an incorrect syntax for the file name, directory name, and/or volume label.

On first glance it would seem that none of these exceptions are worth retrying. It looks like a simple case of "do nothing" or "add value" (for example, log the exception and re-throw it to the layer above). However, there is another possible scenario: clustering.

Clustering provides resilience at an infrastructure/configuration level. An active/passive cluster is typically used to expose the shared drive to offer more resilience. If the active server fails, the passive node would take over and expose the share instead. The application could be trying to access the file right at the very point the cluster is failing over, and the drive isn't actually available. A cluster failover takes a certain amount of time, and it would be a terrible shame to have built in such costly clustering capabilities only for the application itself to fail in the middle of a cluster failover. The wait-retry pattern would certainly alleviate almost all of the potential application failures in this scenario (assuming the wait time and retry count were set to acceptable values and aligned with the cluster failover timings).

Unit testing and proving all the individual scenarios would be very difficult. Thorough and specific tests should be carried out during performance testing and failure and recovering testing. A reasonable selection of tests would need to be defined and carried out during build and unit testing to prove that the retry configuration and retry exception mapping were suitably robust.

The wait-retry pattern, as far as I am concerned, is a "value-added" exception-handling process. It is very possible and necessary on occasion to simply catch any exception and apply the retry logic. However, this doesn't mean to say that it should be abused and used everywhere to catch any and all exceptions. You should apply due diligence when analyzing such situations, although there can be valid cases where there are too many documented and/or undocumented possibilities to support (such as the previous example). Which of the preceding listed exceptions would be thrown in the example scenario? It is actually not possible to tell unless you either prove it by executing a specific test or it has been documented by someone else. I'd still like to prove it myself, and there are a couple of ways to do so by using a simulator. It is possible to use a completely generic approach to the configuration, but because the "retryable" exceptions can pertain to file access, data access, and so forth, it stands to reason that very specific retry configuration wouldn't necessarily be defined in the database. The following simple pseudo code example shows the wait-retry pattern in a file open operation:

```
retryCount = 0;
success = false;

while( !success )
{
    try
    {

        // try to open the file
        open file filename;

        // set the success flag
        success = true;

    }
    catch( Exception e )
    {
        // add value
        // log the exception and raise the necessary events
        // update the relevant diagnostics, monitoring and incident
        // investigation information

        // determine if the exception is retryable
        retryLimit = WACException.GetRetryLimit( e );

        // if the retry limit is zero or we've retried the maximum
        // number of times then simply re-throw
        if( retryLimit == 0 || retryCount > retryLimit )
        {

            // pass on the exception
            throw;

        }
        else
        {

            // the exception is retryable so update the retry count
            retryCount = retryCount + 1;

            // update the relevant diagnostics, monitoring, and
            // incident investigation information

        }
    }
}
```

The missing logic can be filled in along with the correct tracing, event logging, and so on. Private methods would be employed to isolate the various areas of the code to keep it neat and tidy. The pseudo code provides a typical overview of the wait-retry pattern and its relative implementation. What's interesting in the pattern is that it is using a real retry count that doesn't include the initial operation. Furthermore, what the example doesn't specifically highlight is the fact that the exception could potentially be different on subsequent retries. As such, the retry limit could actually be different each time around (assuming the configuration and/or code specified so). There are a few things that you could do in this situation:

❑ **Leave it as-is.** Doing nothing would simply mean the operation would be retried a different number of times, depending on the exceptions. For instance, if the first exception had a retry limit of 3, the second exception had a retry limit of 4, and then the third exception had a retry limit of 2, you would essentially pop the loop at this point with an unsuccessful state, as you would have gone over the retry limit of the last exception. However, if the last exception was greater than or equal to 4, you'd try again. This option would result in an undetermined number of retries, although the minimum would be 1 unless the subsequent exception wasn't "retryable," in which case you'd throw it to the layer above.

❑ **Reset the** `retryCount`. You could reset the `retryCount` based on the fact that the exception was different. This could lead to a potentially never-ending retry cycle, although the chances are quite slim. Nevertheless, you need to consider it as an option. It is possible that the subsequent exception had a retry limit of 0, in which case you'd need to change the logic slightly to ensure that the operation wasn't retied under these circumstances. You would then only ever pop the retry loop either when you successfully performed the processing or when you managed to reach the retry limit of a consistent exception.

❑ **Stick with the first** `retryLimit`. This option would ensure that the operation was carried out only a maximum number of times, a number that would be determined by the very first exception that occurred. Subsequent exceptions would be logged as part of the overall diagnostics, but they wouldn't be considered. However, the subsequent exception could really be fatal, so it is not worth retrying. There's also the possibility that it could be dangerous to try the operation again under these circumstances.

What these options really highlight is that it is the operation that is being retried under certain circumstances. As a rule of thumb, the application should not retry under a fatal exception (for example, `retryLimit == 0`). Therefore, it comes down to a choice between option 1 and option 2. To fully evaluate the choice, you need to understand and evaluate the probability of a different exception occurring each time. This would be a very difficult task, as you would need to examine a number of permutations, although my gut reaction is that the chances of a different exception occurring during the retry would be quite slim. If you think about the situation, if a given operation and exception could (and should) be retried a number of times, then why not option 2? If a subsequent exception were raised with a retry limit, then it is an entirely new situation altogether. It all boils down to the amount of time it takes to complete the transaction (successfully or unsuccessfully). If it were a background file transfer process, the system could suffer from an initial connection timeout. It may then suffer from a file transfer timeout. Irrespective of the number of retries, the system would keep trying until it finally threw an exception or completed successfully. In this situation, it could be a good idea to run with option 2, as long as it didn't create too much unnecessary operational "noise," although it would need to be known by the operators that the process was struggling to complete. It would be a good idea to make all this configurable, or set overall limits and/or timings, or arrange the code in such a way that you could make the choice on a case-by-case basis.

Add Value When You Can't "Handle"

An incident investigation will typically require an examination of trace logs. The `StackTrace` property, of the `Exception` class, contains the individual classes and methods that have been called. The stack trace itself doesn't contain any real contextual information. The `Message` property can provide some value, but the real value is typically in the Data property. This property contains a collection of key/value pairs that the application can use to provide specific contextual information relating to the processing and functionality. For example, an exception could be caught and the method could add the appropriate parameters and values that it was using for processing. This is shown in the following example code snippet:

```
public void TransferFile( string filename, string fromLocation, string toLocation,
  int transerFlags )
{
   try
   {
      // try to transfer the file
      ...
   }
   catch( Exception e )
   {
      // add value
      e.Data.Add( "filename", filename );
      e.Data.Add( "fromLocation", fromLocation );
      e.Data.Add( "toLocation", toLocation );
      e.Data.Add( "transferFlags", transferFlags );

      // re-throw
      Throw;
   }
}
```

The Data property should be output, along with the other properties on the exception, in resulting events and logs. The items added should provide real contextual information that could help in the subsequent incident investigation. Because it is only a simple key/value pairing, different exception handlers could potentially try to add the same key. A consistent naming convention is required across all components. Using a namespace-style convention such as ClassName.MethodName.ItemName would help. For example:

```
catch( Exception e )
{
   // add value
   e.Data.Add( "FileHandler.FileOpen.filename", filename )

   ...
```

The preceding examples are catching any and all exceptions, and although this is typically considered bad practice, if the method is adding value to the exception and re-throwing it in the correct way, I think this is perfectly acceptable. If the method isn't adding any value, then of course it shouldn't catch the generic exception. However, in the case of adding value, the method doesn't actually care which exception has been thrown. Adding value can be more than just specifying additional contextual information and logging and raising events. It can involve performing a variety of different actions including but not limited to:

❑ **Environment cleanup/teardown** — This is probably the most important action or set of actions that should be performed during the exception-handling routine. Different processing will require different clean-up, but in general cleaning up means performing a number of actions, including but not limited to:

- ❑ Roll-back transactions (where required) to maintain data integrity and consistency.

- ❑ Close connections and handles to keep everything in good shape.

- ❑ Stop (and dispose of) separate processing threads and/or processes to ensure that there are no orphan threads/processes.

- ❑ Destroy or dispose of objects (where necessary) or return them to an object pool.

- ❑ When a process is going to exit following an exception, it can often help to call the `Environment.Exit` method to ensure the framework terminates the process correctly. The method also passes the exit code to the operating system. In the case of command-line execution, the exit code can be examined via the `%ERRORLEVEL%` value.

❑ **Setting default behaviors** — It is a fairly typical practice to set default values when configuration values and settings can't be found or perhaps even contain invalid values. Default values and behaviors should be considered very carefully and be understood fully if they are to be implemented. If a configuration value can't be found or isn't set correctly, this could be treated as incorrect configuration. The application could throw an exception detailing all the necessary information and exit. This would allow the operations team to correct the configuration and restart the system. If the application is going to continue with default values under these conditions, the operations team would need to know by way of a warning event. The default values might not be suitable for production running; therefore, the system could operate incorrectly and actually cause more problems.

Exceptions Lead to Operational Procedures

Operations documentation should be very clear and provide step-by-step instructions that almost anyone can follow. You can't assume that the person following the instructions knows as much as you do. Anytime that you are going to throw an exception or raise an event, or if you suspect that an exception can be thrown that will be logged, you should analyze the exception and situation fully. The operational procedures will almost certainly need to include the steps to carry out in the event the exception or situation occurs.

The Operations Manual and procedures are the most important documents the operations and support staff use. The more resilient the application is to failures, the fewer operational procedures and documentation there will be. However, there should always be operational procedures for starting, stopping, monitoring, and supporting the system. The operational procedures need to be robust and quick to execute to ensure that the system can be up and running as soon as possible. Exception handling is not just about what happens in the code; it is about the entire end-to-end process. Each exception and associated event should be fully documented from an operational point of view.

I once had to write an entire Operations Manual for a third-party system that had been heavily customized. I am sure the development team thought I was rather annoying when I kept asking "What would I need to do when this occurs?" A robust system encompasses robust processes and procedures. I had to examine every potential exception that the system could raise and write the exact step-by-step procedure to deal with it. There were more than 200 situations, ranging from fairly simple "File Not Found" exceptions to "Can't Connect to Queue" and "Invalid Message Format." There is always a reason for the exception and there's almost always a way to correct it. Deployment procedures, configuration files, and configuration setting procedures will typically resolve most incorrect configuration issues. This exercise took me nearly 4 months to complete and it always involved talking to the development team to understand what the application did to handle the situation and what the operations team would need to do to correct it in live service. I am not saying that as a developer you should write complete operational documentation; however, the development outputs will be used to produce the operations procedures. The outputs should always include all the exceptions that the application can raise, the reason for it happening, and the corrective actions to take.

When implementing exception handling, and especially when logging, raising, and throwing exceptions (either internally or by re-throwing system exceptions), the exception should be documented in the development outputs. Where possible, all exception conditions should also be thoroughly tested to ensure that the application performs the correct actions and writes out the correct error messages. There is nothing worse than doing an investigation to discover the error message is misleading.

Non-Stop Processing

As discussed previously, hardware clustering and load balancing can help to provide resilience within the overall architecture and infrastructure. There are a few more resilience patterns and practices that you can use to provide a more robust solution:

❑ **Running multiple synchronized processes** — Where possible, it is always a good idea to run multiple processes in parallel. In some cases, the processes could be standing by to perform the exact same processing on the exact same records and data, but the processes are communicating with each other to ensure that they are fully synchronized. The communication mechanisms can range from remoting calls, metaphors, flat files, or the database. The important thing is that when one process fails or stops for some reason, there's another or possibly many others that could assume the work load. This approach of running multiple synchronized processes is nothing more than an internal clustering mechanism that offers even more resilience within the application itself. It is also possible on occasion to run processes in an active/active processing fashion. All the processes are synchronized and performing actions at the same time on different records and data. However, if one fails or stops, one of the other processes will take on the additional work. The processes could be alternative threads, other processes on the local machine, and even processes on another machine.

❑ **Automatic restart** — When a process stops or exits, you should think about whether it should be restarted automatically. A simple controller service can manage and control many different processing threads, each of which can control many more threads. When one thread fails, the controller service would restart it automatically after a specific period of time. If the controller service were to fail, it is even possible that it could also be restarted automatically.

❑ **Quarantine/dead letter queue** — To avoid multiple issues and events and recurring issues, whenever processes come across invalid records, data, messages, and so forth, the records, data, and so forth should be quarantined. This is a simple process of moving problem data, files, and records into another area to prevent the data from being picked up and processed again. When quarantining data, it is important that the appropriate events be raised and logged to ensure that the invalid information can be appropriately reviewed, corrected, and resubmitted to the live processing area.

These are just a few simple tips that you can employ to build robust solutions and applications. Try to think about all the possible scenarios and how the application can essentially provide non-stop processing to reduce the overall amount of downtime.

Summary

This chapter discussed some simple but effective exception-handling guidelines and resilience patterns that can be used to offer more robustness in the application and overall solution.

The following are the key points to take away from this chapter:

❑ **Manage configuration changes appropriately.** Ensure that configuration values are fully documented, especially when they relate to other values and settings, such as throttles.

❑ **Understand the browser behavior.** You should fully understand the browser's navigation controls and what happens "behind the scenes", especially during postback and other browser functions such as forward, back and refresh.

❑ **Validate user inputs and encode them**. You should always validate user input and where necessary encode the values to avoid malicious attacks.

❑ **Protect the system against URL hacking.** The application should not allow users to perform actions that they are not authorized to do.

❑ **Consider implementing a token-synchronization pattern**. The token synchronization pattern helps to ensure that all operations and transactions return to a "known state."

❑ **Don't leave exception handling to the last minute.** Have an exception handling strategy up front.

❑ **Handle exceptions where you can.** You need to consider all the exceptions that could occur in a method and handle each of them appropriately.

❑ **Add value where you can't actually handle an exception.** It is important for incident investigation that you record as much information about the exception and the processing that was being performed at the time. This information will be invaluable when trying to re-create the incident.

❑ **Use wait-retry logic to handle common errors.** The wait-retry pattern can alleviate system downtime by providing a robust mechanism for retrying transactions. Remember, the wait-retry pattern can be used in areas where it is not so obvious at first glance. However, the pattern should not be abused. You should also understand the operational implications during startup and shutdown.

❑ **Consider running multiple synchronized processes.** You should consider running multiple synchronized processes to provide application specific "clustering" and failover.

❑ **Consider automatically restarting after a failure.** When the system stops it will require operator intervention. You should consider where automatic restart would be a viable option to recover from failure.

❑ **Quarantine bad data.** Avoid re-processing bad data by quarantining it when you can't process it properly.

20

Designing for Monitoring

This chapter builds on the messages in Chapter 8 by looking at two of the most important diagnostic features that should be designed into an application for monitoring purposes: performance counters and event logs. Diagnostics also includes trace files and log files, although these are typically used during incident investigation (see Chapter 21). The incident investigation process is triggered from an event being raised during execution and monitoring. System monitoring is primarily performed by the operations team while the system is in live service. For the most part, once the system has stabilized, monitoring system behavior should be a passive activity — that is, the operations team should not have to constantly "watch" the system. While the system is stabilizing, however, the operations team monitors the startup, general execution, shutdown, and batch processes very closely. The diagnostics embedded within the system specify whether any attention is required.

When I refer to "monitoring," I'm focusing on the application-specific diagnostics, rather than all the other monitoring and operability requirements, such as monitoring the hardware and operating system, or monitoring whether services are running, starting, or stopping. The performance counters and events included within the application code are crucial to the monitoring process.

You can also use third-party products to obtain the performance counter data and events from the system, centrally filter them, and display them to the operations team. Consider the following scene: The system's been fully tested and is ready to go. You've just spent all weekend preparing it for a Monday morning launch. Without the appropriate diagnostics and monitoring in place, however, you wouldn't be able to determine how the application was performing. The same would be true if the operating system didn't generate any events or include any performance counters to monitor. You could be monitoring the frameworks, hardware, operating system, and third-party applications to ensure the system was up and running and available, but you still wouldn't know exactly how the application itself was performing.

This chapter is organized into the following sections:

❑ **Performance Counters** — Examines the different categories and types of counters as well as some alternative actions that can provide the same information. It also discusses when and where performance counters can be used and how often data is updated and sampled.

❑ **Events and Event Logs** — Examines events and event logging. An event or alert is typically the trigger for incident investigation, and this section discusses the different types of events and alerts you can include in an application, including when and where to use them and the type of information they should contain.

❑ **Monitoring Configuration** — Examines the monitoring configuration that should be considered for the solution. It is important to note that a critical event in one environment might not be a critical event in another. In addition, some environments may require different contextual information from others. Although you wouldn't want to include sensitive information such as passwords in production events, it might be prudent to do so during development and testing.

Performance Counters

It is generally quite difficult to determine exactly which performance counters are required to effectively monitor a system or application. Once you have a reasonable idea of what the application is going to perform, you can look for areas where performance counters can provide beneficial information for operations. In most cases, during live-service monitoring, performance counters are used to actually generate events by placing thresholds around their values. This is usually implemented via the operational monitoring tools. For example, if a performance counter reaches a certain value, a warning event is raised; if it progresses to another value, an error is raised; and so forth. This is not generally coded into the application, as modern monitoring solutions are usually very good at this kind of "roll up" and rule-based analysis. However, the operating system can also provide its own analysis. For example, when the amount of free disk space is reduced, the system generates a "Low Disk Space" warning event and suggests freeing up more disk space. The operating system doesn't contain a full-blown monitoring solution, of course. The application needs to provide the counters necessary to profile and monitor the application during both testing and live service.

Each performance counter is of a specified type, as follows:

❑ **NumberOfItems(32 or 64 bit)** — This counter type contains a value pertaining to the latest number of items or operations. For example, it could contain the total number of items in a queue or the total number of transactions processed. In the first instance, the value would fluctuate over time as the queue increased and decreased in size. In the second instance, the value would increase only as more transactions were processed.

❑ **RateOfCountsPerSecond(32 or 64 bit)** — This counter type contains a value that relates to the average number of items or operations observed during each second. A counter of this type could be used to record the number of logins per second.

❑ **AverageTimer(32 bit only)** — This counter type contains a value representing the average amount of time taken to perform an operation. A counter of this type could be used to record the average processing time for a login transaction.

It is worth knowing how to incorporate each of the different counter types into the application to provide better monitoring and diagnostics. By examining the application functionality and the various components, you can come up with a good set of performance counter categories and individual counters to include in the application. This is where some of the component diagrams, flows, and other modeling activities already discussed can really help. Figure 20-1 shows the logical architecture and the different components within the case study's conceptual design.

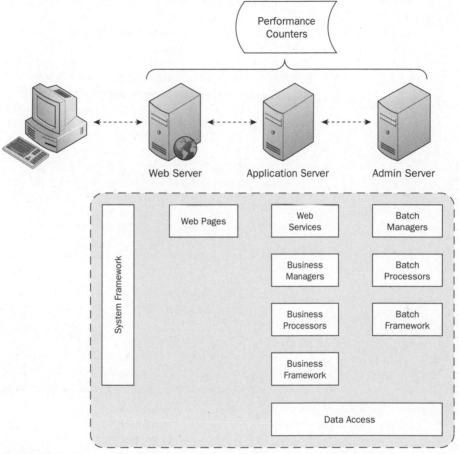

Figure 20-1

An online transaction will flow from the client browser, through the system, and update the database (not shown in the diagram). Average end-to-end performance is typically one of the most wanted performance figures by a business. For example, on average, how long does it take to process a transaction completely from end-to-end? The value is then typically used to determine whether it is within certain tolerances. Although you can use tools to measure this value in a web application during testing, in live service you don't want to be running "sample" transactions through the system, causing additional overhead. You've already seen that there are analytics solutions that can analyze the web server log files, but again, this is typically performed offline at the end of each day, rather than as an intra-day activity (although it is perfectly possible to do this during the day). In most systems it is also often possible to derive this type of data by other means, such as running reports against the database transactions, calculating timings, and so on. These types of solutions are often used to reduce the overhead created by including specific performance counter updates within the application code.

Initializing and updating performance counters in real time impacts an application's overall performance, especially if a number of different processes or threads are updating the same performance counter instance. You need to be very careful that updating performance counters doesn't become a bottleneck in the system. If the counters and updates are implemented effectively, the actual overhead is somewhat insignificant, as it needs to be included within the overall performance requirements and timings. However, it is good practice to include performance counters that provide *real* benefits, and not to overload the application with unnecessary counters that could impact performance. Furthermore, the application's configuration should be suitably flexible to allow you to switch counters on or off and, where necessary, specify sampling rates. Monitoring configuration is discussed later.

In the case study and similar applications, it is very straightforward to include an end-to-end latency value as a series of performance counters that the application updates in real time. The counters could be included in both the online application and the batch components, both of which are shown in Figure 20-1.

The online application would encompass the web server components as well as the application server components shown in the diagram. However, the real questions are: How useful is end-to-end performance for monitoring purposes? In live service, what does it mean if the Create New Account process is taking 2 seconds on average versus 1.5 seconds? What should be done about it? It really means something only when it is totally out of normal tolerances — for example, if, on a normal day, with normal load, it should take no longer than 1.5 seconds. This also means you need to understand the current load on the system to determine whether it is a normal day or whether there is additional load that is causing transactions to take slightly longer, or even perhaps hardly any load, which would be even stranger.

I mentioned earlier that very often performance counters are used to trigger events or alerts that initiate the incident investigation process. The counters themselves need to be in place and updated by the application. The tolerances, thresholds, and rules need to be set accordingly so that the application can be effectively monitored. It's precisely these types of questions and situations that lead to a change in the narrative. The following sections look at the different areas where you can use performance counters to effectively monitor the application without adding unnecessary performance overheads and causing undue noise to operators.

Counters — The Good, the Bad, and the Ugly

You can think of performance counters as windows into the application's internals and processing. A process should use counters to indicate its internal processing state. The individual counters can be categorized into the following classifications:

❑ **Good** — "Good" counters are typically used to measure the system's performance. An application should generally include good counters, as they can often be used during testing to ascertain the system's performance. The counters can also be used to raise events if the value is outside specified tolerances. Good counters include, but are not limited to:

❏ **Transaction counts and throughput** — The transaction counts and throughput give a real indication of the current load on the system and how well it is performing against that load. For example, the case study has a number of flows and you could define a set of counters for each of the high-level transactions within the system, such as Create New Account, Activate Account, and so on. The counters indicate the overall number of transactions and the average speed at which each transaction was being processed. The batch processes would also use similar counters to indicate their overall performance.

❏ **Connection counts** — These counters indicate the current number of connections to and/ or from the system. For example, the application may need to connect to an external system or external systems may be connecting to it.

❏ **Pool counts** — The application may implement object pooling and reuse to limit the amount of garbage collection during high-volume processing. Pool counters indicate the number of items in the pool and the number of items in use.

❏ **Queue counts** — These counters indicate the number of work items in a queue that require processing. A constantly increasing count indicates that a process isn't running or processing the items in the queue.

❏ **List counts and usage counts** — Applications typically load information and retain it in memory — for example, display messages, configuration values, and so forth. These counters indicate the number of items in the list, and how many times each item has been used, respectively. These counters can help to tune the system configuration, assuming it supports the dynamic loading and unloading of items.

❏ **Bad** — Bad counters are used to collect and inform operators of unusual or abnormal behavior. Bad counters can be used to raise events when they reach certain values or breach tolerances. Bad counters include but are not limited to the following:

❏ **Invalid transaction counts/rate** — These counters indicate the number of invalid transactions during processing. They can often be used to detect malicious or improper behavior. As the value and rate of invalid transactions increases, it could indicate that a "black-box" process is sending in invalid transactions. Batch jobs can also use these types of counters during processing.

❏ **Transaction retry counts** — The wait-retry pattern was discussed previously and these types of counters would indicate the retry attempts and counts.

❏ **Ugly** — Ugly counters inform operators of what should be very rare occurrences of a particular incident. For example, a set of counters could be used to indicate a process is stopping and restarting. As the counter increases, it would indicate potential instability in the overall application that might need to be investigated.

Counters — What, When, and Why

Determining which counters to include in an application is difficult and depends entirely on the application and individual processing. With respect to the case study, Figure 20-1 showed the different servers and the various components that reside on them. The counters updated by the components shown in the figure should provide operational (and reporting) benefits and/or benefits during the development and testing phases. The previous section showed the different classifications of counters. Looking at the basic functional processing helps to define a high-level group of performance counters, such as:

- ❑ Online transactions and processing, including:
    - ❑ Create New Account
    - ❑ Activate Account
    - ❑ Re-Request Activation Key
    - ❑ Login/Logout
    - ❑ Update Account
    - ❑ Change Password and Reset Password
    - ❑ Close Account
- ❑ Batch transactions and processing, including:
    - ❑ Account Email Processing (New Activation Key, Resend Activation Key, and Closure)
    - ❑ Account Removal Processing (Aged Account Flagging, Closure, and Removal)

Each high-level performance counter group represents an individual transaction type rather than a single process or component. You can then break down these groups into the types of information you'd like to capture:

- ❑ Information about transaction counts and performance:
    - ❑ **Overall Total** — To help gauge load, each transaction type would benefit from a set of counters recording the minimum, current, and maximum number of transactions.
    - ❑ **Transactions per Second** — The number of transactions being processed per second would be an indicator of performance.
- ❑ End-to-end performance would also be very helpful when gauging system throughput and performance. The online transactions are especially important because they will tell you how long (on average) each transaction is taking across the board. Performance could be measured for all the online and batch transactions previously listed.

The preceding performance indicators would provide the very highest level of internal application performance on a per-transaction type basis. Walking through all the processing and the individual components also helps to define additional counters. Performance counters are actually installed on each server in the farm and are updated by the relevant components on that server. The following list represents some of the high-level server groups and the component types that would be deployed to them:

- ❑ Web servers
    - ❑ ASP pages
    - ❑ Framework components

- ❑ Application servers
    - ❑ Web services
    - ❑ Manager components
    - ❑ Processor components
    - ❑ Provider components
    - ❑ Framework components (including data access)
- ❑ Administration servers
    - ❑ Batch managers
    - ❑ Batch processors
    - ❑ Framework components (including data access)

Each component type could be recording its own internal performance, so it is important to differentiate between the counters and the components. For example, the web servers could have a "Within-a-Click Web" performance object that contains the online counter set, including the following counters:

- ❑ Create New Account Performance
- ❑ Create New Account Transactions (Total)
- ❑ Create New Account Transactions (Unsuccessful)
- ❑ Create New Account Transactions/Sec
- ❑ Activate Account Performance
- ❑ Activate Account Transactions (Total)
- ❑ Activate Account Transactions (Unsuccessful)
- ❑ Activate Account Transactions/Sec
- ❑ Login Transactions (Total)
- ❑ Login Transactions (Unsuccessful)
- ❑ Login Transactions/Sec

The counters would be updated by the web pages and components residing on the web servers. You can't really apply the same pattern to the application servers, however, because there are multiple components, including web services, managers, and processors — all of which might benefit from recording similar counters to indicate performance. The application would need to define different performance objects for the web services, managers, and processors — for example, Within-a-Click Web Service, Within-a-Click Manager, and Within-a-Click Processor, respectively — to differentiate between the counters and their values.

There are many other ways in which the objects and counters could be sliced and diced. The different servers would show the transaction counts, timings, and performance, but the web server values would essentially show the real end-to-end performance from the front-end web page right back to the user.

You might think that some of the performance counters would contain the same values on the application servers — for example, transaction counts. The web service, the manager, and the processor could all have a similar counter. It would really depend on the application and how it is used. The web servers would communicate with the back-end application via the web services (installed on the application servers). However, other "trusted" applications could be using the web services or the managers or the processors. Therefore, the counts and load would be different across the various components and layers.

It is worth thinking about this and how the components interact. You should model the end-to-end flow through the components to determine the best (and most valuable) point where the counters should be updated. It is also important to ensure that the number of counters and their updates doesn't adversely affect the performance of the solution. The counters should provide real value and justify their overhead.

Furthermore, it is also possible to obtain the transaction counts and performance information from the database, assuming it has all the required timestamps. Reports could be developed that show all the required information. This information would be very useful for reporting complete end-to-end transaction counts and timings. However, it is not truly "real-time," so it would be difficult to determine where potential bottlenecks occurred in slow transactions. It wouldn't show whether a particular server or a particular process or group was going "slow." Therefore, the better defined the counters are, the better the monitoring (and reporting) will be.

As a rule of thumb, a set of counters on each server group is a very good starting point. In this example, the web servers are pretty easy, as they only contain the ASP pages (and framework components). They are the best place to record all the "online" transaction counts and latency.

The web services are acting as a pass-through between the online application and the back-end. That said, the web services could also be used by other applications and sources. Although a total "transaction" count might be useful, it may be potentially more useful to have a set of counters "per source." This would allow you to differentiate between transaction counts entering from different sources — for example, if a particular "source" was firing in a large number of transactions. However, it does mean that the web service would need to be passed the "source." In this instance, this is easy because it can simply be added to the `TransactionContext`. It also means that a counter per source is installed or created. This would be a more involved implementation and would require updates as and when new systems used the web services.

The application servers, on the other hand, have a number of different component types, all of which could update similar "transaction" counters. Implementing this would provide the maximum amount of information, but it would also mean that every layer is updating similar performance counters. It is my experience that as soon as you leave out a layer, you find yourself wishing that you'd included it because it becomes a bottleneck sooner or later. The following looks at the top-level layers and what they could potentially record:

❑ The manager components are performing field-level and business-level validation. They, too, could record transaction counts and performance, perhaps on a per-source basis. They could record the number of validation failures on a per-transaction basis or the number of failures on a per-type basis — for example, "Username already exists."

❑ The processor components are performing the actual processing, so they would also be a good place to record the number of transactions and performance, perhaps again on a per-source basis.

It is clear that framework components (base classes and components) would isolate the functionality of implementing and updating the counters. The "application" components would simply specify the particular counter that should be updated.

There are other framework components within the solution that form part of the end-to-end transactions. For example, the queue provider, which is used to enqueue and dequeue e-mail messages, sits between the key online pages and the key batch processes. However, the queue component would again be installed on different machines. Performance counters relating to the number of items being placed on the queue could prove useful during monitoring. However, this information could equally be obtained from the database in this instance.

It is important to look at the individual components to ascertain a reasonable set of counters. It is also important to think about when counters are reset. The counters will be on different servers, so they won't be incremented and decremented by components on other servers, unless, of course, the configuration pointed to a set of counters on a particular server. It could certainly be done, but it would introduce a network transaction each time the counter was updated. You would need to consider this carefully, as it would introduce even more latency into the overall transaction. Monitoring solutions often support "counter aggregation," so counters from different server values can be totaled up and presented as a single figure.

Other internal components include the following:

- ❑ Authentication provider
- ❑ Message provider
- ❑ Cryptography provider
- ❑ Validation provider
- ❑ Data access components

All the code-base components in the logical component model are candidates for updating performance counters and may also benefit from some basic instrumentation, especially during performance testing.

Before closing this section, it is worth looking at alternatives. The end-to-end transaction counters are useful for high-level performance indicators, although the counters for individual components can really highlight bottlenecks. "Diagnostic" logging can also be used to complement (or possibly remove the need for) performance counters. For example, method entry and method exit timestamp logging has long been used to "measure" performance in a method. "Method entry logging" is simply tracing out to a file (or alternative) when a method is entered, and "method exit logging" is tracing out to a file (or alternative) just before the method exits or returns. The following pseudo code demonstrates method entry and method exit tracing within an example Authenticate method that accepts a username parameter and a password parameter:

```
Authenticate( string username, string password )
{
    const string METHOD_NAME = "AuthenticationProcessor.Authenticate";

    // trace method entry
    Trace( CLASS_NAME, METHOD_NAME, TraceType.MethodEntry, username, password);
```

```
        // do method processing
        // ...

        // trace method exit
        Trace( CLASS_NAME, METHOD_NAME, TraceType.MethodExit, returnValue );

        // exit
        return returnValue;
    }
```

Tracing is discussed in more detail in Chapter 21. The trace file would contain the timestamp for the point at which the method was entered, and the trace file would contain the timestamp for the point just prior to method exiting. These are indicated by the `MethodEntry` and `MethodExit` trace statements in the pseudo code. The diagnostics in this instance contain more information than a performance counter would. For instance, the logs would contain the parameters and the return value for the method. The logs would also identify how long the method took to process, although this information could also be included in a "real-time" performance counter.

It is worth looking at all the components in the solution and listing the possible counters that could be implemented. Modeling the end-to-end flow can highlight areas where certain counters might not be required because the information is available elsewhere. In most cases, the counters will be of the typical types already discussed (for example, counts, transactions per second, and latency).

Intermittent Counter Updates

Counters that are updated on a per-transaction basis reflect true values and real averages. In high-volume transaction processing, updating the counters for every single transaction can be a costly exercise simply because of the number of transactions. Therefore, some high-level processing updates a counter only every *n*th transaction. This can lead to somewhat strange graphs and charts because the "sampled" transaction may not represent the norm. To explain, let's say that the counter is updated only every 100th transaction. All the processing conducted for the 99 unrecorded transactions could be of very average timing. However, the 100th transaction could be a particularly fast or a particularly slow transaction, which would lead to graphs showing misleading and confusing peaks and troughs.

Batch processes are a fairly reasonable example of where intermittent updates to performance counters could be performed. The batch processor could be responsible for the counter updates (based on configuration). If the processor was performing bulk operations, the counters would essentially be getting updated for every batch of transactions. If one transaction in the batch was subject to adverse processing conditions, it would color the numbers for the entire batch. In large transaction-processing systems, it is even more important to maintain throughput and reduce overall latency. Intermittent updates can improve performance, but at the cost of potentially reflecting inaccurate information. Although the counters themselves are recording the minimum, maximum, and average values, these would be based only on the batch and might not represent true values. The provider could maintain individual values for minimum, maximum, and peak processing:

❑   **Minimum** — A counter recording a minimum value would be used to record the lowest number of transactions in a processing period and/or the throughput, and so on. If you discount 0, the value can really help when charting, as it shows the true lowest value and can be compared with other days or processing periods. For example, when applied to end-to-end performance, the minimum value would contain the slowest transaction so far. The value could decrease throughout the day, which could also indicate the system was getting progressively slower — although it is not conclusive. A transaction could have been blocked and retried a number of times, contributing to the downturn in end-to-end performance and averages.

❑ **Maximum** — Records the maximum number of transactions in a sampling period and/or the throughput, and so on. Again, discounting 0, the value would show the true maximum value and can be compared with other days or sampling periods. Applied to the end-to-end performance example, the value would record the peak processing so far. The value could also increase throughout the day, which could indicate that the system is getting faster — although again it is not conclusive. It could be particularly fast as there are no other transactions in flight.

❑ **Peak** — This value would be used to record the peak ("optimum") processing in a block of transactions. It is quite similar to the normal average but can discount the minimum and maximum values, or values that are outside particular tolerances, such as retries or limits. The value reflects a truer "peak" average of processing performance by discounting the overly fast and slow transactions. It represents a steady state peak average for the overall processing sequence. If all the transactions were particularly fast or particularly slow, the value would be consistent with the other counter values (minimum and maximum). It is not trying to give "better" performance indications; it is simply trying to provide more realistic data when every single transaction isn't being recorded.

The number of calculations performed on a per-transaction basis also affects performance, so it is really worth focusing on which counters are required and why. There may be other ways of retrieving the same data without overly impacting the application's performance.

Thresholds and Tolerances

The counters will be fluctuating throughout the day, and the values will be sampled by the monitoring application. As the values increase and decrease, there's typically an optimum operating level within which things are considered "normal." However, when the values go outside of normal operating rules, events and warnings are typically raised. The events can be generated by the application itself based on configured thresholds and tolerances. The monitoring solution can also include rules whereby events are raised based on thresholds and tolerances being breached.

When defining counters, it is worth thinking about the tolerances and operating thresholds. It is even more important to think about what could actually be done when the breach occurs. If nothing can be done about it, it is simply information, however useful. Panic sets in when the system is running slow or approaching a critical situation. We've already seen how operational procedures need to be very clear and concise. During performance testing, thresholds and tolerances will be further refined, but it is important to determine whether the application requires specific code to raise events at certain points in the processing or whether the tolerances and thresholds can be solely achieved using the monitoring solution. The application code may be able to provide more contextual information to the event. The application can perhaps also manage the events more appropriately by "canceling" or providing "information" when the counters return to normal. For example, when a counter breaches a certain tolerance, a warning event could be raised; when the counter returns to normal, a further event could be raised indicating so. This does have the potential for creating noise, but it also has the potential to fine-tune the monitoring solution. For instance, it may be possible to include rules that pair the warning and the cancellation within a certain period of time and do not raise an alert. For instance, if a warning and cancellation are raised within the same minute, the monitoring solution will not escalate the event. When thinking about the tolerances and breaches, it's worth thinking about when they return to normal operating tolerances. Some monitoring solutions "learn" the normal processing performance throughout the day, and instead of setting a fixed threshold, it varies throughout the day. For instance, instead of getting alerts at 9am when everyone logs in, the monitoring solution "knows" that this is a particularly busy period. You should understand the capabilities of the monitoring solution and maximize their usage.

Events and Event Logs

Events are probably the most important part of monitoring the application. They provide valuable information to the operations and support teams regarding the application's internal state, especially under abnormal conditions. Although performance counters offer processing performance and other internal state-related information, events can contain far more information than simple values that can be sampled.

Windows-based applications can raise events using the `EventLog` class. An event can be of type Information, Warning, Error, Success Audit, or Failure Audit. The events raised by the application are stored in a specific "event log." An event log is a special type of log file and is not to be confused with debug or trace logs. Applications use the `Debug` and `Trace` classes to output information that helps to trace program execution and assist in debugging activities. The events raised by the application should indicate information that is useful from an operational point of view, not "spam" the event log with unnecessary information. The following simplified pseudo code shows a hypothetical example of a program flow using both event logging and tracing:

```
Trace.WriteLine "Process Started"

// trace execution
Trace.WriteLine "Checking AccountState 'AccountState' for Account 'thisAccount'"

if( thisAccount.AccountState==AccountStates.New )
{
    try
    {
        // process account
        ...
        Trace.WriteLine "Account 'AccountId' Processed Successfully"
    }
    catch( Exception e )
    {
        EventLog.WriteEntry Error "Processing error 'e'"
        throw
    }
}
else
{
    EventLog.WriteEntry Error, "Account 'thisAccount' State Not New"
}
Trace.WriteLine "Process Completed"
```

The preceding pseudo code example snippet shows that the program would output trace information using the `Trace` class and raise events using the `EventLog` class. You'll notice that the events raised in the pseudo code are both of an Error type. Events are not just reserved for errors, however; events can be of other types, as mentioned previously and discussed in more detail later in this section. Before examining the various types of events, I'll cover the actual event logs themselves rather than the events they contain.

Each server has its own event log, which the application components can update. As shown in Figure 20-2, the servers, by default, typically have an application event log, a system event log, and a security event log.

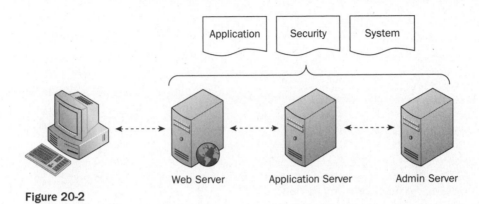

Figure 20-2

An application typically records events in the generic application event log until the application is initialized correctly. Once the application is initialized, it records events in its own application-specific event logs. For example:

- **Within-a-Click Web** — This event log would be used by the components residing on the web servers.

- **Within-a-Click Web Service** — This event log would be used by the web service components residing on the application servers.

- **Within-a-Click Manager** — This event log would be used by the manager components residing on the application servers.

- **Within-a-Click Processor** — This event log would be used by the processor components residing on the application servers.

- **Within-a-Click Provider** — This event log would be used by the provider components residing on the application servers.

It is important to think about the different logs and how they will be used. You can achieve performance improvements by carving up the logs to reduce the load on any particular log. Again, modeling the transaction flow and the events that would be raised can help to produce an initial list. The component model provides the initial basis for this activity.

Figure 20-3 shows a simple example of where you could even have an event log for each component type. The left side shows a typical approach whereby all the manager components are raising their events in a single event log. The right side shows an alternative approach whereby individual managers have their own specific event log.

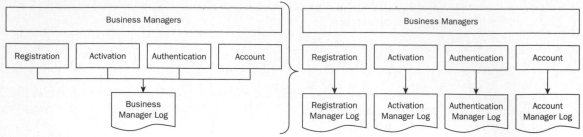

Figure 20-3

There are pros and cons to either approach and there's no right or wrong answer. The application should raise events in the most appropriate place for effective monitoring. The more event logs there are, the more configuration there is in the monitoring solution. However, the application may actually perform better with a larger number of discrete logs, and reading through the events on the local component might be easier because they pertain only to a single component. This pattern can be applied to the processors as well as to the providers.

Finally, framework components may also need to raise specific events. If the events raised by the framework components are going to be stored in the same event log as the component that is calling them (for example, manager, provider, and so on), the calling component will need to pass the framework component a reference to the specific event log it (the caller) is using. Alternatively, each component could have its own specific logs for its events or simply throw exceptions and not raise any events at all.

Event Types

This section looks at the different types of events that the application can raise, what they can be used for, and what contextual information they should contain. The following provides an overview of the different types of events:

❑ **Information** — Good events typically translate to Information event types in the event log. A good event is raised when something significant has been achieved — for example, loading configuration values, establishing a connection with an external source, creating a transaction account, closing an account, and so on. A good event can also be used to cancel a previous warning to inform the operations team that the application has returned to a steady state. Processing milestones in batch are also considered good events — for example, start, percentage complete, and completion.

❑ **Warnings** — Bad events typically translate into Warnings event types, although on rare occasions bad events are raised as Information events. A bad event is generally raised when something happens that can be handled either automatically, or at least handled to a degree by the application, or perhaps even by the user. A transaction retry would typically constitute a Warning event rather than an Information event. Although retrying is considered part of the normal processing, it is in response to an exception or abnormal processing conditions.

❑ **Error** — Unexpected conditions and incomplete processing events usually translate into Error events. Error events almost certainly require some form of incident investigation, corrective actions, and operational procedures. Failure to complete a transaction or processing would constitute an Error event. The shutdown of a process would usually mean an Error event even if the process were under an automatic restart.

❑ **Success audit** — Successful authentication (or security-based) events are typically raised as Success Audit event types — for example, when a user logs in successfully or is granted access to a secure resource.

❑ **Failure audit** — Failed authentication (or security-based) events are typically raised as Failure Audit event types — for example, when a user isn't authenticated successfully or is denied access to a secure resource.

Determining the type of event to raise is generally easier with Error events than the other types because they are typically based on exceptions raised by the underlying system. Even when the application isn't specifically raising its own errors or events, there are still system exceptions that can occur and stop further processing, irrespective of whether they are truly handled by the code. If the application is going to stop further processing and/or exit for any reason, this would typically constitute an Error event.

The case study contains a number of different areas where the event types discussed could be applied. To keep things short, we'll examine a few of the high-level processing areas:

❑ **Authentication success/failure** — The authentication processor is essentially the "gatekeeper" for authentication attempts; all authentication attempts are controlled through it. An influx of Failure Audit events could indicate that someone is trying to "hack" accounts. To reduce noise, the application could be configured to raise only a single failure event if a (configurable) number of invalid attempts were made. This could be coupled with future account-locking functionality. In this instance, it may not be necessary to raise an Audit Success event but to instead concentrate on failures only. And if this was the case, it could also discount the access processor from raising Success Audit or Information events when an account was successfully logged in to.

❑ **Account created/activated/updated/closed or password changed** — These events would indicate positive actions that were completed by the functional processing and would typically be Information. From a *real* monitoring perspective, their actual value is somewhat limited. The sheer number of these events that could be raised during a single day or even an hour could be huge. The events simply indicate that the system is functioning correctly. That doesn't mean that they couldn't be raised, but one needs to question the monitoring value that they add. The performance counters for throughput and performance would indicate the load on the system and how it was performing.

❑ **Resend Activation Key** — A large number of requests for Activation Keys to be resent could indicate that e-mail isn't being sent at all or perhaps is taking too long a time to arrive. The events would complement the performance counters by providing the accounts for which the Activation Keys were being re-requested. These types of events would typically be categorized as Information events. The account details are encrypted, so the only useful piece of information would be the unique account identifier or username. From a monitoring perspective, the performance counters would provide enough information to indicate a high-level of "Activation Key re-request" activity. The account IDs could help to pinpoint a particular queue or e-mail process that wasn't functioning, although these entries could equally be logged in trace files.

❑ **Account not created/activated/updated/closed** — These events are really bad if they are the result of underlying system exceptions. The events would typically be Error events because users can't complete the action through no fault of their own (for example, through simple validation failures or duplicate usernames). It is difficult to determine what operations would do with this information. However, the event should include the exception, which could lead them to perform some form of standard operational procedure. The user would be presented with a technical error and they will likely retry the transaction anyway.

❏ **Batch processes** — The batch processes are truly running in the background. The standard output will help you (and operators) to see how the processes are performing, although this can be complemented with milestone events and performance counter updates during the processing cycle. The following describes a few sample event types:

  ❏ **Batch process started** — These Information events would indicate that a batch process had started. The contextual information should include all the parameters that were passed to the process.

  ❏ **Batch process progress** — These Information events would indicate key processing milestones, such as 25 percent complete, 50 percent complete, and so on. The contextual information could include a synopsis of the processing that has been completed thus far, such as the total number of items processed, the number of items not processed, and the total number of items remaining.

  ❏ **Batch process failure** — These types of events would indicate that an error occurred within a batch process. The error might be fatal and cause the batch process to end, in which case the event would be an Error event and the contextual information should contain all the necessary information regarding the error encountered. In other cases, the error could be associated with a particular item being processed. If the process can "skip" the item and continue processing other items, the event would typically be a Warning or Information event to indicate that the job had not processed a work item. If the process can't continue without processing the work item, the job would need to end and the event would be an Error.

  ❏ **Batch process completed** — These Information events would indicate that a batch process had completed. The contextual information should include the overall outcome of the process and a synopsis of the processing performed, such as the total number of items processed, the number of items not processed, and the end-to-end processing time.

Some of the preceding final error conditions/outcomes could be thrown or caused by system exceptions and failures in some of the following framework components (which can also raise their own events):

❏ **Configuration provider** — The configuration provider may not be able to find the configuration files, in which case it should raise Error events. The application could ask for a configuration value that can't be found, which would indicate incorrect/incomplete configuration. This should also be raised as an Error event. A Warning event could be raised if the configuration file or values were going to "default" to internal values.

❏ **Message provider** — The application could request a message ID that couldn't be found, which would constitute an Error event. You could limit the possibility of this happening by having the database auto-generate the message enumerations and classes. If the database couldn't load or reload the messages, an Error event would result. The messages could be cached in memory and reloaded from the database periodically. Information events would be raised when the messages start and finish reloading. It is possible that even a Warning event could be raised if the values weren't reloaded, as the provider could revert to using the current cache until the next reload period.

❑ **E-mail queue provider** — This component could fail because of database access, so Error events are essentially system exceptions. If the component fails (after suitable retries), the entire transaction would be rolled back and the event would be rippled back up to the top, resulting in an overall failure. The component could raise Information events for each of the items added to the queue, but the operational benefits would have to be considered.

❑ **Cryptography provider** — This component would fail primarily because of system exceptions. The provider has no real knowledge of the expected outcome of the transaction, so it probably wouldn't benefit the monitoring solution by raising any specific events. It is possible that this component updates performance counters to ensure that it can be monitored for performance.

❑ **Validation provider** — The application might try to validate a data element that didn't exist. You could reduce this by leveraging auto-generation techniques. However, it would be a serious issue if the component was unable to truly validate a data element properly. Given the amount of validation being performed, neither events nor even performance counters would necessarily provide any real monitoring benefit (apart from performance), unless they were very specific and could indicate some form of malicious usage or incorrect transactions from an external system.

❑ **Data access provider** — The data access provider is used by the other components in the solution (account data access and e-mail data access) to access the database. The data access provider will implement wait-retry logic, with the retries typically raised as Warning events and ultimate failure resulting in Error events.

The preceding are just a few of the potential Information, Error, and Warning events across the application's layers and components. Working out the most valuable events to raise is a matter of walking through the individual components and the solution. Where possible, the events should be discussed with the support team to ensure that everyone is in agreement, as this will be part of the handover and support activities. The events raised should help to effectively monitor the application and provide real value for the ensuing incident investigation.

Event Log Entries — The Good, the Bad, and the Ugly

A good question to ask yourself is, "Given only the event information, could I put together an idea of what happened?" This is very important, as reducing the number of follow-up actions from the event can save time and money. I'll discuss this subject more in Chapter 21, but for the moment, let's look at some simple guidelines for event log content. Place yourself in the shoes of the support team and think about the information you would require to start an investigation. Undoubtedly, other logs and artifacts will be required, but the event is the starting point. Here are just a few tips for event log entries:

❑ **Good** — A good event log entry contains all the relevant contextual information regarding the event or incident. You've seen how adding contextual data to the error can benefit any further investigation. A good entry would at least point to the class and method where the error occurred and include all the relevant (and agreed to) contextual information. The contextual information should not contain anything that would breach security or privacy. That said, the actual contextual information could be different across environments. The call stack, along with the key parameters, would also greatly help the investigation. Good event entries typically include:

❑ The unique event/error identifier.

❑ The class name and method name where the event occurred.

❑ The action being performed (or line number).

❑   The exact details of the error or error message, including any contextual information.

❑   The appropriate contextual information, such as the parameters passed in the method, the in-memory state such as cached values, the parameters passed to a stored procedure or query. You could also attach the entire `TransactionContext`.

❑   The stack trace, if raised in conjunction with an exception, although this could breach the limit of the event size and could be recorded elsewhere, such as in a log file.

❑   **Bad** — Bad event log entries don't contain the relevant contextual information or even the starting point for the investigation — for example, indicating "File Not Found" without specifying which file wasn't found. Events that contain simple spelling mistakes, incorrect class names and method names, or incorrect contextual data are further examples of shoddy (and untested) event logging. For instance, outputting the `accountID` when it should be the `emailRequestId` might be a very simple mistake but results in a shoddy event context and hinders any incident investigation.

❑   **Ugly** — Not including the class name and method name where the error occurred is a very bad practice. Copy and paste errors are another pet peeve of mine. You can generally always tell when an event or log has been pasted from a previous one because all the information is the same. The event being raised is actually incorrect because it has been copied from somewhere else. These sorts of failings can lead to a lot of wasted effort when trying to resolve issues and problems. Forgetting to specify the correct contextual data can also lead to atrocious context information, such as "The account {0} could not be found."

The monitoring (and support) of an application is much smoother when events are consistently good and provide all the relevant information.

Monitoring Configuration

As you can tell from the discussions so far, nothing is really cast-in-stone, except that things will differ from project to project. Things will actually differ from environment to environment as well. A Warning event in one environment may not necessarily be a Warning event in another; it could be Information or perhaps even an Error event. There's no denying that correctly instrumenting an application has a performance overhead, not to mention development and test overheads. But this needs to be balanced against effective monitoring and support. Where possible, the application should support a flexible approach to monitoring through configuration.

Performance Counter Configuration

The configuration should allow performance counters to be switched on or off. The application shouldn't update counters that have been switched off in the configuration. This greatly helps with testing because the counters can be switched on and the values can be sampled to provide reports. However, the counters can be switched off in production to improve the overall performance of the application. The configuration should also allow the sampling period to be modified where appropriate. For example, if a counter is being updated every 100th transaction, this should be a configurable value. All the performance counters in the system should be well-documented and understood so that the production configuration is optimum. The configuration may change on-the-fly, so a consistent approach to obtaining configuration values should be used.

To save everyone from having to implement the same or very similar code to access and update performance counters, access to performance counters should be performed through a consistent component, such as a diagnostic provider. The diagnostic provider can then control all the relevant locking, loading, and configuration management (using the standard configuration provider). From the calling component's point of view, all it needs to do is call the diagnostics provider — for example:

```
if( DiagnosticProvider.IsCounterOn( Counters.CreateNewAccount ) )
{
    // increment the counter value
    DiagnosticProvider.IncrementCounter( Counters.CreateNewAccount );
}
```

The preceding pseudo code is only an example, but it shows how a component can use the diagnostic provider to check whether a performance counter is actually switched on using the IsCounterOn method (for example, the counter is being recorded based on the configuration). If so, the diagnostic provider would return true and the pseudo code would proceed to increment the CreateNewAccount counter using the IncrementCounter method on the diagnostic provider. If the performance counter is switched off (for example, the counter isn't being recorded based on the configuration), the diagnostics provider would return false (and the code wouldn't execute the statements within the if block.) This is in keeping with the messages for performance in Chapter 18 whereby the code isn't performing any unnecessary updates.

Event Configuration

Events (and their contents) should also be configurable. During unit testing it might be very useful to output all the information for a given exception, such as the username, password, e-mail address, and so forth. However, this may be totally inappropriate for live service, so the configuration would be different. Managing different contextual information is generally quite difficult and can often lead to events being raised with incorrect contextual information. It is very possible to specify the configuration of message and data elements in the database (or other configuration source) and assign different data elements to messages along with an ordinal position to support truly configurable messages. Given that this would need to be designed into the application and accounted for in the timescales, however, a simpler solution is to only raise events that contain the production information and include other testing-related information in the log files or trace files. The basic event configuration should at least support what event types are switched on or off, such as Error, Warning, and so forth. It could be extended to include specific events (or categories) that are switched on or off, such as Activate Account. Most important, the configuration should really allow each event to be associated with a specific event type (Error, Warning, Information and so on). This allows each event being raised to have a different severity in different environments.

The application could use the diagnostic provider to determine whether the particular event is actually being recorded and, if so, raise the event. The following shows an example of this in pseudo code:

```
if( DiagnosticProvider.IsEventOn( Events.DatabaseRetry ) )
{

    // raise event
    DiagnosticProvider.RaiseEvent( Events.DatabaseRetry, … );

}
```

When the events need to be raised will dictate the best place for the configuration. It is quite clear in the preceding example that the application code itself is not concerned with whether the event is an Error, Warning, or even Information. It simply checks whether the event is actually switched on and, if so, proceeds to raise the event with the appropriate contextual information.

Summary

This chapter has looked at two important factors for successful monitoring of a solution, performance counters, and events. To support better monitoring, the solution should support a level of configuration.

The following are the key points to take away from this chapter:

❑ **Identify and use performance counters.** Walk through the solution components and highlight areas where performance counters will provide real monitoring benefit. What may seem like something irrelevant may have real benefit in production running.

❑ **Updating performance counters mustn't affect performance.** Ensure that performance counters are updated only when they need to be and that everyone understands the counter, its sampling rate, and values.

❑ **Think about the events that the system should raise.** Not all events are "bad." There are some very good reasons for raising good events. You should walk through the solution and identify events that should be raised to assist in monitoring and operations.

❑ **Use application specific event logs.** Determine where events will be raised and the logs they will be raised in. You should consider using multiple event logs where necessary.

❑ **Include detailed contextual information in events.** You need to ensure that all events contain all the information they need for the follow-up incident investigation.

❑ **Consider a flexible monitoring configuration.** Remember that not all environments are the same. What might be a warning in one environment may be an error in another. Consider a flexible solution to monitoring configuration to allow easier management. A totally generic and configurable solution could very well impact timescales and costs, but this should be weighed against the benefits in further test phases and live service support.

The next chapter discusses some patterns and practices for incident investigation that build on the messages in this chapter.

Designing for Incident Investigation

Incident investigation will often follow an error or abnormal event being raised. Developers are constantly involved in incident investigation — right through the lifecycle, not just in live service. Defects raised during testing need to be resolved quickly and efficiently. It is often during testing that you find that not only are the events inadequate, but the logging, tracing, auditing, and tooling are, too. Developers often spend so much time trying to get the functionality right that they forget the instrumentation and diagnostics. I've mentioned this before, but there's nothing worse than being awoken at 3 A.M. to investigate a problem and the event itself contains no real information, and then, to add further insult to injury, the logs don't tell anything conclusive, either.

Incident investigation is all about getting to the root cause of the problem, re-creating the issue, analyzing and defining a solution, and, ultimately, implementing that solution. The quicker you can achieve this goal, the sooner you can go (back) to bed. You've seen how good diagnostics provide a great starting point. This chapter looks a little bit further into the actual actions that follow and what you can do to really provide value to this process.

This chapter is organized into the following sections:

❑ **Tracing** — Examines the tracing that should be included in the solution components. It also looks at some important practices that you should consider when implementing tracing to ensure that tracing is configurable for different environments and purposes.

❑ **Investigative Tooling** — Examines some of the tools that could be required during incident investigation and how they could be used to analyze the root cause effectively.

Tracing

Part of establishing a timeline for an incident invariably involves analyzing log files and trace files, as well as other outputs from the solution. The tracing is no different from events for quality purposes. There are good trace entries, bad trace entries, and downright ugly trace entries. When you see a trace entry that doesn't include the most vital piece of information, you hold your head in your hands and cry "WHY?"

An optimal level of tracing should be a part of the production system and included within the performance requirements. Personally, I don't think it's very good to say, "The system runs at 100 miles an hour with everything switched off." There really needs to be tracing to ensure that issues can be resolved when they occur — unless, of course, the event has everything you need. The tracing also needs to maintain code quality and readability while providing adequate output.

In many cases tracing can further demonstrate the 80/20 rule. Consider the following example pseudo code (which is for demonstration purposes only):

```
Authenticate( string username, string password )
{

status = false;

    // method entry trace
    if( DiagnosticProvider.IsTracing( Activity.MethodEntry ) )
    {

        DiagnosticProvider.Trace( TraceType.MethodEntry, CLASS_NAME,
                                  METHOD_NAME, username );

    }

    // obtain user
    if( DiagnosticProvider.IsTracing( Activity.ObtainAccount ) )
    {

        DiagnosticProvider.Trace( CLASS_NAME, METHOD_NAME, Information,
                                  Activity.ObtainAccount, username, password );

    }

    if( AccountProvider.GetUserByUsername( username ) )
    {

        // check if password matches
        if( DiagnosticProvider.IsTracing( Activity.ComparePassword ) )
        {

            DiagnosticProvider.Trace( CLASS_NAME, METHOD_NAME, Information,
             Activity.ComparePassword, password,
             AccountProvider.AccountData( AccountDataElements.Password ) );

        }
```

```
        if( password == AccountProvider.AccountData( AccountDataElements.Password) )
        {

            // check if password matches
            if( DiagnosticProvider.IsTracing( Activity.PasswordMatches ) )
            {

                DiagnosticProvider.Trace( CLASS_NAME, METHOD_NAME, Information,
                    Activity.PasswordMatches, username, password,
                    AccountProvider.AccountData( AccountDataElements.Password) );

            }

            // set status
            status = true;

        }
        else
        {

            // trace password failed
            if( DiagnosticProvider.IsTracing(
                Activity.ComparePasswordFailed ) )
            {

                DiagnosticProvider.Trace( CLASS_NAME, METHOD_NAME, Information,
                    Activity.ComparePasswordFailed, username, password,
                    AccountProvider.AccountData( AccountDataElements.Password) );

            }

        }

    }
    else
    {

        // trace account not found
        if( DiagnosticProvider.IsRaisingEvent( Events.AccountNotFound ) )
        {

            // raise event
            DiagnosticProvider.RaiseEvent( CLASS_NAME, METHOD_NAME,
                Events.AccountNotFound, username );

        }

        // trace account not found
        if( DiagnosticProvider.IsTracing( Activity.AccountNotFound ) )
```

```
            {

                DiagnosticProvider.Trace( CLASS_NAME, METHOD_NAME, Information,
                    Activity.AccountNotFound, username );

            }

        }

        // method exit trace
        if( DiagnosticProvider.IsTracing( Activity.MethodExit ) )
        {

            DiagnosticProvider.Trace( TraceType.MethodExit, CLASS_NAME,
                METHOD_NAME, status );

        }

        // return status
        return status;

    }
```

I've deliberately made this code long because it demonstrates a situation in which you can't see the forest from the trees. It also shows the 80/20 rule because the majority of the code is actually for tracing purposes and simply outweighs the actual functional code. It doesn't even contain any exception handling, performance counter updates, or "proper" commenting. It does somewhat demonstrate why most tracing statements are typically omitted, considering the method would look something like the following without them:

```
Authenticate( string username, string password )
{

    status = false;

    if( AccountProvider.GetUserByUsername( username ) )
    {
      if( password == AccountProvider.AccountData( AccountDataElements.Password ) )
      {
            // set status
            status = true;
      }
    }

    // return status
    return status

}
```

The latter code snippet is also far easier to implement and test than the former because it doesn't require any configuration, and the account provider could also be "stubbed" to provide a particular result based on the username value. Stubbing and simulating are discussed in Chapter 23, "Designing for Testing."

Irrespective of the tracing configuration, the problem with tracing is that it will pepper the code (not to mention the associated comment that says "Trace . . ."). I'm not saying the first example isn't viable; I'm just saying it has a lot of tracing code compared to its actual functionality. In addition, you have to think about what you're really going to trace. The first example actually shows the "password" being written to the trace. The password is considered "secure information" and shouldn't really be traced out. Information that isn't logged raises a potential gap and could hinder incident investigation. Where secure information is omitted, you should consider how it could be logged securely, such as encrypted or encoded so that it is included in the log and can be used later for incident investigation (assuming it can be decrypted appropriately). During testing, it might be possible to log secure information in plain text but this would need to be discussed, agreed on and probably, configurable.

Imagine that you were drawing a sequence diagram or interaction diagram by hand. The diagram would be vastly expanded if all tracing, and events were included. The simple fact is that tracing and diagnostics can often outweigh the functional code, especially when you take a line-for-line approach (for example, one line of trace per line of code).

Consistent use of tracing is encouraged. If a simple method like the one just discussed has so much tracing, a method with far more functionality should have even more. However, it is often not the case because in a simple method, it is generally easier to implement a larger amount of tracing than it is in a complex method. The result is that when you look through the logs, you find lots of entries and information for all the very small methods, but you find only a couple of entries for the really complex ones. And it is typically the really complex ones that go wrong and need investigating.

You should define a tracing strategy that specifies the rules, the necessary configuration, when to trace, and the files where the trace will be contained.

Tracing is typically based on a category (information, warning, error, and debug). The logging approach should first assess each of these categories, and the following provides some examples:

❑   An *information trace* is used to trace the individual use-case steps. From a functional perspective, a very good starting point is the use-case steps.

❑   A *warning trace* is used to trace the fact that the application is "proceeding at risk." You can see a good example of this in the wait-retry pattern. Each time the system encounters an exception, it will be traced out as a warning until the maximum number of retries has been reached, whereupon the exception is escalated to an error trace and the transaction would fail.

❑   An *error trace* is typically used to trace exceptions. When the system encounters an exception that can't be retried or the maximum number of retries has been reached it would typically output the exception to the trace file.

❑   A *debug trace* is used to trace information that is useful during debugging — for example, tracing method entry, method exit, and other internal processing steps within individual methods.

The rules surrounding each category can then be further refined — for instance, to specify what each entry type must contain. Using the rules, you can pull together a high-level tracing model (discussed in Chapter 4 as an input into the construction process). The case study has a transaction model, for example, that is used to determine where core processing should be performed. The transaction model can be used again to highlight trace areas using the preceding trace categories. Figure 21-1 shows an example of this.

Activate Account Page	Activation Manager	Activation Process	Authentication Process	AccountProvider
Debug *Inputs - Username, Password, Previous Transaction* **Information (must contain parameters passed)** 1) The "Activate My Account" page is displayed and the fields blank/pre-populated are enabled/disabled according to the route from which they arrived.				
Debug The system obtains the current date and time using the CalendarProvider and adds it to the request as Activated Date and Time.				
Debug *ActivateAccount - Username, Password, Activation Key, Activated Date and Time*	**Information (must contain the parameters passed)** 3) The system checks that all mandatory information has been specified and that each element is valid and correct according to its individual validation rules (where required).			
	Debug *Authenticate - Username, Password*		**Debug** *GetAccount - Username* **Debug (containing the serialized AccountData)** **AccountData** Information (can contain the hash values being compared) 5) The system authenticates the user by comparing the password entered with that stored on file.	Information (must contain the username being searched for) 4) The system checks that an account exists with the Username specified.
	Debug (containing the serialized account data) **Response includes** **AccountData**			
	Information (should include the account state returned) 6) The system checks that the account is in a state of "New".			
	Information (should contain the Activation Keys being compared) 7) The system checks that the supplied "Account Activation Key" matches that stored on file.			
	Debug *ActivateAccount - AccountData*	Information 8) The system sets the account state to "Active". Information (can include the date and time being set) 8) The system sets the Account Activated Date and Time.		
		Debug *Login - AccountData*	Information 9) **The system logs the user in** to the system and records the date and time the user was logged in.	
			Debug *UpdateAccount - Account Data* **Debug (containing serialized account data)** **Response will include** **Account Data**	Information (should include what is being passed to the database) 9) **The system** logs the user in to the system and **records the date and time the user was logged in.** Information 10) The system removes any "flagged for removal" mark that may be present on the account.
		Debug (containing all the values being populated) Populate and Return Response		
	Debug (containing all the values being populated) Populate and Return Response			
Information 9) **The system logs the user in** to the system and records the date and time the user was logged in.				
Debug (containing the values being placed in the cache)				
Information 11) The system displays the "Account Activated" confirmation message and "Continue" button.				

Figure 21-1

The basic idea is to simply mark each step in the flow with a particular type of trace and any additional notable information.

In this instance, the transaction model doesn't show the low-level components and the tracing they would perform. If all the components were modeled, you'd have a very solid picture. I've also removed the steps that are performed by the user.

The transaction model helps to solidify the tracing approach and provides the basis for further discussion and improvement. For example, the transaction model indicates that the account data will be serialized and outputted by both the account processor and the account manager. This is a bit of a waste, considering that under normal circumstances nothing will have changed. This could be embedded within the account provider itself.

The diagram also indicates "duplicate" steps — for example, Step 9 whereby the system is logging in the user. What's the difference between the two traces? The web server in this instance is actually performing the "functional" login, whereas the processor (at the moment) is simply passing information through. You could simply remove one of the trace statements but this would need to be balanced against end-to-end visibility of the transaction through the application.

You can flatten the information in the transaction model to produce a sample output file. In addition, you can use the model to highlight data and values to include in the file. This would help you to "visualize" the trace and the information it contained. The transaction model also highlights where the components cross over, which is vitally important. For instance, you can't log the use-case step numbers from within the lowever-level components because these would be different depending on where the components were called from. This raises the question of whether to move certain trace entries higher up into the manager and processor. The transaction model is simply being used in exactly the same way as before — to assess the end-to-end flow of the transaction and adjust where certain processing, or in this case, tracing should be performed. We've now used the modeling table for three distinct purposes and in all cases it has provided valuable information. Obviously, you can achieve the same result modeling the application using formal sequence diagrams.

From a technical perspective, when defining the tracing rules, you should start by considering the following questions:

❏ **Are you going to trace method entry / method exit?** These traces can sometimes provide invaluable information during incident investigation. (It is possible to implement aspect-based logging, but that's a whole different conversation.) A method entry trace typically outputs the class name, the method name, and the parameters it has been passed. A method exit trace typically traces out the class name, method name, and the return value or status. Based on the information in the modeling table, you could restrict the method entry and method exit tracing to large functional components and methods only. However, there is a risk associated with this choice: Some incidents might slip through the cracks. For instance, a small component might be altering a value or perhaps using a different value that would not necessarily be obvious as you look through the logs, in which case it might be prudent to implement only method entry tracing. If all traces contained the class name and method name, it would be easy to determine when the called method returned. For example:

```
ActivationManager.Authenticate Method Entry [username]=username,
[password]=password
ActivationManager.Authenticate Calling AuthenticationProcessor.Authenticate with
    username, password
```

```
AuthenticationProcessor.Authenticate Method Entry [username]=username,
[password]=password
AuthenticationProcessor.Authenticate ...
AuthenticationProcessor.Authenticate ...
ActivationManager.Authenticate AuthenticationProvider returned with [status]
```

This does mean that without method exit tracing, the caller may need to output the status returned.

❑ **Are you going to trace method calls in calling components?** Tracing method calls in calling components is typically implemented using the "Calling . . ." style trace. Method A outputs a line of trace indicating that it is about to call Method B, and then it calls Method B. The line of trace would be something along the lines of "[Method A] Calling Class.MethodB with . . ." and listing all the parameters and values. When method entry/method exit tracing is adopted, the trace file typically shows these lines of trace, followed by "[Class.MethodB] Method Entry . . ." and listing all the parameters and values. This is shown in the preceding pseudo code. The example tracing shows that nothing has changed the values between the call from Method A to Method B. It would be somewhat difficult for a process to interfere with the parameters when making a local or perhaps even a remoting call. It would be possible to reduce the amount of trace to only method calls where not all the parameters are being passed — for example, where null is being passed. This approach could also be applied when calling methods that have multiple overloads.

The first level of effective tracing lies in the answers to these questions. And as you've probably guessed, it depends entirely on the circumstances. Once you've decided when and where you're going to do this, you can implement the rules accordingly. Don't forget that tracing is meant to assist in an incident investigation while maintaining code quality and readability. Trawling through reams of duplicated and unnecessary trace is actually a hindrance during an investigation. And reviewing a method and/or updating untold unnecessary trace statements is also counter-productive. The key is to find the right balance between the two.

The level of tracing also depends on whether a component or method could be called from many different locations or applications. If the component was built and designed for total reuse, it would probably include more tracing because its uses are varied. However, if the component is specific to the application and the implementation, the end-to-end flows can be analyzed and the right amount of tracing can be embedded in the appropriate places.

To further reduce the amount of tracing code in the source, you should consider "doubling up" the output. For example, the preceding pseudo code contained the following:

```
// log account not found
if( DiagnosticProvider.IsRaisingEvent( AccountNotFound ) )
{

    // raise event
    DiagnosticProvider.RaiseEvent( CLASS_NAME, METHOD_NAME,
    Events.AccountNotFound, username );

}

// log account not found
```

```
    if( DiagnosticProvider.IsTracing( Activity.AccountNotFound ) )
    {

        DiagnosticProvider.Trace( CLASS_NAME, METHOD_NAME, Information,
        Activity.AccountNotFound, username );

    }
```

You could reduce this code further by embedding the trace statements within the `RaiseEvent` method on the `DiagnosticProvider`. The configuration would map the `AccountNotFound` event to the `AccountNotFound` trace entry, which would be configured as `Information`. The resulting code would simply look as follows:

```
    // log account not found
    if( DiagnosticProvider.IsRaisingEvent( AccountNotFound ) )
    {

        // raise event
        DiagnosticProvider.RaiseEvent( CLASS_NAME, METHOD_NAME,
        Events.AccountNotFound, username );

    }
```

The `RaiseEvent` method would not only raise the event — it would also output the line of trace.

You could take this encapsulation approach even further and apply it when catching and throwing exceptions. The follow code is used for example purposes only:

```
try
{
    // do something
    ...
}
catch( Exception e )
{
    // add value

    // throw
    Throw WACException.Raise( CLASS_NAME, METHOD_NAME, e );
}
```

This snippet is passing the exception to the base `Exception` class's `Throw` method. This method could encapsulate all the event logging and tracing before throwing a wrapped exception. You should handle this approach with care, as the stack trace of the original exception would need to be preserved within an inner exception, and a new `WACException` would be thrown up the stack. This essentially starts a new stack trace from the point at which the exception was thrown. The inner exception, however, would contain the stack trace for the original exception.

It would also be viable to implement the following code, which raises an event prior to actually throwing the exception:

```
try
{
    // do something
    ...
}
catch( Exception e )
{
    // add value

    // raise event/log
    DiagnosticsProvider.RaiseEvent( CLASS_NAME, METHOD_NAME, e );

    // throw
    throw;
}
```

The most important thing is to have an approach for "justified" tracing — that is, tracing that's implemented where it is necessary and that provides value to an incident investigation by ensuring key areas of the code, the pertinent processing steps, algorithms, and values are traced out.

Activity-Based Tracing

Activity-based tracing is used to tie individual tracing outputs together. Individual processes are outputting their trace information. In some cases, a single process may have many threads executing simultaneously and outputting trace information. Furthermore, components reside on different servers, so trace output is spread across multiple trace files (see Figure 21-2).

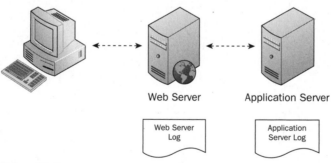

Web Server   Application Server

Web Server   Application
Log   Server Log

Figure 21-2

First, it is important that the trace entries in a single log can be distinguished from one another. Consider the following example trace again:

```
ActivationManager.Authenticate Entry [username]=username, [password]=password
ActivationManager.Authenticate Calling AuthenticationProvider.Authenticate
 with username, password
AuthenticationProcessor.Authenticate Entry [username]=username, [password]=password
```

```
AuthenticationProcessor.Authenticate ...
AuthenticationProcessor.Authenticate ...
ActivationManager.Authenticate AuthenticationProvider returned with [status]
```

The trace shows the primary components involved in a transaction. However, it is difficult to determine whether these trace entries actually apply to the same transaction.

When multiple processes and threads are at work, the tracing typically is not sequential. That means it is even harder to follow because the trace lines are all mixed up. For example:

```
ActivationManager.Authenticate
ActviationManager.Authenticate
ActivationManager.Authenticate
AuthenticationProcessor.Authenticate
AuthenticationProcessor.Authenticate
AuthenticationProcessor.Authenticate
AuthenticationProcessor.Authenticate
```

There are multiple calls and methods at work. Pinning down which relates to which can be difficult because it requires matching up the contextual information. If components are logging only what they are actually interested in, you wouldn't necessarily know which lines related to each other.

The tracing prefix is a set of values that are included in every line of trace — Chapter 4 showed examples of this. The tracing prefix ideally needs to include some form of end-to-end activity identifier to ensure that all the individual trace statements for a particular transaction can be tied together. For example, when a transaction or functional process is started, it is allocated a unique activity identifier. As the transaction or functional process passes through the system, all tracing and events are "stamped" with that activity identifier, making them much easier to follow through each component. The following shows a sample that includes a simple activity identifier:

```
[1] ActivationManager.Authenticate
[1] ActivationManager.Authenticate
[2] ActivationManager.Authenticate
[1] AuthenticationProcessor.Authenticate
[2] AuthenticationProcessor.Authenticate
[2] AuthenticationProcessor.Authenticate
[1] AuthenticationProcessor.Authenticate
```

The sample shows the method calls in the order that they are placed in the log file. With the activity identifier, it is much easier to see which transactions and calls belong to a single transaction. If an exception occurs, it can be logged and raised as an event with the appropriate activity identifier, which will make following the individual logs far easier. It also enables you to collate logs that reside on different servers.

Activity-based tracing requires the activity identifier be passed through the entire system from end-to-end. It could be passed as a parameter on each method call. However, for the case study, the best place to put this is in the `TransactionContext` class. By including the `TransactionContext` class early on in the design and using it to pass information between components, you create a fantastic placeholder for the activity identifier and any other information you might want to include without having to modify any method signatures.

In addition, if you implement the token-synchronization pattern for all transactions, you'd automatically have a unique activity identifier to use for both event logging and tracing. Furthermore, there's even the possibility that you could use this activity identifier as the unique Activation Key for the account, which would enable you to avoid generating another unique key later on. So, you could even reduce the amount of processing required in certain components. Again, it is only by walking through these situations and scenarios that you uncover these areas for further consideration and discussion.

The `TransactionContext` can also be used by background processes and batch jobs. The activity identifier could relate to a single run of the job or even a single "bulk" processing cycle. All the information contained in the `TransactionContext` can be bundled up and added to the events and logs to provide really good and useful logging and tracing information.

Using Multiple Trace Files

To avoid clashes and improve performance, it is often necessary to use multiple trace files. For example, each process could have its own trace file, rather than all processes using a single file. This is rather like the event log discussion. There are certain "internal" actions that need to be logged, such as initialization and so forth. A trace file per component type would help reduce the crossover. A trace file per individual component would break it up even more. Each batch process would almost certainly have its own trace file. This further highlights the need for a consistent activity identifier because the transaction will pass through many different processes and files. Furthermore, different threads may also have their own trace file, which further increases the number of files. A consistent naming convention should be given to the trace files so that they can be easily identified.

This topic raises an interesting question regarding using a trace file per activity and per server. The activity is unique and access to the file would, by nature, be generally sequential (unless multi-threading is implemented). Each component is called in turn and would be writing to the individual trace file. The web servers would have files containing all the trace for the given activity, as would the application servers. Figure 21-3 shows a sample of this.

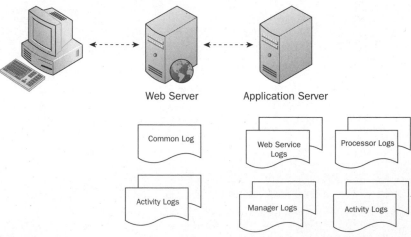

Figure 21-3

590

This approach would generally limit the amount of "noise" in the general trace files. The general trace files would contain any non-activity-based tracing along with the "activity" entry and exit milestones. For example:

```
...
...
[Timestamp][WS001][ActivateAccount.aspx][ActivateAccount] Activity [1] Started
...
...
[Timestamp][WS001][ActivateAccount.aspx][ActivateAccount] Activity [1] Finished
...
...
```

The actual activity trace would be contained in a separate file. You would need to balance this approach against the number of files being opened and closed, which would also affect end-to-end performance and transaction latency. A Web-based application could have thousands of activities being performed, which would potentially create thousands of trace files. The same would be true of a high-volume transaction-processing system. Similarly, the general trace files would also be potentially enormous, given the number of transactions passing through the system.

There are many ways to carve up the trace files. The important thing to remember is that they contain the information required to effectively diagnose issues. They're used to re-create a timeline. An activity log should contain everything required to trace a single transaction right through the system. Having a trace file per application process will limit the number of potential trace files, and the tracing configuration would limit the number of entries contained within them.

Tracing Configuration

The tracing in an application shouldn't adversely affect performance. However, the fact of the matter is that it often does; verbose logging and tracing really slows the system down. That's usually why the production configuration has it switched off, which again is why you can never get the information you need when an exception occurs.

You have already seen in Chapter 18 that performance is improved by surrounding statements with simple if conditions, such as:

```
// log account not found
if( DiagnosticProvider.IsLogging( Activity.AccountNotFound ) )
    {

        DiagnosticProvider.Trace( CLASS_NAME, METHOD_NAME, Information,
         Activity.AccountNotFound, username );

    }
```

Although this is an example and not necessarily the final implementation code, it reduces the amount of unnecessary code being executed. Performing a very fast and simple call to the provider, to check if logging is configured, saves you from executing a number of statements unnecessarily.

The "activity" value used in the pseudo code is simply an example to demonstrate the concept and to show how far you can go with defining activities and configuration values. The activities could actually be at a very high level, such as information, warning, debug, and error, which would mean any trace statement with that activity would be output to the trace file, assuming that the activity's trace was switched on.

The options are too numerous to mention using such an approach, but using the case study, you could break the activities down to the following high-level functional areas:

- ❑ Authentication
- ❑ Registration
- ❑ Activation
- ❑ SolicitedEmail
- ❑ DatabaseAccess

The activities can be further refined to take into account the different error levels, such as:

- ❑ Information (1)
- ❑ Warning (2)
- ❑ Error (4)
- ❑ Debug (8)

The overall tracing level can then be configured and set as usual. In addition, individual activities can be switched on and off separately, allowing a finer granularity of tracing control. The Diagnostic Provider (or similar component) would load and access the configuration using the common Configuration Provider. An example of the configuration is follows:

```
<TraceConfiguration overallTraceLevel=4>
<TraceActivities>
<Authentication traceLevel=7 />
<DatabaseAccess traceLevel=6 />
</TraceActivities>
</TraceConfiguration>
```

The example indicates that the overall trace level has only error tracing enabled (for example, a value of 4). However, the trace activities for authentication and database access are overriding the overall trace level with their own trace levels to provide additional information. In this example, Authentication activity has a value of 7, indicating that information, warnings, and errors would be traced out. The DatabaseAccess activity has a value of 6, indicating that warnings and errors would be traced out. Having finer control over the trace during runtime will help to improve the performance of the application while retaining an optimum configuration for production and any other environment. Furthermore, using a common configuration component can help to ensure that values are reloaded from the configuration location in the event they change on-the-fly.

It is worth looking at what the runtime offers in terms of logging and tracing configuration to determine whether this will meet the necessary requirements. If not, a custom approach may need to be implemented or complemented with the runtime's functionality.

Investigative Tooling

The tooling required during an incident investigation will vary greatly. During testing phases, testers raise defects against the application. In production, incident investigation is triggered following a live service incident, such as the application raising an error event. In either case, pulling together a complete timeline of the transaction and the data being used helps to identify what happened. The following outlines some of the "tools" that can help with piecing together the timeline:

❑ **Event log(s)** — The event logs should point to the heart of the issue and contain all the relevant contextual information about the activity. This is the starting point for most incident investigations. The transaction will be executed through many servers and many components. The timeline needs to be pieced together from all the event entries. The event logs will also show what other "system" and application activity was happening at the same time, which could throw new light on the incident being investigated. A simple script or tool that can extract all the relevant log entries from the relevant servers will come in very handy during testing and live support.

❑ **Trace file(s)** — The trace files will also be distributed across multiple servers. There will probably be trace files for different processes, so it is even more important to ensure that activities can be traced across these individual files. A simple tool that I've always wanted is one that scrapes the files from a number of different servers (based on configuration) and allows the operator or user to specify a set of filters based on date and time ranges, servers, processes, threads, activity identifier, trace activities, and error levels. The filtered items would be based on the general tracing prefix, and would also allow wildcards or exact values to be specified. Tools like this can save so much time during an incident investigation. The trace files could be formatted in such a way that the tool could interpret the entries with them quite easily. Alternatively, a very simple script that gathers the log files from around the production system can also provide a lot of benefit.

❑ **Configuration files and settings** — When trying to re-create an issue, it is important to ensure that you have the same (or very similar) configuration settings as the environment that has the problem. Using tools and scripts to gather the configuration files and settings from the servers and locations will save you a lot of time during an investigation. A single configuration parameter often can be the root cause of the problem and you can use the diff utility to highlight differences between configuration files.

❑ **Test data / scripts (when incidents are raised during testing phases)** — It is very important when trying to re-create an incident that you have the correct test scripts and test data. You might need to implement specific procedures to ensure that testers provide the relevant information.

❑ **Database extracts/backups and logs** — The database and audit tables contain a lot of information regarding the transaction and timeline. You should consider tools and scripts that can extract data from the primary databases and import it into another database for incident investigation. You can even use the generic batch processes, such as the data extraction, data importation, and data comparison processes that were described in Chapter 16. Alternatively, a database backup can be taken and restored in a separate database for incident investigation. It is often prudent to perform live incident investigation in a separate database to avoid any further impact on the production service.

Thinking about the information required to re-create an incident will help to highlight what you need to include in the event logging and tracing.

Summary

Designing an application is a series of incremental improvements. Each step will change existing components and introduce new ones. As you've seen, supporting incident investigation has introduced its own considerations for the design and the components within the solution. The tooling requirements may also cause a change to the way things are done or output. Thinking about these types of problems and design patterns will greatly enhance the application and ensure that it meets all the necessary quality characteristics. The patterns do not need to be followed verbatim because technologies change over time and implementations will differ greatly. However, the principles remain the same. As computing evolves, things will only get more complicated, so you need to ensure that you can effectively support your systems and turn around issues quickly.

The following are the key points to take away from this chapter:

❑ **Tracing needs to provide the relevant information for effective incident investigation.** You should ensure that the trace conforms to good practices. Sloppy tracing can cause huge delays when trying to resolve issues. Tracing should also be thoroughly tested and reviewed.

❑ **Maintain code quality.** Think about how you can improve the overall quality of the tracing while keeping the code "free" of unnecessary information and maintaining readability.

❑ **Link trace entries together.** Consider activity-based tracing to provide better visibility of transactions through the system and various components. This greatly reduces the time it takes to pull together an incident timeline.

❑ **Consider using multiple trace files.** Using multiple trace files can greatly improve incident investigation with a single file containing all the relevant trace steps. However, you need to consider whether this will affect performance.

❑ **Tracing must not affect performance.** An optimal level of trace should be configured and factored into the performance requirements. A configurable tracing approach will help to tune the output in production and other environments.

❑ **Think about the tooling requirements for incident investigation.** You need to consider whether any custom tools or scripts should be implemented during development to help with test phases and live service support. Thinking about the information required to investigate and re-create an incident helps to highlight what you need to include in the event logging and tracing.

22

Designing for Application Maintenance

This chapter examines some of the practices you can employ to ensure that your systems are maintainable. You've seen that application maintenance is not just about live service support and maintenance. During the development and fix activities you are acting as part of an application maintenance team and need to ensure that you can make updates without too much trouble. Application maintenance and development are very closely related. I thought I'd take a different approach for this chapter and actually walk through parts of the development environment. The examples in this chapter are based on Visual Studio 2008, although the practices can and should be applied to any tools and technologies.

Starting out with the right approach will help to ensure that the project continues in a consistent and manageable way. Every developer needs to ensure that what they are doing conforms to the overall approach that's been decided.

This chapter is organized into the following sections:

❑ **Preparing the Solution** — Examines how to prepare the solution folder structure, the individual projects, and the code profiler settings that you should have switched on right from the very start of development.

❑ **Defining the Standards** — Examines some of the best practice standards and guidelines, including XML comments and general commenting and coding standards.

❑ **Supporting Configurability** — Examines a few areas where you can make the application easier to maintain by using configuration settings. It also looks at some options for where configuration settings can be stored, including configuration files, the system registry, and the database.

Preparing the Solution

A well-structured and organized solution is the key to effective development and application maintenance. The solution is the first thing that you see. A poorly organized and structured solution is not only annoying, but it also affects your ability to find things. It may get sorted out eventually, but a little preparation goes a long way. Before a long car journey, you check the oil, water, and tire pressure. These simple checks go a long way toward ensuring a trouble-free journey. In this section, you perform a similar set of readiness activities for the solution.

Defining the Folders and Projects

The solution is nothing more than a simple hierarchical folder structure. Chapter 3, "Preparing for 'Production'," touched on how the folders could be organized to distinguish different configurations and environments. The overall solution structure is intended to distinguish the different projects and components. The solution should be structured in two important ways:

❑   To differentiate what is intended for production vs. testing

❑   To provide a meaningful "at-a-glance" overview of the solution structure, projects, and components

Although defining the solution is a personal choice, keeping the preceding in mind will help to ensure that development and test matter doesn't get mixed up (and deployed) with production elements. The second point will naturally help promote the deployment concept throughout the project. Chapter 14 looked at the high-level architecture for the reference application, and this is a fairly reasonable place to start.

Figure 22-1 shows a sample Within-a-Click solution layout. When you open a solution file in Visual Studio, the Solution Explorer window should be shown, and you can expand the folders to achieve the same view. If the Solution Explorer window isn't shown, you can open it by clicking the Solution Explorer menu option on the View menu.

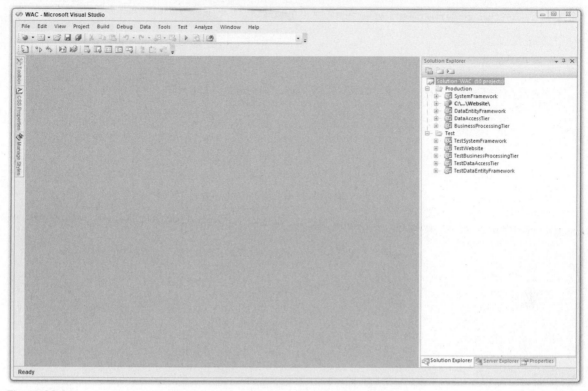

Figure 22-1

The structure is split into two high-level folders:

❏ **Test** — This folder contains all the elements used during testing, such as unit tests, integration tests, stubs, simulators, and so forth.

❏ **Production** — This folder contains the elements of the final state solution — in other words, the "production code."

The Production folder contains the projects according to the deployment concept. This may seem very basic. However, hours can be spent reorganizing solutions for better understanding and readability. When the design isn't straight, neither is the solution. Fleshing out the solution outline is a good way to determine whether there's enough clarity in the design. If you're struggling to create the basic outline, then you probably don't have enough information. So, it is typically back to the drawing board.

The Test folder contains the projects that will be used to test the functionality of the elements in the Production folder. The Test folder contains an individual test project per production component, as listed in the following table.

Test Project Name	Associated Production Project
TestSystemFramework	SystemFramework
TestWebsite	C:\...\Website\
TestBusinessProcessingTier	BusinessProcessingTier
TestDataAccessFramework	DataAccessFramework
TestDataEntityFramework	DataEntityFramework

Again, you may not agree with the exact structure presented here, which I'm using for discussion purposes. You could separate components into subfolders or group various components together. The important thing is to model the hierarchy before diving in and writing code.

The amount of work you do up front clearly depends on the size and scale of the project. Having these "simple practices" in place will make it easier for new developers to understand and follow. It can also help to reduce the amount of formal documentation required. The sample solution uses Visual Studio. However, the messages equally apply to any programming language or technology.

Defining the Project Settings

With a reasonable outline in hand, you can start to define the project settings. You need to ensure that your development starts off on the right foot and continues throughout the project — and beyond.

Figure 22-2 shows the first two key project settings: treating warnings as errors and outputting XML documentation. You can obtain these settings by right-clicking on the project file, selecting Properties on the context menu, and then selecting the Build tab.

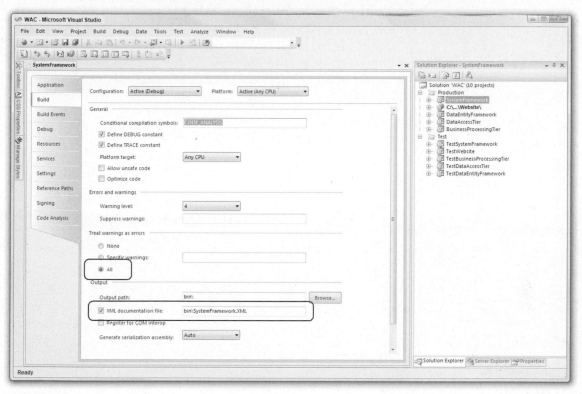

Figure 22-2

I'm a firm believer in leaving nothing to chance. You should treat all Warning events as Error events so that they actually cause you to *stop and think*. Before you know it, you have untold projects and classes that generate long lists of Warning events that haven't been assessed or understood. The other important point is to generate XML documentation files right from the start so that you can easily produce documentation for your solution.

Figure 22-3 shows the next series of important settings: code analysis switched on for all configurations and no rules ignored. This is achieved by selecting the Code Analysis tab on the properties, selecting All Configurations in the Configuration drop-down list, checking the Enable Code Analysis on Build checkbox, clearing the Suppress results from the generated code checkbox, and, finally, ensuring that all rules are enabled and treated as errors.

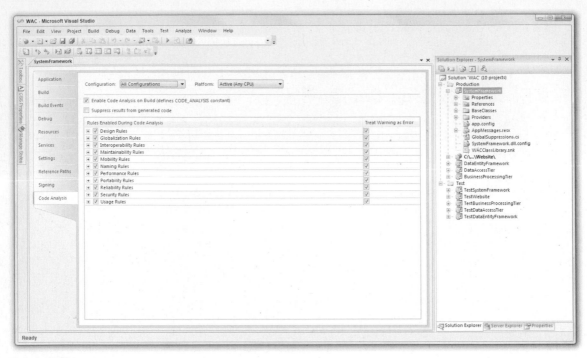

Figure 22-3

I believe whole-heartedly in switching everything on before starting to code because it sets the baseline for the code profiling. The project settings should be applied to all the projects in the solution. As errors (or warnings) are encountered, they can be discussed, documented, and suppressed, as necessary. Chapter 25, "Review and Wrap-Up," presents some of the profiling results from an example solution . It is very important to ensure that profiling results (and suppressions) are captured clearly to avoid any unnecessary discussions and debate later in the lifecycle.

Defining the Standards

You're now armed with a solution outline and a series of profiling rules. This is actually a good place to start to define the following:

- ❑ XML documentation comments
- ❑ Commenting standards
- ❑ Coding standards and practices

Commenting your code and following coding standards and guidelines should be commonplace during development. The rush to code bites us all and before we know it, we have hundreds of classes that don't conform to the required standards. When the out-of-box profiling functionality is enabled you can check the code every step of the way.

XML Documentation Comments

Using XML documentation commenting enables you to comment the code and generate documentation from the comments. In addition, the development environment will also use these comments to display tips during coding. Your code and configuration should be well-documented, and your requirements should be captured and traceable through the code. Throughout the project lifecycle, you'll have numerous meetings and discussions that will change the course of the project. These decision points should be captured in your code so that when you generate your documentation, it forms part of your overall delivery. The comments are the key to understanding the code and the following table contains a representative list of the XML commenting tags you can use in your code and their purpose.

Tag	Purpose	Example

<summary>	The <summary> tag is used to describe the class or class member. The tag should be used to provide exactly what it says. It should be a summary of the class or member describing its intent.	`<summary>`
		`UC-001-08 The system "queues" a`
		`request for an "Activation Key`
		`Email" to be sent to the user's`
		`email address and records the date`
		`and time the request was made.`
		`</summary>`

<param>	The <param> tag is used to describe method parameters.	`<param name="EmailRequest">Email` `request to enqueue.</param>`
<returns>	The <returns> tag is used to describe the return value of a method.	`<returns>EmailRequest object from` `pool</returns>`

<exception>	The <exception> tag is used to describe the exceptions that can be thrown by the method.	`<exception cref="WAC.Production`
		`.BusinessProcessing.Exceptions`
		`.AccountNotFound">Account not found`
		`exception</exception>`

<remarks>	The <remarks> tag can be used to provide supplemental information to the summary.	`<remarks>`
		`UC-001-08a In the background the`
		`email request will be processed and`
		`the system will compose and send the`
		`user an email containing their`
		`account activation key and record`
		`the date and time the email was`
		`sent.`
		`</remarks>`

(continued)

(continued)

Tag	Purpose	Example
`<para>`	The `<para>` tag is used to ensure that the resulting text is paragraph formatted. It is intended for use within the other tags.	```<remarks>` `<para>UC-001-08a In the background the email request will be processed and the system will compose and send the user an email containing their account activation key and record the date and time the email was sent.</para>` `</remarks>```
`<example>`	The `<example>` tag is a great place to comment "usage" scenarios.	```<example>` `To queue an email request simply use the following syntax:` `<c>EmailQueue.Enqueue(request)</c>` `</example>```
`<c>`	The `<c>` tag is used to denote a line of code. The resulting documentation will be marked up as code.	```<c>EmailQueue.Enqueue(request)</c>```
`<code>`	The `<code>` tag is used to specify more than one line of code.	```<code>` `// invoke the diagnostics provider` `diagnosticsProvider.RaiseEvent(...);` `</code>```
`<see>`	The `<see>` tag is used to reference other parts of the solution. The tag is intended for inclusion with other tags, such as `<summary>` and `<remarks>`.	```<remarks>` `UC-001-08a In the background the email request will be processed and the system will compose and send the user an email containing their account activation key and record the date and time the email was sent.` `<see cref="WAC.Production.BusinessProcessing.ApplicationFramework.EmailQueue" />` `</remarks>```
`<seealso>`	The `<seealso>` tag has the same syntax as the `<see>` tag. However, the resulting output is indented.	```<seealso cref="WAC.Production.BusinessProcessing.ApplicationFramework.EmailQueue" />```

There are other commenting tags that you can use. The preceding list contains the most common tags, which can result in quality documentation and quality code when applied effectively. If your tools support them, you really should investigate them further and use them wherever appropriate. You can find out more about XML commenting on the Microsoft Developer Network through the following link: http://msdn.microsoft.com/en-us/library/b2s063f7(VS.80).aspx.

Commenting Standards

You need to encourage good commenting throughout your code. The documentation-generation tools will ease documentation production, although not all languages and technologies are covered. Where possible, you should generate documentation from your source code regularly; your profiling tools should be configured to ensure that comments are included; and "mark one eyeball" reviews should check the comments. While this may seem very familiar to some folks, a large proportion of code is still often undocumented or, worse, incorrectly documented.

Commenting applies to all files, including but not limited to:

- All class files (production, development, test, etc.)
- All configuration files
- All stored procedure and database artifacts
- All scripts

During the incident investigation and fix activities, you need to get to the bottom of the issue. Comments will help you to understand the code and, more important, *why* it was coded in that way. Comments don't just relate to code, however; they can be included in almost all files. Although I refer to code here, you should apply these guidelines elsewhere. The comments help new joiners to understand the code. The following are my Top 10 commenting guidelines:

1. The comments should describe the *function* of the code, not the code itself. Programmers can read code. They need to know what it is supposed to do, not how it does it.

2. Comments should be specified in plain, understandable language. Abbreviations should be avoided to ensure there is no misunderstanding.

3. The comments should map back to the requirements, constraints, and decision points. The identifiers and headlines should be captured along with any other contextual text.

4. Changes and updates should be well-commented to ensure the reason for the change is captured appropriately. Fixes should map back to their defect identifier, and changes should map to their change identifier.

5. Comments that explain the code are often inserted because the code is overly complex. If this is the case, re-factoring the component should be considered.

6. The comments should not clutter the code and make it overly verbose. Too many comments get in the way and too few make it hard to understand.

7. Comments should contain usage scenarios, assumptions, and limitations. Common components and frameworks should be described so that they can be consumed effectively.

8. Comments should describe deviations from standards and guidelines, and the rationale for doing so.

9. Configuration values should be well-documented to avoid incorrect settings or values.

10. Document what's outstanding and needs to be done. Use TODO: comments to ensure that all unimplemented functionality is well-documented and not forgotten.

A good set of commenting standards helps to ensure that your code is readable, usable, and maintainable.

Describing the Function

The function of the code is the most important factor when it comes to commenting. While there may be an abundance of external documentation, the comments are at the heart of the code. The key to understanding the code is either to work through it or to understand the intent. Poorly commented code can really throw the reader off what they are trying to achieve. The comments should be neatly arranged and describe what the intent or function of the code is, not the code itself. Developers understand code. People understand comments. The first step in achieving good comments is to ensure that they can be read by anyone.

It is very easy to write poor comments. It is a lot harder to write good ones. What are you thinking? Why are you doing it? When someone is reading the code, that's what they need to know. This will give them an understanding of why you did something a particular way, not how you did it. It was the same in school when the teacher wanted you to "show your workings" for particularly hard math questions. It gives the reader an indication of the thought process.

The summary comments provide the reader with a snapshot view of the code and its intent or purpose. Think *"problem–design–solution."* Start by documenting the problem; then document the approach; and the solution is the code. The comments don't need to be overly verbose. They should explain what is meant to be happening. A summary of the function is simply a couple of sentences or statements that underpin the essence of the code. Use-case steps are typically described in one or two sentences. Consider the following comment:

```
// call the email queue provider
EmailQueue.Enqueue( request );
```

The comment provides no value whatsoever. It is there simply to "decorate" the code. It doesn't tell *why* it's queing an e-mail request or what the intent is. Is this right? Should it be doing this? It might be better to describe the use-case step and/or requirement. For example:

```
/* UC-001-08 The system "queues" a request for an "Activation Key Email" to be sent
   to the user's email address and records the date and time the request was made.
*/
EmailQueue.Enqueue( request );
```

Comments that span multiple lines can use the /* ... */ block commenting approach instead of starting with //. This comment is quite verbose, but it does describe the step that's being performed. You could even "extend" this comment to include the background processing:

```
/* UC-001-08 The system "queues" a request for an "Activation Key Email" to be sent
   to the user's email address and records the date and time the request was made.
   UC-001-08a In the background the email request will be processed and the system
   will compose and send the user an email containing their account activation key
   and record the date and time the email was sent.
*/
EmailQueue.Enqueue( request );
```

The comment is now very verbose for a single line of code. However, it does describe the intended processing and function of the code. If you were generating code from design tools, it's possible that the resulting code would include verbose comments like these along with TODO: statements, such as:

```
/* UC-001-08 The system "queues" a request for an "Activation Key Email" to be sent
   to the user's email address and records the date and time the request was made.
   UC-001-08a In the background the email request will be processed and the system
   will compose and send the user an email containing their account activation key
   and record the date and time the email was sent.
*/


// TODO: Place implementation here.
```

There's clearly a balance to what is helpful versus a hindrance. Copying the use-case steps verbatim might be a good idea, but you can also summarize the function and make the code clearer. The key is to include the identifier, but the comments should also be consistent across the application. If you're doing the same thing in more than one place, this in itself begs the question of whether the code should be re-factored. The following sample shows the comments along with the other steps involved in queuing the request.

```
// UC-001-08 Queue "Activation Key Email" request
// UC-001-08a Enqueue sends email in the background and updates the account.
EmailRequest newKeyRequest = EmailRequest.Acquire( EmailRequest.NewKeyEmail );

newKeyRequest.AccountId = thisAccount.AccountId;
newKeyRequest.DateTime = CustomCalendar.GetInstance().Now;

EmailQueue.Enqueue( newKeyRequest );

EmailRequest.Release( newKeyRequest );
```

This example is for discussion purposes only. These two comments summarize the exact nature of what's going on and its intent. There's no need to litter the code with additional comments. However, there are additional technical implementation details that are not described. For example, do we know why we're using a pooled object here? What happens when there are no objects available in the pool? Should you be using an object pool? You could answer the first question by including a comment with the appropriate requirements. You could answer the second question by moving the mouse cursor over the Acquire method and reviewing the usage comments associated with it, assuming the method is well-documented, that is. The third question would require a full understanding of the solution architecture.

Commenting the "Requirements"

Capturing the requirements in the comments is a great way to provide visibility and traceability throughout the solution. Requirements can be captured in the <remarks> tag at the class level or the method level. Given the number of requirements that need to be met, it could be a rather long list, although this in itself begs the question of whether the code is split up sufficiently.

The following example shows a fairly short list of requirements captured in the `<remarks>` tag:

```
<remarks>
Requirements:
HFR-ASAA-002 (Close Account only allowed on "Active" accounts)
HFR-AGEDACCFR-004 (Flagged Account not impacting user)
HFR-AGEDACCFR-005 (Removal of flag)
HFR-EMAILPROC-001 (Email sent asynchronously)
</remarks>
```

The requirements can equally be commented inline where they are addressed. In addition, I already mentioned that it's not just the production code that needs to be commented. These comments could also be included in the unit test and integration test classes. They already describe some high-level functional tests that need to be performed.

Commenting the Changes and Changing the Comments

It is very important to maintain a consistent picture throughout the project. When testing begins, defects get raised. As do changes. So, you will need to update both the code *and* the comments. I mentioned previously the infamous "one-line change." It's all too easy to simply change the code without changing the comments. When a fix or change is implemented, it should be recorded in the comments. The following shows an example of an original piece of code including its comments:

```
// check if account created date is less than flag date
if( accountData.CreatedDateTime < flagDate )
```

If a defect is raised because the check should be "less than or equal to," then the fix and comments should reflect this, as follows:

```
// DIN - 15/10/2008
// Defect 1 - CreatedDateTime should be less than or equal to flagDate
// check if account created date is less than or equal to flag date
if( accountData.CreatedDateTime <= flagDate )
```

If the requirement had been included in the comment in the first instance, it is less likely the original code would have been implemented incorrectly. However, if the original requirement was wrong, then the update to the code would actually be a change to the agreed requirements. Although the configuration management system provides "diff" functionality, commenting the code ensures that the updates will not be regressed by accident. For example, when someone else is changing the code, he or she may think "Hey, that shouldn't be less than or equal to," and he or she may change the code back to its original state. The comment clearly states the requirement and why the code has been changed. It's equally important to include the name of the developer and the date the change was made. This helps when you need to talk to the person who made the change.

When commenting code, you could also keep a record of the individual changes at the top of the class. For example:

```
// DIN - 15/10/2008
// Defect 1 - CreatedDateTime should be less than or equal to FlagDate
// DIN - 20/11/2008
// Defect 2 - ...
```

Documenting Non-Conformance

Certain components might need to deviate from standards for a very good reason. Where possible, of course, all the code should meet the standards. If Warnings are raised as Errors, the code will not execute. Each Error should be thoroughly assessed and understood before the Error is suppressed or reduced to a Warning (that is not treated as an Error). You should use the `<remarks>` tag to add comments where it is known that the code will produce profiler warnings. The resulting documentation will show very clearly the non-conformance to standards and appropriate rationale for why it doesn't adhere to the standards.

Commenting the Configuration

This section covers the following two points:

- ❑ The comments should capture where the configuration values are used.
- ❑ The configuration files should be well-commented.

The first point is very important. You must understand which classes and methods are using the various configuration values and the effect that changing the values could have across the system. The second point is to ensure that the configuration values are changed appropriately. Consider the following example:

```
<appSettings>
  <add key="Wait" value="5" />
  <add key="Retry" value="3" />
</appSettings>
```

Although this might mean something to the developer, it means nothing to the outside world. The name doesn't indicate any specific usage, nor does it indicate the time period. One could hazard a guess that it is the wait-retry logic: waiting 5 seconds and retrying 3 times. But what's the effect of changing it? What uses this value? The name should be more meaningful and the entry should be clearly commented with "acceptable" ranges. For example:

```
<appSettings>
  <!-
    The wait-retry default values will be used in the event the consumer
    doesn't specify any particular values. Consumer specific values would be
    specified as:
      ComponentWaitRetryWaitPeriodInSeconds
      ComponentWaitRetryRetryCount
      (where Component would be the specific component name)

    These values are used by:

    WAC.DataAccess.DataAccessFramework.ExecuteStoredProcedure

    A value of 0 (in either value) indicates that Wait-Retry will not be performed.
    DefaultWaitPeriod should only be set between 5 and 30 (inclusive).
    DefaultRetryCount should only be set between 1 and 5 (inclusive).
  -->
  <add key="WaitRetryDefaultWaitPeriodInSeconds" value="5" />
  <add key="WaitRetryDefaultRetryCount" value="3" />
</appSettings>
```

Although this appears quite lengthy (as do the value names), it actually tells you what you need to know. If the configuration needs to change, it really helps to have a good understanding of what to change.

Using "TODO:" Comments

Comments should use a simplistic style and avoid the use of "flower-boxing" and other hard to maintain and hard to read elements. For example, the following example uses a flower box to draw attention to it.

```
// ***********************************
// * MUST IMPLEMENT BEFORE GO LIVE!!!! *
// ***********************************
```

Although this comment says exactly what needs to be done, and stands out from the rest of the code, a simple TODO: comment can achieve the same result. For example, the Task List in Figure 22-4 shows TODO based on a comment in the source code.

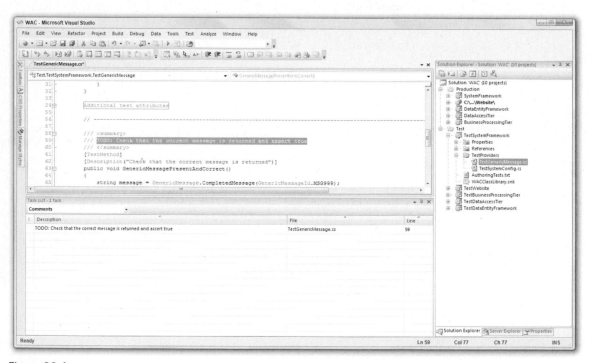

Figure 22-4

Not all editors support this functionality, however, so you might have to use other means to draw attention to certain things. Where TODO: comments are supported, you should use them effectively and complete them all prior to submitting artifacts into a release.

Coding Standards and Practices

The coding standards ensure that all the code in the solution follows good practice. It is actually possible to write an entire book on the subject, and many people have. The key is to have agreed, documented coding standards in place. It is also important to ensure that all code adheres to a set of defined standards, including but not limited to:

- ❑ Class files
- ❑ Stored procedures and database artifacts
- ❑ Scripts

The basic coding standards typically cover the following subjects:

- ❑ **Naming conventions** — The naming conventions generally cover class names, member variable names, method names, and parameter names. They can also include project names, configuration value names, and so forth.

  - ❑ Ensure that all names are meaningful and describe the function or purpose of the class, method, variable, or parameter.

  - ❑ Avoid using abbreviations. If you must use abbreviations, ensure that the comments spell out what they mean.

  - ❑ Avoid using excessively long names. Although the names should be meaningful, excessively long names can be difficult to read and display.

  - ❑ Avoid using short names, such as i, x, y, and z, especially in nested iterations.

  - ❑ Specify names in a consistent case. For instance, specify class and method names in upper camel case, or Pascal case (`EmailRequest.Enqueue`), and parameter and variable names in lower camel case (`emailRequest`).

  - ❑ Avoid using keywords, such as Time, Date, and so on by using prefixes — for example, `AppTime`, `AppDate`, and so on.

- ❑ **Formatting** — The formatting standards state how the code should be laid out and indented for readability. Layout includes classes and methods as well as processing structure.

  - ❑ Use white space judiciously and consistently to separate code statements, comments, and blocks.

  - ❑ Use consistent indentation of code and comments.

  - ❑ Place opening and closing curly braces "{}" consistently in the code.

  - ❑ Use a layout that is straightforward and easy to follow.

- ❑ **Coding style** — Coding style focuses on the use of the actual programming language, including using a particular programming style for iterative and conditional logic. It also covers certain usage guidelines for arrays, collections, and so forth.

  - ❑ Avoid using exceptions to control flow.

  - ❑ Avoid ignoring exceptions.

  - ❑ Avoid empty `if` or `case` conditions.

❏ Avoid `if` conditions without curly braces.

❏ Avoid multiple nested `if` conditions.

❏ Avoid cluttering loops with multiple processing.

❏ Avoid hard-coded values and magic strings or numbers.

❏ Avoid the use of generic types, such as `object`. Use properly defined types and interfaces.

❏ Use abstraction and layering to reduce complexity and promote reuse.

❏ Have only one return point from a method.

❏ . . . and the list goes on.

It is really not actually worth going into a lengthy discussion on this, because the profiling tools (and other sources) will provide an abundance of information on the subject. Suffice it to say that you should have in place, and follow, coding standards that cover all aspects of the system. The standards should be easy to follow and adopt. The easier something is, the more likely it will be used. The simple rule of thumb is to switch everything on in the profiler and continually run it against the code. You can assess Warnings and Errors as they are raised. It is important to understand the capabilities of the profiler and, when warnings arise, to analyze them. If the technologies don't support profiling, seek out, define, document, and agree on a set of coding standards and best practices.

Supporting Configurability

The solution should be modular and organized, as large and unwieldy solutions are often hard to maintain and update. You should consider breaking up the code into small chunks of discrete processing and functionality. Smaller units are easier to understand and maintain. However, if the units are too small, you can end up with too many of them. On the other hand, if they are too large, the code can become monolithic and unmanageable.

Furthermore, things are going to change. Wherever possible you should think about the implementation and try to avoid tight coupling. You can use interfaces and delegates to promote extensibility. Functionality changes should be relatively straightforward to implement; they shouldn't require major re-factoring.

Under normal circumstances, the project criteria will determine how much flexibility and extensibility you can include within the foundation architecture. However, you should certainly "lay the foundation" for future expansion and enhancement, taking it into account during planning, designing, and estimating. The best way to allow for future growth and support change is to store as much information in "configuration" as possible. Configuration values are much easier to change than source code. However, changes need to be managed appropriately.

Consider the following groups of configuration settings:

❏ **Application-specific configuration settings** — This group encompasses the application-specific configuration settings identified by the requirements, such as the New Account Expiry Period and the Closed Account Removal Period. As a project progresses through its lifecycle, additional configuration values will continue to be identified.

❑ **Static page elements** — Static page elements typically include labels and any text that is displayed on a page or screen to the user. Storing these values in configuration allows the application to better support internationalization and localization. Although it is not always a requirement to support internationalization, these values have a tendency to change throughout the project. It can often be a lot easier to change them when they're separated from the source code. Of course, some changes to these values will inherently require you to make changes to the code and rebuild the application.

❑ **Validation rules** — The validation rules encompass all the field- and form-level validation functions performed by the application.

❑ **Messages** — Messages include all messages that are displayed to the user as well as text used in events and logging and tracing. Chapter 13 contained a number of messages that would be displayed to the user in the event of validation failures and invalid operations, such as "Username not specified" and "Account already activated." It also showed the e-mail messages a user would receive after performing certain operations, such as the New Activation Key e-mail message. Messages encompass any textual elements that are read externally. Keeping these values in configuration again supports reuse, flexibility, and ease of change.

Again, the amount of flexibility and configuration within the solution depends entirely on the project's requirements, budget, and timescales.

Application-Specific Configuration Settings

Applications written in .NET typically make use of various web.config and other .config files. Managing multiple configuration files can be a burden on the project. Each server has its own copy of the file, which means the files need to be carefully managed during support and deployment to ensure that they are all in sync.

The .NET Framework allows you to develop specific handlers to custom sections that provide access to the configuration values in the .config files. Custom handlers are invoked by the framework during initialization and can also be re-created whenever the configuration values change. This functionality can be quite useful when you need to change specific values on-the-fly. That said, the application domain might need to be restarted when certain settings are changed. This is not always an issue, but it's worth considering.

It is well worth modeling the configuration sections. The following shows a sample specification of the configSections part of a standard .NET configuration file:

```
<configSections>

 <!-- specific Within-A-Click web settings -->
 <section name="WACWebConfiguration"
  type="WACWeb.WebFramework.ConfigurationProvider, WACWeb.WebFramework"/>

 <!-- specific Within-A-Click trace settings -->
 <section name="WACWebTraceConfiguration"
  type="WACWeb.WebFramework.Diagnostics.TraceProvider,
  WACWeb.WebFramework.Diagnostics"/>
```

```
<!-- specific Within-A-Click event log settings -->
<section name="WACWebEvent
Configuration"
 type="WACWeb.WebFramework.Diagnostics.EventLogProvider,
 WACWeb.WebFramework.Diagnostics"/>

</configSections>
```

Each section listed in the `configSections` contains the specification of the actual configuration settings, as follows:

```
<!-- specific Within-A-Click web settings -->
<WACWebConfiguration>

 <!-- Within-A-Click general settings -->
 <add key="WAC.Web.HomeDirectory" value="D:\WAC\WEB"/>

</WACWebConfiguration>

<!-- specific Within-A-Click trace settings -->
<WACWebTraceConfiguration>

 <add key="WAC.Web.Diagnostics.Trace.Enabled" value="True"/>
 <add key="WAC.Web.Diagnostics.Trace.Path" value=".\Logs"/>
 <add key="WAC.Web.Diagnostics.Trace.Level" value="4"/>
 <add key="WAC.Web.Diagnostics.Trace.Categories" value="*"/>

</WACWebTraceConfiguration>

<!-- specific Within-A-Click event log settings -->
<WACWebEventConfiguration>

 <!-- Within-A-Click web event settings -->
 <add key="WAC.Web.Diagnostics.EventLog.SourceName" value="Within-A-Click"/>
 <add key="WAC.Web.Diagnostics.EventLog.ComputerName" value="."/>

</WACWebEventConfiguration>
```

Again, these values are used for discussion purposes only. However, modeling the configuration helps to flesh out all the configuration values and settings required by the different components. In this example, the configuration file mainly contains diagnostic settings.

The application and administration servers are generally performing far more functional processing. Furthermore, there are tasks continuously running in the background. This presents a bit of a design challenge: caching the values for performance while supporting changes on-the-fly.

Consider the following scenario: A number of multi-threaded processes are running continuously in the background, processing a number of records. For performance purposes, the processes are using a throttling technique to limit the number of records processed in a single iteration and time-slice. A performance degradation issue has been identified as a result of a major influx of new transactions. In short, records are coming in far faster than they are being processed because of the throttles.

A quick but detailed analysis of available memory and CPU indicates that the throttle size can be increased dramatically to improve performance. In this instance, stopping and starting the processes to reload values would have an even bigger impact on the performance of the system, because taking down processes and bringing them back up can often take a while. In some cases, the processes take a while to stop while memory is freed up and connections are closed, and so forth — not to mention the time it takes for the process to start up again.

In situations like this, the configuration values need to be updated without affecting the overall running of the component. In the bygone days of cooperative multi-tasking, applications typically had to release processing time back to the operating system to allow it to perform its tasks. Anyone familiar with Visual Basic programming will be aware of the Do Events statement, which was used for this very purpose.

Most background processes will throttle and/or sleep periodically to avoid excessive CPU usage while processing. These periods of "downtime" can be very useful for performing checks and reloads of configuration values. If the task never stops processing or never has any idle time, I'd have to question what was happening with CPU usage. My personal preference is to periodically reload configuration value changes during any periods of downtime. It is when a process doesn't have any specific downtime as part of its normal processing cycle that one could argue that using a similar approach costs valuable processor cycles unnecessarily (especially for the number of instances where it actually resolves an issue and provides some benefit). The time it takes to reload also depends on where the configuration values are stored. In many cases the system needs to be restarted in order to reload configuration values. This can cause major issues in live service because connections are dropped and have to be re-established, not to mention the time it takes.

When designing the configuration components, you should try to ensure that you, the business, and operations and support fully understand the dynamic reload requirements. This way, configuration values can be changed and it should only be a matter of seconds before they come into effect. The reload logic needs to be highly robust and not cause the application to failover if the settings can't be found or reloaded. It is possible for an operator to be updating the configuration values at the time the application tries to reload them. If any other exception occurs during the reload logic, the system ideally should continue with the existing configuration settings and, where appropriate, raise a Warning event for operational staff. The reload logic is peripheral to the core functionality, so it shouldn't really impact anything else. After all, the whole premise of putting the logic in place is to keep the application up-and-running at all times. It is exactly these types of choices that need to be discussed and agreed.

There are a number of places where configuration values can be stored, as discussed in the following sections.

Storing Configuration Values in the System Registry

The *registry* provides a secure storage area for application settings. It supports String, DWORD, Binary, Multi-String, and Expandable String data types. The registry is a hierarchical structure and organizations should store their configuration settings under the main HKEY_LOCAL_MACHINE\ SOFTWARE key. This main key has many entries under it, some of which are specific to an organization and some of which are specific to a particular application (which I personally find messy). When using the system registry, I've always started by creating a key specific to the organization — for instance, HKEY_LOCAL_MACHINE\SOFTWARE\Wrox. You can then group all of the organization's applications under one roof, such as HKEY_LOCAL_MACHINE\SOFTWARE\Wrox\Within-a-Click. The registry keys should be locked down so that access to them is controlled appropriately.

Storing configuration values in the registry means that the configuration component would need to isolate the functionality for accessing the system registry. The registry also needs to be managed appropriately. It is not simply a question of updating settings by simply dropping a file in a location. Registry settings need to be imported or manually updated when required. The diagnostic settings are likely to change in the event of an incident, so a registry import file could be prepared and run-in to each of the required servers. This is essentially no different from preparing the configuration file and deploying it to each server. The real key is to ensure that the change process is documented thoroughly and tested to iron out any issues.

Where the configuration settings are stored ultimately depends on the system being implemented. However, it's important to weigh the different options when designing the solution. There are pros and cons to each approach. However, the system registry does provide a consistent place-holder that can be accessed by all components residing on the same server.

Storing Configuration Values in the Database

You can also store configuration values in the database. Figure 22-5 shows an example database structure.

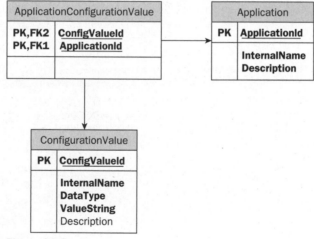

Figure 22-5

The configuration model shown here is totally generic. The `Application` table could contain all the applications within the solution. Using a simple table like this helps to separate and group all the individual entities under a single application entry. Although initially there may be only one application, a future enhancement to the solution could include an Administration user interface, which would follow the same configuration principles. The following provides an overview of the key columns in the `Application` table:

❑ **ApplicationId** — This column contains the unique identifier for the application. It is included in various tables to provide a linkage for entities specific to a particular application.

❑ **InternalName** — This column holds the application name. You could be generating code from the values in this table. The values in this instance couldn't contain any spaces or other "non-compilable" characters.

❑ **Description** — This column contains a brief description of the application.

The following shows a snippet of the enumeration that could be generated from the Application table:

```
public enum Application
{

 // <summary>
 //  Within-A-Click Reference Application
 // </summary>
 WAC = 1

}
```

The configuration values that are globally available to the entire application could be stored in the `ConfigurationValue` table. Its key columns are as follows:

❑ **ConfigValueId** — This column contains the configuration value's unique identifier.

❑ **InternalName** — This column contains the configuration value's internal name.

❑ **DataType** — This column specifies the system base data type for the configuration value (`int`, `decimal`, `boolean` and `string`, and so forth).

❑ **ValueString** — This column contains a string representation of the configuration value, which a specific component converts into the appropriate system data type during runtime. This is exactly the same as the `web.config` approach, although specifying the data type in the database further supports code-generation. The configuration properties of the class could be completely generated from the database.

The specific application configuration values are linked to a particular application entry through the `ApplicationConfigurationValue` table. This allows the configuration values to be separated by application. Using this table structure, it is possible to automatically generate class files that contain enumerated values, which the application can use to obtain the configuration values.

As you can see, there is quite a lot to configuration. Each approach has its own place and its own merits. The database can provide another single source of configuration data. That said, it needs to be coupled with another approach, as the database connection string needs to be stored somewhere else.

Static Page Elements

The ASP.NET Framework supports localization functionality via the culture properties of the page and through the use of specific localization controls. Resource files contain the language-specific values. For example, assume the filename for the following snippet is `Welcome.aspx`:

```
<asp:Localize runat="server" ID="Welcome"
   meta:resourcekey="Welcome">Hello</asp:Localize>
```

The code snippet shows the use of the `Localize` control in the page source. The solution then needs to contain specific resource files for each of the supported cultures. Let's say the application wanted to support French as well as the default language — in this instance, English. The solution would require two separate resource files: one containing the English resources and another containing the French resources. The files would be named according to the culture. The English resource file would simply be called `Welcome.aspx.resx`, whereas the French resource file would be called `Welcome.aspx.fr-FR.resx`. Each resource file would contain a single string resource that is "wired" to the control on the page — in this example, the `Welcome` control. The following snippet shows a sample entry from the resource file's source:

```
<data name="Welcome.Text" xml:space="preserve">

    <value>Hello</value>

</data>
```

The resource `name` is specified as `Welcome.Text` and the `value` would contain either "Hello" or "Bonjour". When the culture properties of the page are changed (and the page is refreshed), the resource is loaded from the appropriate file and displayed. The resource files can either be local (or specific) to the page or global to the entire application.

Even if the application isn't supporting different cultures, you can use this functionality to separate the static elements of the page from the code. Whether you leverage this approach or implement a custom solution, loading resources dynamically will impact the overall application performance. However, it is usually minimal. If the pages or even a portion of the pages were hard-coded or generated using a specific code-generator, this would require separate sites for each of the supported cultures.

Using resource files helps to improve the overall maintainability and extensibility in the solution. For the first version of the application, resources could be produced for a default culture (English). This would at the very minimum establish a base pattern, which you could then extend as appropriate.

Validation Rules

Many applications embed validation rules in the source code. That is, many web pages use `validator` controls to specify the validation rules and the associated validation error messages. The following code snippet shows an example of this usage:

```
<td>
        <asp:TextBox enableViewState="false" id=EmailAddress runat="server"
    MaxLength="24"></asp:TextBox>
        (required)
        <asp:RequiredFieldValidator runat="server"
          controlToValidate=EmailAddress
          errormessage='You must specify an Email Address'
          display=dynamic
          >*</asp:RequiredFieldValidator>
        <asp:RegularExpressionValidator
            runat="server"
            ControlToValidate="EmailAddress"
            ErrorMessage="The email address is incorrectly formatted
    (should be specified as x@y.z)."
```

```
                    ValidationExpression="^\w+((-\w')|(\.\w+))*\@\w+((\.|-)\w+)*\.\w+$"
                      >*</asp:RegularExpressionValidator>
                  <asp:CustomValidator id=EmailAddressUniqueValidator
                    runat="server"
                    ErrorMessage="The specified email address is already in use."
                    ControlToValidate="EmailAddress"
                    >*</asp:CustomValidator>
   </td>
```

Unless this code is generated automatically, it is not very reusable by other consumers — either internal or external. The following points should be noted:

❑ **The page hard codes the error messages that are displayed to the user.** I've mentioned previously that error messages are likely to change throughout the project, so unless this is the only place where these messages are displayed, it could involve updating many different files.

❑ **The page hard codes the physical validation rules, first by using the required field validator and then by using the regular expression validator.** Again, these are likely to change throughout the project. Mandatory fields, which are often dynamic in nature, are more likely to change on large forms. For instance, selecting a particular value in one field means that another field becomes mandatory.

The page is perfectly fine if the application is only ever going to specify the validation rules in one place, and one place only. However, storing these values in configuration (such as resource files or the database) promotes better reuse and can ease their change. In addition, encompassing the validation rules within the business functionality rather than the user interface retains consistency across the application when there is more than one consumer. The ideal situation would be a combination of both approaches to ensure validation is performed at the client end as well as within the business processing. However, this adds a challenge of how to keep the validation in line through the development lifecycle, which needs to be considered.

Messages

The last group of configurable elements is the messages group. The different types of messages that the user sees include:

❑ "Mandatory field missing" error messages

❑ Field-level validation error messages

❑ Form-level validation error messages

❑ Business processing error messages

❑ Business processing confirmation messages

❑ Exception messages

❑ Email messages

Again, storing all these values in resource files allows them to be internationalized and localized along with the static page elements.

Given the wide variety of messages that are used in the application, they generally need to support *contextual elements*. The primary examples are the e-mail messages. Because the e-mail needs to contain the Activation Key, the e-mail message will need to contain "tags" that the `MessageProvider` component can replace with the actual data.

For example, the following represents a sample template for the "Welcome" e-mail:

```
Subject: Welcome to Within-a-Click
Body:

Thank you for registering with us. We are very pleased to provide you with
your new account activation key:

{0}

We hope you enjoy using our site!

The WAC Team.
```

The tags in this case are surrounded by curly braces, exactly as they are when using the string formatter class within C#.

Replacing basic information like this could also be required when displaying certain messages to the user. However, the code and the message need to be kept in sync. Again, it is worth modeling the application to determine whether the "display" messages need to include any context. For instance, at some point a confirmation message might need to include context information, as shown in Figure 22-6.

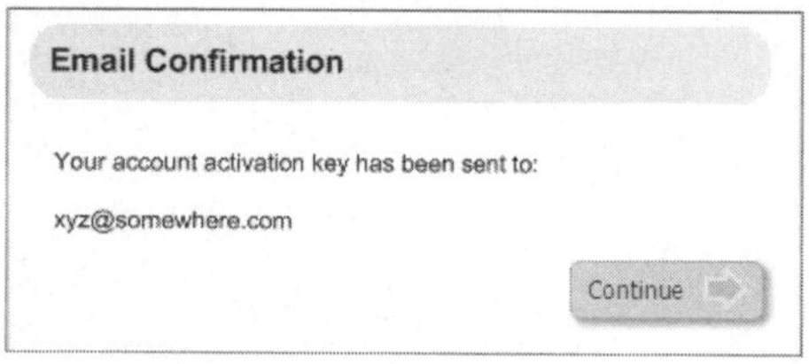

Email Confirmation

Your account activation key has been sent to:

xyz@somewhere.com

Continue ➡

Figure 22-6

This would be pretty useful, as the user could see where the e-mail is being sent. It might indicate that the e-mail address is wrong, which could open up a whole area of design discussion based on when the user could change it. This might mean revisiting the original account state allowable actions or saving this for a later date. Either way, including the contextual information shouldn't be a massive problem to implement.

Summary

This chapter looked at some of the practices to ensure that your code is maintainable and well-commented, and that it conforms to "best practices." It is important to get off to a good start so that you avoid issues later in the process.

The following are the key points to take away from this chapter:

❑ **Prepare the solution.** The solution should be well-outlined. If there are difficulties in doing this, it is probably because you haven't defined the design sufficiently. The solution outline is intended to:

  ❑ Differentiate what is intended for production vs. testing

  ❑ Provide a meaningful "at-a-glance" overview of the solution structure, projects, and components

❑ **Switch on the profiler.** Ensure that all the profiling tools are switched on and configured. When warnings are raised, they can be assessed, documented and suppressed as appropriate. There are many profiling categories and settings, each of which should be evaluated thoroughly.

❑ **Use XML comments.** XML comments are used to generate documentation from the code. There are many tags that can be used to generate a rich set of documentation, however the most commonly used tags include:

  ❑ Summary

  ❑ Remarks

  ❑ Param

  ❑ Returns

  ❑ Exception

❑ **Define and use commenting standards.** A good set of commenting should be in place. The standards and guidelines should be adhered to throughout the project, including:

  ❑ Describing the function or purpose of the code

  ❑ Documenting the requirements

  ❑ Commenting changes and changing the comments

  ❑ Documenting non-conformance

  ❑ Commenting the configuration

  ❑ Using TODO: comments

❑ **Define and use coding standards:** The profiler includes a number of coding standards that should be reviewed and adhered to where necessary. The basic coding standards include:

  ❑ Naming conventions

  ❑ Formatting

  ❑ Coding style

❑ **Support configuration.** The solution should store as much as possible in "configuration" as config changes are far easier than code changes. The groups of configuration settings discussed included:

  ❑ Application specific configuration values

  ❑ Static page elements

  ❑ Validation rules

  ❑ Messages

In addition to the above configuration setting groups, you need to consider where the configuration settings are stored and the following storage options where discussed:

  ❑ Resource files

  ❑ Configuration files

  ❑ The system registry

  ❑ The database

❑ **Use a modular design and extensible solution.** The solution should be broken into small, discrete, loosely coupled components to promote maintainability and extensibility.

23

Designing for Testing

This chapter takes a look at how to design your solutions to incorporate features that will help you test more efficiently and effectively, as well as ensure that the system meets the quality characteristics. From a core development perspective, testing consists of unit testing and integration testing. After the software leaves the development team, it is in the hands of the functional and technical testers. You need to ensure that you've tested as much as possible to avoid an influx of defects that will overly burden the development or fix team. As developers, we have a tendency to feel that we own the components we develop and that we are responsible for them throughout their lifetime. This may be true in some organizations. However, it is not always guaranteed. When the software is released for formal testing and defects are uncovered, it is very possible that someone else will be responsible for implementing a fix. The components should be well-documented and well-tested, as these activities are vitally important as the project progresses. At some point during the project there are typical "wash up" meetings. In these meetings, the participants look at the number of defects raised, their overall severity and, more important, where they could have been caught (and fixed) earlier in the lifecycle — in particular, where defects could have been detected and fixed through thorough unit and integration testing. The outcomes of the meetings provide valuable information that should be understood and folded back into the early design, build, and test activities. Design sign-off and checkpoints are one thing, but ultimately unit testing and integration testing are the first chance of catching issues in the working software. The more issues that can be found and resolved in these early testing activities, the smoother the remainder of the project should be.

This chapter is organized into the following sections:

❑ **Developer Testing Activities** — Examines the types of tests performed during developer testing. It looks at some of the component groups and the high-level conditions and scenarios that could be proven before moving on.

❑ **Examining the Factory Pattern** — Examines the factory pattern, which can be used to facilitate testing. The factory pattern isolates the construction of an object within the software factory itself. There are many different ways in which this can be implemented, and each has its own pros and cons. This section examines two ways in which the factory can determine the object to create and these include:

❏ Using compiler directives

❏ Using configuration and "late-binding" techniques

❏ **Using Stubs and Simulators** — Examines the use of stubs and simulators during testing as well as the differences between them. Stubs and simulators can help to test areas of the application that could otherwise be troublesome to set up and instigate.

Developer Testing Activities

Developer testing is the first chance to identify defects early in the lifecycle. The first thing to do is to define the types of tests you're going to perform and on which components and groups. The conceptual architecture helps to lay out the components and determine the unit tests, integration tests, and possibly smoke tests. Figure 23-1 shows the component groups in the case study laid out in an end-to-end fashion to help with this exercise.

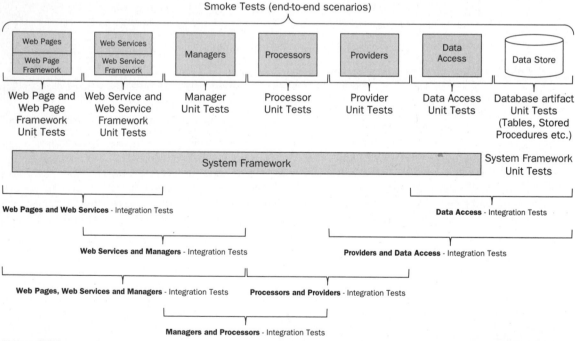

Figure 23-1

I find diagrams like this really useful during early design and planning activities. They allow you to pick out the components and how they could be tested as individual units and as groups. The diagram doesn't show all the components in the solution; it simply shows the high-level component groupings. The following provides an overview of the diagram:

❑ **Unit tests** — Specific units tests are associated with each high-level component group. For instance, web pages are tested in isolation from the other application components. The web pages use the web page framework, so these can also be tested in isolation or as a group. Testing each component group in isolation typically requires stubs or simulators to be in place. For example, most of the components use the system framework, so you can stub out the system framework to allow isolated unit testing. You can also stub out any other components that the unit (the class or method being tested) is using. You can test the system framework (and other classes) in isolation as well as integration test them with other components in the architecture.

❑ **Integration tests** — Integration testing typically identifies collections of components that should work together and are typically referred to as an assembly. Figure 23-1 showed a number of suggested groupings for integration testing, including:

　❑ **Web Pages and Web Services** — These tests ensure that the web pages are calling the right web services and that there are no communication-related issues.

　❑ **Web Services and Managers** — These tests ensure that the web services are calling the correct business manager components.

　❑ **Web Pages, Web Services, and Managers** — These tests ensure that the flow between the web pages and the managers works correctly.

　❑ **Managers and Processors** — These tests ensure that the managers invoke the correct processors and verify the bi-directional communication.

　❑ **Processors and Providers** — These tests ensure that the processors and providers work together correctly.

　❑ **Providers and Data Access** — These tests ensure that the flow between the providers and the database works correctly.

　❑ **Data Access** — These tests ensure that the data access layer works as a complete flow, including the database.

Integration tests can also include conditions for special cases and exceptions that could be thrown during the flow. This differs somewhat from smoke testing, as integration tests actually test exception scenarios and multiple linkages between components. For the purposes of the case study, integration testing, for example, would need to test the different requests and fields between integrated components.

❑ **Smoke tests** — These tests are generally functionality-based and the scenarios map to actual user actions, such as creating a new account, activating an account, and so forth. The tests are conducted through the application's front end and run through the entire application and architecture stack. Smoke testing should be automated to reduce manual effort and the scenarios should cover the core functionality of the application. Smoke tests are a very good way of uncovering functional defects prior to releasing the software for formal testing. However, smoke tests do not always uncover subtle interaction issues between individual components. You can enhance the value of smoke tests by including exception scenarios and covering alternative flows.

The size and scale of the system determines the number of integration points and how they can be tested as a flow. You should model the individual assemblies to ensure the tests are valid and provide real value during developer and early testing.

Over time, unit tests and integration tests can lose their value (see Figure 23-2). And in some cases, they can even provide "negative" value. This typically happens when additional test scenarios, such as smoke tests, are developed that cover the similar functionality to the individual unit or integration tests. The unit tests and integration tests might be using stubs, whereas the additional tests might use the real components. This means the unit and integration tests are being maintained (which costs time and effort) and that they aren't really providing any additional value or benefit. This can also extend to the stubs and simulators used by these tests.

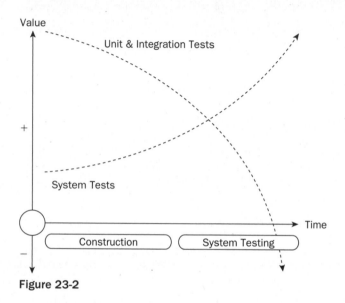

Figure 23-2

I mention this now because you need to be careful when choosing where to implement a stub or simulator. Some of the very early tests and the associated stubs and simulators could become redundant as the project progresses. You must balance the effort to devise the tests, the test data, and the harnesses accordingly. There's no point in wasting time and money maintaining them when they provide no real value. You need to think about where you can use tests, stubs, and simulators to provide true, fully quantifiable value. In my opinion, you should test the solution, not the tests.

At this point in the book, a large number of components, types, and classes that will form part of the case study's final state solution have been identified. Nothing is actually cast-in-stone, as there could be changes, depending on the findings required for testing. The initial component inventory provides the backdrop for the testing analysis and design. Let's look at some of the high-level component groups, working up from the database, to determine the testing requirements:

❑ **Database objects** — The database objects include all the tables, views and stored procedures. When component testing and integration testing these artifacts, it is important to focus on the application-specific functionality and not exhaustively test the database engine's capabilities. For example, if a table includes a NOT NULL column, a very simple test case could be used to try and insert a NULL value. This is essentially testing that the database does, in fact, *throw* an exception and that the table is configured correctly for NOT NULL. As the project progresses through development and testing, the database artifacts can sometimes become out-of-sync — for instance, when a new column is added that is NOT NULL but the stored procedures, views, and test data do not take this into account. Testing the database in isolation requires a suite of tests and a set of tools to:

❏ **Insert, update, select, and delete records from (and using) a "production-like" test data collection** — If the application is going to use stored procedures for all database transactions, then the stored procedures should be used to test the underlying database objects. This requires a test tool that can execute stored procedures, preferably in multiple threads over a number of connections to ensure that locking and isolation is tested. The stored procedures used for batch processes should also be tested.

❏ **Extract and compare expected results with actual results** — The expected results and actual results need to take into account all the tables (including audit updates). The tools (and scripts) need to be sufficiently mature to take into account potentially indeterminate results such as database identity columns, dates and times, and so forth. For instance, when updating a record in the Account table, you expect an audit entry. The audit ID will be generated by the database and may not be able to be used as a key for extraction. In addition, the extraction and comparison tools should highlight any truncation issues or data type conversation issues.

❏ **Test the reporting components** — If the reporting architecture is using views to return specific datasets, a series of reporting extracts needs to be tested (which can typically be done by reusing existing tools). It is simply a question of selecting data based on a view and checking it against the expect results.

❏ **Create, reset, and "tune" the database** — After each test, test cycle, or test suite, the database may need to be re-created (or cleared down) and reset. To achieve realistic performance figures, it is often necessary to re-index the database and re-compile stored procedures after a large data-pump or removal exercise. The tooling should support these administrative tasks, along with the ability to delete transaction logs, reset internal sequence numbers, and so forth.

❏ **C# entity/model classes** — The data entity and model classes are simple components that consist of basic property "getters" and "setters." These should be tested in isolation using production-like test data via C# test harnesses that can be executed automatically. The properties are strongly typed, so there should be no need to test "invalid" types. The test harness should throw an exception if it tries to convert or cast a test data item into an invalid type — for instance, trying to convert the value 1,000,000 into a `byte`. This failure would indicate that the entity property is not suitably typed for production data.

❏ **C# "system" framework components and classes** — These components rely on each other. For example, the diagnostic provider requires configuration, and the configuration provider requires diagnostics. If configuration is stored in the database, then the configuration provider requires the data access provider, which in turn requires configuration and diagnostics. Testing the components in isolation requires the following:

❏ A thorough set of configuration data, including performance counters, message configuration, event configuration, tracing configuration, and application configuration values

❏ A set of C# test harnesses that test each of the properties and methods based on the test configuration data

❏ A set of tools to extract and compare the outputs for expected results vs. actual results, including performance counter updates, events raised, trace output, and values loaded

❏ Stubs for each component to ensure the individual flows and interactions are tested

❏ **C# application framework classes** — The application framework classes are one level above the system framework classes. The application framework classes include the lower-level providers, including `ValidationProvider` and `EmailQueueProvider`, as well as `data-access` components, and so forth. You can test these components in isolation and, where necessary, use stub versions of system framework components. You can also use C# test harnesses to test these components. Testing the components requires the following:

  ❏ A thorough set of application and data entity configuration, including validation rules and associated messages

  ❏ A thorough set of configuration data and test data, including cryptographic configuration settings

  ❏ Tools for extraction and comparison to evaluate the actual results (database updates, diagnostic output, and so on)

❏ **The solicited e-mail provider** — I've called this component out specifically because it is one of the most interesting in the collection. Fully testing this component requires a real connection to an e-mail provider, in addition to a comprehensive set of test and configuration data, of course, and the e-mails would be sent to real e-mail addresses. Automating the comparison of the actual results against the expected results would require a complicated solution that accessed the particular e-mail Inbox and extracted the e-mail for comparison against the expected results. Unless automated testing and comparison is absolutely necessary, it is somewhat overkill and a specific set of "manual" tests might be better. Manual testing needs to be flagged very early on to ensure that it is clearly understood and that resources can be put in place to test the functionality appropriately for each new release. To support automated unit and integration testing, a stub or simulator needs to be put in place that simply outputs the e-mail to a known location (such as a text file), where it can be compared against expected results using standard "diff" tools. There is also another issue here in that the Activation Key generator generates unique Activation Keys. How do you prepare expected results for this value? The test tools would need to extract the key from the e-mail text file for comparison against the expected results. However, the expected results need to be known. Another stub could be used in place of the real generator to simply return a "known" key so that automation and comparison is possible.

❏ **The cryptography provider** — I've also called this component out specifically because it is also one of the most interesting in the collection. It is designed to encrypt one-way or two-way and return a value. Testing this component requires comparing actual results with expected results, as all tests do. The challenge is how to generate the expected results. It's a bit of a chicken-and-egg situation. If you use the component to generate the expected results, you are simply checking "actual" results, not the real functionality. The expected results need to be based on "known" values (for example, "using these specific keys and this algorithm, the expected results are xyz"), proving that the component will produce the same results (every time). It is fairly safe to say that changing the encryption keys will generate the different (but expected) results. Challenges with testing and/or test preparation should again be flagged early. In this example, a specialist security architect may need to be involved to ratify the design and testing. In addition, this component may require a stub counterpart that doesn't perform any encryption at all to support all the other testing efforts that would otherwise be faced with encrypted values in the outputs.

❏ **C# (online) manager/provider classes** — These classes essentially do not overlap each other, although they do complement each other. They make use of application framework components such as the `ValidationProvider` and so on. To test these components in isolation, you can stub the application framework components. C# test harnesses are required to test the properties and methods of these components. If you are using real versions of the framework components, rather than stubs, the tools must be able to extract and compare the outputs of each component.

❏ **C# (batch) shell(s)/manager/provider classes** — All these classes are part of the batch solution, but they also make use of the application framework classes. You can test these components in isolation using C# harnesses and stubs, as appropriate. You can also test them using the batch execution shell. A thorough set of test and configuration data is required to fully test the functionality of these classes. The extract and compare tools verify the outputs (database updates, and so on) from each of these processes. You can confirm the `StdOut` and `StdErr` streams visually, or you can develop a test harness to capture the output and compare it with expected results.

❏ **C# Web services** — You can test the web services in isolation, without using the ASP pages, by developing a simple, web-based test harness that sends an XML message and checks the appropriate response. There are also third-party components that are very good at this and can be used to automate the scripts so that they can be run over and over again. You can also test the web services in isolation from the rest of the application by implementing a set of manager stubs that simulate responses to the requests. This approach can be coupled with the ASP page testing to allow for the basic testing of page elements, flows, and transitions. There are even external websites that offer tests of this nature, which can greatly reduce costs.

❏ **Web pages** — Automating the testing of ASP pages typically requires the use of a third-party testing product. These products enable you to "capture" what you are doing and then replay the script over and over again. The pages typically are not tested in complete isolation, so the tests can be considered as full "link" or end-to-end integration tests, as they test the entire flow from start to finish (unless a stub or simulator intercepts the transaction part-way through). Testing ASP pages also includes visual ("mark-one eyeball") confirmation of adherence to styles and formatting guidelines. The underlying framework components and model classes that the pages use also must be in place to support the testing, although these could be "stubbed", as appropriate.

The preceding list applies only to the core solution. Don't forget that all the scripts and tools in the solution will also need to be tested.

Now that you have the high-level testing inventory and challenges, you need to define the testing strategy. Again, this depends entirely on the situation and requirements. However, armed with the preceding information, you can perform the necessary cost-benefit analysis and lay down the initial ground rules by determining a few simple terms of reference:

❏ **First, do you really need to support parallel development and testing?** That is, does the timeline need to be compressed such that components are built out of their natural dependency order — for instance, building the system framework components at the same time as building other components that are dependent on them. My gut says the answer would be no, given the additional overheads, requirements, and cost implications. However, if and when the project starts to slip, you should revisit this decision; it is very likely that the components will end up being built in parallel. To alleviate the situation, you need to position yourself so that you can be ready if it happens, improve the quality of the testing, and not unduly affect timescales and costs.

❏ **Do you really need all these stubs and simulators?** See the section "Using Stubs and Simulators" later in this chapter.

❏ **Do you really need all these extract and compare tools?** This really depends. They will be very useful during testing and live service. It is typically not long before very similar tools and scripts are developed for (or by) the support team. The logs, events, and diagnostics can always be visually confirmed and the appropriate evidence can be packaged with the build completion.

The automated testing suite would need to at least support the primary tests for the application functionality, which would invariably involve database extract and comparison.

❑ **What's wrong with manual testing?** Manual testing requires effort. Every time a new release is built, it would require manual smoke testing. This will generally increase costs and introduce unnecessary dependencies. It has been my experience that manual regression tests don't cover as many scenarios as they should. The automated tests can test far more scenarios than a manual tester. The tests can also be executed on a periodic basis to ensure that everything works appropriately. The key is to start with automation in mind and build up into a full solution. Getting it right in the first instance will help to build on the foundations. Automated testing does require the appropriate tooling, which is why you need to think about it up front so that it doesn't delay the build and testing phases.

❑ **Won't automated testing increase the impact of change?** In general, automated testing will require the same updates as manual testing when a change is introduced. For example, when a validation rule changes, the test data, test scripts, and expected results will all need to change. It is typically when new scenarios are introduced that specific tests need to be written, rather than it only being updated in documentation.

Automated testing isn't that much more than writing a test harness and automatically comparing expected and actual results. However it does require careful planning and implementation. Testing a component thoroughly requires that the appropriate configuration and test data be in place to ensure a complete set of tests. A reasonable set of test data can be handcrafted. Where appropriate, production data should be used. However you can also generate test data based on the database schema. There also are a number of third-party products that will generate huge amounts of test data based on the database schema.

Examining the Factory Pattern

Chapter 2 touched on the point that unit tests aren't strictly supposed to go outside of their class boundary because a unit is the smallest testable item. Consider the following abridged pseudo code snippet:

```
Public Class AccountProvider
{
    Public AccountData CreateNewAccount( Username, Password, ... )
    {
        AccountData account = new AccountData();
        CryptographyProvider crypto = new CryptographyProvider();
        AccountDataAccess dataAccess = new AccountDataAccess();

        // compile account data object
        account.Username = Username;
        account.Password = crypto.Encrypt( Encrypt.OneWay, Password );
        ...

        // create new account
        dataAccess.CreateNewAccount( account );
    }
}
```

The example is used for discussion purposes only. You can see that the code creates a number of objects to perform its core processing. You can also see that the CreateNewAccount method doesn't include any diagnostic code, either. However, if you followed the rule that unit testing must not go outside its class boundary, you'd have to stub all the components the CreateNewAccount method was calling. I'll discuss whether there is any actual value of doing this later. For the moment, let's simply look at how the creation of both test and real objects could be done to ease testing. There are many ways of doing this, including:

❑ Using conditional compilation to determine the "type" of component to be instantiated.

❑ Implementing software factories to return the right "type" of component, which can also be based on conditional compilation or configuration.

The first option is the most basic (and you saw this approach in Chapter 2 when looking at unit testing). The basic pattern is as follows:

```
Public Class AccountProvider
{
    Public AccountData CreateNewAccount( Username, Password, ... )
    {
        #if UNIT_TEST

            AccountData account = new AccountDataTestStub();
            CryptographyProvider crypto = new CryptographyProviderTestStub();
            AccountDataAccess dataAccess = new AccountDataAccessTestStub();

        #else

            AccountData account = new AccountData();
            CryptographyProvider crypto = new CryptographyProvider();
            AccountDataAccess dataAccess = new AccountDataAccess();

        #endif

        ...

    }
}
```

In this example, the code is determining the object to create using the compiler directive. The issue can be further complicated when different test cycles require different stubs. The code might end up looking something like this:

```
Public Class AccountProvider
{
    Public AccountData CreateNewAccount( Username, Password, ... )
    {

        #if( UNIT_TEST )

            AccountData account = new AccountDataUnitTestStub();
            CryptographyProvider crypto = new CryptographyProviderUnitTestStub();
```

```
        AccountDataAccess dataAccess = new AccountDataAccessUnitTestStub();

    #elif( ASSY_TEST )

        AccountData account = new AccountDataAssyTestStub();
        CryptographyProvider crypto = new CryptographyProviderAssyTestStub();
        AccountDataAccess dataAccess = new AccountDataAccessAssyTestStub();

    #else

        AccountData account = new AccountData();
        CryptographyProvider crypto = new CryptographyProvider();
        AccountDataAccess dataAccess = new AccountDataAccess();

    #endif

        ...

    }
}
```

This implementation makes the consumer code quite messy. Instead, this code could be moved down into an object factory. For example:

```
Public Class AccountProvider
{
    Public AccountData CreateNewAccount( Username, Password, ... )
    {
        AccountData account = AccountDataFactory.CreateNew();
        CryptographyProvider crypto = CryptographyProviderFactory.CreateNew();
        AccountDataAccess dataAccess = AccountDataAccessFactory.CreateNew();

        ...

    }
}
```

This tidies up the consumer code and leaves the factory to determine the type of object that needs to be created during its CreateNew method (this is just a sample method name). The factory could use the previous compiler-directive implementation style. However, this leads down a path where there are going to be multiple releases of the compiled code-base, which will impact the build and deployment processes, especially when you might need even more stubs for functional testing and possibly even technical testing.

It stands to reason that the stubs need to implement the same properties and methods that the real object implements. To ensure that this is adhered to, you should define interfaces for each of the objects. The consumer should communicate with the concrete object through an interface, as shown in the following snippet:

```
Public Class AccountProvider
{
    Public AccountData CreateNewAccount( Username, Password, … )
    {
        IAccountData account = AccountDataFactory.CreateNew();
```

```
        ICryptographyProvider crypto = CryptographyProviderFactory.CreateNew();
        IAccountDataAccess dataAccess = AccountDataAccessFactory.CreateNew();


        ...
    }
}
```

This ensures that all the objects created and returned by the factory must implement the defined interface. For example, the following is an abridged interface definition for the `IAccountData`:

```
Interface IAccountData
{
    string Username
    {
        get;
        set;
    }

    string Password
    {
        get;
        set;
    }

    string EmailAddress
    {
        get;
        set;
    }

}
```

The data entities are very simple classes, and one would naturally have to question what the rationale would be for supporting multiple implementations.

If you consider that every object inherits the `ToString` method, which returns a string representation of the object, you could have different implementations that returned different string representations of the object. During testing you might want to serialize the entire object (which could be quite large) for diagnostic logging. In production you might want to reduce the amount of serialization for performance purposes. You might also use this approach to keep "secure" information from being outputted in plain text format — for example, never return the user's password in the resulting string, whether it's in the clear or not. The factory approach provides these opportunities without impacting any other implementation or purpose.

The final part of the picture is to decide how the factory determines which object needs to be created and returned. You've already seen that you can use compiler directives within the code. However, you could use configuration values instead. If you work on the basic premise that you're more than likely going to have different configuration settings for different test cycles and production, this approach would simply extend the various configuration settings.

All you really need in the configuration is the assembly name and class name. The factory would simply obtain these values and create and return the concrete object. As shown in Figure 23-3, this greatly simplifies the factory's implementation. This is the same approach you saw in Chapter 16 to instantiate batch managers and processes through the use of late-binding techniques.

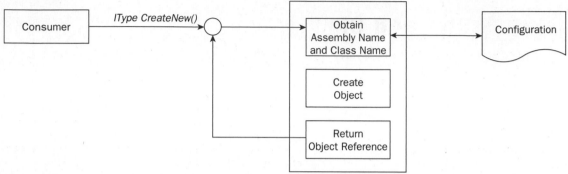

Figure 23-3

The configuration needs to be managed carefully to ensure that the correct configuration is in place for the particular purpose, but this needs to be done anyway for other values in the solution. Using this approach throughout would retain a single, compiled code-base. Only the configuration would need to change for different environments and purposes.

It is also worth considering the performance angle of this approach in various situations. When objects are being created on a per-transaction basis, the overhead of obtaining the configuration setting could be costly. However, this also needs to be considered for other configuration settings. The configuration values should really be cached in memory (and re-loadable) to ensure quick access and support in-flight modification.

You should also consider the code profiling rules when using such an approach. A lot of code profilers, frown upon late binding techniques like this and raise warnings for "unsafe code."

You could even combine the two approaches (if and where required). For instance, you could have two compiled code-bases — one for testing and one for production — as shown in the following snippet:

```
Public Class AccountDataFactory
{
    Public IAccountData CreateNew()
    {
        #if( TEST )
            // obtain assembly name and class name from configuration
            // create object
            // return concrete object
        #else

            return( new AccountData() );

        #endif
    }
}
```

The snippet shows that unless this is a TEST release, the production (default) object will be created and returned by the factory. This approach limits the number of different releases to two; it also provides a standard mechanism for creating the real production objects (rather than returning stubs), and it provides hooks for test releases.

Using Stubs and Simulators

Stubs and simulators, in my opinion, are different entities. I tend to draw the following distinctions:

❑ **A stub is simply an end-point.** Stubs can contain some rudimentary logging to output the various parameters it was passed, and it can return a specific value to indicate success. Stubs are typically used when the real component isn't available and nothing specific in the consumer needs to be tested.

❑ **A simulator is used when a component is either not available or specific "conditions" need to be tested.** The simulator can implement logic based on parameters passed in or through configuration to return specific values or to throw specific exceptions. For instance, during testing, you might want to test your exception-handling routine. To do this thoroughly, you need to get the component you're calling to throw the various exceptions you expect. This can be quite difficult to arrange when using the real component. It might involve specific timing or other complicated environmental set-up. Using a simulator enables you to simulate the various conditions quickly and easily.

Figure 23-4 shows a holistic (cloud) view of the case study. The clouds represent the underlying processing, and the resulting outputs are noted. In this instance, processing output can be presented on the web page, in the database, or represented as diagnostic information as well as solicited e-mails.

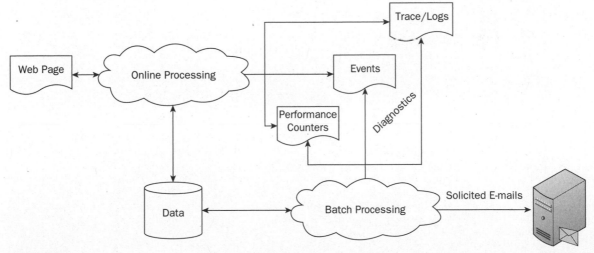

Figure 23-4

The important thing with stubs and simulators is to avoid overkill. Using them all over the place can result in wasted effort by testing only portions of the application.

Each test activity will have its own requirements, and stubs and simulators should be used to provide real value to the testing being performed. When a stub (or simulator) may need to be used to provide development continuation, depends entirely on the construction plan. For example, the case study needs to encrypt various data elements for security purposes. Cryptography is notoriously hard to implement and test thoroughly. You don't want the entire project team to be held up because the crypto component isn't ready. It would make a certain amount of sense to stub the cryptography provider to allow development and testing to continue without its final implementation. The component is well isolated and it is used in every flow, so it is a prime candidate for stubbing.

Testing components in isolation using stubs and simulators helps to cover as many cases and scenarios as possible while reducing the overhead of doing so. For example, another good place to use a simulator is for sending solicited e-mails. Isolating the actual semantics of this into a single component enables you to test the remainder of the application without hindrance from the actual underlying e-mail sub-system. You don't want construction or testing to be held up just because the physical e-mail server is down or not working properly. The simulator can place the e-mail in a separate file so that the necessary parties can verify its content, and also be used as part of the unit, integration, and end-to-end testing results, as shown in Figure 23-5.

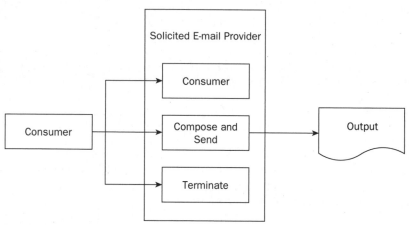

Figure 23-5

In this instance, the `Initialize` method could do what was required to initialize the simulator. Likewise, the `Terminate` method would perform all the cleanup actions. If you modeled the output from the simulator, it might look something like the following:

```
EmailAddress: ide1968@hotmail.com
EmailType: 1 - New Activation Key Request

Subject: Welcome to Within-a-Click
Body:

Thank you for registering with us. We are very pleased to provide you with
    your new account activation key:
```

```
1111-1111-1111-1111-1111

We hope you enjoy using our site!

The WAC Team.
```

The output shows the e-mail address that the mail would be sent to. It also shows the type of e-mail and the final output. Using a purpose-built simulator needs to be balanced against the testing that you would perform on the actual message provider itself. For instance, you might also simulate the message provider to return "canned" data instead of getting it from its final source. Furthermore, if the solicited e-mail provider includes the appropriate diagnostics, do you really need a separate output? The output would actually be the diagnostics, which should tell you all this information anyway. You shouldn't need to go somewhere else for core information like this.

You could even simulate the data access layers. You don't actually need to communicate with a physical database. Instead, the simulator could return canned test data. If you wanted to test the wait-retry logic as an isolated unit, you could simulate failures from the framework's SQL objects. This would prove that the wait-retry logic was working correctly before you passed the component on for further testing. You could also fully automate this type of testing to avoid manual steps. Once again, this needs to be balanced against its use and importance. The wait-retry pattern is initiated only in the event of a failure and it would be tested fully during system testing. The early tests want to make sure that there are no fundamental flaws in the processing logic. Therefore, you don't need to simulate every single type of failure. You could probably reduce the conditions to those that provide a comfort factor before moving forward.

The amount of simulated activity required really depends on the component and its importance within the overall solution. In some cases entire applications might need to be simulated, especially when they are not available when you need to perform testing.

Stubs and simulators can be used to great effect during prototyping activities. A prototype is usually implemented using smoke and mirrors. The components aren't fully working versions; they simply simulate certain actions and processing. You could essentially model the solution end-to-end and you'd end up with a number of class outlines (properties and methods) and some core processing requirements. These classes would provide the basis of the exemplars and templates for moving forward without being held up by implementation-specific details. By implementing the factory pattern, you can easily include the "real" components as and when completed.

At some point, the application needs to be fully tested without stubs or simulators. Therefore, it is important that the isolated tests, stubs, and simulators prove as much as possible, provide real value and benefits, and don't actually impact the proper testing.

Summary

Testing is vitally important and you need to consider all the different types of tests that you are going to carry out. You need to model the application components to determine the unit tests, integration tests, and smoke tests. Using interfaces and factories from the outset enables you to make (and change) decisions as the project progresses without unduly impacting construction. Stubs and simulators can provide real value when developed and used appropriately.

The following are the key points to take away from this chapter:

- **Determine the types of developer tests to carry out.** The tests should be categorized into the following areas:

    - Unit tests should cover complete components or classes, including exception scenarios.

    - Integration tests should cover multiple interactions between components as well as exception scenarios.

    - Smoke tests should cover the core functionality of the application.

- **The value of unit and integration tests can decrease as the project progresses.** The following should be considered when devising unit and integration tests:

    - Maintaining redundant tests and test matter is a waste of time and money.

    - Test the application, not the tests.

- **Have the right tools and processes in place.** To support thorough testing you need to have all the right tools and processes in place, including:

    - Test execution tools.

    - Expected and actual results comparison tools.

- **Use the Factory Pattern.** The software factory pattern that can be used to plug in different components.

    - Interfaces and factories should be used to facilitate testing.

    - Where appropriate the factories should use configuration to reduce the number of code-based releases in the overall solution.

- **Use Stubs and Simulators wisely.** Using stubs and simulators during development and testing can be very beneficial; however, their usage should be considered carefully. Consider the following:

    - Stubs and simulators provide a great way of modeling and prototyping the solution before heading into full-scale development.

    - Stubs should be used to provide basic end-point confirmation or when real components are unavailable.

    - Simulators should be used to help thoroughly test the application where it would otherwise be troublesome to do so.

    - Stubs and simulators should be used to help with "actual" results comparison.

    - It is important to ensure that each test, stub, or simulator provide real benefit and value.

24

Designing for Deployment

Deployment is the art of ensuring the right components are installed on the right servers with the right configuration. You don't want to "flick the switch" on the day of go-live only to find that the application is running in "test mode." Likewise, you don't want to start functional testing when the application is configured for production only to find that you run out of memory when trying to load all the reference data. Each environment (and possibly release) will have its own purpose and deployment requirements. Chapter 3 discussed configuration management and highlighted some of the areas of the solution that are likely to be different for each environment and purpose, including:

- ❑ Data and database scripts
- ❑ Configuration files and settings
- ❑ Core solution libraries (assuming multiple code-bases are used)
- ❑ Test scripts and test data
- ❑ Stubs and simulators
- ❑ Tools (including productivity scripts)
- ❑ Documentation

Limiting the number of different releases will help with deployment. A single compiled code-base is much easier to deploy and manage. In this chapter we're going to briefly look at a couple of the techniques and practices that should be considered during design to ensure that the solution is deployable.

This chapter is organized into the following sections:

- ❑ **Splitting Out Test Materials** — Examines the need to completely decouple all test matter from the solution to ensure that it doesn't get deployed into production. It is probably the most important factor — you saw previously that organizing your solution in the right way can help with this.

❑ **Separating the Components** — Describes how separating the application components can help with deployment and especially patching or hot-fixing.

❑ **Classifying the Releases** — Examines the purpose, content, and configuration of the different types of packaged releases.

This chapter does not discuss the specifics of actual packaging and deployment. There are many different tools that provide packaging and deployment features, all of which will allow you to produce reliable installation mechanisms for your software. Throughout a project, you'll need to deploy your software to various locations; it is a good idea to understand all of these requirements so you can incorporate them into your design.

Splitting Out Test Materials

This subject is close to my heart. It helps not only with application maintenance, but also when deploying to production environments. You need to ensure that all development and test materials are completely separated from the production releases. It is very easy to get carried away during development and forget this and when releases are being compiled for production use, they suddenly contain a lot of test matter. This could be something as simple as including a unit test class in the same library as the core code. Or it could be the inclusion of test configuration settings in the live configuration files. You also need to consider naming conventions to ensure that test items can be easily identified. It would be very easy in a plug-in architecture to accidentally wire-up a test component if it wasn't named correctly. For instance, consider the following simple example:

```
<AccountData assemblyName="DataEntities" className="AccountData" />
```

Is this the real class or a test class? Without it being named correctly, it would also be very easy to wire-up the wrong class. However, when the components are named correctly, this can be avoided. Furthermore, consider the following example:

```
<AccountData assemblyName="DataEntities" className="AccountDataTestStub" />
```

This implies that the DataEntities library contains both a real account data object and one designed specifically for testing. In the early days of modeling, you could have a DataEntities library structure somewhat similar to the following:

```
[Library]
    WACDataEntities.dll

[Namespace]
    WAC.DataEntities

[Classes]
    AccountData
    AccountDataTestStub
    TransactionContext
    TransactionContextTestStub

[Interfaces]
    IAccountData
    ITransactionContext
```

Although this is a simplified example, it demonstrates just how easily things could be included in the wrong library. The situation typically arises when a test class is required and it is unclear exactly where to put it. Organizing the solution outline early helps to avoid these situations. In this simple example, the interfaces are the only common elements. The test class should reference the main library for the interfaces and implement its own version of the component. For instance:

```
[Library]
   WACDataEntityTestStubs.dll

[Namespace]
    WAC.DataEntities.TestStubs

[Classes]
    AccountDataTestStub
    TransactionContextTestStub
```

This model shows a completely separate library for test entities, a completely separate namespace, and each class being clearly named. The library can now be included in different packages to avoid being deployed to production. You can extend this approach for different purposes, such as to specify different unit test classes. For example:

```
[Library]
   WACUnitTestDataEntities.dll

[Namespace]
    WAC.DataEntities.UnitTest

[Classes]
    AccountDataUnitTestStub
    TransactionContextUnitTestStub
```

This library wouldn't be deployed for any purpose other than unit testing. Using different libraries helps to separate the components, and using different names helps to highlight what the component is intended for.

Separating the Components

During testing and even live service, you're required to deploy updated components. Even if this activity is fully automated, it needs to be verified, which can take time. Verification could involve a combination of manual checks as well as running sample transactions through the system (which would need to be cleared out following the verification tests).

In testing, it is not unusual to deploy a patch or a hot fix to an environment. An issue might arise that needs to be turned around quickly, so instead of deploying a full code release, you deploy a discrete subset of components or libraries. Although this is also true in production sometimes, the operations and service delivery teams will generally want all production servers and environments to be in-sync. For example, consider a simple change in the SystemFramework library. This library would need to be deployed to all the servers across the estate, including the disaster recovery site. If it is not, there is the chance that Version 1 could reside on some servers while Version 2 could reside on another server, as shown in Figure 24-1.

Figure 24-1

The operations and service delivery teams are not usually keen to deploy single hot fixes and libraries like this unless it's absolutely necessary for emergency purposes. They'd much rather deploy a full release, knowing that all the components have been built and tested together so there's limited opportunity for errors. Having everything in-sync makes managing the environment far easier and avoids clashes when further deployments are required.

Separating components, configuration, and libraries into mini-packages can sometimes alleviate the need to deploy the release to all the servers. However, when shared components and libraries are required, this is often unavoidable. However, in the case of batch and reporting, the shared components and libraries are likely to change both throughout and after the project. By isolating these components into their own libraries, you can package and deploy them separately. After all, these components don't reside on every server, so a mini-package could be deployed to only the required servers.

Figure 24-2 shows the batch package being deployed only to the administration server. This minimizes the risk of errors and the number of servers affected. It also helps to minimize the amount of post-deployment verification that needs to be performed. This is especially helpful when deploying emergency fixes.

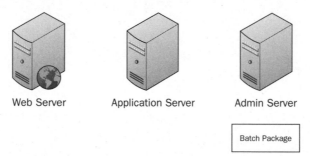

Figure 24-2

Where loose-coupling or late-binding is implemented, it is also possible to deploy a single library outside of a full release, although this needs to be managed carefully in production environments. There are risks associated with deploying a full release into a production environment, so it is worth thinking about how to reduce the risk and potential impact to the live service. You should never release into production environments unless you have a detailed plan of how you are going to roll it back if it fails. So, it is also worth thinking about how the release could be rolled back.

Classifying the Releases

The first step in defining the deployment strategy is to classify the various releases or packages and their purpose. There are many different ways in which the different packages can be sliced and diced, so it is a question of what's the best fit.

I find the best way to organize the release packages is to sit back and imagine a clean machine (or environment) and an installer, like the one shown in Figure 24-3. It doesn't matter if you're using a formal installer or scripts to deploy the software. If there were only two installation options in the drop-down list, "test" and "production," what would you expect to be installed and where would you expect it to reside? Using an installer would essentially be the same as running a script called "Install Test Release."

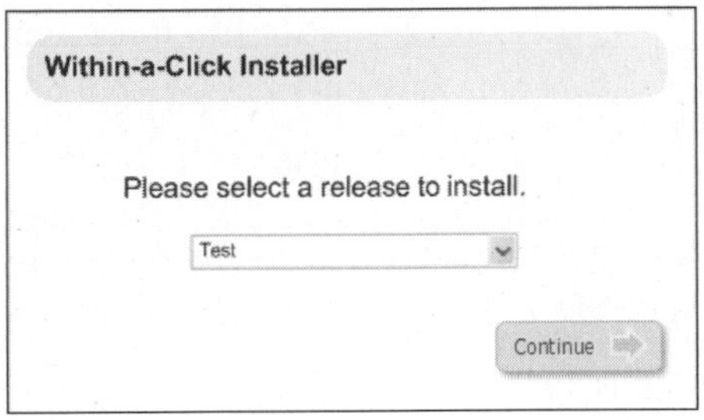

Within-a-Click Installer

Please select a release to install.

Test

Continue

Figure 24-3

One of the simplest ways to build up a candidate list for the release packages is to answer the question, "What is it being installed for?" To answer that question, you must look at the following activities involved in the lifecycle:

- ❑ Unit testing
- ❑ Integration testing
- ❑ Smoke testing
- ❑ Functional testing
- ❑ Technical testing
- ❑ Acceptance testing
- ❑ Production (including Disaster Recovery)
- ❑ Review

This list really just breaks down into two high-level categories: test releases and production releases. However, it provides a very useful starting point for this exercise. The different activities can also have different server environments, such as single server, multi-server, and so on.

I mentioned early on in this book the concept of the "day-one developer," which included thinking about what a developer would need on his or her first day to get up-to-speed on a project. Classifying the releases is a similar exercise. The high-level deliverables of the project are a good place to start and typically include the following items:

- Database scripts (such as Create Database, Create Table, and so on)
- Base data or reference data
- Test data
- Test tools (including stubs and simulators)
- Test scripts
- Documentation (including product documentation, design documents, and so on)
- Configuration files
- Source code (including scripts, unit tests, integration tests, and so on)
- Application binaries

In addition to the preceding core artifacts, there can be other areas of installation and configuration that need to be performed. These can include runtime environment configuration, such as IIS and other technologies.

With respect to the core deliverables, you could physically install all the contents on a single machine or environment (except for the production environment). I previously discussed rapid turn-around scripts that would turn an environment around for different purposes. If all the necessary content were physically on the machine, there would be no need to open the installer and uninstall/reinstall. The result of the installation could look something like the following:

```
Within-a-Click
   bin
   docs
   install
      bin
         unit test
         integration test
      src
         scripts
            unit test
               ut_install.cmd
            integration test
               it_install.cmd
      cfg
         unit test
      data
         unit test
      docs
         unit test
            Unit Test Primer.doc
```

Each directory would contain the various elements of the release. The following provides a brief overview of the example top-level folders:

❑ `Within-a-Click\bin` — This folder contains the solution's core libraries and configuration files.

❑ `Within-a-Click\docs` — This folder contains the documentation for the installed release.

❑ `Within-a-Click\install` — This folder is broken down into individual folders to allow for further installation and configuration of the environment. The sub-folders would contain all the items that needed to be copied to the main folders, such as:

❑ The actual scripts that need to be executed to further install and configure the environment for a specific use.

❑ The core libraries and configuration that would need to be copied to the main location.

❑ The documentation for the associated release. The sample shows the Unit Test Primer documentation, which describes how to write and execute the unit tests.

The preceding folders are used for example purposes only. In this instance, users would click on `ut_install.cmd` to install the unit testing environment on their machine. To turn their environment around for integration testing, they would simply execute `it_install.cmd`.

In this example, the actual installer is doing nothing more than placing all the files on the correct servers. However, it could be extended to include custom options that allow the user to choose which items to install.

In production, the installation would need to be fully automated so that it could be deployed to all the servers without requiring manual intervention. You wouldn't want to deploy all the files to all the servers; rather, you should have multiple mini-packages or releases for various components and/or servers.

Figure 24-4 shows a table of the deliverables and how they could differ between releases and packages.

Package Differences	Unit Testing	Integration Testing	Smoke Testing	Functional Testing	Technical Testing	Acceptance Testing	Production
Database Scripts	Workstation Database Installation	Workstation Database Installation	Workstation Database Installation	Workstation Database Installation	Server Database Installation	Production Database Installation	Production Database Installation
Base Data	Unit Test Base Data	Integration Test Base Data	Smoke Test Base Data	Functional Test Base Data	Technical Test Base Data	Acceptance Test Base Data	Core Reference Data
Test Data	Unit Test Data	Integration Test Data	Smoke Test Data	Functional Test Data	Technical Test Data	Acceptance Test Data (Production)	N/A
Test Tools	Developer Test Tools	Developer Test Tools	Functional Test Tools	Functional Test Tools	Technical Test Tools	Acceptance Test Tools	Verification Tools
Stubs and Simulators	Unit Test Stubs	Integration Test Stubs	Smoke Test Stubs	Functional Test Stubs	Technical Test Stubs	Acceptance Test Stubs	N/A
Product Documentation	Unit Testing Documentation	Integration Testing Documentation	Smoke Testing Documentation	Functional Testing Documentation	Technical Testing Documentation	Acceptance Testing Documentation	Production Documentation
Design Documentation	All Design Documentation	All Design Documentation	All Design Documentation	All Design Documentation	All Design Documentation	All Design Documentation	All Design Documentation
Test Scripts	Unit Test Scripts	Integration Test Scripts	Smoke Test Scripts	Functional Test Scripts	Technical Test Scripts	Technical Test Scripts	N/A
Configuration	Unit Test Configuration	Integration Test Configuration	Smoke Test Configuration	Functional Test Configuration	Technical Test Configuration	Acceptance Test Configuration	Production Configuration
Source Code	Only for Code Review	Only for Code Review	Only for Code Review	N/A	N/A	Only for Code Review	N/A
Productivity Scripts	Unit Test Scripts	Integration Test Scripts	Smoke Test Scripts	Functional Test Scripts	Technical Test Scripts	Acceptance Test Scripts	Production Scripts
Application Binaries	The source code could contain #if statements specifically for Unit Testing.	The source code could contain #if statements specifically for Integration Testing.	The source code could contain #if statements specifically for Integration Testing.	Production Binaries	Production Binaries	Production Binaries	Production Binaries

Figure 24-4

The number of items that would be included in a release depends entirely on the size and scale of the system. However, the values shown in the table represent a starting point. The table helps to identify where there are (or would be) differences in the solution that would essentially require separation. These would be separated in the configuration-management system. The table also highlights areas where the code-base could be different because of specific code embedded in the solution; where possible, this should be reduced and preferably there should only be one code-base — the production one.

You could be installing the components in the packages across a number of different servers, although that would further complicate the packaging requirements. The environment design and the deployment concept both feed into the packaging and deployment solution. As you can see from the table, even on a single server there could be many different components. If you added multiple servers, the table would become even more complex.

Splitting up the components will help you to create discrete packages or scripts that can be used to easily deploy the solution.

Once you have classified your releases and you know the different packages you'll be using, you need to ensure that each and every deployment package includes the appropriate artifacts and a "build" or "release" number. You saw earlier how easy it is to have version 1 of a component on one server and version 2 on another, ensuring that each and every package, irrespective of whether it is a full release, a hot-fix or a patch, is properly identified to ensure that you know what is installed and where.

Summary

Getting the right artifacts on to the right servers is the primary objective of deployment. This brief chapter looked at some simple practices you can employ to support the deployment of your solutions.

The following are the key points to take away from this chapter:

- ❏ **Split out the test materials.** You should completely decouple development and test materials from production:
  - ❏ Test components should be kept in separate libraries.
  - ❏ Non-production matter should be clearly identifiable through its name.
- ❏ **Separate the components and libraries.** Organize the components into libraries and packages that can be easily deployed and verified:
  - ❏ Components should only be deployed to the servers where they are required.
  - ❏ Libraries (and groups) that are likely to change should be separated to ease deployment.
- ❏ **Classify the releases.** There are many different ways in which your deployment strategy can be achieved. The following should be considered when determining the different packages required:
  - ❏ Full production deployment needs to follow the deployment concept.
  - ❏ Partial production deployment could be on a per-server basis or a mini-package basis.
  - ❏ Test releases (where necessary) should deploy all materials to allow quick turnaround of the environment.
- ❏ **Identify every release with a "build" or "release" number.** It is extremely important that each and every package has a release number. Irrespective of whether the package contains a full release, a hot-fix, or a patch, it should be identified to ensure that you know which versions are where.

Part V
Conclusion

Chapter 25: Review and Wrap-Up

25

Review and Wrap-Up

Some of the ideas and concepts discussed in this book will require more formal modeling, and, in some cases, would actually require you to prototype the solution. It is always worth prototyping something to ensure that the design (and implementation) is straight. There's nothing worse than putting something down in a design document only to find that it doesn't work when you come to implement it. This is true for everything and not just the code.

In terms of the case study, it is at this point that you'd start your detailed design and planning activities. The case study has helped to promote the analysis, design, and planning activities. You'd bring everything together and solidify your solution. However, I've simply used the case study to model real world scenarios against a hypothetical development project. It is not about documenting, reviewing, or even implementing the final solution for the case study, it is about learning from the lessons and considerations it has highlighted and applying these to your own projects and solutions.

This final chapter is organized into the following sections:

❑ **Back to the Real World** — This section summarizes some of the patterns and practices discussed in this book and it looks at a couple of them and the implications of implementing them on real-world projects. In doing so, it uses Visual Studio and the code supplied with this book to demonstrate some of the tools and concepts.

❑ **Onwards and Upwards** — This section simply rounds off this book with some final parting messages.

Back to the Real World

I've written a lot about software quality, development practices and application maintenance. Only you know the quality of the code and the quality of the solutions you develop. There are good practices and there are bad practices. You may already be thinking about how you would set about implementing some of the messages in this book on your own projects to improve quality. If it were me, I'd firstly list the key principles and practices and then determine whether the solution employed them. If not, I'd determine whether the practice was required and if so, I'd look at the implications of implementing the practice appropriately.

This section actually looks at performing this exercise against a sample code base. For the purposes of this exercise, the source code doesn't adhere to all the principles discussed. It isn't production-ready, nor is it a complete solution. It is used solely for demonstration and example purposes. There are good points and there are many areas for further development.

I've listed some of the categories and included some of the key principles in the table that follows.

Category	Practices
Application Maintenance	The solution should differentiate what it intended for production vs. testing.
	The solution should provide a meaningful "at-a-glance" overview of the solution structure.
	Switch on the profiler — Treat warnings as errors. When errors are raised these can be assessed, downgraded or suppressed.
	Use XML comments for documentation generation — Commonly used tags include: Summary, Remarks, Param, Returns, and Exception.
	Use commenting standards — Describe the function. Document the requirements. Comment the changes. Comment the configuration. Use TODO comments.
	Use coding standards — Naming conventions, formatting, and coding style.
	Support configuration — Application specific configuration values, static page elements, validation rules, and messages.
	Use a modular design and extensible solution.
Testing	Unit tests should cover complete components or classes, including exception scenarios.
	Integration tests should cover multiple interactions between components as well as exception scenarios.
	Smoke tests should cover the core functionality of the application.
	Interfaces and factories should be used to facilitate testing.
	Stubs should be used to provide basic end-point verification.
	Simulators should be used to help thoroughly test the application where it would otherwise be troublesome to do so.
Incident Investigation	Tracing needs to provide the relevant information for effective incident investigation.
	Tracing must maintain code quality and keep the code "free" of unnecessary information.
	Link trace together using some form of activity or transaction identifier.
	Tracing mustn't affect performance. An optimal level of trace needs to be configured for production running.
	Tracing should be configurable.

Category	Practices
Monitoring	Identify and use performance counters.
	Updating performance counters mustn't affect performance.
	Identify and raise events (including detailed contextual information required for potential incident investigation).
	The events and performance counters should be configurable.
Resilience	Handle exceptions where you can — add value where you can't handle exceptions.
	Use wait-retry to handle common errors.
Performance	Avoid unnecessary method calls. Surround statements with a quick `if` check.
	Implement object recycling.
	Use object pools.
	Cache frequently used/infrequently updated information.
	Perform bulk operations.
	Optimize method processing. The most important statements should be executed first.

You can see from the table that it is rather like a set of code profiling rules or a code quality checklist. The table doesn't include all the patterns and practices discussed in this book. However, you could complete this list for your own purposes. Furthermore, you could even compile a complementary list for all the processes and associated practices outlined at the start of this book and throughout.

The following sections aren't going to be truly exhaustive. You're not going to be updating the solution. However, you can download the solution and execute the exercises. The following sections are simply going to touch on a few key areas of the code and the solution. If you were so inclined, you could complete the exercise for the sample code. However, it would be far more prudent to conduct them against your own projects.

To keep things short, this section only covers the items in the Application Maintenance and Testing categories. I've chosen these two subjects because they also demonstrate a few of the tools included in Visual Studio 2008. On your own projects it is worth performing similar exercises across all of the categories and practices you require.

Application Maintenance

The Within-a-Click solution (WAC.sln) is split into two main folders: Production and Test, as shown in Figure 25-1.

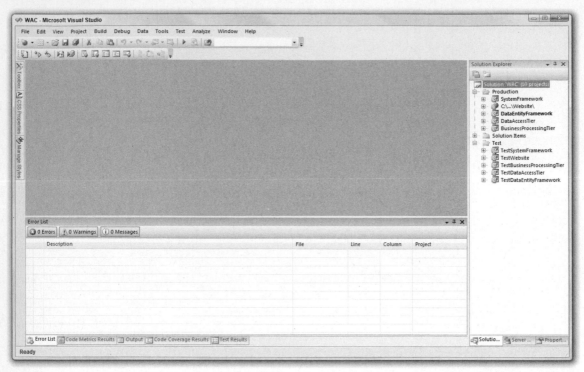

Figure 25-1

According to the first two items in the Application Maintenance checklist, the solution should:

❑ **Differentiate what it intended for production vs. testing** — The Production folder contains the elements that would be deployed to production and the Test folder contains all the test projects.

❑ **Provide a meaningful "at-a-glance" overview of the solution structure** — The solution structure is pretty clear and each library is named appropriately. You can see that there are five production projects and five associated test projects.

The next item in the Application Maintenance checklist is to switch on the profiler. Chapter 21 showed how to do this so I'll not go over this again. Figure 25-2 shows a screen shot containing some of the SystemFramework's profiling output sorted by description.

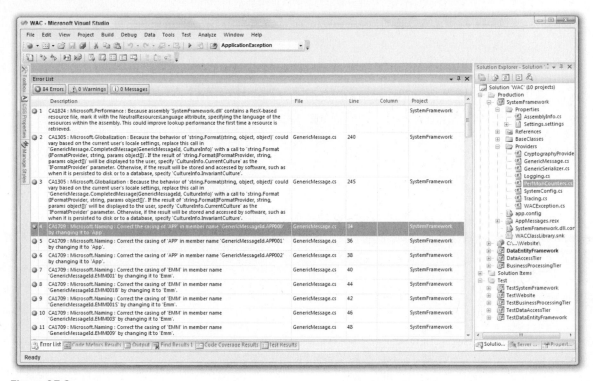

Figure 25-2

The profiler warnings have been treated as errors, as per the recommended practice, and as such the solution will not compile without the errors being downgraded or suppressed. You can see that there are a number of profiling errors so I'm not going to go into every single error listed.

When lists like these are presented to the outside world, there's an instant reaction that the code quality isn't good. The application could actually work like a dream, but these warnings and errors can cause issues with the way someone perceives the solution quality. These issues are sometimes hard to recover from. It is no good just turning the warnings off, as someone will run the profiler at some point and uncover them. The warnings should be addressed and/or discounted, as appropriate.

There are a number of errors that have been raised suggesting we should correct the casing of member names. This is one simple example of where the design can affect the code profiling. The design used capitalized prefixes such as VEM, IOM, MSG, and so forth but the profiler doesn't like them being used in the code. The Application Maintenance checklist states that there should be naming conventions and standards. It is a question of whether the naming conventions are correct for the solution or for the profiler.

The following summarizes the majority of the remaining categories:

❏   Globalization flags up that we must specify which culture is relevant when we are converting or formatting, or declare that the culture is irrelevant.

❏   Design is advising us that the exception handling needs to be improved or updated in a number of classes, including the `CryptographyProvider`.

The Application Maintenance checklist also contains a number of areas regarding commenting code. The comments in the summary for the `CryptographyProvider` are readable in the code. However, they are not correctly formatted for documentation generation because all the comments are contained within the `<summary>` tag. Furthermore, looking at the source code, there is a comment `// other options ?`. This is clearly something that needs to be revisited, but it has been lost among the general commenting. All such items should be clearly marked with TODO comments so they can be quickly located and addressed.

For each of the errors listed in the profiling results, you would need to perform the following general actions:

1. Understand the nature of the profiling error and what it means in terms of the solution.

2. Determine whether the error needed to be corrected, downgraded to a warning, or simply suppressed.

3. If the error needs to be corrected, you need to prioritize it (according to other errors and workload) and create a remediation plan. You would also need to include the costs associated with correcting the error and perform a cost-benefit analysis.

In addition to the code analysis profiler, there is also a code metrics profiler. To calculate the code metrics, select "Calculate Code Metrics for System Framework" from the Analyze menu. Figure 25-3 shows the output (expanded for the next discussion).

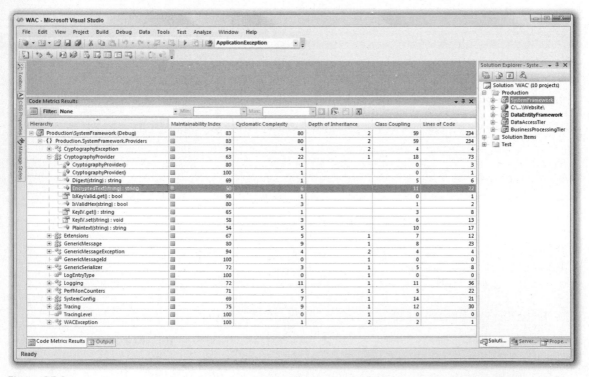

Figure 25-3

654

The Code Metrics Results tab displays a number of metrics. If you drill down to the `CryptographyProvider` then to the `EncryptedText` method, you will see that this has the lowest maintainability index, the highest cyclomatic complexity, and the highest class coupling. maintainability amalgamates cyclomatic complexity, inheritance, and class coupling.

According to the documentation, cyclomatic complexity measures the number of linearly independent paths through the method, which is determined by the number and complexity of conditional branches. A low cyclomatic complexity generally indicates a method that is easy to understand, test, and maintain. The cyclomatic complexity is calculated from a control flow graph of the method and is given as follows:

- ❑ cyclomatic complexity = the number of edges - the number of nodes + 1, where a node represents a logic branch point and an edge represents a line between nodes. The rule reports a violation when the cyclomatic complexity is more than 25.

In our case, the cyclomatic complexity of `EncryptedText` is 6, while for the whole `CryptographyProvider`, it is 22. We should consider dividing the class into smaller units and factoring out some of the code from `EncryptedText`.

The documentation for class coupling states:

- ❑ This rule measures class coupling by counting the number of unique type references that a type or method contains. Types and methods with a high degree of class coupling can be difficult to maintain. It is a good practice to have types and methods that exhibit low coupling and high cohesion.

`EncryptedText` has an unusually high coupling compared to other methods and classes. This would be reduced if we factored out some of the code into separate methods.

For each of the classes and methods listed in the metrics results, you would need to perform the following general actions:

1. Understand the nature of the metric calculation and what it means in terms of the solution.
2. Determine whether the metrics were within an acceptable range.
3. If the code needs to be corrected, you need to prioritize it (according to other corrections and workload) and create a remediation plan. You would also need to include the costs associated with correcting the error and perform a cost-benefit analysis.

Testing

In the previous section we saw the `CryptographyProvider`; it is worth considering how we would test this component and how we might assist in the testing of components which use it. The checklist states:

- ❑ Unit tests should cover complete components or classes, including exception scenarios.
- ❑ Integration tests should cover multiple interactions between components as well as exception scenarios.
- ❑ Smoke tests should cover the core functionality of the application.
- ❑ Interfaces and factories should be used to facilitate testing.

❏ Stubs should be used to provide basic end-point verification.

❏ Simulators should be used to help thoroughly test the application where it would otherwise be troublesome to do so.

Firstly, the Test folder isn't broken out into separate folders for Unit Tests, Integration Tests, or Smoke Tests, which makes it difficult to determine whether the tests included in the solution are simply unit tests or a combination of different types of tests. If everyone knows the testing approach then this isn't a problem.

If you open the `TestSystemFramework` project, you can examine the `TestCryptography` class under `TestProviders`. You will see that a comprehensive set of tests has been authored for this class. However, no evidence is given regarding the origin of the *expected* digest and encrypted strings. The expected results may have been generated by the component itself, but do not properly validate that aspect of the component.

You can open the Test List Editor from the Windows menu item under the main Test menu item. Figure 25-4 shows the Test List Editor with the `CryptographyProvider` tests checked in readiness for the next section.

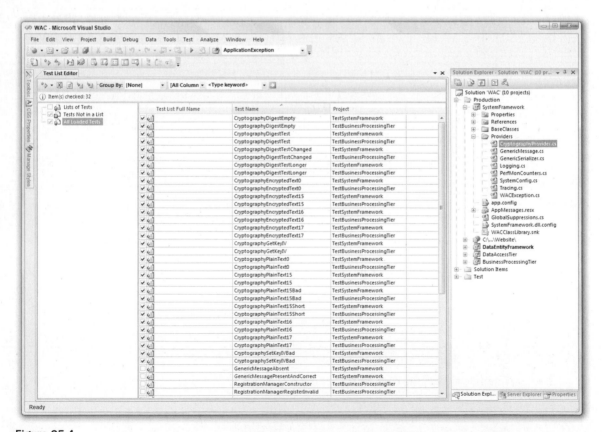

Figure 25-4

You can run the tests by selecting "Tests in Current Context" from the Run menu item under the main Test menu item. They should all pass, but if you select the Code Coverage Results tab, and expand the Hierarchy, you will see that only about half of the code paths have been executed. This is shown in Figure 25-5.

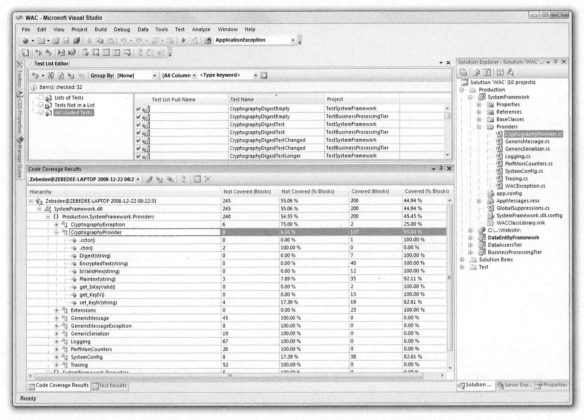

Figure 25-5

Expanding further, we see that the coverage check includes other items in the library, such as `GenericMessage`, `PerfMon` and `Tracing`. At this point, we are only interested in the `CryptographyProvider`, and we see that coverage is approaching 100 percent (93.84 percent), which is a very good statistic.

However, you can see that there are areas of code coverage needing improvement within the overall solution. Again, this breaks down to the following general actions:

1. Understand the nature of why a particular area of code hasn't been covered.

2. Determine whether the code needs to be covered, removed, or exempt.

3. If the code needs to be covered, you need to prioritize the test development (according to other corrections and workload) and create a remediation plan. You would also need to include the costs associated with writing the new tests and perform a cost-benefit analysis.

A number of other components in the solution make use of the `CryptographyProvider`. How can we know that they are using it correctly when all we see is encrypted strings? This is an area where stubs and simulators will be useful. You need to be able to substitute a simplified version of the component.

You can see an example of this in the `SolicitedEmailProvider`, which resides in BusinessProcessingTier, under Providers. In this sample component, e-mails can be sent to the normal database queue or can be diverted to the log. An enumerator contains the different e-mail options and an interface determines how the individual `SolicitedEmailProviders` appear to the consumer. Each time the `ProviderFactory` is instantiated, it checks the configuration to see which actual provider should deal with the e-mail.

Onwards and Upwards

Throughout this book you have seen a variety of patterns, practices, and principles for production-ready software development. This book hasn't covered every single topic, nor has it gone into the nth level of detail, so there will be more to learn and apply. Each chapter has summarized the key points to take away from it and it is up to you to decide what you want to use on your own projects and include in your own solutions. Every project is different and you will need to consider and plan for how you incorporate the points you take away.

You need to think about what you are doing, who you are doing it for, and why you are doing it. The art of software design, development, and implementation lies in your hands. The better you are at it and the more you understand, the better your solutions will be.

Index

SYMBOLS

* (asterisks)
as mandatory field indicator, 145
as standard indicator, 178

A

acceptance testing
defined, 230–232
in production environments, 239
technical, 233
access
design considerations, 154
page specifications, 180
access, data. See data access
accessibility
considerations, 138
design considerations, 149–150
design overview, 145–149
in quality landscape, 38
Account Manager service, 415
accounts
application modeling. See application modeling
event types, 573–574
HFRs (High-Level Functional Requirements).
See HFRs (High-Level Functional
Requirements)
My Account page, 336–337
online application walkthrough, 331–335
partitioning based on, 520
planning architecture. See architecture
planning
Welcome page, 335–336
accounts, storyboard
accounts, 339–342, 344–345
activation, 339–342
changing passwords, 346–348
closing, 349–350
creating new, 337–339
logging in, 344–345

logging out, 345
re-requesting activation key, 342–344
re-requesting key, 342–344
resetting passwords, 345–346
updates, 348–349
accounts, use case
activation, 375–377
changing passwords, 384–387
closing, 390–392
creating new, 372–374
logging in, 379–381
logging out, 381–382
re-requesting activation key, 377–379
resetting passwords, 382–383
updating, 388–390
acquiring objects, 526–527
actions
page specifications, 180
providing audit trail, 510
in use cases, 166–173
Activate Account page
functional requirements, 359–361
modeling flow, 450–452
modeling inputs and outputs, 444
storyboard, 339–342
use case, 375–377
activation
account, 332
Activation service, 415
component responsibility modeling, 435–439
new key processing, 460
reporting components, 463–465
re-requesting activation key. See Re-Request
Activation Key page
sending emails, 424–425
Welcome page, 335–336
active nodes, 209–210
**active-active configurations, 226–227,
238–239**
**active-passive configurations, 223–226,
238–239**